THE LEGACY OF CANAAN

SUPPLEMENTS

TO

VETUS TESTAMENTUM

EDITED BY

VOLUME V

LEIDEN
E. J. BRILL
1965

THE LEGACY OF CANAAN

THE RAS SHAMRA TEXTS AND THEIR RELEVANCE TO THE OLD TESTAMENT

BY

REV. PROF. JOHN GRAY M. A., B. D., Ph. D.
University of Aberdeen

SECOND, REVISED EDITION

LEIDEN
E. J. BRILL
1965

FIRST EDITION, 1957

PRINTED IN THE NETHERLANDS

CONTENTS

Preface vii

Preface to Second Edition viii

Abbreviations x

The Ugaritic Alphabet and Transliteration xii

Chapter I: Ugarit and its Records 1

Chapter II: Myths of the Fertility Cult 20

Chapter III: Saga and Legend 106

Chapter IV: The Religion of Canaan 152

i: The Gods 152
ii: The Cult 192
iii: Cultic Personnel 209

Chapter V: The Social Order 218

Chapter VI: Literary and Linguistic 259

Bibliography 312

Concordance of Ugaritic Texts 326

Index of ugaritic passages 330

Index of ugaritic words 333

Subject index 337

Authors' index 341

Index of scriptural passages 344

PREFACE

The author's studies in the Ras Shamra Texts date from 1936, when as Blackie Travelling Fellow of Edinburgh University his interest in them was engaged in the library of l'École Biblique de St. Étienne in Jerusalem. At that time the historical interpretation of certain of the longer texts had not been seriously questioned, and many striking but hasty conclusions had been drawn after M. CHARLES VIROLLEAUD's prompt publication of the texts. Our initial reserve has been confirmed by subsequent critical study. No longer can we find any specific reference to the fathers of the historical Hebrews or to particular localities in Palestine. The texts, however, are most valuable as documenting the life and culture of Canaan on the eve of the Hebrew settlement, and it is in the belief that they are vitally relevant to the understanding of the Old Testament that we present this study.

To M. CHARLES VIROLLEAUD, the first editor of the texts, to M. CLAUDE F. A. SCHAEFFER, by whose skill the texts were recovered from their archaeological context and so accurately dated, and to M. RENÉ DUSSAUD, who gave the first full synthesis of the texts, all scholars in this field must remain grateful, and, if many of the original views of MM. VIROLLEAUD and DUSSAUD have been exploded, their work is still most stimulating. With the critical reaction against the first interpretation of the texts the initiative passed largely to American scholars, notably C. H. GORDON and H. L. GINSBERG, whose judgement on philological points has always commanded respect. To Professor GORDON Ugaritic scholars owe a particular debt for his *Ugaritic Handbook* and *Manual*, which make the texts so readily accessible. Our debt to Professor GORDON is evidenced by the fact that we have found references to his work too numerous for citation in our authors' index except by '*passim*'. Of other major works we should particularly note our appreciation of T. H. GASTER's admirable anthropological study *Thespis*, and the most recent study of the major texts by G. R. DRIVER. Our MS was already complete and accepted for publication before the appearance of the last work, and, though we were permitted to resume the MS, we must frankly admit that in other circumstances we should have dealt more fully with this fine work. We trust that we have conveyed our just appreciation of the contribution of all other fellow-workers in this field by our citation of their works in our bibliography.

We should like further to express our gratitude to the staff of the library of l'École Biblique de St. Étienne in Jerusalem, where our serious study of the texts began, to the REV. PROFESSOR H. H. ROWLEY M.A., D.D., Theol.D., Ll.D., F.B.A., our former principal in the University of Manchester, whose voluminous library of books and offprints was so freely at our disposal, to PROFESSOR P. A. H. DE BOER of Leiden and the editorial staff of Vetus Testamentum and to the compositors of the house of BRILL for their handling of such intricate matter in so many scripts, and to the REV. GEORGE FARR M.A., B.D., of the Baptist College, Manchester for stimulating discussions in matters of common interest and for his careful reading of our proofs.

King's College,
University of Aberdeen,
April 1957.

PREFACE TO SECOND EDITION

The publishers' request for a second edition of *The Legacy of Canaan* has given the writer the welcome opportunity to develop certain themes, on which he had previously only touched, and to declare more firmly on certain problems, which he was obliged to leave open in the first edition. Since the first edition was already in press when G. R. DRIVER's *Canaanite Myths and Legends* appeared, the writer is glad of the opportunity to consider PROFESSOR DRIVER's work more adequately than was formerly possible. The most useful *Wörterbuch der ugaritischen Sprache* (1963) of the late PROFESSOR J. AISTLEITNER has been a notable advantage in the study of texts still notoriously problematic. The recent death of PROFESSOR AISTLEITNER is indeed a grievous loss to scholarship in this field, and the moment is opportune for our sincere acknowledgement of his achievement and of the unfailing stimulus of his fertile genius and mature scholarship. It is indeed fitting that the work of this notable pioneer in Ugaritic research should be crowned by his comprehensive lexicon and concordance.

It is highly gratifying to see the industry of the indefatigable

PROFESSOR SCHAEFFER rewarded with continued success in the discovery of new texts. By the great courtesy of PROFESSOR SCHAEFFER these are already known to the writer, though, since the most recently discovered alphabetic texts are not yet published, they are omitted from the present edition. In the third edition of this work, however, which the writer and his publishers already project, they will form an important addition together with the political documents from the palace of Ugarit, so far omitted from *The Legacy of Canaan* since they do not so closely relate to the significance of the Ras Shamra discoveries for the study of the Old Testament.

My particular thanks are due to my assistant the Rev. WILLIAM JOHNSTONE M.A., B.D., Lecturer in Hebrew and Semitic Languages in the University of Aberdeen, who has found time in a very full programme of archaeological field work at Ras Shamra, research, and routine work in University and Church to read my proofs with characteristic thoroughness, and to the compositors of E. J. BRILL for their masterly handling of the various difficulties involved in the text of this book with its exacting problems of transliteration and the various scripts involved.

King's College, J. G.
University of Aberdeen,
January, 1965

ABBREVIATIONS

AASOR	*Annual of the American Schools of Oriental Research*
AfO	*Archiv für Orientforschung.*
AJ	*Antiquaries Journal.*
AJSL	*American Journal of Semitic Languages and Literatures.*
AO	*Der Alte Orient.*
ARA	*Ancient Records of Assyria* (D. D. LUCKENBILL, 1927).
ARE	*Ancient Records of Egypt* (J. H. BREASTED, 1906).
Arch. Or.	*Archiv Orientální.*
ARW	*Archiv für Religionswissenschaft.*
AS	*Anatolian Studies.*
ASAE	*Annales du Service des Antiquités d'Égypte.*
AV	*Authorized Version.*
BASOR	*Bulletin of the American Schools of Oriental Research.*
BJRL	*Bulletin of the John Rylands Library.*
BZAW	*Beihefte zur Zeitschrift für die alttestamentliche Wissenschaft.*
CBQ	*Catholic Biblical Quarterly.*
CRAIBL	*Comptes Rendus de l'Académie des Inscriptions et Belles Lettres.*
ET	*Expository Times.*
ETL	*Ephemerides Theologicae Lovanienses.*
FuF	*Forschungen und Fortschritte.*
HUCA	*Hebrew Union College Annual.*
IEJ	*Israel Exploration Journal.*
JAOS	*Journal of the American Oriental Society.*
JBL	*Journal of Biblical Literature.*
JEA	*Journal of Egyptian Archaeology.*
JMUEOS	*Journal of the Manchester University Egyptian and Oriental Society.*
JNES	*Journal of Near Eastern Studies.*
JPOS	*Journal of the Palestine Oriental Society.*
JQR	*Jewish Quarterly Review.*
JRAS	*Journal of the Royal Asiatic Society.*
JTS	*Journal of Theological Study.*
KNUDTZON	J. KNUDTZON, *Die El-Amarna Tafeln*, 1908-15.
JSS	*Journal of Semitic Studies.*
MT	*Massoretic Text.*
NSI	G. A. COOKE, *A Text-Book of North Semitic Inscriptions*, 1903.
NTS	*Norsk Tidsskrift for Sprogvidenskap.*
NTT	*Norsk Teologisk Tidsskrift.*
OLZ	*Orientalistische Literaturzeitung.*
PEF	*Palestine Exploration Fund.*
PEFQS	*Palestine Exploration Fund Quarterly Statement.*
PEQ	*Palestine Exploration Quarterly.*
PG	*Patrologia Graeca* (MIGNE).
RA	*Revue d'Assyriologie et d'Archéologie Orientale.*
RB	*La Revue Biblique Internationale.*
RES	*Revue des Études Sémitiques.*
RHPhR	*Revue d'Histoire et de Philosophie Religieuses.*
RHR	*Revue de l'Histoire des Religions.*
RSV	*Revised Standard Version.*

RV	*Revised Version.*
SEÅ	*Svensk Exegetisk Årsbok.*
TLZ	*Theologische Literaturzeitung.*
TR	*Theologische Rundschau.*
TZ	*Theologische Zeitschrift.*
UH	*Ugaritic Handbook* (C. H. Gordon, 1947).
UL	*Ugaritic Literature* (idem, 1949).
UUÅ	*Uppsala Universitets Årsskrift.*
VT	*Vetus Testamentum.*
ZA	*Zeitschrift für Assyriologie.*
ZAW	*Zeitschrift für die Alttestamentliche Wissenschaft.*
ZDMG	*Zeitschrift der Deutschen Morgenländischen Gesellschaft.*
ZDPV	*Zeitschrift der Deutschen Palästina-Vereins.*

THE UGARITIC ALPHABET AND TRANSLITERATION

𐎀	*ʾa*	𐎎	*m*
𐎛	*ʾe*	𐎐	*n*
𐎜	*ʾu*	𐎒	*s*
𐎁	*b*	𐎝	*ś* (a variant of *s*)
𐎂	*g*	𐎓	ʿ
𐎄	*d*	𐎙	*ġ*
𐎅	*h*	𐎔	*p*
𐎆	*w*	𐎕	*ṣ*
𐎇	*z*	𐎑	*ẓ*
𐎈	*ḥ*	𐎖	*q*
𐎃	*ḫ*	𐎗	*r*
𐎉	*ṭ*	𐎌	*š*
𐎊	*y*	𐎏	*ž* [1]
𐎋	*k*	𐎚	*t*
𐎍	*l*	𐎘	*ṯ*

---

[1]) This consonant corresponds to a variety of sounds ranging through Arab. ث, س, ش, ص, د, and ذ and Hebr. ז and שׂ, probably reflecting non-Semitic influence in the Semitic dialect of North Syria, cf. the sibilant pronunciation of ث in the Aleppo district in modern colloquial Arabic.

CHAPTER I

UGARIT AND ITS RECORDS

Over 30 years have now elapsed since the fortuitous find of a peasant on the North-Syrian coast some 7 miles north of Latakia led to the discovery of a corbel-vaulted tomb and subsequently of a whole necropolis associated with the Mycenaean settlement known to later Greek geographers as *Leukos Limen* (Whitehaven), which persists in the modern Arabic name of the place Minet el-Beida.

Significant as such a discovery was, it is dwarfed by the work on the neighbouring landward mound of Ras Shamra (Fennel Head) which reveals traces of five main periods of occupation from the Neolithic Age before 3500 B.C. to the destruction of the city in the last phase of the Bronze Age, c. 1200 B.C., [1] which coincided with the coming of the 'Sea-peoples' from the coast-lands of Anatolia and the Aegean islands and from even further afield in the regions beyond the Bosphorus. Those peoples, well-known from Egyptian and Hittite sources, included the Biblical Philistines, whose settlement in Palestine coincided with what we regard as the main phase of the Hebrew settlement of the Central Highlands.

The city reached its cultural zenith about 1400 B.C. about the time that the Hebrew tribes associated with the name of Jacob were migrating from North Mesopotamia to Palestine. Ugarit, as Ras Shamra was anciently called, was at that time a sphere of Egyptian influence under the XVIIIth Dynasty. This period was one of relative peace and prosperity in the ancient Near East. The great imperial powers of Egypt and the Hittites had not yet engaged in the battle for Syria. Babylon was under the rule of Cassite conquerors from the highlands of Iran who had little to offer towards cultural progress but did at least preserve peace and decent obscurity. In North Mesopotamia Assyria had not yet embarked on her career of expansion and was, in fact, not yet a nation. The seat of her future empire was

---

[1]) There are certain traces of the resumption of occupation of the site from the Assyrian period c. 700 B.C. to the Hellenic period, especially in a small cemetery with sarcophagus burials. From this period an interesting find was a hoard of Macedonian silver staters of the 6th century, the earliest coined money yet found in Syria. C. F.-A. SCHAEFFER, *Syria* XVIII, 1937, fig. 18.

then occupied by the state of Mitanni whose population was a mixture of Semites and non-Semitic Hurrians under an Indo-Iranian ruling caste and a feudal aristocracy who had introduced the horse and light war-chariot to Western Asia just after 2000 B.C. All those powers, as the Egyptian state archives from Tell el-Amarna indicate, were in amicable correspondence and the royal houses of Egypt and Mitanni were actually affiliated by marriage. [1]) This was the golden sunset of the great empires of the ancient Near East before the irruption of the barbarians in the Iron Age limited their power and disrupted the 'entente cordiale'. The conditions of that more peaceful age are reflected in the material remains of Ugarit about 1400 B.C.

The site thus affords a unique opportunity of studying the interrelationship of ancient cultures, standing as it did near the coast of Syria opposite Cyprus. It was a terminal of trade-routes via the Euphrates from Mesopotamia and from the metal-bearing regions of Anatolia and at the same time a bridge-head of Egypt and Mycenaean Greece in Asia. There were many ethnic groups, too, represented in Ugarit in the Late Bronze Age, as is indicated mainly in the nomenclature of its inhabitants, which has been the subject of a fruitful study by NOTH. [2]) Though this aspect of the culture of Ugarit must be emphasized, it is nevertheless with its native elements that we shall be concerned in this work, since those illustrate the Canaanite culture which confronted the Hebrews when they settled in Palestine. To be sure, there was a reaction against those Canaanite conceptions and practices, but not before they had made a deep impress on the Hebrew way of life. Such reactions take place, as PEDERSEN shrewdly observed in his study of Hebrew prophecy, [3]) only after the system against which the reaction takes place has succeeded in influencing even the forces of reaction to such an extent that they can never quite emancipate themselves. As documents which so intimately illustrate the Canaan of the Hebrew settlement, the Ras Shamra texts ought to command the interest not merely of the few specialists but of all who are really interested in the Old Testament, and this is the justification for the present study.

In such a cosmopolitan city as Ugarit, where the material remains

---

[1]) This relationship, however, was unilateral. Two Mitannian princesses were in the harems of the Pharaohs Amenhotep III and Akhnaten.

[2]) M. NOTH, 'Die syrisch-palästinische Bevölkerung des zweiten Jahrtausends v. Chr. im Lichte neuer Quellen', *ZDPV* LXV, 1942, pp. 9-67.

[3]) J. PEDERSEN, *Israel III-IV*, 1940, p. 131.

demonstrate contacts with Egypt, Mesopotamia, Hittite Anatolia, Crete, Cyprus, and Greece, we are prepared to find various languages and scripts represented. There are Egyptian hieroglyphics, Akkadian syllabic cuneiform on clay tablets, texts in the language of the non-Semitic Hurrians of the Anatolian foothills (the Horites of the Old Testament), and vocabularies of Sumerian-Akkadian and Sumerian-Akkadian-Hurrian words and syllabaries. The linear Cypriot script is also represented and Hittite elements also occur. The most significant find, however, was the local alphabetic script in a Semitic dialect in which the bulk of the literature was written. This script was a new and unsuspected discovery. [1]) The decipherment was accomplished in a remarkably short time by three scholars working independently, the late HANS BAUER of Halle, [2]) and the French scholars ÉDOUARD DHORME [3]) and CHARLES VIROLLEAUD, [4]) the last of whom published, transcribed, and translated the texts from 1929 onwards. [5]) The initial work of these scholars has been modified and supplemented in details with the accumulation of evidence, but in the main it stands. There is less certainty as to the precise dialectic affinity of the language, though it is clear that it is Semitic.

In virtue of the situation of Ras Shamra in the extreme North of Syria and at the Western terminal of a trade-route from Mesopotamia we might have expected the local dialect to show affinities with Akkadian. BAUER regarded Ugaritic as a new language hitherto unattested which lay between Biblical Hebrew and Akkadian, [6]) and this view has been accepted by CANTINEAU, [7]) AISTLEITNER, [8])

---

[1]) Since the discovery of the cuneiform alphabet of Ras Shamra two other cases have been found in Palestine, one a fragment from Bethshemesh (E. GRANT, *BASOR* 52, 1933, pp. 3 ff.), and the other an inscription on a bronze dagger blade from the plateau between Beisan and Kawkab el-Hawa in Lower Galilee (S. YEIVIN, 'An Ugaritic Inscription from Palestine', *Qedem* II, 1945, pp. 32-41). As this edition goes to press Dr. Paul Lapp has just informed the writer in a private communication of the find of 'a 12th century B.C. Canaanite cuneiform tablet' in his excavation at Tell Taʿannek.

[2]) H. BAUER, 'Die Entzifferung einer neuen Keilschrift', *Vossische Zeitung* 182, June 4th, 1930.

[3]) E. DHORME, 'Un nouvel alphabet sémitique', *RB* XXXIX, 1930, pp. 571-577.

[4]) C. VIROLLEAUD, 'Lettre du 1er octobre, 1930, annonçant le déchiffrement des tablettes de Ras Shamra', *CRAIBL*, 1930, p. 265.

[5]) See current volumes of *Syria* and *Annales Archéologiques de Syrie*.

[6]) H. BAUER, 'Safonisches', *OLZ* XXXVIII, 1935, pp. 129-133.

[7]) J. CANTINEAU, 'La Langue de Ras Shamra', *Syria* XIII, 1932, p. 169. XXI, 1940, pp. 59-61.

[8]) J. AISTLEITNER, 'Zum Verständnis des Ras-Shamra Textes ID', *Dissertationes in honorem Dr. Ed. Mahler*, 1937, pp. 38-39.

FRIEDRICH, [1] and GOETZE. [2] There are certainly Akkadian features, especially in verbal forms and tenses, [3] but these are not so extensive as we should expect. In his critical study of the thesis of GOETZE that Ugaritic is an Amorite dialect with North-Eastern affinities DE LANGHE [4] was able to demonstrate that the great majority of Ugaritic peculiarities cited by GOETZE can really be parallelled in Canaanite dialects. Ugaritic can, without undue difficulty, be brought into the Canaanite group of languages including Biblical Hebrew, and all working translations make this assumption. [5] The problem, however, is not simple. We find certain features in Ugaritic, for instance, which are peculiar to Hebrew. Indeed, in morphology, vocabulary, and grammatical and literary structure the Ugaritic texts show striking affinities with Biblical Hebrew, particularly in the poetic passages of the Old Testament. We do not doubt that this is due to the fact that in literature as in other cultural respects the Hebrews assimilated, or consciously drew upon, the legacy of ancient Canaan. While the Old Testament and the Ras Shamra texts elucidate each other, we should be led into glaring errors if we sought to solve linguistic difficulties in the latter by relying exclusively upon Hebrew philology. This preference for Hebrew as a key to the solution of the problems of Ugaritic often led VIROLLEAUD and DUSSAUD far astray in the early days of Ugaritic scholarship, especially in their historical interpretation of the Krt text and that one dealing with the birth of the twin-gods Šḥr and Šlm (GORDON, *Ugaritic Handbook* 52), though both scholars, to be sure, are competent Semitic philo-

---

[1]) J. FRIEDRICH, 'Ras Schamra, eine Überblick über Funde und Forschungen', *Der Alte Orient* XXXIII, 1-2, 1933, p. 27.

[2]) A. GOETZE, *Hethiter, Churriter, und Assyrer*, 1936, p. 142.

[3]) The narrative tense in Ugaritic is commonly the 'imperfect' or, as we suspect, the preterite, as in Akkadian. A survival of this tense is probably the 'imperfect' with *waw* consecutive in Hebrew.

[4]) West-Semitic, or specifically, Canaanite features are noted in detail by R. DE LANGHE, *De Taal van Ras-Shamra-Ugarit*, 1948, p. 24.

[5]) The situation is well stated by J. A. MONTGOMERY and Z. S. HARRIS, though with a tendency to oversimplification. 'The vocabulary is in general Hebrew with the exception of what are mostly cultural words of international use, these chiefly to be identified from Akkadian, with a number demonstrably or presumably of Hurrian or Hittite origin. The inflection of the verb is, it appears, largely that of classical Hebrew, and almost all its phenomena can be parallelled from the latter. Inflectional vocalic endings in noun and verb still survived and are indicated by the alephs, but traces of this primitive condition of nouns may be seen even in the Bible'. 'The Ras Shamra Mythological Texts', *Memoirs of the American Oriental Society* IV, 1935, pp. 16-17.

logists and could on occasion skilfully apply their knowledge of other Semitic languages. Though we appreciate the work of H. L. GINSBERG, he too is often too prone to draw on the reserves of Rabbinical Hebrew to explain obscurities in the Ras Shamra texts. Nevertheless, a controlled use of the Hebrew cognate is fruitful, as may be seen from the work of the late Professor CASSUTO, who was particularly alive to Hebrew affinities, yet did not allow this to lead him into patent absurdities. In this respect his last great work האלה ענת is in our opinion the finest piece of work of this kind yet produced. There are other cases, again, of features in Ugaritic peculiar to, or characteristic of, Arabic, or of the Aramaic dialects, and a thorough familiarity with Arabic morphology and vocabulary is in our opinion essential to the study of the Ras Shamra texts. [1]) Again we should stress that the use of A1abic as that of Hebrew in Ugəritic study should be strictly controlled. Any attempt to force Ugaritic into the mould of any one known Semitic language is disastrous. The Ugaritic scholar must be alive to the affinities of construction and vocabulary with one or another of these dialects, particularly with Hebrew and Arabic. We see no reason to differ from the opinion of C. H. GORDON, who since the pioneer work of VIROLLEAUD has done more than any other to make the texts accessible and intelligible to students, that there was in ancient Ugarit considerable interpenetration of dialects. [2]) This is quite feasible in view of the peculiar situation of Ugarit already noted and the various phases of Semitic penetration and settlement.

The content of the various tablets from Ras Shamra is what we might expect from such a cosmopolitan city. There are business documents from Mesopotamian business houses [3]) which dealt in purple from the *murex* for which the Phoenician coast was famous, legal tablets, mostly in Akkadian cuneiform, [4]) private letters in the

---

[1]) We have demonstrated this at length in an article in the Hebrew journal *Melilah* V, 1955, pp. 1-14. We believe that in addition to having words from roots common to other Semitic languages Arabic absorbed many words from the older attested languages in the Moslem expansion and has preserved them in local dialects, where they may be studied in current usage.

[2]) C. H. GORDON, *UH* 1947, p. 116. The myths and legends are now conveniently available in transliteration and translation with succinct philological notes in G. R. DRIVER's *Canaanite Myths and Legends*, 1956.

[3]) F. THUREAU-DANGIN, 'Un comptoir de laine pourpre à Ugarit d'après une tablette de Ras Shamra', *Syria* XV, 1934, pp. 137-146.

[4]) F. THUREAU-DANGIN, *Syria* XVIII, 1937, pp. 147-254; VIROLLEAUD, *Syria* XXVIII 1951, pp. 54-56; SCHAEFFER, *Syria* XXXI, 1954, pp. 29-32; J. NOUGAY-

local alphabetic script and dialect, [1]) and diplomatic correspondence between the King of Ugarit and the Hittites [2]) which show that the latter, while on occasion able to command the allegiance [3]) and even tribute of Ugarit, [4]) were generally obliged to treat this significant realm with respect. There are also military dispatches from one *Iwerẓarri*, [5]) of which the Iwer element may be a title. [6]) There are offering-lists which contain many technical terms and names of the various deities worshipped at ancient Ugarit. [7]) There are also veterinary texts prescribing treatment for the ailments of horses [8]), in which a concoction of ripe figs, raisins, and beanflour [9]) recalls Isaiah's prescription for Hezekiah's boil (2 Kings xx, 7, Isaiah xxxviii, 21). Texts more recently found in the great palace-complex include an omen-text indicating observation of the stars, [10]) and actual alphabets, the first in the history of man, comprising 30 letters in the following order:

ʾa, b, g, ḫ, d, h, w, z, ḥ, ṭ, y, k, š, l, m, ẓ̌, n, ẓ, s, ʿ, p, ṣ, q, r, ṯ, ġ, t, ʾe, ʾu, ś.

It will be noted that the order of the Hebrew letters in the alphabet coincides with their Ugaritic equivalents. The Ugaritic alphabet, however, has certain extra sibilants and gutturals which are inserted

---

ROL in *Mission de Ras Shamra VI*: *Le Palais Royal d'Ugarit* III (ed. C. F. A. SCHAEFFER), 1955.

1) E.g. GORDON *UH* 89, 95.

2) *Ibidem* 118. This is a letter from Niqmad the King of Ugarit to Šubbiluliuma. Since a King Niqmad is named in the colophon to two of the mythological texts (GORDON *UH* 51, VIII, edge; 62, 56) it might be thought that the redaction of these texts might be dated in the first half of the 14th century B.C. The matter, however, is not so simple since it is known that there were three kings named Niqmad. It is nevertheless probable that the texts in their present redaction do come from this period.

3) As at the battle of Qadesh on the Orontes where Ramses II lists *Ekeret* among the Hittite allies, A. ERMAN, *The Literature of the Ancient Egyptians*, 1927, p. 262.

4) GORDON *UH* 118.

5) *Ibidem* 54, 138.

6) The names Uriah and Araunah, as suggested by J. A. MONTGOMERY (*JAOS* LV, 1935, p. 94 n.), may be Hebrew misunderstandings of the title. In this light we understand the peculiar passage in II Samuel xxiv, 23, *v. infra* pp. 260-261.

7) GORDON *UH* 1, 2, 5, 9, 17, 19, 22, 23, 41, 44, 47, 107, 134.

8) *Ibidem* 55, 56.

9) *dblt yṯnt wṣmqm yṯnm*
wqmḥ bql

The word *bql* might be cognate with the Arabic باقلاء, 'beans'.

10) VIROLLEAUD, 'Les nouveaux textes de Ras Shamra', *Syria* XXVIII, 1951, pp. 22-56, text III. Our translation of this text is published in *PEQ* 1955, p. 182. For our emended translation *v. infra* p. 194.

where we should hardly expect them. Of these the last three are probably added to the basic alphabet as innovations or refinements, and *ẓ̌*, which is an interdental sound, probably represents a local dialectic consonant, perhaps influenced by the Anatolian element in the population and dialect of Ugarit. It is noteworthy that this consonant is particularly common in words of Hurrian origin. [1])

An important body of texts are administrative in purport. The inhabitants of the town and country districts of the realm were listed for purposes of military service or possibly merely for the provision of arms. Either a quota of soldiers with appropriate arms, such as slings and bows, or the arms only, was demanded of each district [2]) or, it might be, of each guild, such as the priests or craftsmen of various categories. [3]) Taxes were levied in silver, produce, [4]) or labour, [5]) recalling Solomon's levies in Israel (1 Kings v, 13 ff., ix, 15 ff., xi, 28). Land grants and money payments were also made to certain classes military and apparently religious. [6]) An interesting feature is that, though there are traces of a social order based on tribes, this was largely replaced for administrative purposes by an order based on territorial or class divisions, a process which we find in operation in Israel in Solomon's time (1 Kings iv, 7-19) and in North Israel in the time of Jeroboam II on the evidence of the Samaritan ostraca. [7]) The guild organization of the population of Ugarit may be a manifestation of the caste system operative in India at the present day, and may well have been introduced by the Indo-Iranian element who penetrated into Western Asia early in the 2nd millennium and organized the state of Mitanni in Upper Mesopotamia. [8]) There is also indication in those texts of a feudal system with a baronial order, the *mariannu*, who were specialists in chariot

---

[1]) E. ULLENDORFF has conveniently listed such words, 'Ugaritic Marginalia II', *JSS* II, 1962, pp. 349-51. Analogous to this dialectic peculiarity at Ras Shamra is the pronunciation of Arabic ث as a sibilant in the district of Aleppo at the present day. See further in the chart on p. XII.

[2]) GORDON *UH* 321.

[3]) *Ibidem* 113.

[4]) *Ibidem* 108-109.

[5]) *Ibidem* 110.

[6]) *Ibidem* 300.

[7]) The stratification of Samaria indicates that those sherds are from the time of Jeroboam II and not, as was first suggested, from Ahab's palace, J. W. CROWFOOT, *Samaria-Sebaste I*, 1942, p. 8.

[8]) The system at Ugarit may also have been influenced by the organisation of crafts and occupations in the temple-state economy of Sumerian Mesopotamia.

warfare. There is a certain amount of archaeological evidence that this system was introduced to Palestine during the Hyksos domination [1]) and was retained by the Egyptians in the XVIIIth Dynasty as the machinery of government in Syria and Palestine. [2]) It seems also to have been adopted by the Philistines, who were probably familiar with the system in the phase of their history as vassals and mercenaries of the Hittites in Anatolia. So much is at least suggested by the case of David who was a feudatory of Achish of Gath with Ziqlag as his perpetual fief (1 Samuel xxvii, 6). We agree with ALT that on a smaller scale the system was employed by Saul and certainly by David and Solomon and their successors in Jerusalem. [3])

More recently a great number of administrative texts in alphabetic and syllabic cuneiform have been published respectively by VIROLLEAUD [4]) and NOUGAYROL [5]). These greatly increase our knowledge of feudal relations and of the law in ancient Ugarit. Unfortunately this is practically limited to the law as administered by the King within his own feudal jurisdiction, and does not supply any evidence of a civil code like the Babylonian, Hittite and Assyrian laws of the 2nd millennium and their Canaanite variation which is reflected in the casuistic law in the Book of the Covenant (Exodus xx, 22-xxiii, 33). These publications contain also economic, and ritual texts, and mythological fragments, private letters and political correspondence, and will be cited ad. loc. throughout this work.

By far the most interesting texts, however, consist of longer pieces in the local cuneiform alphabet and the Semitic dialect. These are written in epic style. They comprise various fragments found in the annual campaigns up to 1939 in the adjunct of the chief temple of Ugarit, the shrine of Baal on the acropolis of the site. They were

---

[1]) W. F. ALBRIGHT, *The Archaeology of Palestine*, 1949, pp. 91-93.

[2]) ALT maintains that the local feudalism in Palestine and Syria was retained by the Egyptians of the XVIIIth Dynasty as a convenient basis for their garrisoning of their Asiatic empire. This system seems to be in force in the Amarna Tablets and in the annals of Thothmes III, where ALT notes in the coastal plain and in the great central plain of Palestine a concentration of towns individually responsible to the Pharaoh. These political units and the system of local administration were in turn utilised by the Philistines in Palestine. *Die Landnahme der Israeliten*, 1925, pp. 7 ff. *Die Staatenbildung der Israeliten in Palästina* 1930, p. 3. 'Völker und Staaten Syriens im frühen Altertum', *Der Alte Orient* XXXIV, 1936, pp. 31-32.

[3]) A. ALT, *Die Staatenbildung* . . . pp. 31 ff.

[4]) C. VIROLLEAUD, *Le Palais Royal d'Ugarit* II, 1957.

[5]) J. NOUGAYROL, *Le Palais Royal d'Ugarit* III, 1955.

published by VIROLLEAUD with transliteration, translation, and commentary in current volumes of *Syria*, and, while this had the advantage of making the material available to scholars at the earliest possible moment, it was not always easy to fit the fragments together and to grasp the main purport of the texts. Many positive 'howlers' were committed by premature efforts to interpret the texts, or rather to use details without a serious attempt to interpret the texts as a whole. The tendency still unfortunately persists to use the Ras Shamra texts as a kind of literary lucky-bag out of which all sorts of odds and ends may be drawn. VIROLLEAUD himself was aware of three main texts among the fragments, one dealing with the vicissitudes of Baal, one with Krt, an ancient king, and another which he published as '*La légende phénicienne de Danel...*' in 1936. A further step in the synthesis of the Baal myths was taken by H. L. GINSBERG in a Hebrew publication on the Ugaritic texts in 1936. The process was continued by DE LANGHE in his very thorough work '*Les textes de Ras Shamra-Ugarit et leurs rapports avec le milieu Biblique de l'Ancien Testament*' (1945), a work which embraced not only the Baal-myths but the whole of the texts so far known. In 1949 all the Ras Shamra texts of any significance were translated, as far as that was possible, and grouped according to subject matter in GORDON's *Ugaritic Literature*, which is so far the most convenient form in which non-specialists may consult the Ras Shamra texts. A similar service was done by H. L. GINSBERG, who similarly treats the longer Ras Shamra texts in PRITCHARD's *Ancient Near Eastern Texts relating to the Old Testament* (1950). A similar synthesis of the Baal-myths and the Dn'el text is offered by T. H. GASTER in his great work *Thespis* (1950), though this is but part of his thesis of a general pattern of seasonal ritual drama and mythology in the Near East. One of the best syntheses of the Baal fragments is that of the late UMBERTO CASSUTO, a Hebrew work on *The Goddess Anat* (1950) with a most valuable introduction, translation, and commentary. Now the most useful translation of the Baal-texts and other longer texts from Ras Shamra is DRIVER's *Canaanite Myths and Legends* (1956), which is characterized by a thorough and most ingenious attempt to restore fragmentary passages and a wealth of philological notes. The texts are prefaced by an introductory summary where the author states somewhat dogmatically that the Baal-myths had no seasonal significance. Thus there is now ample opportunity to study the texts as a whole and to form an opinion of their general import and significance for kindred studies. There is nonetheless, as the numerous articles and monographs show, a great scope for original work on linguistic details, any one of which may vitally affect the general interpretation of the text. This is, however, no field for armchair philologists. The Ras Shamra texts not only demand a knowledge of the range of Semitic languages with a nice sensitivity to the nuances of words and phrases in their actual context in literature and in the spoken dialects of Syria and Palestine; they also demand familiarity with anthropology and a sympathy with primitive modes of thought and behaviour. GASTER is particularly sensitive to this, though often, one feels, his methods are somewhat Frazerian, and he might have made a stronger case had he been more selective in his analogies. We must also have regard to the relation of vocabulary and phraseology to the situation in life according to the methods of form-criticism, where such situations demand given forms of expression.

EISSFELDT [1]) has suggested a convenient division of the long literary texts of Ugarit between those which have as their heroes gods and those where the protagonists are human. The first are myths; the second may be broadly characterized as sagas or legends, though in the latter case modifications have to be made in this definition.

WILLIAM ROBERTSON SMITH has well warned us that in primitive religion myth, where not connected with ritual, which was primary, may be a misleading guide to religion [2]). There is no doubt that at the sophisticated stage which Philo of Byblos had reached, his philosophic reconstruction of Canaanite mythology, while often faithful enough to originals, is a hopelessly inadequate clue to Canaanite religion in the Bronze Age. Mesopotamian mythology too, except in the myth *enuma eliš* and the Descent of Ishtar, reflects rather the merging of the cults of the various city-states in the fluctuations of political life in Mesopotamia, and, but for the many ritual texts from the various archaeological sites in the land, would have given us a very inadequate idea of the religious life of the people. Not so the Ras Shamra myths, which, in spite of their literary development, generally reveal their connection with the rituals they supplement.

The bulk of the mythological poems concern Baal the Mighty,

---

1) O. EISSFELDT, 'Mythus und Saga in den Ras-Shamra-Texten', *Arabistik, Semitistik, und Islamswissenschaft*, 1944, pp. 275 ff.

2) W. ROBERTSON SMITH, *The Religion of the Semites*, 1894, pp. 17-19.

Aleyn Baal, who, incidentally, is not El Elyon of Genesis xiv, as has been stated. He is, as the Ras Shamra texts show, the God Hadad, 'the Thunderer', who is manifest in the violent storms of autumn and late winter. His stock epithet is 'He who Mounteth the Clouds' (*rkb ʿrpt*), a rôle and title which the Hebrews appropriated for Jahweh (Psalm lxviii, 5; civ, 3; Deuteronomy xxxiii, 26). Baal is opposed by two adversaries, the unruly waters, 'Prince Sea, even Judge River', and *Mot*, 'Death', the sinister power of drought and sterility. It is generally thought that there is a unity in the Baal-myths, but of this we are doubtful, for reasons which we shall elaborate in the proper place. [1]) We regard the texts describing the conflict of Baal and Mot as reflecting the progress and recession of growth in the Syrian peasant's year. The myth of Baal and the waters, on the other hand, while probably used at the annual autumn festival of the agricultural New Year, as the analogous Hebrew psalms on the theme of the kingship of Jahweh suggest, seems to have had a different origin. In theme and even in certain details the myth suggests the Babylonian myth *enuma eliš*, which celebrates the conflict of Marduk and Tiamat with her allies, the chaotic powers of the deep. Baal, like Marduk, eventually triumphs, and as champion of the gods he is established as king. This last feature gives the clue to the nature and purpose of the text. It is the Canaanite declaration of faith in Providence, and its regular, probably annual, repetition, with or without ritual acting, served the purpose of relieving the emotional tension felt by the community when the vital autumn rains (the 'early rains' of the Old Testament) were still pending, and of a rite of imitative magic to predispose the cosmic powers to a favourable issue; the community was also reassured and enabled to reassert its faith in the power of cosmos in a world of change and tension. We particularly emphasize this text in the literature of Ras Shamra since the theme of the victory of cosmos over chaos and the establishment of the divine kingship was adapted by the Hebrews after their settlement in Canaan, and, as we shall demonstrate, conditioned their thought on the subject of Providence in nature, history, and the moral order [2]) even to the fulfilment of the hope of the Kingdom of God in the advent of Our Lord.

---

[1]) *Vide infra* pp. 21 ff.

[2]) We agree with MOWINCKEL (*Psalmenstudien* ii, 1922) that the cult was the source of the Hebrew idea of the kingship of God. We believe that their familiarity with this idea dated from the time of their sojourn in Egypt and particularly at

We should distinguish between the myth just described and the rest of the Baal-texts, where the antagonist of the god is Mot, the power of death, drought, and sterility, whose home is appropriately the underworld. While admitting certain common features such as the struggle between Baal and his adversaries for the Kingship, and the building of a 'house' to signalize the supremacy of the god, we find no certain evidence of the unity of the myth of Baal and the Waters and Baal and Mot, which is nevertheless feasible. In the latter texts a prominent, often indeed the leading, rôle is played by the goddess Anat, the sister of Baal. Broadly speaking, those texts describe the tension between fertility and sterility, and thus reflect climatic conditions in Syria where the summer, if not actually a season of sterility, as GORDON has emphasized, [1]) is nevertheless a season of tension. Indeed, with spring rain (the 'latter rains' of the Old Testament) deficient or too long delayed when the corn is coming into ear, or with frequent or sustained siroccos and the absence of the normal heavy dew, the season could well be disastrous.

The chief themes are the death of Baal, his return to life, and the building of his 'house' (palace or temple). There is not yet unanimity among scholars as to the order of those events, and the major question is as to whether the texts refer to the annual cycle of vegetation or, as GORDON has contended, [2]) have no such seasonal significance but are related to the circumstances of the Sabbatical year at the end of a seven-year cycle. Our view is that certain of those texts were so applied, [3]) but our opinion is that the bulk of this mythology, though properly part of the liturgy of the autumnal New Year festival, is related to various phases in the year of the Syrian peasant. There are also, we believe, various quite definite indications of agricultural ritual underlying the myths.

Those myths are not primarily aesthetic nor speculative, but are

---

Baal-Saphon in Goshen, which, as the name indicates and as archaeological remains of the Roman Imperial period and a reference in Philo of Byblos (*Fragmenta Historiarum Graecarum* ed. Müller) show, was a cult-centre of Baal, who in Canaanite mythology won his kingship in conflict with the powers of Chaos typified by the unruly waters. See the writer's article on 'Canaanite Mythology and Hebrew Tradition', *Transactions of Glasgow University Oriental Society* XIV, 1953, pp. 47-57.

[1]) C. H. GORDON, 'Sabbatical Cycle or Seasonal Pattern? Reflections on a New Book' (A. S. KAPELRUD, *Baal in the Ras Shamra Texts*, 1952), *Orientalia* XXII, 1953, pp. 79 ff.

[2]) *Ibidem.*

[3]) *Vide infra*, pp. 38 ff.

functional, as first appreciated by F. F. HVIDBERG [1]). H. and H. A. FRANKFORT have well emphasized that there was for men in the ancient Near East an essential connection between reality and myth with of course its accompanying ritual. In the recurrent cycle of nature, to which no man at any stage of development can be indifferent, the Canaanites like their neighbours in Egypt and Mesopotamia were incapable of intellectual or speculative detachment; they were emotionally involved. 'Hence it seemed wise that man, each year, at the critical turn of the seasons should proclaim the knowledge which he shared with the powers, in order to involve them once more' in what these writers term the 'potent truth of nature which has disclosed itself to him' [2]). The actualization in myth and ritual of the initial establishment of Order against the menace of Chaos was at once a means of preserving the *status quo* and a provision for the future with the effect of relieving the emotional tension of men and of assuring them of the future. This aspect of myth, from the Babylonian point of view, was expressed by Gunkel in his well-known dictum *Endzeit wird Urzeit.* Here is indeed the source of eschatology, which was to become a characteristic of Jewish thought under the impetus of Israel's distinctively historical faith.

Myth then among the Canaanites, as elsewhere in the ancient Near East, was creative, the creative word, which, according to the current conception of the operative force of the spoken word cast in regular measure and graphic language and imagery, could double the efficacy of the ritual act. Both myth and ritual served to actualize the natural order and even, in the case of the royal legends of Krt and Aqht and the myth of the marriage of the Moon-god and Nkl and the actual marriage to which the latter part of that text relates, the social order. They were also instruments of imitative magic, designed to influence Providence by autosuggestion. This articulate expression of his aspirations and desires in myth and ritual was deemed by the Syrian peasant to be as vital as his actual labour on the land. Such rites of imitative magic, together with an intense sympathy with the powers and processes of nature are features of most primitive agricultural societies, and the Syrian peasants were no exception. Here we have, as GASTER has shown, [3]) the origins of the drama as it developed in Greece. It is possible to find elements in the Ras

[1]) F. F. HVIDBERG, *Graad og Latter i det Gamle Testament*, 1938.
[2]) H. and H. A. FRANKFORT, 'Myth and Reality', *Before Philosophy*, 1951, p. 16.
[3]) T. H. GASTER, *Thespis*, 1950.

Shamra myths which were fundamental in Greek drama, both tragedy and comedy, which also, of course, grew from the myth and ritual of seasonal festivals under very similar climatic conditions. While emphasizing the essential connection of myth with ritual, we recognize, nevertheless, that the myths of Ras Shamra have far outgrown their primitive origins. So far are they, indeed, from being the mere mechanical accompaniments of ritual that they have assumed the style and proportion of epics. [1]) Carefully redacted under the authority of the High Priest about 1400 B.C., as we know from colophons to certain texts, they stand as the finished product of a long period of literary development, as is recognized by all Ras Shamra specialists. We may add here that this careful elaboration and balance of thought and diction is a vital aid to the solution of many a hard problem in the vocabulary of the texts, a fact which is not always appreciated even by specialists.

Those then are the main features of the Baal-mythology of Ras Shamra. There is another text, GORDON *UH* 52, which also falls into the category of seasonal liturgy, though its *Sitz im Leben* is hard to determine. The second part of this text, the 'myth' properly speaking, describes in rather coarse terms how El seduced two women and begot the twin-gods *Šḥr* and *Šlm*, 'Dawn' and 'Evening'. [2]) GASTER has not failed to notice here the very broad humour which is characteristic of Greek comedy, [3]) which served the purpose of relief for the emotional tension in the seasonal rites observed by the primitive community. In the first half of this text there is also much

[1]) A similar development may be noted in the case of Greek drama. BAUMGARTNER however, considers that, though religious conceptions and cultic practices formed the material of the myths, these were developed as aesthetic works in their own right 'Ugaritische Probleme und ihre Tragweite für das Alte Testament', *TZ* III, 1947, pp. 89-91. So also EISSFELDT, *El im Ugaritischen Pantheon*, 1951, p. 58. This is also the opinion of DE LANGHE, who is much more reserved on the question of the relation of the Baal-myth to the cult, 'Myth, Ritual and Kingship in the Ras Shamra Tablets', *Myth, Ritual and Kingship*, ed. S. H. HOOKE, 1958, pp. 122-148.

[2]) It is generally suggested that *šlm* means 'peace', i.e. of evening. Peace, however, is a secondary meaning of *šlm*. The root meaning is 'completeness' hence we take *šlm* in the text to signify 'the completion of day', i.e. evening. The Venus star, Aṯtar in Semitic mythology, is, of course, denoted. In this text this astral deity is regarded as twins, so also at Palmyra the Venus star had two hypostases *Azizu* and *Arṣu*, and at Edessa the deity is hypostatised as the twins 'Azizos et Monimos' (Arab. *ʿazîz* and *munāʿim*) according to Julian. For further discussion of this question see the writer's article 'The Desert God ʿAṯtar in the Literature and Religion of Canaan', *JNES* VIII, 1949, pp. 74-75.

[3]) T. H. GASTER, *Thespis*, 1950, pp. 251 ff.

of vital significance. It is divided by a series of horizontal scores into a number of sections, some of which are rubrics relating to seasonal ritual and others are best explained as catchlines of hymns to be chanted at a particular point. This text then plainly demonstrates the close connection between myth and ritual. We believe too that in Psalm lxviii, which ALBRIGHT takes to be a catalogue of early Hebrew lyrics, [1]) we have an analogy to the hymns denoted by their catchlines in the Ugaritic text in question.

In his *editio princeps* of this text with translation and commentary [2]) VIROLLEAUD regarded it as a historical text, seeing references to Ashdod, the desert of Qadesh, and Arabs. He was, however, somewhat reserved in his conclusions. DUSSAUD, [3]) however, though admitting the strong liturgic element in the text, followed VIROLLEAUD and elaborated the theory that it concerned the establishment of a caravanserai between the Mediterranean and the Red Sea in the vicinity of Beersheba. Such historical interpretations [4]) are supported by presumed geographical references and even personal names, such as Etraḫ which was taken to be a form of Terah, the father of Abraham. More critical philology, however, and a fuller understanding of the style and whole context of the texts make such views no longer tenable. This applies also to the historical interpretation of other texts, notably the Krt and Dn'el—or rather 'Aqht—texts. Those two fall into EISSFELDT's second category, where the protagonists are not divine but human.

In his publication of the Krt text VIROLLEAUD [5]) propounded the sensational thesis that this was the historical record of the conflict between Krt, the legendary hero of the Phoenicians, and the people of Terah, the father of Abraham, in the Biblical Negeb, the steppe-land south of Palestine, involving vast numbers, 3,000,000, as the text

---

1) W. F. ALBRIGHT, 'A Catalogue of Early Hebrew Lyric Poems, (Psalm LXVIII)', *HUCA* XXIII, 1950-51, pp. 1-39.

2) C. VIROLLEAUD, 'La naissance des dieux gracieux et beaux, poème phénicien de Ras Shamra', *Syria* XIV, 1933, pp. 128-151.

3) R. DUSSAUD, 'Le commerce des anciens Phéniciens à la lumière du poème des dieux gracieux et beaux', *Syria* XVII, 1936, pp. 58-66.

4) A similar interpretation is that of G. A. BARTON, who appreciates the liturgical nature of much in the text, but elaborates the thesis that it is the liturgy of the spring festival at Jerusalem in patriarchal times. *JBL* LIII, 1934, pp. 61-78. BARTON bases his theory upon the presumed occurrence of geographical names, notably *šlm*, which he takes to be Salem, i.e. Jerusalem. This word, however, where it is not a divine name in the text, is a common noun.

5) C. VIROLLEAUD, *La Légende de Kéret, roi des Sidoniens*, 1936.

states with evident hyperbole. This involved, it was stated, displacement of whole ethnic groups, such as Asher and Zebulun, and occasioned a great social upheaval. The action was continued in Transjordan, where VIROLLEAUD located *ʾudm* of the text, identifying it with Biblical Edom. Most of those particular geographical references, however, and the presumed references to Terah have been explained by GORDON [1]) as common nouns with a quite different significance. Most critical scholars now, though seriously criticising VIROLLEAUD's particular interpretation, maintain that there is a historical nucleus in the text [2]) even though that is merely domestic history. This is our own position. A cultic interpretation was suggested by MOWINCKEL, [3]) who takes the hero King Krt as originally a dying and rising vegetation-deity of the Adonis type. The original god of the myth, however, has become the dynasty-founder of 'a mythic hero legend'. ENGNELL, [4]) on the other hand, as a result of very tendentious exegesis, regards the text as a pure cultic myth with no historical association. He suggests that the text is 'an older Canaanite pattern of the Old Testament sukkot-festival', the Feast of Tabernacles.

The Krt text as it stands does make a consistent whole, [5]) though

---

[1]) C. H. GORDON, 'TRḪ, ṮN, NKR in the Ras Shamra Tablets', *JBL* LVII, 1938, pp. 407-410. So ALBRIGHT, 'Was the patriarch Terah a Canaanite moongod?', *BASOR* 71, 1938, pp. 35-40, GASTER, 'Notes on Ras Shamra Texts, IV', *OLZ* XLII, 1939, cols. 273-276, PEDERSEN, 'Die Krt Legende', *Berytus* VI, 1941, pp. 63-105, and A. HERDNER, (review of Pedersen, *op. cit.*), *Syria* XXIII, 1942, pp. 275-285.

[2]) E.g. EISSFELDT, 'Zum geographischen Horizont der Ras Shamra Texte', *ZDMG* XCIV, 1940, pp. 59-85, ALBRIGHT, *BASOR* 94, 1944, p. 30, DE LANGHE, *Les textes de Ras Shamra-Ugarit et leurs rapports avec le milieu Biblique de l'Ancien Testament*, 1945, II, pp. 122-125, H. L. GINSBERG, 'The Legend of King Keret, a Canaanite Epic of the Bronze Age', *BASOR*, Supplementary studies 2-3, 1946, pp. 15 ff., GORDON, *UH*, 1947, p. 249, all take *ngb* in the Krt text to refer to a Southern locality, though not the Biblical Negeb in the South of Palestine. DE VAUX, while critical of the 'Negebite' theory of VIROLLEAUD and DUSSAUD, proposed to locate the action of the text in Galilee a few miles south-west of the south end of the Sea of Galilee where a number of modern place-names suggest localities which he claimed to find in the text, 'Le cadre géographique du poème de Krt', *RB* XLVI, 1937, pp. 362-372. Here a more scientific philology controlled by appreciation of the style of the texts renders such geographical references extremely unlikely, and it is notable that DE VAUX in his review of the writer's *Krt Text in the Literature of Ras Shamra* declares that he has abandoned this view, which, he states, was too good to be true, *RB* LXIV, 1957, pp. 313-314.

[3]) S. MOWINCKEL, *NTT* XLII, 1941, pp. 129-158. XLIII, 1942, pp. 24-26.

[4]) I. ENGNELL, *Studies in Divine Kingship*, 1943, pp. 149 ff.

[5]) The order of the fragments is as follows; GORDON *UH* Krt (VIROLLEAUD

the numerous lacunae make this somewhat skeletal. It may very well be that what is extant is but a fragment of a much fuller poem. It has been termed an epic rather than a myth. We hesitate to apply the term epic to the Krt text, though there is no doubt that the style here as in the Baal-myths is that characteristic of the epic. Whatever the original nature of the Krt text may have been, it did serve to formulate and so preserve certain customs and institutions in the social order, and so, like the Baal-myths, the Krt text was in effect, and probably also in origin, functional. The text served particularly as a charter for the royal office as leader in war and priest on whom the seasonal rites, such as desacralisation of the new crop, devolved. The primitive belief in the King as the dispenser of fertility, to the fluctuations of whose health nature herself is relative, also finds articulate expression here.

We believe that the historical nucleus of the text is the wedding of Krt, which we take to reflect a decisive stage in the symbiosis of Semite and Hurrian in North Syria about the beginning of the 2nd millennium, and probably also the foundation of a dynasty through the youngest daughter of the King, who is singled out for distinction in the text. Thereafter the text recording the foundation of a dynasty would probably serve on the occasion of royal weddings to give articulate expression to the hopes of the community which were centred in the king, the propagation of the royal line and office. It is, however, well-known that in the ancient Near East important social events were arranged to coincide with appropriate phases of nature. [1]) Thus we believe that Krt's wooing took place between the end of harvest [2]) and the New Year so that his marriage should be consummated at the New Year Festival which, we do not doubt,

---

I K), Gordon *UH* 128 (Virolleaud III K), Gordon *UH* 125, Gordon *UH* 126, Gordon *UH* 127 (Virolleaud II K).

[1]) In ancient Egypt the accession of the new Pharaoh officially coincided with sunrise at the beginning of some new phase in nature. The Zed-festival too, which signified the renewal of kingship, usually coincided with the first day of the first month Tybi in the 'Season of the Coming Forth', H. Frankfort, *Kingship and the Gods*, 1948, pp. 79, 102 ff. Similarly in the late Assyrian period Sargon celebrated the completion and dedication of his palace at Khorsabad in the middle of Tishritu. This was, of course the season of New Year, the beginning of the agricultural year. It was at this time too that Solomon dedicated the Temple at Jerusalem, 1 Kings viii, 2. There the month is named Ethanim, the month of the 'regular rains'.

[2]) This may be supported by the reference to Krt's baking of 'bread of the fifth, food of the sixth month', i.e. possibly a desacralisation rite as well as practical provisioning of his retinue after the barley and wheat harvest.

was associated with sexual licence as a rite of imitative magic on the eve of the new season of growth.

The last long text is that published by VIROLLEAUD as '*La légende de Dan'el*' (1936). Here we notice the spelling of Dan'el, which agrees with the consonantal spelling of the name of the primaeval hero in Ezekiel's denunciation of the King of Tyre (Ezekiel xiv, 14, 20). The text thus immediately invites investigation by any interested in the Old Testament.

The Dn'el, or rather Aqht, text is one of the most problematic in the whole collection. Though the *dramatis personae*, Dn'el and his son Aqht and his daughter *pġt* (the Maiden), are human characters, it is nonetheless true that the substance of the text, the real *agon*, is a conflict of wills between Aqht and the goddess Anat for the possession of a composite bow which had been made by the divine craftsman and destined for gods, but had been presented by him to Dn'el for his son Aqht. Thus myth is intermingled with saga.

The fusion of those two elements, with their respective divine and human figures, is the more natural owing to the fact that the ancient king, as we see from the case of Dn'el, had a sacral character. In the Aqht text, for instance, natural fertility fluctuates with the fortunes of the royal house, and Dn'el's stock epithet is *mt rp'e*, 'the healer', 'dispenser of fertility' [1]), in fact the 'medicine man'.[2]) This text describing the birth of the young prince Aqht, his conflict with the goddess Anat resulting in the death of the young hero, the consequences of his death, the mourning of his father Dn'el, and the blood-revenge sought by his sister make this text a most rewarding study, of foremost significance for our understanding of certain social values among the primitive Canaanites and their conception of the influence of the king on natural forces. It is not easy to determine the category of the text. At the moment we may say that we regard it as a saga which is in the process of becoming a myth, reserving a fuller discussion of the text for a more appropriate point in our work.

Those, then, are the main texts of Ras Shamra recovered in the pre-war phase of the excavation of Ras Shamra. Even from this

---

[1]) We take *rp'e* in the same sense in which it is used in Hebrew in Genesis xx, 17, where Jahweh restores fertility to the harem of Abimelech of Gerar, and in 2 Kings ii, 21, where Elisha restores the fertilising properties of the water of the spring at Jericho.

[2]) See further the writer's articles on this subject, 'The Rephaim', *PEQ* 1949, pp. 127-139, and 'DTN and RP'UM in ancient Ugarit', *PEQ* 1952, pp. 39-41.

general outline their bearing on the Old Testament and the anthropology of the ancient Near East ought to be apparent, and it will be our task to demonstrate this in detail. In many particulars the Hebrew settlers in Palestine served themselves heirs to the heritage of ancient Canaan. The first element to be adopted was no doubt the ritual and accompanying myth appropriate to the seasons of the agricultural year, and particularly to the transitional phases such as the New Year and the beginning and end of harvest. This matter would, of course, be preserved at the various local sanctuaries. The clearest indication of the Hebrew appropriation of a Canaanite myth is in the case of the establishment of God's kingship over the powers of Chaos, the unruly waters, which were later historicised as the political enemies of Israel, a theme which was carried over into Jewish apocalyptic, where it often reappears with many primitive features. This theme was appropriate to the New Year Festival. The next stage of the assimilation of this Canaanite matter was the literary stage when there was a conscious adaptation of Canaanite themes notably in the Psalms, in the later prophets, and in the Book of Job. Here the Canaanite mythology is used in more sporadic fashion, though there is an abundance of isolated motifs. With the themes and the poetic—sometimes epic—style of the Canaanite literary prototypes the Hebrews assimilated also, we believe, the Canaanite dialect, which came thus to supplant their native Aramaic. Thus the study of the Ras Shamra texts elucidates much obscurity in the vocabulary of the Old Testament and is, in fact, an essential instrument in the restoration of many a misunderstood or corrupt passage in the Old Testament.

CHAPTER II

MYTHS OF THE FERTILITY CULT

Of the longer literary texts of Ugarit those which have as their actors only gods fall, by analogy with other literatures, into the category of myths. We recognise, however, two connotations of the term 'myth'. The first is general, signifying, according to the definition of the Oxford Dictionary, a fictitious narrative involving supernatural persons and embodying popular ideas on natural phenomena etc. The second connotation of the term is more specific. Here the 'myth' (literally the 'word') is technically the spoken counterpart of ritual actions and has the purpose of making those explicit to the participants in the rites and of making those rites as acts of imitative magic doubly effective. This latter usage of myth, we think, was primary in the ancient Near East. The 'myth', or articulate expression of the ritual acts, eventually developed into a coherent narrative, and by the time that the Ras Shamra texts were redacted in the middle of the 2nd millennium B.C. we see that the Canaanite myth had assumed the proportions and style of epic. Certain of those myths, we believe, exhibit their close association with seasonal ritual, particularly those dealing with the conflict between Baal and Mot (Gordon *UH* 49, 51, 62, 67, 'nt). Other texts again are apparently less concerned with seasonal ritual than with the cosmic theme of the triumph of Providence over the powers of disorder depicted in the myth of the conflict of Baal and the unruly waters (Gordon *UH* 129, 137, 68). Further, a certain episode might be abstracted from the mythology at a more or less advanced stage of its development and adapted as an aetiological myth with the purpose of explaining or sanctioning some ritual or social practice (e.g. Gordon *UH* 75) [1]. These conceptions of myth in the general and specific senses must be kept clearly in mind as we approach the study of the main body of the myths of Ras Shamra, which are associated with Baal the Mighty ('Al'eyn Baal).

The most active deity in the pantheon of Ugarit, at least on the evidence of the extant texts, is Baal, the Amorite storm-god

---

[1]) *Vide infra*, pp. 75 ff.

Hadad. [1]) His temple with its adjuncts on the most conspicuous site of the city corroborates this impression. This deity was manifest in the thunder, lightning, massed storm-clouds and violent rains of autumn, the 'early rains' (יורה) of the Old Testament, which soften the hard-baked crust of the earth and inaugurate the new season's cultivation. As such Hadad was acclaimed as the Baal, 'lord', par excellence, on whom the life of the community and indeed of all nature in those latitudes depended. He was thus regarded as the almighty power which sustained ordered nature, or Cosmos, against the menace of Chaos or blind caprice and ungoverned violence. Those vital rains of autumn, however, which lash down in solid sheets of water might be a menace in themselves. Indeed we have known a case where a dozen Jewish colonists were engulfed and drowned in the sudden flood of a small wadi in the Galilean foothills which not half-an-hour before had been absolutely dry. The normally insignificant stank of the Qishon played a similar rôle on that memorable day when 'the stars in their courses fought against Sisera'. A glance at the terraced hillsides of Palestine and Syria or the ruins of Nabataean and Byzantine terracing and damming of wadis in the Negeb and Transjordan remind us of the perpetual danger of soil erosion. The vital resources of the land might in fact bleed away unless the god of the autumn storms prescribed a 'hitherto and no further', setting to the waters 'a bound that they may not pass over' (Psalm civ, 9). [2]) More specifically, so far as the Ras Shamra myth of Baal and the waters is concerned, sustained storms at sea might dam back the watercourses in the coastal plain, which we have seen thus inundated in the neighbourhood of Ras Shamra as late as January. In an early season of sowing this could destroy the growing crop, while in a late season it might defer sowing until it was too late for the crop to mature before the siroccos of summer checked the growth.

This theme, as our last citation suggests, was familiar to the Hebrews and finds frequent expression in the Old Testament in the motif of the conflict of God and the unruly waters as, for instance, in Psalms lxxiv, 12-19; lxxxix, 10-15; xciii. [3]) In those instances the

---

[1]) GORDON *UH* 51, VI, 39; VII, 36, 38; 67, II, 22; ʿnt, pl. x, V, 17; 75, I, 41, II, 6, 23.

[2]) GASTER would explain the Ugaritic text as the mythologisation of the natural rivalry between the rain and the river as sources of irrigation. *Iraq* IV, 1937, p. 21. The difficulty in this view is that the Sea is not the source of irrigation.

[3]) In such passages we have instances of the theme of the kingship of God won in conflict with the powers of Chaos in its actual cultic context, which, as

association of this divine conflict with creation, as in Psalms lxxiv and lxxxix, indicates the cosmic significance of the theme. We believe that the Canaanite theme of Baal's conflict with the tyrannical waters of Sea and River, which many of the Old Testament passages verbally re-echo, had a similar significance, though we must emphasize that the creation theme was not part of the Baal-myth, El and not Baal being creator in Canaanite thought. Furthermore, a comparison of the Ras Shamra mythology with the mythology of Mesopotamia shows clearly that, though the Ugaritic mythology is singularly independent of that of Mesopotəmia, [1]) there is an undoubted affinity between the three Ugaritic fragments describing the conflict of Baal and the waters and the myth *enuma eliš* describing the conflict of Marduk and Tiamat. [2]) Handling as it does the themes of kingship among the gods, creation, and the recovery of the tablets of destiny consequent upon Marduk's victory over Tiamat and her chaotic allies, there is no doubt of the cosmic significance of that myth, a fact which is clearly indicated by its use at the Babylonian *akitu*,

---

Zechariah xiv, 16-17 suggests, was the annual Feast of Tabernacles on the eve of the winter rains. This suggests that the Baal-myth too had a similar *Sitz im Leben*, even though, as DRIVER claims (*op. cit.*, p. 20), there is no explicit evidence in the texts of their relation to annual occasions.

[1]) This, of course, applies to the Baal cycle in the main. In the case of the myth dealing with the marriage of the Moon-god *yrḫ* and his consort *nkl* we see the penetration of a Mesopotamian cult, probably from Harran, which was a centre of the cult of the Sumerian Moon-god Sin and of his consort Nin-gal. The cult of this goddess in Harran is indicated in the Syriac '*Doctrine of Addai*', which refers to Beth Nikkal, and also by Clemens Romanus (CHWOLSON, *Ssabier und Ssabismus*, 1856, I, p. 400). It was on his return from the temple of Selene, apparently at some distance from the actual city of Harran, that the Emperor Caracalla was assassinated in 217 A.D., according to Herodian, iv, 13. On the topography and history of Harran see SETON LLOYD and W. BRICE, 'Harran', *Anatolian Studies* I, 1951, pp. 77-111. The cult of Nikkal and Sin is attested in the 7th century in North Syria at Neirab, 5 ml. S.E. of Aleppo and 95 ml. N.E. of Ras Shamra, in the stelae of Sin-zeraban and Agbar, COOKE, *NSI* 64, 65.

[2]) Common features are the helplessness of the gods before the insolent adversary, the emergence of the young god as their champion, and the kingship as the consequence of his victory. In particular the naming of the weapons of Baal to suggest their purpose and potency recalls the naming of the animals which draw Marduk's chariot, 'the Destructive, the Pitiless, the Trampler, the Fleet'. Such similarities, as well as more striking divergences between the Canaanite and Mesopotamian mythologies suggest that CLAY was right in supposing that *enuma eliš* was an amalgamation of Amorite and Sumerian traditions and such features as it shared with the Hebrew creation narratives were the specifically Amorite features already developed in the West before the Amorite expansion into Mesopotamia. *Amurru, the Home of the Northern Semites*, 1909, pp. 53-54. *The Origin of Biblical Traditions*, 1923, pp. 23 ff.

or Spring New Near festival, which is attested at least from the time of Nebuchadrezzar. [1])

The Canaanite myth in question is contained in the three fragments which we have already cited as GORDON *UH* 129, 137, and 68. [2])

The first of these texts (GORDON *UH* 129) is very fragmentary and gives little information beyond the fact that Sea the Prince (*ẓbl ym*) has a 'house', whereas some other deity has none, [3]) but complains: [4])

lblm ʾard bnpšny	'Am I to come down with my offspring [5]) to dampness, [6])
trḥṣn kṯrm bbt ym.	And the Skilly Ones [7]) wash him in the house of Sea?'

The identity of the unfortunate deity is uncertain, but we think he is Baal, though we admit that GASTER may well be right in supposing the deity to be Aṯtar, the deity associated with irrigation. [8]) This deity is certainly mentioned in the text (l. 24), but in the state

[1]) N. H. SNAITH, *The Jewish New Year Festival*, 1947, pp. 212 ff. A. HEIDEL, *The Babylonian Genesis*, 1942, pp. 3-4.

[2]) We agree with G. R. DRIVER (*Canaanite Myths and Legends*, 1956, pp. 11-12) that the text GORDON *UH* ʿnt pl. ix and x (VIROLLEAUD VI AB) is probably an earlier episode of this theme. This very fragmentary tablet contains certain passages peculiar to the text GORDON ʿnt (VIROLLEAUD V AB) and may be restored to a certain extent from the latter text. These, however, are really no more than stock phrases common in similar situations in epic style, and there is no real reason for connecting the two texts. The theme is the inauguration of an era of peace and plenty consequent upon the building of a 'house' for a certain god. This favoured deity is apparently the son of El named Yw, the Beloved of El. From the latter title it would seem that the deity is Ym (Sea), to the building of whose 'house' the text GORDON *UH* 129 refers. In these two texts the inveterate enmity of Baal and Ym is foreshadowed.

[3]) GORDON *UH* 129, 19-20. Aṯtar is mentioned in the fragmentary text and may be the deity in question, as A. CAQUOT suggests ('Le dieu ʿAthtar et les textes de Ras Shamra', *Syria* XXXV, 1958, pp. 45-59), but this is uncertain. This passage is the same as in GORDON *UH* 51, where it is stated that Baal has no temple like the other gods.

[4]) GORDON *UH* 129, 20-21. It will be noted that we read the third letter *l* () instead of *ʾu* () which GORDON reads at this point.

[5]) We connect *npšny* with the Arabic نفاس , 'childbirth'.

[6]) We explain *lblm* as *bl* with the preposition *l* and the final *m* to emphasise the preposition. We suggest that *bl* is the cognate of the Arabic بلّ, 'to be wet'.

[7]) From the texts GORDON *UH* Aqht and 77 we know that the Skilly Women assisted at births. Here, however, the masculine form *kṯrm* is strange, since men did not assist at birth. It is possible that this is a scribal error or even a fault in the clay tablet (*m* = ; *t* = ).

[8]) GASTER, *Thespis*, 1950, p. 133. So also DRIVER, *op. cit.*, pp. 12-13, 77-79.

of the text nothing certain can be stated about the rôle that Aṯtar plays here. It may well be that he is introduced as a foil to the efficacy of Baal, a part which he plays in the text Gordon *UH* 49.

The second fragment (Gordon *UH* 137) is better preserved and more explicit. The Sea sends his two messengers with a defiant message to El and the heavenly assembly on the sacred mount, [1]) and peremptorily demands the surrender of Baal: [2])

tn ʾelm dtqh	'Give up, ye gods, him whom ye guard, [3])
dtqyn hmlt	Even him whom together [4]) ye preserve. [3])
tn bʿl wʿnnh	Give up Baal, even himself, [5])
bn dgn ʾarṯm pǯh.	The son of Dagon that I may inherit his portion.' [6])

The gods receive this delegation in abject submission, which is reminiscent of the attitude of the Babylonian pantheon to Tiamat. They actually agree to surrender Baal: [7])

hlm . ʾelm . tphhm	Lo! the gods saw them,
tphn . mlʾak . ym	They saw the messengers of Sea,
tʿdt . ṯpṭ . nhr	The witnesses [8]) of River the Ruler.

---

[1]) The phrase 'mount of assembly' does not actually occur, but there is reference in this text (ll. 14, 15, 20, 31) to the divine 'convocation of the assembly' (*pḫr mʿd*) on a mountain called *ġr ll*, where they feast, like the Scandinavian gods in Aasgard. The conception of the mountain of god as a sort of Canaanite Olympus is found in Ezekiel xxviii, 14, and the 'mount of assembly in the extremities of Saphon' in Isaiah xiv, 13 is, of course, a specific reference to this. Armageddon of Revelation xvi, 16 may well be a Greek corruption of הר מועד rather than of הר מגדו as is popularly supposed.

[2]) Gordon *UH* 137, 18-19, 34-35.

[3]) We connect *tqh* and *tqyn* with the Arabic وق 'to keep'.

[4]) *hmlt*, literally 'a crowd', is probably used adverbially.

[5]) *ʿnnh* suggests the use of the phrases *ʿnn ʾaṯrt* in Gordon *UH* 51, IV, 59, where El asks indignantly if he and Aṯerat 'herself' are expected to set to work and build a temple with their own hands, and *ʿnn ʾelm ʾatm* in Gordon *UH* ʿnt, IV, 76, where Anat impatiently taunts the messengers of Baal that they are too slow and she will undertake the return journey herself for 'ye are but images of gods'. The sense of those passages is best served by connecting *ʿnn* with the Arabic عنّ, 'to appear'.

[6]) So Driver (*op. cit.*, pp. 79, 163), who cites Syriac and Hebrew cognates (e.g. פסה, Psalm lxxii, 16) which he takes as Egyptian loan-words, a probable solution in view of the peculiar sibilant in the Ugaritic word.

[7]) Gordon *UH* 137, 21 ff., 36 ff.

[8]) *tʿdt* is best explained as an abstract noun used as a collective, cf. *ṣrt* in Gordon *UH* 68, 9 and in Hebrew ארחת, 'travellers', גולה, 'exiles', יושבת, 'inhabitants', Isaiah xii, 6; Micah i, 11 ff., and איבת 'enemies', Micah vii, 8, 10 and possibly Nahum i, 9 לא תקום פעמים צרה. In this case there is no need to read a masculine plural subject with Albright, who claims a case of a masculine plural subject with the imperfect of a verb with preformative *t*, as in Ugaritic, *CBQ* VII, 1945, p. 23.

tġly.ʾelm.rʾešthm	The gods lowered [1]) their heads
lẓr.brkthm	On to their knees,
wlkḥṯ.ẓblhm	Yea, on to the seats of their nobility.
. . . .	. . . .
(wyʿn).ṯr.ʾabh.ʾel	(Then answered) the Bull his father El.
ʿbdk.bʿl.y ymm	'Thy servant is Baal, O Sea,
ʿbdk.bʿl.(y ym)	Thy slave is Baal, O Sea.
bn.dgn.ʾasrkm	The son of Dagon is thy bondman; [2])
hw.ybl.ʾargmnk	He will be given as thy tribute. [3])
kʾelm ( )ybl	When the gods give [4]) thee tribute,
wbn.qdš.mnḥyk	The Sons of Holiness [5]) are thy tributaries.' [6])

Baal, however makes a spirited reply. He plucks up courage (*ʾanš*) [7]), seizes weapons, and makes an onslaught on the insolent messengers, [8]) but is forcibly restrained for the sake of decorum by

---

[1]) *ġly*, as we know from the opposite *nšʾu* in l. 29, means 'to lower'.

[2]) Literally 'thy prisoner'.

[3]) *ʾargmn* is found with this sense in Niqmad's letter to his Hittite overlord Šubbiluliuma, GORDON *UH* 118, 18, 24. In view of the general connotation of the word here DRIVER (*op. cit.*, p. 81) is hardly right in rendering it 'purple' in the Baal-text, though he has regard to the general meaning of *ʾargmn* in the letter cited in translating '(tribute of) purple', taking 'purple' as the primary meaning of the word, which is the only sense it bears in Hebrew and Akkadian. We prefer, with DRIVER, to take *ybl* as passive. As a slave Baal will be handed over as tribute.

[4]) In Hebrew the root יבל is found with this same technical sense in Zephaniah iii, 10, and Hosea xii, 2. We follow DRIVER in taking *k* in *kʾelm* (   ) *ybl* in the temporal rather than the causal sense.

[5]) The question arises here as to whether *qdš* denotes the goddess Aṯerat as mother of the gods in her hypostasis as Qodšu who is known from inscribed Egyptian steles of the XIXth Dynasty, as DUSSAUD maintains, *Les Découvertes de Ras Shamra* . . . 2nd ed., 1941 pp., 106-109, or simply denotes holiness as the essential attribute of divinity. The phrase *bn qdš* probably means simply 'holy ones'.

[6]) מנחה bears this specific sense in 2 Samuel viii, 2, 6.

[7]) DRIVER takes *ʾanš* as cognate with the Arabic أنس, 'to be sociable' or 'gentle', the passage being El's attempt to allay the suspicion of Sea that Baal would not readily surrender. *op. cit.*, pp. 13, 81. AISTLEITNER's proposal 'plucks up courage', lit. 'plays the man' (*Die mythologischen und kultischen Texte aus Ras Shamra*, 1959, p. 37; *Wörterbuch* 318) is also a possibility, which, in view of the phrase והיו לאנשים (1 Samuel iv, 9, cf. 1 Kings ii, 2), we adopt.

[8]) GORDON *UH* 137, 39 ff.

( ) *yʾuḫd byd*	A ? he seizes in his hand,
mšḫṭ bm ymn	A knife in his right hand.
mḫṣ ġlmm.	He has smitten the servants . . . .

the goddesses Anat and Aṯtrt. So Baal, like Marduk in *enuma eliš*, becomes the champion of the gods. [1])

The third text after a mutilated beginning continues: [2])

wʿn kṯr wḫss	Then up spake the Skilful and Percipient One.
lrgmt lk lẓbl bʿl	'Have I not told thee, O Prince Baal,
ṯnt lrkb ʿrpt	Have I not repeated, O thou who mountest the clouds? [3])
ht ʾebk bʿlm	Behold, thine enemy, O Baal,
ht ʾebk tmḫṣ	Behold, thine enemy thou shalt smite:
ht tṣmt ṣrtk	Behold, thou shalt subdue thine adversaries. [4])
tqḥ mlk ʿlmk	Thou shalt take thine eternal kingdom,
drkt dt drdrk	Thy sovereignty everlasting.' [5])
kṯr ṣmdm ynḥt	The Skilful One hews out a double mace, [6])
wypʿr šmthm	And proclaims [7]) its name. [8])

1) Gordon *UH* 137,

(24) *bhm.ygʿr.bʿl*	Among them Baal cries out:
. . . .	. . . .
(27) *šʾu.ʾelm.rʾaštkm*	'Lift up, O gods, your heads
lẓr.brktkm	From (the top of) your knees.
ln.kḥṯ.ẓblkm	Take your ease on your princely thrones.
wʾank.ʿny.mlʾak.ym	And I will answer the messengers of Sea,
tʿdt.ṯpṭ.nhr	Even the witnesses of River the Ruler . . .'

2) Gordon *UH* 68, 7-32.

3) The verb *rkb* means just this and not 'rider', or even, as Kapelrud has recently translated it, 'driver', *Baal in the Ras Shamra Texts*, 1952, pp. 61 ff., cf. De Langhe, 'De Betekenis van het Hebreeuwse Werkwoord רכב', *Handelingen van het XVIIIe Vlaamse Filologencongres*, 1949, pp. 89-96. The imagery is reproduced almost verbatim in Psalm lxviii, 5 סלו לרכב בערבות, where the Ras Shamra texts support the Massoretic reading with the meaning suggested by the emendation עבות for ערבות. The same imagery, with שמים for ערבות is found in v. 34 and in Deuteronomy xxxiii, 26. The imagery, with the secondary meaning of רכב is found in Psalm civ, 3. ערבות may be a dialectic variant for ערפות, though it may also be a simple scribal error for ערפות, the regular form of the word in the cognate Semitic languages, as Ginsberg proposes, *JBL* LXII, 1943, pp. 112-113.

4) *ṣrt* is a case of the abstract noun used as a collective. *Vide supra*, p. 24, n. 8.

5) The 'everlasting sovereignty' of God, familiar in the Old Testament, is now seen to rest, at least in its liturgic context, on a Canaanite cliché. We agree with Mowinckel (*Psalmenstudien* ii, 1922) that the conception of the kingship of Jahweh among the Hebrews had its root in the cult. See the writer's articles on 'Canaanite Mythology and Hebrew Tradition' in *Transactions of Glasgow University Oriental Society* XIV, 1953, pp. 55-57, 'The Hebrew Conception of the Kingship of God: its Origin and Development', *VT* VI, 1956, pp. 268-285.

6) *ṣmdm* is in form a plural, but, as the sequel shows, a single weapon is denoted. This was probably thought of as having a dual aspect; the mace-head may have been in two halves, or have had a groove, a vestige of the thong-groove, which gave it this aspect.

7) The verb *pʿr* is always found in this context of naming in the Ras Shamra texts, cf. Gordon *UH* 75, I, 28-29; ʿnt, pl. x, IV, 15, 17, 19.

8) On the plural suffix see n. 6. The noun *šmt* is reminiscent of the Akkadian

šmk ʾat ygrš	'Thy name is Driver;
ygrš grš ym	Driver, drive Sea,
grš ym lksʾeh	Drive Sea from his throne,
nhr lkḥṯ drkth	Even River from the seat of his sovereignty.
trtqṣ bd bʿl	Thou shalt soar and swoop in the hand of Baal,
km nšr bʾuṣbʿth	Even as an eagle in his fingers. [1]
hlm ktp zbl ym	Strike the shoulders of Prince Sea,
bn ydm ṯpṭ nhr	Even the breast [2] of River the Ruler.'
yrtqṣ ṣmd bd bʿl	Then soars and swoops the mace in the hand of Baal,
km nšr bʾuṣbʿth	Even as an eagle in his fingers.
ylm ktp zbl ym	It smites the shoulders of Prince Sea,
bn ydm ṯpṭ nhr	Even the breast of River the Ruler.
ʿz ym lymk	Sea is strong; he does not subside; [3]
ltngṣn pnth	His strength [4] is not impaired; [5]
lydlp tmnh	His dexterity [6] fails not. [7]
kṯr ṣmdm ynḥt	The Skilful One hews out a double mace
wypʿr šmthm	And proclaims its name.
šmk ʾat ʾaymr	'Thy name is Expeller. [8]

šimtu, 'destiny', and this may be the meaning here, though the name could, and generally did, declare the destiny or purpose of the object. In connection with *kṯr*'s naming of the weapon, itself an act of imitative magic, we may note the tradition transmitted by Philo that Χουσορ was the inventor not only of crafts but of magic and incantation.

[1]) Gaster supposes that *ʾuṣbʿt* refers to the talons of the eagle, *Thespis*, p. 157. The parallelism with *bd*, 'in the hand', however, indicates that the word means 'fingers'.

[2]) We translate *bn ydy* (literally, 'between the hands') as 'in front', i.e. 'on the breast', on the analogy of the Arabic بين يدى .

[3]) For the meaning of *ymk* cf. Ecclesiastes x, 18 בעצלות ידים ימך המקרה ובשפלות ידים ידלף הבית. The root is found in the Hophal in Job. xxiv, 24, and is plausibly conjectured in Deuteronomy xxxiii, 3 in והם תכו ברגלך, reading וְהָמְתְּכוּ ברגליך, F. Cross and D. N. Freedman, 'The Blessing of Moses', *JBL* LXVII, 1948, pp. 193-200. TheIfteʿal (reflexive) form is well attested in Ugaritic and occurs in the Mesha inscription (c. 830 B.C.).

[4]) *pnt* suggests the Arabic فَنَّة, 'abundance', hence our translation, 'strength'.

[5]) *tngṣn* seems a cognate of the Arabic نغص, 'to be interrupted' (as camels at water). The final *n* is the energic ending of the imperfect. Driver's equation of the verb *ngṣ* with the Arabic نغث, 'to oscillate', flagrantly flouts the principles of phonetic correspondence in Semitic dialects (*op. cit.*, p. 156).

[6]) *tmnh* is usually taken as 'his form', Hebrew תמונה. We connect it with *ymn*, 'right hand', hence 'dexterity'. The formation with initial *t* to a root with initial י or ו is well known in Hebrew, e.g. תודה from ידה, תורה from ירה, and תימן from ימן, etc.

Our conjecture is corroborated by the parallel *pnth*, 'his strength'.

[7]) On *ydlp* see the Hebrew passage cited in n. 3.

[8]) On the analogy of the former name, which has the form of the imperfect *ygrš*, *ʾaymr* should be an imperfect. The initial *ʾa*, however, is a problem. This

'aymr mr ym	Expeller, expel Sea,
mr ym lks'eh	Expel Sea from his throne,
nhr lkḥṯ drkth	Even River from the seat of his sovereignty.
trtqṣ bd b'l	Thou shalt soar and swoop in the hand of Baal,
km nšr b'uṣb'th	Even as an eagle in his fingers.
hlm qdqd zbl ym	Smite the pate of Prince Sea,
bn 'nm ṯpṭ nhr	Between the eyes [1]) of River the Ruler,
yprsḥ ym wyql l'arṣ	That Sea may collapse and fall to the ground.'
wyrtqṣ ṣmd bd b'l	Then soars and swoops the mace in the hand ot Baal,
km nšr b'uṣb'th	Even as an eagle in his fingers.
ylm qdqd zbl ym	It smites the head of Prince Sea,
bn 'nm ṯpṭ nhr	Between the eyes of River the Ruler.
yprsḥ ym yql l'arṣ	Sea collapses and falls to the ground;
tnġṣn pnth	His strength is impaired;
wydlp tmnh	His dexterity fails.
yqṯ b'l wyšt ym	Baal drags Sea away [2]) and disperses him; [3])
ykly ṯpṭ nhr	He annihilates River the Ruler.
bšm tg'rm 'ṯtrt	Exultantly [4]) Aṯtarat [5]) cries out.

---

is probably an interjection; an instance of its use with the verb (optative perfect probably) is Gordon *UH*, krt, 201. Here it is vocalized *'e*, probably by assimilation, e.g. *'e'eṯt*. Another possibility is that in *'aymr* we have an imperative of the verb *mrr* with the initial interjection *'ay*, which is actually found with the imperative in Gordon *UH* 52, 6

lḥm blḥm 'ay	'Ho, eat of the meat,
wšty bḥmr yn 'ay	Ho, drink of the ferment of wine '

The verb is, of course, cognate with the Arabic مرّ, 'to pass', and is attested in the Amarna Tablets in the causative in the correspondence of Ribaddi of Byblos referring to the repulse of the predatory bands GAZ, *tušamriru GAZ*, J. A. Knudtzon, *Die El-Amarna Tafeln*, 1908-15, 77, 1. 24.

1) There is most likely a word-play here between the two meanings of *'n*, 'eye' and 'spring'.

2) *yqṯ* suggests the Arabic قثّ, 'to drag'.

3) *yšt* is probably the cognate of the Arabic شتّ, 'to scatter', so J. Obermann, *JAOS* LXVII, 1947, p. 205. The scattering of the conquered enemy dragged out of his native element seems to have been known to Ezekiel who twice (xxix, 5 and xxxii, 4-5) refers to such treatment of תנים (*sic* according to certain Hebrew MSS). Both of these passages refer to the victory of God over the unruly waters symbolized in certain aquatic monsters, and the stereotyped diction and imagery strongly suggests the influence of myth fixed by cultic usage.

4) We explain *bšm* as *bš*, cognate with the Arabic بشّ, 'to rejoice', with final *m* used as a substitute for a preposition, tantamount to an adverbial usage as in Hebrew יומם, פתאם, חנם, and ריקם.

5) Only in this myth is this goddess really active. It is noteworthy that in an Egyptian papyrus from the early XIXth Dynasty there is preserved a myth in which the Sea appears as an arrogant tyrant demanding tribute (cf. Gordon *UH* 137, 37, and *supra*, p. 22) and is appeased by the giving of Aṯtrt as a bride. The papyrus, unfortunately, is too fragmentary to permit of any certain reconstruction, but there are sufficient motifs in common with the three Ras Shamra

bṯ lʾalʾeyn bʿl	'Scatter him, O Mighty Baal,
bṯ lrkb ʿrpt	Scatter him, O thou who mountest the clouds,
kšbyn ẓb(l ym	For Prince Sea has held us captive,
k) šbyn ṯpṭ nhr	He held us captive, even River the Ruler.'
wyṣʾa b( )	Then B(aal) goes out,
ybṯ nn ʾalʾeyn bʿl	Baal the Mighty scatters him, [1]
w( ) ym lmt	And ( ) Sea to death.
bʿlm yml (k)	Let Baal [2] reign! [3]
....	....

The end of the text is unfortunately fragmentary: [4]

ḥm. lšrr ( )	Eager to reign ( )
yʿn. ym lmt ( )	He answered, Sea is indeed dead ( )
lšrr. wtʿ(n ʿṯtrt)	( ) to reign, and (Attrt) replied,
bʿlm hmt ( )	( ) for ever(?) ( )
brʾešh. ( )	( ) on his head ( )
(bn) ydh ( )	His breast ( )
(b)n ʿnh ( )	Between his eyes ( )

DRIVER is probably right in giving the meaning of *ḥm. lšrr*, *brʾešh*, and *bn ydh* after the translation we have given. [5] KAPELRUD tentatively proposes on the basis of the reference to bodily parts in the last three lines to see a parallel to the dismemberment of the corpse of Tiamat as a prelude to creation in *enuma eliš*. [6] This, if he is right, would be the only association with creation in the Baal-myth of Ras Shamra. We think it more likely that after the references to the kingship of Baal the fragmentary passage refers to the investiture of Baal with

fragments we are now considering to suggest to us that the papyrus fragments are the local version of the myth of the conflict of Baal and the unruly waters, and probably the cult-legend of a Canaanite shrine in or near the Delta, most likely Baal Zaphon, where there was an influx of Canaanite influence towards the end of the XVIIIth Dynasty and especially in the XIXth, A. H. GARDINER, 'The Astarte Papyrus', *Studies presented to F. Ll. Griffiths*, 1932, pp. 74-85.

[1]) In view of the probable significance of *nn* as a pronominal suffix Driver's translation 'he is ashamed of her' (*op. cit.* p. 83) is barely feasible. We propose to take *bṯ* as cognate with the Arabic بثّ, 'to scatter', *v. supra*, p. 28, n. 3.

[2]) The final *m* in *bʿlm* is probably an emphatic enclitic. The phrase was probably a cultic exclamation to be voiced by the worshippers, cf. *mardukma šarru*, 'Marduk is king' in *enuma eliš*.

[3]) This is probably the acclamation of the worshipping community, as יהוה מלך was in the Hebrew community. In such Hebrew psalms as this phrase is found in we note that the theme is the same as in the Baal-myth, the conflict between the powers of Cosmos and Chaos and the victory and kingship of God.

[4]) GORDON, *UH* 68, 33-40.

[5]) DRIVER, *op. cit.*, pp. 82-83.

[6]) A. S. KAPELRUD, 'Baal's Kamp med Havets Fyrste i Ras Sjamra-Tekstene,' *NTT* 1960, pp. 249-50.

the crown and pectoral of royalty, including perhaps the counterpart to the 'tablets of destiny' of Babylonian mythology.

The fragmentary nature of this text naturally invites speculation as to its full content. Would the full text, for instance, reveal closer correspondence with the Mesopotamian text *enuma eliš*, an important feature of which was the creation of nature and man by the victorious god Marduk respectively from the dismembered corpse of Tiamat and the blood of her ally Kingu ? To this question KAISER replies in the negative, [1]) noting that in the Ras Shamra text the earth with its seas and rivers is already created and the conflict between Baal and the Waters is for sovereignty over the earth. The same, however, might be said of the Babylonian myth, and KAISER's argument is altogether too naive in view of the fact that cultic myth of this type cannot be limited by logic, as KAPELRUD well observes. [2]) The myth here is not speculative but creative. It is not the first stammerings of a scientific cosmology, but the means whereby the community sacramentally experienced the triumph of their god over chaos, sustaining their faith in the power of Providence in the present and in the future with all its hazards.

Sharing our own caution against seeking too close analogy with *enuma eliš* in spite of striking echoes of its major themes, KAPELRUD propounds his view of the Canaanite counterpart to the dismemberment of Tiamat with commendable reserve. With like caution KAPELRUD cites the references to the slaughter of certain monstrous adversaries of Baal, notably *ltn* and *tnn*, in which we recognize Leviathan and Tannin of the Old Testament. In the only passage in which *ltn* is actually named [3]) Baal is given the credit of slaying the

---

[1]) O. KAISER, *Die mythische Bedeutung des Meeres in Ägypten, Ugarit, und Israel*, *BZAW* LXXVIII, 1962.

[2]) KAPELRUD, *op. cit.*, p. 248.

[3]) GORDON *UH* 67, I, 1-7.

ktmḫṣ.ltn.bṯn.brḥ	'Though thou didst smite Ltn the Primaeval Serpent,
tkly.bṯn ʿqltn	And didst annihilate the Crooked Serpent,
šlyṭ.dšbʿt.rʾašm	The Close-coiling One of Seven Heads,
ṯṯkḥ.ttrp.šmm	The heavens will dry up, yea, languish;
krs.ʾepdk.ʾank.ʾespʾe	I shall pound thee, consume thee, and eat thee,
ʾuṭm.šrqm.ʾamtm	Cleft, forspent, and exhausted.
lyrt.bnpš.bn.ʾelm.mt	Thou shalt indeed go down into the throat of Mt the son of El.'

Those words are addressed by Mot through his emissaries to Baal. In this passage *ttrp* may be connected with the Arabic root ترف, 'to be softened by luxury', or may be the reflexive of the intensive form of *rpy*, cognate with the

monster. In another passage, however, among various monsters which Anat claims to have slain [1]) 'the crooked serpent, the Close-

Hebrew רפה, 'to droop', as DRIVER suggests (*op. cit.*, pp. 105, 155). For *krs* DRIVER reads *krks*, postulating haplography of the sign *k*, an easy error after *k* (⊏⊢) and *r* (⊏⊏⊢). His translation of *krks ʾepdk* is 'like the belt of thy mantle'. The reference to the drooping of the heavens like the slackening of Baal's belt is not easily understood. We prefer to read *krs*, taking it as a participle, cognate with the Arabic كرص, 'to pound'. We suggest that *ʾepd* is the imperfect of the verb *npd*, cognate with the Arabic نفد, 'to consume'. We take *ʾuṭm*, *šrqm*, and *ʾamtm* as adverbs, the final *m* lending this force to the verbal nouns, which we connect with the Arabic أطّ, 'to split', سرق, 'to be enervated', and أمت, 'weakness, emptiness'. DRIVER's association of *ʾuṭm* with the Arabic وطم, 'funeral meat' does violence to the principle of phonetic correspondence in Semitic dialects, though, to be sure, we have heard the initial *hamza* supplanted by *w* in very vulgar colloquial Arabic pronunciation of أُذْن, 'ear'. In *yrt* the final *d* of the root *yrd* is assimilated to *t*, as regularly in Ugaritic, e.g. GORDON *UH* 52, 53, 60, *ʾeṯt ʾel ylt*. The word *npš* means in Ugaritic the breath-vapour and also the throat. The latter meaning suits better in Habakkuk ii, 5, where, incidentally, the imagery re-echoes the passage we have just cited from the Ras Shamra texts. In *ltn bṯn brḥ* we recognize quite clearly לויתן נחש ברח of Isaiah xxvii, and נחש ברח of Job xxvi, 13. The verb *brḥ* is used here apparently in its primary sense of 'to pass on', cf. Arabic ألبارح, 'yesterday', 'to flee' being a secondary meaning. In view of the Arabic usage it is difficult to understand DRIVER's resolute rejection of the meaning 'primaeval', proposed by ALBRIGHT, in favour of 'slippery', which is a conjecture based on parallel terms in the passage. Though generally the principle of parallelism obtains in these texts, this is not so absolutely mechanical as to admit of no variation. We propose that *šlyṭ* is a Šafʿel formation expressing an appellative, cf. *šʿtqt* (GORDON *UH* 127, 2), from the verbal root *lwṭ* or *lyṭ* cognate with Arabic لاط(و) 'to cleave to' and Hebrew לוט ,'to envelope'.

[1]) On being approached by the emissaries of Baal, Anat replies (GORDON *UH* ʿnt, III, 34 ff.):

mn.ʾeb.ypʿ.lbʿl	'What enemy rises up against Baal?
ṣrt.lrkb.ʿrpt	What foes against him who mounteth the clouds?
lmḫšt.mdd.ʾel.ym	Have I not smitten Sea Beloved of El?
lklt.nhr.ʾel.rbm	Have I not annihilated River the great god?
lʾeštbm.tnn.ʾešbmnh	Have I not put a muzzle on *tnn*?
mḫšt.bṯn.ʿqltn	Have I not smitten the Crooked Serpent,
šlyṭ.dšbʿt.rʾašm	The Foul-fanged with Seven Heads?
mḫšt.mdd.ʾelm.ʾarṣ.mt	I have smitten the Darling of the Earth-deities Mt,
ʿgl.ʾel.ʿtk	Who strideth with prodigious haste.
mḫšt.klbt.ʾelm.ʾešt	I have smitten the Bitch of the gods Fire,
klt.bt.ʾel.šbb	I have annihilated the Daughter of El Flame'.

CASSUTO seems right in taking *mdd ʾel* as a euphemistic title of Mt, האלה ענת, p. 49, cf. *Pontus Euxinus* of the Greeks and *daoine sith* of Celtic folklore, the fairies against whose ill potential it was necessary to guard by terming them 'men of peace'. We see no reference in *ʿgl ʾel ʿtk* to some monstrous 'calf of El', though etymologically this would be possible. We take *ʿgl* as the Arabic عجْل, meaning 'haste'. The noun is used, we suppose, adverbially, qualified by *ʾel* in the sense

coiling One, with Seven Heads' is listed. This, of course, is the exact description of *ltn*. In the latter passage *tnn* is also mentioned as having been 'muzzled', this being the only clear reference to *tnn* as a monstrous adversary of the gods in the Ras Shamra texts[1]). We note the association here of *tnn* and the serpent with the unruly waters, 'Sea beloved of El', and 'River the great god'. It must be frankly admitted that in the texts dealing with Baal's conflict with the Sea there is no mention of his victory over *tnn* and *ltn* such as the Ugaritic passages just cited and certain Old Testament passages imply. Here, of course, we must bear in mind that we are dealing with fragments of the whole Canaanite literature, so that the *ltn* episode may yet prove to be connected with the fragments concerning Baal and the waters. The impressive list of monstrous adversaries cited by Anat, several of which are otherwise quite unknown in the extant texts, serves to remind us that we are dealing with but a fragment of a much larger whole. At the same time, the manifest uncertainty as to whether Baal or Anat slew the serpent indicates that here we have older material which has never been properly and consistently integrated into the main mythological tradition of Ras Shamra. The figure of Rahab, so familiar in the Old Testament in association with the unruly waters, is never found in the Ras Shamra texts.

But though the passages Gordon *UH* 67, I, 1-7 and ʿnt, III, 34 ff. give us no clue to the significance of the victory over the monsters, nor indeed to the relation if any of this episode to others in the extant texts, the context of references to *tnn* and *ltn* in the Old Testament in such passages as Psalm lxxiv, 12 ff., Isaiah xxvii, 1; li, 9 ff. and to Rahab in Psalm lxxxix, 6-18, definitely suggests an eschatological victory which will repeat the triumph of Cosmos over Chaos in the beginning, which has been sacramentally experienced in the cult. Here, and especially in Psalm lxxxix, 6-18, it is possible to see a connection with creation, which is the result of the triumph of God over the forces of Chaos. Again, however, we must be careful about drawing too close an analogy between the myth among the

---

of 'divine', 'supernatural', or 'awful'. This usage of *ʾel* has been noted by Gaster in the phrases *ʾudr ʾel*, 'mighty *ʾudr*-trees' in Gordon *UH* 51, V, 102, and *mdbr ʾel*, 'the awful desert' in Gordon *UH* 75, I, 21-22, cf. Hebrew הררי אל. Gaster, *Thespis*, p. 448. The word *ʿtk*, which Gordon leaves untranslated (*Ugaritic Literature*, p. 20), and Gaster transcribes (*Thespis*, p. 214), we take as the participle of the verb *ʿtk* connected with the Arabic عتك, 'to rush upon, assail'.

[1]) The fragmentary text *PRU* II, 1,1 appears to attribute the smiting of *tnn* to Baal.

Canaanites and among the Hebrews. The ascription of creation to El, creator of heaven and earth (אל עליון קנא שמים וארץ) in Genesis xiv, 22 and in the Phoenician inscription of Azitawadd [1]) indicates that, whatever was the significance of Baal's victory over the unruly waters and primaeval monsters, the predominant belief among the Canaanites was that El was the creator, and in fact, one of his stock epithets in the Ras Shamra texts is *bny bnwt* ('creator of created things'). The association of the kingship of Yahweh won in conflict with the unruly waters and other adversaries with that of creation in the Psalms, Prophets, and Wisdom Literature of the Old Testament may simply be an instance of the syncretism in the Jerusalem cult between the ideology of the Canaanite New Year festival and that of the pre-Israelite cult of El Elyon as creator, which according to Gen. xiv was localized in Jerusalem.

On the question of the *Sitz im Leben* of the myth of Baal and the waters, its cultic relevance, and also, we believe, of its connection with the main body of the rest of the Baal mythology, the clue is given in the phrase, which we take to be a cultic exclamation, *b'l-m ymlk* ('Let Baal be King !'). The theme of God's conflict with the unruly waters resulting in his establishment as King recurs in certain of the Psalms, e.g. xxix, 10; xlvi, 2-4; lxxiv, 12-15; lxxxix, 8-18, and in the Prophets, explicitly in Nahum ii, 1 (Hebrew text; EVV. i, 15), which in our opinion, taken in conjunction with Isaiah lii, 7, conclusively determines the *Sitz im Leben* of the liturgy of God as King in the New Year festival in Israel, as MOWINCKEL has consistently argued since the publication of his monumental *Psalmenstudien* II in 1922. After the acclamation of Yahweh's victory over the waters in language and imagery which strikingly recall the imagery of the Baal-myth at Ras Shamra the prophet proceeds (ii, 1, EVV. i, 15):

> Behold upon the mountains the feet of him that bringeth good tidings,
> That publisheth peace.
> O Judah, keep thy solemn feasts (חָגִּי ... חַגַּיִךְ).

The reference is surely to the New Year festival (החג). Referring almost certainly to the same occasion, the prophet in Isaiah lii, 7 declares:

> How beautiful upon the mountains are the feet of him that bringeth good tidings,
> That publisheth peace,

---

[1]) Col. III, 18. GORDON, 'Azitawadd's Hebrew Inscription', *JNES* VIII, 1949, pp. 108-115.

That saith to Jerusalem,
Thy God reigneth!

This suggests that the New Year festival was the *Sitz im Leben* of the cult of Yahweh as King, a conclusion which is supported by the post-Exilic text Zech. xiv, 16-17. The New Year festival, the most significant crisis in the agricultural year in Canaan, was the natural occasion for the sacramental celebration of the triumph of Cosmos over Chaos, the Kingship of God, won in conflict with his cosmic adversaries, and, though the three Ugaritic fragments we have cited give no specific indication of this seasonal festival, the Hebrew analogy certainly suggests it. On this important occasion, when order and prosperity in nature and the community were in the balance and were ardently anticipated, ancient Israel stayed her faith in the power of her God by entering again into the experience of Yahweh's original triumph over the forces of Chaos in nature and in history in the great saving act of the Exodus, which was the basis of Israel's faith. This was the ground of her hope in the present and in the indefinite future, and is the origin of the particular eschatological hope in Israel. [1]) Here as in Christian eschatology the same mythological imagery is characteristic.

These mythological motifs recur with a similar significance, though divorced from actual cultic experience, in Exilic and post-Exilic passages in the Old Testament, e.g. Ezekiel xxix, 3 ff. and xxxii, 2 ff. and Isaiah li, 10 in the Exilic period, and in the Book of Job and in post-Biblical writings, where a minority of Israel express themselves in face of the domination of heathen world-powers which raises the problem of the providence of God in nature and in history, the very subject which in monarchic times had been expressed in terms of the ancient Canaanite myth of Baal and the unruly waters. So now we find a recurrence of the themes of Conflict and Kingship in Daniel vii, 7 ff. (cf. 2 Esdras xii, 11 ff.), Daniel xi-xii, Book of Jubilees xxiii, 11 and 2 Esdras viii, 63-xi, 6, where it is explicitly stated that the pre-

---

[1]) We agree with MOWINCKEL (*Psalmenstudien* II, p. 223) that the Hebrew view of the operation of God in history resulted in a more sharply defined eschatology, a view of τα ἐσχατα in the strict sense of the term, a view to which the ancient Canaanites, with their interest in the recurring cycle of nature apparently never attained. Nevertheless to separate myth from eschatology as S. B. FROST has done (*Old Testament Apocalyptic*, 1952, pp. 32-34) is to prejudge the matter with a logic unknown to the ancient Near East and to ignore the evidence of the Enthronement Psalms, which reiterate in the Hebrew adaptation the Canaanite theme of the triumph of Cosmos over Chaos.

liminary of the consummation of God's absolute order will be a re-enactment of the primaeval emergence of Cosmos from Chaos. The influence of the old Canaanite providence myth which we have cited is indicated by the fact that the various beasts in the Book of Daniel which represent the world-empires come up *from the sea.* So in the Apocalypse of Baruch after the establishment of the Messiah as King (2 Baruch xxxix, 7) and before his final judgement on all peoples (2 Baruch lxxii, 1 ff.) the earth is threatened by a flood of black waters (2 Baruch lxx, 1 ff.). In the Psalms of Solomon (ii, 28 ff.) the providence of God is vindicated in the downfall of Pompey which is described in the categories of the ancient Baal-myth:

> But thou, O Lord, delay not to recompense them on their own heads,
> To cast down the insolence of the dragon.
> . . . .
> For he said, 'I will be lord of land and sea',
> And knew not that the lord is God,
> Great, mighty and powerful,
> And he is King over heaven and earth,
> And he judges kingdoms and princes.

We repeat that in apocalyptic the features of the Canaanite myth are divorced from their cultic association in a way that they probably were not in the whole monarchic period in ancient Israel, and are now used consciously as imagery. There is, we claim, an organic connection with their *Sitz im Leben* in the cult in pre-Exilic Israel and ultimately in Canaan. It is not fortuitous that this imagery is associated with the activity of the Messiah. We agree with MOWINCKEL that the Messiah of apocalyptic was unknown in pre-Exilic Israel [1]). This figure, however, was a development of the earlier historical king, the anointed of Yahweh, who represented the people before God and mediated the divine blessing to the community. The installation of such a prince was itself a manifestation and warrant of the triumph of Cosmos over Chaos, and the king's ascendancy was the counterpart of the Kingship of God, a conception which is expressed in the royal psalms ii and cx. Again the good order of God was sustained by regular seasonal festivals, where the king played a vital rôle. Thus the theme of the triumph of God over the unruly waters and other powers of Chaos, which is proper to the psalms of the enthronement of Yahweh, is also appropriate to the royal psalms. After the abolition of the Hebrew monarchy the royal psalms were retained, no doubt

---

[1]) S. MOWINCKEL, *Han som Kommer*, 1951, p. 13.

for the sake of the doctrine of providence which they expressed. The figure of the anointed king, however, now obsolete in its original significance, acquired a new significance in the absolute eschatology of apocalyptic. The anointed agent of God came to be what he had never been before, the supernatural Messiah of apocalyptic, the agent of the absolute consummation of God's order when the present world order has been abolished. Thus we may say that the Messiah and the conquest of the powers of Chaos, unruly waters, sea-monsters, or world-powers, are not the fusing together of originally independent elements, but originally belong together in the Hebrew monarchic period and probably also in pre-Israelite Canaan. In this connection the Apocalypse of Baruch is particularly instructive, associating as it does the various features of the ancient theme, the kingship of the Messiah (2 Baruch xxxix, 7), the rout of the armies of the last inveterate enemy and the judgement of this ultimate enemy in Zion (2 Baruch xl, 1), the menace to the earth of the black waters (2 Baruch lxx, 1 ff.) the judgement of the Messiah on all peoples (2 Baruch lxxiii, 1 ff.), the Messianic banquet on the flesh of Leviathan and Behemoth (2 Baruch xxix, 4), and the establishment of the Golden Age (2 Baruch lxxiii, 1 ff.).

In the Christian realization of the faith of Israel the same hope in the Reign of God is dominant, and follows generally the same pattern. Standing in the forefront of the proclamation of Jesus (Matthew iv, 12-17; Mark. i, 15) and of his disciples (Matthew ix, 35; Luke ix, 2), the faith in the Reign of God assumes victory after conflict, as notably in the famous Beelzebub controversy (Matthew xii, 25 ff.; Mark. iii, 23 ff.; Luke xi, 17 ff.). The main theme, if not the actual imagery of the old Canaanite myth, adapted by Israel, has now been baptized into Christianity. The rich imagery here recedes into the background. It reappears, however, with full force, together with scraps of imagery from less well known native mythologies, in the Apocalypse in the imagery of the serpent which belched floods from his mouth to engulf the woman and child (Revelation xii), the beast out of the sea (c. xiii), and in the prospect of the final victory of God, when there shall be a new creation, but with 'no more sea' (Revelation xxi).

The cosmic significance of this eschatological theme of the re-enactment of the primaeval victory of Cosmos over Chaos in the Hebrew adaptation of the Canaanite myth strongly suggests that it is to the category of cosmic mythology relating to the *Urzeit* that the three fragments describing Baal's victory over the waters is to be assigned. [1]

The major problem in the Ras Shamra texts is the order in which the Baal-complex should be arranged. The difficulty may be appreciated when it is realized that we have to deal with at least eight tablets in twelve or thirteen fragments. Nor is the text thus recovered undamaged. Since we are concerned with the content rather than with the form of the texts, we shall in passing refer the reader to a section in DE LANGHE's *magnum opus* where the dimensions and extent of these fragments are carefully described and the bibliography cited to date. [2] Suffice it to say that the largest text, GORDON *UH* 51, when complete consisted of some five hundred lines, most of which are either extant or may be restored with a high degree of certainty, thus yielding a text in epic style about the length of one of the smaller books of the Iliad.

The Baal-complex consists first of the texts GORDON *UH* 129, 137, and 68, which we have just considered. To these we should probably add as introduction GORDON *UH* ʿnt, and ʿnt, pl. ix and x and at some later point GORDON *UH* 133. These texts possibly once stood apart from the rest of the Baal-cycle as a cosmic, rather than as a seasonal, myth, [3] and our opinion of the comparative independence of this myth is apparently shared by DE LANGHE, who admits the texts into the main Baal-cycle only secondarily. [4] Whatever their original significance, however, they can be integrated with the main Baal-cycle. MOWINCKEL apparently regards the Baal mythology as a unity. [5] KAPELRUD takes the same view, regarding the myth of Baal and the Waters and that of Baal and Mot as both related to the Enthronement Festival at the autumnal New Year. KAPELRUD proposes the feasible view that the phases of the agricultural year were anticipated in the vicissitudes of Baal on this occasion as rites of imitative magic or, to use his own felicitous phrase, 'creative

---

[1] We have elaborated this theme at length in our papers, 'The Hebrew conception of the Kingship of God: its Origin and Development', *VT* VI, 1956, pp. 268-285, and 'The Kingship of God in the Prophets and Psalms', *VT* XI, 1961, pp. 1-29.

[2] DE LANGHE, *Les textes de Ras Shamra-Ugarit et leurs rapports avec le milieu Biblique . . .*, I, pp. 153-162.

[3] GASTER takes this myth to refer to 'the grey beginning of years', *Thespis*, p. 115.

[4] DE LANGHE, *op. cit.*, p. 153.

[5] MOWINCKEL, 'Psalm Criticism between 1900 and 1935', *VT* V, 1955, pp 13-33.

analogy'. [1]) Gordon admits the difficulty of arranging the texts, in which we may not, after all, be justified in seeking a consistent unity. With this caveat he suggests that the fragments of the myth of the conflict of Baal and the Waters served as an introduction to the rest of the Baal mythology, [2]) and this view has lately been propounded by Driver. [3])

Of the rest of the Baal-texts there is one which is somewhat difficult to place in its context. That is the text published by Virolleaud as V AB [4]) and by Gordon in *UH* as ʿnt.

The text opens with a banquet, where Baal is entertained (ʿnt I), probably in the 'house' of El, the doyen of the Ugaritic pantheon: [5])

ʿbd.ʾalʾeyn bʿl	...'Serve Baal the Mighty,
sʾed.ẓbl.bʿl.ʾarṣ	Satisfy [6]) the Prince, Lord of the earth.
qm.yṯʿr.wʾašlḥmnh	Rise, let preparation be made [7]) that I may feed him,
ybrd.ṯd.lpnwh	Let them cut up [8]) a brisket [9]) before him
bḥrb.mlḥt	With a goodly knife; [10])
qṣ.mrʾe.ndd	Apportion [11]) slices of fatlings.'
yʿšr.wyšqynh	They feast him and give him to drink;
ytn.ks.bdh	They give him a cup in his hand,
krpnm.bklʾat.ydh	A flagon in his clasped [12]) hands,

---

[1]) Kapelrud, *Ras Sjamra Funnene og det Gamle Testament*, 1953, pp. 76 ff.

[2]) Gordon, *Ugaritic Literature*, 1949, p. 9.

[3]) Driver, *op. cit.*, pp. 11 ff.

[4]) Virolleaud, *Syria* XVII, 1936, pp. 335-345; XVIII, 1937, pp. 85-102, pp. 256-270; *La Déesse ʿAnat*, 1938.

[5]) Gordon, *UH* ʿnt, I, 2 ff.

[6]) *sʾed.* This verb is found as a parallel to *šlḥm* ('feed') and *ššqy* ('give to drink') in Gordon *UH* 2 Aqht, V, 20.

[7]) *yṯʿr* is found in the same sense in Gordon *UH* 77, 35 and in Hebrew as שׂער, e.g. Proverbs xxiii, 7 כי כמו שׂער בנפשו כן הוא (?) *v. infra*, p. 266, n.

[8]) Driver proposes to connect the verb *brd* with the Hebrew פרד, 'to divide', giving the feasible translation of *ybrd ṯd*, 'they carved breasts'. *op. cit.* pp. 83, 164.

[9]) *ṯd* lit. 'breast', cf. Arabic ثدى.

[10]) Our original interpretation 'with knife unsheathed', cf. Arabic لحت 'to strip', e.g. the bark of a tree, must be given up in view of the adjective *mlḥt* in the phrase *ʾuz mrʾat mlḥt*, 'Geese fat and well-looking', cited by S. A. Loewenstamm, טכסטים חדשים בלשון אוגרית, *Tarbiz* (in Hebrew), XXVIII, 1959, p. 245; Eissfeldt, *JSS* V, 1960, p. 67, from the text published by Virolleaud in *PRU* II, 289, 30. Ullendorff makes the feasible suggestion 'a salted knife', citing an Abyssinian custom, 'Ugaritic Marginalia II', *JSS* VII, 1962, p. 346.

[11]) *ndd* may best be taken as an active participle, cognate with the Arabic ندّ, 'to apportion'.

[12]) We should connect *klʾat* with the root כלא, 'to enclose' here, cf. *llʾa klʾatnm*, 'a sheep from the pens' in Gordon *UH* krt, 68, 161.

bk rb. ʿẓm.rʾe	A large goblet, [1]) of mighty draught, [2])
dn.mt.šmm.	A jar of the folk of heaven, [3])
ks.qdš ltphnh.ʾaṯt	A cup proper [4]) to gods, which women might not look upon,
krpn ltʿn.ʾaṯrt	A flagon which a goddess might not regard,
ʾalp kd.yqḥ.bḫmr	A thousand jars he takes with wine,
rbt.ymsk.bmskh	Ten thousand he mixes; as he mixes (them)
qm.ybd.wyšr	There has arisen to improvise [5]) and sing,
mṣltm.bd.nʿm	Cymbals in hand, a gracious one,
yšr.ġẓr.ṭb.ql	A lad, good of voice, sings
ʿl.bʿl.bṣrrt.ṣpn	Of Baal on the cliffs of Saphon,
ytmr.bʿl.bnth	How Baal looks [6]) upon his girls,
yʿn.pdry.bt.ʾar	Watches the Plump damsel [7]) the girl of Mist, [8])
ʾapn.ṭly.bt.rb...	Also Dewy, the girl of Rain ... [9])

Here it will be noticed that not Baal but some other deity, probably El, takes the initiative. Nevertheless Baal is very much alive and not, as Dussaud believes, [10]) in the underworld. We believe that Baal, though *redivivus*, has not quite emerged from his seasonal eclipse—later to be described—and we should explain this feast as an initial rite, whereby the god, once dead, was reintegrated into the living society of the active fertility powers. [11])

---

[1]) We accept the proposal of Gaster (after Cassuto) that *bk rb* should be read, meaning 'a great beaker'. Gaster cites the Greek transliteration of what was admitted to be a Phoenician word βικος, *Thespis*, pp. 210, 449.

[2]) *V. infra*, p. 285.

[3]) Again accepting Gaster's arrangement of the text, which is complicated by the absence of the word-divider between *bk* and *rb* and between *rʾe* and *dn.*

[4]) We take *qdš*, properly 'sacred', as 'special', i.e. sacrosanct in the widest sense, with Ullendorff, *op. cit.*, p. 346. Driver feasibly suggests a more specialized meaning of *qdš*, 'shining', translating (*op. cit.* p. 83) 'A shining cup which a woman would verily regard, A flagon on which a deity would verily gaze (with envy)'.

[5]) *ybd* is found in parallelism with *yšr* also in Gordon *UH* 2 Aqht, VI, 31. The verb seems a cognate of the Arabic بده 'to extemporise'.

[6]) *ytmr* as a synonymn of *yʿn* suggests the Akkadian cognate *amâru*, 'to consider', so Aistleitner, 'Die Anat-Texte aus Ras Shamra', *ZAW* LVII, 1939, p. 210.

[7]) Cf. Arabic افزر, 'To be fleshy', usually describing a woman according to Oriental taste.

[8]) So Driver, *op. cit.* pp. 85, 135, connecting *ʾar* with the Arabic أرى, 'dew, rain'.

[9]) *rb* is Hebrew רביב. The association of *ṭl* and *rb* recalls the parallelism רביבים//טל in Micah v, 6 (Evv. 7).

[10]) Dussaud, 'ʾAlʾeyn Baal et ses messages d'outre-tombe', *RHR* XCVI, 1937, pp. 121-135. *Les découvertes de Ras Shamra (Ugarit) et l'Ancien Testament*, 2nd ed., 1941, pp. 116-117.

[11]) Instances of a meal as marking the end of the period of mourning or ritual separation are found in 2 Samuel xii, 20-21 (David after the death of his son by Bathsheba) and 2 Samuel iii, 35 (David after his mourning for Abner).

After a lacuna at the end of column I and the beginning of column II a remarkable passage occurs where Anat gathers certain people into a 'house' and indulges in an orgy of slaughter: [1]

kl'at.ṯġrt.bht ʿnt	(Anat) has closed the gates of the house;
wtqry.ġlmm.bšt.ġr	She gathers [2] (her) ministrants into the inmost recesses [3] of the inner shrine. [4]
whln.ʿnt.tmtḫṣ bʿmq	Then [5] Anat smites in the open plain; [6]
tḫtṣb.bn.qrytm	She cuts down (her) foes between the walls; [7]
tmḫṣ.l'em.ḫp y(m)	She smites the princes [8] by the sea-shore; [9]

[1]) Gordon *UH* ʿnt, II, 3 ff.

[2]) *tqry* seems here to have the sense of the Arabic قرى, 'to gather', e.g. قرى 'ponded water'. Elsewhere the root may have the sense 'to confront' in a hostile sense, e.g. Gordon *UH* 2 Aqht VI, 43, *l'aqryk.bntb pšʿ*, 'Verily I will confront thee on the path of rebellion', cf. Hebrew קרי, Leviticus xxvi, 21.

[3]) We take *št* as cognate with the Hebrew שׁת, 'base, foundation', hence here 'inmost recess'.

[4]) *ġr* might mean, as elsewhere in the Ras Shamra texts, 'mountain', here referring to the mount of assembly of the gods, namely Sapon, the Canaanite Olympus. Here it may be cognate with the Arabic غور, 'hollow' or 'cave', cf. Hebrew מערה, used by the goddess as a temporary refuge for her own devotees in the day of her vengeance on worshippers of a rival cult. In 2 Kings x, 25, however, עיר בית בעל, describing a feature of the Baal Temple at Samaria, suggests the inmost shrine of the temple, reflecting an original cave sanctuary, as the most ancient shrine of Apollo at Delos. Klostermann, in fact, proposed to read דביר for עיר, *Die Bücher Samuelis und der Könige, Kurzgefasste Kommentäre*, 1887, ad. loc.

[5]) *whln* is unattested except in this passage, where it marks a new step forward in the narrative.

[6]) *bʿmq* has been taken as adverbial, meaning 'with violence', after Akkadian *emuqu*, a sense which the word bears in Gordon *UH* 2 Aqht VI, 45. Here, however, we prefer to take the word in the locative sense, meaning 'plain' in parallel with *bn qrytm*, meaning 'between the walls'.

[7]) *bn qrytm* is generally taken as 'men of the city' and even as 'men of the two cities', Ginsberg in *Ancient Near Eastern Texts*, (ed. J. B. Pritchard), 1950, p. 136 and Cassuto, האלה ענת, pp. 64, 76. Our rendering 'between the walls' would, of course, refer to the slaughter of the goddess in the city, *bʿmq* referring to her slaughter in the open country. Cf. Job xxxix, 21, where בעמק means not 'in the valley' (EVV), but 'violently', as the parallel בכח indicates, so Albright, *CBQ* VII, 1945, p. 26.

[8]) *l'em* immediately suggested to commentators the Hebrew לאמים, which is universally translated as 'people'. The word occurs in the phrase *ybmt l'emm* which we translate as 'the sister of the Prince', i.e. Baal. The word *l'em* may be, connected with the Assyrian *limmu*, as suggested orally by G. R. Driver. On this rendering of *l'em* we see the possibility that the LXX may be right in rendering the Hebrew לאמים by ἄρχοντες in Genesis xxvii, 29; Isaiah xxxiv, 1; xli, 1; xliii, 4, 9 and lv, 4, *v. infra* p. 271. In the present passage, of course, *l'emm* might be 'people' just as well as 'princes'. We favour the latter translation, however, and suggest that the parallel *l'emm/'adm* is reminiscent of the Phoenician ממלכת/אדם in Cooke, *NSI* 4, 10 ff; 5, 11.

[9]) The picture is thus a comprehensive one including country (*bʿmq*) and town

tṣmt.ʾadm.ṣʾat.špš	She annihilates [1]) the folk in the direction of the sunrise. [2])
tḥth.kkdrt.rʾe(š)	Under her are heads like balls; [3])
ʿlh.kʾerbym kp	Above her (fly) hands like locusts,
k.qṣm.ġrmn. kp	Yea, hands like lots of corn [4]) in piles [5])
mhr.ʿtkt ( )	Swiftly attacking [6]) ( ).
rʾešt.lbmth.šnst.	The heads [7]) she has tossed [8]) on to her back, [9])
( ) *kpt.bḥbšh*	( ) all together [10]) in her bundle; [11])
brkm.tġ(ll).bdm.ẓmr	Her knees she plunges in the blood of the soldiers, [12])

(*bn qrytm*), princes (*lʾemm*) and commoners (*ʾadm*), and West (*ḫp y (m)*) and East (*ṣʾat špš*). The description, of course, is hyperbolical.

[1]) *tṣmt* from the root *ṣmt* as in Hebrew.

[2]) *ṣʾat špš*, 'the outgoing of the sun', i.e. sunrise, East, and not West as translated by GASTER, *Thespis*, p. 211.

[3]) The word כדור meaning 'ball' is familiar in post-Biblical Hebrew, but is found only once in the Old Testament, in Isaiah xxii, 18. The occurrence of the word in the Ras Shamra texts, redacted about 1400 B.C., indicates that the single occurrence of this and other such words in the Old Testament is a matter of chance and does not render the context open to suspicion of late insertion.

[4]) We prefer to take *qṣm* as cognate with the Arabic قصم, 'piece, fragment', rather than to follow CASSUTO (*op. cit.*, p. 77) in referring the word to locusts on the strength of the parallelism. We think that it refers not to 'cut' corn, as DRIVER suggests (*op. cit.* p. 85), but to the lots of each peasant on the common threshing-floor, a familiar sight in the Arab East to the present day.

[5]) The final *n* of this word is an adverbial ending, the word itself being cognate with the Hebrew ערמה, 'a heap' of corn, familiar in the Old Testament, especially in the Book of Ruth.

[6]) The root عتك is attested with this meaning in Arabic. It occurs again in the next column in the phrase *ʿgl ʾel ʿtk* a reference to the onset of the sinister god Mt with prodigious haste.

[7]) These were tokens of her prowess as the foreskins of the Philistines which Saul demanded of David, or the hands which the Egyptian warriors cut off from the enemies they killed in battle.

[8]) *šnst* is the Causative of a verb cognate with the Arabic ناش found in the IVth form with the same meaning.

[9]) *bmt* is the regular Ugaritic word for the back of the body, suggesting the etymology of the Hebrew במה 'a high place'. *v. infra*, p. 259.

[10]) An adverb from the root found in Arabic as كفّ, 'to roll up in a bundle'.

[11]) cf. Hebrew חבש, 'to bind up'.

[12]) The meaning of *ẓmr* must be conjectured through its association here with *mhrm*, which is found in parallel with *ṣbʾem* and *ġẓrm*, 'soldiers' and 'heroes' in l. 12. The word is probably cognate with the Arabic ذمير, 'brave', cited by DRIVER, *op. cit.*, p. 149, and by AISTLEITNER, *Wörterbuch* 2717. This is possibly also the root of the Hebrew proper name Zimri, as AISTLEITNER suggests.

ḥlqm.bmm(ʿ).mhrm	Her loins [1] in the gore [2] of the warriors. [3]
mṭm.tgrš.šbm	With a staff she drives the young men, [4]
bksl.qšth.mdnt	Her bent bow [5] at her back.
whln.ʿnt.lbth.tmġyn	Then Anat reaches her house,
tštql.ʾelt.lhklh	The goddess comes to [6] her palace,
wl.šbʿt.tmtḫṣh.bʿmq	Yet has she not had her fill of slaughtering in the open plain,
tḫtṣb.bn.qrtm	Nor of cutting down between the walls.
tṯʿr.ksʾat.lmhr	She prepares [7] seats for the warriors,
ṯʿr.ṯlḥnt lṣbʾem	Dressing [8] of tables for the soldiers,
hdmm.lġzrm	Footstools for the heroes. [9]
mʾed.tmtḫṣn.wtʿn	Violently she smites and gloats,
tḫtṣb.wtḥdy ʿnt	Anat cuts them down and gazes; [10]

---

1) We connect *ḥlqm* with the Hebrew חלצים, 'loins', as suggested by the parallel *brkm*. For the dialectical variation between *ṣ* and *q*, cf. Hebrew ארץ and Aramaic ארק.

2) The meaning of *mmʿ* is indicated by its parallel *dm*. The word seems best connected with the Arabic مع or ماع, 'to melt', or 'exude'.

3) That these are cultic functionaries is suggested by the texts Gordon *UH* 123, 7 and 124, 8, where there is mention of *mhr bʿl* and *mhr ʿnt*. Gaster cites a reference in Assyrian literature to *mu-i-ir-ru ekalli*, which obviously has the same implications, *Iraq* VI, 1939, p. 133, n. 117.

4) Cassuto takes *šbm* as the participle of a verb cognate with the Hebrew שבה 'to take captive', *op. cit.*, pp. 64, 77. If this were so, as may well be the case, this would be an instance of the goddess 'leading captivity captive'. We prefer, however, to connect the word with the Arabic شباب, 'young men'. Driver's translation 'old men' from the root *šyb* (*op. cit.*, pp. 85, 149) is also possible.

5) *mdnt* agreeing with *qšth*, 'her bow', suggests the Arabic cognate دن 'to be crooked', i.e. Anat's bow was ready for further action.

6) The word *tštql* is taken by Gordon (*UH*, p. 274) as an Ifteʿal of the root *šql* which, however, is not otherwise attested in the Ras Shamra texts. The general meaning of *tštql* is indicated by the parallel *tmġy*, 'she arrived', here and in Gordon *UH* 1 Aqht, 170-171 and 2 Aqht, II, 25. We prefer to regard the form as an Ištafʿal from *qll*, the common verb in Ugaritic for 'to fall'. The idea of 'arriving' as 'coming down' (i.e. from one's camel) is found also in Arabic in the verb نزل.

7) Driver connects the verb with the Arabic ثعر, 'to break', *op. cit.* pp. 85, 151.

8) We take *ṯʿr* as a verbal noun, meaning 'to arrange', *v. supra*, p. 38, n. 7.

9) *ġzr* regularly occurs in Ugaritic for a mettled young man. The word appears in Hebrew also in the phrase עזרי המלחמה in 1 Chronicles, xii, 1. Driver (*op. cit.*, p. 142) after Albright equates the word with Arabic غزر (IV) 'to treat generously'. Hebrew usage of the root עזר in 1 Chron. v, 20, ויעזרו עליהם, and 1 Chron. xii, 1, עזרי מלחמה, however, suggests that the root is rather cognate with Ethiopic *ʿẓr* adduced by Ullendorff (*JSS* VII, 1962, p. 347), 'to attack impetuously'.

10) The verb *ḥdy* seems best taken as 'gaze' rather than 'rejoice', which would

tġdd . kbdh . bṣḥq	Her liver exults [1]) in mirth,
ymlʾu . lbh . bšmḫt	Her heart is filled with joy,
k bd . ʿnt . tšyt	For in the hand of [2]) Anat is victory, [3])
kbrkm . tġll bdm . ẓmr	For she plunges her knees in the blood of the soldiers,
ḫlqm . bmmʿ . mhrm	Her loins in the gore of the warriors
ʿd . tšbʿ . tmtḫṣ . bbt	Till she has had her fill of slaughtering in the house,
tḫtṣb . bn . ṯlḥnm	Of cleaving among the tables.
ymḫ . bbt . dm . ẓmr	The blood of the soldiers is wiped [4]) from the house; [5])
yṣq . šmn . (š)lm . bṣʿ	The oil of peace [6]) is poured out on the walls. [7])
trḥṣ . ydh . btlt . ʿnt	The Virgin Anat washes her hands,
ʾuṣbʿth . ybmt . lʾemm	Even her fingers the Sister of the Prince; [8])

---

be cognate to the Hebrew חדה. In the Ras Shamra texts *ḥdy* regularly appears as a dialectic variation of the Hebrew חזה, 'to see'.

[1]) *tġdd* is connected by GORDON (*UH*, p. 259) with the Late Hebrew התעדד.

[2]) We follow GASTER (*Iraq* VI, 1939, p. 134) in reading *k bd* for Virolleaud's *kbd*, also read by DRIVER who translates most hazardously 'A. gave herself up to rejoicing', lit. 'set her liver' (*kbd ʿnt tšyt*), *op. cit.* 85.

[3]) VIROLLEAUD (*La déesse Anat*, 1938, *ad. loc.*) felicitously suggested the Hebrew תּוּשִׁיָּה, though wrongly in the sense of 'safety, salvation, or power'.

[4]) We take *ymḫ* as cognate with the Hebrew מחה, 'to wipe', so AISTLEITNER, *ZAW* LVII, 1939, p. 207, and CASSUTO, *op. cit.*, pp. 65, 78, rather than with the Akkadian *maḫâḫu*, 'to be soaked', GASTER, *Iraq* VI, 1939, p. 135, n. 141.

[5]) Reading *bbt* (𐎁𐎁𐎚) for GORDON's *-dt* (-𐎄𐎚), cf. DRIVER (*op cit.* p. 84), who reads *bt* taking it as the direct object of *ymḫ*. For the usage of the preposition *b* in Ugaritic cf. the stock phrase *bph rgm lyṣʾa bšpth hwth*, 'from his (her) mouth the word had not quite gone forth, nor from his (her) lips the speech (when . . .) 'GORDON *UH* I Aqht, 75, 113 etc., and *wyqḥ bhm ʾaqht*, 'And he takes A. from them', GORDON *UH* 1 Aqht, 145. See GORDON *UH*, pp. 83-84.

[6]) Here *šlm* is not a peace-offering, but signifies the state of peace and normality after Anat's slaughter. As we take the slaughter to relate to some rite of separation after the period of sterility just past, this unction would represent a rite of 'aggregation' to indicate that life had resumed its normal tenor after the transitional period of suspense.

[7]) There are various possibilities in the case of *bṣʿ*. It is taken as a cognate with the Hebrew צעה and the Arabic صواع, meaning 'bowl', so GORDON, *UL* 1949, p. 18, GASTER, *Thespis*, p. 212, GINSBERG, *op. cit.*, p. 136 and DRIVER, *op. cit.*, p. 85. This meaning would suit quite well, but in view of the mention of the cleansing of the house in the parallel stichos, we prefer GASTER's suggestion (*Iraq* VI, 1939, p. 135, n. 142) that *ṣʿ* might be cognate with the Hebrew יצוע meaning 'something spread'. This might signify a carpet or couch (so CASSUTO, *op. cit.*, pp. 65, 78), or perhaps, as in 1 Kings vi, 5, 10, a side-chamber of the 'house' or even a partition.

[8]) On *lʾemm v. supra*, p. 40 n. 8. The word *ybmt* is found in Hebrew used of a widowed female relative. As an epithet of Anat it may refer to her estate as Virgin, *btlt*, her stock epithet. This might describe her state of dependence upon her brother Baal, 'the Prince'. DRIVER takes the word literally as 'sister-in-law of rulers', *op. cit.* p. 85.

(t)rḥṣ.ydh.bdm.ẓmr	She washes her hands from [1]) the blood of the soldiers,
(ʾu)ṣbʿth.bmmʿ mhrm	Even her fingers from the gore of the warriors,
.lksʾat.	(Chairs) by chairs,
ṯlḥnt.(l)ṯlḥn(t)	Tables by tables,
hdmm.ṯṯʿr lhdmm	Footstools by footstools she arranges,
(t)ḥspn.mh.wtrḥṣ	She scoops [2]) up water and washes,
(ṭ)l.šmm.šmn.ʾarṣ	Even dew of heaven the fatness of earth, [3])
rbb.rkb.ʿrpt	The rain [4]) of Him who Mounts the Clouds,
ṭl.šmm.tskh	The dew which the heavens pour forth,
(rbb) nskh.kbkbm	(The rain) which is poured forth by the stars,
ttpp.ʾanhb(m dʾalp šd)	She sprays [5]) herself with the ? of a thousand mountains, [6])
ẓuh.bym ( )	Her slops [7]) in the sea (are cast).

In seeking an explanation of this strange and striking passage we are, of course, obliged to consider the passage in its context. Later in the text we learn that negotiations were set afoot for the building of a 'house' for Baal. This anticipates Baal's rehabilitation and his readiness to consummate his *hieros gamos* and demonstrate his virility, which would have its counterpart in the fertility of flock and field.

---

[1]) See p. 43, n. 5. In the context we judge it better to take *b* as meaning 'from', so AISTLEITNER, *op. cit.*, p. 205, GASTER, *Thespis*, p. 212, GINSBERG, *op. cit.*, p. 136, CASSUTO, *op. cit.*, p. 65. GORDON takes *b* as meaning 'in', *UL*, p. 18.

[2]) The word *tḥspn* (energic imperfect as in Arabic) is from the root *ḥsp*, which is found in Gordon *UH* 1 Aqht, 51, 55, 199, 200 in a passage describing the industry of the daughter of Dnʾel, *ḥspt lšʿr ṭl*, 'she sweeps the dew off the barley', i.e. rises early. The word is used for scooping up water from a well, Isaiah xxx, 14 לַחְשֹׂף מַיִם מִגֶּבֶא.

[3]) The conception of dew as 'fatness of the earth' immediately suggests Isaac's blessing of Esau in Genesis xxvii, 28, וְיִתֶּן־לְךָ הָאֱלֹהִים מִטַּל הַשָּׁמַיִם וּמִשְׁמַנֵּי הָאָרֶץ.

[4]) *rbb* is the Hebrew רביבים, 'showers'. The parallelism *ṭl*/ /*rbb* here suggests the same parallelism in Deuteronomy xxxii, 2 and Micah v. 6 (Evv., 7).

[5]) We take the word *ttpp* as the Ifteʿal imperfect of *npp*, the initial *n* being assimilated to the infixed *t*. The passage obviously refers to Anat's toilet, so we connect the verb with the Arabic نفّ, 'to sow, scatter', from which is derived نفناف, 'a spray'.

[6]) *ʾanhb dʾalp šd* is always found in a similar context, and there are various interpretations. The most feasible of the suggestions which we reject is that of GASTER, who takes *ʾalp šd* on Akkadian analogies as 'wild ox' of the sea, whose excrement, *ẓʾuh*, is used as a cosmetic as ambergris, *Iraq* VI, 1939, p. 136, n. 157. We think that *ʾalp šd* should be rendered as 'thousand mountains'. The gods of ancient Ugarit act on the grand scale in cups or cosmetics. Whatever the etymology of *ʾanhbm*, the context indicates that *ʾanhbm* is not a cognate of Arab. نهب, 'to plunder', as CASSUTO (האלה ענת, 1950, pp. 64, 76) claims, but a cosmetic.

[7]) In our rendering of *ẓʾuh* we agree with CASSUTO (*op. cit.*, pp. 65, 79) who most appositely cites Isaiah iv, 4, אם רחץ אדני את צאת בנות־ציון.

Hence we should explain the bloodbath of the goddess Anat as relating to a rite proper to the season of transition between the sterility of the late Syrian summer and the new season of fertility. It seems to us to indicate at once a rite of separation from the phase of sterility and a rite of imitative magic to stimulate a liberal outpouring of fresh vitality, the blood being to the ancient Semite the life-essence. [1]) In the latter respect the copious blood-letting has its ritual analogy with the self-laceration of the 'prophets' of Baal at the ordeal with Elijah on Mount Carmel which, as the sequel shows, was associated with the breaking of a drought. [2])

There seems to be a reference to the *hieros gamos* in the beginning of column III, where, however, there is a lacuna, after which there is a reference [3]) to:

mšr.l.dd.'al'eyn.b'l	'A love-charm [4]) for the love of Baal the Mighty,
yd.pdry.bt.'ar	The love of the Plump Damsel, daughter of Mist,
'ahbt.ṭly.bt.rb	The affection of Dewy, daughter of Showers,
dd.'arṣy.bt.y'bdr	The love of the Earth-maiden, [5]) daughter of the Wide World.' [6])

The consequence of this *hieros gamos* is, furthermore, anticipated by the message of Baal to his sister Anat in a passage which is a real *crux interpretum* in the texts: [7])

qryy.b'arṣ.mlḥmt	'Effect [8]) unions [9]) in the land,
št.b'prm.ddym	Diffuse [10]) love [11]) in the earth;

---

[1]) Genesis ix, 4; Leviticus xvii, 14; Deuteronomy xii, 23. We do not believe with Dussaud that the slaughter of Anat is immediately followed by a prayer to Baal to pour out dew and rain. *Les découvertes* . . . 2nd ed., 4. 117; *Les origines cananéennes du sacrifice israélite*, 2nd. ed., 1941, p. 328.

[2]) I Kings xviii, 44-45.

[3]) Gordon *UH* 'nt, III, 2 ff.

[4]) *mšr* seems to be derived from the verbal root *nšr*, probably cognate with the Arabic نشر, 'to charm'. Driver (*op. cit.*, pp. 87, 160) suggests the meaning 'token' or 'confirmation', citing the Akkadian and Syriac verbs *šrr*.

[5]) Alternatively *'arṣy* may mean the Fruitful One, cf. Arabic أريض, 'fruitful'.

[6]) So Driver after Albright. He explains the word as *y'b dr* 'is spacious (Arabic وعب) in circuit'. *op. cit.*, pp. 87, 165.

[7]) Gordon *UH*, 'nt, III, 11-17.

[8]) We take *qryy* as the intensive (causative) of *qry*, 'to cause to happen'.

[9]) For *mlḥmt* we suggest affinity with the Arabic root لحم, 'to consolidate, solder up'. In the IIIrd form it means 'to ally through marriage'.

[10]) We suggest that this verb is cognate with the Arabic شتّ, 'to scatter', as in Gordon *UH* 68, 27, where Baal 'scatters' Sea.

[11]) *dd* is sexual love and not amity or affection.

sk.šlm.lkbd.'arṣ	Pour out well-being [1]) into the midst of the earth,
'arb.dd.lkbd.šdm	Increase love amidst the fields.
ḥšk.ʿṣk.ʿbṣk	Forbear [2]) to gainsay [3]) and grudge [4])
ʿmy.pʿnk.tlsmn	To me may thy feet run, [5])
ʿmy.twtḥ.'ešdk	To me may thine impulse [6]) hasten.'

The seasonal significance of the text is definitely indicated in the sequel, where Baal sends a message to Anat that he has created a wonderful new weapon, lightning. [7])

dm.rgm.'eṯ.ly.w'argmk	'For lo! I have a communication and I shall tell it to thee,
hwt.w.'aṯnyk	A word, and I shall declare it to thee,
rgm.ʿṣ.wlḥšt.'abn	A word ot the tree, yea the whisper of the stone,
t'ant.šmm.ʿm.'arṣ	Which the heavens murmur to the earth,
thmt.ʿmn.kbkbm	And the deep to the stars.
'abn.brq.dl.tdʿ.šmm	I will create lightning which the heavens do not know,
rgm.ltdʿ.nšm	A matter [8]) that men do not know, [9])

[1]) *šlm* in the context ought, we suggest, to be taken in its primary sense of 'wholeness' in the sense of 'well-being' and not in the pacifist sense.

[2]) Cf. Hebrew חשך, 'to restrain'.

[3]) Cf. Syriac ܚܪܝܢܐ (= ἀντιλογία in Jude 11), Arabic عصى, 'to rebel', 'refuse to acquiesce'.

[4]) We suggest that *ʿbṣ* is cognate with the Arabic عبق, 'to be niggardly, cling to'. For correspondence between *ṣ* and *q* which our derivation demands see p. 42, n. 1.

[5]) The verb is cognate with the Akkadian *lasamu*, 'to run'.

[6]) We connect the noun *'ešd* with the Arabic أسد, meaning 'courage', hence 'impulse'. The verb *twtḥ* we take to be the Ifteʿal of a root *wḥy* cognate with the Arabic وحى which means in the Vth form 'to hasten'.

[7]) Gordon *UH* ʿnt, III, 17-28.

[8]) M. D. Cassuto (*From Adam to Noah*, 1953, pp. 50-51), followed by Pope (*El in the Ugaritic Texts*, 1955, pp. 99-100) and Ginsberg (ANET, p. 126), takes *'abn brq* as 'stones of lightning', which F. C. Fensham takes to be 'flints', 'Thunder-stones in Ugaritic', *JNES* XVIII, 1959, pp. 273-4. The problematic אבני אש of Ezekiel xxviii, 14 is cited. Albright, in a private communication cited by Fensham, supports this interpretation, taking *rgm* in the following line as a parallel to *'abn brq*, citing Akkadian *rigmu*, 'stone'. In view of the repetition of *rgm* earlier in the passage in the obvious sense of 'word', this is a hazardous suggestion. The announcement of a proclamation more naturally suggests a verb *'abn brq*, 'I will create lightning', than a noun. Driver well observes that the lightning was the prelude to the rain (*op. cit.*, p. 87), cf. 1 Kings xviii, 38, 45, and the modern Palestinian folk-saying, البرق علامة المطر, 'The lightning is the announcement of the rain'. The lightning shaft is the shaft of the spear of Baal in sculpture.

[9]) Here we have a case of the Canaanite idiom of the masculine plural of the imperfect with the preformative *t*. Driver (*op. cit.*, p. 87) thinks that the sounds were intended to give notice to heaven and earth of the impending rain, *l* in this case not being the negative particle. This is possible, though the word-divider between *dl* and *tdʿ* rather suggests that *l* is the negative particle.

wltbn.hmlt.ʾarṣ	Nor the multitudes of the earth understand.
ʾatm.wʾank.ʾebġyh	'Come now [1]) and I will show [2]) it to thee,
btk.ġry.ʾel.ṣpn	I, god of Sapon, in the midst of my mountain,
bqdš.bġr.nḥlty	In the sanctuary, in the mountain of mine inheritance
bnʿm.bgbʿ.tlʾeyt	In the pleasant place, in the Hill of Power.'

Violent thunder and lightning, the peculiar manifestation of the presence of Baal or, as he is named, Hadad, is a feature of the beginning of the New Year of the Syrian peasant in autumn, the season of the 'early rains', יורה of the Old Testament, to which indeed there is a further reference in this text in column IV, 70, 'Let Baal drive up his clouds.' [3]) The fact, however, that Baal's lightning is a novelty suggests that perhaps this text should be considered a cosmic myth in the same category as the texts Gordon *UH* 129, 137, 68. In this connection Anat's reply to Baal's messengers is significant: [4])

ʾek.mġy.gpn.wʾugr	'In what case come 'Vine' and 'Field'?
mn.ʾeb.ypʿ.lbʿl	What enemy rises up against Baal,
ṣrt.lrkb.ʿrpt	What adversary against Him who Mounts the Clouds?
lmḫšt.mdd.ʾel.ym	Have I not slain Sea beloved of El?
lklt.nhr.ʾel rbm	Have I not annihilated River the great god?
lʾeštbm.tnn.ʾešbmnh	Have I not muzzled [5]) *tnn*, holding her in a muzzle?
mḫšt.bṯn.ʿqltn	I have slain the Crooked Serpent,
šlyṭ.d.šbʿt.rʾašm	The Close-coiling One with Seven Heads.
mḫšt.mdd ʾelm.ʾar(ṣ)	I have slain the beloved of the earth-deities,
mt.ʿgl.ʾel.ʿtk	Even Mot who passes on his way with prodigious haste.
mḫšt.klbt.ʾelm ʾešt	I have slain the Bitch of the gods, Fire.
klt.bt.ʾel.ẕbb	I have annihilated the Daughter of El, Flame,
ʾemtḫṣ.wʾetrṯ.ḫrṣ	Smiting and dispossessing the Flood, [6])
ṭrd.bʿl.bmrym.ṣpn	Who would drive [7]) Baal from the crags of Sapon,
mšṣṣ.kʿṣr.ʾudnh	Who would repel [8]) like a bird his lordship,

1) *ʾatm* is the imperative of *ʾaty*, 'to come', with the emphatic enclitic *m*.

2) This verb seems a cognate of the Arabic بغى, which in the IVth form means 'to help to attain'.

3) *bʿl mdlh ybʿr*. The noun *mdl* is found in modern Arabic as مزن, meaning 'cloud'.

4) Gordon *UH* ʿnt, III, 33 ff.

For philological notes on this passage *v. supra*, p. 31, n. 1.

5) There is a more specific reference to this exploit in the fragment from the palace of Ras Shamra, *PRU* II, 1, l. 7, where an iron collar (*ʾaṭm prṯl*) is imposed on the head of the serpent (*bṯn*), and in *PRU* II, 3, ll. 8-9, where it is stated that 'she muzzled *tnn* with a muzzle' (*tnn lšbm tšt*).

6) *ḫrṣ* is better taken as a cognate with the Arabic خريص, 'flood', the notorious adversary of Baal.

7) *ṭrd* seems best read as a participle.

8) *mšṣṣ* may be a participle connected with the Akkadian *šaṣu*, 'to be refractory'.

gršh.lks'e.mlkh	Would drive him from the seat of his kingship,
lnḫt.lkḥṯ.drkth	From the dais, [1]) from the throne of his sovereignty.
mnm.'eb.ypʿ.lbʿl	What enemy rises up against Baal?
ṣrt.lrkb.ʿrpt	What adversary against Him who mounts the Clouds?'

This passage obviously connects the text with Gordon *UH* 129, 137, 68. In those texts, however, there is no mention of any adversary but the Waters, Sea and River, and there the victor is Baal and not Anat. It should, however, be noted that elsewhere one of those monsters namely *ltn*, the Crooked Serpent, is said to have been slain by Baal. [2]) This indicates to us that this was an old theme readapted, the text Gordon *UH* ʿnt being used to bridge the gap between the cosmic mythology describing the conflict of Baal and the primaeval monsters and the unruly waters and the seasonal mythology where the storm-god Baal has become identified with the vegetation which he has promoted.

Nevertheless the main theme of the text is fertility, and after Anat has agreed to

> 'effect unions in the land,
> diffuse love in the earth,
> pour out well-being into the midst of the earth,
> increase love amidst the fields',

the text goes on to deal with her negotiations with El and his consort Aṯerat for the building of a 'house' for Baal, [3]) and eventually the divine craftsman, the Skilful and Percipient One, or Hyn, is approached [4]). This theme is the keynote of the text Gordon *UH* 51, which describes the actual building of the 'house', which is dedicated

---

[1]) *nḫt* is used in the description of the throne and dais of El. It is derived from a root cognate with the Arabic ناخ, 'to level', hence its meaning 'platform' or 'dais'. We suggest that the phrase והיה מנוחתו כבוד in Isaiah xi, 10 should be translated 'And his dais shall be glory'. This may also be the meaning of מנוחה in Psalm cxxxii, 14, especially if the verb ישב in the parallel phrase has the pregnant meaning 'to be enthroned', which the context certainly suggests.

[2]) Albright maintains that, even though Baal seems to be indicated in the text Gordon *UH* 67 as the slayer of the dragon *ltn*, that was actually the exploit of Anat, whom Albright takes to be the representative of Baal, her name signifying 'the sign or indication' of Baal's will, *From the Stone Age to Christianity*, 1940, pp. 286, 339, n. 51, *BASOR* 84, 1941, p. 15. Our explanation is that this is either a survival of some more primitive cosmic myth which has been only imperfectly integrated with a later mythology proper to the cult of Baal and Anat or the version of the Baal myth which was current at a shrine of Anat.

[3]) Gordon *UH* ʿnt pl. vi, IV, V.

[4]) *Ibidem*, VI, 9 ff.

with a great feast which recalls the hecatombs of Solomon on his dedication of the temple (1 Kings viii, 5, 62 ff.).

Here again there is an analogy with *enuma eliš*, where after the acclamation of Marduk as King upon his triumph over Tiamat the gods proceed to erect him a temple in Babylon. In the Ugaritic text, Aṯerat, in urging upon El the building of a temple for Baal, declares:

mlkn.'al'eyn.b'l
ṯpṭn.w'en.d'lnh (GORDON, *UH* 51, IV, 43-44)
Our King is Baal the Mighty,
Our ruler, above whom there is none.

The association of the building of the temple of Baal in late autumn with his royal estate is significant in view of the association of Enthronement Psalms in the Old Testament with the New Year festival, which, we claim, may be securely established for the monarchic period on the evidence of Nahum ii, 1 (Hebrew text) taken in conjunction with Isaiah lii, 7 and Zechariah xiv, 16-17, *v. supra* p. 33.

With this text GORDON *UH* 51, [1]) which we should definitely place in the category of pure seasonal myth, the connection with a particular phase of the agricultural year is not difficult to establish. To be sure, the action moves slowly in the regular epic style, which cites the mandate of the gods to messengers, retails the actual message, and often cites the agreement of the addressee in identical terms. The work of the craftsman-god is described in great detail, and the whole weary business of entreaty of El—this time *per* Aṯerat—to sanction the building of the 'house' for Baal is repeated in columns IV and V with almost verbatim agreement with GORDON *UH* 'nt pl. vi, V, 38-51. This passage in the text GORDON *UH* 51 gives us a clue to the '*Sitz im Leben*' of the text, which we are able to place in the autumn or New Year Season. This is particularly clear in column V, 68 ff.: [2])

wn'ap.'dn.mṭrh.b'l.y'dn 'Moreover [3]) Baal will send abundance [4]) of his rain,

[1]) First published by VIROLLEAUD as II AB, 'Un nouveau chant du poème d'Alein-Baal', *Syria* XIII, 1932, pp. 113-163.

[2]) GORDON *UH* 51, V, 68 ff.

[3]) *wn'ap* is a *hapax legomenon* in the Ras Shamra texts, the meaning of which, however, is hardly in doubt. The *n* (►►►) may be a dittograph of *'a* (►►). Or it may be inserted *metri causa* as we suspect elsewhere in the texts. We prefer the latter suggestion.

[4]) So DRIVER, *op. cit.*, p. 97. The root appears in the Arabic عدانة, 'a crowd'.

ʿdn.ṯrt.bglṯ — Abundance of moisture [1]) with snow, [2])
w(y)tn qlh.bʿrpt — And he will utter his voice in the clouds,
šrh.lʾarṣ.brqm — (He will send) his flashing [3]) to the earth with lightning.'

Another feature which, in the opinion of the writer, relates the myth to a seasonal ritual is the installation of a shutter in the 'house' of Baal. When the divine craftsman Kṯr wḪss, 'the Skilful and Percipient One', is entertained by Baal and discusses the building he suggests: [4])

bl.ʾašt.ʾurbt.bbhtm — 'Nay but I shall put a shutter [5]) in the house,
ḥln.bqrb.hklm — Even a window in the midst of the palace.'

To this Baal replies: [6])

ʾal.tšt.ʾurbt.bbhtm — 'Put not a shutter in the house,
ḥln.bqrb.hklm — A window in the midst of the palace.'

---

[1]) Reading *ṯrt* (𐎘𐎗𐎚) with DRIVER (*op. cit.*, p. 96) for Gordon's *ṯkt* (𐎘𐎋𐎚). Following GORDON's reading, AISTLEITNER (*MKT*, p. 41) translates

Von nun an möge Baal die Zeit seines Regens festsetzen,
Die Zeit des Erstarrens zu Eis.

His interpretation of *ʿdn* is feasible, but in connecting *ṯkt* with Arabic وَثِقَ, 'to be firm', cf. Akkadian *ešequ*, 'to make firm', and *glṯ* with Arabic جلّى, 'to freeze', cf. Syriac ܓܠܝܕܐ, 'frost, ice' (*Wörterbuch* 657), he assumes two irregular phonetic correspondences in two successive words, the first being really serious.

[2]) With DRIVER (*op. cit.*, pp. 97, 146) after DUSSAUD, connecting the word with the Arabic ثلج, 'snow'. Such metathesis of a letter is not unknown as a dialectic variation, e.g. Hebrew נחש and modern Arabic حناش, 'snake'.

[3]) *šr* seems to be cognate with the Arabic شرّة. There is also a word شرار, 'sparks', which might suit the context here. In Job xxxvii, 3

תַּחַת־כָּל־שָׁמַיִם יִשְׁרֵהוּ
וְאוֹרוֹ עַל־כַּנְפוֹת הָאָרֶץ,

which is quite intelligibly translated,

Under the whole heaven he lets it loose,
And his light is unto (read אֶל) the edges of the earth,

ישרהו, parallel by position to אורו, 'his light', may be a corruption of שָׁרֵהוּ from a root cognate with Ugaritic *šr*, 'flashing', as GINSBERG tentatively suggested ('The Ugaritic texts and Textual criticism', *JBL* LXII, 1943). We should therefore read שָׁרֵהוּ for יִשְׁרֵהוּ and translate:

Under the whole heaven is his flashing
And his light to the edges of the earth.

[4]) GORDON *UH* 51, V, 123-124.

[5]) The word *ʾurbt* is that used in the Flood story in Genesis for the 'windows of heaven' which were opened, Genesis vii, 11; viii, 2.

[6]) GORDON *UH* 51, V, 126-127.

The Skilful and Percipient One, however, will not abandon his project, but persists: [1])

> ‘Hear, I beseech thee, O Mighty Baal,
> Let me indeed put a shutter in the house,
> A window in the midst of the palace.’

Baal persists: [2])

’al.tšt.’urbt.bbhtm	‘Put not a shutter in the house,
ḥln.bqrb.hklm	A window in the midst of the palace.
’al.td.pdry.bt.’ar	Wet [3]) not the Plump damsel the daughter of Mist,
(*ṭl)y.bt.rb*	Dewy the daughter of Showers . . .’

The divine craftsman meanwhile acquiesces but adds: [4])

tṯb.b‘l.lhwty	‘Thou wilt return, O Baal, to my suggestion.’

Eventually, the ‘house’ being completed and a great feast held for all the gods, doubtless as a rite of ‘aggregation’, Baal asks for a window to be installed: [5])

’aštm.kṯr bn.ym	‘I should instal it, O Skilful One Master of Design, [6])
kṯr.bnm.‘dt	O Skilful One Master of Tools, [7])
yptḥ.ḥln.bbhtm	Let a window be opened [8]) in the house,
’urbt.bqrb.hklm	A shutter in the midst of the palace.’

The repetition of this theme is a literary device to emphasize the significance of a certain feature in the accompanying ritual, the

---

[1]) *Ibidem* VI, 4-6.

[2]) *Ibidem*, VI, 8-11.

[3]) The jussive *td* is best taken as from the root *ndy*, cognate with the Arabic ندى, ‘to be wet’. GASTER conjectures a connection with the Hebrew נדה ‘to be abducted’, the point being that Baal’s girls would abscond and he would be ridiculed by his rival Mot (*Thespis*, pp. 176, 448). CASSUTO, ALBRIGHT, GINSBERG and DRIVER maintain that Baal’s objection to the window is that Mot (Death) should climb in. They cite Jeremiah ix, 20 (Evv. 21), ‘For Death has come up into our windows . . .’ In any case this passage shows that the Plump damsel, Dewy, and the Earth-girl, were Baal’s consorts and suggests that the purpose of building the ‘house’ was that Baal, restored to life and virility, might celebrate the *hieros gamos*.

[4]) GORDON *UH* 51, VI, 15.

[5]) *Ibidem*, VII, 15-18.

[6]) *bn ym* is generally taken as ‘the son of a day’, so ‘this very day’, so GASTER, *JAOS* LXX, 1950, p. 14. We take *ym* as a verbal noun from *ymm*, cognate with the Arabic يمّ, ‘to purpose’.

[7]) GASTER takes *‘dt* as ‘now’ and renders the compound phrase *bnm ‘dt* as ‘this very moment’, which is quite a feasible translation. Our own view is that in *‘dt* we have the root cognate with the Arabic عدّة, which is used in the Syrian dialect for ‘tools’.

[8]) *yptḥ* is best taken as a passive imperfect.

opening of the said shutter as a rite of imitative magic. This is apparent from the sequel: [1])

wyptḥ . bdqt . ʿrpt	'And cause the clouds to be opened with rain [2])
ʿl p(tḥ) . kṯr wḥss	When the Skilful One opens the window.'

Then the text goes on: [3])

yptḥ . ḥln . bbhtm	He opens a window in the house,
ʾurbt . bqrb . hklm	A shutter in the midst of the palace.
ptḥ . bʿl . bdqt . ʿrpt	"Open, O Baal, the clouds with rain".
qlh . qdš . b(y)tn	He utters his holy voice . . . [4])

A fragmentary passage ensues, where the effect of Baal's thunder recalls Ps. xxix, and the text continues: [5])

ʾeb . bʿl tʾeḥd yʿrm .	The foes of Baal occupied the forests
šnʾu . hd . gpt ġr .	The enemy of Hadad the inmost recesses [6]) of the mountains,
wyʿn . ʾalʾeyn bʿl .	Then up spake Baal the Mighty,
ʾeb . hd(d) . lm . tḫš	O enemy of Hadad, why art thou dismayed?
lm . tḫš . nṯq . dmrn	Why dismayed at our solid strength? [7])
ʿn . bʿl . qdm . ydh	The eyes of Baal anticipate his hands
ktġẓ . ʾarẓ . bymnh	When the cedar(spear) is brandished in his right hand,
bkm . yṯb . bʿl . lbhth	Now that Baal returns to his house
ʾumlk . ʾubl mlk	Shall any, king or no king,
ʾarṣ . drkt yštkn	Make the earth his dominion?

Here, then, obviously is a myth associated with the construction of a 'house' in the season of the Syrian New Year when the violent

---

[1]) Gordon *UH* 51, VII, 19-20. We see a reference to a similar rite of imitative magic in the Krt text, Gordon *UH* 126, IV, 11 ff., where El bids the 'water-pourer of the house of Baal' (*ngr bt bʿl*) and his consorts ascend to the roof and perform their office. We connect *ngr* here with the Hebrew נגר, and our conjecture is supported by the fact that the waterpourer and his consorts are called by El *mṯrry*, 'my water-providers' (from *ṯrr*), cognate with the Arabic ثرّ, 'to be abundant in water'.

[2]) *dqt* is a verbal noun from a root *wdq* cognate with the Arabic ودق, 'to drip rain'.

[3]) Gordon *UH* 51, VII, 25 ff.

[4]) The voice of Baal is, of course, thunder, which often accompanies the heavy rains of autumn in Syria. The phrase נתן קול is used of thunder in 1 Samuel xii, 17, and probably has the same significance in Amos i, 2.

[5]) Gordon *UH* 51, VII, 35-44.

[6]) So Driver (*op. cit.*, p. 146), who cites Arabic جنف, 'the inside of a house.

[7]) Lit. 'the solidity of our strength', cf. Hebrew הר קדשו, 'his holy hill'. Driver connects *nṯq* with the Arabic وثق 'to be firm', and *mr* with the Arabic مرة, 'firmness, strength', *d* being the relative particle.

rains and thunderstorms were expected. It is connected with a rite of imitative magic to induce the rain, and the building of the 'house' was probably the preliminary to the *hieros gamos*, though that is not explicit.

The myth of the building of the house of Baal has, thus, certain essential features which have their counterpart in the dedication of Solomon's Temple in Jerusalem, which was dedicated in the same season, the seventh month, Ethanim, the month of 'the regular rains' (1 Kings viii, 2), and in the Feast of Tabernacles, which fell in the same period. Indeed the rite of imitative magic which we have pointed out in the Canaanite myth suggests the water-pouring rite at the Hebrew Feast of Tabernacles, when water was drawn from the Pool of Siloam and poured out on the altar. [1]) The 'house of Baal', in fact, may well have been the mythical prototype of the tabernacles or bivouacs which the Hebrews, doubtless following the peasants of Canaan, erected at this festival. If we are right in our supposition that the 'house of Baal' was erected for the great *hieros gamos* we may suppose that his activity was abetted by the worshippers in those 'tabernacles' and, indeed, such sexual licence is noted in Amos (ii, 7) [2]) and more explicitly in the Mishnah, where we read that eventually the sexes had to be separated in worship.

At the height of his power, a king with a castle, having made a round of his realm, asserting his lordship and compelling his enemies to shrink back to the inmost recesses of forest and mountain, Baal ventures to hope that he may subject his inveterate enemy Mot, the destructive power of drought, sterility and death itself. Here the vicissitudes of Baal in the vegetation he promotes and the tensions of fertility and sterility in the agricultural year are anticipated. Baal declares: [3])

---

[1]) The blowing of trumpets on the same occasion probably indicates an original rite of imitative magic to induce the thunder which was the harbinger of rain, Mishnah, *Sukkah* IV, 9; V, 5.

[2]) The fact that other sins mentioned in the same context are the more condemned because they are done 'by every altar' and 'in the house of their God' indicates that the reference is to ritual prostitution, as is suggested by the phrase 'to profane my holy name'. It cannot be conclusively demonstrated that the ritual prostitution here was an element in the New Year festival, but the preoccupation of Amos with 'the day of Jahweh' probably signifies that the appearance of the prophet at Bethel was on the occasion of the New Year festival of the Enthronement of Jahweh, which was an adaptation of the Canaanite New Year festival celebrating the rehabilitation of Baal as King.

[3]) GORDON *UH* 51, VII, 45-52. So DRIVER (*op. cit.*, p. 101), instead of our

dll.ʾal.ʾelʾak.lbn ʾelm.mt	I shall indeed send a guide for the god Mot,
ʿdd lydd ʾel ġẓr	A herald for the Hero, beloved of El
yqrʾa.mt.bnpšh	To call Mot to his grave. 1)
ystrn ydd.bgngnh	To conceal that 'darling' in his tomb. 1)
ʾaḥdy.dymlk.ʿl.ʾelm	I alone am he who will reign over the gods,
lymrʾu.ʾelm.wnšm	Yea, be leader 2) of gods and men,
dyšb(m).hmlt.ʾarṣ	Even marshal 3) the multitudes of earth.' 4)

Baal's response is to send his messengers, Vine and Field (*gpn w ʾugr*),5)

---

original translation. 'Adulation (cf. Arabic دلّ, 'blandishments') shall I not send to Mot the son of El, Nor compliments (cf. Arabic عدّى 'to eulogize the dead') to the Hero beloved of El etc.'; *ʾelʾak* suggests an embassy, hence DRIVER's personal objects *dl*, 'guide' and *ʿdd*, 'herald', cf. Arabic عدّاد, 'One who repeats' (*op. cit.*, p. 141). DRIVER's translation is much more congruous with the context.

1) This couplet and the parallels *npšh* and *gngnh* exemplify the difficulty of interpreting these texts. *npš*, in the Ras Shamra texts as in Hebrew regularly means 'throat' and *ggnh*, of which *gngnh* could be the unassimilated form, means 'inwards' in GORDON *UH* 127, 26, where the phrase occurs *ywsrn ggnh*, 'his inwards instruct him'. In the present passage the verb cannot be the derivative of *wsr*, since the infixed *t* would appear before *s*. Hence DRIVER rightly takes it as *str*, 'to hide' (*op. cit.*, p. 157), in which case *gngnh*, means 'his tomb', of Arab. جنجن, 'chest', cited by DRIVER (p. 157) after al-YASIN, and *npšh* means 'grave', cf. Aramaic נפשא, cited by DRIVER.

2) *lymrʾu* should possibly be read *dymrʾu*. The verb would be a *hapax legomenon*, but its meaning is suggested by the parallel *ymlk*. It is apparently a denominative verb from the noun *mrʾu*, which denotes a member of a military class at Ugarit in the administrative texts.

3) For the doubtful final letter of *yšb* (   ) we read *m* enclitic instead of ʿ read by GORDON and DRIVER. The verb, in parallelism with *ymlk* and *ymrʾu* might be cognate with the Arabic نسب, 'to arrange, regulate'.

4) The earth, as often in the Ras Shamra texts and usually in such a context as the present, possibly signifies the underworld.

5) The nature of Baal as a fertility deity is plain from his relation to his messengers Vine and Field, whom he addresses (VII, 53-56):

ʿn.(gpn).wʾugr	'Look, Vine and Field,
b(n).ġlmt.(ʿmm)ym	Ye large-limbed sons[i]; of the maiden (or Dusk),[ii]
bn.ẓlmt.r(mt prʿt) ʾebrtn	Ye sons of Shadow high and lofty [iii] whom I impregnated.'[iv]

i. The text actually reads *bġlmt*, which we suppose to be a scribal error for *bn ġlmtʾ ʿmmym* is the dual masculine. The root is cognate with the Arabic عمم, 'large-limbed'.

ii. *ġlmt* could mean either 'maiden', Hebrew עלמה, or 'dusk', Hebrew צלם. In the latter sense the root is found in GORDON *UH* Krt, 19, *ġlm ym* 'darkness of day', as first appreciated by GASTER, *JQR* xxxvii, 1947, pp. 289 ff. The imagery which makes Vine and Field the offspring of Baal the Storm-god by the darkness (i.e. of storm-clouds) is particularly appropriate.

iii. *prʿ* seems cognate with the Arabic فارع, 'lofty'.

iv. In the last two letters we have re-grouped the four horizontal strokes to

to the underground realm of Death, which is graphically described: [1])

'edk.'al.ttn.pnm	'Then, indeed, set face
'm.ġr.trġzz	To the mountain of *Trġzz*
'm.ġr.ṯrmg	To the mountain of *Ṯrmg* [2])
'm.tlm.ġṣr.'arṣ	Even to the twin mounts which hem in the earth. [3])
š'a.ġr.'l.ydm	Take the mountain on your hands,
ḫlb.lẓr.rḥtm	The hill on the top of your palms, [4])
wrd.bt ḫpṯt.'arṣ	And descend to the House of the Corruption [5]) of the earth,
tspr.byrdm.'arṣ	And be numbered with those who go down into the earth.
'edk.'al.ttn.pnm	Then, indeed, shall ye set face
tk.qrth.hmry	Towards his city Ruin. [6])
mk.ks'u.ṯbth	Dilapidation is [7]) the throne on which he sits,
ḫḫ.'arṣ.nḥlth	Loathsomeness [8]) is the land of his inheritance
wnġr.'tn.'elm	But be on guard against [9]) the most ruthless of the gods;

---

read *-tn* instead of *-nt* read by Gordon. We have thus the perfect of the verb *'ebr* with the energic form of the 3rd fem. sing. The verb. seems cognate with the Arabic أبر, 'to impregnate'.

[1]) Gordon *UH* 51, VIII, 1 ff.

[2]) The names of those mountains, visualised no doubt beyond the area of Semitic occupation in Anatolia, are non-Semitic.

[3]) So Gaster, *Thespis*, p. 183.

[4]) *rḥtm* is found in parallelism with *ydm* in Gordon *UH* 67, V, 14 in the same couplet describing entry into the underworld. *rḥt* is cognate with the Arabic راحة, 'palm of the hand'. In the context of the visit to the underworld we take this odd phrase to mean 'grope' in the darkness.

[5]) The complex *btḫpṯt* is usually divided into two words *bt ḫpṯt*, and this suggests to some commentators the Hebrew בית החפשית, the 'isolation ward' in which lepers like King Uzziah were confined (2 Kings xv, 5 = 2 Chronicles xxvi, 21). Gaster takes *tḫpṯt* as one word from the root *ḫpṯ* which he connects with the Arabic خبث, 'to be filthy', *Thespis*, p. 448. The cognate in Arabic may signify 'corruption' or 'sterility', either of which is suitable in the context. We prefer the division *bt ḫpṯt*, though there is no word-divider in the original text. The word-divider is occasionally omitted where it obviously ought to stand. Our principle is to deal with a long complex of letters as we have done with *btḫpṯt*, taking liberty with the word-divider where it is not marked, but observing it rigidly where it is noted. *arṣ* as often in the Ras Shamra texts, has the connotation of 'the underworld'.

[6]) *hmry*, the name of Mot's stronghold, is cognate with the Arabic همرة appropriately enough meaning 'confusion'.

[7]) We connect *mk* with *mkk*, 'to collapse', cf. Gordon *UH* 68,17 and Hebrew מכך, e.g. יִמַּךְ הַמְּקָרֶה, 'the roof-tree collapses', Ecclesiastes x, 18.

[8]) *ḫḫ* has been connected with the Akkadian *ḫabḫu* meaning 'mere trash' by Ginsberg and this meaning is admitted by Gaster, *Thespis*, p. 452. It is used to describe lies in Gordon *UH* 2 Aqht VI, 35.

[9]) *nġr* is cognate with Hebrew נצר, 'to watch', the participle being used of the guardian of the crops in Gordon *UH* 52, 68-70.

'al.tqrb.lbn.'elm mt	Come not near to Mot the son of El
'al.y'dbkm k'emr.bph	Lest he make you like a sheep in his mouth,
kll'e.bṯbrn qnh tḫt'an	And ye be carried off [1]) in his jaws. [2])

Unfortunately the end of this column is lost and we do not know the full content of Baal's message to Mot beyond the announcement that he has had his 'house' built. This is tantamount to the announcement that he is king. Thus the stage is set for the drama of the life-and-death conflict between Baal and Mot which is an expression of the perpetual tension between fertility and drought throughout the whole of the husbandman's year in Syria.

Here we note that Baal's adversary is no longer the unruly water and its associate monsters, but Death, Mot. It is true that this dread deity is associated with the corruption of the underworld, but he is nevertheless also manifest in the drought and menacing desolation of the Syrian summer. In a passage which apparently connects the text GORDON *UH* 67 (VIROLLEAUD I* AB) [3]) with that we have just discussed, Baal's messengers to Mot are sent back with the message: [4])

ktmḫṣ.ltn.bṯn.brḥ	'Though thou didst smite Ltn the primaeval serpent,
tkly.bṯn.'qltn	And didst annihilate the Crooked Serpent,
šlyṭ.dšb't.r'ašm	The Close-coiling One of Seven Heads,
ṯṯkḥ.ttrp.šmm	The heavens will dry up, yea languish;
krs.'epdk.'ank.'esp'e	I shall pound thee, consume and eat thee,
'uṭm.šrqm.'amtm	Cleft, forspent and exhausted
lyrt.bnpš.bn.'elm.mt	Lo thou art gone down into the throat of the god Mot,
bmhmrt.ydd.'el.ġẓr	Into the gullet [5]) of the Hero, Beloved of El.

---

[1]) After DRIVER (*op. cit.*, p. 139), who takes the verb as a cognate of Arabic خَتَأَ (VIII), with the same meaning. The verb appears in the same context in GORDON *UH* 49, II, 23.

[2]) Lit. 'breach of his throat'. *qn* is probably the cognate of the Arabic قَنَاةٌ, 'conduit, pipe, spout of jug', hence 'wind-pipe'.

[3]) VIROLLEAUD, 'Le mort de Baal', *Syria* XV, 1934, pp. 305-336.

[4]) GORDON *UH* 67, I, 1-8, 12-26. This is a very difficult passage, as may be realized by the number of italicised words in GORDON's translation (*UL*, p. 39) and that of DRIVER (*op. cit.*, p. 105), and the very different interpretation in the rather paraphrased version of GASTER, *Thespis*, p. 187. For philological notes in support of our own translation *v. supra*, p. 30, n. 3.

[5]) The word *mhmrt* in this context suggests *hmry* which we have already noted as the name of the stronghold of Mt. In form it might be a local name like the Hebrew מזבח, 'place of sacrifice, altar', or the intensive participle feminine singular or plural from a verbal root *hmr*, cognate with the Arabic همر, 'to pour

....	....................................'
tḫm.bn.ʾelm.mt	The message of Mot the son of El,
hwt.ydd.bn.ʾel.ġẓr	The word of the Hero, Beloved of El,
pnh.š.npš.lbʾet.thw	Whose face is (that of) a sheep, his spirit (that of) an onrushing lioness. [1]
hm.brlt.ʾanḫr.bym	"Lo (my) throat (gapes like that of) the dolphin [2] in the sea;
hm.brky.tkšd.rʾumm	Lo my knee prevails over (that of) wild oxen;
ʿn.kẓd.ʾaylt	(My) eye has the intensity [3] of the hind.
hm.ʾemt ʾemt.npš	If my throat is indeed athirst [4]
blt.ḫmr.( )ḫt	It must be slaked with the draught [5] of an ass.
bklʾat.ydy.ʾelḫm	My hands shall clutch [6] and I shall eat.
hm.šbʿ.ydty.bṣʿ	Yea indeed sate my desire [7] with the bowl,
hm.ks.ymsk.nhrk l(y)	Yea let thy river mix me a cup.
ṣḫn.bʿl.ʿmʾaḫy	Call [8] Baal with my brethren,
qrʾan.hd.ʿm.ʾaryy	Invite Hadad [8] with my kinsmen?
wlḫmm.ʿm.ʾaḫy.lḫm	Though food has been eaten with my brethren,
wštt.ʿm.ʾaryy yn	And wine has been set forth with my kinsmen,
pnšt.bʿl.ṭʿn.ʾeṭʿnk	I have forgotten this, O Baal; I shall certainly pierce thee..."

The particular reference to the thirst of Mot is of course an allusion to the summer drought.

---

down' with the suggestion of confusion, cf. همّار, 'a babbler'. Its position in parallelism with *npš*, 'throat', indicates a part of the body, the throat, as 'the place of pouring down', which Driver rather paraphrases as 'miry gorge' (*op. cit.* p. 105). For the bearing of this passage on Old Testament exegesis *v. infra* p. 273.

[1]) *thw* is a relative clause (antecedent *lbʾet*) without the relative particle, as occasionally in Hebrew poetry and in Arabic after an indefinite antecedent. *thw* is from the verb *hwy*, probably cognate with the Arabic هوى, 'to rush'.

[2]) *ʾanḫr* is generally taken as cognate with the Akkadian *naḫeru*, 'dolphin'.

[3]) We suggest tentatively that *ẓd* is cognate with the Arabic شدّ, 'to be strong, or intense'. It would be strange if *kẓd* were written as a variant spelling of *kšd*, as Driver suggests (*op. cit.*, p. 145), in the space of a couplet. We take *kšd*, in the previous line as cognate with the Akkadian *kašadu*, 'to subdue'.

[4]) We take *ʾemt* as the perfect of the stative verb cognate with آم, 'to be thirsty'. The second *ʾemt* is probably a verbal noun.

[5]) *blt* is a verbal noun of either *bll* or *ybl*, respectively cognate with the Arabic بلّ, 'to be wet', and وبل, 'to flow'.

[6]) Lit. 'in the confining of my hands'.

[7]) We connect *ydty* with the Arabic ودّة, 'desire'.

[8]) Following the reading of A. Herdner, *Corpus*, 1963, p. 33. The point of the passage as we have taken it is that the enmity of Mot was not mitigated by social convention where kinship and the partaking of a common meal were double securities against violence in primitive Semitic society as among the Bedouin today.

In the same context there may be another clue to the seasonal significance of the myth. In what appears to be the end of Mot's communication to Baal we read: [1])

....	....
(špt l'a)rṣ.špt.lšmm	'One lip to earth, one lip to heaven,
(wl)šn.lkbkbm	(And the tongue) to the stars [2])
y'rb.(b')l.bkbdh	That (Baal) may go into his inside,
bph.yrd	Yea go down into his mouth,
kḥrr.ẓt.ybl.'arṣ	As the choicest of olive oil which the earth produces [3])
wpr.'ṣm	Even as the fruit of the trees'.

This apparently anticipates the death of Baal sometime during the summer when the fruits begin to mature. The languishing of vegetation is implied in Baal's fear and his submission to his redoubtable adversary to whom he sends again his messengers. [4])

yr'a'un.'al'eyn.b'l	Baal the Mighty fears him
ṯt'.nn.rkb 'rpt	He who Mounteth the Clouds is adread of him. [5])
tb' rgm.lbn.'elm mt	Depart, tell the god Mot,
ṯny.lydd.'el ġẓr	Repeat to the Hero, Beloved of El,
tḥm.'al'eyn.b'l	The decision of Baal the Mighty
hwt.'al'ey qrdm	The word of the Mightiest of Heroes.
bhṯ.bn.'elm.mt	'Hail [6]) god Mot,
'bdk.'an.wd'lmk	I am thy servant and thy substitute.' [7])

---

[1]) Gordon *UH* 67, II, 2-6, . . .

[2]) The same phrase is used to describe the gargantuan appetite of the twin-gods *Šḥr* and *Šlm* in Gordon *UH* 52, 61-62.

[3]) The seasonal reference we suspect would be established beyond doubt if we were to admit Dussaud's translation (*Les découvertes* . . ., 2nd. ed., p. 130) 'When the olive . . . feels the heat' (*kḥrr ẓt*). The difficulty of the translation of Driver, who is as determined against any seasonal reference in the Baal-myth as Dussaud is for it, is the very doubtful Arabic cognate نَحْر, 'throat', which he cites (*op. cit.*, p. 138) in support of his translation 'as the olive . . . is swallowed' (*op. cit.*, p. 105). We regard *ḥrr* as a noun, cognate with the Arabic حُرّ, 'choice part'.

[4]) Gordon *UH* 67, II, 6-12.

[5]) So Driver (*op. cit.*, p. 151), who cites the root *št'* in the Karatepe inscription, col. II, l. 4, with this meaning.

[6]) The translation 'Hail' for *bhṯ* is suggested by the Arabic بهث, 'to welcome', cited by Driver, *op. cit.*, p. 163.

[7]) *d'lmk* obviously has some relationship to *'bd*. It is natural to think that perpetual servitude is denoted. It is, however, possible that *d'lmk* means 'thy substitute', *'lm* being connected with Hebrew צלם, which is phonetically possible. In this case such a relationship might be denoted as that between Ahab and his

Here there is a large lacuna in the text and the following two columns are extant only in the first halves of the lines with a final complete lacuna of some 10 lines. When we find the text complete again Baal is peremptorily summoned to the underworld: [1])

w'at.qḥ.'rptk	'And thou, take thy clouds,
rḥk.mdlk.mṭrtk	Thy wind, thy rain-cloud, [2]) thy rain,
'mk.šb't.ġlmk	With thee thy seven lads, [3])
ṯmn.ḫnẓrk	Thine eight swine, [4])
'mk.pdry.bt.'ar	With thee the Plump damsel, girl of Mist,
'mk.ṭly.bt.rb	With thee Dewy, girl of Rain.
'edk.pnk.'al.ttn	Thy face thou shalt surely set
tk.ġr.knkny	Towards the Mountain of Concealment. [5])
š'a.ġr.'l.ydm	Take the mountain on thy hands,
ḫlb.lẓr.rḥtm	The hill on the top of thy palms,
wrd.bt ḫpṯt.'arṣ	And descend to the House of Corruption in the underworld,
tspr.byrdm.'arṣ	And thou shalt be numbered with those that go down into the earth;

---

vassal Jehoshaphat of Judah at Ramoth Gilead when the latter acted as 'stooge' in his royal robes while Ahab went disguised (1 Kings xxii, 30). The ancient Near East was familiar with substitute kings who bore the burdens of kingship in national emergencies and even underwent death for the community *vice* the king. This may be the meaning of *'bd 'lm* in the text Gordon *UH* krt, 55, 127, 252. Driver, who does not regard the passage as signifying Baal's submission to Mot, regards this declaration as polite deference if not sarcasm (*op. cit.*, pp. 17, 105).

[1]) Gordon *UH* 67, V, 6-17.

[2]) *mdl* seems to us obviously the Arabic مَزْن, 'rain-cloud', as the context suggests, rather than a cognate of دلْوة, 'bucket', as Driver proposes, *op. cit.*, p. 161.

[3]) The numbers seven and eight are perhaps without precise significance, being used to express an indefinite number. As the number of Baal's attendants, however, seven may have significance as a cultic number, e.g. seven days of the Feast of Tabernacles among the Hebrews.

[4]) *ḫnẓr* may mean swineherds as well as swine. There is no mention of swine as sacrificial animals in the offering-lists from Ras Shamra, and we do not know the precise connection of Baal with swine. One recollects the tradition that Adonis, the vegetation deity, was killed by a wild boar, which might suggest that *ḫnẓr* (vocalised *ḫanāẓir*) should be translated 'boar-hunters'. If the pig were associated with the cult of Baal, we might understand the Hebrew taboo on pigs as a protest against the religion of Canaan. On the other hand, as the lack of evidence in the offerings-lists suggests, the pig may have been taboo also in Canaanite religion, the Adonis legend of the boar-hunt being an aetiological myth to explain this taboo, which was adopted automatically by the Hebrews. Another possibility is that *ḫnẓr* is the same word as *ḫẓr*, which denotes a craftsman, probably a smith, in the administrative text *PRU* II, 24, rev. 4-6, 9.

[5]) *knkny*, the final *y* indicating a place-name, suggests the Arabic كنّ, 'a place of concealment'.

wtdʿ.ʾell.kmtt	Yea thou shalt know annihilation [1]) as the dead.'

At this juncture Baal mates with a heifer: [2])

yšmʿ.ʾalʾey.bʿl	Baal the Mighty hears.
yʾuhb.ʿglt.bdbr	He loves a heifer in the Back of Beyond, [3])
prt.bšd.šḫlmmt	A cow in the tracts of the Strand of Death, [4])
škb.ʿmnh.šbʿ.lšbʿm	He lies with her seven times and seventy times,
( )ly.ṯmn.lṯmnym	Yea ( ) eight times and eighty times;
w(th)rn.wtldn mṯ	And she conceives and bears a male...

The purpose of this may be, as GASTER has suggested, [5]) to leave issue in case he did not return from the underworld, or perhaps to gain the strength of a bull for his forthcoming conflict with Mot. This would be a case of contactual magic. We feel that the first suggestion is the more suitable. The fact that the actual birth of a calf is mentioned may seem at first sight to deprive the passage of any seasonal significance. The birth, however, seems to be mentioned in anticipation. The conception may have been regarded as the earnest of fulfilment, and as such of value as a rite of imitative magic. Here too we may see a seasonal reference. In the Syrian desert DOUGHTY notes that the camels were mated so as to calve in the *rabiʿa* or season of pasture which springs from the 'early rains'. [6]) Thus the mating season for cattle in Palestine might conceivably fall in April-May. That is just before the sirocco winds, before which vegetation wilts. That is indeed the time of Baal's eclipse and the ascendancy of Mot which is anticipated here. Here there may well have been

---

[1]) *ʾell* seems cognate with the Arabic أَلّ, and the adjective أَلِيل, 'bereaved'. A closer cognate is the Hebrew אליל, 'nothingness', happily adduced by DRIVER, *op. cit.*, p. 136. The last letter, however, is effaced, and read as *m* by A. HERDNER, *Corpus*, p. 36.

[2]) GORDON *UH* 67, V, 17-22.

[3]) *dbr* may be cognate with Hebrew מדבר, grazing-land. But *dbr* may also be cognate with Hebrew דביר, 'the inmost shrine' or 'hindmost part' and with Arabic دُبْر 'back'. DRIVER's translation (*op. cit.*, p. 154) 'decease', citing Arabic دَبَرَ and Aramaic דְּבַר, 'to take away', is also feasible.

[4]) So DRIVER (*op. cit.*, p. 107) after DUSSAUD, who adduces the Arabic phrase سَاحِل مَمَاتِين 'plain of death'.

[5]) GASTER, *Thespis*, p. 192.

[6]) C. M. DOUGHTY, *Travels in Arabia Deserta*, 1936, p. 261.

a ritual mating behind the myth. In fact the beginning of the breeding season may have been so marked and the whole enterprise thus put under the aegis of Providence.

After a long lacuna of some 30 lines, which must have described the death of Baal, we again pick up the thread of the narrative with a vivid description of El's mourning for the dead Baal. Here, incidentally, comes the theme of the search for the dead god by a goddess, which recalls the search of Isis for the dead Osiris, Ishtar's search for Tammuz, Demeter's search for Kore, and that of Aphrodite for Adonis. [1]) The text continues: [2])

l.bʿl.npl.lʾarṣ	'Verily [3]) Baal has fallen to the earth,
mt.ʾalʾeyn.bʿl	Dead is Baal the Mighty,
ḫlq.ẓbl.bʿl ʾarṣ	Perished [4]) is the Prince, Lord of the earth.'
ʾapnk.lṭpn.ʾel.dpʾed	Then the Kindly One, El the Merciful
yrd.lksʾe.yṯb.lhdm	Comes down from his throne, he leaps [5]) to the footstool,
wl.hdm.yṯb.lʾarṣ	And from the footstool he leaps to the ground.
yṣq.ʿmr.ʾun.lrʾešh	He lets down [6]) his turban [7]) in grief [8]) from his head;
ʿpr.plṯt.l.qdqdh	On his head is the dust in which he wallows. [9])

---

[1]) Here we may cite Bion's *Lament for Adonis* 19 ff., quoted with other relevant material by GASTER, *Thespis*, p. 194 n., 'And Aprodite unbinds her locks, and goes wandering through the woodlands, distraught, unkempt and barefoot. The thorns tear her as she goes, and gather her holy blood, but she sweeps through the long glades, shrieking aloud and calling on the lad, her Assyrian lord'. 'Assyrian', of course, to the Greek author signified 'Syrian'. GASTER has justly interpreted the recurrence of these motifs of the seasonal ritual as expressing a vital psychological experience of the Mediterranean peasantry.

[2]) GORDON *UH* 67, VI, 8-25.

[3]) This is not the preposition *l*, but the enclitic, cf. Akkadian *lû* and Arabic لَ. Here it may introduce a cultic cry taken up at this point by the worshippers.

[4]) These verses are, in our opinion, a cultic cry to be taken up by the worshippers. This is suggested by the verbal repetition in GORDON *UH* 49, I, 13-14. *ḫlq* in parallelism with *mt* seems cognate with the Arabic خلق, which in the IVth form means 'to wear out' (of clothes).

[5]) *yṯb* could mean, of course, 'sits'. It might also be cognate with the Arabic وثب, 'to hop'.

[6]) *yṣq* might be cognate with the Hebrew יצק, 'to pour out', hence 'to loosen'.

[7]) *ʿmr* is the Arabic عمرة, 'turban', with which El is depicted probably on the well-known sculpture from Ras Shamra. *ʿmr ʾun* in this context suggests לֶחֶם אוֹנִים of Hosea ix, 4, cf. Deuteronomy xxvi, 14, with reference to a funeral feast.

[8]) *ʾun* is best taken as cognate with the Hebrew אוֹן, 'affliction'.

[9]) *plṯt* is the verbal noun from *plṯ*, 'to wallow (in the dust)', cf. Micah i, 10 עפר התפלשי (*Qere* for *Kethibh*, התפלשתי).

lpš.yks.mʾeẓrtm	He tears asunder [1]) the knot [2]) on his girdle,
ǵr.bʾabn.ydy	He makes the mountain re-echo [3]) with his lamentation, [4])
psltm.byʿr.yhdy	And with his clamour [5]) the forest to resound [6])
lḥm.wdqn.yṯlṯ	Cheeks [7]) and chin he rends [8])
qn.ẓrʿh.yḥrṯ	The humeral joint of the arm [9]) he scores,
kgn.ʾaplb.	The chest [10]) as a garden plot,
kʿmq.yṯlṯ.bmt	Even as a valley-bottom his back he lacerates.
yšʾu.gh.wyṣḥ	He raises his voice and cries.
bʿl.mt.my.lʾem.bn.dgn	'Baal is dead. What is become of [11]) the Prince [12]) the son of Dagon?
my.hmlt.ʾaṯr.bʿl	What of the multitudes, the followers of Baal?'

The end of this text describes Anat's search for Baal: [13])

ʾard.bʾarṣ	'I shall go down to the earth.'

---

[1]) We take *yks* as passive of a verb *nks* cognate with the Arabic نكص, 'to withdraw'. There is a reference to loosening of fastenings of clothing as an element in mourning and fast rites in Isaiah lviii, 6,

'Is not this the fast I have chosen
To loose the bands of wickedness?'

[2]) *lpš* might be cognate with the Arabic لفت, 'to twist' and Hebrew לפת with the same meaning, hence our translation 'knot'.

[3]) *ydy* is probably from *ndy*, cognate with the Arabic ندى, 'to re-echo'.

[4]) *ʾabn* suggest the Arabic ابن, meaning in the IInd form 'to compose elegies'.

[5]) *psltm* seems cognate with the Arabic صلطة, 'clamour', the initial *p* being the conjunction (Arabic ف) and the final *m* the substitute for the preposition. as also in Akkadian, see De Langhe, *Muséon* LIX, 1946.

[6]) *yhdy* seems to be cognate with the Hebrew הדה, 'to stretch out, be prolonged'. In Isaiah xi, 8 it is used of a child stretching out his hand on the hole of the asp. Here in parallelism with *ndy*, 'to re-echo', we can see the force of the verb meaning 'to prolong sound', 'to resound'.

[7]) *lḥm* is obviously cognate with the Hebrew לחי, 'cheek'.

[8]) *yṯlṯ* stands in parallelism with *yḥrṯ*, he ploughs, i.e. 'furrows', and is taken by Gaster on the strength of Akkadian parallels as being a synonym, on the hypothesis of a custom of threefold ploughing (*Thespis*, p. 194). In the present context, however, the reference is rather to three furrow-like scores drawn by the three fingers of a mourner in laceration. T. Worden felicitously cites Ps. cxxix, 3, על גבי חרשו חרשים, 'The Literary Influence of the Ugaritic Fertility Myth on the Old Testament', *VT* III, 1953, p. 288 n.

[9]) So A. Herdner, *RES* 1942-43, p. 49, who cites Job xxxi, 22, *v. infra* p. 268.

[10]) *ʾaplb*, lit. 'front of heart', hence 'chest'.

[11]) *my* suggests the usage in Ruth iii, 16 מי את בתי, 'In what condition art thou, my daughter?'

[12]) *lʾem* is usually taken as 'people', and in view of *hmlt ʾaṯr bʿl* in the parallel *stichos* this is quite possible. We prefer to take *lʾem* as Baal's title 'the Prince', *v. supra* p. 40, n. 8.

[13]) Gordon *UH* 67, VI, 25-31.

'ap.'nt ttlk.wtṣd	Anat too goes and ranges [1])
kl.ġr.lkbd.'arṣ	Every mountain to the heart of the earth,
kl.gb'.lkbd.šdm	Every hill to the midst ot the fields.
tmġ.ln'my.'arṣ.dbr	She comes to the pleasant land of the Back of Beyond
ysmt.šd.šḥlmmt.	The fair tracts of the Strand of Death;
tmġ.lb'l.npl.l'arṣ	She comes upon Baal fallen to the ground.

The text breaks off with a reference to Anat's mourning, and this connects it with the fragment Gordon *UH* 62 (Virolleaud I AB). [2]) Here the mourning of Anat is described, the same rites being followed as by El. The repetition of the details may well indicate an accompanying ritual, such, in fact, as the weeping for Tammuz practised by the women of Jerusalem witnessed by Ezekiel, presumably in the sixth month (Ezekiel viii, 14) or the public mourning for Hadad-Rimmon in the Valley of Megiddo (Zechariah xii, 11). A closer analogy is the mourning of the Israelite virgins on the mountains of Gilead, which was rather artificially invested with a historical significance and attached to the tradition about Jephthah and his daughter (Judges xi, 37-40).

After duly performing the mourning rites, 'the rites of separation', the goddess recovers the body of Baal: [3])

'd.tšb'.bk	When at length she was sated with weeping,
tšt.kyn.'udm't	Drinking tears like wine, [4])
gm.tṣḥ.lnrt.'elm.špš	Aloud she shouts to *Špš* the Light of the Gods, [5])

[1]) The same parallelism between *hlk* and *ṣw/yd* is found in the text Gordon *UH* 52, 67-68.

[2]) Virolleaud, *Syria* XII, 1931, pp. 193-224; *ibidem*, pp. 350-357; *Syria XV*, 1934, pp. 226-243. De Langhe, however, suspects that there is no connection between Gordon *UH* 67 and 62, *Les Textes de Ras Shamra-Ugarit et leurs rapports avec . . . l'Ancien Testament* I, p. 157.

[3]) Gordon *UH* 62, 9-18.

[4]) The conception is familiar in Hebrew, e.g. Psalm lxxx, 6 ותשקמו בדמעות, and in Babylonian literature, e.g. *dimtu maštiti* in penitential psalms.

[5]) Cf. in Mesopotamian mythology, where the Sun-god is 'the Illuminator of the Igigi and Anunnaki'. The role of *špš* in the recovery of the dead Baal is significant. A. Caquot ('La divinité solaire ougaritique', *Syria* xxxvi, 1959, pp. 93 ff.) has adduced evidence from Mesopotamian texts, which are borne out particularly by this passage and the sequel in Gordon *UH* 49, IV, 30-44, that the sun, as traversing the sky and the underworld, was a fitting agent in the presentation of the dead. More particularly in the present passage Caquot sees the mythological expression of the phenomenon of evaporation by the agency of the sun, which is probably reflected in Isaiah lv, 10,

For even as the rain and the snow
Descend from the sky return not
Without having watered the earth . . .

cf. Genesis ii, 6.

ʿms mʿ.ly.ʾalʾeyn.bʿl	'Lift [1]) upon me, I pray thee, Baal the Mighty.'
tšmʿ.nrt.ʾelm.špš	*Špš* the Light of the Gods hearkens;
tšʾu.ʾalʾeyn.bʿl	She lifts up Baal the Mighty
lktp.ʿnt.ktšth	Upon the shoulder of Anat and she sets him there. [2])
tšʿlynh.bṣrrt.ṣpn	She takes him up to the crags of Sapon;
tbkynh.wtqbrnh	She weeps for him and buries him;
tštnn.bḫrt.ʾelm.ʾarṣ	She puts him in the niche [3]) of the divinities of the earth.

The text then closes with the description of the funeral feast which Anat prepares for Baal: [4])

tṭbḫ.šbʿm.rʾumm	She slaughters seventy wild-oxen
kgmn.ʾalʾeyn.bʿl	As a funeral due [5]) to Baal the Mighty;
tṭbḫ.šbʿm.ʾalpm	'She slaughters seventy oxen
kgmn.ʾalʾeyn.bʿl	As a funeral due to Baal the Mighty;
tṭbḫ.šbʿm.ṣʾen	She slaughters seventy sheep
kgmn.ʾalʾeyn.bʿl	As a funeral due to Baal the Mighty;
tṭbḫ.šbʿm.ʾaylm	She slaughters seventy deer
kgmn.ʾalʾeyn.bʿl	As a funeral due to Baal the Mighty;
tṭbḫ.šbʿm.yʿlm	She slaughters seventy wild-goats
kgmn.ʾalʾeyn.bʿl	As a funeral due to Baal the Mighty;
tṭbḫ.šbʿm.ḥmrm	She slaughters seventy asses [6])
kgmn.ʾalʾeyn.bʿl	As a funeral due to Baal the Mighty.'

Here it may be recalled that after Ishtar's mourning for the dead Tammuz a funeral feast was an important feature of the Tammuz cult. [7]) This is, of course, a procedure well known to anthropologists as a rite of 'aggregation', to signify that Baal is duly separated from the company of the living and united with the dead. There are many indications that those myths reflect in many instances human institutions and this may be a simple case of anthropomorphism. The funeral feast was of course a familiar convention in Israel, being

1) *ʿms* is cognate with the Hebrew עמס, 'to load' or 'carry a load'.

2) We suspect that *ktšth* should be read *wtšth*, i.e. *w* (𐎆) for *k* (𐎋), but the enclitic *k* is often used as a strong asseverative introducing the predicate, which in that case is reserved till the end of the hemistich, GORDON *UM*, 1955, II, p. 46, citing Genesis xviii, 20 זעקת סדם ועמרה כי רבה וחטאתם כי כבדה and Psalm xlix, 16 אך אלהים יפדה נפשי מיד שאול כי יקחני

3) *ḫrt* seems cognate with the Hebrew חור, 'cave'.

4) *Ibidem*, 18-29.

5) We take *gmn* as cognate with the Hebrew and Aramaic גמל, and may cite the Aramaic phrase חֶסֶד גְּמַל, 'to show pious duty to the dead'.

6) Asses were actually used as sacrificial animals in a covenant-ceremony by the Amorites of Mari on the mid-Euphrates in the Middle Bronze Age.

7) E. EBELING, *Tod und Leben nach der Vorstellungen der Babylonier*, 1931. M. WITZEL, *Tammuz-liturgien und Verwandtes*, 1935.

expressly forbidden in Deuteronomy xxvi, 14. It is, however, uncertain if this rite was one for the dead member of the community or the survival of a funeral feast for Baal in the fertility cult [1]). The connection with harvest, however, suggests the connection with the fertility-cult. The myth, then, probably reflects here the actual ritual of mourning for Baal, which we know to have been practised in Hebrew Palestine and Hellenistic Syria.

The text Gordon *UH* 49 (Virolleaud I AB) [2]) obviously follows Gordon *UH* 62 since the text opens with the statement by some goddess, doubtless Anat: [3])

'That Baal the Mighty is dead,
That the Prince, Lord of the Earth is perished.'

This raises the question of a substitute for Baal, the dead king-god, and Aṯtr, the deity manifest in the bright Venus-star, is put forward as a candidate, his qualifications being the fact that as the brightest star in those latitudes he might match in some degree the lightning-flash of Baal: [4])

gm.yṣḥ.ʾel	Aloud El cries
lrbt.ʾaṯrt.ym	To Lady Aṯerat of the Sea,
šmʿ.lrbt.ʾaṯrt.ym	'Hear, O Lady Aṯerat of the Sea,
tn.ʾaḥd.bbnk.wʾamlkn	Give one among thy sons and I will make him king'
wtʿn rbt.ʾaṯrt.ym	And Lady Aṯerat of the Sea answered,

[1]) Deuteronomy xxvi, 14 certainly reflects the struggle of Yahwism with the local fertility-cult. H. Cazelles ('Sur un rituel dans Deutéronome', *RB* LV 1948, pp. 54-71) suggests that on this occasion offering was made to Mot, who was treated as an Adonis-figure. We are not convinced by any of the Ras Shamra texts cited by Cazelles, who, in our opinion, might have greatly strengthened his case by the citation of the above passage.

[2]) Virolleaud, 'La lutte de Mot, fils des dieux, et d'Alein, fils de Baal', Syria XII, 1931, pp. 193-224. 'Note complémentaire', *ibidem*, pp. 350-357. 'Fragment nouveau du poème de Mot et d'Aleyn Baal', *Syria* XV, 1934, pp. 226-243.

[3]) Gordon *UH* 49, I, 13-15. The fact that this would be welcome news to Aṯerat the consort of El (I, 11-13) suggested to D. Nielsen (*Ras Shamra Mythologie und Biblische Theologie*, 1936) that the substitute Aṯtr belonged with El and Aṯerat to a different stratum of religion than the cult of Baal. We agree with Nielsen in seeing here the amalgamation of an astral cult and the fertility-cult proper, the former being associated with the Amorites before their settlement in Syria. The matter, however, cannot be so simply solved as Nielsen suggests, taking the Baal-cult as chronologically younger than the astral cult. It is rather a matter of the astral cult being associated with the desert, and the fertility-cult with the settled land. There were so many invasions and infiltrations from the desert to the sown that it is impossible to say when the astral cult was introduced or how far the cult of Baal or Hadad was assimilated to a fertility-cult already established in Syria.

[4]) Gordon *UH* 49 I, 15-27.

bl.nmlk.ydʿ ylḥn	'Yea let us make king one who knows how to flash.'[1]
wyʿn.lṭpn.ʾel.dpʾed	Then answered the Kindly One, El, the Merciful,
dq.ʾanm.lyrẓ	'Is it a light thing[2] to contend,
ʿm.bʿl.lyʿdb.mrḥ	To prepare a spear[3] against Baal,
ʿm.bn.dgn.ktmsm	Against the son of Dagon as (?) ?
wʿn.rbt.ʾaṯrt.ym	Then answer, O Lady Aṯerat of the Sea,
blt.nmlk.ʿṯtr.ʿrẓ	Shall we indeed make 'Aṯtr the Luminous[4] king?'
ymlk ʿṯtr. ʿrẓ	Let 'Aṯtr the Luminous be king![5]

The text continues:[6]

ʾapnk.ʿṯtr.ʿrẓ	Thereupon Aṯtar the Luminous
yʿl.bṣrrt.ṣpn	Goes up to the crags of Sapon;
yṯb.lkḥṯ.ʾalʾeyn.bʿl	He takes his seat on the throne of Baal the Mighty.
pʿnh.ltmġyn.hdm	His feet do not reach the footstool,
rʾešh.lymġy.ʾapsh	His head does not reach the top thereof.
wyʿn.ṯtr.ʿrẓ	Then Aṯtar the Luminous declares.
lʾamlk.bṣrrt.ṣpn.	'I may not be king on the crags of Sapon.'
yrd.ʿṯtr.ʿrẓ	Aṯtar the Luminous comes down,
yrd.lkḥṯ.ʾalʾeyn.bʿl	Down from the throne of Baal the Mighty,
wymlk.bʾarṣ.ʾel.klh	And he reigns in the ground, god of it all . . .[7]

GASTER in our opinion is right in seeing here that Aṯtar, having proved a sorry substitute for Baal, the god of the rain-storms, is limited to the sphere of irrigation-culture.[8]

---

1) We take *ylḥn* as energic imperfect from a root cognate with the Arabic لاح, 'to flash', which is actually used of the shining of a star. DRIVER (*op. cit.*, pp. 111, 158) proposes to connect it with the Arabic لحن 'to have understanding', but is obliged to postulate the conjunction *w* (and), which is not in the text.

2) Is *ʾanm* the Ugaritic conjunction equivalent to the Arabic انّ, with the enclitic *m*? DRIVER (*op. cit.*, pp. 111, 135), after ALBRIGHT, proposes to take *ʾanm* as the plural of *ʾan*, the Canaanite adaptation of the Egyptian *ʾiwn*, 'pigment', and translates 'Let the finest of pigment(s) be ground from Baal' (*dq ʾanm lyrẓ ʿm bʿl*). While this is a feasible translation of the first three words, *yrẓ* being the passive imperfect of *rẓẓ*, cognate with Hebrew רצץ, the preposition *ʿm* is never found elsewhere in Ugaritic meaning 'from', but always 'to' or 'against', in which sense we propose to take it here.

3) GORDON (*UH*, p. 247) cites this word meaning 'spear' in Egyptian and Coptic. Agreeably with his interpretation of the couplet as signifying the use of the corpse of Baal to prepare pigments and unguents for the anointing of the new king DRIVER translates *mrḥ* as 'unguents'.

4) *ʿrẓ* is generally taken as cognate with Hebrew עריץ, 'terrible', 'awe inspiring'. In view of the manifestation of Aṯtar in the Venus-star, the brightest star in Near Eastern latitudes, we suggest the connection rather with Arabic عرض, 'to flash' (of lightning).

5) Here the devotees possibly echoed the proclamation that Aṯtar should be king.

6) GORDON *UH* 49, I, 28-37.

7) So DRIVER (*op. cit.*, p. 111), most felicitously, in our opinion.

8) GASTER, *Thespis*, p. 198.

There is, unfortunately, a lacuna at this point, and the text resumes with a graphic description of Anat interceding with Mot for the restoration of Baal: [1])

klb.ʾarḫ.lʿglh	As the heart of the cow after her calf,
klb.ṯʾat.lʾemrh	As the heart of the ewe after her lamb,
km.lb.ʿnt.ʾaṯr.bʿl	So the heart of Anat (yearns) after Baal.
tʾeḫd.mt.bsʾen.lpš	She seizes Mot by the hem [2]) of his clothing,
tšṣq( ).bqṣ.ʾall	She restrains him by the border of his mantle; [3])
tšʾu.gh.wtṣḥ .	She raises her voice and cries:
ʾat.mt.tn.ʾaḫy	'Thou Mot give me my brother.'

Here we remember that the body of Baal had already been recovered and buried. There is thus an apparent inconsistency in Anat's intercession with Mot for the recovery of Baal. Ritual texts, however, are not limited by logic, and there is no insuperable difficulty here. Insofar as we may seek consistency, it may be possible to discriminate here between the mortal physical body and that part of a person which remained indestructible at death and was capable of reincarnation. These myths, however, are not metaphysical speculations, but are the outgrowth of ritual, where the fact of the death and burial of Baal and his revival corresponded to rituals relating to the death and revival of vegetation.

Mot, however, is not to be entreated. He boasts of his freedom to extend his desolating influence over the earth and of his destruction of Baal: [4])

wʿn bn.ʾelm.mt	Then answered the god Mot,
mh tʾršn.lbtlt. ʿnt	'What dost thou wish, O Anat?
ʾan.ʾetlk.wʾaṣd	I go about and range over
kl ġr. lkbd.ʾarṣ.	Every mountain to the heart of the earth,
kl gbʿ lkbd.šdm	Every hill in the midst of the country,
npš ḫsrt bn.nšm	Life has failed among men,
npš hmlt.ʾarṣ.	Even life among the multitudes of the earth.
mġt.lnʿmy.ʾarṣ dbr	I came to the pleasant land of the Back of Beyond,
ysmt.šd.šḥlmmt	The fair tracts of the strand of Death,
ngš.ʾank.ʾalʾẹyn bʿl	It was I who rounded up [5]) Baal the Mighty

---

[1]) GORDON *UH* 49, II, 6-12.

[2]) We take *sʾen* as parallel to *qṣ* ('extremity') and meaning thus 'edge', or 'hem'. We propose the cognate سأى, 'to tear a garment', thus 'make a fringe', though DRIVER's translation 'boot' (Hebrew סאון), after MONTGOMERY, is seriously to be considered.

[3]) *ʾall* is found in parallelism with *lpš*, 'clothing', in GORDON *UH* 75, II, 48, and with *kst*, 'covering', in GORDON *UH* 1 Aqht, 37, 48.

[4]) GORDON *UH* 49, II, 13-25.

[5]) Cf. Arabic نجش, 'to beat for game'.

ʿdbnn ʾank.(k)ʾemr.bpy	It was I who made him as a lamb in my mouth,
kllʾe.bṯbrn q(n)y ḫtʾu hw	He was carried off like a kid in my jaws.
nrt.ʾelm.špš.ṣḥrrt	Shepesh, the Luminary of the gods was burning hot.
lʾa.šmm.byd.bn ʾelm mt	Glowing [1]) in heaven because of the god Mot.

Mot remaining obdurate, Anat continues to importune him, during which some lapse of time is visualised,

ym.ymm.yʿtqn	One day, two days pass,
lymm.lyrḫm	From days to months,
rḥm.ʿnt.tngṯh	The Maiden Anat importunes him...

Eventually the redoubtable goddess resorts to force: [2])

tʾeḫd.bn.ʾelm.mt	She seizes the god Mot;
bḥrb.tbqʿnn	With a blade she cleaves him;
bḫṯr.tdrynn	With a shovel she winnows him;
bʾešt.tšrpnn	With fire she parches him;
brḥm.tṭḥnn	With a millstone she grinds him;
bšd.tdrʿnn	In the field she scatters [3]) him;
šʾerh.ltʾekl.ʿṣrm	His remains [4]) the birds eat,
mnth.ltkly.npr	The wild creatures [5]) consume his fragments,
šʾer.lšʾer.yṣḥ	Remains from remains are sundered. [6])

Here we have clearly a connection between the myth and a seasonal ritual. There is no doubt that this was a rite of desacralisation of the new grain-crop to make it available for common use. Such a rite is recorded in Hebrew legislation in Leviticus ii, 14 (P), which refers

---

[1]) Cf. Arabic لألأ, 'to glow brightly'.

[2]) GORDON *UH* 49, II, 30-37.

[3]) Cf. Judges ix, 45 and Zechariah x, 9, where, as S. E. LOEWENSTAMM points out, the meaning is not 'sow' but 'scatter', 'The Ugaritic Fertility Myth—the Result of a Mistranslation', *IEJ* XII, 1962, pp. 87-88. The point of the rite was that the grain was disposed of to the wild creatures and not sown. CASSUTO, in his eagerness to dissociate this myth from seasonal rituals in the agricultural year, observes that the scattering of Mot for the birds to eat was the reverse of an agricultural ritual, 'Baal and Mot in the Ugaritic Texts', *IEJ* XII, 1962, p. 79. He misses the point that this was not a rite of imitative magic, but of desacralization, as in Leviticus ii, 14. G. FOHRER also mistakes this as a rite of imitative magic, 'Wie das Korn wird er (Mot) zerhauen (gedroschen) ,geworfelt, aufs Feldt gesät, um wiederaufzuleben', 'Die wiederentdeckte kanaanäische Religion', *ThLZ* LXXVIII, 1953, col. 197.

[4]) *šʾer*, as perceived by GASTER (*Thespis*, p. 200), is the Hebrew שאר, 'remnant', and not 'flesh', which in Ugaritic is *ṯʾar*.

[5]) *npr*, in parallelism with *ʿṣrm* ('birds'), seems cognate with the Arabic نفر 'shy', i.e. 'wild creatures'. It is actually used of birds in the modern Syrian dialect.

[6]) We take *yṣḥ* as imperfect passive of a verb *ṣwḥ*, cognate with the Arabic صاح(و), 'to split'.

to the offering of the first sheaf, 'green ears of corn, dried by the fire, even corn beaten out of full ears'. This rite in the Hebrew community is described more fully by Philo, [1]) Josephus, [2]) and in the Mishnah. [3]) The fact that all date the rite on the 10th of Nisan and that Philo and Josephus state that the sheaf was of barley indicates that the rite in Hebrew usage was the offering of the first sheaf which set the new crop free for public consumption, as noted specifically in Josephus and the Mishnah. [4]) We know, however, that not until the last sheaf had been offered was it legitimate to use the new crop in the Temple service. This took place at the end of the wheat harvest at the Feast of Weeks, or Pentecost, fifty days after the offering of the first sheaf, hence in Siwan, about the end of May. Now a similar rite is described by the mediaeval writer Ibn en-Nedim [5]) who writes that at Harran in the middle of Tammuz there was held a ceremony of weeping for Tammuz who had been done to death by his lord (ربه) by having his bones ground with mill-stones, then scattered to the winds. Whence the women [6]) ate nothing ground in mill-stones, but wheat, lentils sodden, dates, raisins, etc. This rite at Harran fell in the month Tammuz, which falls in July. We had been previously rather impressed with the correspondence between Anat's treatment of Mot in the text GORDON *UH* 49 and the rites of the offering of the first sheaf in the Hebrew sources above cited. We feel now, however, that, though the sources contain nothing to suggest that the rite of the offering of the last sheaf resembled the offering of the first in details, this is no argument that there was no such correspondence. The offering of the last sheaf was but the consummation of the desacralisation rites inaugurated on the 10th of Nisan, hence we believe that DUSSAUD may after

---

[1]) PHILO, *De Sept.* II, 20.

[2]) JOSEPHUS, *Antiquities* III, 250.

[3]) Mishnah, *Menaḥoth* X, 3-4 ET (London, 1948) 65a-66a.

[4]) An earlier reference to the desacralisation of the new crop by fire is the reference to the use of unleavened bread (מַצּוֹת) and parched corn (קָלוּי) of the produce of the land in Joshua v, 11.

[5]) *Ibn en-Nedim*, *El-Fihrist*, Cairo, A. H. 1348, p. 449.

[6]) We note especially the part played by women in such 'rites of transition'. The reversal of the normal rôles of men and women at such seasons is, of course, an anthropological common-place. Thus when we find a goddess, such as Anat, the protagonist in the Ras Shamra texts we immediately suspect that the text is related to seasonal crises. Ammianus Marcellinus (XXII, ix, 15) attests a similar rite of weeping for Adonis by the women of Antioch on the 19th of July. During the seven days ascendancy of the Dog-star women tended their Adonis-gardens according to Plato, *Phaedrus*, p. 276.

all be right in seeing in the passage in GORDON *UH* 49 a reference to the rite of the last sheaf at the end of harvest. [1])

The revival of Baal and the consequent restoration of fertility is anticipated by a dream of El: [2])

kḫlq ( )	Though (Baal) had perished ( )
whm.ḥy.ʾa(lʾeyn bʿl)	Lo! Baal the Mighty is alive
whm.ʾeṯ.ẓbl.bʿ(lʾarṣ)	Lo! the Prince, Lord of the earth exists
....	....
bḥlm.lṭpn.ʾel.dpʾed	In a dream of El the Kindly One, the Merciful,
bẓrt.bny.bnwt	In a vision [3]) of the Creator [4]) of Created Things,
šmm.šmn.tmṭrn	The skies rain oil,
nḫlm.tlk.nbtm	The wadis run with honey. [5])
šmḫ.lṭpn.ʾel.dpʾed	El the Kindly One, the Merciful rejoices,
pʿnh.lhdm.yṯpd	His feet on the footstool he sets; [6])
wyprq.lṣb.wyṣḥq	And he opens his throat [7]) and laughs;
yšʾu.gh.wyṣḥ	He raises his voice and cries.
ʾaṯbn.ʾank.wʾanḫn	'I shall sit and take my ease,
wtnḫ.bʾerty.npš	And the soul shall repose in my breast,
kḥy ʾalʾeyn bʿl	For Baal the Mighty is alive,
kʾeṯ ẓbl bʿl ʾarṣ	For the Prince, Lord of the Earth exists.' [8])

---

[1]) DUSSAUD, *Les découvertes* . . . 2nd ed., p. 137.

[2]) GORDON *UH* 49, III, 1-21. Here the text resumes after a lacuna of c. 30 lines.

[3]) As we see from parallel passages in the Krt text 36 and 297, *ẓrt* is a variant spelling of *shrt*, which connects with the Syriac ܫܗܪܐ, 'the vigil of a saint, a waking vision', or possibly with the Arabic ظهر, 'to be manifest'.

[4]) We note that the creator in Ugaritic religion is not Baal, but El. The verb *bny* is found in this sense also in Hebrew, Genesis ii, 22, ויבן... את־הצלע... לאשה.

[5]) This general conception of preternatural fertility in Nature associated with rehabilitation after conflict (so eschatology, though limited) was familiar to the Hebrews, probably from liturgy associated with seasonal festivals, as the almost identical language of Amos ix, 13 and Joel iv, 18 (Hebrew text) suggests.

[6]) *yṯpd*, apart from the general sense of the passage, may be determined by its Arabic cognate ثفد, 'to set on, superimpose'.

[7]) This phrase *yprq lṣb wyṣḥq* is found again in a similar context in the text GORDON *UH* 2 Aqht II, 10, where the ancient king Danʾel, on the news of the birth of his son and at the pleasant prospect of ultimate relief from the weight of responsibility, feels the tension relaxed. The word *lṣb* is possibly cognate with the Arabic لصب, 'to stick', as a sword in the scabbard or a ring upon the finger, hence the verbal noun لصب, 'straitness'. The present passage may indicate the relaxation of the tension of anxiety or the reserve of royal dignity, but ULLENDORFF is probably right in translating more literally 'he opens his gullet', citing the Arabic لِصْب, from the root we have quoted, in the sense of 'strait'.

[8]) Since this passage obviously visualises the absence of Baal who must still be sought by Anat and Špš, *ʾeṯ* must mean 'exists' and not 'is present', contrary to the opinion of ALBRIGHT à propos of the text GORDON *UH* krt, 201, *BASOR* 94, 1944, p. 31. The final couplet is, in our opinion, a cultic cry to be voiced by the

Baal, however, must still be sought, and this is the joint concern of a pair of female deities, his sister Anat and the sun-goddess Špš, who, as traversing the sky and the whole region under the earth, naturally knew all the secrets of life and death. [1])

ttbʿ.btlt.ʿnt	The Virgin Anat departs;
ʾedk.lttn.pnm	Then she sets her face
ʿm.nrt.ʾelm.špš	Towards Špš the Light of the Gods.
tšʾu.gh.wtṣḥ	She raises her voice and cries:
tḥm.ṯr.ʾel.ʾabk	'The message of the Bull El thy father,
hwt.lṭpn.ḥtkk	The word of the Kindly One thy sire. [2])
pl.ʿnt.šdm.yšpš	"Arbiter for [3]) the furrows [4]) of the field, O Špš,

---

worshippers, cf. *ʾey zbl*, אי זבול, which, we claim was the original form of the name Jezebel, corrupted by Hebrew scribes to אִיזֶבֶל. We propose that the cultic cry which was the real name of Jezebel reflected the season of her birth.

[1]) Gordon *UH* 49, IV, 30-44.

[2]) *ḥtk* is used either of father or offspring. Here in parallelism with *ʾab* it obviously means 'father', but in Gordon *UH* 76, III, 34-35 in the phrase *ḥtk dgn*, who is generally described as *bn dgn*, it means 'offspring', as also in Krt, 21-22. Ullendorff, more explicitly, sees a reference to circumcision, citing חתך in the Mishnah, *Shabbath* xviii, 3, this being originally, presumably, the father's duty, 'Ugaritic Marginalia II', *JSS* VII, 1962, p. 341. In this passage חתך might refer to the cutting of the navel-string rather than circumcision. Driver (*op. cit.*, p. 138) regards the word in the first sense as an active participle, 'begetter' and in the second as a passive participle, 'begotten'.

[3]) *pl*, like *ʿnt*, is patient of several interpretations. It may be the passive of the verb *pll* or a by-form *pwl* or *pyl*, cognate with Arabic فلّ, 'to be notched' (of a sword), which Driver apparently accepts, taking the reference to be to the cracking of land in drought. It may also be cognate with Arabic فَلٌّ, 'parched land'. In this case *ʿnt* would naturally signify 'furrows', which is philologically possible, and is accepted by Driver and Gordon. *yštk*, restored from the parallel passage in l. 26, requires *pl* as a noun or prepositional phrase, either as a noun or participle or as a prepositional phrase. Gordon (*UL*, p. 46) takes *pl* as Arabic ل + ف, and translates 'Over the furrows of the field let El set thee'. Alternatively *pl* may be cognate with a root akin to Hebrew פליל, meaning 'arbiter, intercessor'. It might have been possible to take *ʿnt* as cognate with Arabic عان, 'to help', translating 'Now as succour for the fields El appoints thee'. The occurrence of *ʿnt* in the following line *bʿl ʿnt mḥrṯ*, however, precludes this meaning, the combination of *ʿnt* with *šdm* and *mḥrṯ*, making it almost certain that the meaning is 'furrows', Hebrew מענה and Arabic معنة. We prefer to take *pl* as cognate with Hebrew פלל, 'to intercede for', translating 'arbiter'. The reference may be to fallow land, cf. the term أرض شمسية, 'sun's land', describing common grazing land in the Belqa at the end of last century, A. Jaussen, *Coutumes des Arabes au pays de Moab*, 1908, p. 237.

[4]) See n. 3.

pl. ʿnt. šdm. ʾel. y( )	Arbiter for the furrows of the field El (appoints thee)[1]
bʿl. ʿnt. mḥrṯh	As for the Lord of his ploughed furrows,
ʾey. ʾalʾeyn bʿl	Baal the Mighty, where is he?
ʾey. ẓbl. bʿl. ʾarṣ	Where is the Prince Lord of the earth?"
wtʿn. nrt. ʾelm. špš	Then answers Špš the Light of the Gods.
šd yn. ʿn. bqbt (k)	Pour sparkling wine[2] from (thy) vat[3]
bl lyt. ʿl. ʾumtk	Without anxiety[4] on account of thy kinsman,[5]
wʾabqṯ. ʾalʾeyn. bʿl	And I will seek Baal the Mighty.'

After a lacuna we encounter Baal *redivivus*. He avenges himself on his adversaries:[6]

yʾeḫd. bʿl. bn. ʾaṯrt	Baal lays hold of the sons of Aṯerat
rbm. ymḫṣ bktp	Repeatedly[7] he smites them with a scimitar;[8]
dkym. ymḫṣ. bṣmd	He pounds them;[9] he smites them with a club.
ṣḥr mt. ymṣʾe. lʾarṣ	He makes vast desolation[10] of death to light upon[11] the underworld,

[1]) See n. 3, p. 71.

[2]) So DRIVER (*op. cit.*, p. 113), who feasibly connects *šd* with Aramaic שְׁדָא cf. Syriac 'ܫܕܐ (*op. cit.* p. 148). For his interpretation of *yn ʿn* he cites Proverbs xxiii, 31

אל תרא יין כי יתאדם
כי יתן בכוס עינו

Look not upon the wine when it is red
When it gives forth its sparkle in the cup.

We may further cite the Arab poet al-Aʿsha, who compares wine to 'the eye of a cock' كعين الديك.

[3]) So DRIVER, who takes *qbt* as cognate with Hebrew יָקַב. The general sense is 'to make an end of mourning', which is symbolized by the use of normal food and conduct.

[4]) We read this letter complex as *bl lyt*, connecting *lyt* with Arabic لوى, 'to twist, writhe' cf. لوية, 'stomach gripes'.

[5]) *ʾumt* suggests the Arabic امة, 'people'. The Ugaritic word may be an abstract noun.

[6]) GORDON *UH* 49, V, 1-6.

[7]) Or '(He smote them) though many', DRIVER, *op. cit.*, p. 113.

[8]) *ktp* in these texts generally means 'shoulder'. Here the fact that it stands in parallelism with *ṣmd* suggests that a weapon is indicated, and R. T. O'CALLAGHAN in fact has adduced evidence from Egypt that this was indeed the name of a weapon, 'The Word *ktp* in Ugaritic and Egypto-Canaanite Mythology', *Orientalia* XXI, 1952, pp. 27-46.

[9]) *dkym* may be a verbal noun from *dky*, cognate with the Arabic دكّ, 'to pound', with the adverbial *m*. Or the verb may be a perfect from *dkk*, the *ym* being a dittograph of *ym* which begins the next word *ymḫṣ*. An alternative translation is DRIVER's '. . . though resplendent', taking *dkym* as cognate with the Arabic ذاكى, 'brilliant' (*op. cit.*, p. 154), after GASTER.

[10]) In this difficult passage we take *ṣḥr* as a verbal noun, cognate with the Arabic صحر, found in the IVth form meaning 'to be wide', and secondarily, as صحراء, 'desert'.

[11]) *ymṣʾe*, as the final vowel indicates, is Causative in the context, the verb

(	)*ṣ.lks'e.mlkh*	(	) to (or from) [1] the throne of his kingship,
(	) *lkḫṯ.drkth*	(	) to (or from) the seat of his governance.

Baal's triumph over Mot, however, was apparently only temporary, since we read that after a space of seven years Mot emerges from his eclipse to challenge Baal to a final combat to avenge his injury at the hands of Anat: [2]

....	....
l(ymm).lyrḫm	From days to months,
lyrḫm.lšnt	From months to years;
mk.bšbʿ šnt	Then in the seventh year
w( ).bn.'elm.mt	Mt the son of El...
ʿm.'al'eyn.bʿl	To Baal the Mighty.
yš'u.gh.wyṣḥ	He raises his voice and cries.
ʿlk.bʿlm.pht.qlt	'Thy fault, [3] O Baal, was my humiliation; [4]
ʿlk.pht.dry.bḥrb	Thy fault my being scattered with the blade;
ʿlk.pht.šrp.b'ešt	Thy fault my being burned with fire;
ʿlk.pht.t)ḥn.brḥm	Thy fault my being ground with the millstone;
ʿlk.p(ht.dr)y.bkbrt [5]	Thy fault (my being winnowed) in the sieve;
ʿlk.ph(t)bšdm	Thy fault ( ) in the fields;
ʿlk.pht.drʿ.bym.( )n	Thy fault my being scattered on the day of(?).' [5]

The mention of years here seems at first sight to militate against the reference of the mythology to an annual agricultural cycle. We think, however, that behind it lies the practice, known in Hebrew ritual, of a seven-year agricultural cycle culminating in the Sabbatical year. The seventh year was a 'season of passage', a transitional period, during which the land was allowed to lie fallow (Exodus xxiii, 10-11 (E), Leviticus xxv, 3-7). We suggest that coupled with the notion that a regular period of transition should be observed between the two cycles of normal agriculture, the period may have had a certain cathartic significance. The power of sterility may have been allowed full scope in the hope that its power might be exhausted before the next six-year period. This may have been ex-

---

being cognate with the Hebrew מצא, which means 'to light upon' as well as 'to find'.

1) The preposition *l* can have both meanings.

2) GORDON *UH* 49, V, 7-19.

3) *ʿlk*, literally 'upon thee', i.e. 'Thou art responsible for', as in Hebrew and Arabic.

4) *pht* seems cognate with the Arabic فَهّت, 'weakness'. We are obviously referred back here to Anat's rough handling of Mot.

5) So A. HERDNER, *Corpus*, p. 42. The slight lacuna after *bym* suggests that this can hardly mean 'in the sea', but 'on the day of . . .', i.e. 'when . . .'. We may restore *bym ('u)n*, 'on the day of grief', or even *bym (d)n*, 'on the day of reckoning'.

pressed at Ras Shamra by the emergence of Mot in the seventh year to challenge the supremacy of Baal. Since, however, primitive religion 'is something not so much thought out as danced out' the ancient Canaanite community required some visual representation of this vital conflict between the powers of fertility and sterility. We feel sure that some ritual combat lay behind the vivid description of the conflict between Baal and Mot.

The conflict opens with verbal exchanges, Mot threatening: [1])

ʾaḫ ym.ytnt.bʿl	'Baal, thou shalt be made a fellow of Sea,
lpʾuy.bnm.ʾumy.klyy	Smitten [2]) indeed for my mother's sons, yea destroyed'.

Then battle is joined. [3])

ytʿn.kgmrm	They glare at each other like glowing coals; [4])
mt ʿẓ.bʿl.ʿẓ	Mot is strong, Baal is strong;
yngḫn.krʾumm	They thrust at each other like wild-oxen;
mt.ʿẓ.bʿl.ʿẓ	Mot is strong, Baal is strong;
ynṯkn.kbṯnm	They bite like serpents;
mt.ʿẓ.bʿl.ʿẓ	Mot is strong, Baal is strong;
ymṣḫn.klsmm	They kick like stallions; [5])
mt.ql.bʿl.ql ʿln	Mot is down, Baal is down on top of him.

The conclusion of this 'battle royal' is unfortunately lost in a lacuna, but in all probability it ended in a triumph for Baal since Špš, the sun-goddess, intervenes to rebuke Mot, who is evidently dismayed: [6])

špš.tṣḫ lmt	Špš calls to Mot,
šmʿ.mʿ.lbn.ʾelm.mt	'Hear now, O god Mot,

---

[1]) GORDON *UH* 49, VI, 14-15. The first complex of letters is usually given as *ʾaḫym*, but we have divided this into *ʾaḫ ym*, which we think legitimate in the absence of the word-divider. The point is that as Baal has treated Sea, so Mot proposes to treat Baal.

[2]) *pʾuy* seems to be a cognate of the Arabic فأى, 'to smite'. In this case we should take it as a passive participle with emphatic initial *l* as before the predicate in Arabic. It is possible, however, that *lpdy*, for 'a ransom', should be read, i.e. *d* (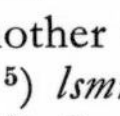) for *ʾu* (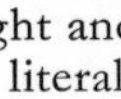).

[3]) GORDON *UH* 49, VI, 16-22.
The forms of the verbs are interesting in this passage; *ytʿn* is reciprocal, with preformative *t*, the other imperfects are Nifʿals.

[4]) *gmr* seems obviously the Arabic جمرة, 'glowing coal', and is found in the Syrian dialect meaning the stone carbuncle. DRIVER equates *gmr* with the Hebrew גמר, and *ytʿn* with the Arabic عان (*op. cit.*, p. 141), rendering 'They attacked one another with might and main' (*op. cit.*, p. 115).

[5]) *lsmm* means literally 'coursers', from Akkadian *lasamu*, 'to run'.

[6]) GORDON *UH* 49, VI, 23-31.

ʾek.tmtḫṣ.ʿm.ʾalʾeyn.bʿl	How fightest thou with Baal the Mighty?
ʾek.ʾal.yšmʿk.ṯr.ʾel.ʾabk	How will thy father the Bull El not hear thee?
l.ysʿ.ʾalt.ṯbtk	Nay [1] he will pluck up the spear of thy tribunal [2]
lyhpk.ksʾa.mlkk	He will overturn the throne of thy kingship,
lyṯbr.ḫṭ.mṯpṭk	He will break the staff of thy rule.'
yrʾu.bn.ʾelm.mt	The god Mot is afraid,
ṯtʿ.ydd.ʾel.ġẓr...	Terrified [3] is the Hero, Beloved of El...

The text as this point is badly damaged but from what remains it seems that Mot admitted Baal's claim to kingship.

The last part of the text GORDON *UH* 49 culminating in the combat with Mot, which we should relate to the observance of a Sabbatical year, is possibly the ground from which the text GORDON *UH* 75 (VIROLLEAUD *BH*) [4] developed. This text has always presented a problem to interpreters, as we have indicated in a special study of it. [5] To be sure, the protagonist is Baal, yet we have the greatest difficulty in admitting the text into the Baal-cycle which we have just discussed, and our reserve is shared by DE LANGHE who admits it as belonging to the main Baal-cycle only secondarily, [6] and by GASTER, who regards it as a variant version of the downfall of Baal. [7] From the mention of a seven-year cycle and the fact that Baal as the power of fertility is out of his element in the desert we have argued that the text relates to a Sabbatical year. [8] The suffering of Baal is depicted

---

1) It is possible that *l* in *l.ysʿ*,*lyhpk*, and *lyṯbr* is the interrogative negative rather than the emphatic particle.

2) *ʾalt* is taken by GORDON (*UH*, p. 212) as 'throne' since he takes it as parallel to *ksʾa*. The parallelism, however, is between the compound phrases *ʾalt ṯbtk* and *ksʾa mlkk*. The word *ʾalt* may be a variant of *ʾahlt*, 'tent', cf. *ẓrt*/*ẓhrt*, *bt*/*bht*. There is, however, an Arabic word أَلَّة meaning 'a broad-headed spear'. The spear was the symbol of royal authority in the case of Saul, 1 Samuel xxii, 6, xxvi, 7 ff. In the last instance the spear stuck in the ground signified the royal presence as it marked the place where the chief of an Arab tribe was to be found, W. R. SMITH, *Kinship and Marriage in Early Arabia*, 1903, p. 171. In the Krt text also the spear signifies princely status.

3) The verb *ṯtʿ* is found here in parallelism with *yrʾa*, 'to fear', and must be a synonym, cf. p. 58, n. 5.

4) VIROLLEAUD, 'Les chasses de Baal: poème de Ras Shamra', *Syria* XVI, 1935, 247-266.

5) J. GRAY, 'The Hunting of Baal: Fratricide and Atonement in the Mythology of Ras Shamra', *JNES* X, 1951, pp. 146-155.

6) DE LANGHE, *Les textes de Ras Shamra-Ugarit et leurs Rapports avec . . . l'Ancien Testament*, I, p. 153.

7) GASTER, *Thespis*, p. 217.

8) GRAY, *op. cit.*, p. 152.

as the expiation of fratricide, and we relate this feature to the passage in the end of the text GORDON *UH* 49, specifically VI, 11, where Mot threatens Baal with vengeance for the death of his brothers, and in the same text V, 1-4, where Baal smites the sons of Aṯerat. An apparent difficulty in the identification of the sons of the mother-goddess Aṯerat with the brothers of Baal is that he is not the son of Aṯerat the consort of El, nor is he named the son of El, but of Dagon. Against this, however, our reply is that we are not dealing with strict genealogy here but with cultic relationships complicated by the settlement of Syria by strata of population at various periods. If Baal is called the son of Dagon in the texts it is equally true that he is the brother of Anat, who is uniformly called the daughter of El, and in relating Baal thus to El we find ourselves in agreement with KAPELRUD. [1]) Thus we regard the sons of Aṯerat, whom Baal smote, as his half-brothers, having El as a common father, and this serves, we think, as a key to the problematic text GORDON *UH* 75.

In this text after a lacuna a certain female, an attendant of Aṯerat herself is sent, pregnant by El, to the desert to bear certain monsters which shall lure Baal to hunt them, so that by some means which, through the damaged state of the text, is uncertain he may be brought to his downfall. Our translation of this text is as follows: [2])

ʾel.yẓḥq.bm lb.	El laughs in his heart,
wygmẓ.bm kbd	Yea, is convulsed with mirth [3]) in his liver.
ẓʾe.ʾat.ltlš	'Humble thyself [4]) that thou mayest deceive (him); [5])
ʾamt.yrḫ ldmgy.	O Maid of the Moon-god, [6]) do thou cozen him. [7])
ʾamt ʾaṯrt.qḥ	O Maid of Aṯerat take [8])

---

1) A. S. KAPELRUD, *Baal in the Ras Shamra Texts*, 1952, pp. 64-65.

2) GORDON *UH* 75, I, 12-41.

3) So GASTER, *Acta Orientalia*, XVI, 1937, p. 45, after Ethiopic *gamasa*.

4) *ẓʾe* is not 'Go out', which would be *ṣʾe*. Phonetically it corresponds to the Arabic طأطأ, 'to stoop'.

5) *tlš* is imperfect of *wlš* in our opinion, cognate with the Arabic ولس, which in the VIth form means 'to deceive or conspire'.

6) The Moon-god is possibly El himself, whose consort is Aṯerat.

7) We take *dmgy* as an imperative from a verb *dmg*, cf. Arabic دماج, 'clandestine'.

8) We had previously taken *ʾamt* and *ʾaṯrt* as being in apposition, *op. cit.*, p. 148 n. We now emphasize the repetition of the word *ʾamt*, which we take in its literal sense. Here we have an analogy with the story of Hagar's banishment into the desert with Ishmael (Genesis xvi).

ksʾank.ḥdgk ḥtlk.	Thy stool, [1]) thy settle, [2]) thy swaddling-bands, [3])
wẓʾe bʾaln.tkm	And stoop, couch [4]) in pain [5])
btk.mdbr ʾel	In the midst of the awful desert. [6])
šʾey kry ʾamt	Bear [7]) my burden, [8]) O Maid,
ʿpr.ʿẓm yd	Tremendous, [9]) strong of limb, [10])
ʾugrm.ḥl.ld	On the ground [11]) writhe, give birth;
ʾaklm.tbrkk	Thou shalt be brought to thy haunches [12]) with the Devourers
wld ʿqqm	Yea, bear the Voracious Ones,
ʾelm ypʿr šmthm	Divine shall their names be called;
bhm qrnm km.ṯrm	On them shall be horns like steers
wgbṯt km.ʾebrm	And humps like bulls.

---

[1]) Gaster reads *ksʾan* as a diminutive, cf. the Hebrew ending ־ון, *Thespis*, p. 450. This is probable, since the *n* of nunation would, on the Arabic analogy, be dropped before the pronominal suffix.

[2]) *ḥdg* suggests the Arabic حداجة, 'the woman's riding-litter'.

[3]) The root חתל in this sense is familiar in the Old Testament, e.g. Ezek. xvi, 4, לא המלחת והחתל לא חתלת.

[4]) For *tkm* Gaster first suggested the derivation from a root *wky*, cognate with the Arabic وكى, the final *m* being enclitic. We suggest that the root is *wkm*, cognate with the Arabic وكن, 'to sit down', or 'brood', of a hen.

[5]) *ʾaln* has been variously read. Virolleaud and Dussaud suggest 'oak', cf. Hebrew אלון. Ginsberg notes that אלון is occasionally rendered '*convallis*' by Jerome and מישר in the Targum, *JPOS* XVI, 1936 p. 141 (after F. Stummer, 'Convallis Mambre und Verwandtes', *JPOS* XII, 1932, pp. 6-21). This is now followed tentatively by Gaster, *Thespis*, p. 219. The rendering of אלון as 'valley', however, seems to rest not on a forgotten Semitic root *ʾaln*, but on Aquila's literalistic rendering of אלון as ἀυλων, which means, of course, 'a valley'. Gaster once suggested that *ʾaln* in the Ugaritic text was a scribal error for *ʾabn*, 'stones', but has now apparently abandoned this theory. We suggest that *ʾaln* is connected with the Arabic ألم, 'pain'.

[6]) Literally 'divine desert'. Gaster has noted several instances of nouns qualified by *ʾel* in the sense of 'supernatural, awful', cf. Hebrew הררי אל. The desert in Mesopotamian myth and ritual was the place inhabited by evil and unclean spirits, hence beyond the control of man. This notion is expressed in the phrase which recurs in Akkadian ritual texts, *ṣeru ašru ellu*, 'the desert a pure place', indicating a place remote from human contacts convenient for rites of purification.

[7]) Here we make a rather different division of the letters than is usually done.

[8]) We connect *kry* with the Arabic كارة, 'a bundle'. The possessive suffix indicates El's paternity.

[9]) *ʿpr* seems cognate with the Arabic عفر, e.g. أسد عفر, 'tremendous lion'.

[10]) Literally 'strong of hand'.

[11]) The word *ʾugrm* is the noun *ʾugr*, which we have already encountered as the name of one of Baal's two messengers Vineyard and Field (*gpn wʾugr*). The word is cognate with the Akkadian *ugaru*, 'plain'. The final *m* is prepositional.

[12]) Literally 'the Devourers will make thee kneel'. The squatting posture is adopted by Oriental women in childbirth.

wbhm.pn .bʿl	And against them Baal will set his face, [1]
bʿl ytlk wyṣd	Baal shall go forth and hunt,
yḥ pʾat.mdbr	Making haste [2] to the desert marches.
kn.ymġy.ʾaklm	So shall he come upon the Devourers,
wymẓʾa.ʿqqm	Yea, light upon [3] the Voracious Ones.
bʿl.ḥmdm.yḥmdm	The desire of Baal will be roused,
bn dgn.yhrrm	The son of Dagon will be excited, [4]
bʿl.ngṯhm.bpʿnh	Even Baal as he approaches [5] them on foot,
wʾel hd.bḫrẓh	Yea, the god Hadad in his haste. [6]

The actual circumstances of this hunt which brought Baal to his downfall are lost in a damaged piece of the text. But when the text resumes we read that Baal by El's appointment is suffering a 'long-term sentence': [7]

šbʿ.šnt.ʾel.mlʾa( )	Full seven years has El allotted
wṯmn.nqpt.ʿd ( )	And the eighth anniversary as well.

The reason for this is clearly given. It was the penalty of fratricide: [8]

klbš.km lpš.dm (ʾaḫh)	For he is covered with his brothers' blood as with a garment,
km.ʾall.dm.ʾaryh	With his kinsmen's blood as with a robe.
kšbʿt.lšbʿm.ʾaḫh.ym(d)	For seven (years) is appointed [9] (corresponding to) his seventy brothers, [10]
wṯmnt.lṯmnym	Yea, eight (years) for (his) eighty (kinsmen).

---

[1]) For this expression of hostility Gaster cites the Hebrew פני יהוה בעשי רע *Thespis*, p. 450.

[2]) We agree with Gaster in taking *yḥ* as imperfect of a root *wḥy*, cognate with the Arabic وحى, 'to hasten', *JAOS* LXX, 1950, p. 13.

[3]) The Hebrew cognate מצא also means 'to light upon' as well as 'to find'.

[4]) The verb seems best taken as cognate with the Arabic هرهر, 'to shake, move', as the parallel *yḥmdm*, 'desires', suggests.

[5]) *ngṯ* with the pronominal suffix *hm* is best taken as a participle, cognate with the Hebrew נגש, 'to approach'.

[6]) The last word of this column is usually read *bḫrẓʿh*, which has not at all the appearance of a Semitic word. We postulate an error of dittography resulting in 𐎑𐎓 (*ẓʿ*) instead of 𐎑 (*ẓ*), and so read *bḫrẓh*, 'in his haste', cognate with the Arabic خرط, which is used in the VIIth form in Syrian Arabic, meaning 'to rush rashly into an enterprise'.

[7]) Gordon *UH* 75, II, 45-46.

[8]) *Ibidem*, II, 47-50.

[9]) This incomplete word might be restored *ym(lʾu)*, 'filled', i.e. 'allotted in full'.

[10]) The 'seventy brothers' of Baal are doubtless 'the seventy sons of Aṯerat' the mother-goddess of whom we read in Gordon *UH* 51, VI, 46. In this passage, incidentally, those 'seventy sons of Aṯerat' are almost certainly the 'brothers' and 'kinsmen' of Baal whom he invites to his 'house-warming'.

This theme is repeated later in the text: [1])

ttpq lʾawl	'Thou art appointed as satisfaction [2]) for (thy) kinsmen; [3])
ʾešttk . lm . ttkn	I appoint thee to be spent [4]) for them.'

Meanwhile another figure appears whom we take to be 'the avenger of Baal's brothers', namely Mot: [5])

šr . aḫyh . mẓʾah	The avenger [6]) of his brothers found him,
wmẓʾah . šr . ylyh .	Yea the avenger of his kinsmen [7]) lighted upon him
bskn . sknm . bʿdn . ʿdnm	In his utmost jeopardy, [8]) in his critical hour. [9])
kn . npl . bʿl( )	So had Baal fallen ( )
( ) *km . ṯr*	( ) as a bull
wtkms . hd	And prostrate lay [10]) Hadad
p( ) *km ʾebr*	And ( ) as a steer
btk . mšmš dšʾe	In the midst of the miry [11]) swamp. [12])

---

[1]) GORDON *UH* 75, II, 57-58.

[2]) In the first word of this line we connect the first letter of Gordon's reading, *ʾe*, with the previous word and proceed to read *ttpq*, which we connect with the Arabic وفق, 'to fit', here anIfteʿal with the initial *w* assimilated to the infixed *t* as in Arabic.

[3]) We take *ʾawl* either as connected with the Arabic آل, 'family', or as a broken plural of a noun from the root *wly* cognate with the Arabic ولى, 'to be near'.

[4]) We take *ttkn* as the imperfect energic Ifteʿal of *ntk*, 'to pour out'.

[5]) GORDON *UH* 75, II, 51-56.

[6]) *šr* is taken by GASTER (*Thespis*, p. 223) as 'the chieftain (of his brothers)'. He is obviously thinking of the Akkadian *šarru*, 'king'. We connect the word rather with the Hebrew root שור 'to watch intently', whence שורר in the psalms, the enemy who continually watches for his opportunity, an apt description of the avenger of blood. In GORDON *UH* 52 Mot is known as *šr* in the double title *mt wšr* (1.8). While *šr* possibly means 'the enemy' in this passage, we prefer DRIVER's proposal that there it means 'dissolution', *v. infra*, p. 95 + n. 8.

[7]) *ylyh*, parallel to *ʾaḫyh*, must mean 'kinsmen', and is probably cognate with the Arabic ولى, 'to be near'.

[8]) *skn* is surely connected with the Hebrew סכן 'to incur danger', e.g. Eccles. x. 9, cf. Arabic صكم 'to hit' (of misfortune), صكمة, 'a shock'.

[9]) *ʿdn* suggests the Akkadian *edinnu*, which indicates crises in seasons or illness, as pointed out by B. LANDSBERGER, *JNES* VIII, 1949, p. 257. The construct singular with the absolute plural is, of course, the familiar Hebrew superlative e.g. שיר השרים.

[10]) *kms* must mean 'lie prostrate', since it is parallel to *npl*, and is cognate with the Akkadian *kamasu* with this meaning.

[11]) The normal phonetic correspondence of *mšmš* would be with the Arabic مشمش, 'to be intricate', as suggested by VIROLLEAUD, hence in the text it might mean 'in the toils'. We prefer GASTER's equation however, with the Arabic مشاشة, indicating soft ground about a waterhole, the last refuge of Baal in the time of drought. We recollect that in a similar emergency Ahab scoured the country about the waterholes for grass to save his horses, 1 Kings xviii, 5.

[12]) DRIVER (*op. cit.* 147) on GORDON *UH* 75 I, 22 cites Hebrew שאיה, 'waste land',

The avenger pronounces the sentence:
'Thou art appointed as satisfaction for (thy) kinsmen...'

In this most difficult text the clue to its meaning seems to be in the passages from the second column which we have just cited. The theme is Baal's punishment for fratricide. The enormity of this crime causes barrenness and this is expressed by the fact that Baal, the spirit of fertility, languishes almost extinct 'in the midst of the miry swamp'. The connection between fratricide and sterility is, of course, familiar to anthropologists and is expressed in the Old Testament in God's curse on Cain: 'And now thou art cursed from the earth which hath opened her mouth to receive thy brother's blood from thy hand. When thou tillest the ground it shall not henceforth yield unto thee her strength...' (Genesis iv, 11-12). This suggests to us that the text may have been related to the observance of the artificial sterility of the Sabbatical year.

As we have indicated, the vicissitudes of Baal described in this text were conditioned by his experiences in the main body of the Baal mythology. Here, however, it seems to us that we have an episode elaborated in isolation until the text becomes an aetiological myth. The seven- or eight-year cycle of the eclipse of Baal suggests to us a connection with the Sabbatical year. Perhaps the sufferings of Baal were related to some final expiatory sacrifice which ended the period of sterility, as the scape-goat of Hebrew ritual driven out into the wilderness on the 10th of Tishri may originally have done. The text, however, was adapted, we believe, to a specific sociological occasion and served to explain and sanction the punishment of fratricide. [1]) We are led to this conclusion by the final passage of the text, which seems to visualize just such an occasion, relating to the judicial and ritual functions of the king: [2])

šṯk.mlk.dn	'So may the king dispense [3]) judgement;
šṯk.š'ebt.ʿn	May he pour out what is drawn [4]) from the well; [5])

'ruin'. He cites also Akkadian *še-'u*, 'running water', which might better suit the context. The last two letters, however, are doubtful, and HERDNER (*Corpus*, p. 55) reads tentatively *ṣ* or *l* for our *š*.

[1]) The effect of fratricide, of course, was not confined to the individual, but was felt by the whole community.

[2]) GORDON *UH* 75, II, 59-62.

[3]) *šṯk*, which we take as the Šafʿel of *ntk* 'to pour', is a precative perfect. The reference is to judgement with water as a medium, probably some kind of ordeal as in Numbers v, 17-27.

[4]) *š'ebt* seems best taken as a verbal noun.

[5]) The connection between springs and judgement is well-known in the

šṯk.qr.bt.'el	May he pour out the well-spring of the temple of El, [1]
wmṣlt.bt.ḫrš	Even the deep [2] of the House of Divination.' [3]

The text Gordon *UH* 76 (Virolleaud IV AB) [4] presents another problem. Concerning as it does the birth of a bull-calf to, or for, Baal, it might refer to the passage in Gordon *UH* 67, V, 18-22, where in view of his forthcoming encounter with Mot Baal mates with a heifer either to secure the strength of a bull for his ordeal by the process of contactual magic or perhaps, by an act of imitative magic, to inaugurate life in view of his apprehended death. In that passage we have seen that the actual birth of the calf is mentioned immediately after the mating, and have indicated the difficulty, suggesting that the birth may have been mentioned merely in anticipation. This being so, it may have been felt necessary to elaborate the theme of the birth and the result would be the text Gordon *UH* 76. Again the prominent rôle which Anat plays in this text, in spite of the fact that Baal is not yet in eclipse, may indicate that this text belonged to a cycle centring about the goddess, and in use as a cult-legend at one of her shrines. This may well have been elsewhere than in Ugarit, as is perhaps indicated in the text, where a certain locality *'aḫ šmk* is mentioned, which may well be far south of Ras Shamra.

This text is very fragmentary. It consists of three columns, the first of which has the first half of every line missing. The second describes an encounter between Anat and Baal, who is absent from his usual residence on Mount Sapon on a hunting expedition in *'aḫ šmk*, the haunt of wild oxen (*ml'at r'umm*). This is apparently a great distance from Mount Sapon on the Northern horizon of Ugarit, since Anat flies there. The text goes on to mention Anat's selection of a cow, doubtless the dam of the bull to be born to or for Baal, but the text breaks off here. In the third column with frequent lacunae

Exodus tradition, e.g. Meribath Qadesh and Massa, both of which signify law-suit and ordeal, and 'Ain Mishpat, 'the Well of Judgement', in the same vicinity (Genesis xiv, 7).

1) The association of spring and sanctuary is well known, e.g. in Psalm xlvi. The Well of Zamzam at Mecca is another instance.

2) This word seems to be connected with the Hebrew מצולה; at least it is natural so to connect it in the context where *'n* and *qr* are mentioned. It means 'basin' or 'deep reservoir'.

3) The most feasible suggestion we can offer for *bt ḫrš* in such a context is to connect *ḫrš* with the Hebrew חֶרֶשׁ, 'divination'.

4) Virolleaud, 'Anat et la génisse', *Syria* XVII, 1936, pp. 150-173.

and much apparently inconsequential prolixity we are told that Anat brought the news of the birth of the calf to Baal, who had meanwhile returned to his palace on Sapon.

There is little of significance in this text. Our own opinion is that it relates to the birth of a sacred bull, which in the ritual of ancient Ugarit typified Baal in procreation, as is described in GORDON *UH* 67, V, 18 ff., when Baal (*scilicet* the sacred bull in which he is incarnate) mates with a heifer, and in his death, as is suggested in GORDON *UH* 75, II, 54-55 where it is said:

So had Baal fallen ( ) as a bull
And prostrate lay the god Hadad ( ) as a steer.

The text is of interest to Old Testament scholarship mainly because of the theory of DUSSAUD that it relates to the cult of the bull at a shrine at the headwaters of the Jordan at Dan, and that in sponsoring this cult Jeroboam the son of Nebat was not innovating but building on a cult already established. [1]) As far as concerns the cult promoted by Jeroboam that is probably true enough. DUSSAUD's theory, however, is based upon the identification of *'aḫ šmk* of the text with the swamps (*'aḫ*, Hebrew אחו) north of the shallow Lake Huleh. Certainly this lake was known to Josephus as Σεμαχονιτις. [2]) and is called in the Talmud אגמא דסמכא. [3]) The description 'abounding in wild oxen' suits the locality, the formerly inaccessible reed-jungles of which were well known to the writer and his colleagues in the Palestine Police under the British Mandate as hunting-grounds for wild pig. Nevertheless, though we might admit that this locality is visualised in the Ugaritic text, the centre of interest remains Mount Sapon, Jebel el-Aqra, on the Northern horizon of ancient Ugarit. In insisting on this, however, we do not exclude the possibility—indeed, we should say, the probability—that those cult-legends and the ritual behind them were known in Palestine as well as in Syria, as the seasonal rituals and much of the liturgy of Israel suggests. After all, to say nothing of the probability of DUSSAUD's view that Dan was a centre of the cult of Baal before its occupation by the

---

[1]) DUSSAUD, 'Cultes cananéens au source du Jourdain d'après les textes de Ras Shamra', *Syria* XVII, 1936, pp. 283-295.

[2]) Josephus, *Antiquities*, XV, x, 3.

[3]) Talmud Babli, *Yebamoth* 121a. One notes the discrepancy between the ס of the Talmud and the *š* of the Ras Shamra text. This, however, is the less significant perhaps owing to the lapse of time between the two and the known vagaries of the Babylonian Talmud in the spelling of place-names in Palestine.

Israelites, there was a place Beth Anath in Upper Galilee not far distant from the Huleh basin, [1]) and this, as the name suggests, was probably a shrine of the goddess whose exploits are celebrated together with those of her brother Baal in this and the rest of the Baal-cycle in the mythology of Ras Shamra. Further than this we cannot follow DUSSAUD in his efforts at particularisation. [2])

The view that we have presented that the myth of the conflict of Baal and Mot related to the agricultural year has not gone unchallenged. GORDON [3]) points out that the summer, which is generally assumed to be the season of drought and sterility by those who regard the myth as having a seasonal relevance, is actually a season of growth and ripening of fruit, when moisture is supplied by heavy dew. This may be freely admitted, but, with the possibility of early and late siroccos, drought was still a serious menace in the Syrian summer. No one who has lived a year in those regions is unaware of the general suspense of the peasants till the coming of the 'early rains' of late autumn or the anxiety lest the sirocco should strike in April before the 'latter rains' have sufficiently swelled the corn in the ear.

In a study published posthumously U. CASSUTO [4]) admits the seasonal reference in the passage describing Anat's slaying of Mot (GORDON *UH* 49, II, 30-37). But of the myth in general he states: 'It is hard to suppose that in an epic of such large and comprehensive proportions, so rich in colourful episodes and stories of all kinds, which presents us with a whole assortment of gods and heroes,

---

[1]) Joshua xix, 38; Judges i, 33. This place has been located by GEORGE ADAM SMITH at ʿAinetha 10 miles north-north-west of Huleh (see map to *A Historical Geography of the Holy Land*), and by F. M. ABEL at Al-Baʿaneh 12 miles north-north-east of Acre. Whether we agree with one location or the other the fact remains that Beth Anath was in the orbit of Naphtali and so within easy reach of Huleh.

[2]) Colour is lent to DUSSAUD's thesis by the fact that when the tribe of Dan settled in Upper Galilee they found the locality already settled by the Phoenicians, who were apparently sensible of the economic value of the rich corn-lands of the Hauran. Judges xviii, 7.

DRIVER considers that the young bull was born to Anat (sired probably by Baal), and that this is the token of Baal's revival and the inauguration of a new era of peace and plenty, when even the wild beasts will become gentle (*op. cit.*, pp. 19, 115-119). This is an interesting thesis, but depends too much upon conjectural restoration of damaged text to be entirely convincing, though one must admire the ingenuity of the scholar.

[3]) GORDON, *UL*, 1949, pp. 3-5.

[4]) U. CASSUTO, 'Baal and Mot in the Ugaritic Texts', *IEJ* XII, 1962, pp. 77-86.

monsters and beasts, creatures and buildings, is no more than an allegory of a single, clearly-defined natural phenomenon such as that of the drying up of vegetation in the hot summer and its renewal in the rainy season... The nature myth... may have been one of the elements that went into the making of the epic of Baal and Mot, but it certainly cannot have been the only one'. Now there is an element of truth in what CASSUTO observes, and we freely admit that the development of the myth in epic style and proportions has been embellished far beyond the scope of a strict accompaniment of seasonal ritual. In our detailed study, however, we hope that we have shown the seasonal bearing of the myth relative to such significant crises as the coming of the early rains, when the house of Baal was completed, and the desacralization of the new crop, to which Anat's slaughter of Mot refers. In this particular episode, to be strictly consistent, Mot ought not to be the victim, but in the ascendant at the season of harvest, when Baal was in eclipse. We need not, however, look for strict logical consistency in myth, as we see from the fact that after his death at the hands of Anat Mot is still able to challenge Baal (GORDON *UH* 49, V, 7-19). Here Mot as the enemy of Baal was a convenient victim as a substitute for the ripe corn in the rite of desacralization. CASSUTO, of course, is right in seeing that the significance of Mot was wider than the drought and the threat of sterility in summer, and that he symbolizes the general power of decay and death. In the desacralization rite whereby the new crop was set free for the nourishment and enjoyment of the community the end of Mot was appropriate to the occasion.

The length, literary elaboration, and rich variety of themes in the myth of Baal and Mot need not militate against the relevance to the progress of the agricultural year. The frequent verbal repetition of passages serves the double purpose of accentuating an episode or a ritual, and may be as strong evidence of a related ritual as an actual rubric. Such episodes and others, such as Baal's conflict with his various monstrous adversaries, serve the purpose of sustaining and intensifying dramatic suspense as well as occupying the worshippers while the ritual was performed. Here the poet has developed the primitive myth beyond its mechanical relation to ritual. CASSUTO, in our opinion, misrepresents the case by treating such passages as episodes in themselves, whereas they are reminiscences, strictly secondary to the main theme of the conflict of Baal and Mot. The first time that Baal's conflict with these monstrous adversaries is mentioned Anat receives Baal's messengers by asking what adversary has risen against Baal, since she has slain his monstrous adversaries, which are then detailed. These conflicts, it should be noted, are not described, and in the second case where they are mentioned Mot replies to Baal's challenge by sending his defiance to him though he had slain the various monsters, which are then detailed. Here the recital of Baal's conquests emphasizes the power of his immediate enemy Mot and intensifies dramatic suspense in view of the coming conflict between him and Baal.

In the texts which describe the conflict of Baal and Mot we should again note the relevance of various passages to seasonal rituals and festivals. The house of Baal is completed on the eve of the heavy autumn rains and storms, and Anat's slaughter of Mot is obviously related to rites of desacralization of the new corn-crop. The texts however, as they stand cannot relate severally to such seasonal rituals. They are in fact tightly interlocked. GORDON *UH* 51, which describes the building of the house of Baal, describes also Baal triumphant, and most clearly relates to the autumnal new year on the eve of the heavy rains. Here Baal's conflict with Mot is already anticipated (GORDON *UH* 51. VII, 47 ff.). GORDON *UH* 67 gives Mot's defiant reply to Baal (I, 1-8, 12-26), announces the death of Baal (VI, 8-10), and describes the mourning of El and Anat, and the latter's search for the body of Baal (VI, 11-31), which, as parallels from the Near East suggest, is related to Tammuz-rites of early summer. GORDON *UH* 62 continues the theme of the mourning of Anat (1-8), and the recovery and burial of the corpse of Baal (I, 8-29), which recalls the same Tammuz ritual. GORDON *UH* 49, dealing with the substitute on the throne of the dead Baal (I, 15-37), obviously continues the theme. The same text, which describes Anat's slaughter of Mot (II, 30-37), with obvious relation to a harvest rite, proceeds immediately to describe the revival of Baal (III, 1-21), obviously referring to the new season of fertility, when

> The skies rain oil,
> The wadis run with honey.

With that indifference to strict logic which characterizes myth in its relation to ritual, the same text, which has described Anat's annihilation of Mot (II, 30-37) describes the final battle between Baal and Mot after 'days, months, then in the seventh year...'

It is obvious then that these texts form one complete whole and cannot be detached and related to rituals at different seasons of the agricultural year. We believe that they reflect those rituals, and are probably elaborated from myths severally related to those occasions, but as the text stands, if, as we believe, it is functional rather than simply aesthetic, it relates directly to one single ritual occasion.

This occasion may be a great festival at the end of a seven-year cycle, which was observed in Israel in a different way as the year of release. This may be suggested by the final battle between Baal and Mot 'in the seventh year'. Again, however, the number seven may be simply a case of literary convention, signifying 'eventually'. If, on the other hand, as the obvious references to seasons and rites in the peasant's year seem to indicate, the text may be related to an annual occasion that is without doubt the autumnal New Year. This, as Gordon *UH* 51 indicates, is the season when Baal comes to the fulness of his power as king, which is symbolized by the building of his house. This *Sitz im Leben* of the whole Baal-complex is further suggested by the fact that the texts are dominated by the theme of Baal as king. In pleading with El to sanction a house for Baal, Aṯerat declares [1]):

Baal the Mighty is our king,
Our ruler, over whom there is none.

As he sits in his house and defies Mot Baal asks indignantly with reference to the claims of Mot [2]):

Shall any, king or no king
Have the earth as his dominion?

The kingly function of Baal is admitted even in his eclipse, when his throne is filled by a substitute Aṯtar (Gordon *UH* 49, I, 15 ff.). Finally, in his defeat in the supreme conflict, Mot admits the sovereignty of Baal (Gordon *UH* 49, VI, 33-35). These texts, of course, are naturally connected with the three fragments Gordon *UH* 129, 137, and 68, which describe how at the outset Baal won his kingship in conflict with the unruly waters.

The great significance of the Baal-myth of Ras Shamra for Old Testament scholarship is its relevance to the question of the Kingship of God, particularly as that is expressed in certain of the Psalms, passages in the Prophets, and in Apocalyptic, both Jewish and Christian. In Psalms xlvii, xciii, xcvi, xcvii, xcviii, and xcix, which,

---

1) Gordon *UH* 51, IV, 43.
2) Gordon *UH* 51, VII, 43.

with their specific declaration יהוה מלך, are admitted by all to have a special relevance to the Kingship of God, the pattern of the Ugaritic ideology of the Kingship of the god won in conflict with the powers of Chaos is reproduced. In these psalms, if Yahweh emerges as King, he has proved himself so against the forces of chaos in nature, the arrogant waters (Psalm xciii, 3-4), which must then acclaim his triumph (Psalm xcviii, 7-8); or he subdues all peoples, the political enemies of Israel (Psalm xlvii, 3, 8; xcvi, 10; xcix, 2), and has consequently proved himself more effective than their gods (xcv, 3; xcvi, 4; xcvii, 7-9). Yahweh is King over all the earth (Psalms xlvii, 2, 7; xcvi, 1; xcvii, 9), he has established order in nature, 'the world is established that it cannot be moved' (Psalm xciii, 1; xcvi, 10), and he created the heavens (Psalm xcvi, 5), and even the sea, which particularly typifies the forces of Chaos (Revelation xxi, 1), in his creation (Psalm xcv, 5). He has secured the moral order too; he who chose Israel as his people and revealed his nature and will to her fathers is true to his own revelation, and the principles of that revelation, his order (משפט) shall be established in Jacob (Psalm xcix, 4); 'his testimonies are very sure' (Psalm xciii, 5). He shall maintain the order which he established by judgement of all the earth and its people and rulers (Psalms xcvi, 13; xcviii, 9), and by his vindication of his people Israel (Psalms xcvi, 10, 13; xcviii, 9). Here it is well to remember the evidence of the Ras Shamra texts that the verb שפט means 'to rule' as well as 'to judge', a fact which is of great moment insofar as it extends the category of enthronement psalms and relevant passages in the Prophets to much nearer the proportions for which Mowinckel contends. Nor is this ideology confined to such psalms; it is reflected in other categories of psalm also.

The recognition of the essential features of the conception of the Kingship of God in the light of the Canaanite prototype, where these are thrown into bold relief, enables us to lay the proper emphasis on these essentials in Hebrew passages on this theme, and even where all the features are not expressed we know what is implied by the mention of one or another of the main motifs.

The *Sitz im Leben* of psalms on the subject of the Kingship of God, as suggested by Zechariah xiv, 16-17 and Nahum ii, 1 (Hebrew text) taken in conjunction with Isaiah lii, 7, is certainly the autumnal New Year festival. The determination of the *Sitz im Leben* of such passages in the Old Testament must strengthen the probability that the Canaanite prototype also was relevant to this occasion.

The Ras Shamra analogy makes a further valuable contribution to the solution of a burning controversy on the Kingship of God in the Enthronement Psalms xlvii, xciii, xcvi-xcix and others which are not universally admitted as enthronement psalms. That is the significance of the key words יהוה מלך, where grammatically the verb may be either stative or narrative perfect. Contending for the former interpretation, EISSFELDT [1]) notes the fact that kingship was the normal attribute of all the gods in the ancient Near East. Now this latter proposition must be freely admitted and is corroborated by the Ras Shamra texts, where El is King, and the antagonists of Baal Sea-and-River and Mot are also of royal status. We believe that MOWINCKEL [2]) is right in contending against EISSFELDT that, on the analogy of a similar phrase acclaiming Absalom (2 Sam. xv, 10), Adonijah (1 Kings i, 11, 18), and Jehu (2 Kings ix, 13), which obviously refers to a single action, יהוה מלך in the Enthronement Psalms refers to a definite cultic act signifying the assumption of royal power or the epiphany of Yahweh as King. This conclusion is supported by Ps. xlvii, where just before the call to praise Yahweh as King it is said:

עלה אלהים בתרועה   יהוה בקול שופר

Since the blast of the trumpet is well known as the concomitant of the act of enthronement (cf. 2 Sam. xv, 10; 1 Kings i, 39; 2 Kings ix, 13; xi, 14) עלה אלהים בתרועה is a variant of יהוה מלך. Now since עלה does not admit of a stative meaning the suggestion is that יהוה מלך is not stative, but narrative perfect. The conclusion is fully supported by the Baal myth of Ras Shamra. Here the kingship of Baal is not a state, but a function. In GORDON *UH* 129, 137, and 68 it is won after critical conflict.

In GORDON *UH* 51, VII, 43 in the declaration

Shall any, king or no king
Have the earth as his dominion?

Baal admits that others such as Mot may have royal estate, but effective rule over the earth is a definite function. This is likewise implied in the reign of the substitute Aṯtar on the vacant throne of Baal. Aṯtar was obviously of kingly status, but in effect he was

[1]) O. EISSFELDT, 'Jahwe als König', *ZAW* XLVI, 1928, pp. 81 ff.
[2]) S. MOWINCKEL, *Offersang og Sangoffer*, 1951, pp. 523-526.

inadequate for the exercise of Baal's royal office. When finally Mot admits the supremacy of Baal he declares: [1])

Let Baal be enthroned ( )
( ) of his kingship,
( ) of his governance.

Baal's supremacy, as in his conflict with Sea-and-River, has been contested and has been won in conflict. As a result he assumes his throne and is ready for active rule. Surely the close parallels between the Enthronement Psalms and kindred passages in the Psalms and Prophets of Israel and in Jewish and Christian Apocalyptic and the Ras Shamra myth of Baal as king indicate that in such passages in the Old Testament the Kingship of Yahweh is more than a state, that it is in fact a dramatic epiphany, a dynamic function rather than a stative attribute. When this is appreciated EISSFELDT's argument that the Kingship of Yahweh in the Psalms simply denotes an attribute which Yahweh shared with all Semitic deities, true though it is, misses a vital point and does less than justice to the evidence of the Psalms, though to be sure we must consider in this connection many more passages than those which include the obvious key words יהוה מלך.

Against the view that the ideology of Yahweh as King with the implications we have noted was introduced to Israel in her assimilation of the Canaanite New Year festival with other seasonal rituals of the settled land in the two centuries of the settlement [2]) and in the development of the cult in Solomon's Temple [3]) BUBER has contended that the conception was native to Israel. [4]) He would see it implied in the Sinai covenant, which, at least according to the Decalogue in Exodus xx. 2-17, has indeed the form of the treaties imposed by the Hittite kings on their vassals in the 14th century. This form-

---

[1]) GORDON *UH* 49, VI, 33-35.

[2]) A. ALT, 'Gedanken über das Königtum Jahwes', *Kleine Schriften zum Alten Testament* I, 1953, pp. 345-357, esp. pp. 348, 353 ff., where the cult of Yahweh as King is associated with the worship of *Yahweh Ṣebaoth*, enthroned on the ark at Shiloh.

[3]) H. SCHMID, 'Jahwe und die Kulttraditionen von Jerusalem, *ZAW* N.F. XXVI 1955, pp. 169-197. Schmid, however, ignores all but the traditions of El as creator, undoubtedly incorporated in the Solomonic Temple cult from the pre-Israelite local tradition, and so does not do justice to the strong affinities between the liturgy of the Jerusalem New Year festival and that of the seasonal festival of Canaan, so strongly indicated by the Ras Shamra Baal-myth.

[4]) M. BUBER, *Königtum Gottes*, 1932.

critical argument seems in the nature of the evidence sound, the peculiar style of treaty probably reflecting the general Near Eastern usage in the Late Bronze Age. The fact that the style of the treaty is not reproduced in detail after this period has suggested the historicity of the Covenant, and, for BUBER, the origin of the royal status of Yahweh in Israel in the Covenant [1]). His argument, however, seems to carry us no further than EISSFELDT's observation that all gods in the ancient Semitic world have the attribute of King. Yahweh as supreme authority in Israel could not have less than royal authority. What is in question, however, is the source of the dynamic expression of God's royal power in its most common function in the Old Testament, his triumph over the powers of Chaos in nature, in history, and in the moral sphere. Here we encounter the pattern of the epiphany of God as King after conflict, which is already familiar in the Canaanite fertility-cult and its Babylonian counterpart, both related to the respective New Year seasons. Granted that this theme with its affinities in language, thought, and imagery with the seasonal mythology of Canaan is bound up in certain psalms with the peculiarly Israelite themes of *Heilsgeschichte* and Covenant, no relevant passage in the Old Testament may be conclusively demonstrated to antedate the foundation of the Temple and its cult, when, on the evidence of the Psalms, both themes were related to the liturgy of the New Year festival. No passage earlier than this dealing only with the *Heilsgeschichte*, the theme of Yahweh's election and preservation of Israel and the revelation of the Covenant, mentions Yahweh as King, with the possible exception of the problematic Blessing of Moses (Deuteronomy xxxiii), where, to be sure, it is not certain whether 'מלך in Israel' in v. 5 means 'king' and whether it refers to Yahweh or Moses. In this connection it may be noted that EISSFELDT, who certainly has no purpose to subserve here, asserts boldly 'Die älteste sicher datierbare Stelle, die Jahwe das Königsprädikat beilegt, ist Jes. 6. 5'. [2])

We may, in concluding, summarize our view of the mythology of ancient Ugarit which centres round Baal. There is a cosmic theme represented by the myth of the conflict between Baal and the Unruly Waters, by which Baal secured kingship and established Cosmos. Echoes of this survive in other texts which are not primarily cosmic

[1]) G. E. MENDENHALL, *Law and Covenant in Israel and the Ancient Near East*, 1955.

[2]) 'Jahwe als König', *ZAW* XLVI, 1928, pp. 81-105.

myths, namely GORDON *UH* ʿnt, III, 35-IV, 47 and 67, I, 1-3 where, together with the Unruly Waters, various monsters are mentioned as the enemies of Cosmos. This is that part of the literature of ancient Canaan which shows the closest affinity with the cosmic mythology of Mesopotamia, particularly with the myth *enuma eliš*. It too was that element in the Canaanite literature which was particularly appropriated by the Hebrews, being peculiarly adapted to express their conception of Divine Providence, and with various modifications finds expression in the psalms celebrating the kingship of God. Apart from its general suitability to express Hebrew conceptions and hopes, we believe that this theme more than any other in the mythology of Canaan finds expression in the Old Testament, being perhaps known to the Hebrews as the cult-legend of the Baal-shrine of Baal Saphon in the Eastern Nile Delta in the days before Moses led the 'mixed multitude' out of the land of bondage. [1]) The same myth, again, suggested the imagery of Hebrew eschatology in the Prophets and later Jewish and Christian apocalyptic.

Here, however, the Hebrew adaptation of the Canaanite ideology of the Kingship of God at the New Year festival invests the old conception with an entirely new significance. The Canaanite myth and its accompanying seasonal ritual, insofar as it was limited to nature, had a purely cyclical significance. The kingship of Baal was menaced by the same chaotic forces with calendrical regularity. In Israel, however, though the theme of conflict, victory, and the rule of God was annually celebrated with stereotyped ritual and oral expression, the particularization of his victory in the overthrow of the Pharaoh's army and the establishment of his order in the giving of the law referred to something which in spite of its recurring sacramental appropriation by Israel could not be repeated. In her home in the cockpit of nations too Israel always encountered the unprecedented crisis. The forces of Chaos were regularly identified with political enemies of Israel and her God, as in Psalm xlvi, for instance, and notably, we believe with P. HUMBERT [2]), with Assyria

---

[1]) We do not suggest that the Hebrews had ever actually been worshippers of Baal at this shrine, but simply that they were familiar with the local cult-legend of Baal's triumph over the Unruly Waters, just as Muhammad knew and used Jewish and Christian traditions. We have suggested further that this local cult-legend may have coloured the Exodus tradition of the crossing of the Sea of Reeds. 'Canaanite Mythology and Hebrew Tradition', *Glasgow University Oriental Society Transactions* XIV, 1953, pp. 55-57.

[2]) P. HUMBERT, 'Le problème du livre de Nahoum', *RHPhR* 1932, pp. 1-15.

in the year of the fall of Nineveh (612), in which the prophet Nahum particularized God's triumph over the powers of Chaos in the New Year festival in that year. The New Year festival presented both Canaanites and Israelites with the opportunity to express their faith that their God, their help in ages past, would be their hope for years to come. Israel, however, as soon as she particularized the theme of the festival in history projected her faith into the future, not as a recurring cycle, but as a progressive development. No doubt in pre-Exilic days men's hopes, nourished by this regular cultic experience, were set on a speedy vindication of God's power and purpose. But when the cult was abolished with the destruction of the Temple in 586 hopes so nourished looked beyond the bounds of history for the establishment of the Kingdom of God, to which possibly more sober spirits like the pre-Exilic prophets had also begun to turn. [1]) This view of the origin and development of eschatology in Israel seems to find confirmation in the recurrent use of the imagery and sequence of thought in this particular myth in the eschatology of the Prophets and in later Jewish and Christian Apocalyptic.

The text GORDON *UH* ʿnt serves to bridge the gulf between this cosmic myth and the myth of Baal's conflict with Mot, which we believe to be related to seasonal agricultural ritual. The fact that the text GORDON *UH* ʿnt seems to overlap GORDON *UH* 51 to a considerable degree and to suggest a different version of the conflict between the powers of Cosmos and Chaos where not Baal, but Anat, is triumphant may be explained by supposing the myth to have come originally from an Anat shrine. The myth of the conflict between Baal and Mot, on the other hand, betrays an unmistakable relation to agricultural ritual within the scope of the year. [2]) The text GORDON *UH* 49, which deals with the theme of Baal *redivivus*, leads up to the myth and ritual conflict possibly connected with the Sabbatical Year. Here we are outside the scope of myth and ritual relating to the various phases of the husbandman's year, but are still on the fertility theme. [3]) Finally in the text GORDON *UH* 75 we have the case of a

---

[1]) A. R. JOHNSON, *Sacral Kingship in Ancient Israel*, 1955, p. 54 n. in contention with MOWINCKEL, *Psalmenstudien* II, pp. 190-202.

[2]) Referring to a harvest rite either in anticipation or in retrospect within the context of the New Year liturgy. The myth proper to the harvest rite was certainly abridged in its incorporation into the New Year liturgy, and possibly transformed somewhat in the process.

[3]) Those who dispute the ritual significance of these myths commonly object

myth centring upon the ritual of the Sabbatical Year as the penalty of Baal's blood-guiltiness. The last element is taken over from the main body of the Baal-myth and is emphasized. The myth is then taken out of its original context in the fertility-cult to be used as a myth explaining and authorising the social rite of atonement for fratricide.

To be reckoned also in the category of myths of the fertility cult is the problematic text GORDON *UH* 52, and here, thanks to the obvious criterion of rubrics, there is little doubt of the relation to seasonal ritual. This text is fairly well preserved on a tablet consisting in all of 76 lines. The obverse consists of a number of passages comprising invocations (ll. 1-7, 23-27) catchlines of hymns (l. 13, 16-18, 21-22, 28-29), and ritual rubrics (ll. 8-11, 12, 14-15, 19-20), which are divided by horizontal lines. The reverse consists of 46 unbroken lines of a myth. This passage, though describing the begetting and birth of the twin-gods *šḥr* and *šlm*, Dawn and Sunset (lit. 'completion', i.e. of day), the god manifest in the Venus-star, is also closely related to ritual. It opens, for instance, with a water-drawing rite (ll. 30-31, 35-36), which can be paralleled from the cult at Hierapolis in the Roman imperial period. [1]) In the sequel, where El shoots and cooks a bird over the fire (ll. 37-39), a ritual prelude to a *hieros gamos* is apparently described (ll. 33-49). The *hieros gamos* and birth of the twin-gods is then described (ll. 49-59), a comic strain being introduced by the suggestion of the husband of the two women seduced by El that the children are his (ll. 52-53, 59-60). The text goes on to describe the growth of the pair on the desert confines (ll. 60-76).

The main interpretations of the significance of the text have depended upon the construction put upon the reverse part. The historical hypothesis of DUSSAUD [2]) that the text refers to the development of a Phoenician caravanserai in the Negeb depended upon the assumed proper names Terah (Etraḫ), Ashdod, and the Desert of Qadesh in ll. 64-65, and on the translation 'I will make a division

---

that rubrics are notably lacking. It must be frankly admitted that rubrics are practically non-existent, and, where they may be suspected, are never beyond doubt. It is a fair presumption that occasional phrases at critical points in the text noted in our study are probably cultic exclamations for public expression. The use of these as proper names, as possibly אי זבול and עמנואל in the Old Testament, indicate the relation of the texts to public worship and their essentially dramatic character, whatever ritual may have accompanied them.

[1]) Lucian, *The Goddess of Syria* (Loeb ed.), § 13.

[2]) R. DUSSAUD, 'Les Phéniciens en Negeb et en Arabie après un texte de Ras Shamra', *RHR* CVIII, 1933, pp. 5-49.

between sea and sea' (*'agẓrym bn ym*, reading *'agẓr ym* in the first complex of letters.) This view is long since exploded and is held no longer by any scholar who has worked at first hand on the texts. Though R. LARGEMENT [1]) has, in our opinion, presented a more balanced view of the subject of the reverse of the text as the birth and nurture of the gracious gods, we doubt if he is right in including the theme of their fertilization of the desert, where they have built their sanctuary.

Though certain phrases, notably the invocation of the gods gracious and fair (*'elm nʿmm wysmm*), 'who delimit the day, two born on the same day, who suck at the teats of the breasts of Aṯerat' (*'agẓr ym bn ym ynqm b'ap ẓd 'aṯrt* (var. *šṯ*)) (ll. 23-24, cf. 58, 61) connect the myth with certain passages in the obverse of the tablet, we cannot agree with LARGEMENT that the continuous text in the reverse is the myth accompanying the rubrics and catchlines of the obverse. The passages in the obverse are not all related to the reverse, and the latter itself, as we have already indicated, implies a good deal of ritual not mentioned in any passage in the obverse. The matter, in fact, is a good deal more complicated than LARGEMENT suggests, as we now proceed to demonstrate by a more detailed study of the text.

By a convention common in liturgics in the ancient Near East the presence of the gods is invoked by their titles, 'the gracious and fair, the shining ones', and perhaps 'the exalted': [2])

'eqr'a . 'elm . nʿ (mm)	I will invoke the gods gracious
wysmm . bn . šr(m)	And fair, the Shining Ones ( ). [3])
ytnm . qrt . lʿly(nm)	Let them give honour [4]) to the Exalted Ones
bmdbr . špm . yd( )	In the desert of the bare heights [5]) let them ( )

We note here that the gods in question are associated with the desert, which is perhaps their cult-place. The gods then are not primarily associated with the fertility-cult, and are in all likelihood

---

[1]) R. LARGEMENT, 'La naissance de l'Aurore, poème mythologique de Ras Shamra-Ugarit' *Analecta Lovaniensia Biblica et Orientalia*, Ser. II, Fasc. ii, 1949.

[2]) GORDON *UH* 52, 1-4.

[3]) Cf. Arabic شرى, 'to flash' (lightning), cf. DRIVER (*op. cit.*, p. 121), who takes *šrm* as plural of *šr* cognate with Akkadian *šarru*, 'king'. On the possible occurrence of the root, meaning 'to flash' in Psalm lxxxii, 7 see pp. 272-273.

[4]) Taking *qrt* as a verbal noun from *yqr*, after GINSBERG.

[5]) There is no reference here to ים סוּף as DUSSAUD proposed. *špm* is better taken as cognate with Hebrew שְׁפָיִם, 'bare, windswept', cf. Jeremiah iv, 11; xii, 12, as VIROLLEAUD proposed (*Syria* XIV, 1933, p. 137).

astral deities. This would accord with their title 'the Shining Ones' (*bn šrm*) and is corroborated by the identity of 'the gods gracious and fair' with *šḥr* and *šlm*, the Venus-star, which was particularly venerated as Aṯtar by the Arabs.

Next follows an injunction to crown the statues of the gods: [1])

lr'ešhm.wyš (t)m ( ) on their heads, and let them place ( )

There follows an invitation to a sacred meal: [2])

lḥm.blḥm 'ay	Eat of the food, Ho!
wšty.bḫmr yn 'ay	And drink of the ferment of wine, Ho!

This meal effects the integration (*šlm*) of the participants one with another and with the gods invoked. Apparently, however, the community do not partake in person, but only through their representatives, the king, queen, and ministrants who have direct access to the sanctuary (*'rbm*), and their attendants (*ṯnnm*): [3])

šlmt mlk.	Mayst thou be at one [4]) O King!
šlm.mlkt. 'rbm.wṯnnm	May queen, choristers [5]) and singers of responses [6]) be at one.

After the invocation and ritual introduction a passage ensues which is obviously connected with vine-pruning and grafting, probably the ceremonial inauguration of that operation. This is connected with the mutilation of Death-and-Dissolution (*mt wšr*), the analogy with Anat's mutilation of Mot in the rites of desacralization of the first or last sheaf (Gordon *UH* 49, II, 30-37) being immediately suggested: [7])

mt.wšr.yṯb	Death-and-Dissolution [8]) sits,
bdh.ḫṭ.ṯkl	In his hand is the sceptre of sterility,

---

[1]) Gordon, *UH* 52,5.

[2]) *Ibidem*, 6.

[3]) *Ibidem*, 7.

[4]) We take *šlmt* and *šlm* as optative perfects.

[5]) *'rbm* are equated by Gaster (*Thespis*, p. 240) with the Mesopotamian *erib biti*, who have access to the temple after the chief ministrant in the Babylonian New Year ceremonies. On this analogy the king would seem to have been the officiating priest in the ritual behind this Ugaritic text. The *'rbm*, as is apparent from l. 12 have the specific function of singing in antiphonal chorus, their counterparts being *ṯnnm* (lit. 'responders').

[6]) See n. 5.

[7]) Gordon *UH* 52, 9-11.

[8]) Driver (*op. cit.*, p. 148) aptly cites the Syriac expression ܫܪܝܐ ܕܡܘܬܐ, 'the dissolution of death'.

bdh.ḫṭ.ʾulmn	In his hand is the sceptre of widowhood; [1]
yẓbrnn.ẓbrm.gpn	In pruning the vine it is him they prune, [2]
yṣmdnn.ṣmdm.gpn	In binding the grafts of the vine it is him they bind,
yšql.šdmth.km gpn	He is laid low on the level plot [3] as a vine.

There seems to be no necessary connection between this passage and the main body of the text concerning the birth of the twin gods manifest in the Morning and Evening Star. Its inclusion seems to indicate that the ceremonial pruning and grafting of the vines coincided with the season at which the birth of *šḥr* and *šlm* was celebrated. These operations are commonly carried out in January-February in modern Syria, though DALMAN [4] attests pruning in the Merj Ayyun as late as March. The probable reference in another rubric in the text (ll. 13-14) to the cooking of a kid in milk suggests a season as late as March or even later. Indeed the Gezer tablet lists vine-dressing (*ẓmr*) in the two months between wheat-harvest and the in-gathering of summer fruit, hence in June-July-August. The reference in ll. 25-26, however, to the fructification of vine-tendrils, which is equated with the growth of the gracious gods, suggests the earlier date in March, when the vines begin to burgeon, 'when the bud is perfect and the sour grape is swelling in the flower' (Isaiah xviii, 5).

After this passage a rubric follows: [5]

šbʿd.yrgm. ʿl. ʿd.wʿrbm.tʿnyn

Seven times shall it be recited to the accompaniment of the lute, [6] and the choristers shall respond. [7]

wšd.šd ʾelm	And the effluence [8] is a divine effluence,
šd ʾaṯrt.wrḥm	The effluence of Aṯerat and the Maid [9]

With the sequel GORDON 52, 14-15 the chant in l. 13 is divided off from what precedes and follows. The sequel is a rubric relating to the cooking of a kid in milk and a calf in butter-milk as milk-charms, and almost certainly connects with the chant in l. 13.

---

1) Cf. the association of שכול ואלמון in Isaiah xlvii, 9. The root שכל signifies 'bereavement', but cf. 2 Kings ii, 19, where it signifies 'sterility'.

2) Alternatively 'emasculate', GASTER, *Thespis*, p. 241.

3) Perhaps there is a word-play on *šd mt*, 'field(s) of death'.

4) G. DALMAN, *Arbeit und Sitte in Palästina* I, i, p. 264 ff.

5) GORDON *UH* 52, 12.

6) Cf. על in Psalm headings indicating the musical accompaniment.

7) GORDON *UH* 52, 13.

8) So DRIVER (op. cit. pp. 121, 148), who cites the Aramaic שְׁדָא and the Syriac ܫܕܐ.

9) I.e. probably Anat, alluding to her sexual potential, cf. Judg. v, 30 רחם רחמתים לראש גבר and רחמות in the Moabite Stone, l. 17. The literal meaning of *rḥm* is 'womb'.

ʿl.ʾešt.šbʿd.ġzrm.ṭb(ḫ g)d.bḥlb.ṯʾannḫ bḫmʾat wʿl ʾagn šbʿdm.dġ (ṣt yṣq)
Over the fire seven times the sacrificers [1]) cook a kid in milk, a calf [2]) in butter-milk, and over the cauldron seven times (pure water is poured) [3])

Here in incantation (l. 13) and ritual (ll. 14-15) is a milk-charm which recalls the Biblical prohibition against boiling a kid in its mother's milk (Exodus xxiii, 19: xxxiv, 26; Deuteronomy xiv, 21), which Maimonides [4]) recognized as a Canaanite rite. The passages in Exodus associate this rite with the offering of first-fruits at the Feast of Weeks. If this had independent significance as a milk-charm it may have been performed at this time in order to promote a flow of milk from the goats and cattle which was already failing in the summer drought after the plentiful flow after parturition in the spring. On the other hand a Karaite source cited by GASTER [5]) associates the practice with a ritual for fructifying trees, fields, gardens, and orchards. In view of the reference to the burgeoning of the vines in ll. 25-26 the rite to promote the flow of milk may also have been adapted to promote the flow of sap in the vine at the swelling of the fruit. If the Canaanite rite may be dated, as in the Book of the Covenant, to the end of the grain-harvest that is the season when the Bedouin drive in their flocks to graze on the aftermath, and the boiling of a kid in milk, still the common native way of cooking mutton, may be associated with a fellowship meal between nomads and peasants of the settled land, as well as serving as a rite to promote a fresh flow of milk on the new pastures, which itself was held to have homoeopathic influence on the fertility of crops. The *Sitz im Leben* of the bulk of this text, in fact, may be the annual reunion of peasants and the nomad herdsmen after pasture. It may be noted that the gods *šḥr* and *šlm* are associated with the desert in l. 4 and ll. 68 ff., and the honouring of these manifestations of the Venus-star, which was worshipped by the Arabs in later times as el-ʿUzza, fittingly united the peasants and nomads for the season.

---

1) LARGEMENT (*op. cit.*, p. 35) felicitously cites אדר עזרים '*magister sacrorum*' in a Punic-Latin bilingual inscription.

2) Perhaps rather a plural (broken) from a noun cognate with Arabic نخة, 'beast of burden'. DRIVER (*op. cit.*, p. 120) and AISTLEITNER (*Wörterbuch* 1794) take it as cognate with Akkadian *nanaḫu*, 'mint', cf. Syriac ܢܢܚܐ.

3) So restored by DRIVER conjecturally (*op. cit.*, p. 120), who cites the Arabic داغصة, 'pure water' (*op. cit.*, p. 153).

4) *Moreh Nebukhim*, iii, 48, cited by GASTER, *Thespis*, p. 244.

5) *Thespis*, p. 244.

With such an occasion the broad and bawdy hilarity of the myth in the reverse of the tablet is in keeping. This may reflect *connubium* between the two social groups and the reunion of nomad husbands with wives wed in a *ṣadiqa* union, where the wife continues to live with her father's people and is visited occasionally by the husband.

The next passage probably refers to the parade of the statues of the Maid (*rḥmy*) Anat and another goddess, almost certainly Aṯerat, and ends with a rubric: [1])

tlkm . rḥmy . wtṣd	The Maid goes to and fro and ranges
( ) [2])	( )
tḥgrn . gẓr . nʿm	They are girt in might and beauty,
( )	( )
wšm . ʿrbm . yr( )	And the choristers (?)

Next comes a rubric: [3])

mṯbt . ʾelm . ṯmn	The thrones of the gods are eight,
ṯ(bt) pʾamt . šbʿ	(The thrones) of the great goddesses [4]) are seven.

A declaration of devotion follows, which may be the catch-line of a hymn to the astral deities *šḥr* and *šlm*: [5])

ʾeqnʾu . šmt b(n) . šrm	I am zealous for the names of the Shining Ones.

The invocation of the gracious gods is renewed, and reference is made to their nurture at the breasts of Aṯerat the mother of the gods, this suggesting the burgeoning of the vines, which probably coincided with the season to which the text was relevant: [6])

ʾeqrʾan . ʾelm nʿmm	I invoke the gracious gods,
ʾagẓr ym bn ym	Who delimit the day [7]), two born in the one day,

---

[1]) Gordon *UH* 52, 16-18.

[2]) Probably describing the activity of Aṯerat.

[3]) Gordon *UH* 52, 19-20.

[4]) Largement (*op. cit.*) cites the Arabic فأم, 'to fill', cf. فئامة, 'a large party'.

[5]) Gordon *UH* 52, 21-22. [6]) *Ibidem*, 23-27.

[7]) Aistleitner (*Wörterbuch* 643) connects the word with the root *gẓr*, which is well known in Hebrew, Arabic, Aramaic, and Syriac, meaning 'to cut', and takes it to mean 'figures', so Driver (*op. cit.*, p. 121), who cites the Syriac ܓܙܪ meaning 'to cut out a shape' (*op. cit.* 134). Aistleitner (*Die mythologischen und kultischen Texte aus Ras Schamra* 1959, p. 59) translates *ʾagẓrym* as 'die Ebenbilder *Jm*-s', 'images of (the god) Ym'. We think rather of the Morning and Evening Star 'cutting off', i.e. delimiting the day. In its context, which refers to the voracious appetite of the gods, Gaster (*Thespis*, p. 253) translates 'two little gluttonous boys', citing Isaiah ix, 19 (Evv. 20) ויגזר על־ימין ורעב ויאכל על־שמאל ולא שׂבעו איש בשׂר זרעו יאכלו׃ (*op. cit.* p. 451). In spite of the remarkable association of ideas and language in this passage and that in Gordon *UH* 52, 61-64, גזר in Isaiah, meaning 'to snatch', means basically 'to cut off'.

ynqm.b'ap zd.'aṯrt	Who suck at the teat of the breast of Aṯerat.
špš myprt[1]*).dlthm*	Špš makes their tendrils to abound,
( ) *wġnbm*	( ) and grapes.
šlm. ʿrbm.ṯn(nm)	Peace to the choristers (and) those who make responses,
hlkm.bdbḥ nʿmt	Who go with a sacrifice for favour.

The last short passage before the myth proper repeats the incantation of l. 13.

The text continues fairly well preserved on the reverse except for the concluding passage (ll. 71-76), which describes the encounter of the young gods *šḥr* and *šlm* with the warden of the crops between the desert and the sown. This is the myth proper describing the birth and nurture of the twin gods. It differs from the rest of the mythological texts of Ras Shamra, however, in that here the narrative style is much less fully developed, and the myth is much more obviously related to rites of imitative magic. The rituals, in fact, relating mainly to concupiscence, appear to be the more significant element, and the myth is related to the ritual in a way so forced as to require explicit notice, e.g. ll. 41-42, 44-46:

h(l) ʿṣr tḥrr l'ešt	Lo, the bird is being roasted at the coals,
ṣḥrrt.lpḥmm 'a(ṯ)tm	But what are being inflamed at the coals are two women,
'aṯt.'el.'aṯt.'el wʿlmh	The wives of El, the wives of El, even the eternal.

We shall emphasize this particularly close, if forced, relationship between the myth and ritual in our more detailed presentation of this part of the text.

The passage opens with a short lacuna, and El is presented as drawing water from the sea to fill a cooking cauldron. This recalls the water-drawing rite noted by Lucian of Samosata in the fertility-ritual of Hierapolis in the 2nd century A.D. The water is taken to the 'house' of El, which is probably his temple. The quasi-domestic activity of El, who is generally depicted as an old man full of dignity, who influences affairs in nature and society by his final sanction rather than by his personal activity, has possibly a burlesque purpose, El becoming a figure of comedy, which, from the Greek analogy, we know to have been an essential feature of the fertility myth and ritual. In this respect El's rôle is analogous to that of Herakles in Attic comedy. The activity of the aged god excites the admiration of certain women, whom El is later to excite sexually and then

[1]) A. Herdner (*Corpus*, p. 99, n. 4) suggests that for *p*, which is indistinct, *ṣ* or *s* may be read.

seduce. In anticipation El is himself sexually excited. This is the first strophe (30-35):

( ) b ( ) gp ym	( ) the shore of the sea,
wysġd . gp . thm	And proceeds to the shore of the deep.
( ) mšt'ltm	( ) in cupped handfuls, [1]
mšt'ltm . lr'eš . 'agn	In cupped handfuls to the top of the cauldron.
hlh tšpl hlh trm	Lo, this maid bows down, lo, this one rises up,
hlh . tṣḥ 'ad 'ad	This one shouts, 'Daddy! Daddy!'
whlh . tṣḥ 'um . 'um	And this one shouts, 'Mother! Mother!'
t'erkm . yd . 'el . kym	The organ [2] of El grows long as the sea,
wyd 'el . kmdb	Yea, the organ of El as the flood. [3]
'ark . yd . 'el . kym	The organ of El is long as the sea,
wyd 'el . kmdb	Yea, the organ of El as the flood.

The next strophe or 'act' (ll. 35-49), the ladling of water into a cauldron, continues; this is then taken into the 'house' of El. He lays aside his sceptre and staff, respectively symbols of dignity and age, and shoots down a bird from the sky, which he roasts as a rite of imitative magic with the purpose of inflaming the desire of two of the women whose admiration he had already excited. The passage ends with their admission (ll. 46-49) that the rite has had this effect: [4]

yqḥ . 'el . mšt'ltm	El takes cupped handfuls,
mšt'ltm . lr'eš . 'agn	Cupped handfuls till the cauldron [5] is full,
yqḥ . yš(t) . bbth	He takes it and puts it in his house;
'el . ḫṭh . nḥt	El lays down his sceptre,
'el . ymnn . mṭ . ydh	El puts aside [6] the staff of his hand,
yš'u yr . šmmh	He lifts up (his hand), he shoots into the sky,
yr . bšmm . 'ṣr	He shoots a bird in the sky.
yḥrṭ . yšt lpḥm	He plucks it and sets it on the coals.
'el . 'aṯtm . kypt	El indeed entices two women;
hm . 'aṯtm . tṣḥn	Lo, the women cry out.
ymt . mt . nḥtm . ḫṭk	O goodman, goodman, thy sceptre is laid down,
mmnnm . mṭ ydk	The staff of thy hand is laid aside.
h(l) 'ṣr . tḫrr . l'ešt	Behold a bird is roasted at the fire,
wṣḥrrt . lpḥmm 'a(ṯ)tm	But what are being inflamed fire, are two women,
'aṯt . 'el . 'aṯt . 'el . w'lmh	One wife of El, another wife of El, even the Eternal.
whm 'a(ṯ)tm tṣḥn	And lo, the two women cry out

[1]) *mšt'ltm* is probably cognate with Hebrew שעל cf. Isaiah xl, 12, מי מדד בשעלו מי ים (Qumran Isaiah).

[2]) For this sense of *yd* cf. Isaiah lvii, 8.

[3]) As the parallel suggests *mdb* is best taken as the derivative of a root *dwb*, as Dussaud suggested, for which Driver cites the Mandaean *ẓaba*, 'a stream' and South Arabian *mẓf* (*op. cit.*, p. 161).

[4]) Gordon *UH*, 52, 35-49.

[5]) *'agn* suggests the Arabic إجانة, 'washing-tub'.

[6]) Driver cites the Ethiopic *mannana*, 'to reject' (*op. cit.*, p. 161).

y.ʾad ʾad.nḥtm ḥṭk	O Dad! Dad! thy sceptre is laid down.
mmnnm.mṭ ydk	The staff of thy hand is laid aside.
hl.ʿṣr.tḥrr.lʾešt	Behold a bird is being roasted at the fire,
wṣḥrrt.lpḥmm btm	But what are being inflamed at the coals are two girls,
bt.ʾel.bt ʾel wʿlmh	One girl of El, another girl of El, even the Eternal.
whn.ʾaṯtm.tṣḥn	And lo, the two women cry out,
y.mt mt nḥtm.ḥṭk	O goodman, goodman, thy sceptre is laid down,
mmnnm.mṭ ydk	The staff of thy hand is laid aside.
hl.ʿṣr tḥrr lʾešt	Behold a bird is being roasted at the fire,
wṣḥr(r)t.lpḥmm ʾaṯtm	But what is being inflamed are two women.
ʾaṯt ʾel ʾa(ṯ)t.ʾel.wʿlmh	One wife ot El, another wire of El, even the Eternal.

Here the threefold allusion by the women to the analogy of the roasting of the bird to sexual excitement certainly indicates that this is a rite of imitative magic and an element in the main theme of the text, which is a *hieros gamos*. The 'goodman' (*mt*) or Dad (*ʾad*) are possibly burlesque references to El in his domestic capacity, but in our opinion the reference is probably to the husband of the two women or perhaps to several husbands in a common rite of sexual rejuvenation, where the women in ritual coitus with their husbands or those who are declared to be such sacramentally unite with El the Creator (*bny bnwt*) and first progenitor. In 'the sceptre laid down and the staff of the hand laid aside' there may be a *double entendre* referring to the failing virility of the males whom it is the purpose of the myth to rejuvenate.

The next passage (ll. 49-57) relates to the sexual act, resulting in the birth of the twin-gods *šḥr* and *šlm* (ll. 52-53). The broad, bawdy humour of comedy is sustained by the report of the fond husband of the two women to El that his wives have borne twins. There are probably two rubrics in the passage. At l. 54 the mention of the birth of *šḥr* and *šlm* the Morning and Evening Star occasions the call to 'Take up and prepare (an offering) to Lady Sun and to the fixed stars.' The beginning of the description of the sexual act described in ll. 49-51 is repeated in ll. 55-56, this being part of the rubric that this passage 'shall be repeated five times . . . by the singers of the assembly' (ll. 56-57). We may well suppose that this activity of El was sacramentally experienced by the community in the sexual orgies of the fertility cult which the Hebrew prophets so vehemently denounced.

yhbr.špthm.yš(q)	He stoops down and kisses their lips.
hn.špthm mtqtm	Lo their lips are sweet! [1])

[1]) The form is dual.

mtqtm klrmn(m)	Sweet as pomegranates. [1]
bm.nšq.whr	By kissing and conceiving,
bḥbq.ḥmḥmt.tqt(nṣn)	By embracing and desire they travail. [2]
tldn šḥr wšlm	They bear *šḥr* and *šlm*
rgm l'el ybl	Word is brought to El,
'a(ṯty) 'el.ylt	My two wives have borne children. [3]
mh ylt	What have they borne?
yldy šḥr wšl(m)	Two are born, *šḥr* and *šlm*
š'u ʿdb.lšpš rbt wlkbkbm kn(m)	Take up (and) prepare (an offering for Lady Sun and the fixed stars.
yhbr špthm yšq	'He stoops down and kisses their lips.
hn špthm.mtqt(m)	Lo their lips are sweet
bm.nšq.whr	In kissing and conceiving,
(b)ḥbq wḥ(m)ḥmt	In embracing and desire'
yṯbn( ) yspr.lhmš.lṣb(r ?.wl) šr pḥr	To be repeated five times by the company [4] and by the singers [5] of the assembly.

The repetition of this passage, possibly seven times, reflects the mood of the festal assembly and possibly also the sexual licence in which they indulged on this occasion. It certainly emphasizes the primary ritual association of the myth, which is narrative only relatively to the chants and rubrics of the tablet. In such a text then we do not expect the strictly logical development of narrative. Hence we do not find it strange that the labour of the two women seduced by El and the birth of the gods, which has already been described in ll. 49-53, is again described in practically the same words in ll. 57-60. This is the end of the passage to be recited five times according to the rubric, which notes the passage for repetition by citing only the opening. Now after the rubric the next passage, concerning the nurture of the gods (ll. 59 to the end), is introduced

---

[1]) So DRIVER, who cites the Assyrian *lurindu matqu*, 'sweet pomegranate' (Hebrew *rimmon*) (*op. cit.* p. 123). AISTLEITNER prefers to take the word as a cognate of Akkadian *lurimtu*, 'grapecluster' or even *lurinu*, 'fig-tree' (*Wörterbuch* 1483).

[2]) So DRIVER, who cites Ethiopic *qanaṣa*, 'to leap', so presumably to crouch in the posture of one about to leap, the crouching position being that of childbirth in the East, cf. GORDON *UH* 75, I, 26 (*tbrkk*, 'they will bring thee to thy knees'). The derivation and meaning, however, is uncertain, and AISTLEITNER feasibly translates 'conceive' citing the Arabic قنيصة, the lower part of the belly of a bird, after LANE.

[3]) *ylt* is an instance of the assimilation of the *d* of the root to the final *t*.

[4]) We conjecture *ṣbr*, 'band', or possibly *ṣbrt*, the feminine form being regular in the Ras Shamra texts, cf. DRIVER *ṣb'e*, with the same meaning (*op. cit.* 1. 122).

[5]) Alternatively *šr pḥr* may mean 'leader, lit. 'king', of the assembly', as DRIVER proposes (*op. cit.*, p. 123).

by the citation of the end of this passage, which had been repeated. The gods, however, are no longer named *šḥr* and *šlm*, as in l. 53, but 'the gods gracious, who delimit the day, two born in the one day', which obviously refers to the twin-gods *šḥr* and *šlm*.

klʾat tqtnṣn.wtldn	Both of them squat down and give birth,
tld ʾelm nʿmm	They bear the gods gracious,
ʾagzr ym bn.ym	Who delimit the day, two born in one day,
ynqm.bʾap (ž)d.št	Sucking at the teat of the breasts of the two (goddesses),
rgm.lʾel.ybl	Word is given to El,
ʾaṯty.ʾel.ylt	My wives, O El, have given birth.
mh.ylt	What have they borne?
ʾelm.nʿmm ( )k	The gods gracious,
ʾagzr ym.bn ym	Who delimit the day, two born in one day,
ynqm.bʾap.žd.št	Who suck at the teat of the breasts of the two (goddesses).
špt lʾarṣ.špr lšmm	One lip to the earth, one lip to the sky,
wlʿrb.bphm.	And into their mouths go [1])
ʿṣr.šmm wdg bym	The birds of the heavens and fish from the sea;
wndd (lg)zr.lgzrm	And they flit [2]) from morsel to morsel,
yʿdb ʾu ymn ʾu šmʾal.bphm	Putting [3]) right or left into their mouth,
wlʾu šbʿny	But are not satisfied.
ʾaṯt.ʾetrḫ ybn ʾašld	O wives (whom) I wed, O sons (whom) I begot,
šʾu ʿadb tk mdbr qdš	Take equipment into the awful desert [4])
ṯm.tgrgr.lʾabnm.wlʿṣm	There go around [5]) from stones to bushes.

[1]) *ʿrb* is probably an infinitive absolute with the sense of the finite imperfect, like *ndd* in the following line.

[2]) So Driver (*op. cit.*, p. 123), who cites Job xv, 23 where the verb is used as here of shifting about for food. We may cite Isaiah xvi, 2, where the verb is used of a wandering bird.

[3]) *yʿdb* may possibly be the verb in a relative clause where the relative particle is omitted after the antecedent *gzrm*.

[4]) Lit. 'the holy desert' (*mdbr qdš*), not the Desert of Qadesh (Barnea), as proposed by Virolleaud in his *editio princeps* (*Syria* XIV, 1933, pp. 128-151), Dussaud (*RHR* CVIII, 1933, pp. 5-49), nor Qadesh on the Orontes (Ginsberg, cited by Albright, *BASOR* 71, 1938, p. 37, n. 24). *qdš* here may either be a synonymn of *ʾel*, the qualificative which signifies supernatural or awful, or it may indicate the ritual significance of the desert in the period of ritual separation of mother and offspring after birth, 'the seven, yea eight' year period perhaps having a ritual significance. In both particulars the passage recalls the birth of the monstrous adversaries of Baal in the desert in Gordon *UH* 75. Albright appositely cites the phrase *ṣeru ašru ellu*, 'the desert a pure place' from Akkadian ritual texts (*JPOS* XIV, 1934, p. 137). Driver translates 'in the glaring wilderness', citing the Assyrian phrase *ina šadani elluti quddušuti*, 'on the bright, glaring mountains' (*op. cit.*, p. 125).

[5]) Cf. Driver (*op. cit.*, p. 125), 'run to and fro', citing Ethiopic *gargara*, 'to roll' (*op. cit.*, p. 146), so Aistleitner, *Die mythologischen und kultischen Texte aus Ras Schamra*, 1959, p. 61.

šbʿ šnt tmt	Seven whole years,
ṯmn nqpt.ʿd	An eighth circuit besides
ʾelm nʿmm.ttlkn šd	The gracious gods go about in the open country,
tṣdn.pʾat.mdbr	Scouring the desert marches.
wngš.hm.nġr mdrʿ	Lo, they draw nigh to the warden of the sown land, [1])
wṣḥ hm. ʿm.nġr.mdrʿ	Lo, they cry aloud to the warden of the sown land,
ynġr nġr pt(ḥ)	O warden, warden, open up (thy stores) [2])
wptḥ hw.prṣ.bʿdhm	And he opens up and grants a favour [3]) for their sakes.
wʿrb.h( )g	And they come into
hm.(ʾeṯ dgn.l) [4]) *lḥm*	If there is (corn for) eating,
tn wnlḥm	Give that we may eat
hm.ʾeṯ (yn dšrb) [5])	If there is wine (to drink),
(w)tn.wnšt	Then give that we may drink.
wʿnhm.nġr mdrʿ	And the warden of the sown land answers them
(ʾeṯ dgn llḥm)	(There is corn to eat)
wʾeṯ.yn d šrb	And there is wine for drinking
bṯk( )	In ( )
mġʾept lhn	(?) titbits [6])
lg yn h)	A *log* [7]) of wine ( )
wḥbrh.mlʾa yn	And his companion was full of wine.
( )	( )

It is not easy to appreciate the relevance of this passage to the narrative of the myth or to its ritual *Sitz im Leben*. The reference to *mdbr qdš*, especially in connection with the new-born gods and their mothers suggests the seven-days ritual quarantine for mother and child after childbirth (cf. Leviticus xii). This may be supported by the reference to 'seven years, yea eight circuits', during which the gracious gods and their mothers are in the desert. On the other hand this period may simply, in the common Semitic literary convention, denote an indefinite period of time. The 'warden of the sown land'

---

[1]) This office is actually mentioned in the administrative text *PRU II*, 16.

[2]) *ptḥ* may be used in the technical sense of exposing corn for sale or dole, cf. Joseph's distribution of corn as subject of the verb in Genesis xli, 56, cf. Amos viii, 5. The usage may refer originally to the opening of storage pits.

[3]) *prṣ* is generally taken as a noun, the object of *ptḥ*, 'a chink' or the like. We suggest that it is the conjunction *p* (Arabic فَ) and the perfect of the verb *rṣy*. (Hebrew רצה, Arabic رضى), which we consider to give better sense in conjunction with *bʿdhm*.

[4]) Probable restoration according to Driver (*op. cit.*, p. 124).

[5]) Restored by Driver from l. 74.

[6]) Cf. Arabic طفن , 'to take hors d'oeuvres'. A. Herdner (*Corpus*, p. 101) reads *mġ hw, lhn*, possibly meaning 'He came to them ...'

[7]) The *log* is known in Lev. xiv, 10, 24 as the smallest liquid measure, about a pint.

may be paralleled by the wardens of the Egyptian frontier posts in the Isthmus of Suez, who kept a check on the seasonal migrations of nomads to and from the settled land, as the Tale of Sinuhe and various dispatches from these frontier forts indicate. A closer parallel is probably the guards of corn-crops, who used to be a feature of the rural economy between the desert and the steppe in Palestine, [1] where signals used to be set up on heights to give notice to nomadic herdsmen that crops were growing, which must not be destroyed by grazing. [2] The final passage suggests, in fact, that the *Sitz im Leben* of this obviously ritual text may have been the annual reunion of peasants and nomads at the season after harvest when the latter moved over to enjoy their grazing rights on the aftermath of the cereal crops. These local relationships and the rights they involve are often secured in the case of modern Arab communities by connubium between particular nomad tribes and peasant communities, somewhat after the relationship between the people of Bethlehem and the Moabites of the region of the perennial wadis in 'the Plains of Maob' Northeast of the Dead Sea in the Book of Ruth. The exercise of this connubium probably involving *ṣadiqa* marriage, may underly the repeated reference to the sexual act in the text, and the description of the nurture of the gods who range the desert marches may have served as the charter of the nomads' grazing rites from the distant past of the Canaanites of Ugarit.

---

1) G. DALMAN, *Arbeit und Sitte in Palästina* II, 1932, p. 59.

2) A. JAUSSEN, *Coutumes des Arabes au pays de Moab*, 1908, p. 251. Alternatively *nġr mdrʿ* may be not the warden of the sown land, but the guard, modern Arabic ناطور, of the crop on the threshing-floor, or even of the grain after it was finally stored in grain-pits as the verb *ptḥ* in the text suggests.

CHAPTER III

SAGA AND LEGEND

Besides the pure myths which we have just considered the Ras Shamra literature contains two long texts the protagonists of which are not divine but human. One of these deals with the vicissitudes of one Dn'el and his son Aqht; the other has as its hero the King Krt. Both Dn'el and Krt were kings [1]) and thus in their sacral capacity stand in a peculiar relation to the gods. The latter, however, though not absent from the Krt text, play a much more prominent part in the Dn'el, or rather the Aqht, text as we shall call it, following GORDON's designation. In this text it is by no means easy to determine whether we are dealing with myth or legend.

Where we are dealing with the fortunes of human beings we naturally expect that there is a historical element in the text. This is true even though the gods are numbered among the actors, as, for instance, in the Iliad. In the Aqht text, however, opinion differs as to the extent of the historical element. G. A. BARTON notably committed himself rather too hastily to a historical view of the text, [2]) and even E. DHORME did not hesitate to see in Dn'el the eponymous

---

[1]) Though Dn'el is nowhere explicitly entitled 'king' there seems little doubt that he was a king. In the passage describing the curse upon the localities adjacent to the scene of Aqht's murder (GORDON *UH* I Aqht, 152) the first curse is pronounced by the king (*mlk*). As there is no reference in this context to any actor besides Dn'el, the king in question is probably Dn'el. In two other passages (GORDON *UH* 2 Aqht I, 26-27 and II, 24-25) we find *hklh* in parallelism with *bth*, both pertaining to Dn'el. The context indicates that the meaning of *hkl* here is not 'temple' but 'palace', hence we conclude that Dn'el was a king. See further our paper 'The *Goren* at the City Gate; Justice and the Royal Office in the Ugaritic Text 'Aqht'. PEQ 1953, pp. 118-123.

[2]) BARTON would locate the action of the text in Galilee and finds reference to *qdš* in 2 Aqht I, 44 ff., II, 16 ff. which he takes as Qadesh Naphtali. In 3 Aqht rev., 31 he takes *mgdl* as Magdal at the south end of the Plain of Kinnereth. In 1 Aqht, 163-165 and 3 Aqht, II, 30 he takes *qrt 'ablm* as 'the city of Abel', i.e. Abel beth Maacah of 2 Samuel xx, 15 (Abel Maim of 2 Chronicles xvi, 4). Barton after Virolleaud (*op. cit.* p. 122) sees further reference to Galilee in what he supposes to be a reference to 'the women of Asher' in 2 Aqht VI, 36, and to Dor on the coast in 1 Aqht, 154, 162, 168. He notes *ẓbl* as a title of Dn'el and conjectures that Dn'el was the ancestor of the Zebulonites. He would find further reference to Galilee in 1 Aqht, 147 where he claims to find 'the fishing places of Kinnereth'. 'Danel, a pre-Israelite Hero of Galilee', *JBL* LX, 1941, pp. 213-225. Those bold conjectures are not supported by the context, *v. infra*, ad loc.

hero of the Israelite tribe of Dan. [1]) Even where no such historical particularisation is made it is generally stated that Dn'el was an ancient Canaanite king pre-eminent for his justice. This supposition is based on the passage where it is stated of Dn'el [2]) that

ytšʾu.yṯb.bʾap.ṯġr	He rises to sit at the entrance of the gate
tḥt.ʾadrm.dbgrn	In the place of the notables who are in the public place; [3])
ydn.dn.ʾalmnt	He decides the case of the widow;
yṯpṭ.ṯpṭ.ytm	He judges the suit of the orphan.

We should not admit even this, however. All that is indicated in this passage is that the king has revived or rather that he has emerged from ritual seclusion and is therefore able to discharge all his kingly function including justice. Dn'el was no more noted for his justice than any other ancient king in the Near East, and indeed in the Krt text there is an almost identical definition of the judicial powers of the king. Ezekiel's impression of Dn'el as pre-eminently righteous (Ezekiel xiv, 14, 20) and wise (*ibidem*, xxviii, 3) is probably due to the etymology of the name rather than to anything in the Ugaritic text.

The last reference and the fact that the prophet spells the name of the primeval hero exactly as in the Ugaritic text suggests that the text, first published by Virolleaud as 'La Légende de Dan'el' (1936), ought to be investigated.

Dn'el, an ancient king, is pre-occupied with the problem of

---

[1]) E. Dhorme, *Syria* XVIII, 1937, pp. 105-106, n.

[2]) Gordon *UH* 2 Aqht, V, 6-8//1 Aqht, 21-25.

[3]) The word *grn* is generally taken as 'threshing-floor', the meaning which it most often has in Hebrew and Arabic. This, however, does not appear to be the primary meaning of the word. The verb جرن in Arabic means 'to fray, or rub', and الجارون is found meaning 'the worn track'. Hence we think of *grn* in the Aqht text as a space rubbed by public concourse and so kept clear. This is an apt description of the open space immediately within the city gate familiar from the excavation of various sites in Palestine and Syria. See our article 'The *Goren* at the City Gate . . .', *PEQ* 1953, pp. 118-123 in reply to Sidney Smith, 'On the Meaning of *Goren*', *PEQ* 1953, pp. 42-45 and 1946, pp. 5-14, where it is contended that *goren* means threshing-floor and *ʾadrm* is cognate with the Aramaic אדרא, 'threshing-floor' (actually wicker fences set up on the leeward side of the threshing-floor to catch the chaff). This sense of *ʾadr* is not attested in the Ras Shamra literature. The root means 'noble'. The preposition *tḥt* need not mean 'under' as S. Smith translates, but 'in place of', as regularly in Hebrew, a king being said to accede תחת אביו, cf. more specifically Isaiah x, 4 תחת הרוגים יפלו. 'They will fall in the place of (i.e. among) the slain'.

progeny. The text introduces him in a ritual vestment ministering to the gods in the sanctuary: [1])

'uẓr.'elm.ylḥm	Veiled [2]) he offers food to the gods,
'uẓr.yšqy.bn.qdš	Veiled he offers drink to the holy ones.

During this period of seven days in the holy precinct he resorts to ritual incubation with the purpose of receiving in dreams divine assurance that his wish for progeny would be granted. Then 'on the seventh day' Baal presents Dn'el's supplication to El and outlines the ideal son the king would desire to maintain the status of his person in society and in the sanctuary: [3])

mk bšbʿ ymm	Then on the seventh day
wyqrb.bʿl.bḥnth	Baal proffers [4]) his intercession
'abynt.dn'el.mt.rp'e	For the impotence [5]) of Dn'el the Dispenser of Fertility,
'anḫ.ġẓr.mt.hrnmy	Even for the groaning of the hero, the man of Hrnm,
d'en.bn.lh.km.'aḫh	That he has no son like his brother
w.šrš.km.'aryh	Nor root like his kinsman,
bl.'eṯ.bn.lh.km.'aḫh	'Nay but may he have a son like his brother,
wšrš.km.'aryh	Even a root like his kinsman'.
'uẓrm.'elm.ylḥm	Veiled he offers food to the gods,
'uẓrm.yšqy.bn.qdš	Veiled he offers drink to the holy ones;
ltbrknn.ltr.'el.'aby	Then bless him, O Bull El my father,
tmrnn.lbny.bnwt	Grant him thy benediction, [6]) O Creator of Creation.

---

[1]) Gordon 2 Aqht I, 3-4, 8-9, 10-11, 13-14.

[2]) We connect this problematic word with the Arabic ازارة, 'a veil'. One naturally thinks of Moses veiled in the Divine presence on Sinai (Exodus xxxiv, 33). Driver (*op. cit.*, p. 134) suggests as a cognate the Arabic وذْرة, 'meat without bones', in spite of the improbable phonetic correspondence between hamzate aleph and *w*. His translation 'nectar' seems to us no more felicitous, since it is as unsuitable to 'eat' as 'meat without bones' is to 'drink'.

[3]) Gordon 2 Aqht I, 16-34.

[4]) Lit. 'approaches with his supplication', cf. the Arabic idiom أتى بـ, 'to bring' (lit. 'to come with'), cf. the divine intercessor who presents a devotee (and his prayers) to a seated god in a type of cylinder-seal common in Mesopotamia in the beginning of the 2nd millennium, e.g. A. Parrot, *Abraham et son Temps*, 1962, Pl. 11a, pp. 28-29.

[5]) We may cite the Arabic مأبون, 'effeminate', which we take to be a cognate of *'abynt* of our text.

[6]) Here as in Gordon *UH* 128, II, 15 the verb is found in parallelism with *brk*, 'to bless', so that its meaning is beyond doubt. This is probably the root of the Syriac ܡܪܢ which is used as a title of the saints. We note enclitic *l* before the

wykn.bnh.bbt	And may there be a son for him in the house,
šrš.bqrb.hklh	Even a root in the midst of his palace,
nṣb.skn.ʾelʾebh	One who may set up the stele [1] of his ancestral god [2]
bqdš.ztr.ʿmh	In the sanctuary which enshrines [3] his forefather,
lʾarṣ.mšṣʾu.qṭrh	Who may pour out his liquid-offering to the ground, [4]

---

jussive as in Arabic. In the phrase *ltr ʾel* and *lbny bnwt l* is, of course, the vocative particle, as commonly in Ugaritic, and not the preposition introducing the dative, as it is taken by GORDON *UL*, p. 86.

[1]) The same word is found on a stele erected to Dagon at Ras Shamra, GORDON *UH* 69, 1.

[2]) The word *ʾelʾebh* has been the subject of considerable speculation and is still surrounded by obscurity. GORDON takes it to refer to ancestral gods (*UL*, p. 86), GASTER (*Thespis*, p. 272) to departed ancestors, and ALBRIGHT connects the second element *ʾeb* with Hebrew אוֹב, and Arabic أَبَ, 'to return' (*Archaeology and the Religion of Israel*, 1942, p. 203), so also EISSFELDT, *El im Ugaritischen Pantheon*, 1951, p. 42. In connection with the last interpretation it may be noted that the incident of Samuel conjured up by the witch (בעלת אוב) of Endor (1 Samuel xxviii) indicates the belief that the spirits of the departed could return and that such were called אלהים (v. 13). G. R. DRIVER 'Ugaritic and Hebrew Problems', (*Archiv Orientalni* XVII, 1949, pp. 153-157) cites an instance of *ʾelʾeb* as apparently a deity in a theophoric name עבד אלאב on a Hebrew seal published by D. DIRINGER. *Iscrizioni antico-ebraiche palestinese*, 1934, pp. 233 ff. In our opinion a less likely theory is that of A. VAN SELMS (*Marriage and Family Life in Ugaritic Literature*. 1954, pp. 100-101) that *ʾelʾeb* is connected with the Arabic لأَّب, 'to be erect', hence *nṣb skn ʾelʾebh* is translated by VAN SELMS 'he sets up his standing stela'. This root is not attested in the best Arabic lexicons. In spite of the vocalization of *ʾeb* we find it difficult not to connect *ʾelʾeb* with worship of ancestral gods. This being so, it is likely that the parallel *ʿm* means here not 'people' or 'clan', as we formerly read, but 'kinsman', the founder of the family or clan, who lives in its rulers, who inherit his *beraka*, or blessing. That *ʿmh* has such a personal significance is suggested by the pronominal suffix *qṭrh* and *ʾaṭrh*. The renewal of the solidarity of the community through its living head with a sacrifice and communal meal (*šelamim*) at the clan shrine, where the standing-stone (here *skn*, OT מצבה) stands as a memorial to the founder of the community or to some notable ancestor signalized by the manifest possession of the *beraka*, like the *weli* in primitive Arab society, was a well-established institution even in Israel. We should emphasize the primary significance of *bamoth* ('high places') as raised platforms for such memorial stelae, as ALBRIGHT has argued ('The High Place in Ancient Palestine', *V.T.* Supplement IV, 1957, pp. 243-258). Such places were incidentally also shrines. It was probably the social significance of these *bamoth* which gave them their appeal to the Israelites, though in such local centres it would be much more difficult to keep the assimilation of Canaanite seasonal rituals in check. *ʿm*, lit. 'uncle', is common as a predicate of deity in Amorite theophorics and in Hebrew proper names such as עמיאל and ירבעם.

[3]) Lit. 'which shelters', taking *ztr* as a dialectic form of Hebrew סתר. Such orthographical variation is attested in Hebrew, e.g. עלז, עלס, GESENIUS-KAUTZSCH, *Hebrew Grammar* 1898, § 19,1. We take *ztr* in apposition to *qdš*.

[4]) The word *qṭr* is found once again in the Aqht text meaning 'smoke'. Here

lʿpr.ẓmr.ʾaṯrh	Even to the dust wine after him. [1]
ṭbq.lḥt.tʾeṣh	Who may heap [2] up the platters [3] of his company,[4]
grš.dʿšy.lnh	Who may drive away any who would molest [5] his guest, [6]
ʾaḫd.ydh.bškrn	Who may hold his hand when he is drunk,
mʿmsh.kšbʿ.yn	Who may carry him when he is sated with wine, [7]
spʾu.ksmh.bt.bʿl	Who may eat his slice in the temple of Baal,
(w)mnth bt.ʾel	His portion in the temple of El. [8]
ṭḫ.ggh.bym.ṯʾeṭ	Who may plaster his roof when it is muddy, [9]
rḥṣ.npṣh.bym.rṯ	Who may wash his garment when it is dirty.' [10]

---

we take it as cognate with the Arabic قطر, 'dripping of water'. The preposition, *l* may mean 'from', in which case the meaning of *qṭr* would be the smoke of sacrifice. In view of the meaning of the following line, however, we prefer the former meaning for *qṭr*.

[1]) We agree with VAN SELMS (*op. cit.*, pp. 100-101) in taking *ẓmr* as the Hebrew שמר (Isaiah xxv, 6), 'wine left to settle on the lees'. The parallel stichos shows that the reference is to funerary offerings, for which installations were provided in the Late Bronze Age tombs excavated at Ras Shamra, SCHAEFFER, *The Cuneiform Texts of Ras Shamra-Ugarit*, 1939, pp. 46-56.

[2]) The word *ṭbq* suggests the Arabic طبق, 'to heap up layer upon layer'. We visualize entertainment on the grand scale as among the Bedouin, where a great wooden dish is set before the guests. This dish is actually called طبق.

[3]) The world *lḥt* has been taken as tablets, after the Hebrew לוח. We prefer to take it in the sense of flat boards or plates, probably of wood.

[4]) The word *tʾeṣ* may be an abstract verbal noun from the root *wʾaṣ*. This root is found in Arabic in the Vth form meaning 'to gather round', as, for instance, about a waterhole. The crowd about a waterhole suggests the guests and others about the common dish.

[5]) The word *ʿšy* seems best taken as a cognate with the Hebrew עשה which is found in Ezekiel xxiii, 3, 8 in the phrase עשׂו דדי בתוליהן, and with the Arabic غسى, 'to compress a woman'.

[6]) Lit. 'him who spends the night with him'.

[7]) This filial duty to a mother is noted by GINSBERG in Isaiah li, 18 ff., *JBL* LXII, 1943, p. 111, after U. CASSUTO, *REJ* cv, 1940, p. 129.

[8]) The reference here is to the communion meal (שלמים) by which the various members of the community asserted their solidarity as a social and religious body. A man lived in his son who performed this office for his family.

[9]) The word *ṯʾeṭ* suggests the Arabic ثئط, which, however, means 'to have a bad smell'. Black and stinking mud, however, is called ثأطة. The reference in the Ugaritic text is no doubt to mud mixed with dung for the sake of consistency. There is no doubt as to the general meaning of the passage, as the verb *ṭḫ* indicates, this being cognate with the Arabic طخّ, 'to smear, or spread'. The small roof-roller on the roofs of modern Arab village houses indicates the importance of this operation where the roofs are of beaten mud.

[10]) The word *rṯ* is cognate with the Arabic رثّ, 'to be old or dirty' (of clothes), as VIROLLEAUD perceived. The point here is that the clothes through contact with a man's body had a particular significance in relation to himself, hence one

El accedes to Baal's intercession and Baal communicates this decision to Dn'el. The fact that the duties characteristic of the ideal son are listed four times in identical terms suggests to us that the text had, though perhaps merely incidentally, the social function of formulating, and so preserving, such social values.

The actual birth of this son is not described. Indeed when he does appear (GORDON *UH* 2 Aqht) he is already a grown youth. The text describes how the artisan-god, 'the Skilful and Percipient One', passes by with a stock of bows and, being entertained by Dn'el, gives one to the king who hands it over to his son Aqht [1] GASTER emphasizes the bow. [2] This was no ordinary weapon, but one destined for a god, or rather for the goddess Anat, who strives without scruple to secure it. She invites Aqht to a feast and uses all female charms and wiles to induce him to part with the bow: [3]

lʾarṣ kst.tšrm	She raises her skirt [4] from the earth.
tšʾu gh wtṣḥ	She lifts her voice and cries.
šmʿ.mʿ lʾaqht ġzr	'Hear now, O hero Aqht,
ʾe)rš.ksp.wʾatnk	Ask [5] silver and I will give it thee,
(ḫrṣ wʾaš)lḥk	(Even gold and I will freely) give it thee, [6]
wtn.qštk ly	But give me thy bow,
tq)ḥ (q)ṣʿtk.ybmt.lʾemm	Let the Sister of the Prince take thine arrows.'

In a passage which shows that the bow in question was a composite one, as perceived by ALBRIGHT and MENDENHALL, [7] Aqht replies: [8]

---

must be careful that no ill-disposed person should handle them and so 'put a ju-ju upon one'. This office might safely be entrusted to a son.

1) The name probably signifies 'ruler', cf. Genesis xlix, 10 עד כי יבא שילה ולו יקהת עמים and the name קהת, Genesis xlvi, 11; Exodus vi, 16 ff.

2) GASTER, *Thespis*, p. 279.

3) GORDON *UH* 2 Aqht, VI, 15-19.

4) *kst* suggests the Akkadian *kušitu*, 'skirt'. Alternatively we may cite DRIVER (*op. cit.*, p. 53), 'She hurls the cups to the ground'. In support of this translation we should note that in the fragmentary passage immediately preceding a feast is described.

5) *ʾerš* is the imperative of *ʾarš* which occurs in the text GORDON *UH* krt, 42.

In Arabic أرش means 'bloodprice', i.e. that which is demanded. The Akkadian cognate is *erešu*, cf. Psalm xxi, 3, תאות לבו נתתה לו וארשת שפתיו בל־מנעת.

6) The parallel *ʾatnk* suggests that this word means 'give', and is not connected with לֵחַ, 'life force' or 'sexual power' (cf. Deuteronomy xxxiv, 7) as ALBRIGHT suggests. *BASOR* 94, 1944, pp. 32-35. The word in this sense suggests the Hebrew שִׁלּחים, 'parting gift'.

7) ALBRIGHT and G. E. MENDENHALL, *JNES* I, 1942, pp. 227 ff.

8) GORDON *UH* 2 Aqht, VI, 20-25.

ʾadr.ʿqbm.dlbnn	'There are goodly [1] tendons in Lebanon (?); [2]
ʾadr.gdm.brʾumm	There are goodly sinews in the wild oxen;
ʾadr.qrnt.byʿlm	There are goodly horns on the mountain-goats;
mtb( )m bʿqbt.ṯr	(?) in the tendons of the bull;
ʾadr.bġlʾel.qnm	There is abundance of reeds in the vast cane-brakes; [3]
tn.lkṯr.wḫss	Give them to the Skilful and Percipient One;
ybʿl.qšt.lk	Let him make [4] thee a bow,
qṣʿt.lybmt.lʾemm	Even arrows for the Sister of the Prince.'

Anat, however, persists: [5]

ʾerš.ḥym.lʾaqht.ġzr	'Ask life, O hero Aqht,
ʾerš.ḥym.wʾatnk	Ask life and I will give it thee,
blmt.wʾašlḥk	Immortality and I will freely grant it thee.
ʾašsprk.ʿm.bʿl.šnt	I will make thee number years with Baal,
ʿm.bn ʾel.tspr.yrḫm	Even with the sons of El wilt thou tell months.
kbʿl.kyḥwy.yʿšr	As Baal, even as he lives and is fêted,
ḥwy yʿšr.wyšqynh	He lives and is fêted and they give him to drink,
ybd.wyšr.ʿlh.	Singing and chanting about him,
nʿmn.wtʿnynn	Singing of him, [6] even the Gracious One, [7]
ʾap ʾank.ʾaḥwy.ʾaqht.ġzr	Even so will I give thee life, O hero Aqht.'

Aqht, however, is under no delusions and repulses the goddess with scorn: [8]

ʾal tšrgn.ybtltm	'Fabricate [9] not, O Virgin;

---

1) *ʾadr* has been variously interpreted. The least likely is the reading of Albright and Mendenhall (*op. cit.*, p. 228) 'I have vowed'. Gaster understands it to mean 'strength' (*Thespis*, p. 284), and Gordon tentatively suggests 'mightiest . . .' (*UL*, p. 90). Ginsberg (*BASOR* 97, 1945, p. 19) reads 'plenty'. It seems to be connected with *ʾadr*, 'noble' and we take it as 'goodliness'. It may well be used in an exclamatory sense like the Hebrew אשרי.

2) We should expect here the name of some animal, and we are not at all sure that *lbnn* should not be so rendered rather than as the place-name. The reference may be to sucking-animals, the cartilage of which, before it set into bone, was in demand for the making of composite bows.

3) Here we follow Gaster, *Thespis*, pp. 285, 452. The complex *ġl ʾel* may be a broken plural of *ġl.* which in any case seems an obvious cognate of the Arabic غيل, 'a marsh or cane-brake'. We prefer to take the *ʾel* element as qualifying *ġl*, reading 'divine cane-brakes', hence 'vast . . .'.

4) We note the spelling of the familiar verb 'to make' with *b* instead of *p*.

5) Gordon *UH* 2 Aqht, VI, 26-33.

6) The subject of the verb is feminine.

7) This is the title of Adonis in the Graeco-Roman period in Syria.

8) Gordon *UH* 2 Aqht, VI, 34-40.

9) Albright takes *šrg* as the Šafʿel of a root *rgg* or *rgy* found in Aramaic with the meaning 'to covet', cf. Arabic رجو, 'to hope', *BASOR* 94, 1944, pp. 33-34. In l. 35, however, the verbal noun *šrgk* indicates that the root is *šrg*, as perceived by Ginsberg, *BASOR* 97, 1945, p. 20. This seems best taken as cognate with the Arabic سرج which in the IInd form means 'to fabricate a story'.

dm . lġẓr . šrgk . ḫḫm	To a hero thy lies are trash. [1]
mt . ʾuḫryt . mh . yqḥ	As for mortal man, [2] what does he get as his latter end? [3]
mh . yqḥ . mt . ʾaṯryt	What does mortal man get as his inheritance? [4]
spsg . ysk . (l)rʾeš	Glaze [5] will be poured out on my head,
ḥrṣ . lẓr . qdqdy	Even plaster [6] upon my pate,
(w)mt . kl . ʾamt	And the death of all men will I die,
wʾan . mtm . ʾamt	Yea I will surely die.
(ʾap mṯ)n rgmm . ʾargm	And moreover [7] I tell thee.
qštm . (qšt m)hrm	The bow is the bow of warriors. [8]
ht . tṣdn . tʾenṯt	Are women [9] now taking up hunting?'

Anat affects to be amused by this reply, but she is nevertheless mortally offended and marks the young prince down as a victim. Repairing to the presence of El she slanders Aqht and seeks—and eventually extorts—his sanction to destroy Aqht: [10]

ʾedk(lttn pn)m	Then she sets face
ʿm ʾel . mbk . nhrm	To El at the well-head of the two streams, [11]

---

[1] Gaster (*Thespis*, pp. 286, 452) suggests the reading *ḫẓm*, which is quite feasible (𐎑 = *ẓ* for 𐎃 = *ḫ*). He would take *ḫẓm* as cognate with the Arabic خزى, 'to insult'. Ginsberg cites the Akkadian word *ḫabḫu*, meaning 'rubbish', which we accept.

[2] Note the emphatic position of *mt* in *casus pendens.*

[3] In *ʾuḫryt* Virolleaud saw a reference to 'Hurrian women', *La légende . . . de Danel*, p. 116.

[4] In *ʾaṯryt* Barton, endeavouring to find historical references in the text, sees a reference to 'the women of Asher', *op. cit.* The parallelism with *ʾuḫryt*, however, confirms our translation. For the meaning of *ʾaṯryt* we may cite the administrative text from the palace archives *PRU* III, 16.257 IV, 21, which mentions a class *murʾu ʾušriyanni*, otherwise known as *murʾu ʾibirana*, retainers of the heir-apparent Ibiranu.

[5] Ginsberg proposed this reading and on the basis of it emends Proverbs xxvi, 23 to כספסג מצפה על חרש instead of .... כסף סיגים of the MT, *BASOR* 97, 1945, p. 22; 98, 1945, pp. 20-21, n. Albright cites the Hittite term *ẓapẓagu.*

[6] The word *ḥrṣ* in parallelism with *spsg*, 'glaze', suggests the Arabic حرض, 'potash'.

[7] Lit. 'Also repeating . . .'

[8] *mhrm*, 'warriors' is found in the text Gordon *UH* 'nt, II, 11, 35.

[9] *tʾenṯt* appears to be an abstract noun in the singular, used collectively, probably in a derogatory sense, 'women-folk'.

[10] Gordon *UH* 2 Aqht, VI, 46-54; 3 Aqht rev, 11-19.

[11] This is the conventional description, found also in the Baal-cycle, of the abode of El. It may denote the source (*nbk*) of the great rivers, cf. the source of the great rivers of Paradise in Genesis ii, 10-14. Pope, however, (*El in the Ugaritic Texts*, 1955, pp. 73-81), following J. A. Montgomery (*JAOS* LIII, 1933, p. 11), who connects the name Membij (ancient Hierapolis) with Ugaritic *mbk*, suggests the more specific location of the seat of El at Aphqa on the Nahr Ibrahim near Beirut,

(qrb 'apq).thmtm	In the midst of the source of the two deeps.
tgly.žd 'el.wtb'u	She clears [1]) the threshold [2]) of El and enters
qrš.mlk.'ab.šnm	To the seat [3]) of the King, the Father of the Exalted Ones [4])
(lp'n 'el t)hbr.wtql	At the feet of El she does obeisance [5]); she falls down,
tšṭḥ(wy wtkbdnh)	Bowing down and honouring him.
tlšn.'aqht ǵzr	She slanders [6]) the hero Aqht,

well-known in Graeco-Roman times as the seat of the Adonis-cult with its licentious rites, with which Pope connects the sexual ritual of the text Gordon *UH* 52. On the other side of the mountain from the source of the Nahr Ibrahim, and connected with it in popular tradition, there is a remarkable intermittent lake El-Yammunah which lends colour to Pope's identification. We do not feel, however, in spite of his analogy of the specific location of the seat of Baal at Mount Saphon (Jebel el-Aqra), that it is necessary to press for a definite location of the seat of El, and certainly, apart from this fanciful and questionable location of the seat of El, there is no evidence for the chthonic character of El in the Ras Shamra texts, for which Pope (*op. cit.*, p. 61) and Kaiser (*Die mythische Bedeutung des Meeres in Ägypten, Ugarit und Israel, BZAW* 76, 1962, pp. 48 ff.) contend. The imagery of the throne of God from which waters flow (Psalm xlvi, 5, cf. Ezekiel xlvii and Joel iv, 18 (Hebrew text)), which is localized in Jerusalem, reflects the survival of the tradition of the Canaanite El there, which in turn is reflected in the conception of the Davidic King reigning 'from the river to the ends of the earth' (Psalm lxxii, 8; Zechariah ix, 9). The imagery of El, the King of the gods, enthroned at the source of the waters probably underlies Ezekiel's tirade on the King of Tyre, 'I sit in the seat of God (אלהים) in the midst of the seas' (Ezekiel xxviii, 2).

[1]) Here we seem to have a usage akin to the Hebrew, where גלה means 'to clear' (transitive) and 'to pass into captivity'.

[2]) We take the doubtful word *žd* as cognate with the Arabic سدّة, 'a barrier', though we admit that the two words do not exactly correspond phonetically.

[3]) This word is admittedly difficult. If we may take it as a cognate of the Hebrew קרש and Arabic قرس, it would mean 'that which is firm', the dais or seat of El. It is used of the deck of a ship in Ezekiel xxvii, 6, and on this analogy we may visualize the word in the Ugaritic passage as signifying El's firm seat amid the welter (*mbk*) of the waters.

[4]) We are very doubtful of the conventional rendering of *'ab šnm* as 'Father of Years' and prefer Pope's suggestion 'Father of the Exalted Ones', i.e. gods. *v. infra*, pp. 155, 156, n. 3.

[5]) The general sense of this passage being obvious, *thbr* was taken as the synonymn of *tql* and the etymology was not seriously considered. Driver (*op. cit.*, p. 137) accepts al-Yasin's etymology (cf. هبر, 'depressed ground'), but Ullendorff rightly indicates (*JSS* VII, 1962, p. 339-40) that in this passage the parallelism is chiastic, *thbr* being parallel to *tkbd*. Hence he accepts Driver's translation 'did homage' (*op. cit.*, p. 109), citing Isaiah xlvii, 13, where הברי שמים, a *hapax legomenon*, is parallel to החזים בכוכבים. He proposes to read 'worshippers of heavens', 'star-gazers'. The primary meaning of *hbr*, however, is 'to bow down', as Gordon *UH* 52, 55 clearly indicates.

[6]) This denominative verb has this sense also in Arabic and Hebrew, e.g. Psalm ci, 5; Proverbs xxx, 10.

(*kdd dn)'el mt.rp'e*	(the offspring of Dn)'el the Dispenser of Fertility.
wt'n (btlt 'nt)	Then up speaks (the Virgin Anat)
tš'u g)h.wtṣḥ	She raises her) voice and cries
hwt ( )	'The word ( )
'aqht	( ) Aqht ( )
	.... [1])
ašhlk (šbtk dmm)	I will make (thy grey hairs) to run (with blood),
(šbt dqn)k.mm'm	(The grey hairs of) thy (beard) with gore [2])
wypltk.bn.(dn'el)	And let the son of (Dn'el) rescue thee,
wy'ẓrk.byd.btlt.('nt)	Yea, let him succour thee [3]) from the hand of the Virgin (Anat').
wy'n.ltpn.'el.dp('ed)	Then answers El, the Kindly One, the Merciful.
yd'tk.bt k'anšt	'I know, my daughter, that thou art kindly
w'e(n b'elht ǵ)lṣ	And there (is no) roughness (in goddesses).
wtb'.bt.ḫnp lb	If one haughty of heart [4]) has risen [5]) against thee, my daughter,
ḫd.d'et.bkbdk	Hold the matter as it is in thine heart,
tšt.b(qrb).'ertk	Lay it up within thy breast.
dt.ydt.m'qbk	The one who has deluded [6]) thee shall be trampled down.' [7])

To this end the goddess lures the youth to a hunting-party at a place called 'Ablm, where she has him ambushed by her hired thug Yṭpn: [8])

tqḥ.yṭpn.mhr	She takes, the henchman Yṭpn;
št.tštn.knšr.bḫbšh	She makes him as a vulture in her mantle, [9])
km.d'ey.bt'rth	Even as a bird in her quiver.
'aqht.km.ytb.llḥ(m)	As Aqht sits down to eat,
bn.dn'el.ltrm	Even the son of Dn'el to meat,
'lh.nšr(m).trḫpn	Vultures hover above him,
ybṣr.ḫbl.d'ey(m)	A flock of birds watches (him).
(bn).nšrm trḫp.'nt	Among the vultures Anat hovers;

---

[1]) GORDON *UH* 3 Aqht, rev. 11-19. The lacunae in this text are easily filled from a similar passage in the text GORDON *UH* 'nt.

[2]) For the meaning of *mm'* in parallelism with *dm v. supra*, p. 42.

[3]) The verb *'ẓr*, the middle radical of which is probably a dialectical variation of *ẓ*, is obviously cognate with Hebrew עזר, 'to help'.

[4]) The phrase *ḫnp lb* is found in Job xxxvi, 13.

[5]) This is a case of the conditional perfect without the conditional particle. For the meaning we follow GASTER (*Thespis*, pp. 289, 452), who connects the verb with the Akkadian *tebu*.

[6]) *m'qbk* is the participle of *'qb*, connected with the Hebrew עקב, 'to over-reach', Genesis xxvii, 36.

[7]) *dt ydt* is a case of the infinitive absolute with the passive of the verb, which is probably medial *y*, cf. Arabic مديثة, 'beaten track'.

[8]) GORDON *UH* 3 Aqht, 27-37.

[9]) *ḫbš* is something which 'confines'. It may well mean 'bag' rather than 'mantle'.

ʿl (ʾaqht) tʿdbnh	She releases [1]) him above Aqht;
hlmn.ṯnm (qdqd)	He smites him twice (on the head),
ṯlṯʾed.ʿl.ʾudn	Three times on the ear,
š(pk km)šʾey.dmh	Shedding his blood as an assailant, [2])
km.šḫṭ.lbrkh)	(Bringing him) to his knees as a slayer.
yṣʾat.km.rḥ.npš(h)	His breath has gone out as wind,
(km ʾeṯl)brlth	(Even as a gust) [3]) his spirit,
km qṭr.(bʾaph)	As vapour (from his nostrils).

The bow is thus procured, though at the cost of Aqht's life, a result which Anat had apparently not intended. [4]) On his return from the expedition, however, the assassin drops the bow into the sea. [5])

The sister of Aqht, 'the Maiden', notices a flight of vultures, which are, of course, the harbingers of death in those lands ('where the body is there do the vultures gather'): [6])

(bn)šʾe.ʿnh.wtphn	As she raises her eyes she sees
bgrn.yḫrb ( )	On the threshing-floor [7]) ( ) is wasted,
yġly.yḫsp.ʾeb( )	The verdure [8]) droops [9]) and languishes.
ʿl bt.ʾabh.nšrm.tr(ḫpn)	Above her father's house fly vultures;
ybṣr.ḥbl.dʾeym	A flock of birds keeps watch.

With fine intuition the maiden apprehends the death of her brother and initiates mourning rites: [10])

tbky.pġt.bm.lb	The maiden weeps in her heart;
tdmʿ.bm.kbd	Inwardly she sheds tears.

---

1) In the verb *ʿdb* here we seem to have a parallel usage to that of the Hebrew עזב in Exodus xxiii, 5, where one is enjoined to free an ass which has fallen under his burden.

2) *šʾey* is the participle active of the verb *šʾay*, which we take as a cognate of the Arabic شأى, 'to precede'. Here the verb means to take the initiative as an aggressor.

3) The sense of *ʾeṯl* is suggested by the parallelism. Aistleitner, however (*Wörterbuch*, 473), proposes that *ʾeṯl* is a broken plural of a noun cognate with Arabic ثول, 'a swarm of bees'.

4) Anat concludes her instructions to Yṭpn by saying (Gordon *UH* 3 Aqht, 26, 27): 'Howbeit I shall quickly revive him' (*ʾuʾap mhrh.ʾank.lʾaḥwy*).

5) The passage, however, (Gordon *UH* 1 Aqht, 2-3) is very fragmentary.

6) Gordon *UH* 1 Aqht, 28-33.

7) The summer crops and fruits in the Arab villages lie on the threshing-floor till they are solemnly 'gathered in', cf. Hebr. אסיף.

8) *ʾeb* is probably connected with the Akkadian *ebbu*, 'flourish', and with the Hebrew. אֵב, 'fresh verdure'.

9) The verb *ġly* is used of the gods 'lowering' their heads in the text Gordon *UH* 137, 23-24.

10) Gordon *UH* 1 Aqht, 34-47.

tmẓʿ.ḳst.dnʾel.mt.rpʾe	She rends [1]) the robe of Dnʾel the Dispenser of Fertility,
ʾall.ġẓr.mt.ḫrnmy	Even the mantle of the hero, the man of Hrnm.

It is a conception familiar to anthropology that blood shed violently and uncovered by the earth occasions sterility, as is indicated by the instance of Cain and Abel (Genesis iv, 11-12) and elsewhere in the Old Testament. [2]) So, anticipating such a case, Danʾel offers prayers for rain and dew: [3])

ʾapnḳ.dnʾel.mt.rpʾe	Thereupon Dnʾel the Dispenser of Fertility
yṣly.ʿrpt.bḥm	Prays for the clouds in the heat:
ʾun.yr ʿrpt tmṭr	In the season [4]) of heavy rain [5]) may the clouds rain,
bqẓ ṭl.yṭll.lġnbm	In the season of summer fruit may the dew fall on the grapes.

His prayers, however, do not avail, for his precipitate grief in

---

[1]) The verb *tmẓʿ* is cognate with the Arabic مزع, 'to divide' (IInd form.) We take it as feminine singular as the verbs in the preceding couplet. It may, however, be 3rd masculine singular perfect, the initial *t* being the augment of the reflexive form, as Driver (*op. cit.*, p. 59) suggests, after Cassuto.

[2]) E.g. Numbers xxxv, 33, and other instances in the Old Testament and post-Biblical literature cited by Gaster, *Thespis*, p. 296.

[3]) Gordon *UH* 1 Aqht, 38-42. Our former conclusion was that this was an imprecation rather than a prayer, being connected with a mourning rite (ll. 36-37, 46-48), so Gordon (*UL*, pp. 94-95), Gaster (*op. cit.*, p. 297) and Ginsberg (*ANET*, p. 150). David's curse on the mountains of Gilboa after the death of Saul and Jonathan (2 Samuel, i, 21) in language which closely re-echoes ll. 44-45 seemed to confirm this interpretation. *yṣly* is, of course, cognate with Arabic صلا, which, however, is not found in the sense 'to imprecate, curse'. This interpretation demands the following arrangement of the text:

ʾapnḳ.dnʾel.mt.rpʾe	Thereupon D. the Dispenser of Fertility
yṣly.ʿrpt.bḥm.ʾun.yr	Imprecates the clouds with heat in the season of heavy rain,
ʿrpt.tmṭr.bqẓ	The clouds which rain in the season of summer fruits.

The great difficulty is the last line. *qẓ*, the season of summer fruits, is noted in the Gezer tablet as falling in August-September, the month following the late pruning (*ẓmr*). Rain, of course is rare in Palestine and Syria in summer, though the heavy dew may fall as heavily as rain and is heralded by clouds. Dalman attests such a dew-fall which he experienced near Hebron on July 10th, 1921, *Arbeit und Sitte in Palästina* I, 2, 1928, pp. 517 ff. Rain may be experienced any time after August, as is indicated by the folk-saying cited by Dalman, 'As for Elul its verge is soaked by rain' (أيلول طرفه بالشتاء مبلول), *op. cit.*, p. 514. Nevertheless this interpretation is strained. Though we now take *yṣly* in the sense 'to pray' we cannot agree with U. Cassuto (*Orientalia* VIII, 1939, p. 239) in translating 'He prays the clouds for the heat of the season'.

[4]) *ʾun* may be cognate with Arabic أوْن, 'season'. Here it is apparently used adverbially.

[5]) *yr* is the Hebrew יורה, the heavy rains of late autumn.

rending his robe has of itself set in operation the curse on nature after bloodshed, which must now run its course: [1])

šbʿ.šnt.yṣrk.bʿl	For seven years Baal is restrained [2])
ṯmn.rkb.ʿrpt	Yea eight he who mounteth the clouds,
bl.ṭl.bl.rbb	Without dew, without showers,
bl.šrʿ.thmtm	Without upsurging [3]) of the lower deep.
bl.ṭbn.ql.bʿl	Without the drum-roll, [4]) the voice of Baal,
ktmẓʿ.kst.dnʾel.mt.rpʾe	For the robe of Dnʾel the Dispenser of Fertility is rent,
ʾall.ġẓr.mt.hrnmy	Even the mantle ot the hero, the man of Hrnm.'

Here we have an instance of the close association of the primitive king with the fertility of nature, which is a feature also of the Krt text. Accordingly in the next episode Dnʾel makes a round of his territory and performs the strange rite of kissing and embracing odd stalks of grain when the harvest is over: [5])

ydn (dn)ʾel.ysb.pʾalth	Dnʾel investigates; [6]) he goes round his parched land; [7])

---

[1]) GORDON *UH* 1 Aqht, 42-48.

[2]) The first instinct is to take the final *k* in *yṣrk* as a pronominal suffix, but in this case it is difficult to connect the pronoun with anything in the context. In this case it seems better to take the verb as passive of *ṣrk*, cognate with the Hebrew צָרַךְ, 'to restrain or constrain'.

[3]) The word *šrʿ* seems best taken as a verbal noun of a verb cognate with the Arabic شرع, 'to open out, or debouche', like a house-door on to the street. GINSBERG has used this passage to elucidate 2 Samuel i, 21, which he emends to read אל טל ואל מטר עליכם ושרע תהומות 'A Ugaritic Parallel to 2 Samuel i, 21', *JBL* LVII, 1938, pp. 209-213. We admit the general affinity of sentiment between the two passages, but agree with GORDIS (*JTS* XLI, 1940, p. 35) in retaining MT. שדי, read שְׁדִי 'effluence', an alternative reading for MT שְׂדֵי תְרוּמוֹת being שְׂדֵי הַמָּוֶת 'plains of death', *v. infra* pp. 280-281.

[4]) We take *ṭbn* as a cognate of the Arabic طَبْل, 'a drum', a suitable meaning in our text especially in association with *ql bʿl*, which refers to the thunder. In this connection we may further cite the name *Ṯblhddi* in the Egyptian Execration Texts of the 19th century B.C., G. POSENER, *Princes et pays d'Asie et de Nubie, textes hiératiques sur des figurines d'envoûtement du Moyen Empire*, 1940, (E 16), p. 73.

[5]) GORDON *UH* 1 Aqht, 61-74.

[6]) For *ydnʾel* of the text, an error of haplography, so A. HERDNER, *Corpus*, p. 88. CASSUTO connects the verb with the Arabic دنا, 'to draw near' and renders 'he draws near'; *Orientalia* VIII, 1939, p. 240. We should cite the Arabic phrase دنى فى الأمور, and so render 'he investigates'.

[7]) *pʾalt* like *yġl* obviously means some sort of a field. DRIVER after CASSUTO suggests the translation we have adopted, citing Arabic فَأَلَ, 'to be dried up' (*op. cit.*, p. 162). AISTLEITNER *Wörterbuch* 2184) suggests the affinity of *pʾalt* with Arabic بَؤُلَ, 'to be poor or paltry'.

bṣql yph bp'alth	He sees a plant [1] in the parched land,
bṣql.yph.byǵlm	A plant he sees in the scrub. [2]
bṣql.yḥbq.wynšq	He embraces the plant and kisses it. [3]
'aḥl.'an bṣ(ql)	'Ah me [4] for the plant!
ynp'.bp'alt.bṣql	Would that the plant might flourish [5] in the parched land,
yp'.byǵl.'ur	That the herb might flourish in the scrub,
t'espk.yd.'aqht.ǵẓr	That the hand of the hero Aqht might gather thee in,
tštk.bqrbm.'asm	That it might put thee in the granary.'
ydnh.ysb.'aklth	He investigates it; he makes a round of his blasted land;
yph.šblt.b'aklt	He sees an ear of corn in the blasted land,
šblt.yp'.bḥmdrt	An ear of corn growing in the parched land. [6]

1) We see from the parallel *'ur* (Hebrew אוּר), 'plant', that *bṣql* must have a similar meaning. It is tempting to apply this meaning to the problematic בְּצִקְלֹונוֹ in 2 Kings iv, 42, ויבא לאישׁ האלהים לחם בכּוּרים עשׂרים־לחם שׂעורים וכרמל בְּצִקְלֹונוֹ. Here LAGARDE, following the Vulgate, proposed to read בקלעתוֹ for בצקלונוֹ, meaning 'in his wallet'. This presupposes an error of haplography, and in the proto-Hebraic script this is very feasible. Our own view is that the text was originally בְּצִקְלוֹן כַּרְמֶלוֹ and the rare word בצקלון was forgotten and the initial *b* taken as a preposition, the whole complex בצקלון being transposed to the end of the phrase. We should take בצקלון as a singular collective and read 'And he brought plants of his orchard' (כּרמֶלוֹ).

2) So DRIVER (*op. cit.*, pp. 61, 165) after AISTLEITNER, cognate with the Arabic وغل, 'dense tree'.

3) The kissing of grain-heaps by passers-by is attested in *Midrash Rabba* on The Song of Songs vii, 3.

4) CASSUTO (*Orientalia* VIII, 1939, p. 240) takes *'aḥl* as the Hebrew interjection אַחֲלַי, 'Would that...', so also GORDON, tentatively, (*UL*, p. 95), GASTER, (*Thespis*, p. 298), GINSBERG (*Ancient Near Eastern Texts* . . ., p. 153), and DRIVER (*op. cit.*, p. 61).

5) *ynp'* is apparently the Nif'al of *wp'*, the cognate of the Arabic وفع, 'to be big, or lofty'. The Nif'al must have a reflexive rather than a passive sense here as the verb is used intransitively in the simple form in the same passage.

6) The meaning of *bḥmdrt*, in parallelism with *b'aklt*, is very doubtful. GASTER (*Thespis*, p. 452) follows GOETZE in connecting it with an Akkadian cognate meaning 'swathe, dried grass'. VIROLLEAUD cites the Akkadian *ḫamadiratu*, 'drought'. Neither of these suggests a good parallel to *'aklt*, a difficulty which CASSUTO apparently felt in proposing to translate *'aklt* as 'blasted land' (*op. cit.*, p. 240). In this proposal to treat *'aklt* as a passive participle of the simple form of the verb CASSUTO is followed by GASTER (*Thespis*, p. 298) and DRIVER (*op. cit.*, p. 61), who cites אכל describing the effect of drought and cold on a man in Gen. xxxi, 40. Neither the passive of the simple form nor this sense of *'akl* is well enough attested in Ugaritic to put the interpretation of the passage beyond doubt, but the relative position of *'aklt* and *p'alt* in the parallel passage in ll. 61, 62 indicates that CASSUTO was right. GINSBERG follows VIROLLEAUD in translating *ḥmdrt* as 'unwatered land', but tentatively reads 'grainfields' for *'aklt* (*op. cit.*, p. 153).

šblt.yḫbq.wynšq	He embraces the ear of corn and kisses it.
ʾaḫl ʾan.šblt	‘Ah me for the ear of corn!
tpʿ.bʾaklt.šblt	Would that the ear of corn might grow tall in the crop,
tpʿ.( ).ʾur	That the herb might grow tall ( ),
tʾespk.yd.ʾaqht.ġzr	That the hand of the hero Aqht might gather thee in
tštk.bm.qrbm.ʾasm	And put thee into the storehouse.’

This rite is probably intended by a process of homoeopathic magic to transmit fertility to the next crop, and is associated by GASTER with the agricultural rite of the wedding of the ‘corn-maiden’ symbolizing the last sheaf and a male counterpart. [1]) This rôle of Dnʾel suggests to us the significance of his stock epithet in the text, *mt rpʾe*, ‘the healer’ or ‘dispenser of fertility’, an office peculiar to a king. [2]) The mention of Aqht as the one who was to inaugurate the next harvest may indicate the author’s desire to lend pathos to the plight of Dnʾel who knows that bloodshed is the cause of the drought but does not yet know that the slain man is his own son. This is made known to Dnʾel in the next passage.

Dnʾel then seeks to recover the remnants of his dead son from the gizzards of the vultures in order to bury them and so to cover the unburied blood which brings disaster on the land: [3])

bnšʾe.ʿnh.wyphn	Lifting up his eyes he beholds;
yḫd.ṣml.ʾum.nšrm	He sees *Ṣml* [4]) the mother of the vultures.
yšʾu.gh.wyṣḥ	He lifts up his voice and cries.
knp.ṣml.bʿl.yṯbr	‘May Baal break the wing of *Ṣml*,
bʿl.yṯbr.dʾey.hyt	May Baal break her pinion; [5])

[1]) GASTER, *Thespis*, p. 298.

[2]) This office may pertain to Krt, who is numbered *btk rpʾe ʾarṣ* (GORDON *UH* 128, III, 2-4/13-15), but see p. 146. The verb *rpʾa* has the sense of ‘restoring fertility’ in Genesis xx, 17, where Jahweh restores the fertility of the harem of Abimelech of Gerar, and in 2 Kings ii, 21, where Elisha restores the fertilizing properties of the water of the spring of Jericho. Hesiod also (*Works and Days* II, 109-126) speaks of the provision of fertility and wealth as a ‘kingly prerogative’ (γέρας βασιλήιον). This finds expression in the conception of the Golden Age of preternatural fertility in the Old Testament and other ancient Near Eastern royal texts, which was developed as an element in the Messianic ideology.

[3]) GORDON *UH* 1 Aqht, 134-147.

[4]) GASTER (*Thespis*, p. 300) translates ‘Toughy’, taking *ṣml* correctly, we think, as the cognate of the Arabic صمل, ‘to be hard’.

[5]) This meaning is suggested by the Hebrew דאה, ‘to fly’, possibly, but not certainly, attested in the Ras Shamra texts. DRIVER (*op. cit.*, pp. 63, 153) connects the word with Arabic دأى, ‘ribs of breast’, and translates ‘breastbone’.

tql.tḥt.pʿny	May she fall at my feet
ʾebqʿ kbdh.wʾaḥd	That I may split open her inwards and look
hm.ʾeṯ.šmt.ʾeṯ.ʿẓm	If there is any fat, if there is bone,
ʾabky.wʾaqbrnh	That I may weep and bury him,
ʾaštn.bḫrt.ʾelm.ʾarṣ	Placing him in the cavities [1]) of the deities of the earth.'
bph.rgm.lyṣʾa	Scarcely has the word gone forth from his mouth,
bšpth.hwth	Even from his lips his speech,
knp.ṣml.(b)ʿ(l yṯbr)	When Baal breaks the wing of *Ṣml*,
bʿl.ṯbr.dʾey.hyt	Yea Baal breaks her pinion.
tql.tḥt.pʿnh	She falls at his feet;
ybqʿ.kbdh.wyḥd	He splits open her inwards and looks.
ʾeṯ.šmt.ʾeṯ.ʿẓm	There is fat, there is bone.
wyqḥ.bhm.ʾaqht	Thereupon he takes Aqht;
(yb.llqh) ybky.wyqbr	Emptying him from the eagle; [2]) he weeps and buries him,
yqbr.nn.bmdgt.bknkn	He buries him in the darkness [3]) in concealment. [4])

The coincidence of the death of Aqht with the harvest has often been noticed, and it has been suggested that in Aqht we have the personification of the genius of harvest who was symbolically killed to make the new crop available for common use. In the Baal-cycle the death of Mot at the hands of Anat (*v. supra* p. 68 ff.) seems on the evidence of Leviticus ii, 14 to reflect such a rite. In this connection we should draw attention to the fact that just as the body of Aqht was dismembered and eaten by vultures, so Mot was torn in pieces and

---

1) The word is attested in the Akkadian *bit ḫiriti*, the synonym of *eqlati ša ʾuḫraya*, 'fields of destiny', indicating the meaning 'graveyard', GORDON, 'Ugaritic *Ḫrt*/*Ḫiritu* "Cemetery" ', *Syria* XXXIII, 1956, pp. 102-3.

2) If we follow DRIVER's reading (*yd*) for GORDON's (*yb*) *llqh* suggests the Arabic verb لقى, 'to meet'. The passage is not clear, but it would mean probably that D. brings piece(*yd*) and piece together. ULLENDORFF's translation of GORDON's reading, 'he empties him' (*yb* from *nbb*) 'out of the eagle' (*lqh* cognate with Arabic لقو) is also feasible (*JSS* VII, 1962, pp. 342-3), and ought probably to be followed.

3) BARTON proposed to read *mdgt* as 'fishing-places' *v. supra*, p. 106, n. 2. We suggest that *mdgt* is cognate with the Arabic دجة, 'darkness'.

4) The reading is not certain here and VIROLLEAUD (*La légende . . . de Danʾel*, pp. 164-165) proposed to read *bknkn*, 'in a great jar'. Actually the readings *knkn* (𐎋𐎐𐎋𐎐) and *knrt* (𐎋𐎐𐎗𐎚) are very much alike. In support of VIROLLEAUD's reading we can cite the archaeological evidence of burials in large store-jars both from Syria and from Mesopotamia. We prefer to connect *knkn* with the Arabic كَنَّ, 'to conceal'. There is some doubt about the Arabic cognate كنارة, with which we formerly connected our reading *knrt*, being a true Arabic root. Reading *knrt*, BARTON found a reference to Kinnereth by the Sea of Galilee.

'the birds ate his portions'. This suggests to us that the Aqht text, in spite of its human protagonists, was a composite work where an originally historical theme had already passed into a myth with a variety of seasonal themes incorporated. A similar confusion of myth and history, but with the emphasis finally laid on the historical element, is seen in the Joseph story, where indeed the fate of Pharaoh's baker suggests the fate of Mot and Aqht.

As in the Old Testament (Deuteronomy xxi, 1-9) in the case of homicide where the guilty party is unknown a curse is pronounced upon the localities nearest to the scene of bloodshed: [1])

qr.m(ym) mlk.yṣm	The King curses [2]) the Source of Water: [3])
ylkm.qr.mym	'Out upon thee, O Source of Water,
dʿlk.mḫṣ.ʾaqht.ġẓr	For upon thee lies (the guilt) [4]) of the slaughter [5]) of Aqht the hero,
ʾamd.gr.bt.ʾel	Perpetually [6]) seeking sanctuary [7])
ʿnt.brḫ.pʿlmh	A fugitive [8]) now and for ever,
ʿnt.pdr.dr	Now and for every generation!"
ʿdb.ʾuḫry mṭ.ydh	(So says he), the staff in his hand signifying finality. [9])

[1]) GORDON *UH* 1 Aqht, 151 ff.

[2]) *yṣm* seems best taken as the imperfect of *wṣm*, cognate with the Arabic وصم, 'to spoil'. We note the title *mlk*, 'king', which can hardly refer to anyone other than Dnʾel.

[3]) This has been taken as the name of a city, which, of course, would be sited by a spring. We see no reason to take it as other than a natural feature, like the myrrh tree in the second curse, the reference to the root and crown of which surely indicates that an actual tree is meant and not a city.

[4]) *ʿl* here refers to liability as in Hebrew and Arabic.

[5]) *mḫṣ* is best taken a verbal noun, subject of *ʿlk*.

[6]) Cf. Arabic على الآمد, 'eternally'.

[7]) Lit. 'a refugee at the temple of god' cf. Arabic جار الله, a fugitive from blood vengeance who finds sanctuary in another tribe. The 'source of water' includes human inhabitants who are spoken of collectively in the singular.

[8]) Pursuing the theme of the curse of perpetual banishment GASTER takes *brḫ* to refer to the flight of the criminal, like Cain a fugitive and a wanderer, an apt parallel to *gr bt ʾel*. It is astonishing to find GINSBERG translating 'tomorrow' (*Ancient Near Eastern Texts*, p. 154) in view of the Arabic meaning of البارح, 'yesterday'.

[9]) This indicates a gesture, the 'ritual' accompanying the 'myth' of Dnʾel's curse. The significance of the staff as the instrument of curse and blessing is well known in the Old Testament from Moses' staff to the sceptre of 'Ahasuerus'. ULLENDORFF would connect the phrase with the succeeding line in each of its three incidences, indicating the resumption (cf. S. Arabic *ʿdb*, 'to restore') of his staff preparatory to proceeding elsewhere, and he translates:
'Thereupon (אחרי) he picks up the staff of his hand' or
'Finally he takes the stick in his hand' . . . 'and proceeds' (*ymġ*).

ymġ.lmrrt.tġll.bnr	He proceeds to the Myrrh-tree [1]) which emits its perfume [2]) when burned.
yšʾu.gh.wyṣḥ	He lifts up his voice and cries:
ylk.mrrt.tġll.bnr	'Out upon thee, O Myrrh-tree which emits its perfume when burned,
dʿlk.mḫṣ.ʾaqht.ġẓr	For upon thee lies the guilt of the slaughter of Aqht the hero,
šršk.bʾarṣ.ʾal.ypʿ	May thy root never grow big in the ground,
rʾeš.ġly.bd.nsʿk	Thy crown be brought low by the hand of him who plucks thee up.
ʿnt.brḥ.pʿlmh	Away with thee now and for ever,
ʿnt.pdr.dr .	Now and for every generation!'
ʿdb.ʾuḫry.mṭ.ydh	(So says he), the staff in his hand signifying finality.
ymġ.lqrt.ʾablm.ʾablm	He proceeds to the City of Running Waters Abilum,
qrt.ẓbl.yrḫ	The city of his lordship the Moongod. [3])
yšʾu gh.wyṣḥ	He lifts up his voice and cries:
ylk.qrt.ʾablm	'Out upon thee O city Abilum,
dʿlk.mḫṣ.ʾaqht.ġẓr	For upon thee lies the guilt of the slaughter of Aqht the hero,
ʿwr.yštk.bʿl	May Baal make thee [4]) blind [5])
lht.wʿlmh	From now [6]) and for ever,
ʿnt.pdr.dr	Now and for every generation.'
ʿdb.ʾuḫry.mṭ.ydh	(So says he), the staff in his hand signifying finality.

It may well be that here we have the elaboration of a certain element in the myth to adapt it as a means of sanctioning and preserving a social practice.

Aqht is duly mourned: [7])

dnʾel.bth.ymġyn	Dnʾel reaches his house,
yštql.dnʾel.lhklh	Dnʾel lights down at his palace.
ʿrb.bkyt.bhklh	He has caused weeping women to enter his palace,
mšspdt.bḥẓrh	Even mourning women [8]) his court,

1) *v. supra*, p. 122, n. 3.

2) For the meaning of *tġll* we may cite what appears to be the Arabic cognate غلّ (V), 'to perfume oneself', غلية 'perfume'. The myrrh was well known as an aromatic plant, e.g. Song of Songs iii, 6, מקטרת מר ולבנה.

3) I.e. a centre of his cult.

4) Note the singular pronominal suffix, indicating the collective responsibility of the community for the conduct of any one of its number, the familiar basis of ancient Hebrew morality.

5) Gaster (*Thespis*, p. 304) aptly cites the curse of blindness in Deuteronomy xxviii, 28, and in Genesis xix, 11.

6) *l* seems here the preposition 'from' and *ht* means probably 'now', cf. *wht*, 'and now', in letters Gordon *UH* 18, 17 and 138, 10.

7) Gordon *UH* 1 Aqht, 170-179.

8) These are, of course, the professional mourners familiar in the East to the present day. The role of women in those 'seasons of passage' is particularly noteworthy.

p( )pẓġm ġr	And ( ) men who bruise their skin. [1])
ybk lʾaqht.ġẓr	They weep for Aqht the hero,
ydmʿ.lkdd.dnʾel.mt.rpʾe	They shed tears for the offspring of Dnʾel the Dispenser of Fertility,
lymm.lyrḫm	From days to months,
lyrḫm.lšnt	From months to years,
ʿd.šbʿt.šnt	Until seven years
ybk.lʾaqht ġẓr	They weep for Aqht the hero,
ydmʿ.lkdd.dnʾel.mt.rpʾe	They shed tears for the offspring of Dnʾel the Dispenser of Fertility.

This 'seven-years' mourning for Aqht raises a problem. The number seven is, of course, a common motif in the Ras Shamra texts. It may, as in the Krt text, be simply a literary device to give a description of indefinite time or distance. We maintain, however, that it has a more particular application, signifying a period of ritual separation between one phase and another. [2]) It has a reference to what the anthropologist VAN GENNEP terms 'rites de passage', and so it has in the present context. The real problem in the present passage is whether 'years' is to be taken literally. So taken it would refer to the theme of a seven-year famine which plays a conspicuous part in the Joseph-story in Genesis, where, indeed, there are many features characteristic of seasonal ritual and myth. [3])

The social duty of blood-revenge is undertaken by the sister of Aqht, who is un-named, being termed simply 'the maiden' (*pġt*): [4])

wtʿn.pġt.ṯkmt.mym	Then up speaks the maiden, who bears water on her shoulder:
qrym.ʾab.dbḥ.lʾelm	'Appoint, O father, a sacrifice to the gods,
šʿly.dġṯ( ) bšmym	Cause an evening-oblation [5]) to ascend into the heavens,

---

[1]) We accept GASTER's translation of *pẓġm ġr* (פצעים עור) with considerable hesitation, and only in default of any feasible suggestion we have to offer. We do not, however, think that MONTGOMERY is right in taking those two words as the name of Dnʾel's palace. Laceration as a mourning rite is well attested in the Old Testament (e.g. Deuteronomy xiv, 1; Jeremiah xvi, 6) and in the Ras Shamra texts, where Anat and El mourn in this fashion, *v. supra*, p. 62.

[2]) This point has been missed by DE VAUX (*RB* XLVI, 1937, pp. 367 ff.) and DE LANGHE (*Les textes de Ras Shamra . . . et . . . l'Ancien Testament* II, pp. 130), who works out an itinerary on the basis of the statement concerning the seven days journey of Krt to the home of his bride.

[3]) We think, however, that Bo REICKE over-presses his evidence in finding his analogies, 'Analogier mellan Josefberättelsen; Genesis och Ras Shamra-texterna', *SEÅ* X, 1945, pp. 27 ff.

[4]) GORDON *UH* 1 Aqht, 190-197.

[5]) The fact that the offering (indicated by the verb *šʿly*) was to the stars suggests

dġṯ.hrnmy.dkbkbm	The evening-oblation of *Hrnm* proper to the stars.
ltbrkn.ʾalk.brkt	Bless me that with thy blessing I may go;
tmrn.ʾalkn mrrt	Grant me thy blessing that I may go with thy benediction,
ʾemḫṣ.mḫṣ.ʾaḫy	That I may smite him who smote my brother,
ʾakly.mkly.(ʿ)l.ʾumty	Yea, make an end of him who destroyed the offspring of my mother.

It is somewhat surprising to find this grim duty discharged by a female, but this is what we find also in the case of Anat, who avenges the death of her brother Baal. The prominence of the female and even the reversal of normal rôles of the sexes is not unfamiliar in primitive societies at seasons of transition, and in our opinion nothing in the Aqht text so much as this indicates the association of the text with seasonal ritual.

The doughty damsel decks and disguises herself either as the goddess Anat or as a common harlot [1]) and so penetrates into the presence of Yṭpn. The latter entertains the maiden with drink and she in turn plies him with liquor [2]) until in his cups he boasts that he has slain Aqht. At this point the text breaks off, but doubtless vengeance was done by this Canaanite Judith.

The general interpretation of this text is by no means simple. GASTER supposes that the stage is long past when it could be applied strictly as the mythic accompaniment of any seasonal ritual. There are certain characteristic features of this *genre* of literature in the text, but we agree with GASTER that the primitive myth has now become literature. In process of development many elements, perhaps having nothing originally to do with the main theme, have become incorporated. Broadly considered the text turns about the sacral office of the ancient king as the dispenser of fertility. In the death of Aqht, coinciding as it does with the harvest, there may be a

---

that AISTLEITNER was right in connecting *dġṯ* with Arabic دغشة, 'the oncoming of darkness' (*Wörterbuch* 777).

[1]) This turns to a large extent on our interpretation of *ʾagrtn* in l. 213. This is taken as 'she who hired us', i.e. Anat, who employed Yṭpn to strike down Aqht (GASTER, *Thespis*, p. 310), and as 'our hired woman' (GINSBERG, *Ancient Near Eastern Texts . . .*, ed. PRITCHARD, p. 155). In view of Yṭpn's reference to the maiden as 'maiden', (*pġt*) in l. 217 we think it unlikely that he mistook her for Anat. The maiden won admission to Yṭpn by posing as a harlot (*ʾagrtn*). We should suggest that the final *n* of this word is a survival of the nunation signifying, as in Arabic, the indefinite article.

[2]) Have we here the prototype of 'the cup of the Lord's fury'? (Isaiah li, 17; Jeremiah xxv, 15, 28; Lamentations iv, 21; Psalm lxxv, 8 (Hebr. text, 9); Habbakuk ii, 16).

reminiscence of the primitive custom of putting to death a victim, originally the king, whose vitality was thought to be intimately bound up with that of the growing corn. [1]) The fact that the death of Aqht apparently occurred at the end of harvest suggests to GASTER that the myth is related to a phase in the Bow-constellation, which would, of course, explain the prominence of the bow, which occasioned the death of the hero. That there is an astral element in the text is suggested by the known fact of the astral significance of analogous myths from elsewhere in the Mediterranean world, especially that of Orion the huntsman done to death for his presumption. [2]) In considering the subject of such a theme common to Syria and to Greece we should note the Mycenean contacts with Ras Shamra which are demonstrated in the ceramics and tomb architecture at Ras Shamra in the Late Bronze Age particularly at the sea-port of ancient Ugarit at Minet el-Beida which was, in fact, an Aegean 'factory' on the Syrian coast.

No one interpretation of the text by itself seems adequate. Whatever the original purport and significance of the text may have been, it seems to have attracted to itself many elements adapted to various purposes in seasonal ritual, certain of which tended to be more or less emphasized, so that it is not easy to fit these into the context of the text as a whole once that was finally redacted as a literary text in the fragmentary form now extant.

Connected with the Aqht text is certainly one of the fragments published by VIROLLEAUD as Rp [3]) (GORDON *UH* 121). Here we have the problem of fragmentary texts and linguistic difficulties which have so far defied solution. In the text GORDON 121, however, Dn'el plays a part and this serves to connect the text with the Aqht cycle.

Here Dn'el, himself *mt rp'e*, is associated with certain figures called *rp'um* who visit the threshing-floors and plantations (*grnt*, *mṭ't*). These are apparently eight in number (GORDON *UH* 121, II,

---

[1]) The Old Testament preserves what may well be a tradition of this gruesome practice in the account of the execution of human victims at Gibeon at the beginning of the barley harvest (2 Samuel xxi, 1-9). These are represented as the survivors of the house of Saul, but it seems a case of the tradition of some harvest-ritual associated with the Canaanite shrine of Gibeon which has been given a historical explanation after it has fallen into abeyance and become only a vague memory.

[2]) GASTER, *Thespis*, pp. 260 ff.

[3]) VIROLLEAUD, 'Les Rephaim. Fragments de poèmes de Ras Shamra', *Syria* XXII, 1941, pp. 1-30. He designates the fragments Rp I, Rp II, and Rp III.

1, *ṯmn bqrb hkly*) [1]), and make their journey by horse and chariot (*ibidem*, II, 3-4),

'asr.sswm.tṣmd.d ( )	They harness the horses, they couple up ( ).
t'ln.lmrkbthm	They mount their chariots.

By this we conclude that they are human rather than divine, noble, and probably of royal family. We regard the *rp'um* as a sacred guild closely associated with the king in his office as a dispenser of fertility (*mt rp'e*). Such a religious fraternity is termed *mrz'*, as we know from an administrative text which records a royal grant of land to *bit amel M marza(ḫ)i* (*PRU* III, 15. 88, cf. *ibidem*, 15. 70) [2]). This word occurs in the fragmentary text GORDON *UH* 122.

The language of the texts GORDON *UH* 122, 123 connects these fragments with the preceding, the *rp'um* being called probably into a palace (*hkl*// *bt*) and possibly a sanctuary, where a coronation takes place. It is uncertain whether the anointment is that of Baal (VIROLLEAUD, DRIVER, AISTLEITNER) or of the prince, conceivably Aqht revived (CAQUOT). In any case the passage is interesting as evidence of the right of consecration of a king: [3])

šm'.'atm. (*'eln*)	Hear ye (div-)
ym.lm.qdq)*d*)	ine. On his head ( )
šmn.prst ( )	Oil of ? ( )
ydr.hm.ym(*lk*)	He shall be consecrated, [4]) lo, he shall become king,
'l 'amr.y'u(*ḫd ks'a mlkh*)	At my command he shall (take the throne of his sovereignty)
nḫt.kḫṯ d(*rkth*)	Even the dais of the seat (of his dominion)

The text GORDON *UH* 124 is connected with the last by language. This text is better preserved but no less difficult. In our opinion the first ten lines concern the restoration of Dn'el's family after the death of Aqht: [5])

( )	( )
hn.bnk. ( )	Lo thy son ( )

---

[1]) In this fragmentary text the phraseology might run 'seven in my house, yea eight in my palace', in which cases we should not be entitled to take the number literally.

[2]) *marza*(*ḫ*)*u* is known to have a religious significance because of its relation to Šatarna in *PRU* III, 15.70, who is known by the divine determinative in *PRU* III, 16.157 to have been a god.

[3]) GORDON *UH* 123, 13-18.

[4]) We take *ydr* as the passive imperfect Qal of *ndr*, cognate with Hebrew נזר, cf. נזיר אחיו, Deuteronomy xxxiii, 16.

[5]) GORDON *UH* 124, 1-10.

bn bn.ʾaṯrk	A son's son after thee.
ḫn ( ) ydk	Lo thy hand ( )
ṣġr.tnšq.šptk	Thy lips will kiss a little one
ṯm.ṯkm.bm.ṯkm	Then[1]) head above shoulders, each above the other[2])
ʾaḫm.qym.ʾel blsmt	May El raise up[3]) brethren without a check.[4])
ṯm yʿbš.šm.ʾel.mtm	Then the lads will use the name of god aright.[5])
yʿbš.brkn.šm.ʾel ġzrm	The young men in blessing will rightly apply the names of god.
ṯm.ṯmq.rpʾu.bʿl	Then (?[6])) a healer of Baal,
mhr.bʿl.wmhr.ʿnt	A devotee[7]) of Baal, even a devotee of Anat.
ṯm.yḥpn.ḥyly	Then will he surrounded[8]) by my power,
zbl.mlk.ʿlmy	Even my (?) with kingly nobility.'[9])

Then follows a reference to the activity of Anat,[10]) the significance of which we do not understand, and the text goes on to describe a seven-day feast of the *rpʾum*, at the conclusion of which there is a

---

[1]) We take *ṯm* as the Arabic ثمّ, 'then', indicating a new phase of action.

[2]) In *ṯkm* VIROLLEAUD saw a local reference to Shechem (*Revue des études sémitiques*, 1940, pp. 782 ff.) It is again suggested that the phrase *ṯkm bm ṯkm* is reminiscent of the adverbial phrase שכם אחד in Zephaniah iii, 9, which apparently means 'with one accord'. We think that the phrase in the Ugaritic text indicates the family of Dnʾel at various stages of growth.

[3]) This may be either an optative or a prophetic perfect (intensive). The usage of the intensive of *qwm* suggests the Arabic قيّم, 'to resurrect'.

[4]) This is undoubtedly difficult, and our suggestion is no more than tentative. We regard *smt* as a verbal noun cognate with the Arabic صمّ, 'to stop up'.

[5]) We accept Gordon's suggestion (*UH*, p. 255) that *yʿbš* is to be read rather than *yṯbš*, as in l. 7 (ʿ = 𐎓 for ṯ = 𐎘), عبش, 'to arrange'. A stage of development is indicated when the lads, no doubt after proper instruction and initiation, might safely use the divine name without risk of blasphemy.

[6]) *ṯmq*, probably a verb, suggests no cognate. AISTLEITNER takes it as the proper name of a god on the evidence of the proper name *bn-ṯmq* (*Wörterbuch* 2888).

[7]) *mhr* is found in this sense in the text GORDON *UH* ʿnt II, where *mhrm* are the victims of the goddess' bloody orgy, *v. supra*, p. 34 ff. It occurs to us that this problematic passage may refer hyperbolically to some rite of initiation, where partly as an ordeal, partly in order to be marked as devotees, the subjects were incised, as the modern Sudanese.

[8]) This word is possibly cognate with the Arabic حوف, 'to surround'.

[9]) Reading *ʿlmy* after DRIVER (*op. cit.*, p. 68) for *llmy* (VIROLLEAUD, GORDON). DRIVER and A. HERDNER, *Corpus*, p. 96 actually read *ʿllmy*, possibly a case of dittography of *l. mlk ʿlmy* lit. 'royalty of my eternity', cf. Hebrew הר קדשי, is parallel to *ḥyly*, hence is an internal accusative after *yḥpn*, which suggests that *zbl* is the subject.

[10]) GORDON *UH*, 124, 10-11,

km.tdd.ʿnt.ṣd	As Anat ranges to hunt,
tštr.ʿpt.šmm	Scanning the birds in the heavens'.

In this passage *tštr* may be the Ifteʿal of *šwr*, cf. Hebrew שור, 'to watch'.

reference to *'al'eyn b'l*, though here again the fragmentary state of the text does not permit us to particularize.

Mutilated though these texts are, they are not without their value. It seems to us that they indicate the *Sitz im Leben* of the Aqht text. We consider this text to be, at least originally, the myth associated with the ritual performed by the king, or perhaps the relics of an ancient royal house, in connection with harvest or famine. The fragments we have just considered are probably vestiges of the conclusion of the Aqht text describing how with the ritual help of the *rp'um* the famine described in 1 Aqht was brought to an end and perhaps the potency of the king restored, either by the revival of Aqht or the birth of another to play the rôle Aqht had played. The text is thus of great importance to those interested in the office of king as the channel of divine blessing in nature as well as in politics.

In view of the limited number of the *rp'um* in these texts and their apparent fertility function, which agrees with the etymology of the word [1]) we gravely doubt Virolleaud's opinion that the term, as in certain Old Testament passages, is an ethnic one. On this Hebrew tradition indeed is not unanimous. In the Prophetic books and in the Wisdom literature the term is synonymous for the dead, as also in Phoenician funerary inscriptions of the 5th and 4th centuries, [2]) cf. the bilingual inscription of the 1st century A.D. from el-Amruni, where *'elnym rp'ym* is rendered by *diis manibus*. In the fragment of the hymn to the Sun-goddess (Gordon *UH* 62, 45-46), where the journey to the underworld is described, there is a similar equation of *rp'um* and *'elnym*. The latter term, as indicated by the Ras Shamra texts and the Phoenician inscriptions, signifies inferior supernatural beings of chthonic character, e.g. Gordon *UH* ʿnt, IV, 78-80. The Old Testament does not use the term through motives of orthodoxy, though such beings seem to be referred to in the description of the apparition of Samuel to Saul at Endor (אלהים עלים מן־הארץ 1 Sam. xxviii, 13). It remains for us to find if possible a connection with cultic functionaries, which we consider the *rp'um* to be in the three Ugaritic fragments in question, as distinct from Gordon *UH* 62, 45-46.

---

[1]) רפא, which means generally 'to heal' in Hebrew, has the more specific meaning of 'to restore fertility', e.g. to the harem of Abimelech of Gerar (Genesis xx, 17) and to the spring at Jericho by Elisha (2 Kings ii, 21).

[2]) E.g. of Tabnith and Eshmunazzar of Sidon, G. A. Cooke, *NSI*, pp. 26 ff., 30, ff.

In an excellent and penetrating study of the subject CAQUOT [1]) also denies the ethnic significance of *rp'um*, agreeing with us in interpreting the term as 'healers', though not in the sense of dispensers of fertility, but as the dead ancestors who had an influence on the survival of the family, and were present on the occasion noted in the text as the attendants of Baal in a seven day ritual of mourning combined with rites to provide for the survival of the family of Dn'el. Provided that emphasis is laid upon the function of the king and his family as dispensers of fertility, which CAQUOT is not prepared to do, [2]) we could agree with CAQUOT's view of the objective of the action of the *rp'um* in the three fragments. We maintain still, however, for the reasons we have stated that the *rp'um* here were human agents, though we freely admit that the collocation of *rp'um* and *'elnym* in GORDON *UH* 62, 45-46 is a strong argument for CAQUOT's view that the *rp'um* were not human but supernatural, the dead ancestors, with whom communion was sought through a communion meal. Whether the *rp'um* were human or supernatural, the ultimate objective of the rites was the restoration of the king's potency, the re-establishment of his family, and the fertility of the land (the threshing-floors and plantations).

The influence of the dead, particularly the notable dead, in fertility was familiar to the Greeks, and underlay the mythology of Pluto and Persephone, and is expressed by Hesiod, who ascribes a fertilizing function to the departed of the golden age (*Works and Days*, 109-126). It was familiar also in ancient Egypt, where the dead Pharaohs were regarded as assimilated to the fertility god Osiris. In the Djed festival too, when the royal virility and fertilizing virtue was renewed, the Pharaoh ceremonially walked over a field, accompanied in every phase of the ceremony by the *upwant*, or wolf-standard, which is known from the Pyramid texts to symbolize the royal ancestors and was carried by a priest of the ancestral spirits of the royal house. [3])

---

[1]) A. CAQUOT, 'Les Rephaim ougaritiques', *Syria* XXXVII, 1960, pp. 75-93.

[2]) Our difference with CAQUOT turns largely on the weight we lay on the limited number of the *rp'um*, their function in the palace, and their use of horses and chariots, and on the emphasis he lays on the supernatural significance of *'elnym*, the parallel to *rp'um*, and further the fact that he takes *rp'e* in *mt rp'e* as a verbal noun expressing the objective experience of Dn'el as one who has had his potency restored, while we take it as Subjective referring to the king as a dispenser of fertility. As so often in the Ras Shamra texts, both interpretations of the last phrase are possible grammatically and both accord with the content of the Aqhat text, where the title is commonly applied to Dn'el.

[3]) H. FRANKFORT, *Kingship and the Gods*, 1948, pp. 85-89.

Similar instances of the belief in the potency of dead rulers in the fertility of nature are cited from modern Sudanese peoples, the Dinka [1]) and the Shilluk, among whom the dead chief Nyakang is the most active force in the religious life of the people and is believed to be the dispenser of rain and fertility. [2]) In Israel this might explain the popularity of the cult at the tombs of dead ancestors (*bamoth*), but in the Old Testament the conception is reflected rather in its negative aspect in the belief that blood violently shed and not duly 'covered' brought the curse of infertility, as the curse of Abel's blood (Genesis iv, 11-12) and the drought ensuing on the unavenged massacre of the Gibeonites (2 Samuel xxi, 1 ff.). As this belief in the influence of the dead over fertility lost ground in Israel, or was eliminated from the Old Testament by orthodox editors, רפאים ('dispensers of fertility') became the term for the prehistoric inhabitants of the land, as in Genesis xiv, 5; xv, 20; Deuteronomy iii, 11; Josh. xii, 4; xiii, 12; xvii, 15.

The other major text where the protagonists are human is the Krt text. In the Aqht text we have seen that, though Dn'el, Aqht, and his sister are human, the goddess Anat plays a major rôle, so that it may be said that here we have a case of a legend developing into a myth. In the Krt text it is true that deities are active. El and the Ugaritic pantheon are represented as present at a feast to bless the union of Krt and his bride, and the king's illness is due to his omission to fulfil his vow to Aṯerat. Here, however, the gods are much less active, and not really essential to the action of the poem, and we are in no doubt, for our part, that this text concerns the actual vicissitudes of the king and his house. We have already stated the various views of the nature of this text and have indicated our own position. [3]) The text, in our opinion, does deal with historical persons and events, though not on the scale that VIROLLEAUD suggests. We have noted also MOWINCKEL's view that the text was originally a myth with the dying and rising vegetation-deity as hero, but the divine hero has eventually become the mythical founder of a dynasty and the text is 'no longer a pure myth, but a mythical hero-legend'. We cannot accept this view, though we do think that it recognises certain features in the text which we regard as quite vital to its interpretation, that is the sacral office of the king in its various aspects.

---

[1]) C. G. SELIGMAN, *Egypt and Negro Africa: A Study in Divine Kingship*, 1934, p. 22.
[2]) J. G. FRAZER, *The Golden Bough*, Part IV, vol. II, pp. 166-174.
[3]) *V. supra*, p. 15 ff.

The text, however, must speak for itself. The king Krt [1]) is in dire affliction. He had had numerous progeny, all legitimate princes born of his official wife and so potential heirs who might perpetuate his name. One after another, however, they were cut off, and with them perished the hope of the dynasty: [2])

	....
bt (m)lk. ʾetdb	The house of the king was destroyed, [3])
dšbʿ (ʾa)ḫm. lh	The house which had seven brothers,
ṯmnt. bn ʾum	Yea eight sons of one mother.
krt. ḥtkn. rš	Krt our sire was crushed, [4])
krt. grdš. mknt	Yea, Krt [5]) was stripped of (his) establishment.
ʾaṯt. ṣdqh. lypq	His legitimate wife [6]) did he find [7])

---

[1]) We think that *krt* should be vocalised *Karut*, a passive participle, signifying 'He who is cut off', possibly a reference to the ritual seclusion of the afflicted king.

[2]) Gordon *UH* krt, 7 ff.

[3]) *ʾetdb* is possibly a scribal error for *ʾetbd*, which is found in a similar context in l. 24.

[4]) *rš* is generally taken as cognate with Hebrew רשש (Jeremiah v, 17; Malachi i, 4) with a Syriac cognate, 'to crush', so Virolleaud, Ginsberg, Driver, Aistleitner. We accept this as the probable reading.

[5]) *grdš*, taken by Aistleitner as a proper name (*Wörterbuch* 698) and by Virolleaud as a Semitization of Hittite *gurtaš*, 'a fortress', is probably cognate with Syriac ܓܪܕ, 'to skin, denude', meaning 'to be destroyed' in the Ethpaal. The verb is passive. That *grdš* is a verb is suggested by the fact that *mknt* must be a noun, as is indicated by the parallel passage (l. 23), where *ṯbth* appears in place of *mknt*.

[6]) We note the parallelism *ʾaṯt ṣdqh*, *mtrḫt yšrh*. Both *ṣdq* and *yšr* are abstract nouns. Both are technical terms for 'legitimacy', cf. the Phoenician inscription of Yehimelek of Byblos, ll. 6-7, M. Dunand, *RB* XXXIX, 1930, pp. 321-331. *ṣdq* has this connotation in the inscription of Yehawmelek of Byblos, l. 9, G. A. Cooke, *NSI*, 1903, p. 18 ff. The emphasis on succession through the legitimate queen as distinct from concubines suggests that the royal house of Krt was under the influence of Hittite culture where great importance was attached to succession through the *sakuwassar* or 'legitimate queen', G. Contenau, *La Civilisation des Hittites*, 2nd ed., 1948, pp. 109 ff. *mtrḫt*, in parallelism with *ʾaṯt*, is a passive participle of the intensive of the verb *trḫ*, 'to pay the bride-price' (Akkadian *terḫatu*), hence 'to marry'. Gordon was first to explode Virolleaud's theory that this word referred to the Biblical Terah and his wives, Gordon, *JBL* LVII, 1938, pp. 407-410.

[7]) Albright rendered 'whose rectitude *truly befits* (*ypq* from *wpq*, cognate with the Arabic وفق) a spouse, whose virtue (befits) a wedded wife', *BASOR* 71, 1938, p. 38; so too Pedersen, 'Die Krt Legende', *Berytus* VI, 1941, pp. 66-67. We follow Ginsberg ('The Legend of King Keret . . .', *BASOR Supplementary Studies* 2-3, 1946, pp. 14, 33) and Gordon (*UL*, p. 67) in taking *ypq* as meaning 'he got'. Ginsberg cites the Phoenician inscription of Tabnith, Cooke, *NSI* 4, l. 3, pp. 26-28, and Proverbs xviii, 22

מצא אשה מצא טוב ויפק רצון מיהוה

To this we might add Proverbs iii, 13, and viii, 35. where הפיק appears in

mtrḫt yšrh	Even his rightful spouse.
ʾaṯt.trḫ.wtbʿt	He married a wife and she gave him issue, [1])
ṯʾar ʾum. tkn lh	He had offspring of (one) mother.
mṯlṯt.kṯrm.tmt	At three years old [2]) they were perfect in health, [3])
mrbʿt.ẓblnm	At four, princes (all); [4])
mḫmšt.yʾetsp ršp	At five Rešef [5]) gathered them unto himself,
mṯdṯt.ġlm ym	At six their day was darkened. [6])

---

parallelism with מצא. The prefix *l* is best taken as an emphatic particle as ل with the jussive of the verb or the predicate of a nominal sentence in Arabic; so Albright, Pedersen, and Ginsberg.

[1]) *wtbʿt* is generally taken as 'she departed', a euphemism for 'she died', or literally 'she deserted him', Driver, *op. cit.*, p. 29. The word regularly means 'to depart' in the Ras Shamra texts. Here we note the parallelism with *ṯʾar ʾum tkn lh*, 'he had offspring (lit. flesh) by one mother', which suggests to us that *tbʿt* is probably the intensive of the root here cognate with the Arabic تبع 'to follow' cf. تَبِعِيَّةٌ, 'succession', تَبَاعَةٌ, 'issue'.

[2]) The numerals have been taken variously as fractions (Ginsberg, *op. cit.*, p. 33, and Gordon, *UL*, p. 67, and Driver, *op. cit.*, p. 29), ordinals referring to the seven wives of Keret (Cassuto, *BASOR* 119, 1950, p. 19), or multiplicatives (Virolleaud, La Légende de Kéret . . ., 1936, p. 35, and Pedersen, *op. cit.*, p. 68). We suggest that the numbers are passive participles of the intensive of verbs and refer to the age of Krt's family, cf. 1 Samuel i, 24, בפר מְשֻׁלָּשׁ (after LXX ἐν μόσχῳ τριετίζοντι), Genesis xv, 9, עגלה מְשֻׁלֶּשֶׁת, עז משלשת, and איל משלש. In those passages the reference is certainly to the age of the animals.

[3]) We take *tmt* as the perfect stative of *tmm* and not, as is generally thought, the imperfect of *mt*. Up to this point it is the poet's purpose to emphasize the prosperity of Krt and his family in order to make his calamity the more poignant. We take *kṯrm* as an adverb, following Gaster who cites the Syriac ܟܫܝܪܐ in this sense, *JQR* XXXVI, 1947, p. 291.

[4]) We cannot agree that in *ẓblnm* we have a reference to the tribe of Zebulon (so Virolleaud, *op. cit.*, p. 35, Dussaud, *Syria* XXI, 1940, p. 173 and De Vaux, *RB* XLVI, 1937, pp. 446 ff.), nor even to a class in the community along with *kṯrm* (so Albright, *BASOR* 71, 1938, pp. 38-39). We suggest that as *kṯrm* refers to physical perfection *ẓblnm* refers to royal dignity, *ẓbl* being the regular epithet of Baal in the texts.

[5]) Rešef is the Canaanite god of pestilence and the underworld. He does not play any significant rôle in the extant Ras Shamra mythology, though his name appears in theophoric names in administrative texts and he ranks in the Ugaritic pantheon in the offering lists. He is depicted with his insignia of gazelle-horns in Egyptian sculpture from the XIXth Dynasty (Leibovitch, *ASAE* XLVIII, 1948, pp. 435 ff., fig. 1) and on a stele from the same period or a little earlier at Bethshan, where he is named Mekal (A. Rowe, *The Topography and History of Bethshan*, 1930, pl. XXXIII). He was worshipped in the Aramaean states of Syria in the 8th century (Cooke, *NSI* 61, l. 2) and is named in the Phoenician inscription of Azitawwad from Karatepe as *ršp ṣprm*, which Gordon has translated, correctly in our opinion, as 'Reshef of the Bucks', *JNES* VIII, 1949, pp. 110, 115.

[6]) *ġlm ym* in the parallel stichos to the one including *yʾetsp ršp* suggests that it bears a similar meaning, and so *ġlm ym* has been taken in apposition to *ršp* with

mšbʿt hn.bšlḥ.ttpl	At seven, lo! they fell one after the other by the sword. [1]
yʿn.ḥtkh.krt	Krt sees his progeny,
yʿn ḥtkh rš	He sees his progeny crushed
mʾed.grdš.ṯbth	Entirely stripped of his dwelling.
wbtm hn.špḥ.yʾetbd	And lo! the whole [2] family is perished
wbpḫyrh.yrṯ	And in their entirety [3] (his) heirs. [4]

Like Dnʾel in similar case he goes into ritual seclusion: [5]

yʿrb.bḥdrh.ybky	He enters his chamber, he weeps;
bṯn rgmm.wydmʿ	Repeating (his) words he sheds tears.
tntkn.ʾudmʿth	His tears are poured out
km.ṯqlm.ʾarṣh	Even as shekels to the ground,
kmḫmšt.mṭth	As pieces-of-five [6] on the bed.

---

the same predicate *yʾetsp*. It is generally taken as 'the youth or child (Arabic غلام) of the Sea', which cannot be satisfactorily elucidated by anything we know of Canaanite mythology. GINSBERG opens a fresh approach in translating 'the sea engulfed' (lit. 'hid', cf. Hebrew עלם), *op. cit.*, p. 34. GASTER seems to us nearer the truth in translating 'darkness of day', this being the subject of *yʾetsp* understood in the second stichos of the couplet, *JQR* XXXVII, 1947, pp. 289 ff. We agree with GASTER in taking *ġlm* as cognate with the Arabic ظلم, but not in taking *ġlm* as an abstract noun, which would not be suitable as the subject of *yʾetsp* ('gathered to itself'). We suggest that *ġlm* is either a stative or passive verb and *ym* the subject, meaning 'the day was darkened'.

[1]) *bšlḥ* is usually translated 'they fell by the sword'. The Ifteʿal of *npl* may have a reflexive or reciprocal sense, cf. *tntkn* in l. 28 and Hebrew התהלך, being explained possibly by *bšlḥ* 'seriatim', cf. Arabic سلح, Syriac ܫܠܚܐ, 'a row', hence 'fell one after the other'. If this were the meaning of *šlḥ*, however, it would probably have the adverbial ending *-m*, hence it is probably cognate with Arabic, سلاح, 'sword'. The parallelism in the context demands that the means of death is denoted.

[2]) We take *btm* as parallel to *wbpḫyrh*, 'in its entirety'. *hn* after *btm* might be a full form of the pronominal suffix including both the familiar elements of *h* and *n* energic. We take it, however, as the Hebrew הן, which generally occurs in Ugaritic as *hm*, 'lo ', *btm* would thus be an adverbial expression.

[3]) The word *pḫr* is common in the Ras Shamra texts meaning 'entirety', or 'full assembly', e.g. *pḫr ʾelm*, GORDON *UH* 17, 7; *mpḫrt bn ʾel*, *ibidem* 2, 17, 34; 107, 3, cf. the inscription of Yehimelek of Byblos, l. 4 מפחרת אל גבל, DUNAND, *RB* XXXIX, 1930, pp. 321-331. Later in the Krt text GORDON *UH* 128, III, 4, 15, the root occurs in the phrase *bpḫr qbṣ dtn*. In the present passage we suggest that the form *pḫyrh* with the *y* between the two final radicals is a diminutive, familiar in Arabic, e.g. بحر, بحيرة and جنّ, جنينة.

[4]) *yrṯ* is taken by GINSBERG (*op. cit.*, pp. 14, 34) as 'a succession', cf. Hebrew ירש, Arabic ورث, 'to inherit', this being the subject of *yʾetbd* understood as repeated from the previous stichos and in apposition to *špḥ. yrṯ* is a singular used collectively.

[5]) GORDON *UH* krt, 26-30.

[6]) The photographs of the text seem to us to support GORDON's reading *kmḫmšt mṭth* rather than *tmḫ mšt mṭth* which is read by VIROLLEAUD (*op. cit.*,

The king receives divine assurance in a dream that he shall find another wife and have progeny. This assurance is given with a very detailed divine directive describing how Krt should proceed to win his bride: [1])

wbḥlmh ᵓel.yrd	And in his dreaming El comes down,
bẓ̌hrth ᵓab ᵓadm	Yea in his vision [2]) the Father of Men,
wyqrb bšᵓal.krt	And approaches, asking Krt:
mᵓat krt.kybky	'Who is Krt that he should weep,
ydmᶜ.nᶜmn.ġlm.ᵓel	The Gracious One, [3]) the Lad of El, that he should shed tears?
mlk ṯr ᵓabh yᵓarš	Is it the kingship of the Bull, his father, that he desires? [4])
hm.drk(t) kᵓab.ᵓadm	Or government like the Father of Men?
	....
t(r)tḥṣ.wtᵓadm	Thou shalt wash, and make thyself red. [5])

p. 67, Pl. I), PEDERSEN (*op. cit.* p. 69), GINSBERG (*op. cit.*, p. 14), GASTER (*OLZ* XL, 1937, col. 672), CASSUTO (האלה ענת, 1950, p. 21) and DRIVER (*op. cit.*, p. 29), who find the figure of moistening one's bed with tears, cf. Psalm vi, 7. In support of GORDON's reading we should cite 1 Aqht, 82-83, where tears are said to be shed *kmrbᶜt ṯqlm*, 'like pieces of four'. This interpretation is further supported by the parallel stichos *km ṯqlm ᵓarṣh*, 'even as shekels to the ground'. We have probably to visualise shekels (lit. 'weights') as metal rings of a certain weight which were told off on a stick. Coinage became current in Syria in the Persian period, though the earliest coined money yet found in Syria was a hoard of Macedonian silver staters of the 6th century which was found at Ras Shamra, SCHAEFFER, *Syria* XVIII, 1937, fig. 18.

[1]) GORDON *UH* krt, 35-152.

[2]) The parallelism *bḥlmh/bẓ̌hrth* suggests that in *ẓ̌hrt* we have a cognate with the Arabic سهرة, 'sleeplessness', and Syriac ܥܗܪܐ, 'the vigil of a saint'. A closer phonetic correspondence, however, would be with the Arabic ظهر, 'to appear'.

[3]) *nᶜmn* and *ġlm ᵓel* have been claimed as titles of the king as a divine person (PEDERSEN, *op. cit.*, p. 72 and MOWINCKEL, *NTT*, 1942, pp. 24-26). MOWINCKEL takes *nᶜmn* as a title of Adonis, the dying and rising vegetation deity, with whom he identifies Krt in the cult. He associates *ġlm* with *ᶜbd*, another epithet of Krt which refers to his relation to El. The epithet *nᶜmn* is also applied to Aqht the son of Dnᵓel, another royal person. We would take the epithet to refer to the physical beauty or power to excite desire, as we should refer *ġlm* to his sexual potency, so important in one who was expected to propagate his line and office. *ġlm* is cognate with the Arabic noun and verb غلم which means 'to be lustful' or 'to be sexually mature'. This is the root of the Hebrew עלמה in Isaiah vii, 14. For a fuller discussion of those titles see our *Krt Text in the Literature of Ras Shamra, Documenta et Monumenta Orientis Antiqui*, Volumen Quintum, 1955, p. 30, 2nd ed. 1964.

[4]) *yᵓarš* suggests a root *ᵓarš* cognate with the Arabic أرْش, 'blood-price', i.e. something demanded, cf. Psalm xxi, 3, תַּאֲוַת לִבּוֹ // אֲרֶשֶׁת שְׂפָתָיו, the request of his lips' // 'the desire of his heart'.

[5]) *wtᵓadm* (lit. 'thou shalt redden thyself') may simply mean 'freshen up' (PEDERSEN, *op. cit.*, p. 73) or may refer to the use of henna as a cosmetic on the palms

rḥṣ (y)dk.ʾamt	Wash thy hand, thy forearm,
ʾuṣb(ʿtk) ʿd ṯkm	Thy fingers, up to the shoulder.
ʿrb (bẓl ḫmt)	Go into the shelter [1]) of the pens, [2])
qḥ ʾem(r bydk)	Take a lamb in thy hand,
ʾemr.d(bḥ bm).ymn	Even a lamb for sacrifice in thy right hand,
llʾa.k(lʾatn)m	A kid from the enclosures, [3])
klt.l(ḥmk) dnẓl	The whole of thy meat of seclusion, [4])
qḥ.ms(rr) ʿṣr dbḥ	Take a *msrr*, a bird of sacrifice,
ṣ(q bg)l.ḥtṯ yn	Pour wine into a cup of silver, [5])
bgl (ḫ)rṣ.nbt	Honey [6]) into a cup of gold.
ʿl.lẓr.(mg)dl	Go up to the top of the tower,
wʿl.lẓr.(mg)dl	Yea, go up to the top of the tower,
rkb ṯkmm .ḥm(t)	Mount the rampart of the wall.
šʾa.ydk šmm	Raise thy hands to the sky.
dbḥ.lṯr ʾabk.ʾel	Sacrifice to thy father the Bull El;
šrd.bʿl.bdbḥk	Serve [7]) Baal with thy sacrifice.

---

of the hands at the present day in the Near East. We prefer Dussaud's interpretation that here we have the use of blood as a means of consecration of the king for his priestly functions, as Aaron and his sons were consecrated by blood, Exodus xxix, 20-21 (P), Leviticus viii, 22-24, Dussaud, *Les Origines Cananéennes du Sacrifice Israélite*, 2nd ed., 1941, pp. 328-330.

[1]) *ẓl*, 'shadow' or 'shelter', suggests a roof, nevertheless we prefer to visualise the sanctuary consisting of courts open to the sky where *ẓl* might refer to an enclosing wall, perhaps with temporary covering.

[2]) *ḫmt* has been taken as 'tent' or 'pavilion', cognate with the Arabic خيمة. The difficulty, felt by Pedersen (*op. cit.*, p. 74), is that it is apparently from the *ḫmt* that the king gets the sacrificial animals. We suggest that *ḫmt* is cognate with the Arabic خُمّ, 'a coop' (for hens or domestic animals).

[3]) *klʾatnm* is usually taken to signify both hands, *llʾa klʾatnm* meaning a kid that required both hands to hold. We would connect it with the Hebrew verb כלא, 'to confine'. We take *klʾatn* as a dual signifying enclosures. The dual refers to a pair of converging entry-walls to facilitate the corraling of the beasts, a feature noted in the desert marches of Transjordan, cf. A. S. Kirkbride, *JPOS* XX, 1946, pp. 1-5 and Eissfeldt, 'Gabelhürden im Ostjordanland', *F Und F* XXV, 1/2, 1949, pp. 9-11, and probably depicted on the Narmer palette. We may also note the screened entry to the outer court of the Baal temple at Ras Shamra by which sacrificial beasts were probably run into the court.

[4]) For *nẓl* we suggest a connection with the Arabic نذل, 'to pick out' so 'to isolate', the reference being to Krt's 'bread of affliction' which he ate in his ritual seclusion as a mourner. Now that this ritual seclusion is past he is required to sacrifice all (*klt*) this food and so break all association with his ritual isolation.

[5]) Like many names of metals and precious stones in Semitic languages *ḥtṯ*, 'silver', is an Anatolian word.

[6]) *nbt* is the Hebrew נפת 'honeycomb', cf. the prohibition against honey (דבש) in Hebrew sacrifice, possibly a protest against Canaanite usage.

[7]) As far as the form is concerned *šrd* could be a causative (Shafʿel) from *yrd* and is so taken by Driver, *op. cit.*, p. 31. In view of the direct object *bʿl* and the parallel *dbḥ* in the parallel stichos we agree with Virolleaud in seeing in *šrd* a

bn.dgn bmṣdk	The son of Dagon with thy food.
wyrd.krt.lggt	Then let Krt come down from the roof,
ʿdb.ʾakl lqryt	Preparing food from the granaries,
ḥtt.lbt.ḫbr	Even wheat from the storagepits, [1])
yʾep lḥm dḫmš	Let him parch bread of the fifth,
mġd ṯdṯ.yrḫm	Food of the sixth month. [2])
ʿdn ngb.wyṣʾe	Let the crowd muster [3]) and come forth,

cognate with the Hebrew שׂרד which is found in the phrase בִּגְדֵי הַשְּׂרָד (Exodus xxxi, 10) which is translated στόλαι λειτουργικαι, 'vestments of service' in the LXX.

[1]) lqryt//lbt ḫbr is a classical instance of the difficulty of interpreting these texts. qryt regularly means 'a fortified city', and the name of Krt's city in GORDON UH, 128, IV, 8 is ḫbr. But qryt may also be the cognate of the Akkadian qarītu, 'a granary', and bt ḫbr may be cognate with Akkadian ḫuburu, 'a storehouse' (so GINSBERG, ANET, p. 143), cf. Syriac ܚܒܪ, 'a pit'. This is possibly the significance cf. בֵּית חֶבֶר in Proverbs xxi, 9; xxv, 24, cited by DRIVER (Canaanite Myths and Legends, p. 31)

טוֹב לָשֶׁבֶת עַל פִּנַּת גָּג
מֵאֵשֶׁת מִדְיָנִים וּבֵית חָבֶר

[2]) mġd in parallelism with lḥm surely means 'food', cognate with the Arabic غدو 'to nourish', and not 'fortresses' (Hebrew מָעוֹז) as VIROLLEAUD suggested, op. cit., p. 72. In yrḫm the final m is enclitic and the form is singular. 'Bread of the fifth, food of the sixth month' refers probably to the double crop of barley and wheat. We formerly suggested that this referred to a rite of desacralization of the new crop by fire, as in Leviticus ii, 14. But the new crop would have been desacralized before it was brought in from the threshing-floors to the grainsilos and storehouses, an operation which till recently was formally observed with prayer in Arab villages. We now suggest that yʾep denotes the preparation of food for the campaign, denoting parching of grain, which, as קָלִי or קָלִיא, is noted as field rations in 1 Samuel xvii, 17; xxv, 18; and 2 Samuel xvii, 28. The word ṯdṯ, of course, clearly indicates that the numbers are ordinals, cf. DRIVER, op. cit., p. 31.

[3]) The crucial word ngb has been variously taken as the Biblical Negeb or steppe-land in the South of Palestine (VIROLLEAUD, DUSSAUD), the South in general (ALBRIGHT, BASOR 63, 1936, p. 29; 94, 1944, p. 30), the South, probably in Syria (EISSFELDT, ZDMG XCIV, 1940, p. 81), an indefinite locality Negba (DE LANGHE, Les Textes de Ras Shamra-Ugarit et leurs Rapports avec . . . l'Ancien Testament, 1945, II, pp. 122-125). GINSBERG (op. cit., p. 15) and GORDON (UH, p. 249) take ngb as the Negeb though not that of Palestine. PEDERSEN after AIST-LEITNER (op. cit., p. 78) takes the word as meaning 'noble' (Arabic نجيب); so also ENGNELL, Studies in Divine Kingship in the Ancient Near East, 1943, p. 157. We agree with Mlle. A. HERDNER in taking ngb as a Nifʿal participle or perfect of a verb gbb cognate with the Aramaic גבב, 'to gather, rake together, accumulate', Syria XXIII, 1942, p. 278. The question has been opened again since the discovery of the phrase ṣabu-šu ṣi-di-tam na-gi-ib in a letter in the Mari texts, where the sense is probably 'his troops are provisioned with food'. It is noteworthy that Mlle. HERDNER is now disposed to reckon seriously with this interpretation in her review of the writer's first edition of The Krt text . . ., Syria XXXIV, 1957, p. 359, so also A. JIRKU, Kanaanäische Mythen und Epen aus Ras Schamra-Ugarit, 1962, p. 87. The word ʿdn has also been variously taken as 'occupied' (VIROLLEAUD,

ṣbʾu.ṣbʾe.ngb	The élite of the fighting men [1]) mustered;
wyṣʾe.ʿdn.mʿ	Let the crowd come forth together, [2])
ṣbʾuk.ʾul mʾad	Thy host abundant [3]) in freemen, [4])
ṯlṯ.mʾat.rbt	Three hundred times ten thousand, [5])
ḫpṯ.dbl.spr	Peasant levies [6]) without number,

---

after the Arabic عدن, 'to abide'), 'armament' (PEDERSEN, after the Arabic عدّ, 'to prepare'), 'then' (ALBRIGHT, *BASOR* 63, 1936, p. 29, n. 29), after the Aramaic עדנא, 'time', used adverbially as 'then'. Again we follow Mlle. HERDNER in seeing the cognate of the Arabic عدانة, 'crowd'.

[1]) In the phrase *ṣbʾu ṣbʾe* the case endings should be noted. Here, as Mlle. HERDNER preceives, we have the expression of the superlative as in the Hebrew שיר השרים.

[2]) *mʿ* is an adverb meaning 'all together'. cf. Arabic معاً, and معيّة 'a crowd'.

[3]) It seems best to take *mʾad* here as a perfect stative verb and not as an adverb.

[4]) *ʾul* seems an accusative of respect. We follow ALBRIGHT in seeing in *ʾul* a reference to the highest class in the state, *awilum* of the Mesopotamian social order. The word has been connected with the Hebrew אול, 'strength' (PEDERSEN, *op. cit.*, p. 78, GINSBERG, *op. cit.*, p. 16, and DRIVER, *op. cit.*, p. 31). GINSBERG admits the possible connection with *awilu* (p. 37). With the two popular elements *ḫpṯ* and *ṯnn* (*v. infra*) this would give a three-fold social division in the army roughly corresponding to the situation in the Alalakh Tablets (D. J. WISEMAN, *The Alalakh Tablets*, 1953, pp. 10-112).

[5]) A possible translation here is '*ṯlṯ*-men, many hundreds', *ṯlṯ* being possibly the class of warriors known in the Old Testament as שלישים. These were closely attached to the king (2 Kings vii, 2, 17, 19; ix, 25; xv, 25, and x, 25, where they are associated with רצים and are the agents of Jehu's massacre of the Baal-worshippers at Samaria). MONTGOMERY suggests (*Commentary on Kings*, ICC, ed. GEHMAN, 1951, p. 210) that the שליש, or 'thirdling', was the bearer of the shield and the bodyguard of the king, third with him and his driver in the chariot. The office developed into a formal court honour. The original office certainly had to do with horses and chariots, but there may be no connection with the number three. The word may not be Semitic at all, being originally connected with the non-Semites who introduced the horse and light war-chariot into the Near East c. 1800 B.C.

[6]) *ḫpṯ* denotes a class of people, the *ḫubšu* of the Akkadian census-lists from Alalakh, where they are also called *ṣabē namē* (D. J. WISEMAN, *The Alalakh Tablets*, 1953, p. 10). There they are apparently communities living on the outskirts of settlements, having the right to cultivate small plots of land and occasionally possessing a few cattle, but not fully integrated into the sedentary population. As such they made excellent mercenaries. The Alalakh Tablets indicate that they were subject to the levy for military service and state labour. The designation was apparently known in ancient Israel, since after the death of Goliath Saul offered to attach David to his person and make his family חפשי in Israel. The etymology of the word is 'to separate', and we find later in the Krt text (GORDON *UH* 128, I, 5) the phrase *bn ḫpṯ* which we translate 'weanlings' (lit. sons of separation'), *v. infra*. The view of DRIVER should be noted that *ḫpṯ* here means 'pioneers' (*op. cit.*, p. 31), *v. infra*, pp. 235-236, but this is suggested by Assyrian usage in the 1st millennium B.C. It is likely that the significance of *ḫpṯ* in the Ras Shamra texts was the same as in the texts from neighbouring Alalakh about a century earlier rather than in the much later Hebrew and Assyrian texts.

ṯnn.dbl.hg	Trained regulars [1]) without reckoning,
hlk.lʾalpm.ḫẓẓ	Marching [2]) in thousands, clanking, [3])
wlrbt.kmyr	Yea in tens of thousands like a dust storm, [4])
ʾaṯr.ṯn.ṯn.hlk	Two marching after two, [5])
ʾaṯr.ṯlṯ.klhm	After three all of them,
yḥd.bth.sgr	The solitary man shutting up his house,
ʾalmnt.škr.tškr	The widow hiring a substitute. [6])

---

[1]) As a military class *ṯnn* suggests *ṣabē šananna* of the Alalakh Tablets (Wiseman, *op. cit.*, pp. 11-12). These are members of raiding parties or regular striking forces and far outnumber the charioteers in such units, which indicates their popular character. They are apparently regulars, and the word is feasibly connected by Albright in a private communication to Wiseman (*op. cit.*, p. 11, n.) with the Akkadian *šananu* 'to contest, strive', hence 'to train'. We are doubtful of Albright's suggestion that the noun means 'bowmen', which he makes on the basis of his view that the letter *shin* in the Sinaitic inscriptions represents a composite bow. Driver proposes a connection with the Arabic ثَنَّ, 'to be worn out with old age' (*op. cit.*, p. 152) and translates 'veterans'. We previously suggested that the term might mean 'second-rankers', hence 'veterans' or 'reserves', cf. Latin 'triarii', 'third-rankers', 'veterans', but now prefer in the light of the evidence from Alalakh to translate 'trained regulars'.

[2]) Since this is still Krt's vision of what is to happen, we should understand *hlk* as a participle. Since, however, this is divine revelation this might be a case of prophetic perfect.

[3]) The meaning of *ḫẓẓ* is determined by the parallel *kmyr*. For the latter Aistleitner proposed to read *km yr*, 'like early rain' (Hebrew יורה) and Gaster proposed to connect *ḫẓẓ* with חזיזים, which is found in parallelism with מטר in Zechariah x, 1, so also Driver (*op. cit.*, p. 31). In view of the peculiar Ugaritic sibilants of *ḫẓẓ* any equation with another Semitic cognate is hazardous. In view of the want of the preposition *km* we cannot take *ḫẓẓ* in the sense proposed by Gaster, but regard it is a participle, suggesting tentatively that it is cognate with Arabic خَشّ, 'to rustle'. While admitting the feasibility of Aistleitner's interpretation of *km yr*, we propose to read *k myr*, 'like a dust storm', Arabic مور.

[4]) See previous note.

[5]) The reference which Virolleaud claimed to find to Asher is unlikely because of the repetition of *ʾaṯr* and because of the general interpretation of the whole text, where one after another of Virolleaud's ethnic identifications have been eliminated. Ginsberg, in our opinion, is right in reading for *ʾaṯr* 'after', cf. Arabic أَثَرَ, 'to follow in the footsteps'. The word is used as a preposition in Gordon *UH* 49, II, 28-30.

klb ṯʾat lʾemrh 'As the heart of a cow to her lamb,
km lb ʿnt ʾaṯr bʿl So the heart of Anat after Baal'.

[6]) This has been interpreted as a reference to the licence of a cultic occasion and has been translated 'the widow verily gets drunk' (De Langhe, *op. cit.*, II, p. 516; Engnell, *Studies in Divine Kingship . . .*, pp. 157-158), which is quite a feasible translation, but is, in our opinion, not so suitable in the context as the alternative translation, 'the widow hires a substitute'. In this fiction of a military expedition to 'snatch the bride' every house and class is represented.

ẓbl. ʿršm. yšʾu	Let the sick man [1]) be carried on [2]) his bed,
ʿwr. mẓl. ymẓl	Even the blind man will be excited. [3])
wyṣʾe. trḫ ḥdṯ	And even if the bridegroom has paid the bride-price, [4])
ybʿr. lṯn ʾaṯth	He will endure his ardour to claim his wife, [5])

[1]) Here again there are various translations. Virolleaud and Albright (*BASOR* 63, 1936, p. 29) see a reference to a social upheaval where the nobility, *ẓbl*, do menial service. De Langhe (*op. cit.*, II, pp. 516-517) after Aistleitner takes *ẓbl* to mean 'young husband', a sense suggested by the sexual connotation of זבל in Genesis xxx, 20, the point being that the young husband rises (*yšʾu*, cf. Arabic نشأ) from the bed. If this were the interpretation we should have a reflection of the custom noted in Deuteronomy xx, 7; xxviii, 30 which exempted a newly-wed bridegroom from the military levy. Engnell takes a similar line, *op. cit.*, p. 157. The parallelism with *ʿwr* in the following stichos indicates that *ẓbl* refers to a disabled person, hence we translate 'sick man', following Gordon (*UL*, p. 69) and Ginsberg (*op. cit.*, p. 16). The word is associated with the Arabic زبل, 'to bear'. So, tentatively, Driver, *op. cit.*, p. 31.

[2]) 'Carries beds' (Virolleaud, Albright). We take *yšʾu* as passive imperfect of *nšʾa*, the final *m* in *ʿršm* being the substitute for the preposition *b*, as in Akkadian.

[3]) For *ʿwr mẓl ymẓl* we can see no point in the blind man (*ʿwr*) divining by the stars (מזלות = Zodiac), while Ginsberg's translation 'the blind man blinks with one eye' (*mẓl* = late Hebrew פזל, 'to squint') is simply ludicrous. We formerly suggested that *mẓl* is a cognate of the Arabic مزن, 'to praise, *favere linguis*'. Phonetically this is not impossible, but in view of the difficulty of two phonetic variants from the assumed Arabic cognate in one word we prefer to take *mẓl* as cognate with Arabic مذل, 'to be restless'.

[4]) This is another disputed passage. First the variant verb *ybl*, 'gives', in the parallel passage fixes *yṣʾe* as Causative or Intensive and indicates that either *trḫ* or *ḥdṯ* or both is a predicate. Since this stichos must be taken with what follows, *trḫ* must be connected with the Akkadian *terḫatu* 'brideprice' and mean either 'he who has paid the brideprice' i.e. 'the bridegroom', or simply 'the brideprice'. This leaves the problem of *ḥdṯ*, which has been taken as 'new', the reference being to a new brideprice, which is not easily intelligible. De Langhe (*op. cit.*, II, p. 510) cites the Akkadian *ḫadaštu*, 'marriage', so that it might be possible to take *ḥdṯ* as 'bridegroom'. The meaning of *yṣʾe trḫ*, 'produce the brideprice' seems virtually certain in the light of the variant in l. 189 *ybl trḫ*, which appears as a technical phrase in the Amarna Tablets, happily cited by Gaster, *OLZ* XLII, 1929, col. 275. The clue to the meaning of the passage in our opinion is that *yṣʾe* is the perfect intensive with conditional, or concessive, force. The passage reflects the exemption of a newly-wed bridegroom from the military levy (Deuteronomy xx, 7; xxiv, 5).

[5]) According to Hebrew etymology *ybʿr* could mean either 'he burns (i.e. 'is eager') or 'he drives away'. Gaster (*OLZ* XL, 1939, col. 275), Ginsberg (*op. cit.*, p. 16), and Gordon (*UL*, p. 69) take it in the latter sense, as in Gordon *UH* ʿnt IV, 70, and understand *lṯn* as 'to another', to which they take *lnkr* in parallelism as 'to a stranger'. The verb *bʿr* elsewhere in the Ras Shamra texts means 'to burn' (Gordon *UH* 51, IV, 16). If we translate *ybʿr* as 'he burns' *lṯn* must be translated 'to claim', from *ṯny*, cognate with the Akkadian *šananu*, which is found as a parallel to *ragamu*, 'to announce' or 'stake one's legal claim'. Driver's translation (*op. cit.*, p. 31) 'to lie again with' is awkward in view of the direct object *ʾaṯth*.

lm.nkr mddth	Yea, to acquire [1]) his beloved.
kʾerby tškn.šd	As grass-hoppers which occupy the field,
km.ḫsn.pʾat.mdbr	As locusts the desert marches,
lk.ym.wṯn	Go a day, a second (day),
ṯlṯ.rbʿ ym	A third, a fourth day,
ḫmš.ṯdṯ.ym	A fifth, a sixth day,
mk.špšm bšbʿ	Then with the sun on the seventh day
wtmġy.lʾudm rbt	Thou wilt reach Udm the Great,
wlʾudm.ṯrrt	Yea Udm Abundant in Water. [2])
wgr.ʾan.ʿrm	Then abide, be at ease [3]) at the city,
šrn pdrm	Hold council [4]) at the town.

[1]) Gordon (*JBL* LVII, 1938, p. 409) cites Hosea iii, 2 where נכר is used of the purchase of a wife or concubine, and this meaning of *nkr* would give us a good parallel to *ṯn*, meaning 'to claim'. The root occurs again apparently in 1 Samuel xxiii, 7 where Saul says of David נכר אתו אלהים בידי and the verb is, translated by πέπρακεν in the LXX. On the analogy of the Aramaic זַבֵּן, 'to sell', זְבַן, 'to buy', *nkr* in the present passage might be in the Qal meaning 'to buy'.

[2]) We find the same qualification of a city as *rbt* . . . *ṯrrt* in the case of Krt's city *ḫbr*. Albright has proposed that *ṯrrt* is cognate with the Akkadian *šerru*, 'small' (*BASOR* 63, 1936, p. 30, n. 47). This is feasible and has been accepted by Pedersen (*op. cit.*, p. 90), De Langhe (*op. cit.*, II, p. 147), Gordon (*UL*, p. 69), but is less likely when we consider that the root *ṯrr* is found in the intensive later in the Krt text meaning 'to supply with water' (Gordon *UH* 126, IV, 16), see *ad loc.* Eissfeldt in our opinion is right in associating this word with the Arabic ثَرَّ, 'to be abundant in water' (*ZDMG* XCIV, 1940, pp. 59-85), an apt description of a city in the Near East. For *ʾudm* we have no location to suggest. It is obviously a city and not a region, Biblical Edom, as Virolleaud first thought. De Vaux's identification of the place with the twin-site Ḫirbet ed-Damiyeh in Southeast Galilee, possibly the ʾItmm, ʾIdmm, or ʾAd-ma-am of Egyptian inscriptions of the XVIIIth and XIXth Dynasties (Jirku, *Klio*, Beiheft, 1937, I, 36, XXV, 128; Breasted, *ARE* IV, § 714), and of אֲדָמִי of Joshua xix, 33 ('Αδαμμει of Eusebius *Onomasticon*, ed. Klostermann, p. 30, l. 18) is possible, especially as surface sherds indicate that this site was occupied continuously from c. 3000 to c. 1000 B.C. (A. Saarisalo, 'The Boundary between Issachar and Naphtali', *Finnish Academy of Science Publications* XXI, 3, 1927, pp. 39-41). His other geographic particularisations in the same passage, however, though ingenious, are highly improbable on linguistic grounds and we prefer not to particularise on the matter of *ʾudm* either. De Vaux has now given up his view, *RB* LXIV, 1957, pp. 313-314.

[3]) Reading *ʾan* for *nn* which is generally read here. *nn* suggests the energic ending, which would be proper after the imperative here but not after the perfect *gr* in the parallel passage at l. 212. We take *ʾan* as a verb cognate with Arabic آنَ, 'to go gently, be at ease'. The collocation here of *gr. ʾan* suggests to us that in Judges v. 17 ודן למה יגור אניות may be translated 'And why does Dan abide at ease?' rather than 'Why does Dan remain in ships?', taking the feminine plural adverbially.

[4]) The verb *šrnʾa* in the parallel passage at l. 213 indicates that the *n* in *šrn* is not the energic ending, but a radical letter. This suggests to us a Šafʿel (causative) of a root *rnʾa*, which is unattested elsewhere in Ugaritic, but is possibly cognate with the Syriac ܪܢܐ, 'to consider'.

sʿt.bšdm.ḥṭbt	The wood-cutting women will be rushing [1]) from the open country,
bgrnt.ḥpšt	(Likewise) those who congregate [2]) in the thoroughfare; [3])
sʿt.bnk.šʾebt	The water-drawing women [4]) will be rushing from the well,
bbqr mmlʾat	Even from the spring those who fill (their jars)
dm.ym.wṯn	Tarry a day, a second day,
ṯlṯ.rbʿ.ym	A third, a fourth day,
ḫmš.ṯdṯ.ym	A fifth, a sixth day,
ḫẓk.ʾal.tšʿl qrth	Shoot not thine arrow up at his fortress
ʾabn.ydk mšdpt	Nor thy sling-stone [5]) at his lofty burg. [6])
whn.špšm bšbʿ	Then with the sun [7]) on the seventh day

[1]) The repetition of *sʿt* in the first position in the stichos two lines later indicates that this word is a verb and not a place-name. We take it as a feminine participle, the predicate of the feminine *šʾebt* in the latter case and with *ḥṭbh* (possibly 'its woodcarriers', *ḥṭb* being a broken plural), or rather *ḥṭbt*, 'the women carrying wood'. We suggest that *sʿt* is from a defective verb cognate with the Hebrew סָעָה, cf. רוּחַ סֹעָה, 'rushing wind' (Ps. lv, 9).

[2]) We follow GINSBERG in reading the last letter *t* (𐎚), not *h* (𐎅). The verb, however, is not *ḫpṯ* (Arabic cognate خفث), but *ḥpš*, the Arabic cognate of which is حفش, which means 'to gather, congregate'.

[3]) The meaning 'threshing-floor', which generally attaches to *grn* is secondary. We propose to take the word in its primary sense which according to Arabic analogy means 'a place rubbed clear', hence 'an open space'. We think the word has this sense in the text GORDON *UH* 2 Aqht, V, 6 ff., where it is the scene of justice, and again in 1 Kings xxii, 10, where it is the scene of Ahab's muster and the activity of the prophets on the eve of the expedition against Ramoth Gilead, *v. supra*, p. 107, n. 3 الجارون actually means 'the beaten track', specifically the space outside the city-gate where all tracks converge and which is a public market.

[4]) This is another feminine plural participle. The references throughout this passage are to women (*sʿt*, *ḥpšt*, *šʾebt*, *ḥṭbt*, *mmlʾat*). This reference to the activities of the females may be a means of indicating their age, as among the modern peasants of Palestine, who still refer to a girl approaching puberty as 'a gatherer of wood' (حطّابة) and 'a drawer of water' (مالئة). For a full list of such activities appropriate to various ages, see H. GRANQUIST, 'Marriage Conditions in a Palestinian Village', *Societas Scientiarum Fennica, Commentationes Humanarum Literarum* III, 8, 1931, pp. 35-36.

[5]) Here the parallelism with *ḫẓk* ('thine arrow') demands that *ʾabn ydk* must be taken to mean 'sling-stone'. Slings were still in use at Ugarit in the Late Bronze Age, as we know from the mention of them in an administrative text, GORDON *UH* 321, and from stocks of sling-stones from the palace.

[6]) The word *mšdpt*, in parallelism with *qrt*, fortress, must have a similar meaning. We suggest a connection with the Arabic verb شدف, 'to be tall'.

[7]) In *špšm* we have another case of the use of *m* final as a substitute for the preposition. The phrase means 'with the sun' and on the evidence of the Krt text apparently may mean either 'at sunrise' or 'at sunset'.

wl.yšn.pbl mlk	*Pbl* [1]) the king will not (be able to) sleep [2])
lqr.ṯ'egt.'ebrh	For the rumble of the bellowing of his bull,
lql.nhqt.ḥmrh	For the sound of the braying of his ass,
lg'ṭ.'alp.ḥrṯ	For the lowing of his ploughing-ox,
ẓġt klb.ṣpr	For the howling of his starving hound. [3])
wyl'ak ml'akm.lk	And he will send messengers to thee,
'm.krt.mswnh	Even to (thee) Krt to the camp, [4])
tḥm.pbl.mlk	The word of *Pbl* the king:
qḥ.ksp.wyrq	"Take silver and yellow metal, [5])
ḥrṣ yd.mqmh	Gold in token of her value, [6])
w'bd.'lm ṯlṯ.sswm	And a perpetual henchman, three horses,
mrkbt btrbṣ.bn.'amt	A chariot with yoke-fellows well-matched. [7])

---

[1]) We regard *pbl* not as a real proper name but as an onomatopoeic name as the Hebrew בּבל in the popular etymology of Genesis xi, 7, or the Greek βαρβαρος. The reference is to the non-Semitic character of the king in the Krt text, which we regard as commemorating a decisive phase in the amalgamation of Semite and Hurrian in North Syria which documentary and material evidence from the various archaeological sites in Syria clearly attest in the Middle and Late Bronze Ages.

[2]) *l* may be the enclitic emphasizing the verb *yšn*, which Pedersen (*op. cit.*, p. 94) takes as cognate with the Akkadian *šananu* which occurs as a synonym of *šmr* in the Taanach Tablets. The meaning would then be 'pay attention'. We prefer to take *l* as the negative particle and *yšn* as cognate with the Hebrew ישן, 'to sleep'. The various noises of the domestic animals, of course, indicate hunger, as a result of the siege of Udm, cf. Job vi, 5. 'Doth the wild ass bray when he hath grass or loweth the ox over his fodder?'

[3]) So Driver (*op. cit.*, p. 150), who suggests the Arabic cognate صَفِرَ, 'to be empty'. Other possible cognates are the Arabic صَفَرَ, 'to whistle' i.e. 'whine' (Driver, *op. cit.*, *ibidem*), or أَصْفَرُ, 'tawny', lit. 'yellow'.

[4]) This is the locative noun from a verb *swn*, cognate with the Arabic صون, 'to surround'.

[5]) The metre demands that *yrq*, 'pale, yellow', be taken as an absolute, and not as a construct before *ḥrṣ*, a synonym of Hebrew חרוץ.

[6]) Gordon (*UL*, p. 70) suggests for *yd mqmh* the meaning 'a share of her estate'. This meaning of *yd* is found in Genesis xlvii, 24 and 2 Samuel xix, 44, and 2 Kings xi, 7, but Gordon does not particularise on his interpretation of *mqmh*. We cite the Arabic مقام, meaning 'value', and see a reference to a ransom-price. For *yd* we propose the meaning 'in token of', *yd* having this sense in Hebrew, where we read that Absalom set up a יד in the King's Dale at Jerusalem, this being a token of his son, whom, we believe, he would have sacrificed there to 'Molech' if he had not been childless.

[7]) While admitting that *bn 'amt* may be a term of deferential address, cf. Psalm lxxxvi, 16. בן אמתך // עבדך, we suggest that *bn 'amt* denotes the horses. We take *'amt* as a cognate of the Arabic root أَمَّ, 'to agree with'. The noun أُمَّةٌ denotes a regular measure e.g. طول الأمّة 'tallness of stature', مُؤَمٌّ, 'conforming to the

qḥ.krt.šlmm šlmm	Take, Krt, peace-offerings in peace,
wng.mlk.lbty	And depart, [1] O king, from my house,
rḥq.krt.lḥẓry	Withdraw far, O Krt, from my court.
ʾal.tṣr ʾudm.rbt	Beset not Udm the Great,
wʾudm ṯrrt	Even Udm Abundant in Water.
ʾudm.ytnt.ʾel	Udm is the gift of El,
wʾušn.ʾab.ʾadm	The present of the Father of Men."
wṯṯb mlʾakm lh	Then send the messengers back to him (saying):
lm.ʾank.ksp.wyrq	"For what purpose are silver and electrum to me,
ḫrṣ yd.mqmh	Gold in token of her value,
wʿbd.ʿlm.ṯlṯ sswm	And a perpetual henchman, three horses,
mrkbt btrbṣt.bn ʾamt	A chariot with yoke-fellows well-matched?
pd.ʾen.bbty.ttn	Nay, but what I have not in my house do thou give,
tn.ly.mṯt.ḥry	Give me the damsel Ḥry,
nʿmt.špḥ.bkrk	The fair, thy first-begotten,
dknʿm .ʿnt.nʿmh	Whose grace is as the grace of Anat,
km.tsm.ʿṯtrt.ts(m)h	Whose beauty [2] is as the beauty of Aṯtarat,
dʿqh.ʾeb.ʾeqnʾe	Whose eye-balls [3] are as the sheen of lapis-lazuli, [4]
ʿp(ʿp)h.sp.ṯrml	Whose eye-lids are bowls of carnelian. [5]
tḥgrn ( ) b-dm	She is girded with.....
ʾašlw.bṣp.ʿnh	I shall repose in the clear glance [6] of her eyes,
dbḥlmy.ʾel.ytn	For in my dream El has granted,
bẓrty.ʾab.ʾadm	In my vision the Father of Men,
wld.špḥ.lkrt	Offspring shall be born [7] to Krt,
wġlm.lʿbd.ʾel	A lad to the servant of El."

---

mean'. We propose to translate *bn ʾamt* as 'well-matched', an important factor in the swift manoeuvres of chariot warfare. This meaning would best accord with our explanation of *trbṣ* as 'yoke-team', cf. Arabic ربق, 'to tie by the neck'. For the dialectic shift of the consonant *ṣ* to *q* cf. ארץ / ארק.

1) *ng* is the imperative of *ngy*, cognate with the Arabic نجا, 'to escape.'

2) This word is from the root *ysm*, the participle of which is found in parallelism with *nʿm* in the text GORDON *UH* 52. The Arabic cognate is وسم, 'to bear the impress' (usually of beauty).

3) The meaning of 'eyeball' for *ʿq* is suggested by the parallelism with *ʿpʿp*, 'eyelids' (Hebrew עפעפים) in the following stichos. GINSBERG (*op. cit.*, p. 17) cites Psalm vi, 8 where עיני is found in parallelism with עתקה, which he supposes to be an error of metathesis for עקת. The Greek translators and Jerome read the Massoretic text but read עתקתי as the 1st person singular of the verb עתק. GINSBERG's solution seems correct.

4) *ʾeb ʾeqnʾe*, lit. 'flower of lapis lazuli'.

5) *sp ṯrml* might mean either 'bowls of carnelian', which were so finely hollowed out as to be translucent, or 'gleam of carnelian', in which case *ʿpʿp* could not mean eyelids but pupils. The word *ṯrml*, like other names of precious stones and metals from the Anatolian mountains, is non-Semitic.

6) *ṣp* here is probably cognate with the Arabic صفى, 'to be clear'.

7) We follow PEDERSEN (*op. cit.*, p. 103) in taking *wld* as a prophetic perfect, passive.

The text goes on in epic style to describe in almost identical terms how Krt carried out the directions of El. He emerges from his ritual seclusion and, freed from this restraint, he provisions his retinue, which he heads on his journey with military show. His journey to the home of the bride, however, is interrupted by a visit to the shrine of Aṯerat. Here he makes a vow to the goddess: [1])

ʾeʾeṯt.ʾaṯrt.ṣrm	'By the presence [2]) of Aṯerat of Tyre, [3])
wʾelt.ṣdynm	Even the Goddess of Sidon,
hm.ḥry.bty.ʾeqḥ	If I take Ḥry into my house,
ʾašʿrb.ġlmt.ḥẓry	If I bring the damsel into my court,
ṯnh.kspm.ʾatn	Two-thirds of her will I give in silver,
wṯlṯth.ḥrṣm	Yea, a third in gold.' [4])

This vow is rather important, since Krt apparently forgot it, *hinc illae lacrimae.*

Eventually, after a seemly hesitancy on the part of her father the

---

[1]) Gordon *UH* krt, 201-206.

[2]) *ʾeṯt*, precative perfect of a verb medial *y* ,cognate with Hebrew יֵשׁ and Aramaic אִית, with the interjection *ʾe*, cf. Arabic إِيا. The verb elsewhere in the Ras Shamra texts means 'existence' rather than, but not excluding, the idea of 'presence'. Ugaritic seems to have had a verb *ʾeṯ*, probably medial *y*, as is indicated in a passage in a letter of a King of Ugarit to his mother (*PRU* II, 13, 13-14, Gordon *UM*, 117, rev. 14-15), where in a context referring to a vow it is said *mlk bṯy ndr ʾeṯt*, 'the King is in the condition for which you made a vow'. The verb may be derived from the formula of the vow 'By the presence of' (*ʾeʾeṯ*), as in the present passage.

[3]) *ṣrm* and *ṣdynm* are usually taken as 'of the Tyrians' and 'of the Sidonians', and this has been the basis of De Langhe's reckoning of the location of Udm which he takes to be located four days march beyond the district of Tyre and Sidon. Of such geographic particularisations we are very doubtful (*v. supra*, p. 124). We formerly proposed to take *ṣrm* and *ṣdynm* as common nouns, *ṣrm* being cognate with the Arabic صُرَّة, 'a sealed bag of money' and *ṣdynm* with the Arabic صدى (IV), 'to return, re-echo', hence 'oracular responses'. Ancient shrines were used for the deposit of money, as, for instance, the temple of Baal at Shechem, where Abimelech, the son of Gideon, got the money to hire his 'vain and light fellows' (Judges ix, 4). In view of the close association of Ugarit and Beirut attested in a political tablet from the archives of Ras Shamra in the 14th c. from the King of Beirut to his son the governor of Ugarit (Virolleaud, *Syria* XXI, 1940, pp. 214-250), and a deed of redemption from the palace archives (Virolleaud, *PRU* II, 6), the Krt text may refer to the Southern Lebanon, thus making the reference to the goddess of Tyre and Sidon more probable.

[4]) We have already expressed a doubt as to whether this was in the nature of an endowment or a deposit of the bride-price (*The Krt Text in the Literature of Ras Shamra*, p. 43). In virtue of the anger of Aṯerat at Krt's breach of vow we now conclude that the vow must have concerned an endowment to the shrine.

King of Udm, the damsel is won, and to the great sorrow of her people leaves her old home to become Krt's queen.

The king's wedding is blessed of the gods. They are depicted as feasting in Krt's palace and it falls to El to bless the union: [1])

ks.y'eḫd (b)yd	He took a cup in his hand,
krpn.bm (ymn)	Even a flagon in his (right hand);
brkm ybrk ( )	A double blessing he gave,
ybrk 'el.krt	So El blessed Krt,
( ) *m.n'mn ġlm 'el*	( ) the Gracious One, the Lad of El.
'a(ṯt tq)ḥ.ykrt	'The wife thou takest, O Krt,
'aṯt tqḥ btk	The wife thou takest into thy house,
ġlmt tš'rb ḥẓrk	The damsel thou bringest into thy court,
tld.šb' bnm lk	Will bear thee seven sons,
wṯmn tṯtmnm lk	Yea, eight times will she bear unto thee.
tld.yṣb.ġlm	She will bear the lad *Yṣb*
ynq ḥlb 'a(ṯ)rt	Who sucks the milk of Aṯerat,
mṣṣ ṯd btlt ('nt)	Who sucks the breasts of the Virgin (Anat).' [2])

So El further wishes: [3])

m'ed.rm (krt)	'Greatly exalted be [4]) Krt
btk.rp'e.'ar(ṣ)	Among the congregation [5]) of the land,
bpḫr.qbṣ.dtn	In the assembly of the clan of Dtn.' [6])

1) Gordon *UH* 128, II, 16-27.

2) This conception is expressed in the ivory relief from the royal bed from the palace of Ugarit, cf. the Egyptian sculpture of Seti I sucking the breast of a goddess, Pritchard, *ANEP*, pl. 422. The Egyptian analogy suggests that this was related either to the birth of a prince or the accession of a king, E. Kutsch, *Salbung als Rechtsakt im Alten Testament und im Alten Orient*, *BZAW* LXXXVII, 1963, pp. 49-50.

3) Gordon *UH* 128, III, 2-4/13-15.

4) This is another instance of the precative perfect.

5) We must take *rp'e* as parallel to *pḫr* or *qbṣ*, cf. Arabic رفاء, 'union', cited by Driver (*CML*, p. 155 n.), after Ginsberg, who associates *rp'e* with رفأ, 'to darn', hence, 'to join' (*LKK*, pp. 23, 41). It is tempting to translate *rp'e 'arṣ* as 'dispensers of fertility' (*v. supra*, p. 120 ff.), especially after the mention of the King's virility, which was convincing evidence that he was a worthy dispenser of fertility to the people, a conception common among modern primitives in Africa, where drought and famine are associated with the waning virility of the paramount chief. The provision of the young Shunamite for the aged David (1 Kings i, 1-4) may reflect the same conception, and Absalom in appropriating his father's harem may have been publicly declaring his physical fitness to discharge the office of King according to primitive expectations. Notwithstanding, the parallelism which we have noted suggests that *rp'e* in this case means 'congregation'.

6) *Dtn* is found in the administrative texts Gordon *UH* 400, II, 9, where *bn dtn* are equestrian feudatories, *mrynm*, and *ibidem*, VI, 28, where they are priests, *khnm*. In both cases they were rated higher for state payment than any other class or family except *bn ṯ'*. *Dtn* may be the family of an older royal house with priestly functions, specifically that of agrarian ritual.

In the blessing of El it is declared that the youngest of Krt's progeny should have the birthright, which suggests to A. VAN SELMS that the poem may have been written to legitimize the succession through Krt's youngest daughter. [1]) In the text as it has been recovered, however, this theme is not followed out. [2]) With typical epic ellipsis the family of Krt is described, seven sons to the king, seven daughters to the queen. [3])

All is not well, however, and the king falls sick. He has forgotten his vow to Aṯerat, and now the goddess takes vengeance. Here, unfortunately, the text is fragmentary, but we do know that in the absence of the king his queen presides over a feast in the palace to which she calls 'his seventy bulls, yea eighty gazelles'.

It is not easy to determine the significance of this apparently domestic episode, or to know who the 'bulls' and 'gazelles' were. Perhaps they were barons of the realm, as Ginsberg proposes, translating 'barons' and 'peers', citing the analogy of Hebr. אילים, 'chiefs,' lit. 'rams' (Exodus xv, 15) and עתּוּדים, lit. 'he-goats,' but used of dignitaries (Isaiah xiv, 9) [4]). But they were more likely priests. It may be that they represented Baal, whose cult animal was the bull, and Rešef, who is represented with a head-dress mounted with gazelle-horns. [5]) It may well be that the presence of the votaries

---

[1]) A. VAN SELMS, *Marriage and Family Life in Ugaritic Literature*, 1954, p. 16 n.

[2]) The text as it stands certainly ends with a signature colophon which seems to mark the end. On the other hand, there are such colophons in the Baal cycle which do not mark the end of the text, so that the Krt text may after all be only a fragment. Certainly we should expect that such a long text in epic style should lead up to some dramatic catastrophe, which is lacking in our text.

[3]) The association of sons with the king and daughters with the queen is simply a literary convention, cf. GORDON *UH* 51, VI, 47 ff.,

špq ʾelm kṛm yn
špq ʾelht ḫprt yn
špq ʾelm ʾalpm yn
špq ʾelht ʾarḫt yn . . .

[4]) GINSBERG, 'The Legend of King Keret', *BASOR*, Supplementary Series, Nos. 2-3, 1946. If this is so there may be a reference to such an order in 2 Samuel i, 19 in צבי ישׂראל if the text is correct. In this case the 'bulls' would denote the substantial, but not always active, men of property and the 'gazelles' the active younger men.

[5]) He is so represented in Egyptian sculpture of the XIXth Dynasty, J. LEIBOVITCH, *ASAE* XLVIII, 1948, pp. 435 ff., fig. 1. The god Mekal of Bethshan, who is depicted on the celebrated relief, is also so represented, A. ROWE, *The Topography and History of Bethshan*, 1930, Pl. xxxiii. This deity is doubtless Rešef, appropriately worshipped at fever-ridden Bethshan. This data makes GORDON's translation of רשף צפרם as 'Reshef of the Bucks' in the inscription of Azitawwad most feasible, C. H. GORDON, 'Azitawadd's Phoenician Inscription', *JNES* VIII, 1949, pp. 110, 115.

of the vital Baal and of Rešef the god of pestilence indicated some ritual drama in connection with the restoration of the king to health. [1]) We may indeed visualize such a scene as the classic encounter on Carmel between Elijah and the prophets of Baal in the days of Ahab. [2])

The text here is much mutilated, most unfortunately, since the crisis between life and death in the case of the king could not fail to have contained matter of vital interest for social anthropology. As it is, isolated words such as 'dispenser of fertility' (*rp'e*) and phrases such as

'Krt will reach the sunset,
Even our lord the sundown' [3])

are suggestive in view of the hypothesis of divine kingship. The latter couplet recalls the Egyptian belief that immortality awaited the king 'in the West, in the abode to the gods', a hope held out by the Egyptian envoy Wenamon to Zakarbaal the king of Byblos. [4]) If we could press the Egyptian analogy this would be the first emergence in Canaan of the belief in personal immortality. There is other evidence from the texts, however, that the contrary view prevailed. [5])

The text (Gordon *UH* 125) resumes with the mourning of one of Krt's family in somewhat extravagant terms:

tbkyk.'ab.ǵr.bʿl	'The mountain of Baal, O father, will weep for thee,
ṣpn.ḥlm.qdš	Even Sapon the holy precinct;
'any.ḥlm.'adr	The awful precinct bemoans (thee),
ḥl rḥb.mknpt.	The precinct broad of span.
'ap (k)rt.bnm.'el	Is Krt the son of El,
špḥ.lṭpn.wqdš	The offspring of the Kindly One and the Holy?' [6])
....	....

---

[1]) Virolleaud suggests that there may be a reference to priests dressed for a ritual in animal masks, and cites seals from Ras Shamra with such a design, 'Le Mariage du Roi Kéret (III K)', *Syria* XXIII, 1942-43, p. 161, n. 2, cf. Schaeffer, *The Cuneiform Texts of Ras Shamra-Ugarit*, 1939, Pl. X, 2. A closer analogy is a bronze plaque from Mesopotamia depicting an actual exorcism from a sick man by priests in animal masks attendant on two priests dressed in skins of fish, obviously the priests of Ea, the god of the waters and sorcery. The final scene in this plaque depicts the evil spirit or demon of sickness being carried off in the boat of Ea, G. Contenau, *La magie chez les Assyriens et les Babyloniens*, 1947, pl. 8, pp. 228-30.

[2]) 1 Kings xviii, 19 ff.

[3]) Gordon *UH* 128, V. 19-20, *ʿrb špš lymǵ krt*
ṣb'e'a špš bʿlny

[4]) Golenischeff Papyrus, 59-60, H. Gressmann, *Altorientalische Texte und Bilder zum Alten Testament*, 1909, p. 229.

[5]) *v. supra*, p. 113.

[6]) Gordon *UH* 125, 6-11.

'ekm.yrgm.bn 'el krt	How say they Krt is the son of El,
špḥ.lṭpn.wqdš	The offspring of the Kindly One and the Holy?
'u'elm.tmtn	Or do gods die,
špḥ.lṭpn.lyḥ	The offspring of the Kindly One not live?' [1]

The mourning for the sick king is taken up by his youngest daughter 'the Eighth', who had already been singled out for pre-eminence in the family of Krt. Beyond mourning for her father, however, she plays no rôle in the text as that is extant, a fact which may indicate that the Krt text is but a fragment of a much larger whole.

In the text GORDON *UH* 126 the theme is the anticipated revival of Krt. According to the primitive conception the vitality of the king was related to the fertility of nature and so we learn of the dire consequences of the king's sickness: [2]

nš'u r'eš ḥrṯm	The ploughmen have raised their heads,
lẓr ( )db dgn	After [3] (those who pre)pare the corn.
kly lḥm.(b)dnhm	Spent was the bread in their jars.
kly yn.bḥmthm	Spent was the wine in their bottles.
k(l)y šmn bq( )	Spent was the oil in their cruses.
bt krt.t ( )	To the house of Krt they c(ome).

In this passage, which is unfortunately mutilated, the king is regarded apparently as the intermediary between god and man. A rite of imitative magic ensues, wherein one *'elš* [4] and his two wives, all cultic functionaries, [5] are dispatched up to the roof to pour out

---

[1] *Ibidem*, 20-23.

[2] GORDON *UH* 126, III, 12-17.

[3] *lẓr*, for *lẓhr*, 'to the back', may be literal here. Not only was the food supply short but the ploughmen are so anxious that they cannot keep their heads down as they plough, but keep glancing anxiously after those who sow the corn apprehensive lest the seed should be insufficient. In many districts in Syria and Palestine the corn is first sown and then ploughed in, an operation which has the same effect as harrowing in the west.

[4] We have connected *'elš* with the Arabic لسّ, meaning in the IVth form 'to sprout'. *'elš* may be a verbal noun of the IVth form of a verb medial *w* or *y*, a byform of the Arabic root. Alternatively the name may be connected with ألس, 'to be mad', and refer to the propensity to frenzy which characterized such cultic officials as the 'prophets' of Baal, who engage in the rain-inducing rites, on Carmel (1 Kings xviii).

[5] *ngr 'el*, the title of *'elš*, might mean 'waterpouring deity', though *'el* and the feminine form *'elht* may mean those attached to the cult. A parallel usage may be the term *'elm* in the late Phoenician inscription from Ma'sub applied to human agents, actually envoys of the goddess Mlk-Astarte, G. A. COOKE, *NSI* 10, pp. 48 ff.

water. [1]) The text, however, does not inform us of the result of this rite.

Eventually El, the doyen of the pantheon, undertakes the healing of the sick king. He determines to resort to magic and moulds an image of 'goodly dung' (*nʿm rṯ*) into which the sickness of the king is to be transferred. This treatment of illness was well known in Mesopotamia, though the disease was usually transferred to an animal. It is, of course, the idea behind the scapegoat, on which the ritual and moral disabilities of Israel were concentrated. The image in question is apparently manipulated by a female called *Šʿtqt* ('May she cause to pass over') [2]) and in the sequel (Gordon *UH* 127) we learn that the treatment was successful.

Meanwhile, Krt's eldest son Yṣb, apparently unaware of his father's recovery, deems the time ripe to realize his ambitions and addresses his father: [3])

ʾeštm(ʿ) wtqǵ (ʾudn)	'Hear and may thine ear be alert!
(kǵẓ ǵẓm) tdbr.	By slow degrees thou art growing old,
w(ǵ)rm (ṯṯwy)	And in the sepulchral cave thou wilt abide.
šqlt.bǵlt.ydk	Thou hast let thy hands fall into error.
ltdn.dn.almnt	Thou dost not uphold the case of the widow,
lṯṯpṭ.ṯpṭ.qṣr npš	Nor decide the suit of the oppressed.
km.ʾaḫt.ʿrš.mdw	Sickness is as thy bedfellow,
ʾanšt.ʿrš.ẓbln	Disease as thy concubine. [4])
rd.lmlk.ʾamlk	Descend from thy rule that I may become king,
ldrktk.ʾaṯbnn	From thy government that I may be enthroned.'

Yṣb, however, has misjudged the state of his father's health, and the latter retaliates with a hearty curse on this Canaanite Absalom: [5])

yṯbr ḥrn.ybn	'May Horon break, O son,
yṯbr.ḥrn rʾešk	May Horon break thy head,
ʿṯtrt.šm.bʿl qdqdk	Even Aṯtarat the Name-of-Baal thy pate!
tqln.bgbl šntk	Mayst thou fall in the exuberance of thy years!
bḫpnk wtʿn	Even in the fulness (of thy strength) and be troubled.'

[1]) The root *ngr* is found also in Hebrew in the Hiphil. Water-pouring as a rite of imitative magic on the eve of the 'early rains' was a feature of the Hebrew New Year Festival. Talmud B., *Rosh hash-shanah* 16a.

[2]) Alternatively 'She who prolongs (life)' (Driver, *op. cit.*, p. 147, Aistleitner, *Die mythologischen und kultischen Texte aus Ras Schamra*, 1959, p. 103).

[3]) Gordon *UH* 127, 29-38. For philological notes of this and the following passage see our work *The Krt Text in the Literature of Ras Shamra*, 1955, pp. 55-59.

[4]) Cf. Job xvii, 14, 'I have said to corruption, thou art my father; to the worm, thou art my mother, yea, my sister'.

[5]) Gordon *UH* 127, 54-58.

Here the text breaks off and bears the signature of a scribe. This last fact may indicate that this was the end of the text, though it need not signify this, since other texts bear such colophons, which do indeed end the tablet but not the narrative, e.g. GORDON *UH* 62, 53-57.

Such then is the Krt text. It is not, as the first commentators thought, a historical text bearing directly upon the first stages of the Hebrew penetration of Palestine. It has been termed an epic, and the style of the text is undoubtedly the epic style. The poem can only be admitted into this category, however, if we assume that what is extant is but a fragment of a much larger whole, which may well be the case. That, however, is a matter of conjecture. What is certain, however, is that the Krt text and the Aqht text also are documents of first grade importance for the study of Canaanite institutions such as the kingship in its various aspects, and of social practices and values in general. Indeed it is our opinion that the need to express and conserve those values conditioned the preservation of these texts, if it did not occasion their origin.

CHAPTER IV

THE RELIGION OF CANAAN

i. THE GODS.

The material evidence for the religious situation in Canaan before the Hebrew settlement cannot be said to be abundant or impressive. Not until recently was there any documentary evidence except from a later period. Of this the most direct objective testimony is the Phoenician inscriptions, but few of these antedate the latter half of the first millennium. The Old Testament has many references to the religion of Canaan, but is avowedly inimical to such beliefs and practices. The work of Lucian of Samosata on the cult of the Syrian goddess at Hierapolis (Bambyce, modern Membij) dates from the middle of the 2nd century A.D. and relates to little more than the Tammuz-Adonis cult, and Philo of Byblos (fl. 100 A.D.), though claiming the authority of Sanchuniathon, reputed to have flourished at the time of the Trojan War, handled his source rather tendentiously, reflecting Epicurean ideas current in his own time. Now, however, our knowledge of the religion of Canaan has vastly increased as the result of archaeological research. The material evidence, particularly from Palestine, is still comparatively scanty, but such matter as has come to light may be better appraised in the light of such documentary evidence as the Ras Shamra Texts and the Egyptian Execration Texts, neither indeed from Palestine, but both intimately connected with the land and its culture.

From the study of the Execration Texts it is possible to trace the social and religious development of the Amorites [1]) in Palestine and Southern Syria from a stage when they retained a political organization and religion characteristic of a tribal state to the stage when they had finally settled down to the sedentary life of farmers. In the Execration Texts, which date from c. 1850 to 1800 B.C. [2]) the religion of the people is indicated by the theophoric names of the chiefs,

---

[1]) The personnel of the texts is indicated by the similarity of their names to those of the First Amorite Dynasty of Babylon.

[2]) There are two sets of such texts. The first, on fragments of pottery, from Luxor, were published by KURT SETHE ('Die Ächtung feindlicher Fürsten,

several of whom are found in the one locality. [1]) The common type of name comprises the name of the deity and a predicate, such as *Ḥoronabi*, 'Horon is my father', or a predicate and a kin-name in place of a proper name, such as *Ḫalubariḫ*, 'the Uncle (maternal) is noble' and *Ammuyakin*, 'the Uncle establishes'. Here the prevailing conception of the deity as a kinsman is noteworthy. This reflects tribal conditions, where social relations are of paramount importance and religion is essentially moral. Here we recognize the distinctive feature of Hebrew religion and the genesis of the social morality upheld by the Prophets. In the texts published by POSENER, as distinct from those of SETHE, the kinship conception of deity is less prominent and now the deity Hadad makes his appearance in the theophoric names. Hadad is, of course, the deity who became Baal *par excellence* in Canaan (v. supra, p. 78), but there is no reason to suppose that he was originally other than the god manifest in the violent rain- and thunder-storms of autumn and late winter. This is the rôle he seems to play in the Execration Texts, as indeed also in the Ras Shamra myth of the conflict with the Unruly Waters. It was only later that he was identified with the vegetation which was stimulated by the winter rains and he became a dying and rising god, as in the Ras Shamra myth of his conflict with Mot. The Hadad-theophorics in the Execration Texts [2]) do not suggest that the conception of Hadad had developed beyond that of the Amorite storm-god, and the total absence in these texts of any female deity indicates surely that the familiar fertility-cult of Canaan was not yet fully developed.

With the Ras Shamra Texts we pass from the 19th or 18th century to the 14th or 13th. The documents hẹre vary in date and significance and fall into four categories. There are pure myths, the protagonists of which are deities. Other texts, such as the Aqht and Krt texts, concern the fortunes of human beings but reflect their attitude to

---

Völker, und Dinge auf altägyptischen Tongefässscherben des Mittleren Reiches', *Abhandlungen der preussischen Akademie der Wissenschaft, Phil.-Hist. Klasse*, 1926). The second are on figurines from Saqqara, and were published by G. POSENER (*Princes et Pays d'Asie et de Nubie, textes sur des figurines d'envoûtement du Moyen Empire*, 1940). Palaeographical considerations and the archaeological context of the texts at Saqqara led POSENER to conclude that they dated c. 1800 B.C. SETHE's texts, first dated much earlier, were shown in the light of POSENER's texts to date about a generation earlier.

[1]) Askalon had three chiefs and Jerusalem two.

[2]) *Itnhddw*, ('Hadad gives'), *Ibshddw*, ('Hadad fattens'), *Iṯphddw*, ('Hadad increases' or 'Hadad gathers'), *Ṯblhddw*, ('Hadad beats the drum'), *Yndmhddw*, ('Hadad marks the seasons'), and *Rwrhddw*, ('Hadad moistens').

the gods. Both of these categories are of uncertain date though the *terminus ante quem* can be certainly fixed, at least for the Baal-Mot cycle and the Krt text, towards the middle of the 14th century according to colophons to certain tablets. There are, however, no primitive crudities in the texts, which have been elaborated over a considerable period. Then there are theophoric names of people living at Ugarit in the 14th or 13th centuries, and, fourthly, offering-lists which reflect the latest stages of religious development at Ugarit as distinct from the myths, which reflect the heroic past. We propose to treat the subject of the deities of Canaan and their cults as far as possible chronologically, though in an area like Syria and Palestine, which was populated by repeated irruptions from the desert, we cannot posit an absolute evolutionary process.

In the myths the senior god of the Ugaritic pantheon was El. This appears in the texts as the proper name of a particular deity, and is not merely a common noun for the divine. This is apparent from the mythological texts and from the offering-lists, where El is named with his appropriate offering together with the other deities of Ugarit. [1])

In the myths there are certain traces of a complex situation, with an earlier and a later pantheon, [2]) not, indeed, always quite distinct, since there was often a community of function, which led to assimilation as well as conflict. The element of conflict between El and Baal has, we think, been greatly over-emphasized by Nielsen, Kapelrud, Cassuto, and Pope. There is admittedly a certain amount of evidence in the texts for such a conflict. In the preliminary to the conflict between Baal and Sea, for instance, El seems to support Sea rather than Baal, while in the text Gordon *UH* 75 he impregnates the female who is to give birth to the monsters by which Baal is to be lured to his downfall. Elsewhere in the texts, however, El shows no antipathy to Baal, and, in fact, apprehending the news of Baal's revival, El resigns himself gladly to *otium cum dignitate*. Pope, much influenced by the theme of divine conflict in Philo's account of Phoenician religion, and by the Hurrian myth of Kumarbi, who

---

[1]) Gordon *UH* 1; 3.

[2]) It would be more accurate to speak of a primitive and developed stratum of religion, since the former may have been introduced by invaders c. 2000 B.C. represented by the chiefs named in the Execration Texts, but socially and culturally more primitive, hence 'earlier' than the sedentary population of Ugarit, who had a temple to Baal by that date.

deposed his father and was himself deposed, [1]) has recently, after CASSUTO, [2]) suggested on the basis of certain avowedly obscure and fragmentary texts in the Baal-myth (GORDON *UH* ʿnt, pl. x, IV, V) that the Ras Shamra texts dealt with this theme in greater fulness, of which the extant texts give only hints and reflections. [3]) This is possible, but in this case we must suppose that *all* the speculative myths of Ras Shamra have been lost. The Baal myths are patently functional and quite different in character from the Hurrian myth which CASSUTO and POPE cite. The offering-lists and the legends of Krt and Aqht show distinctly that El, though admittedly not so active as Baal in the fertility-cult, was the paramount authority in social affairs. We are in complete agreement with W. SCHMIDT [3]) in regarding the relationship between El and Baal as one of peaceful coexistence, Baal sustaining in conflict with the forces of chaos and sterility what had been created by El. Though El is permanently King among the gods, the manifestation of Baal as King and the declaration of Aṯerat (GORDON *UH* 51, IV, 43), 'Our King is Baal the Mighty', far from implying a defection from El, visualizes the triumph of El's order through Baal. If not so active in the myths of the fertility-cult, El is still the final authority. His royal status, unlike that of Baal was never menaced nor eclipsed. As W. SCHMIDT has so clearly pointed out, the Kingship of El was static while that of Baal was dynamic. Here we have an attempt to express the paradox of the omnipotence of God and the obvious fact of the real menace of evil and chaos in the world. It is not the statement of the theological proposition of the sovereignty of God which gives men assurance in the vicissitudes of life, but the knowledge that their God has engaged the forces of death and dissolution and has passed from conflict to victory.

El is signalized by various titles. He is termed *ʾab šnm*. This is generally taken as 'the Father of Years', which, if correct, would suggest 'the Ancient of Days' of Daniel vii, 13. DUSSAUD [5]) would explain the title as referring to the function of El in regulating the seasons. If *šnm* means 'years' this is possible. DUSSAUD suggests

---

[1]) A. GOETZE, *Ancient Near Eastern Texts* . . . (ed. PRITCHARD), 1950, pp. 120 ff.

[2]) U. CASSUTO, האלה ענת, 1950, pp. 42 ff.

[3]) M. H. POPE, *El in the Ugaritic Texts*, 1955, pp. 30 ff., 93 ff.

[4]) W. SCHMIDT, Königtum Gottes in Ugarit und Israel, *BZAW* 80, 1961, pp. 52-54.

[5]) DUSSAUD, *RHR* CIV, 1931, p. 358.

that in this capacity El is a solar deity. NIELSEN, on the other hand, regards El not as a solar, but as a lunar, deity, [1]) and it is just as likely that the moon should regulate the seasons as the sun. [2]) The plural of the Ugaritic word for year, however, is invariably *šnt* and not *šnm*, so that it may well be that *šnm* in the phrase *'ab šnm* has a different significance. POPE, though pointing out that in Hebrew the word for 'years' has both the masculine and the feminine forms, suggests that *šnm* may be the masculine plural participle from a root *šny*, cognate with the Arabic سنى, 'to be exalted'. [3]) The title *'ab šnm*, then, would refer to El's status as the father of the divine family, to which there is frequent reference elsewhere in the Ras Shamra texts. This is a most feasible suggestion, which we provisionally accept.

El is also entitled *mlk*, 'king', a title which is applied to deities in general, and to Jahweh in the Old Testament. [4]) The title may originally indicate 'possession', if we press the etymology of the Arabic cognate ملك, and thus express the relation between the god and his worshippers as master and slaves. On the other hand, the term in its actual context expresses regular government, order as against disorder, and signifies the supremacy of El among the various gods of Ras Shamra.

Matters affecting the cosmic order, the question of a palace for Yamm or Baal or the substitution of Aṯtar for Baal as the chief power of fertility, are referred to the final authority of El, who is approached in these matters with deference in his remote palace, as for instance by the Mother-goddess, his consort Aṯerat: [5])

'edk.lttn.pnm	Then indeed she sets her face
'm.'el.mbk.nhrm	Towards El at the well-head of the two streams,
qrb.'apq.thmtm	In the midst of the source of the two deeps.

---

[1]) NIELSEN, *op. cit.*, pp. 27 ff.

[2]) In the Babylonian myth *enuma eliš* the moon-god is assigned the function of 'determining days', and the Semites without exception had, as the Arabs still have, not a solar, but a lunar, year.

[3]) POPE, *op. cit.*, p. 33. POPE, as D. WINTON THOMAS, but independently, finds this root in Hebrew in Proverbs xxiv, 21 where שׁוֹנִים in this sense is an apt parallel to 'the Lord and the King' (D. WINTON THOMAS, *ZAW* LII, 1934, pp. 236-238). The conventional translation of *šnm* as 'years' is suspected also by EISSFELDT, who proposed that *šnm* is from the root *šny*, 'to change', *'ab šnm* meaning 'Father of Mortals', *El im Ugaritischen Pantheon*, 1951, p. 31, n. The Ugaritic verb for 'change', however, is not *šny*, but *ṯny*.

[4]) EISSFELDT, '*Jahweh* als König', *ZAW* XLVI, 1928, p. 84. To EISSFELDT's evidence we may now add the Ras Shamra data.

[5]) GORDON *UH* 51, IV, 20-26.

tgly . ẓd . ʾel . wtbʾu	She clears the threshold of El and enters
qrš . mlk . ʾab . šnm	To the throne of the King, the Father of the Exalted Ones.
lpʿn . ʾel . thbr . wtql	At the feet of El she does obeisance and bows down
tštḥwy . wtkbdh	Prostrating herself and honouring him

In this royal figure, who is at the same time the Creator of Created Things (*bny bnwt*), we may recognize 'El Elyon, called the Most High', who according to Eusebius' citation from Philo of Byblos was senior god in the Canaanite pantheon, or El Elyon, El the Most High, Creator of Heaven and Earth (אל עליון קנה שמים וארץ), who was locally worshipped in Jerusalem before David occupied the city. [1]) We may well believe that many of his attributes were inherited by Yahweh through local association, the phraseology and imagery of many of the old hymns finding new expression in the liturgy of the cult of Yahweh. No doubt certain of the Enthronement Psalms such as Psalms xxiv, xxix, xlvi, xcv, xcvi, xcvii, xcix etc. re-echo such litanies, though the Psalms are also enriched by motifs from the liturgy of the Canaanite New Year festival, which celebrated the triumph of Baal over the forces of Chaos, and particularly from Israel's own *Heilsgeschichte*, which particularized such a Divine triumph in history. The imagery of the supreme God in his heavenly court appears in the vision of Micaiah ben Imlah (1 Kings xxii, 19),

[1]) Rightly noting the silence of the Baal-myth as extant at Ras Shamra on the subject of creation, which is a regular feature of the Hebrew Enthronement Psalms, which he rightly takes to reflect the Canaanite Baal-myth, MOWINCKEL suggests that the ultimate origin of the theme of the conflict of God with the powers of Chaos was Mesopotamian mythology, the Ugaritic myth happening to omit the creation theme, and the Israelite emphasis indicating direct Mesopotamian influence, presumably in the Assyrian ascendancy after the 9th c. ("Psalm Criticism between 1900 and 1935" (Ugarit and Biblical Exegesis)', *VT* V, 1955, p. 25). Though we cordially agree with MOWINCKEL's main thesis in this most important article, we differ from him in the last proposition. We would see the source of the creation theme in the passages in the Old Testament relating to the Kingship of God in the ideology of the Kingship of El in the liturgy of the local cult of the Canaanite El Elyon at Jerusalem, which influenced the Hebrew adaptation of the Baal-myth in the Canaanite New Year liturgy, as W. SCHMIDT has contended ('Königtum Gottes in Ugarit und Israel', *BZAW* 80, 1961, cf. H. SCHMID, 'Jahwe und die Kulttraditionen von Jerusalem', *ZAW* N.F. XXVI, 1955, pp. 168-197, who, though rightly stressing the influence of the pre-Israelite cult of El Elyon, ignores the significance of the Baal-myth in the New Year liturgy). The assimilation of the ideology of El Elyon in the local cult in Jerusalem must post-date David's occupation of the city and its development as a cult-centre, and is probably to be dated in the time of Solomon. The Hebrew adaptation of the Canaanite New Year liturgy and the Baal-myth dated from the time of the settlement in Palestine.

in Isaiah's inaugural vision (Isaiah vi), and probably also in the conception of the Davidic king as ruling

'from sea to sea,
Even from the river to the ends of the earth (Psalm lxxii, 8).

This surely reflects the Canaanite conception of El reigning

At the well-head of the two streams,
In the midst of the two deeps

The royal status of El is reflected in the conception that the human king stands in a peculiar relation to him. Krt for instance is termed the son of El, a conception which, *mutatis mutandis* found expression in Israel under the Davidic monarchy, where the king as the adoptive son of God was the temporal warrant and agent of the sovereignty of God (Psalms ii, cx) [1]).

El is, again, termed 'the Bull', *ṯr 'el*. This may refer either to his strength or possibly to his procreative vigour. However we may explain the title *ṯr 'el*, it is remarkable that the God of Jacob is spoken of as אביר, [2]) which also means 'a bull'. Since we find the fertility-god Baal in the Ras Shamra texts mating with a heifer, presumably as a bull, this may be a point at which El and Baal were assimilated, as Jahweh and Baal were at Dan in the time of Jeroboam and possibly earlier. That the title *ṯr 'el* indicates the procreative power of El may be suggested by the fact that El is father of the divine family, and in the only text in the extant literature from Ras Shamra where El is really active he begets offspring, of whom the first are the divine twins Šḥr and Šlm, the deities manifest in the star of dawn and the close of day. [3]) A reminiscence of this mythology is found probably in Genesis vi, 1-4 (J), which describes the amours of the 'sons of God' with the daughters of men. The same tradition again appears in Job xxxviii, 7, which mentions the 'sons of God' in parallel with

[1]) Again we should emphasize the influence of the Canaanite ideology of Baal as King as well as of the sovereignty of El in the new royal ideology in Israel under the House of David. We should further stress that the reflection of the ideology of the Kingship of God in such psalms as Pss. ii and cx is more than mere imagery, as V. Maag has pointedly observed (*Malkût Jhwh*, *VT Supplement* VII, 1960, pp. 146 ff.).

[2]) Genesis xlix, 24 (J).

[3]) Here Pope emphasizes the recourse to magic to stimulate the potency of the aged El, and suggests that this is his 'last fling and farewell to sex' (*op. cit.*, pp. 37-42). He cites a Hittite text the theme of which is the impotence of the old god Elkunirsa (*'el qny 'arṣ?*) who was supplanted in the affections of his consort Ashera by the younger Storm-god (After H. Otten, 'Ein kanaanäischer Mythus aus Bogazköi', *Mitteilungen des Instituts für Orientforschung* I, 1953, pp. 125-150).

'morning-stars'. [1]) That the bull, however, in this connection symbolized not procreation but simply strength, as W. SCHMIDT contends (*op. cit.*, p. 5), is suggested by such passages in the Old Testament as Deuteronomy xxxiii, 17 and 1 Kings xxii, 11 and by the fact that even goddesses are depicted with horns, as the goddess who suckles two youths in the ivory panel from the royal bed of Ugarit (*Syria* XXXI, 1954, pl. VIII).

Another title of El which appears at first sight to support the view that *ṯr ʾel* indicated his procreative powers is *ʾab ʾadm*, 'the Father of Men'. Here, however, as in the case of Jahweh when he is regarded as the father of Israel [2]) or of the king, [3]) we should emphasize not the physical but the social relationship between God and man. Again, we consider it questionable that *ʾab ʾadm* is universalistic in its application. The term *ʾadm* here may mean simply 'community' and *ʾab ʾadm* may thus mean 'He in whom the community is integrated'.

In the main in the Ras Shamra mythology El gives place to Baal as an active deity. He is indeed consulted and gives his final consent in crises in the fertility-drama, as when, for instance, he agrees to the suggestion of Aṯerat that her son Aṯtar should reign in place of Baal who has been overcome and has not yet risen from the underworld. [4]) Again he is consulted by Aṯerat in the question of building a temple to Baal. [5]) In another passage he allows himself to be wheedled and even threatened by the redoubtable Virgin Anat. [6]) Apart from this, however, he is *deus otiosus*, though here we must remember the nature of the documents. Those are the myths appropriate to the fertility-cult, which was properly Baal's province. In such a text as Krt, which concerns not nature so much as society, El is notably more prominent than Baal.

Apart from the treatment he receives from Anat, El is always respectfully addressed. He is *mlk*, 'king', and *bny bnwt*, 'Creator of Created Things'. Before him the gods prostrate themselves and acknowledge his word to be eternal wisdom,

tḥmk ʾel ḥkm	'Thy word, O El, is wise,
ḥkmt ʿm ʿlm [7])	Thou art eternally wise...'

[1]) In both of these passages, however, אלהים is used and not אל.
[2]) E.g. Isaiah i, 2; Hosea xi, 1.
[3]) E.g. Pss. ii; cx. [4]) GORDON *UH* 49.
[5]) *Ibidem* 51, IV.
[6]) *Ibidem* ʿnt, V. 32-33.
[7]) *Ibidem* 51, IV, 41; ʿnt, V, 39.

In the Krt text we see the relationship of El to man. There is probably some ritual bond between El and the king, who addresses him as his 'father'. Again, there is a definite ethical aspect of the nature of El, who is repeatedly termed *lṭpn 'el dp'ed*, 'The Kindly One, El, the Merciful' which could be practically transliterated into Arabic الله اللطيف ذو فؤاد and recalls الله الرحمان الرحيم of the Qur'an. Here we are very close to the God of the patriarchs who called Abraham to be his friend. [1]) Quite as in the patriarchal narratives, too, El reveals his purpose to Krt in a dream [2]) and the final purport of that revelation was, as in the case of the patriarchs, the promise of progeny. The moral aspect of the character of El is seen again in his directive to Krt to do no violence to the town of *'udm.* [3]) This suggests the forbearance of God who allows himself to be entreated by Abraham to spare the cities of the plain if but a quorum of just men should be found there. In the Ras Shamra texts as in the patriarchal narratives there is a kindly tolerant note with no suggestion of the fierce, uncompromising faith of the Hebrew invaders which laid Arad and Jericho in total ruin *ad maiorem dei gloriam.*

The clear evidence of the Ras Shamra Texts that El was not the general conception of divinity, but a particular deity, opens up the whole question of the significance of the *'el* or *ilu* element in theophoric names. [4]) In Palestine the Egyptian Execration Texts attest the worship of El, though it must be admitted that the *'el* element as a proper name in the theophoric compounds in these texts is less frequent than we should expect. There are cases here, as in the Ras Shamra Texts, of the generic use of the term *'el*, but on the other hand in such cases as Yanki-ilu and Yrpi-ilu, where El appears with a verbal predicate, the noun is almost certainly to be read as a proper name. Those instances, however, tell us little about man's conceptions of El, nothing being predicated of him which might not be said of any other god. Indeed, in the later texts of Posener the field is already being occupied by Hadad who appears in the Ras Shamra texts as the Baal of Canaan.

---

[1]) The expression is not actually found in the patriarchal narratives but in Isaiah xli, 8.

[2]) *bḥlm/bẓhrt*, Gordon *UH* krt, 35-36.

[3]) *Ibidem*, 116-117.

[4]) In the data of this nature from Mesopotamia it emerges now as probable that, though *ilu* is found as a generic term, as also at Ras Shamra, there are undoubted cases of its use as the proper name of a particular deity, specifically the supreme god of the old Amorite pantheon.

In the Old Testament in personal names where *ʾel* appears with the afformative *y* (1st person singular possessive suffix) we may have the noun as a generic term. Where it appears, however, in place- and personal names without such a suffix and with the other element as a verb or predicate we are probably justified in treating *ʾel* as a proper name. Such cases are the place-names Yibneel, Yizreel, Yiphtaḥel, Yirpeel, and El roi, and the personal names Yishmael, Paltiel, Reuel, and Israel. Another case of *ʾel* as a proper name which might be established even without the help of the new evidence is that of אל אלהי ישׂראל, where the common noun אלהי is obviously used to define the proper noun אל. Such instances definitely relate the worship of the patriarchs and their contemporaries in Palestine to the particular deity El, whom we now know as the supreme god of the pantheon of ancient Ugarit.

Here the natural assimilation of the attributes of El by Yahweh without the antipathy which Israel felt to the cult and character of the Canaanite Baal [1]) certainly supports the conclusion of EISSFELDT [2]) that El, acknowledged or worshipped by the patriarchs at Jerusalem (Genesis xiv), Beerlahai roi (Genesis xvi, 7-14), Bethel (Genesis xxviii), Penuel (Genesis xxxii, 23-33), and Shechem (Genesis xxxiii, 18-20), was the high god of Canaan under different hypostases rather than different local numina, as held by GUNKEL [3]) and BAUDISSIN. [4]) The easy assimilation of the features of El by Yahweh again indicates that the cult of El was already familiar to more of those who later comprised Israel than isolated individuals or groups in the patriarchal period, and EISSFELDT aptly adduces the known fact of the settlement of Hebrew elements in Canaan before the later militant stages of the settlement, with which he is probably right in associating Yahwism. [5]) These may well be the real mediators of

---

[1]) Even where the writers of the Old Testament are conscious of the distinction between Yahweh and El there is no antipathy, e.g. Genesis xiv, where Abraham recognizes El the Most High at Jerusalem by paying a tithe to his priest Melchisedeq, and Deuteronomy xxxii, 8-9 (after LXX, cf. Psalm lxxxii, 6), where the supremacy of (El) Elyon is acknowledged and Yahweh receives Israel as his portion when Elyon assigns the peoples to their respective gods. It is now recognized by an increasing number of responsible scholars that Yahweh, the god of a militant tribal group, was first subordinated to El the Canaanite high god before he took over his attributes and functions as King and Creator.

[2]) O. EISSFELDT, 'El and Yahweh', *JSS* I, 1956, pp. 25-26.

[3]) H. GUNKEL, *Genesis*, 3rd ed., 1910, p. 187.

[4]) W. VON BAUDISSIN, *Kyrios*, 1929, p. 124.

[5]) EISSFELDT, *op. cit.*, p. 35.

the cult of El, and in this connection we may mention the folk-elements Jacob-el and Joseph-el attested in central Palestine in the inscriptions of Thothmes III at Karnak (1479).

How much El as the high god of Canaan may have had in common with Yahweh to facilitate this assimilation is perhaps impossible to determine. As Creator of nature with all her rich and beneficent variety which the Psalmists praised in the Jersusalem cult, El can have had little if anything in common with Yahweh as the god of a militant group of nomads living at subsistence level in the desert marches, and in fact the descriptions of the theophany of Yahweh associated with this phase of his cult and the Sinai theophany (Exodus xix, 16 ff., Deuteronomy xxxiii, 2, Judges v, 4, and the Psalm in Habakkuk iii, 3 ff.) all emphasize the destructive rather than the creative power of Yahweh. Nor indeed is the conception of kingship natural in the tribal socialism of the desert, while the conception of sovereignty over a divine court is repugnant to the religious particularism of the tribes and obviously implies a long experience of the settled land, reflecting experience of various forces of nature in cooperation and contention and also of much assimilation of immigrant groups. Our conclusion is that the affinity between El and Yahweh lay in the interest of both in human relations. Here to be sure the Ras Shamra texts and the Old Testament, though both attesting this human or moral interest of El and Yahweh, seem, beyond this broad generality, to have little if anything in common.

The Ras Shamra texts fully attest the mercy and tolerance of El, whose stock epithets are 'the Kindly', the Merciful (*lṭpn 'el dp'ed*), but say nothing of his severity, whereas the traditions of primitive Yahwism attest Yahweh as severe even to a fault, 'a jealous God, visiting the iniquity of the fathers upon the children unto the third and fourth generation of them that hate me' (Exodus xx, 5). If he 'shows mercy unto thousands of them that love him' his mercy seems at that early stage to be confined to his peculiar people, to whom the poor unfortunates of Jericho and Hormah and the hapless Agag the Amalekite stand in sharp contrast. Doubtless the divine qualities of mercy and kindliness were still appreciated by a humanity in early Israel which defied the regimentation of the 'holy war', but this larger humanity seems not to have been sanctioned by the cult. The forbearance of God to Sodom and Gomorrah in the patriarchal tradition (Genesis xviii) is no exception since, insofar as it is historical, it concerns El and not Yahweh, to whom it is applied artificially in the J tradition of the Pentateuch, cf. Exodus vi, 3 (P), where the divine name Yahweh is said to have been unknown to the patriarchs. On the common basis of moral interests the cults of El and Yahweh were mutually enriched. The former cult by the particular, historical character of Yahwism and by its uncompromising hatred of sin and wrong was redeemed from the broad tolerance of a vague and indiscriminate universalism. Yahwism was itself, however, greatly enriched. If F. LØKKEGAARD's statement is somewhat exaggerated that El is 'the special contribution of Canaan to the world', [1]) it at least invites the appreciation of the Canaanite conception of El, which is expressed by EISSFELDT, [2]) 'He (sc. Yahweh) received from him (sc. El) the impetus to an evolution which meant the supplementation of the traits originally belonging to him... a dangerous, and bizarre character and jealous vehemence... by the qualities of discretion and wisdom, moderation and patience, forbearance and mercy'.

Baal, known in his various local manifestations in the Old Testament as the fertility-god *par excellence*, is first the god Hadad, whose power is shown in the rainstorms and thunder of autumn and winter, and secondarily the deified principle of fertility manifest in the growing crops, a theme we have elaborated already. The pre-eminence of Baal in Ugarit is signified by the fact that one of the two temples discovered there was dedicated to him, the other being to Dagon whose son Baal is termed. [3]) In the mythology of Ras Shamra the cult of Baal is more explicitly documented than that of any other deity, a subject to which we need not revert. [4])

As we study the attributes and functions of Baal, especially in his hypostasis as Hadad, the god of storm and rain-cloud who utters his voice in the heavens, who mounts the clouds (*rkb ʿrpt*), and whose temple is completed at the same season as, and with rites recalling, the dedication of Solomon's Temple in Jerusalem, we conclude that the cult of the Syrian Baal must have been well-established in Palestine

---

1) F. LØKKEGAARD, 'A Plea for El, the Bull, and other Ugaritic Miscellanies', *Studia Orientalia Joanni Pedersen Dicata*, 1953, p. 232.

2) EISSFELDT, *op. cit.*, p. 37. G. FOHRER also sees in the character of El in the Ras Shamra texts the signs of a monotheistic tendency in Ugarit. He emphasizes the royal title of El, which, he claims, was applied to other gods only insofar as they reflected the divine nature of El ('Die wiederentdeckte kanaanäische Religion', *ThLZ* LXXVIII, 1953, cols. 196-7).

3) *ʾalʾeyn bʿl//bn dgn*, GORDON *UH* 76, III, 11-15 etc.

4) *V. supra*, pp. 20-93.

and have left its impress upon the cult of Jahweh when the Israelites settled the land. No doubt much of this assimilation was due to Solomon and his Phoenician craftsmen and allies, but most probably this phase of the cultural development of Israel in Palestine was but the crystallization of a tendency to conform to the Baal-cult which was almost inevitable when the tribes of Israel crossed over from the desert to the sown. The Book of Judges in spite of its late composition is in all probability correct in accusing Israel of 'a-whoring after the Baalim', language which is not mere invective but probably reflects rites of imitative magic designed to influence Providence by autosuggestion and so to promote prolific vitality in nature. Such a cult in some form or other, but identical in principle, is found among all primitive agricultural communities.

Much of what we have said of Baal and his cult assumes the identity of ʾAlʾeyn with Baal in the Ras Shamra Texts. This is not universally accepted, and it is contended that ʾAlʾeyn Baal is not a composite title, but means 'A. the son of Baal', a theory which really relies on the support of only one passage where the phrase *ʾalʾeyn bn bʿl* occurs. [1]) This at first sight seems to mean 'A. the son of Baal'. H. BAUER, however, as early as 1933 suspected that not two figures, but one, might be denoted. He would explain ʾAlʾeyn as a derivative of the verb *lʾy* 'to be strong'. We agree with BAUER and take ʾAlʾeyn as an adjective with prosthetic *aleph* and final *n*, meaning 'the Mighty'. The phrase *ʾalʾeyn bn bʿl* in the sense 'the Mighty Son, Baal' is unusual perhaps but not impossible. On the other hand the phrase may be suspect as a *hapax legomenon*. Textual corruption in the Ras Shamra cuneiform is comparatively rare, but is not unknown, and in *bn* we may have a dittograph of the final *n* of the preceding *ʾalʾeyn* and of the initial *b* of the following *bʿl*. The explanation of the phrase *ʾalʾeyn bn bʿl* which we offer is that here we have a trace of the assimilation of the mighty warrior, the storm-god Hadad, to Baal, the fertility-god of the settled land. The title *ʾalʾeyn* is found in a variant form, again applied to Baal, as *ʾalʾey qrdm*, generally translated 'the wielder of the axe'. [2]) We suggest, however, that we retain the root

---

[1]) GORDON *UH* 67, II, 17-18.

[2]) *Ibidem* 51. VIII, 34-35; 67, II, 10-11; ʿnt, III, 11. H. BIRKELAND ignores this evidence in associating *ʾalʾeyn* with אלין, 'terebinth' and maintaining that the reference is to the god as a vegetation-deity, specifically a Tammuz figure, 'Zur Erklärung von ʾAlʾeyn in den Texten von Ras Schamra', *Norsk Tidsskrift for Sprogvidenskap* IX 1938, pp. 338-345.

meaning of the word as derived from *l'y* and translate 'Mightiest of heroes'. [1])

The cult of Baal as a fertility-deity is well enough attested in Palestine, where he was worshipped in various local manifestations throughout the period of the Hebrew occupation. As we trace the cult of Baal back beyond this period we have the abundant evidence of proper names in the Amarna Texts for the cult of Baal or Addu-Hadad in Palestine as early as the end of the 15th century B.C. There are other more concrete traces in the shape of copper statuettes of the god in a conical cap mounted with bull's horns and a short kilt. The deity strides out, his right hand raised to wield a mace or battle-axe, and the left holding a second weapon, which we know from an archaic relief of Baal from Ras Shamra [2]) to be a spear. A similar figurine has been found at Tell ed-Duweir (Lachish) [3]) reproducing the features of the figurines from Ras Shamra [4]) and the sea-ward settlement of Minet el-Beida. [5])

Dussaud has noticed the total absence of Baal from the patriarchal legends in Genesis, which have been shown by archaeological research in Mesopotamian law to depict very faithfully the conditions of an early age, which could scarcely have been due to the imagination of later writers. In view of such verisimilitude Dussaud argues that the absence of Baal in these narratives really indicates that Baal was a stranger to patriarchal Palestine. This, of course, begs the question of the date of the patriarchs. If, however, we argue from the known to the unknown, we may date Jacob in the Amarna Age, and, if we are disposed to accept the historicity of Abraham, he obviously cannot antedate the 19th century, if indeed he can have flourished so early. This, then, at the earliest, was the time of the Execration Texts, and, while it is true that the texts published by Sethe do not contain any reference to Baal or Hadad, those of Posener do contain many Hadad-theophorics, though, as we have pointed out, none suggests that Hadad—or Baal—was other than the warrior-god manifest in the storm and thunder. The theophoric names in Addu

---

[1]) We take *'al'ey* as the construct of an elative and derive *qrdm* from the Akkadian *qaradu*.

[2]) Schaeffer, *The Cuneiform Texts of Ras Shamra-Ugarit*, 1939, Pl. XXXII, fig. 2.

[3]) This was found in the ruins of the first temple in the fosse outside the wall dated by J. L. Starkey c. 1480-1420 B.C., *PEFQS* 1936, p. 185.

[4]) Schaeffer, *Syria* XIV, 1933, p. XVI.

[5]) *Idem, Ugaritica I*, 1939, p. 116, pl. XXV.

in the Amarna Texts, which are still in the patriarchal period, attest the fertility-cult in Palestine, and the Ras Shamra myths now amplify this evidence. The absence of any reference to Baal or Hadad in the patriarchal narratives, far from reflecting the actual conditions in the land, is due rather to the nature of the evidence. Neither the nationalist and orthodox source P nor the earlier narrative sources J and E have any interest in even naming the offensive Baal in what was, after all, a somewhat idyllic reconstruction of Israel's past, which is dominated by the theme of the election of Israel and the promise to the patriarchs.

In contrast to El as permanent king and final authority in matters of cosmic moment and affairs of society, Baal, as a nature-god manifest in the winter storms and secondarily in the vegetation thereby promoted is obliged always to fight for his kingship. This is contested by the Unruly Waters (*ym*), possibly 'in the beginning', and by a host of enemies besides, including the Crooked Serpent, Fire, Flood, *tnn*, and others,

> Who would drive Baal from the crags of Saphon,
> Who would repel like a bird his lordship,
> Who would drive him from the throne of his sovereignty. [1])

It is disputed either annually or septennially by Drought and Sterility (*mt*). Baal's royal status is always at stake, and his character as king, as W. Schmidt has so well expressed it, is dynamic rather than static. [2])

In view of the prevalence of the conflict theme in passages in the Old Testament relevant to the Kingship of Yahweh, which otherwise reflect the motifs of the Baal-myth, this seems to us very strong evidence indeed for the influence of the seasonal ritual and myth of the Canaanite New Year festival in the Hebrew conception of the Kingship of God. The Ras Shamra evidence certainly supports Mowinckel's contention that the motif words יהוה מלך in the Enthronement Psalms refer to Yahweh's manifesting himself, or asserting himself, as king in a cult-act rather than, as Eissfeldt contends, to a permanent attribute of sovereignty. The latter view is, of course, implied, for the ideology of the local cult of El the Most High was incorporated in the cult and theology of Yahwism. But in the liturgical deposit of the syncretistic Yahweh-cult of Solomon's

---

[1]) For a list of these adversaries *v. supra*, pp. 30-31 n.
[2]) W. Schmidt, *op. cit.*, p. 22.

temple in the Psalms it is not only the systematic theology enumerating the divine attributes that finds expression. The Psalms reflect the dramatic experience of the cult, where it is not enough for Yahweh to have the attribute of sovereignty, but he must be seen to be King for the assurance of the worshippers.

The supremacy of Baal after conflict with his adversaries is acclaimed at various points by the declaration that he is king (*mlk*), or is exalted (*ẓbl*) or that he has no superior (*'en d'lnh*). A synonymn of these terms is *ṯpṭ*. The last term, also applied to the Unruly Waters in parallelism with *ẓbl*, is the Hebrew שׁפט. This term admittedly means in Hebrew and Ugaritic 'deciding a case as a judge', but this is a secondary meaning. The Ras Shamra data just cited clearly demonstrates that the word had a wider connotation 'ruler', of which 'judgement' was but one function. The order imposed or upheld by the *ṯpṭ*, or ruler, was *mṯpṭ* (Hebrew משׁפט), which is just as wide in its connotation. To *mt*, for instance, who ventures to dispute the rule of Baal, it is stated:

> Nay, he will pluck up the spear of thy tribunal
> He will overturn the throne of thy kingship *(mlkk)*,
> He will break the staff of thy rule *(mṯpṭk)*.

With the recognition that שֹׁפֵט and מִשְׁפָּט have this connotation of 'ruler' and 'rule', or 'order', the class of Enthronement Psalms in the Old Testament and relevant passages in the Prophets becomes very much larger than the psalms characterized by the key phrase יהוה מלך, which critics of MOWINCKEL's view of the *Sitz im Leben* and ideology of the Enthronement Psalms so often admit alone as evidence.

In keeping with his character of the god manifest in the rain- and thunder-storms of winter, Baal's throne in the Ras Shamra mythology is located on Mt Saphon, Mt. Kasios of Greek geographers, the conspicuous mountain over 5000 feet which dominates the realm of Ugarit at a distance of some 20 ml. N. of Ras Shamra. This prominent feature was the fitting seat of 'Him who Mounteth the Clouds', its cloud-cap in the rainy season heralding the victory of Baal in his perpetual conflict with Drought and Sterility and declaring that he had assumed his kingship. This feature also of the Baal-mythology of Ras Shamra survived in the Israelite adaptation of the seasonal cult of Canaan in the Temple-cult where Zion as the throne of Yahweh is identified with 'the extremities or heights of Saphon', ירכתי צפון,

(Psalm xlviii, 3, EVV, 2). The close association between the Baal-myth of Ras Shamra and the Hebrew New Year liturgy is maintained in the theme of the establishment of the 'house' of the god. The building of a 'house' for the god symbolizes the establishment of his status as king. The preparation of a 'house' for *ym*, for instance (GORDON *UH* 129, 19-20), leads up to a conflict between him and Baal, the issue at stake being said explicitly to be the kingship (GORDON *UH* 68, 7-32). Baal's revival and resumption of power necessitates the building of a 'house' (GORDON *UH* 51, VII, 25 ff.). The establishment of the 'house' of Baal, which, significantly enough, is completed like Solomon's temple on the eve of the heavy autumn rain, provokes the conflict with *mt* for the kingship (GORDON *UH* 51, VII, 47-52). In the Old Testament an examination of passages referring to the establishment of the 'house of God' on Mt Zion as the place where the 'house' was built (e.g. Psalms xlvi; xlviii; Isaiah ii, 2-4; Micah iv, 1-3) shows that their theme is the triumph of God in conflict with the powers of Chaos and his establishment of order (משפט), the theme of the liturgy of the New Year festival, of which the manifestation of Yahweh as King is the highlight.

Though the mythology and iconography of Canaan represent Baal as the deity manifest in winter storms and the vegetation thereby promoted, there are three texts which suggest that Baal was not merely an impersonal nature-deity. When Krt ends his ritual seclusion, which has, of course, a social significance, it is to Baal that he sacrifices as well as to El (GORDON *UH* krt 169-70). When Dn'el mourns his childless condition it is Baal who presents his supplication to El (GORDON *UH* 2 Aqht I, 16-34), and the duty of the king, and after him his son, is to preside at the *šlmm* or sacrifice of integration,

> Eating his slice in the temple of Baal,
> His portion in the temple of El.

Baal of Mt. Saphon, moreover, is regularly invoked in oaths which sanction royal deeds from the palace archives of Ras Shamra, which indicate the social significance of Baal by the end of the Bronze Age.

From such passages we may see that in spite of the multiplicity of gods attested by the offering lists and theophoric names from Ras Shamra the practical faith of men was centred on the cult of El and Baal. It may even be that such passages indicate a step in the direction of practical monotheism, El representing God transcendent and Baal God immanent, as G. FOHRER tentatively suggests. [1]) Here we may see in El the Creator, the transcendent, who can be reverenced and supplicated, and in Baal the god who, according to Canaanite conceptions, was the projection of men's natural aspirations and who might be influenced by imitative magic.

A rather interesting figure in the Ugaritic pantheon is that of Aṯtar, who appears as the rival of Baal, or at least a temporary substitute on his throne during his absence in the underworld. He is the son of Aṯerat the consort of El, and at her suggestion he rules by consent of El in the place of Baal. He bears the stock epithet *ʿrẓ*, 'the Luminous', [2]) and *mlk*, 'the king', in which character he is the natural substitute for Baal.

His relation to El is not immediately apparent, but he is definitely the son of Aṯerat, the consort of El, and would thus seem to belong to the more primitive category of gods at Ugarit, and as such to bear an astral character. NIELSEN would identify Aṯtar of the Ras Shamra texts with the deity of the same name in the South Arabian pantheon, who is the first-born of the moon-god Il and the sun-goddess Aṯerat, and is the Venus-star, the brightest luminary in these latitudes after the sun and moon. On the data at our disposal from South Arabian inscriptions and Byzantine sources and from the Ras Shamra evidence a good case can be made out in spite of the apparent difficulty of correlating evidence from periods so widely separated. We accept NIELSEN's theory on the grounds that the lapse of time in this case is discounted by the isolation and natural conservatism of the Semitic communities of South Arabia and the oases, where life was for so long immune from extraneous influences.

In the Ras Shamra texts the god Aṯtar is not conspicuous except in the text where he occupies for a season the vacant throne of Baal. [3]) He does not actually rule in Baal's stead for he does not measure up to the stature of the latter,

> He takes his seat on the throne of Baal the Mighty;
> His feet do not reach the footstool,
> His head does not reach the canopy thereof.

Unable to fill the exalted place of Baal, Aṯtar vacates the throne and comes down,

---

[1]) G. FOHRER, 'Die wiederentdeckte kanaanäische Religion', *ThLZ* LXXVIII, 1953, col. 197.

[2]) Cf. Arabic عرص, 'to flash', rather than Hebrew עריץ.

[3]) GORDON *UH* 49, I.

Down from the throne of Baal the Mighty
And reigns in the ground, god of it all. [1]

This indicates probably that, whereas Baal sent the seasonal rains, the province of Aṯtar was irrigation. [2] It is significant that even in his relative degradation Aṯtar still 'reigns' (*ymlk*).

In the offering-lists from Ras Shamra Aṯtar is never mentioned by name and in the mythological texts he appears only once besides the passage we have cited and in fragmentary passages in the texts Gordon *UH* 129, 137, namely in the myth of the marriage of the Moon-god, *yrḫ*, and his consort *nkl*, where Aṯtar is mentioned, possibly as a prospective father-in-law of the Moongod. [3] Here, though the passage is somewhat obscure, the astral significance of Aṯtar is indicated. In view of this astral character of Aṯtar, the Morning and Evening Star, it is possible that he was assimilated in Ugaritic thought to *Šḥr* and *Šlm*, the twin deities manifest in the star of Dawn (*šḥr*) and Completion (*šlm*) of Day, whose birth is celebrated in the text GORDON *UH* 52.

The *locus classicus* for the character and cult of Aṯtar in the ancient Near East is a passage in the Greek 'Life of St Nilus' from the 5th century A.D. [4] Here there is a vivid description of a Bedouin raid on the monasteries of Sinai. Nilus and his son Theodulus are taken, and the lad is reserved as a sacrifice to the Venus-star. He escapes providentially through the raiders having overslept until the morning-star had faded after sunrise. The practice of child-sacrifice to Aṯtar the Venus-star is particularly significant. It should, however, be noted that neither in this connection nor in any other is there any reference

1) For the possible reflection of this incident in the fall of הלל בן שחר in Isaiah xiv, 12 ff. see p. 288.

2) The Arabic for irrigated ground is أرض عثور. J. MAUCHLINE had already associated عثور and Aṯtr before the new material from Ras Shamra, *Transactions of the Glasgow University Oriental Society* X, 1943, pp. 11-20. A. CAQUOT ('Le dieu 'Aṯtar et les textes de Ras Shamra', *Syria* xxxv, 1958, pp. 45-60), who has conveniently summarized epigraphic evidence for the significance of the cult of Aṯtr, male and female, from S. Arabia, Mesopotamia, the N. Syrian steppe, and Canaan, admits the astral character of the deity, but suggests that this was secondary to fertility functions. The fertility function of the deity is not to be doubted, but in view of the pre-eminence of the cult of Aṯtar in oases and lands bordering on the desert it seems more natural that the fertility-function of the deity in the settled lands is secondary.

3) GORDON *UH* 77, 28-29.

4) NILUS, *Narrative* iii (MIGNE, *PG* LXXIX, 1865), 612, C-D; *Narrative* vii, 681, A; 684, C.

to such deliberate human sacrifice at Ugarit unless in the text GORDON *UH* 'nt, II, where the goddess Anat is depicted as indulging in a veritable blood-bath.

The inscription of Mesha of Moab gives us clear evidence for the worship of Aṯtar beyond Jordan in the middle of the 9th century B.C. [1]) The king of Moab in his war of independence reduced certain Israelite fortresses and shrines and dragged his victims and trophies before his god Aṯtar-Kemosh. Kemosh is the most familiar form of the name of the national god of Moab, but it may be that this is only an epithet of Aṯtar or perhaps the most common hypostasis of that god. In any case the passage in the Moabite inscription suggests that Aṯtar and Kemosh, if not actually identical, could be assimilated without difficulty. In view of the astral character of Aṯtar and his identity with the Venus-star, *Šḥr* and *Šlm*, NIELSEN notes as significant the fact that the dedication to Aṯtar-Kemosh followed the reduction of the Israelite fortress of Nebo after a night-march. [2])

Further North in the kindred state of Ammon the national god was 'Milcom', which was probably not a proper name but a title *mlk* with the suffix *m*, which appears in South Arabian dialects as the definite article [3]) The indentity of the national god of Ammon with Kemosh of Moab is implied in the reply of Jephthah to the Ammonites, 'Wilt thou not possess that which Kemosh thy god giveth thee to possess?' (Judges xi, 24). Thus we arrive at the identification Aṯtar=Kemosh = Mlk-m = Šlm. It is submitted that the god was worshipped in one or other of those hypostases in Palestine and even in Israel in the period of the monarchy.

Leaving aside the comparatively few and indeterminate theophorics with *mlk* in the Amarna Tablets [4]) we read in the Old Testament that Solomon built high places for Kemosh of Moab and 'Molech' of Ammon 'in the hill that is before Jerusalem' (1 Kings xi, 7), probably the Mount of Olives East of the city. Here, of course, no more might be meant than private chapels of Solomon's wives from Moab and Ammon, and he is reported to have done no less for his

---

[1]) G. A. COOKE, *NSI*, 1903, 1, pp. 1-12.

[2]) *Ibidem*, 11. 14-15.

[3]) The name is possibly attested in this form in the offering list GORDON *UH* 17.11.

[4]) E.g. Abi-milki and Ili-milki, where the termination of *mlk* indicates the first person possessive suffix, so that here the noun is common. In the case of Milkilu, who seems by the correspondence of Abdi-ḫepa to be domiciled near Jerusalem, the *mlk* element is probably a proper name.

other foreign wives (1 Kings xi, 8). It seems significant, however, that only Kemosh and 'Milcom' are mentioned by name in the passage. We may well suppose, therefore, that Kemosh and 'Milcom', hypostases, as we believe, of the same deity, were not now for the first time introduced to the land, but were already domiciled there. [1])

The next reference to the worship of 'Molech' is in the account of Josiah's reformation describing how he 'defiled Tophet which is in the Valley of the son of Hinnom, that no man might make his son or his daughter to pass through the fire to Molech'. [2]) In this passage we may note further that there is reference to the worship of the sun, moon, and stars (2 Kings xxiii, 5), while a certain official who had his chamber in the Temple adjacent to the portion dedicated to astral worship is named Nathan-Melech (2 Kings xxiii, 11). The same passage notes the desecration of the precincts of Kemosh and 'Milcom' which had apparently survived from the time of Solomon.

Among the Hebrews, as also among the Arabs on the evidence of St. Nilus, this deity was worshipped with human sacrifice. It is first explicitly attested in Judah under Ahaz (2 Kings xvi, 3) and in Israel under Hoshea (2 Kings xvii, 17), and, though 'Molech' is not named, the parallel passage in Chronicles (2 Chron. xxviii, 3) adds that the scene of those grim rites was the Valley of the son of Hinnom, specifically Tophet, which is associated with *Mlk* in Jeremiah xxxii, 35. From Moab comes the classical case of the sacrifice of the eldest son of Mesha (2 Kings iii, 27), which would certainly be made to Kemosh the national god of Moab, with whom Aṯtar is associated, if not identified, in the Moabite inscription which we have cited.

There is a certain amount of evidence that the worship of this deity was localized at Jerusalem. In the late period of the Monarchy Zephaniah stigmatizes the inhabitants of Jerusalem who 'worship the host of heaven upon the housetops... and they that swear by Malcham' (Zephaniah i, 5). There are certain places about Jerusalem

[1]) There is further reference to the worship of the gods of Ammon and Moab by the Israelites in Judges x, 6, but, as the gods of Syria, Sidon, and the Philistines are included and the whole passage bears the obvious traces of Deuteronomic revision, it cannot be treated as authoritative.

[2]) We note the view of EISSFELDT that in this phrase: לַמֹּלֶךְ means 'for a sacrificial vow', *Molk als Opferbegriff im punischen und hebräischen und das Ende des Gottes Moloch*', 1935, cf. DUSSAUD, *Les origines cananéennes du sacrifice israélite*, 2nd. ed., 1941. While admitting the significance of the term in the Punic inscriptions cited by EISSFELDT, we regard the evidence of a deity *mlk* in the ancient Near East as rendering EISSFELDT's thesis not conclusive as far as the Hebrew phrase is concerned. See ALBRIGHT, *Archaeology and the Religion of Israel*, 1942, pp. 162-164.

which are designated as 'the king's', such as 'the king's garden' (2 Kings xxv, 4), which the Book of Nehemiah (iii, 15) locates more precisely by the Pool of Siloam. As this is near the confluence of the Kidron Valley and the Valley of Hinnom, the scene of human sacrifice to 'Molech', it is possible that 'the king's garden' was the precinct of the god Melech or Aṯtar or Šḥr-Šlm, the Venus-star. This feature may be identical with 'the garden of Uzza' where the apostate kings Manasseh and Amon were buried (2 Kings xxi, 18, 26). We recollect that Uzza was the title of the Venus-star in pre-Islamic Arab paganism. [1]) Similary 'the king's dale' was in the same vicinity, as is suggested by the account of Absalom's monument, and this may be associated with the same deity. The fact that the names of two of David's sons, Absalom and Solomon, should both contain the element *šlm*, which appears again in the name of the city itself, suggests the probability that Šalem was the local god of Jerusalem domiciled there since the time of the Egyptian Execration Texts at least, which cite the name of the city *Urušlmm*.

A. CAQUOT uses the scanty evidence for Aṯtar in the Ras Shamra texts to demonstrate that he is a deity who has fallen in estimation. [2]) In the text regarding the marriage of the Moongod and Nikkal he is honourably mentioned, with his title 'the Lion', as with Baal a possible father-in-law of the Moongod. He next appears as a possible substitute, though an inadequate one, for Baal, and finally he may appear in the fragmentary text GORDON *UH* 129, 20-21 as an immature god, who has no 'house' of his own. The last text is too fragmentary to base much upon, and it must be added that the complaint that the god has no 'house' of his own is also made on behalf of Baal in other texts, where it denotes merely a temporary eclipse of power. The degradation of Aṯtar in the cult of Ras Shamra, however, for which CAQUOT argues seems to be established by the fact that the god is not mentioned by name in the offering lists. He might, however, be alluded to there by his title *mlk*, or as the Morning and Evening Star *šḥr* and *šlm*. The fact is, however, most probably, that in the settled land the significance of Aṯtar as an astral deity declined or was adapted to local agricultural conditions, as in the case of Ishtar in Mesopotamia. In Canaan, where less respect was paid to the stars than in Mesopotamia Aṯtar did not acquire

[1]) J. WELLHAUSEN, *Reste des Arabischen Heidentums*, 1897, pp. 40-45.
[2]) A. CAQUOT, 'Le dieu ʿAthtar et les textes de Ras Shamra', *Syria* XXXV, 1958, pp. 45-60.

the same fertility function, which was fulfilled by Baal and the goddesses Anat and Aṯerat.

Anat, though apparently one of the younger deities in the Canaanite pantheon, is actually the most active goddess in the agricultural ritual and mythology of Ras Shamra. She is closely associated with Baal in his vicissitudes as the dying and rising vegetation-god, and is designated as his sister. [1]) As the counterpart of Baal in the hypostasis of the god of violent storms who roars in thunder and hurls the lightning Anat appears as the warrior-goddess and shows her mettle on gods, men, and primaeval monsters. She cuts to pieces Mot the god of drought and desolation, winnows, parches, and grinds him and scatters his flesh to the birds. [2]) In a scene reminiscent of Jehu's massacre of the scions of the House of Omri in the temple of Baal in Samaria she lops off heads and limbs and wades to the thighs in the blood of the slain. [3]) She recalls her triumph over various monstrous enemies, probably powers of Chaos. [4]) Thus we are not surprised to find Anat adopted into Egypt as one of the Syrian deities whose worship was affected by the warrior-Pharaohs of the XIXth Dynasty. [5]) She is found again appropriately assimilated to Athene in a bilingual inscription of the 4th century B.C. from Larnax Lapethos in Cyprus. [6])

In the last inscription Anat is termed עז חיים, 'the strength of life'. [7]) As a life-giving power she is the fitting companion of Baal. It is precisely to restore Baal to life and vigour that Anat visits the underworld and deals so drastically with Mot, the inveterate enemy of Baal. She is named with Aṯerat, the consort of El, the foster-mother of the sons of El, Šḥr and Šlm, and also in the nurture of the eldest son of King Krt. [8]) Thus in a very pointed sense Anat was a deity who 'kills and makes alive again'.

---

[1]) Gordon *UH* 49, II, 12 ff., *ʾat mt tn ʾaḫy*
'Thou, O Mot, give me my brother'.

[2]) *Ibidem*, 30-36.

[3]) *Ibidem*, ʿnt, II.

[4]) *Ibidem*, III, 34-IV, 48.

[5]) Her cult had already in the 18th century penetrated to Egypt with Semitic elements among the Hyksos, one of the rulers of whom is named Anat-har. The favourite chariot-team of Seti I was named 'Anat is content', a sword of Ramses II was called 'Anat is victorious', and a dog of the same Pharaoh was called 'Anat protects', Albright, *AJSL* XLI, 1924-25, pp. 82 ff.

[6]) Cooke, *NSI*, 1903, 28, pp. 80-82.

[7]) The Greek translation here is Σωτειρα Νικη.

[8]) Gordon *UH* 128, II, 27. It is from this case that we infer the rôle of Anat as

There are definite traces of the cult of Anat in Palestine in the patriarchal period in the place-names Beth-Anath in Naphtali (Joshua xix, 38), Beth Anoth in Judah (Joshua xv, 59), and possibly Anathoth, the home of Jeremiah, in Benjamin just North of Jerusalem. At Bethshan in one of the temples excavated by the University of Pennsylvania a basalt panel was found, the dedication of a certain Egyptian Hesi-Nekht to 'Antit, Queen of Heaven and Mistress of the Gods'. [1]) It must be admitted, however, that beyond these instances there are no clear traces of the cult in Palestine and the Old Testament never names her except in place-names and in the proper name Shamgar the son of Anath (Judges v, 6), which probably means 'Shamgar the man of Beth Anath'.

It is thought that there is a late occurrence of the cult of the goddess Anat in the Elephantine Papyri of the 5th century B.C. where the terms ʿanath-Bethel and ʿanath-Yahu occur as divine names. This, it is claimed, signifies that Anat was regarded by those military colonists from Israel as the consort of Jahweh. [2]) ALBRIGHT, however, is much more cautious, and feasibly suggests that the terms signify no more than the deification of the 'will' or 'purpose' (*ʿanath*) of Jahweh.[3])

Closely associated with Anat probably is the goddess Aṯtarat, the Canaanite Astarte deliberately misvocalized by Jewish scribes as Ashtoreth. She is known from the Old Testament as the fertility-goddess. Her fertility functions at Ugarit were apparently usurped by Anat, as were also her warlike characteristics, which remained with the goddess in her Babylonian character as Ishtar. This deity plays but little part in the mythology of Ras Shamra, but has a definite place in the pantheon since her name appears in offering-lists, [4]) and she is conspicuous in later Phoenician inscriptions. In the Keret text the king on recovering from his grievous illness rebukes his over-sanguine son and curses him: [5])

---

wet-nurse to Šḥr and Šlm in the text GORDON *UH* 52, where the goddess is not named but designated by the title *rḥmy*.

[1]) A. ROWE, *The Topography and History of Bethshan*, 1930, pp. 32-33, pl. 50, no. 2.

[2]) DUSSAUD, *Syria* XXIII, 1942-3, p. 286. A. VINCENT, *La Religion des Judéo-Araméens d'Éléphantine*, 1937, p. 652.

[3]) ALBRIGHT, *BASOR* 84, 1941, p. 15. *From the Stone Age to Christianity*, 1940, pp. 333 ff. pp. 286 n. 51.

[4]) GORDON *UH* 5 1; 17, 3; 19, 16; 22, 6; 23, 4. The goddess is named also in the ritual text 5,1, and in the Krt text (146/293) the beauty of the king's bride is compared to that of Aṯtrt.

[5]) GORDON *UH* 127, 54-57, *yṯbr ḥrn ybn*
yṯbr ḥrn rʾešk
ʿṯtrt šm bʿl qdqdk

'May Ḥoron break, O son,
May Ḥoron break thy head,
Yea Aṯtarat the hypostasis of Baal thy skull.'

The designation of Aṯtarat as *šm bʿl*, the name, or hypostasis, of Baal, indicates that she was a fertility-deity. In the myth of the conflict between Baal and the Unruly Waters (GORDON *UH* 129, 137, 68) Aṯtarat makes a brief appearance as apparently the ally of Baal. The fragmentary nature of the text, however, does not permit us to particularize, though we do believe that this is the Canaanite original of a myth extant in an Egyptian papyrus from the XIXth Dynasty where Aṯtarat plays a more conspicious rôle as the bride who is claimed by the tyrant Sea. [1]) Beyond isolated references, however, the goddess stands definitely in the background in the Ras Shamra myths.

In Palestine, on the other hand, the relative position of Aṯtarat and Anat seems to be reversed. Though the cult of Anat was not unknown, as the Bethshan inscription of Hesi-Nekht indicates, it was Aṯtarat who was more prominent. Her fertility functions in the Old Testament are never in doubt. Her warlike propensity, like that of the Syrian Anat, is perhaps indicated by the fact that it was in her temple (at Bethshan?) [2]) that the Philistines hung up the armour of Saul and his sons as trophies of the victory of Gilboa.

In the account of the reform of Josiah there is notice of 'the Ashera' associated with the cult of Baal (2 Kings xxiii, 4, 6). This, for which the women wove 'hangings', is translated in the AV 'the grove'. There are admittedly passages in the Old Testament where the word does seem to signify some object such as a sacred pole, so called perhaps because it stood erect or straight (אשׁר). Again, however, the word seems to be a proper noun referring to the name of a goddess or, where the definite article is used, an image or symbol of this goddess, the sacred pole, originally no doubt a tree as the repository of life and fruitfulness which it yields under the stimulus of Baal, the male deity of storm and autumn rain. In this case any doubt on the reading of Ashera as a proper name rather than as a common noun is resolved by the Ras Shamra texts which show 'Aṯrt as an active goddess in the fertility-cult. As such she is associated with Baal in Palestine in the period of the Judges (Judges iii, 7).

---

[1]) A. H. GARDINER, 'The Astarte Papyrus', *Studies presented to F. Ll. Griffiths*, 1932, pp. 74-85, cf. the Greek myth of Perseus and Andromeda, localized at Jaffa.
[2]) 1 Samuel xxxi, 10.

To her Maacah the mother of Asa made a 'horrid image', מפלצת, (1 Kings xv, 13); Ahab made 'the Ashera' at Samaria (1 Kings xvi, 33), the image of the goddess, or her symbol, which is noted as still standing after the revolt of Jehu (2 Kings xiii, 6). At Carmel Elijah challenged the prophets of 'the Ashera' to trial by ordeal (1 Kings xviii, 19). At Jerusalem Manasseh set up an image (פסל) of Ashera in the Temple (2 Kings xxi, 7) which was removed by the reformers in the time of Josiah. The issue here is admittedly complicated by the double significance of 'Ashera' as the goddess herself and her image or symbol. In the light of the Ugaritic evidence, however, we must insist on her definite personality alongside Baal and Aṯtarat with whom, as at Ras Shamra, she may tend to be assimilated. In Palestine, however, it would seem that she has almost yielded her identity to Astarte and is known mainly by her symbol, the sacred pole or stylized tree. [1])

In the Ras Shamra texts Aṯerat is quite active. Her regular sacrifice is noted in the offering-lists and she figures frequently in the myths, though her fertility functions seem to a certain extent to have been taken over by the younger Anat. Aṯerat is the consort of El, the senior god of the Ugaritic pantheon, and with him and her son Aṯtar, the Venus-star, may belong to an older stratum of religion at Ras Shamra. She has the alternative title *ʾelt*, 'the goddess', e.g.: [2])

> 'Aṯerat and her sons will indeed rejoice,
> Even *ʾelt* and the band of her progeny.'

This may signify her status as the goddess *par excellence* or allude to her as the consort of El. She is regarded as the mother of the gods who are 'seventy' in number, and as such is probably entitled *qnyt ʾelm*, 'Creatrix of the gods' [3]), though this meaning of the phrase

---

[1]) The sacred tree as a fertility symbol is one of the most familiar motifs in native Canaanite art, being represented as a palm-tree, natural or stylized, often flanked by rampant caprids which reach up to its fruits. That the tree represents the mother-goddess is indicated by the fact that on the relief on the lid of an ivory unguent-box from Minet el-Beida (14th c.), the mother-goddess is represented between the two caprids, to whom she offers plants, C. F. A. SCHAEFFER, *Ugaritica* I, 1939, Pl. I.

[2]) GORDON *UH* 49, I, 11-13, *tšmḫ.ht ʾaṯrt wbnh*
ʾelt wṣbrt ʾaryh

[3]) The root *qny* is found in this sense in the words of Eve, 'I have gotten a man' (Genesis iv, 1). Connecting the root with a South Arabian cognate, however, GASTER renders 'mistress of the gods', 'Baal is Risen, an ancient Hebrew Passion-play from Ras Shamra-Ugarit', *Iraq* VI, 1939, p. 129. NIELSEN, on the other hand, renders 'the possession of El', i.e. El's wife, *Ras Shamra Mythologie und Biblische Theologie*, p. 32.

is not certainly established. This, however, does not alter the fact that Aṯerat stood in a very intimate relation to El and was regarded as the mother of the divine family, e.g.: [1])

'No house has Baal as the gods,
No precinct as the sons of Aṯerat.'

Baal, however, is apparently no son of Aṯerat, and his death is thought to be naturally welcome to the goddess and her sons. [2]) While Baal languishes in the underworld it is Aṯtar her son whom, on the invitation of El, she nominates to fill the vacant throne. Her enmity to Baal is further indicated by the fact that the voracious monsters before which Baal was to fall in the text GORDON *UH* 75 are engendered either by Aṯerat herself or her maidservant. [3]) All this suggests to NIELSEN that in the Baal-cult we have a different stratum of religion from the cult of El and his consort Aṯerat.

In spite of the apparently natural hostility of Aṯerat to Baal she does agree, at the request of Anat, to intercede with El for his consent that a 'house' should be built for Baal in the text GORDON *UH* ʿnt. This activity of female deities in the Ras Shamra texts should be noted. It is always related to some crisis in nature or in the experience of Baal. This prominence of the female beyond her normal rôle can be paralleled in the experience of primitive societies at seasons of crisis in nature or in society. This suggests the *Sitz im Leben* of the Ras Shamra texts. They were related to ritual appropriate to seasonal crises, and were in no sense purely literary productions.

Other deities less conspicuous in the Ras Shamra texts are Dagon and Horon, who are attested in Palestine in the place-names Beth-Dagon and Beth-Horon.

The former is known to have had a temple and cult at Ashdod in the Early Iron Age (1 Samuel v, 1-7). He is not named in the theophoric names in the Egyptian Execration Texts relative to Palestine, but appears in the Amarna Tablets in the name Dagan-takala which is associated with Southern Palestine. [4]) We cannot determine when and in what circumstances Dagon was introduced to Palestine, but from

---

[1]) GORDON *UH*, 51, IV, 50-51, *ʾen bt lbʿl km ʾelm*
wḥẓr kbn ʾaṯrt

[2]) GORDON *UH* 49, I, 11-13.

[3]) The mother of the monsters is *ʾamt ʾaṯrt*, which might be rendered 'O maid of A.' or 'O maid A.'

[4]) KNUDTZON, *Die El-Amarna Tafeln* 317, 318.

the frequency of the name in theophorics from Mesopotamia in the First Amorite Period it is likely that he was an Amorite deity. In the Ras Shamra texts he is named as the father of Baal, which suggests the antiquity of his worship, and also, perhaps, the fact that he has been superseded. His temple was discovered, and it compares very favourably in size with the temple of Baal, with which it was contemporary until the destruction of Ugarit in the early 12th century. Dagon is named in the offering-lists of Ugarit [1]), generally together with, but after, El and Baal. It is remarkable that he plays no part in the mythological texts, and probably he had been superseded by Baal.

Horon, who is named in an imprecation in the Krt text and in a proper name in an administrative tablet, [2]) is better attested in Palestine, occurring thrice in the Egyptian Execration Texts in the proper name Horon-abu, the name of chiefs at Ṯ'pw, Arqa, and Laish, and presumably in the place-name Beth-Horon. The deity is found named as the protector of Ramses II in an inscription from his capital at Tanis in the North-East of the Delta. That Horon on this inscription was a Semitic deity is strongly suggested by the known predilection of Ramses for Syrian deities, [3]) and by the association of Horon with Rešef and Anat in the Harris Papyrus cited by ALBRIGHT. [4]) That he was worshipped already in the XVIIIth Dynasty in Egypt is demonstrated by POSENER [5]) who cites the Papyrus Ermitage, and by ALBRIGHT on the evidence of certain foundation deposits of faience tiles from the temple in the proximity of the great sphinx at Gizeh. A further connection between this deity and Palestine may be suggested by an inscription from Delos in the 2nd century B.C. where the god 'Αυρωνας is associated with Heracles as a deity of Jamnia. [6]) Now the companion of Heracles is normally Iolaos, who appears at Carthage as Asclepius the healing

---

[1]) GORDON *UH* 9, 3; 17, 16; 19, 5. Two inscriptions on votive stelai are extant, GORDON *UH* 69, 2; 70, 2.

[2]) GORDON *UH* 322, VI, 1.

[3]) Anat and Astarte are also named in contemporary inscriptions, P. MONTET, *RB* XLIV, 1935, p. 154. *Le Drame d'Avaris*, 1941, p. 142. Seth was worshipped in the guise of the Syrian Baal Saphon, SCHAEFFER, *Syria* XII, 1931, pl. VI.

[4]) ALBRIGHT, *AJSL* LIII, 1936-37, pp. 1-12.

[5]) G. POSENER, *JNES* IV, 1945, pp. 240-242.

[6]) VIROLLEAUD, *Revue des études sémitiques*, 1937, pp. 39. There is a good deal of evidence to suggest that there were several Phoenician colonies at this time in the coastal plain of Palestine. Heracles was usually identified with the Phoenician Baal.

deity. [1]) As one with power over life and death, then, Horon, if the identification Auronas-Horon is correct, is quite in character in Krt's imprecation on his rebellious son. We note further in this connection that in the vicinity of Beth-Horon there was a site Yirpeel 'God heals', (Joshua xviii, 27). [2]) ALBRIGHT, on the other hand, believes that Horon was a chthonic deity identified with Rešef or Šulman, the Canaanite hypostasis of the Babylonian Nergal, the deity of pestilence and the underworld. [3]) As a further explanation it may be noted that in Arabic حور is found referring to the planet Jupiter, which refers in Mesopotamian incantation texts to Nergal.

It has been claimed that Jahweh himself is mentioned in the Ras Shamra texts.

Scholars have already been conscious of problems raised by the occurrence of the element *Jw*, *Ja'u*, or *Jawi* in theophoric names either from before the period of the Hebrew occupation of Palestine or from areas, such as Syria, which Israel did not occupy. In this case the Ugaritic deity *Yw* has been welcomed as a solution of the problem. DE GROOT, for instance, would so explain the name *Aḫi-yawi* which he reads on a tablet from Taanach (c. 1400) [4]). Here, however, the text might as well be read *Ahi-yami* and the reference be to the god Yamm, far better attested than *Yw* in the Ras Shamra texts. H. BAUER admits the reading *Yw* in the Ras Shamra text and suggests that the *Yw* element in theophoric names on the Samaritan ostraca may refer to this Canaanite deity rather than to Yahweh, [5]) a thesis which we think most improbable. If we accept *Yw* as a Canaanite deity he is more likely to be the Syrian deity Ιευω, who is mentioned by Eusebius [6]) as the god of Byblos, whose priest Hierombalos is cited as the authority behind Sanchuniathon, whom Philo of Byblos quotes. Here, however, the evidence is insufficient to permit any conclusion as to the nature or function of the god.

---

[1]) Thus Horon might be the Phoenician Eshmun, who is not named in the Ras Shamra texts. For citation and review of fuller evidence see our article 'The Canaanite God Horon', *JNES* VIII, 1949, pp. 27-34.

[2]) Identified with Rafat, 5 miles East of Beit ʿUr el Fauqa (Beth-Horon the Upper), F. M. ABEL, *Géographie de la Palestine* II, 1938, p. 92.

[3]) ALBRIGHT, *op. cit.*, pp. 10 ff.

[4]) J. DE GROOT, *De Godsdiensten der Wereld*, ed. G. VAN DER LEEUW, 1948, p. 2. A. VINCENT also accepts the reference to *Yw* in the Ras Shamra texts (*La Religion des Judéo-Araméens d'Éléphantiné*, 1937, pp. 27 ff).

[5]) H. BAUER, 'Die Gottheiten von RS', *ZAW* LI, 1933, p. 94.

[6]) *Praeparatio Evangelica*, ed. E. H. GIFFORD, 1903, 31a.

Further evidence of a deity *Ya'u* or *Yah* in Syria comes from certain theophoric names of rulers of the Aramaean states of the interior in the 8th c. The Assyrian inscriptions mention *Ya'ubi'di* of Hamath on the mid-Orontes, also called *Ilubi'di*, [1]) *Azriya'u* of the northern state of Ya'udi or Sam'al, [2]) who assassinated King Barsur and usurped the throne, and possibly *Ga'yah*, the father of the King of Katka. [3])

Who is this deity venerated by the Aramaeans? Is he identical with the hypothetical *Yw* of the Ras Shamra texts? Or is he Ιευω of the Phoenician Hierombalos? On this we cannot positively declare since, beyond the usage in the names, there is nothing in the texts to give any clue to the nature or function of the deity. It has been claimed that in those Aramaic names we have a form of Yahweh, and DRIVER has suggested that Azriya'u may have been a Jew who founded a small state in N. Syria, which he called Ya'udi after his homeland [4]) a view which we do not think very probable. We would nevertheless agree with DRIVER in seeing a reference to the same Yahweh as had become the national God of Israel. In their original settlement and political development the Aramaeans are not to be considered apart from Israel. Both were of the same general kinship, both had and maintained close links with the desert hinterland, and both stood on much the same cultural level. Among them there may well have been elements jealous of their desert antecedents, like the Rechabites in Israel. Those may have been the core of resistance to political submission and cultural assimilation to Assyria, and indeed that is what the texts imply. It may well be that these had contact with the Qenites, from whom the Hebrew fathers probably adopted, and adapted, the cult of Yahweh. The Qenites as itinerant smiths were, as we know from the instance of Jael the wife of Heber, very mobile. In the case of Azriya'u of Ya'udi, who assassinated the king and usurped the throne, we may have a parallel instance to Jehu of Israel. As Jehu had the backing of the Rechabites Azriya'u in Ya'udi may have represented a similar group with desert ideals. Thus we have no

---

[1]) Inscription of Sargon II, D. D. LUCKENBILL, *Ancient Records of Assyria* II, § 55.

[2]) Inscription of Tiglath-pileser III from Nineveh, *ibidem*, I, § 770.

[3]) In an inscription found at Sefireh, but removed by the natives from Sujin about a mile away and about 12 miles from Aleppo, A. RONZEVALLE, *Mélanges de l'Université de St. Joseph* XV, 1930, p. 235 ff.

[4]) G. R. DRIVER, *ZAW* XLVI, 1928, p. 8. Such a case must have been exceptional, yet we find that in Hamath also a case of such a theophoric *Ya'ubi'di* occurs.

hesitation in accepting the possibility that *Ya'u* or *Yah* in Syria was Yahweh. We insist, however, that the worship of this god was probably confined to a minority among the Aramaeans, who came to power in political crises, and was probably more akin to the worship of Yahweh among the Qenites than to the Mosaic development of Yahwism.

In his first study of the Ras Shamra text presumably containing the name *Yw* [1]) DUSSAUD supposed that Moses did not introduce Israel to a new god, but simply caused them to adopt the Canaanite god *Yw*, who was a son of the high god El. In his latest study on this question [2]) he limited himself to demonstrating that certain of the attributes and funtions of Yahweh in prophetic monotheism were the result of the assimilation of the attributes and functions of Canaanite El and Baal by Yahweh. In the latter proposition we should in the main agree with DUSSAUD, but we question if this was on the basis of kinship of Yahweh to El in Canaanite religion as he claimed on the questionable basis of the genealogy of Philo of Byblos and of Deuteronomy xxxii, 8-9;

> When Elyon apportioned the nations,
> When he distributed the sons of men,
> When he fixed the boundaries of the peoples,
> According to the number of the sons of El, [3])
> Verily the portion of Yahweh was his people,
> Jacob the portion of his inheritance.

In taking this to mean that Elyon is the supreme god, El a god distinct from him, and Yahweh one of the sons of El, DUSSAUD seemed to overpress literalism in the interests of his theory. We do not doubt that the passage represents a stage in the assimilation of the particularist Yahweh-cult to the cult of the universalistic god El Elyon in the settled land, as EISSFELDT has already claimed, [4]) but the term בני אל does not necessarily mean, as DUSSAUD maintained, 'the sons of El', but, in the context, probably 'divine beings', a generic expression, like בני אדם.

The recognition of the fusion between Yahwism and the cult of the Canaanite El and Baal accounts for elements in the Canaanite cult

---

[1]) DUSSAUD, *CRAIBL* 1940, p. 370.
[2]) *idem*, 'Yahwé, fils de El', *Syria* XXXIV, 1957, pp. 233-242.
[3]) Reading בני אל for MT בני ישׂראל with the Versions.
[4]) EISSFELDT, 'Partikularismus und Universalismus in der israelitisch-jüdischen Religionsgeschichte', *ThLZ* LXXIX, 1954, cols. 283 ff.

adopted by Yahwism, but fails to account for the particular nationalistic and ethical elements of Yahwism which persisted in Israel, where the prophets and the Rechabites hark consistently back to a desert tradition. [1]) The vitality and distinctive nature of Israel's primitive Yahwism is evidenced by its survival, by its conscious and unremitting conflict with the grosser elements of Baalism, and also by its power to transform such elements of the cult and theology of the worship of El and Baal which it adopted. In enabling us to determine the extent of this transformation and so to assess the distinctive significance of Yahwism the evidence of the native cult of Canaan in the Ras Shamra texts is of great value for Old Testament study.

Such a view as that propounded by DUSSAUD shows total misunderstanding of the whole ethos of Hebrew religion. Israelite faith and religious practice were conditioned not by relations with an impersonal fertility-deity but by the adoption of Jahweh the God of a certain social group, the Qenites, which involved a clear definition of social obligations in his name and recognized his unique act of grace and power in the Exodus as the genesis of the faith. The Covenant with its essentially moral implications is the basis and essential expression of Hebrew religion. Between the broad universalism and nature-worship of Canaanite nature religion and the essentially ethical particularism of tribal religion there is a whole world of difference.

Actually, even if we accepted the reading Yw in the fragmentary passage [2]) where it is alleged to occur we really gain no elucidation

---

[1]) V. MAAG aptly contrasts the permanence of the desert tradition in Israelite religion with the readiness with which nomads forget their desert antecedents on sedentary settlement, e.g. among the Babylonians, and the Phoenicians, *op. cit.*, pp. 134-137.

[2]) After GORDON *UH* ʿnt, pl. x, IV, 13-20,

wyʿn lṭpn ʾel d(pʾed ....)
šm bny yw ʾel(m ....)
wpʿr šm y(m ....)
tʿnyn lẓntn (....................................)
ʾat ʾadn tpʿr (..................................)
ʾank lṭpn ʾel (dpʾed ....)
ʿl ydm pʿrt (...................................)
šmk mdd ʾel (..................................)

We suggest the following translation, which can be but tentative in the condition of the text:

Then up spake El the Kindly, the Merciful (............)
'The name of my son is "He whom the gods love (.......)
And he declared a name (...........................)

of Hebrew, or even Canaanite, religion. Actually we may well question the reading *yw.ʾelt*, which was read by VIROLLEAUD, DUSSAUD, and GORDON and translated 'Yw the son of Elat'. DRIVER and AISTLEITNER read tentatively *yw ʾelm*, and we adopt this reading. Now the theme of this passage, however obscure it is, is the naming of a young god, a subject which is mentioned specifically probably five times. This indicates either the birth and naming of the young god or his adoption as King and the conferment of a throne-name. In either case the name had symbolic significance with the force of an oracle, consisting of a sentence where the relationship of the god to the nominee was stated. We should thus expect the name to consist of a finite verb with *ʾel* or *ʾelm* as subject. This suggests that *y* in *yw* may be the preformative of the imperfect of a verb, and we suggest that the verb in question is *hwy*, with the elision of the weak initial *h*. This, we suggest, is the cognate of Arabic هوى, 'to love, desire', cf. the Hebrew noun הוה, and propose that the name of the son of El was 'He whom the gods love'. This is supported by the statement that the god's name was *mdd ʾel*. This may be an abridgement or paraphrase of the larger oracular name *yw ʾelm*. The phrase *wpʿr šm y(m*), we suggest, does not mean 'And he declared his name *ym*', but that *y* is here also the preformative of an imperfect, probably of the verb *mlk*, and that it may be an alternative suggestion of a name or perhaps a supplementary oracle. In any case, beyond the relationship to El, the passage reveals nothing of the identity or nature of the god in question.

From two other mythological texts we learn of the gods Šḥr-and-Šlm, the Dawn- and Evening-star [1]) and of Yrḫ the Moon-god and his consort Nkl, [2]) who is, of course, the goddess known in Mesopotamia as Ningal. Šlm, who is mentioned in the offering-list GORDON *UH* 17, 12, and Šḥr, who is not elsewhere attested, are probably but the two hypostases of the one deity manifest in the Morning- and Evening-star. This deity, known otherwise as Aṯtar, played a very important part in the mythology and religion of the

---

She answered him: 'Indeed thou hast beautified me (.......)
Thou, O lord, dost declare (..........................)
I am El the Kindly, (the Merciful... and on my hands .....)
I have declared (.................................)
Thy name is the beloved of El (.......................)

[1]) GORDON *UH* 52.
[2]) *Ibidem*, 77.

desert if we may judge from the later texts cited by NIELSEN and from certain texts and inscriptions from the caravan centres of Edessa and Palmyra. These 'heavenly twins' Šḥr-and-Šlm are termed in the text GORDON *UH* 52 *'elm n'mm wysmm*, 'gods gracious and fair'. H. INGHOLT cites a certain relief from Palmyra depicting a pair of mounted deities named ארצו and עזיזו and termed 'beneficent deities'. [1]) Bearing in mind the affinities of the Aramaic dialect of Palmyra, ארצו might correspond to the Arabic رضو, 'gracious'. [2]) Julian attests the worship of a similar pair at Edessa whom he terms 'Azizos et Monimos'. 'Monimos', like 'Azizos', is obviously a transliteration of a Semitic word, probably מנעם, 'gracious', while Azizos is obviously עזיזו of the Palmyrene inscription. This word, while meaning in Arabic 'noble', has in Akkadian the connotation 'fierce' (*ezezu*), as also in Hebrew. [3]) In this deity manifest in the Morning- and Evening-star we have the beneficent luminary which refreshes men after the heat of the day and guides them on their desert paths; at the same time we have the fierce power who gives light and guidance for the *ghazzia*.

The deity Šlm was known in Palestine as early as the 19th century B.C. as we may perhaps infer from the theophoric name *Kšḥr'ib'i* in the Egyptian Execration Texts published by G. POSENER. [4]) He is thus associated with the Amorites who were just then emerging from a nomad and tribal way of life to the settled life in Palestine. The same texts note Jerusalem as one of the centres of this settlement, [5]) and here again the *šalem* element denotes the god who was thus particularly associated with the city, a fact which seems to be reflected in the names of David's sons Absalom and Solomon. Similar evidence of the cult of Šlm in Moab in the middle of the 8th

---

[1]) H. INGHOLT, *Studier over Palmyrensk Skulptur*, 1928, pp. 42 ff.

[2]) D. NIELSEN, *Handbuch des altarabischen Altertumskunde* I, 1927, pp. 228 ff.

[3]) עז is found as the epithet of a lion (Judges xiv, 18), of an enemy (2 Samuel xxii, 18; Psalm xviii, 18) and of the destructive rage of Simeon and Levi in the 'Blessing of Jacob' (Genesis xlix, 7). It stands in parallelism with אשר לא ישׂא פנים in Deuteronomy xxviii 50 and to קשׁה in Isaiah xix, 4. In Isaiah xxv, 3 עם עז is parallel to עריצים.

[4]) G. POSENER, *Princes et Pays d'Asie et de Nubie* . . ., 1940, p. 74, assuming of course, that, as in the Ras Shamra text GORDON *UH* 52, *šḥr* and *šlm* were inseparable.

[5]) In the texts published by K. SETHE Jerusalem ('Urušalimm) had apparently two chiefs in the vicinity. The fact that the city was settled by various Amorite tribes may well explain the fact that the Venus-star was worshipped under various names and titles, Šlm, Mlk-m, Uzza, and Aṯtr.

century is the truncated theophoric Šalamanu, the name of the king of Moab mentioned in an inscription of Tiglath-Pileser III. [1]) Šlm occurs again as the divine element in a theophoric name on an ostracon from Tell el-Kheleifeh from the 5th or 4th century B.C. when this place, ancient Ezion-geber, was a station on the important trade-route from the oases of Arabia to the Mediterranean and Egypt. [2]) In the orthodox redactions of the Old Testament, of course, the association of Jerusalem with the Amorite deity Šalem has been as far as possible obliterated. Tradition, however, dies hard, and there are many traces of the cult of the Venus-star in Jerusalem, particularly under his titles as 'the king', deliberately misvocalized as 'Milcom', and 'Uzza', which we know to be a title of the Venus-star. [3]) The tradition of a local god Šalem and another Ṣedeq [4]) could, on the other hand, be conveniently revived and applied as when the psalmist visualizes Ṣedeq and Šalem ('Righteousness' and 'Peace') kissing each another. Again, long after the suppression of the cult of the Venus-star, alias Šlm, or 'the king', in Jerusalem popular memory cherished sporadic fragments of his cult-legend which survived locally until they were caught up and worked into the tradition of the new era of peace (*šalom*) with the birth of a king at nearby Bethlehem to which the wise men were guided by a star of exceptional brilliance.

Yrḫ, or the Moon-god, is known from the mythological text celebrating his marriage with Nkl the Moon-goddess, [5]) and from the offering-lists which attest the worship of both Yrḫ and Nkl at Ras Shamra. [6]) There was a great temple of Ningal at Qatna c. 11 ml. N.E. of Homs, and Harran was the cult-centre of the Moon-god Sin and his consort Ningal. The trace of the influence of Harran in an area where the Hurrians predominated may be seen in the ortho-

---

[1]) E. Schrader, *Die Keilinschriften und das Alte Testament*, 1903, p. 475.

[2]) N. Glueck, *BASOR* 82, 1941, pp. 7-9. The name is *ʾapšlm*.

[3]) We have argued for the identity of the various hypostases of this deity about Jerusalem in our article 'The Desert God ʿAṯtr in the Literature and Religion of Canaan', *JNES* VIII, 1949, pp. 73-83.

[4]) The cult of Ṣedeq, a local god of Jerusalem, is postulated by Mowinckel who regards the name Ṣadoq, the chief priest in the time of Solomon, as a hypocoristicon of a theophoric name (*Ezra den Skriftlaerde*, 1916). We note that the names Melchiṣedeq (Genesis xiv, 18 ff.) and Adoniṣedeq (Joshua x, 1, 3), both pre-Israelite kings of Jerusalem, suggest the same conclusion. H. H. Rowley associates Ṣadoq with the pre-Israelite cult at Jerusalem, probably localized at the Stone of Zoheleth, *JBL* LVIII, 1939, p. 123.

[5]) Gordon *UH* 77. This text is an excellent document for evidence of social practice at Ugarit, *v. infra* pp. 248 ff.

[6]) Yrḫ is mentioned in Gordon *UH* 1, 14 and Nkl in 3, 26.

graphic peculiarities of this text which GINSBERG [1]) and GOETZE [2]) have noted as Hurrian features.

The sun was worshipped as a goddess, as we know from the offering lists and from GORDON *UH* 52, 54:

š'u ʿdb lšpš rbt	Take an offering to the Lady Sun

She plays a distinctive part in the myth of Baal, as we should expect from the association of these texts with the fertility-cult. As illuminating the sky and earth, the sun is termed the Luminary of the Gods (*nrt ʾelm*) and as such, and as, according to ancient cosmology, disappearing nightly under the earth, she assists Anat in her search for Baal and in the recovery of his corpse from the underworld. This suggests the Sun's rôle of conductor of the dead, so happily adduced by CAQUOT. [3]) This is the theme of the few lines written on the margin of the text GORDON *UH* 62, which are probably the fragment of a solar myth used as an incantation; [4])

ʾap.ltlḥm (l)ḥm.trmmt	Yea verily thou didst eat the meat of corruption [5])
ltšt yn.tġẓ yt	Didst drink indeed diluted wine [6])
špš rpʾem.tḥtk	O Sun, thou didst hasten [7]) to the shades,
špš.tḥtk.ʾelnym	O Sun thou didst hasten to the ghosts, [8])
ʿdk.ʾelm.hn.mtm	Thine allies [9]) are gods, yea men,
ʿdk.kṯrm.ḥbrk	Thine ally is the Skilful One, thine associate,
wḫss.dʿtk	Even the percipient One, thy friend.

1) GINSBERG, *Orientalia* 1939, pp. 317-327.
2) A. GOETZE, *JBL* L, 1941, pp. 353-374.
3) CAQUOT, *Syria* XXXVI, 1959, pp. 93 ff.
4) GORDON *UH* 62, 42-52.

5) Cf. Arabic رمّ, 'to decay', Hebrew רמה, 'worms'.

6) Cf. Arabic غضّ, 'to abate'.

7) *tḥtk* is generally taken as 'under thee' or 'in thy place', which does not render good sense in the passage. We propose that it is rather the imperfect of the verb *ḥtk*, cf. Arabic حتك, 'to hasten'.

8) There is a similar collocation of *rpʾum* and *ʾelnym* probably in GORDON *UH* 123, 5, 6, and certainly in the bilingual Punic inscription from el-Amruni (1st c. A.D.), where *ʾelnym rpʾym* is rendered by *diis manibus*. *ʾelnym* are therefore chthonic beings, probably supernatural rather than divine.

9) Perhaps *ʿd* is the verbal noun, an abstract with the force of a collective noun, cf. *tʿdt*, 'witnesses' (GORDON *UH* 137, 22, *v. supra*, p. 24 n.), from a root *wʿd*, 'to appoint', meaning 'associates, allies' or the like, cf. Hebrew עדה, as VIROLLEAUD tentatively suggested (*Syria* XV, 1934, p. 239). We admit that we should expect the feminine ending, as in עדה, but this is not an insuperable difficulty.

bym. ʾarš. wtnn	On the day (of battle) [1]) with the Many-headed [2]) and *tnn*,
kṯr. wḫss. yd	May the Skilful and Percipient One drive them away. [3])
ytr. kṯr. wḫss	May the Skilful One rend them asunder. [4])

We suggest that this is a little imprecation, suggested by the mention of the sun-goddess. It may stem from the priest Atnprln, who dictated (*lmd*) the text according to the colophon. The Atn element in the name indicates that the solar cult of Akhnaten had penetrated to the Syrian coast, and probably Atnprln considered that his patron goddess, playing a comparatively minor rôle in the Baal myth, deserved further notice. The reference to *špš* among the shades and the dead is to the nightly disappearance of the sun, after which the imprecation was felt to be necessary. The enemies of the Sun, *tnn* and the Many-headed One (*ʾarš*), already notorious in the Baal myth as the enemies of Cosmos, suggest the well-known myth of the dragon which swallows the sun at an eclipse. We have an echo of this myth in the passage in Revelation xii in the menace of the dragon to the woman clothed with the sun and the stars.

This hymn gives a hint of a mythology of the Sun-cult, which, however, has not survived in the Ras Shamra texts. The Sun, however, is an object of worship, to which the dedication of a votive stele (*pgr*) was recorded (Gordon *UH* 1, 12, 17), and to her with the Moon a shekel of gold was offered (Gordon *UH* 5, 10-11, 13-14). With the Sun is possibly associated a 'heavenly host' (*ṣbʾu*) in Gordon *UH* 3, 47, 53, but on this fragmentary text it is impossible to base much.

Other deities play a prominent part in the myths but were not, apparently, regularly worshipped, if we may judge from their absence from the offering-lists and other ritual texts. Such were Mot, the sinister power of drought and death, whose habitation is 'Corruption' (*ḫpṯt*) [5]) in 'the City of Ruin' (*qrt hmry*) [6]) in the underworld. His

---

1) We suggest that *ym ʾarš* is analogous to יום מדין and يوم اجنادين, 'the day of (the battle) of Midian, Ajnadain'.

2) After Caquot, who feasibly suggests that *ʾarš* is connected with *rʾaš*, 'head' (*Syria* XXXVI, 1959, p. 99). The association with the primaeval enemy of Cosmos *tnn* suggests that *ʾarš* is *šlyṭ dšbʿt rʾašm*, 'the Close-coiling One with Seven Heads' of Gordon *UH* ʿnt III, 39; 67, I, 3.

3) We take *yd* here as in Gordon *UH* 126, V, 11, 18, 21 as the imperfect (here jussive) of *ndy*, 'to drive out', cf. Akkadian *nadu*, Hebrew נדד (Piel).

4) We take *ytr* as the jussive of *ntr*, cf. Arabic نتر, 'to rend' (a garment).

5) Gordon *UH* 51, VIII, 7; for philological note *v. supra* p. 55, n.

6) *Ibidem*, VIII, 11-12, *v. supra* p. 55, n.

rôle is a merely negative one as the antagonist of Baal in the sacred drama. The craftsman-god Kṯr wḪss, who is associated with Memphis, the cult-centre of the Egyptian craftsman-god Ptah, [1]) is similarly limited to the mythological texts, [2]) where he builds the temple of Baal and is the fabricator of the bow which was the bone of contention between Anat and Aqht, and furnishes Baal with the weapons to overcome Sea-and-River, which he symbolically names to make their function effective. In this particular there is a striking correspondence between the Ras Shamra myths and the tradition recorded by Philo of Byblos. Other deities, again, though merely named in the myths, appear regularly as recipients of sacrifices in the offering-lists. Ršp is the power of pestilence and death, like the Babylonian Nergal. He is signalized by his headdress surmounted by gazelle horns as on the Mekal-stele at Bethshan from the 14th century. He is named in ritual texts at Ras Shamra [3]) and in theophoric names. [4]) Dagon, who is obviously connected, as his name implies, with corn (*dgn*), is mentioned in ritual texts [5]) and in two votive inscriptions [6]) and in a theophoric name. [7]) In spite of the fact, therefore, that Dagon is mentioned in the mythological texts only as the father of Baal, he was still independently worshipped at Ras Shamra in the Late Bronze Age, and his temple rivals that of Baal. In the ritual texts there are certain other deities who never appear in the mythological texts. Ṯkmn and Šnm, for instance, named in four texts, [8]) are probably the Lofty and the Exalted, [9]) the attendants of El, and Ddmš, possibly a Hurrian deity, as the termination implies, is mentioned once. [10])

These, then, were the deities of Ugarit in the Late Bronze Age on the evidence of the Ras Shamra texts. There are deities representing various natural forces, and gods of various racial elements in the

---

[1]) GORDON *UH* 2 Aqht V, 23-31.

[2]) *Ibidem* 51; 68; Aqht.

[3]) *Ibidem* 1, 4, 7; 3, 13, 16; 17, 5, and in a mythological text discovered in 1954 (VIROLLEAUD, *PRU* II, 1, 3), where he is termed 'Lord of the Arrow' (*bʿl ḥẓ*), The text, however, is too fragmentary to base much upon.

[4]) *Ibidem* 64, 12; 301, I, 17; 321, III, 45; 400, I, 22.

[5]) *Ibidem* 9, 3; 17, 16; 19, 5.

[6]) *Ibidem* 69, 2; 70, 2.

[7]) *Ibidem* 306, 7.

[8]) *Ibidem* 1, 3; 2, 35; 3, 31; 107, 4. These are identified with the Kassite deities Thukamuna and Shumalia, who, EISSFELDT conjectures, may have been introduced to Ugarit as the result of the accession of a Kassite prince or intermarriage with a Kassite princess, *El im Ugaritischen Pantheon*, 1951, pp. 66-68.

[9]) For etymology see pp. 156 n.; 205, n.

[10]) GORDON *UH* 17, 6.

heterogeneous population of Ugarit. So long as the crises of the peasant's year were celebrated with the rites of the sacred drama implied in the Baal-mythology it is difficult to conceive of any general advance from polytheism to monotheism. Nor, in view of the evidence of the mythological texts and the offering-lists, where El is one among many, is there any apparent ground for the theory of practical monotheism, though this theory has been held, mainly on the ground that the native Canaanite pantheon is the offspring of El. [1]) To this view POPE objects that the disrespectful attitude of Anat to El does not suggest the harmony of the divine family that the monotheistic view demands. [2]) This, however, we feel to be no compelling objection, though it does rather suggest that a purely polytheistic situation obtained. Our own view is that, so far from all other deities in the Ugaritic pantheon being expressions of provinces of the activity of the one original deity, El, there is a fundamental diversity of nature and interest in the case of El, the paramount authority in social affairs, and of Baal and the others, whose province was nature. The family relationship of El and the nature-deities in the Baal-mythology strikes one as artificial, and the comparative superfluity of El in those texts is an indication of this. The titular supremacy of El in the Baal-mythology may be an acknowledgement of the supremacy of some invading tribal element to whom the worship of El was proper, but the fact remains that El expresses the omnipotence of God above the menace of evil, while Baal expresses the dynamic power of God in the struggle to preserve order in Nature.

In Ugarit in the Late Bronze Age, which enjoyed close political and cultural contacts with Egypt of the Amarna Age, it is quite conceivable that certain enlightened men had advanced to the position of at least theoretical monotheism, and this view is held by no less an authority than EISSFELDT. [3]) Indeed, on the basis of a certain text (GORDON *UH* 107), which we believe to be an invocation, [4])

---

[1]) J. AISTLEITNER in a Hungarian publication cited from a private communication to EISSFELDT, *op. cit.*, p. 71.

[2]) POPE, *op. cit.*, pp. 90 ff.

[3]) EISSFELDT, *op. cit.*, pp. 59-70.

[4]) GORDON *UH* 107, *ʾel bn ʾel*
dr bn ʾel
mpḫrt bn ʾel
ṯkmn wšnm
ʾel wʾaṯrt
ḥnn ʾel
nṣbt ʾel

El was apparently hypostatized in his various attributes, such as his Mercy (*ḥnn*, and possibly *mrḫ*), [1] his Exaltation (*nṣbt*), his Perfection (*šlm*), his Transcendence(?) (*n'et*), [2] his Eternity (*ṣmd*) [3] his Nobility (*šrp*), [4] and his Vigour (?) (*ġdyn*). [5] This is a notoriously controversial text, and not all specialists who have studied it would agree with the translation and interpetation we have offered. [6] In the case of the first three elements, however, Mercy, Exaltation, and Perfection,

---

šlm 'el
'el ḫš 'el 'ad'u
b'd/l ṣpn b'd/l
'ugrt
rev. *bmrḫ 'el*
bn'et 'el
bṣmd 'el
bdṯn 'el
bšrp 'el
bknt 'el
bġdyn 'el
'ad'u 'el

Our interpretation of this text as an invocation depends upon the reading *b'd* instead of *b'l* in the last two lines of the obverse. If *b'l* is the proper reading we should regard the text as an oath-formula. The apparent imperatives *ḫš* and *'ad'u*, however, suggest that the text is an invocation 'on behalf of' (*b'd*) Ugarit and Saphon ('the ashes of our fathers and the temples of our gods'). In this case we should emphasize the supremacy of El in history and the social order.

[1]) We suggest the connection of *mrḫ* with the Arabic root راح, the verbal noun of the VIIIth form of which, إرتياح, means 'mercy'. On the other hand *mrḫ* is found in the Krt text (Gordon *UH* 125, 47, 51), meaning 'a spear', and *ṣmd* is found in the text Gordon *UH* 68 meaning 'mace', so that these words and *n'et* may signify weapons of El, of which, however, neither the texts nor sculpture give us any indication.

[2]) The word may be cognate with the Arabic نأى, 'to be remote'.

[3]) This suggests to us the Arabic epithet of Allah الصمد, for which, however, no derivation is suggested which is unanimously accepted by scholars.

[4]) If *šrp* is indeed an aspect of the character of El it might be cognate with the Arabic شرف, 'to be noble'. It is suggested, however, that here as in offering-lists *šrp* may be 'burnt-offerings', or even divine attendants on El, like the Hebrew שׂרפים, H. Ringgren, *Word and Wisdom*, 1947, pp. 74-78.

[5]) If our tentative translation of this very difficult word is correct the root may be cognate with the Arabic غزا, 'to direct oneself to an object with purpose' The word may even mean 'the purpose of El' in the text we cite. It would thus correspond to ענת יהו in the Elephantine Papyri according to Albright's view, *From the Stone Age to Christianity*, 1940, p. 286, n. 51.

[6]) Cf. especially J. Obermann, *JBL* LV, 1936, pp. 21-44, who regarded the various words we have cited as verbs, and Eissfeldt, *op. cit.* p. 61 n., who regards them as predicates of nominal sentences, 'El is Mercy', 'El is Stability', 'El is Wellbeing' etc.

there would seem little room for substantial disagreement. Here, then, is surely a significant indication of the extent to which the ancient Canaanites were capable of spiritualizing the conception of the highest authority in the social realm, whom we believe to be specifically El.

ii. THE CULT

Among the Ras Shamra tablets there are a number which relate directly to current ritual. These are generally either mere catalogues or are in such a mutilated condition that it is impossible to make a complete translation. Moreover they contain many terms which, even if deciphered correctly, still defy translation. Nevertheless, there is sufficient material for a fair reconstruction of the cult at Ugarit in the Late Bronze Age.

The text Gordon *UH* 1 gives a list of the gods worshipped and their appropriate sacrifices. The gods are those we have already noted with the addition of others such as 'the lords of the threshing'(?), *bʿlm dṯt*, [1]) and the deities of certain localities such as *ʾelt mgdl* and *ʾelt ʾasrm*. Other words in this text such as *ʾušḫry*, *ṣml*, *ṯrmn*, *ʿrṯ*, and *ǵlmt*, by their position, probably signify deities. We note also that the sun-goddess, *špš*, and the fertility-goddess, *pdry*, are also recipients of offerings. The last-named is known from the Baal-cycle as the daughter or/and consort of Baal.

The offering, *ṯʿ*, is generally classified as 'great', *gdlt*, or small, *dqt*. The two adjectives are used in the feminine, the precise significance of which eludes us. Otherwise the offering is specified as an ox, *ʾalp*, or sheep, *š*, which must, of course, be 'perfect', *tm*, and 'approved' *nkbd*. We see in *šrp*, the 'burnt offering', and *šlmm* in l. 4 of this text a reference to the two categories of sacrifice familiar in the Hebrew cult, *šrp* being the whole burnt offering, the Hebrew עולה, none of which was consumed by the worshippers, and *šlmm* the communion offering, of which worshippers and deity partook, thus realizing the solidarity (*šlm*) of the worshippers and of the community and its god. We may note the same association of *šrp* and *šlmm* in the text Gordon *UH* 9, 7. There is, we think, a reference to a meal-offering to the gods of the threshing-floor (*bʿlm dṯt*) in Gordon *UH* 1, 9, which apparently consisted of one third (*šnpt ḥṣt*) [2]) of a shekel's weight for every fifteen measures (*ḫmš ʿšrh mlʾun*). There is further

---

[1]) Cf. Hebrew דוש, Arabic داس, 'to thresh'.

[2]) 'Two-thirds of a half', so Gordon *UL*, p. 111.

reference in the text Gordon *UH* 3, 19 to wine, oil, and other produce for the 'house of El', but whether this was an offering to the god or provisions for his ministers is uncertain. We think, however, that the provisions in question furnished the material for a ceremonial meal in which the king was involved. [1]) This was in a given month (l. 1) and on the 'day of the new moon' (*ym ḥdṯ*). This, however, was more than a new moon feast such as we hear of in ancient Israel. It apparently lasted at least seven days since there is a reference to oracles given (*rgm yṯṯb*) [2]) on the sixth and seventh days. Here again, however, our information is gleaned sporadically from a fragmentary text.

Another text fragmentary but suggestive is Gordon *UH* 9. This concerns a ritual in which the king is involved in the 10th month (*yrḫ ʿšrt*). In l. 10 the king washes himself (*yrtḥṣ*) [3]) from spittle (*rr*), and sacrifices, both wholly burnt (*šrp*) and communion offerings (*šlmm*), are made to El, Baal, Dagon, Aṯerat and Ym and doubtless other gods whose names are lost in lacunae. In the first line there is reference to *slḫ npš*, 'forgiveness of soul', and it may well be that here we have the Canaanite counterpart to the Hebrew Day of Atonement, the solemn occasion when the community through its representative, king or priest, laid its life (*npš*) [4]) in the hand of the gods and after due ritual received it back again as a divine favour. Such a text as this, fragmentary as it is, suggests that the religion of ancient Canaan was much fuller and deeper than the imitative magic of the fertility-cult. Gordon regards this as a New Year ceremony, [5]) a view which must be modified by the reading '10th month' [6]) for Gordon's 'the month Tishri').

From the text just cited we see that the Canaanites of Ugarit no less than the Babylonians observed times and seasons. Like the Babylonians too they observed and worshipped the heavenly bodies. We have already noted their veneration of the Venus-star, Aṯtar, hypostatized as Šḥr and Šlm. One of the more recently discovered

---

[1]) ll. 48-50.

[2]) ll. 45-46.

[3]) The text actually reads *yrtḥl* which we take to be a scribal error or perhaps a misreading for *yrtḥṣ*, i.e. 𐎍 (*l*) for 𐎕 (*ṣ*). This reading is confirmed by a fuller copy of Gordon *UH* 3, which also mentions this rite, A. Herdner, 'Un nouvel exemplaire du rituel RS 1929, no. 3', *Syria* XXXIII, 1956, pp. 104-112.

[4]) We must be careful not to spiritualize the term *npš* in a way foreign to early Semitic thought.

[5]) Gordon *UL*, p. 108.

[6]) So A. Herdner, *Corpus*, p. 122.

texts, which we believe to be an omen-text, clearly refers to astrology:[1])

> During the six days of the new moon of the month Ḫyr, the sun setting and Ršp being her porter, then let the devotees divine [2]) danger [3])

The translation and interpretation of this text is not certain, and the last three words may mean 'let the devotees seek out [4]) a substitute'. [5]) In this case we may have an instance of the practice known in Assyria in later times whereby a substitute for the King as the representative of the community was appointed when the stars were particularly unfavourable. [6])

A similar text is GORDON *UH* 5, which, in spite of many doubtful words, indicates that certain duties, offerings and imposts, were incumbent on the royal house at such a crisis.

Now that there is evidence for such fully developed cults in ancient Canaan as early as the age of the Hebrew patriarchs it has been maintained that one of the main bases of WELLHAUSEN's hypothesis of the evolution of Hebrew religion, so vital for this view of the growth and composition of the Pentateuch, has been severely shaken. According to the evolutionary view characteristic of the age of

---

[1]) VIROLLEAUD, 'Les Nouvelles Tablettes de Ras Shamra', *Syria* XXVIII, 1951, pp. 25-27, text III, *b ṯṯ ym ḥdṯ*
ḫyr ʿrbt
špš ṯġrh
ršp
wʿbdm tbqrn
skn

[2]) The root in the Piel has certainly this sense in 2 Kings xvi, 15, where it refers to divination by 'inspection' of entrails, cf. Leviticus xxvii, 33, where the verb means 'to discriminate' between good and evil. The phrase לבקר בהיכלו in Psalm xxvii, 4 probably refers to divination, in this case by consulting the oracle, so MOWINCKEL (*The Psalms in Israel's Worship* II, 1962, p. 54) and in Prov. xx, 25,

מוקש אדם ילע קדש
ואחר נדרים לְבַקֵּר

It is a snare for a man to say rashly 'It is holy',
And after vows to take auspices.

[3]) We propose that *skn* has this meaning in GORDON *UH* 75, II, 5, *v. supra*, p. 79 n. 8 for etymological notes.

[4]) This sense of *bqr* is attested in Leviticus xiii, 36 and Ezekiel xxxiv, 11-12.

[5]) In GORDON *UH* 69, 1 *skn* means a 'stele', something set up as a substitute for something else, probably in this case a votive offering. *zukinu* occurs in the Amarna Tablets (J. A. KNUDTZON, *Die El-Amarna Tafeln*, 1908-15, no. 64, 9) as a Canaanite gloss on Akkadian *rabiṣu*, the representative or substitute of the suzerain power. Akkadian *šakanu* also means 'vizier', with a like significance.

[6]) Cf. J. GRAY, 'Royal Substitution in the Ancient Near East', *PEQ* 1955, pp. 180-2.

WELLHAUSEN an elaborate cult presupposing an established sanctuary is inconsistent with nomadic conditions and the ascription of such ordinances to Moses before the settlement of Canaan is an anachronism. DUSSAUD, having already undertaken to demonstrate on the evidence of technical terms in Phoenician and Punic inscriptions that the Hebrew sacrificial system as elaborated in Leviticus was not necessarily post-Exilic, welcomed the Ras Shamra material as confirmation of his thesis. [1])

The theory that the Ras Shamra texts illustrate the Levitical system is based largely on the occurrence of the familiar technical terms. T. H. GASTER follows DUSSAUD in developing this theme, and maintains that the same technical terms of the cult found in later Phoenician and South Arabian inscriptions indicate a common origin in 'that primitive Hebrew civilization from which those cultures severally developed'. [2]) Of the terms in question GASTER has given a full list in the DUSSAUD memorial publication [3]) and we must now examine these in relation to their context in the Ras Shamra texts.

There are undoubtedly many technical terms common to Hebrew and Ugaritic and we are prepared for this, especially as regards the more general terminology. Thus *dbḥ*, 'sacrifice', corresponds to זבח, *mtn*, 'gift', to מתן, *ndr*, 'vow', to נדר, while, of the verbs, *šqrb* corresponds philologically to הקריב and in meaning to הגיש, 'to bring up a victim for sacrifice'; *šʿly*, 'to offer the victim' corresponds to העלה and *ybl*, 'to offer', found in I Aqht 214, corresponds to הוביל of Psalm lxviii, 30 and Zephaniah iii, 10, while *ʿdb*, 'to do, prepare' may possibly be used in the sense 'to sacrifice', as עשׂה in Hebrew. These, however, are general terms, which might belong to the common matrix of Semitic language in the ancient Near East. They are not

---

[1]) DUSSAUD, *Les Origines cananéennes du sacrifice israélite*, 2nd ed. 1941, pp. 325 ff. DUSSAUD does not disagree, however, with the work of WELLHAUSEN as a literary critic; his objection is that the Wellhausenist school confuses purely literary with historical issues. While accepting the Wellhausenist view of the literary composition of the Pentateuch, DUSSAUD maintains that simply because certain terms and practices are a specific feature of the Priestly Code they need not necessarily date from the time of that code. The fact is that the Ras Shamra texts attest a developed cult, with many points in common with the Hebrew cult, several centuries before the time of Moses. On purely chronological grounds there is no reason why the Hebrews should not have practised such a cult as early as the time of Moses. Socially, however, and economically it is highly improbable that the Hebrew nomads observed such usages, which were quite irrelevant to their desert environment.

[2]) GASTER, *Mélanges syriens offerts à M. René Dussaud*, 1939, p. 577.

[3]) *Ibidem*, pp. 578-580.

sufficiently specific to establish a necessary connection between the cult of Ugarit and that of the Hebrews.

To turn to more specific terms, *šlm* or *šlmm*, which GASTER renders as 'payment offerings', occurs frequently in the Old Testament, though there is diversity of opinion as to the exact significance of the term. It is taken variously to mean 'peace-offering' whereby a man is reconciled to God, and 'welfare-offering', a feature of which was a communal meal. [1]) Here, as in other practices and terminology, we have to reckon with a development in language and usage over a considerable period of time and in varying circumstances. In the Old Testament the term in question is found in 1 Samuel xi, 15, Exodus xx, 24, xxiv, 5 (E), Amos v, 22, Joshua viii, 31 (D), Deuteronomy xxvii, 7, and Leviticus x, 14 (P), in sources, that is to say, ranging over a period of half a millennium. The basic sense of the term, however, is 'communion', the making whole (שׁלם) of the relationship between the community and its God. In the offering-lists from Ras Shamra the letter-complex *šlmm* is found, as we have already seen. In GORDON *UH* 1, 4 and 9, 7 its association with *šrp* suggests the association in the Old Testament of עוֹלה and שׁלמים. The latter term as distinct from the first, which denotes sacrifice exclusively devoted to the deity, denotes a sacrifice which was consumed by both deity and worshippers, thus effecting communion between them. The exiguous nature of the ritual texts of Ugarit, however, does not permit of further particularization on this *terminus technicus*.

GASTER claims to find a reference to the 'wave-offering', תְּנוּפה, which is established as a technical term in the Priestly Code in Exodus xxix, 27, Leviticus vii, 34, x, 14, xxiii, 15, 17, and Numbers xviii, 11. The Ugaritic evidence, however, proves on examination to be fragmentary and disjointed. In a certain offering-list, GORDON *UH* 23, 6 [2]), a term *šnpt* occurs which GASTER reads as a causative (Shaf'el) from a root *npy*. The verb, however, with the meaning GASTER assumes is not otherwise attested in Ugaritic. [3]) Actually GORDON seems to us nearer the truth in taking the word as a local form of the Akkadian *šinipu*, a corruption of the Sumerian *šanabu* meaning 'two-thirds of a shekel'. [4])

---

[1]) DUSSAUD, *op. cit.*, pp. 301-313.
[2]) Another case not cited by GASTER is GORDON *UH* 1, 10.
[3]) The Hebrew root is עׂיו, possibly a by-form of a לׂ״ה verb.
[4]) E. A. SPEISER, 'Of Shoes and Shekels', *BASOR* 77, 1940, pp. 15-20.

Another such technical term listed by GASTER is אשם. The word is found in the Priestly Code indicating a restitution-offering. [1]) It is probably not confined to that late source, however, as it is found applied to the tumours and golden mice which the Philistines returned with the Ark [2]) and again in 2 Kings xii, 17, where it consisted apparently of money and was the perquisite of the priests. [3]) In the Ras Shamra texts, however, the letter complex *'aṯm* is found in only two texts, GORDON *UH* 27 and 45. In the first of those the word occurs no less than eleven times, but never in a whole line, and eight times it is the only word in the line. Apart from the quite possible phonetic correspondence of *'aṯm* and אשם suggested by the Arabic cognate أَثِمَ, 'to commit a crime', the evidence that there was a Canaanite counterpart to the Hebrew אשם is inadequate. In a letter to the high priest (GORDON *UH* 18) in a fragmentary passage (l. 18), *yhbṭ b'aš*(   ) there is a possible appeal for rebatement (Arabic هبط) of assessment for compensation (אשם), but again the evidence is not really adequate.

The term פטר, 'that which opens the womb', the first-born, attested in Exodus xiii, 1-12 (J) and in Numbers viii, 16 (P), is thought to have its counterpart in Ugaritic sacrificial practice and terminology on the evidence of one text, Gordon *UH* 71, 9. Here again the text is fragmentary and, as the context refers to offerings to the sun, *pṭr* may refer to the dawn. In the case of the presumed Ugaritic prototype of תמיד, the regular morning and evening sacrifice attested in Ezekiel xlvi, 15, Ezra iii, 5, and Numbers xxviii, 6(P), there is no etymological counterpart in Ugaritic, but GASTER cites a passage from the text GORDON *UH* 52,

š'u 'db lšpš rbt
wlkbkbm kn(. . . . .)

rendering:

'Take an offering to the Lady Sun and the stars, a perpetual offering'.

GASTER takes the fragmentary *kn* (. . .) as from כון, 'to establish', which is possible but dubious. In any case, even admitting GASTER's reading, the text tells us absolutely nothing about the rite at Ugarit.

We are more than sceptical about GASTER's claim to find reference

---

[1]) G. B. GRAY maintains that the idea of commutation or fine is present in the term even in P, *Sacrifice in the Old Testament; its Theory and Practice*, 1925, pp. 37-38.

[2]) 1 Samuel vi, 3, 4, 8, 17.

[3]) In both those cases we must reckon with the possibility of expansion of the earlier historical record by commentary reflecting later conditions.

to libation (*nsk*) in the Ras Shamra texts. [1]) The verb is certainly used in Ugaritic but only in a general sense of casting metal, or overspreading glaze and the like.

The term מַעֲשֵׂר, which may mean a tenth part in general without any ritual connotation, appears as a technical term for a special offering in Amos iv, 4, Deuteronomy xiv, 22 and in the Priestly Code in Leviticus xxvii, 31 and Numbers xviii, 24, 28. GASTER cites a certain ritual text GORDON *UH* 5, 1-2,

> *kt'rb 'ṯtrt ḫr...*
> *bt mlk 'šr 'šr.*

He translates:

> When the sacred bride enters the cave...
> Tithe tithes ...

Here again it is a case of an obscure passage in a short text. The word *'šr* here as elsewhere in the Ras Shamra texts may mean 'feast' rather than 'tithe'.

The term אִשֶּׁה, occurring in 1 Samuel ii, 28, Deuteronomy xviii, 1, Joshua xiii, 14 (D), and Leviticus vi, 10 and generally in the Priestly Code, is commonly taken as an offering made by fire, being derived from אש. G. B. GRAY, however, suggests that it was derived ultimately from the root אנש, cf. Arabic أنيس, 'sociable', and meant originally a fellowship-offering, though this sense has been quite lost by the time of its literary usage in the Old Testament. [2]) The word does occur in the Ras Shamra texts (GORDON *UH* krt, 135, 278) in the form *'ušn*, but this means probably 'a gift' with no implication of sacrifice.

The word מנחה, the bloodless offering of cereals or oil, may be mentioned in the text GORDON *UH* 120, 1, 4, but its association with *brẓl*, 'iron' in that short text suggests that *mnḫ* means rather 'tribute' than an offering to a shrine, a sense in which מנחה is used in the Old Testament (Judges iii, 13 ff. and 2 Samuel viii, 2 ff.).

From such sporadic evidence it is very precarious to assume a sacrificial system such as is found in the 'Mosaic' law. Even if GASTER's and DUSSAUD's assumption of technical terms were admitted, it would be impossible from the short and fragmentary texts to deter-

---

[1]) There is a reference to libation of wine and honey in GORDON *UH* Krt 71-72/164-5, the verb being not *nsk* but *nṣq* or better *yṣq*.

[2]) G. B. GRAY, *op. cit.*, pp. 9-13.

mine their precise significance. Moreover, since we find a development in the meanings of the terms in the course of the history of the Hebrews themselves, it is likely that there would be a further variation of meaning and application in the case of terms in use in Ugarit in the 14th century B.C. and the same terms in the Priestly Code almost a millennium later.

Actually the equivalence of mere technical terms is the weakest argument for a correspondence between the cultic systems of Israel and Ugarit. DUSSAUD himself, in fact, opened a far more fruitful field in citing certain passages in the longer texts which imply cultic practices which were established in Palestine early in the Israelite settlement and described in detail in the Priestly Code.

This evidence is twofold, being direct, as in the Krt and Aqht texts, and indirect, as in the mythological texts, particularly the Baal-cycle. Since we have touched upon this subject in our treatment of these texts, a brief recapitulation will suffice, with special reference to affinities with Hebrew ritual.

We have emphasized the significance of the principle of imitative magic in ritual supplemented by a verbal accompaniment in the crises and changes of the Canaanite peasant's year. When the Hebrew tribesmen settled down to the new life of agriculture it was natural for them to adopt with the new technique of agriculture those rites of imitative magic. Thus in all innocence Israel adopted one of the most significant features of Canaanite religion. The extent to which this element pervaded Hebrew religion is indicated in all the pre-Exilic prophets, particularly Hosea. It is no less apparent, though perhaps less obvious, in the ritual passages in the Pentateuch and in liturgical literature such as the Psalms.

In the latter we have already seen that the theme of the conflict of God and the powers of Chaos, elemental and political, resulting in the victory of God and the establishment of his kingship is the adaptation of the Canaanite declaration of faith in Providence expressed in the myth of Baal and the unruly waters Sea-and-River, which, by analogy, we may well suppose to have been accompanied by a ritual combat. In the Ras Shamra text there is no indication of the season of the year to which this was appropriate, but the Hebrew adaptation of the myth was traditionally associated with the autumnal New Year and there is good reason to credit tradition here. Thus, then, in all probability, began the year of the Canaanite peasant with an act and a declaration, ritual and myth, which at once predisposed the result of the conflict between Cosmos and Chaos and gave the community the opportunity of voicing, and thereby strengthening, their faith.

The phases of the peasant's year with the alternate progress and recession of the growth of vegetation were attended by their appropriate rites and myths expressing the antagonism between Baal and Mot, the tension between vitality and sterility, with Baal a dying and rising god such as Tammuz in Mesopotamia, Osiris in Egypt, and Dionysus in Greece.

The text Gordon *UH* ʿnt anticipates Baal's rehabilitation. He is alive but not yet active and is still without a temple or 'house'. The most striking passage in this text describes a blood-bath in which his sister and champion the goddess Anat indulges, apparently in her temple. [1]) We have suggested that underlying this text is some bloodletting rite to induce the 'early rains' of which we may have a reminiscence in the self-laceration of the prophets of Baal in the ordeal with Elijah on Carmel (1 Kings xviii).

In this text the question of a 'house' for Baal is raised and after further negotiation this materializes (Gordon *UH* 51). We have already pointed out internal evidence for the building of this 'house' on the eve of the 'early rains' of the Syrian New Year, and have noted that the Hebrew Feast of Tabernacles fell at this season. Now among the Semites the setting up of a house signifies the founding of a family, so it is likely that the building of the 'house' of Baal is connected with his renewed virility. This, of course, was stimulated further by sympathetic licence on the part of the worshippers, possibly in tabernacles or bivouacs raised for this purpose. There is, to be sure, no actual evidence for this in the Ras Shamra texts, but analogies with fertility-cults ancient and modern make this likely, and unless there were such practices it is difficult to account for the stigma of the Hebrew prophets on the sexual licence of the fertility-cult. Direct evidence for the affinity between Canaanite and Hebrew religion in the particular of the building of a temple at this season is the fact that Solomon dedicated the Temple in Jerusalem in the month of Ethanim the month of the 'regular rains'.

On the death of Baal at the hands of Mot the myth describes the familiar details of mourning on the part of El and Anat (Gordon *UH* 67, VI). The repetition of stereotyped phraseology suggests that we

---

[1]) Gordon *UH* ʿnt, II, 5-15, *v. supra* p. 40 ff.

have here the reflection of a well-established rite. Analogies with the practice of modern primitives lead us to suppose that this was a crisis in which the community was bound to take a sympathetic part, and we suppose that here we have the Canaanite prototype of the weeping for Hadad which Zechariah mentions in Palestine (Zechariah xii, 11) and the weeping for Tammuz in which the women of Jerusalem indulged in the time of Ezekiel (Ezekiel viii, 14).

The rôle of women in this rite is reminiscent of the part that the goddess Anat plays in mourning and searching for the dead Baal (GORDON *UH* 67 VI, 25-31). There is probably a reminiscence of those rites in the mourning of the virgins of Israel mentioned in the Jephthah saga (Judges xi, 37-40).

Like the Hebrews the Canaanites had ceremonies connected with the desacralization of the new crop, reflected most obviously in Anat's slaughter of Mot in revenge for the death of her brother Baal. The reference here is to the grain-harvest which begins in April and ends in May or early June. This was inaugurated in Hebrew ritual by the offering of the first sheaf on the morrow of the Feast of Unleavened Bread associated with the Passover and was consummated by the offering of the last sheaf seven weeks later at the Feast of Weeks or Pentecost. We may well suppose the myth of Anat's slaughter of Mot by sickle, winnowing-shovel, fire, and millstone to have been accompanied by such a rite as that described in Leviticus ii, 14 which describes the offering of the first sheaf, 'green ears of corn, dried by the fire, even corn beaten out of full ears'. [1])

The Baal-cycle goes on to describe an epic combat between Baal and Mot after seven years. This passage may reflect an annual ritual combat between the forces of fertility and sterility for, in spite of the heavy dew which is a feature of the Syrian summer, famine and disease were a constant menace in those lands exposed to the siroccos and locust plagues from the desert. In this case the 'seven years' would be figurative, which is quite possible. On the other hand we think that this reference should be taken literally to refer to a septennial rite connected with the Sabbatical Year among the Hebrews. The Ras Shamra text is fragmentary here, but from the scraps that remain it is not unreasonable to conclude that Baal was victorious

---

[1]) *v. supra* p. 68 ff. There may be a further reference to this desacralization of the new crop in GORDON *UH*, Krt, 79-84/171-175, where the king qua priest desacralizes the barley and wheat crops ('bread of the fifth, food of the sixth month') by ceremonial baking or parching, *v. supra* pp. 137.

and the fertility of the ensuing septennium thereby secured on the principle of imitative magic. In the Hebrew practice on the other hand the Sabbatical Year was an artificial famine, the land being abandoned to the power of sterility. Though there is no suggestion in Hebrew usage of a ritual combat, Hebrew and Canaanite practice agree in the principle that the power of sterility must be given free scope for a season in the belief that it will exhaust itself in the crisis.

In mediating the fertility-cult to Israel the ancient sanctuaries of Palestine each played its rôle no doubt. Ophrah, Mizpah, Hebron, and even Beersheba might all have reflected in some degree the Canaanite cult as we now know it from the Ras Shamra texts. Samaria too had a shrine of Baal as is apparent from the incident of Jehu's massacre of the devotes of the fertility-cult (2 Kings x, 18 ff.). Nor is there any reason to suppose that the cults of Dan and Bethel, though known to us particularly only after the Disruption, were pure innovations of Jeroboam. In the case of Dan it is expressly stated that it was a Phoenician settlement (Judges xviii, 7), and it seems likely that Jeroboam's calves were connected with the cult of Baal-Hadad, whose cult-animal was the bull. The significance of Gibeon must have been great, since even the Chronicler, for all his devotion to the orthodox tradition of Jerusalem, cannot suppress the association between the cult and cult-officials of Gibeon and that of the Temple. [1]) The Old Testament evidence reveals more Jahwistic than Baalistic features in the cult at Gibeon, but traces of the fertility-cult do appear, notably in the incident of the immolation and exposure of the sons of Saul (2 Samuel xxi). DUSSAUD has noted the association of this human sacrifice with the beginning and end of harvest [2]), and it may well be that this is the survival—at least in tradition—of a crude practice where a human being was sacrificed either as a propitiation to the spirit of harvest or as embodying the corn-spirit who, as the fate of Mot and Aqht in the Ras Shamra texts indicate, was killed at that crucial season. The narrative of Josiah's reforms gives direct evidence for the cult of Baal at Jerusalem, [3]) and we have already noted that the Hebrews had already had the opportunity to familiarize themselves with the cult and cult-legend of Baal at

---

[1]) 1 Kings iii, 4; 2 Chronicles i, 3, 13.

[2]) DUSSAUD, *Les Origines cananéennes du sacrifice israélite*, 2nd ed., pp. 288-289.

[3]) The cult of Šlm, however, attested also at Ras Shamra, was apparently the specific local cult of Jerusalem, the name of the city being a theophoric compound containing the name of this deity.

Baal Saphon, East of the Delta, in Egypt. [1]) For the fertility-cult in Palestine we may further cite evidence from various archaeological stations in the Late Bronze Age. The bronze figurine of Baal-Hadad from Tell ed-Duweir [2]), which is identical with figurines and reliefs from Ras Shamra and Minet el-Beida, [3]) and the stele in honour of Anat at Bethshan, [4]) attest the worship of Baal and kindred deities in Palestine. The mythology, institutions, and cult-terms of the fertility-cult of Canaan may well have been known also in Palestine. This conclusion, however, must always be qualified by the fact of the comparatively provincial culture of Palestine.

We hope that, in spite of our qualification of the views held by DUSSAUD and GASTER, we have made it plain that there were considerable correspondences between Hebrew and Canaanite religion. Not every feature, however, of the religion of Canaan had equal influence on Hebrew thought. What is really impressive in such a comparative study as we have undertaken is not the superficial correspondences, but the essential differences. The Hebrew genius is characterized particularly by the selective principle on which it worked, by what it appropriated from ancient Canaan, and how it adapted that material. The abiding heritage of Canaan to Israel was the theme of the triumph of God over the powers of Chaos not only in the natural sphere—with which the Canaanites apparently were mainly concerned—but in the realm of history and morality. By the appropriation of this theme, sustained by seasonal ritual and myth, the tribal particularism of primitive Israel matured to a sublime philosophy of history which transcended all national and territorial limitations. The great theme in fact develops steadily through Israel's history and spiritual growth until it reaches full fruition in the Gospel of the Kingdom. No less is the Hebrew genius characterized by what it rejected of the legacy of Canaan. The rest of Canaanite mythology, particularly the conflict of Baal with Mot, never moulded Israelite thought. This is significant in view of the fact that it was associated with seasonal rites and festivals also observed by the Hebrews after their settlement of Palestine. For the Hebrews Jahweh was not, like Baal in his

---

[1]) *v. supra*, pp. 11, n. 2; 28, n. 5.

[2]) J. L. STARKEY, *PEFQS* 1936, p. 175.

[3]) SCHAEFFER, *Syria* XIV, 1933, pl. XVI; *Ugaritica* I, p. 116; pl. XXV.

[4]) This stele was found in the North temple of Ramses III and inscribed to 'Antit Queen of Heaven and Mistress of all the Gods'. A. ROWE, *The Four Canaanite Temples of Bethshan*, 1940, pl. LXV, A, 1.

conflict with Mot, a dying and rising god. He was not the impersonal life-force in nature, but a God who lived with the life of his people. So the mythology of Baal's perpetual conflict with Mot, where he was alternately victor and vanquished, passed into Hebrew tradition merely as literary material, as pagan and classical mythology may be freely used by Milton or any other Christian poet, without influencing his thought.

À propos of the ritual text for 'forgiveness of soul' (Gordon *UH* 9) we have already entered the caveat that we must not assume that what the bulk of the extant texts from Ras Shamra reveal is necessarily all that is to be known of Canaanite religion.

In this connection we may cite the text GORDON *UH* 2, 12 ff.:

ʾulp.ddmy	May the Didymites be pacified, [1]
ʾulp.(ḫry)	May the Hurrians be pacified,
ʾu)lp.ḫty	May the Hittites be pacified,
ʾulp(ʾalṯy)	May the Cypriots be pacified,
(ʾulp.) ṯbr	May the Subaru be pacified,
ʾulp.ḫbtkn	May those who plunder you [2] be pacified,
ʾulp.md(llk)n	May those who impoverish you be pacified.
ʾulp.m( )	May those who ( ) be pacified.
( ) *ʾutḫṭʾen*	( ) or you sin
bʾapkn.db( )	In harm you have suffered [3] ( ).
( ) *tqṭṭn ʾutḫṭʾen*	( ) crime you have committed [4] or you sin,
l(d)bḥ(m).wlṯʿ	With sacrifice and offering. [5]
d(bḥn ndbḥ)	Our sacrifice is slaughtered.
hw.ṯʿ.nṯʿy	It is the offering offered.
hw nkt.nkt	It is the sacrifice slaughtered. [6]
ytšʾe (lʾab bn ʾel)	Let it be taken up to the Father of the gods,
ytšʾe.ldr bn ʾel	Let it be taken up to the divine family,
lmpḫrt.bn (ʾel)	to the seat of the divine assembly. [7]

---

[1]) We take *ʾulp* as a perfect optative passive of a root *ʾalp*, cf. Arabic أَلِفَ, 'to become tame'.

[2]) cf. Akkadian *ḫabatu*, 'brigand', but AISTLEITNER's proposal that the word is cognate with Arabic خبت, 'to be humble, low' (*Wörterbuch* 1002) is also feasible, though in that case we should expect the Intensive with the preformative *m*.

[3]) We take *ʾap* in this context as cognate with Arabic آفة, from the root آف, 'to cause damage', assuming that 'your damage' is objective rather than subjective.

[4]) cf. Hebrew קוץ, 'to do harm in despite of', e.g. 1 Kings xi, 25.

[5]) For *ṯʿ*, 'gift' in the sense of sacrifice AISTLEITNER (*Wörterbuch* 2907) cites the Old South Arabic *mṯʿy*, 'sacrifice'. See further p. 215, n. 3.

[6]) For *nkt* AISTLEITNER adduces Aramaic נכא as a cognate. This may be known in Hebrew in the Hiphil הִכָּה.

[7]) After AISTLEITNER (*Die mythologischen und kultischen Texte aus Ras Schamra*, 1959, p. 106), taking *m* with local significance. See further 205, n. 8.

wšqrb.ṯr	And offer a bull,
mšr mšr bn.ʾugrt	Put on vestments, [1] ye men of Ugarit,
w(npy) tmhnš	And may atonement be made [2] for *Tmhnš*, [3]
wnpy ymʾan	And may atonement be made for *Ymʾan* [3]
wnpy ṯrmn	And may atonement be made for *Ṯrmn*, [3]
wnpy ( ) ʾugr(t)	And may atonement be made for the ( ) of Ugarit,
wnpy nqmd	And may atonement be made for Niqmad.
ʾušn ypkm	May a gift effect your atonement.
ʾulp q(ṭš)	May Qadesh [4] be pacified,
(as ll.12-13, 28-30)	
ʾušn ypkm	May an offering effect your atonement
ʾubʾ apkm.ʾubqṭt. npškm	Whether for the harm you have suffered or for your secret crime [5]
ʾubqṭt.tqṭṭ	Or for crime you have (openly) committed
ʾušn ypkm	May an offering effect your atonement
ld(b)ḥm wl.ṯʿ	With sacrifices and with offering.
dbḥn.ndbḥ	Our sacrifice is slaughtered,
hw ṯʿ nṯʿy	It is the offering made,
hw.nkt.nkt	It is the sacrifice slain.
(yt)šʾe.lʾab.bn.ʾel	Let it be taken up to the Father of the gods,
ytšʾe.ldr bn ʾel	Let it be taken up to the family of the gods,
lṯkmn (w)šnm	To the Lofty [6] and Exalted [7].
hn.ʿr	Here is an ass-load. [8]
wṯb.lmspr.m(š)r mšr.bt ugrt	And again in like number, ye women of Ugarit, put on vestments,

---

[1] We take *mšr* as cognate with Arabic مشر, 'to rejoice' or 'to dress'.

[2] Connecting *npy* with *ypkm* in l. 24 and *ypkn* in l. 31, we propose that it is the Nifʿal of a verb *wpy*, cognate with Arabic وفى, 'to pay in full', cf. وفى عن ذنبه 'he atoned for his fault'.

[3] These are districts of the realm of Ugarit, as is indicated by the fact that in the colophon to Gordon *UH* 62, 56-57 Niqmad is styled 'King of Ugarit, Lord of *yrgb*, Lord of *ṯrmn*'.

[4] Probably a variant spelling of Qadesh, the Amorite city on the Upper Orontes.

[5] *qṭt npškm*, lit. crime of your (inmost) self. For this sense of *npš*, cf. Hebrew usage in Prov. xxiii, 7, כמו שער בנפשו כן הוא 'As one secretly purposes so he is'.

[6] Aistleitner (*op. cit.*, p. 105) takes *ṯkmn*, like *šnm* as names of the heavenly dwelling of the gods. *ṯkmn* and *šnm* are listed as objects of worship in conjunction with *dr- bn ʾel* and *mpḫrt bn ʾel* also in Gordon *UH* 107, 2-4. They are listed with the various gods of Ugarit in the offering lists in Gordon *UH* 1, and are generally taken as gods, so Eissfeldt, citing the Kassite god *Šuqamuna*, 'Ugaritisches', *ZDMG* XCIX, 1945, pp. 29-42. In a forthcoming publication we shall adduce certain evidence that these figures were attendants of El. *ṯkm* means a 'battlement' in Gordon *UH* krt, 75.

[7] *šnm* may be a case of a plural used as an abstract, the word being derived from *šny*, see p. 156 n. 3.

[8] cf. Gordon *UH* 12, 6, 12, 18, which appears to enumerate '50 ass loads' of produce.

wnpy gr ḥmyt ʾugrt	And may atonement be made for the sojourner under the protection [1]) of Ugarit,
w(np)y nṯt	And may atonement be made for Nṯt [2])
ʾušn ypkn [3])	May an offering effect your atonement.
bʾap(kn ʾubq)ṭt npškn [4])	Whether for any harm you have suffered or for your secret crime,
ʾubqṭt tqṭṭn	or for crime which you have (openly) committed
ʾušn ypkn	May an offering effect your atonement.
(ll. 32-35 as ll. 24-26)	

It must be admitted that much in this text is highly controversial. The reference to sacrifice for the king and community, and the admission of sins of various degrees as the reason for defeat by various peoples is, however, quite certain. This text recalls the incident in 1 Samuel vii, 3-9, when Samuel assembled all Israel to a fast at Mizpah, and with libation and sacrifice made intercession to God. That this occasion at Ugarit was no exception in Canaan is indicated in the letter of Ribaddi of Byblos in the Amarna Tablets, who writes: [5])

> And may the King my lord know that the gods of Byblos are angry and the bitter consequences thereof are grievous. So I have confessed my sins to the gods.

Yet Ribaddi was more sinned against than sinning. Both passages reflect the conception common in ancient Assyria and Israel and expressed in fast-liturgies that calamity implied sin in some degree, witting or unwitting, moral or ritual, which must be confessed and expiated. Here we see that there was another aspect of Canaanite religion which went deeper than the amoral worship of the fertility-

---

[1]) *ḥmyt* could mean 'walls', but in view of the final *y* in the root Dhorme is probably right in associating it with the Akkadian *ḥamatu*, 'asylum' (*RB* XL, 1931, p. 39), cf. Virolleaud, who cites the Arabic حمى, 'to protect' (*La légende phénicienne de Danel*, 1936, p. 37).

[2]) The parallel passage, l. 20 in ll. 18-26 suggests that *nṯt* occupies among the women of Ugarit in this ceremony the same position as King Niqmad among the men, hence she is the Queen, as in fact is confirmed by the administrative text *PRU* III, 12.33, where J. Nougayrol (*op. cit.*, p. 14) reads *ne-e-še*(?)-*ti*(?) *belet* ^{mat}*u-(g)a-r(i-it)*, Neshet the Queen of Ugarit.

[3]) The text actually reads *ʾušny.pkn*, our emendation being suggested by the parallel passage.

[4]) Here again in the text *npš.kn* the parallel passages indicate the same scribal irregularity in the placing of the word-divider.

[5]) J. A. Knudtzon, *Die El-Amarna Tafeln*, 1908-15, no. 137, 33.

cult and was much more akin to the historical faith of Israel expressed in such a psalm as Psalm lxxviii.

The mention of singers in the temple personnel in the administrative texts is particularly significant in view of the question of psalmody in the cult in Canaan. More specifically an inscription on a pen-case among the Megiddo ivories (c. 1350-1150 B.C.) mentions a female Kerker, or Kurkur, or Kulkul, the singer of Ptah, who had at that time apparently a temple at Askalon, [1] and the Prince of Byblos in the time of Wen-Amon had also an Egyptian female singer Ta-net-Not, but she is mentioned only in a secular capacity. [2] The Hebrew Psalter also conserves the memory of Canaanite psalmody. Apart from obvious Canaanite influence in form, motif, and imagery, the 'natives' Heman and Ethan are mentioned as authors respectively of Psalms lxxxviii and lxxxix. They are already legendary figures together with Chalcol [3] and Darda when the saga of Solomon's wisdom and greatness was recounted (1 Kings v, 11, EVV iv, 31), so that there is little reason to doubt that 'native' in this case means 'Canaanite'. To be sure the tradition in 1 Kings v, 11 esteems them rather as sages than as poets, but, as MOWINCKEL emphasizes, wisdom and poetic skill were both manifestations of the spirit and both gifts were often combined, especially in such a serious calling as that of the temple singer. [4] The description of these persons in 1 Kings v, 11 as 'the sons of Maḥol' is suggestive. This does not refer to their family affinity, but means 'of the guild of choristers' or the like, as ALBRIGHT first proposed. [5] Through Egyptian singers such as Kerker or Kulkul of Askalon and Ta-net-Not of Byblos such pieces as Akhnaten's hymn to the Sun, known in its Hebrew adaptation in Psalm civ, may have been introduced to Canaan, and the short colourful love-lyrics in the Song of Songs seem to owe something to Egyptian originals. But there was also a native Canaanite tradition of psalmody.

In addressing the Pharaoh in the Amarna Tablets the Canaanite princes tend to lapse into lyric passages, which are definitely not in the epistolary style. These might have been taken as instances of

---

[1]) G. LOUD, *The Megiddo Ivories, Oriental Institute Publication* LII, 1939, Pls. 62-63, with translation by J. A. WILSON, pp. 11-13.

[2]) J. A. WILSON in J. B. PRITCHARD, *ANET*, 1950, p. 28.

[3]) The name is identical with Kerker or Kulkul of the Egyptian inscription from Megiddo.

[4]) MOWINCKEL, *The Psalms in Israel's Worship* II, 1962, pp. 96-97.

[5]) *Archaeology and the Religion of Israel*, 1942, so also R. DE VAUX, *Ancient Israel*, 1961, p. 382, and MOWINCKEL, *The Psalms in Israel's Worship* II, 1962, p. 96.

fulsome hyperbole, but they recur in the same style and stereotyped figures from various localities often very far apart, which suggests a common source in a well-established literary tradition subjected to the uniformity characteristic of the cult.

Biriawaza, for instance, probably the King of the land of Ubi with its capital at Damascus, writes of himself [1] as

> ..... thy servant
> The dust of thy feet
> And the ground on which thou treadest,
> The seat on which thou sittest,
> And the footstool of thy feet...

Ruṣmanya of Saruna in Northern Palestine writes: [2]

> ...... thy servant,
> The dust of thy feet,
> The clay on which thou treadest,
> The footstool of thy feet...

and Ammunira of Beirut uses the last figure. [3] In these passages we note the poetic parallelism and the figures which reflect the cadence and diction of hymns of praise.

Biriawaza further writes in language and cadence recalling Psalm lxxxix, 37 EVV 36: [3]

> My lord is the sun in heaven,
> And as for the rising of the sun of heaven
> So thy servants wait for the coming forth of the words
> From the mouth of their lord...

Tagi writes in language recalling Amos ix, 2: [4]

> See, as for us, my two eyes are upon thee.
> Whether we rise up to heaven
> Or go down to the underworld,
> Our head is in thy hands...

and again: [5]

> I have looked here and I have looked there
> But there is no brightness.
> And I have looked to the King my lord
> And it has become bright.

---

[1] J. A. Knudtzon, *Die El-Amarna Tafeln* 1908-15, 195, 5-10.
[2] *ibidem*, 241, 4-7.
[3] *ibidem*, 195, 16-23.
[4] *ibidem*, 264, 14-19.
[5] *ibidem*, 266, 11-25.

And see, I have set my face thereto
To serve the King my lord,
And a brick may slip from under its building timber,
But I shall not slip from under the feet of the King my lord.

This figure is repeated in letters from the Palestinian chiefs Addudani [1]) and Iaḫtiri. [2])

Apart from several hymns of praise in Akkadian cuneiform transliterated in the Ugaritic alphabet, [3]) which are unfortunately too fragmentary to be fair specimens, and the rubrics and catchlines of Gordon *UH* 52, which clearly allude to chants and hymns, we have already noted an incantation which probably incorporates part of a hymn of praise to the Sun-goddess. [4]) Here, as in the Hebrew hymns of praise, the goddess is invoked by allusion to her exploits, here mythological. The marriage of the Moon-god and the Moon-goddess Ningal is similarly the theme of song. For the Canaanites, then, as for the Hebrews ritual was accompanied by psalmody as well as by descriptive myth. If instead of these few sporadic fragments we had been given fuller specimens of such litanies what wealth of religious experience might not have been revealed?

iii. CULTIC PERSONNEL

A cult implies a priesthood and we must now turn to an investigation of the holy office in ancient Canaan. Here we must consider the priesthood as a developing institution, maintaining our principle that in our evidence we must distinguish between the situation revealed in such texts as Gordon *UH* Krt and Aqht, which describe the heroic past, and that implied in the administrative texts which reflect actual contemporary conditions in the Late Bronze Age.

In the Krt and Aqht texts priestly functions are discharged by the kings Krt and Dn'el and by no other. Doubtless there would be ministers of less degree, but there is no indication of them. Indeed when Krt sacrifices he is depicted as personally taking

... a lamb for sacrifice,
In his hand a kid from the enclosures. [5])

---

[1]) *ibidem*, 292, 8-17.
[2]) *ibidem*, 296, 11-22.
[3]) E. Dhorme, 'Textes accadiens transcrits en écriture alphabétique de Ras Shamra', *RA* XXXVII, 1940, pp. 83-96.
[4]) *v. supra* pp. 187-8.
[5]) Gordon *UH* Krt, 66-68, 159-161.

Again, in what may be a rite of desacralization of the new crop, Krt himself

> ... prepared food for the city,
> Wheat for Beth Ḫbr;
> He parched bread of the fifth,
> Food of the sixth month. [1])

The fact is that in the primitive community—which is, of course, a sacral body—the king is the one member who concentrates in his person the life of his people and relieves the community from practical embarrassment by realizing himself this sacral status. This is the onus of royalty. The king, then, is the one particularly qualified to approach the deity on behalf of the community. He is by his very nature priest. As representative or the embodiment of the society, he maintains perpetual communion with the god of the community, a situation which is characterized by the description of the king as the son of god. This and similar extravagant language, however, must be understood in its own context. The title 'son of god' denotes not a natural, but a sacramental relationship; it is a social category. Here again we should emphasize that in the Krt text El is not only termed the father of the king, but he is also *'ab 'adm*, 'the father of the community' which the king embodies. Thus the king represents the people before the deity as their priest in sacrifices and he mediates to them the divine influence. There is a polarity in this sacramental relationship; now the emphasis falls on the status of the king as the representative of the god, now it falls on his identity with his people. The one aspect of his status, however, never absolutely excludes the other.

In virtue of his peculiar sacramental status the king mediates divine revelation to his people. In the Krt and Aqht texts Krt and Dn'el receive divine revelation concerning their progeny. Here we must beware of regarding this matter as a private concern of the individual kings; the royal succession, guaranteeing stability to society and even, according to the conceptions of the time, affecting the natural order, was a matter affecting the whole community. As mediator of oracles, then, the king concentrated in his person the offices of prophet and priest, a condition exemplified in the case of Moses and Samuel in the Hebrew community and in the case of Solomon, who was the recipient of divine revelation in what was probably ritual incubation at the sanctuary of Gibeon and who as priest dedicated the Temple in Jerusalem.

---

1) *Ibidem*, 80-84, 172-175.

The priestly status of the king and his sacramental communion with the deity explains the conception common in antiquity and in primitive society and current in Britain until the time of Queen Anne that the king had peculiar gifts of healing and of conferring fertility. [1]) Thus in the Krt text the condition of the crops varies with the fluctuations of the king's health. [2]) King Dn'el makes a round of the crops in a time of drought and embraces and kisses the various plants, [3]) a rite designed to promote fertility. [4]) In the three fragmentary texts GORDON *UH* 121, 122, 123 [5]) certain functionaries *rp'um* are indicated who are obviously a guild or association of limited number. [6]) They are sacral figures since they are associated with a shrine, *hkl*//*'aṯr*, and are occupied with threshingfloors and plantations, and thus have an agricultural function, which in accordance with their name we take to be that of dispensing fertility. [7]) In the light of these texts we should explain the title *mt rp'e*, which is one of the stock epithets of Dn'el in the 'Aqht text. In the Krt text there is nothing which so explicitly describes the king as the dispenser of fertility, though in GORDON *UH* 126 III, 12-17 the fertility of the land seems to depend on the King.

When we pass from the heroic past, however, to the contemporary scene in the administrative texts in the Late Bronze Age we find evidence of a not unnatural process of devolution. The colophon to the text GORDON *UH* 62 (ll. 54-56) names the high priest Atnprln alongside the king Nqmd, and the lists of state grants mention no less than twelve different families of priests (*khnm*). [8]) Among these the clan *Ṯ'*, possibly the clan of King Krt, is rated among

---

[1]) Dr. Samuel Johnson records that he was 'touched' by Queen Anne for scrofula.

[2]) GORDON *UH* 126, III, *v. supra* p. 149.

[3]) GORDON *UH* 1 'Aqht, 61-74, *v. supra* p. 119 ff.

[4]) *v. supra* p. 119, n.

[5]) VIROLLEAUD, 'Les Rephaim, Fragments de poèmes de Ras Shamra', *Syria* XXII, 1941, pp. 1-30. We have studied this text in an article 'The Rephaim', *PEQ* 1949, pp. 127-139 where we have questioned VIROLLEAUD's view that the Rephaim were a race rather than a guild.

[6]) They are said to be 'seven, yea eight', GORDON *UH* 121, II, 1.

[7]) The verb רפא is used in the sense of conferring fertility in Genesis xx, 17, where the Lord 'heals' or restores fertility to the harem of Abimelech of Gerar, and in 2 Kings ii, 21, where Elisha 'heals', or gives fertilizing properties to, the spring of Jericho which had previously brought sterility (משכלת) and death (מות) to the land.

[8]) GORDON *UH* 400, VI, 21 ff.

the highest of the various priestly families at Ugarit in the list of state payments, which may suggest that, though the priestly authority of the king had largely devolved from him by the Amarna Age, it may have still been invested to a large extent in once royal families. Here we note that the clan *Dtn* appears alongside the clan of *Ṯ*ʿ as a priestly family, being rated more highly than any other except that of *Ṯ*ʿ and another, *bn mglb*. [1]) In spite of this devolution of priestly authority, however, the king in all probability retained some vestige of his priestly office, as is in fact indicated by the text GORDON *UH* 5 which mentions the king in the cult. [2]) Here, however, it is not quite clear what part he plays. In spite of the paucity of evidence of the king's priestly rôle in the administrative texts of Ugarit in the Late Bronze Age we may fairly assume this on the analogy of other communities in the ancient Near East at a time much more removed from the heroic age when the king was the priest *par excellence*. In Israel Saul personally performed public sacrifice (1 Samuel xiii, 9; xiv, 35), while David officiated at the installation of the ark in Jerusalem (2 Samuel vi) and his sons were priests (2 Samuel viii, 18, Hebr. text). In the 9th century Mesha of Moab sacrificed his eldest son (2 Kings iii, 27), and Ittobaal of Sidon, the father of Jezebel was, according to Josephus, the priest of Astarte. [3]) In the Persian period Tabnith king of Sidon in his inscription refers to the priestly office which he and his father Eshmunazar exercised. [4])

Those numerous priestly families of Ugarit were all employed presumably in offices of varying importance, suggesting a cultic establishment such as that outlined in Chronicles and implied in the headings of the Psalms, a departmentalization of office which stands in sharp contrast to the situation implied in the Krt text where the king himself took the offerings and sacrificed them, and personally parched the grain, possibly in the rite of desacralization.

---

1) Nothing further is known of this family. In this list the Ugaritic *bn* is plural.

2) This text, beginning 'When Aṯtrt enters (?)...' seems to us to refer to some ritual in an astral phase, a conjecture which is supported by references to the sun and moon (ll. 12, 14). From l. 2 it appears that the king's house was implicated, and, since there is reference to payment of silver and gold (ll. 10, 12-14), perfume (*ṭb*) and scent (*npš*), we suppose that this was incumbent on the royal family as well as the provision of a ceremonial meal, ʿ*šr* (l. 2). The attendance of the king at the shrines, probably of several gods, is apparent (ll. 23-26), and he has apparently to make these visits on foot (l. 25), probably in a certain kind of vestment (l. 22).

3) Josephus, *Contra Apionem* i, § 18.

4) COOKE, *NSI* 4, 1-2.

In the administrative texts [1]) there are certain obvious references to cultic functionaries, such as priests (*khnm*) and consecrated persons (*qdšm*). These texts are of various, and not always certain, purport, and it must be admitted that the artisans mentioned in them may quite as well have been secular as sacred. Nevertheless the way in which certain trades are listed together with holy offices suggests that the artisans were dedicated to the temple service. Thus in the text GORDON *UH* 113, a conscription-list noting the number of bowmen which each tradesguild or member thereof was required to furnish in addition to, or as a substitute for, themselves, the priests (*khnm*) were listed together with consecrated persons (*qdšm*) [2]) as liable for one bowman, and similarly the singers (*šrm*), [3]) presumably temple-singers, are listed with the makers of vestments (*yṣḥm*) [4]) and the sculptors (*pslm*). In the case of the latter two classes it is not unreasonable to assume that we have to do with makers and maintainers of priestly vestments [5]) and those who sculptured images, many of which in stone and precious metals have been recovered at Ras Shamra. [6]) The same text groups together *nqdm* and *ṯnnm*. The former, though possibly meaning here shepherds in general, is found as a title of the high priest Atnprln and thus had a sacral significance [7]) as also, no doubt, in the case of Mesha King of Moab, who is termed נֹקֵד (2 Kings iii, 4), and possibly even Amos (Amos i, 1), though we think this less likely. [8]) The term *ṯnn* certainly

---

[1]) GORDON *UH* 113 (a conscription-list), 114, 115 (fiscal lists), 300 (lists of grants of lands to various classes or guilds and allocation of fields to certain guild-members), 301 (list of families serving as *ytnm*), 303 (lists of families serving as *ṯnnm*).

[2]) GORDON *UH* 113, 72-73.

[3]) *v. supra*, p. 204.

[4]) We connect *yṣḥ* with the Arabic ناصح 'to sew', on the analogy of the correspondence between *ytnm* and Hebrew נתן.

[5]) There were such officials in the pre-Exilic Temple in Jerusalem, 2 Kings xxii, 14.

[6]) SCHAEFFER, *Ugaritica I*, 1939, Pls. XXVIII-XXXII, figs. 114-118.

[7]) Those who purveyed the victims for the priest-king when he personally sacrificed may have been the first to take over the office of sacrifice. The title *nqd* as applied to the high priest may be a vestige of this process, but see n. 8.

[8]) In his reply to Amaziah Amos, in denying any status as a cultic prophet, seems certainly to state that he was literally a herdsman (בקר) (Amos vii, 14-15). M. BIČ (*VT*, I, 1951, pp. 293 ff.) feasibly suggests that *nqd* might mean 'hepatoscopist' cf. Akkadian *naqâdu*, 'to probe', i.e. liver in augury. The reputation of Mesha as an augurer might well explain the panic of his enemies on the sacrifice of his son on the wall of Qir Hareseth (2 Kings iii, 27). The interpretation of נֹקֵד

has a sacral connotation in the rubrics to the text Gordon *UH* 52, where it is associated with *ʿrbm*, which in turn has been connected by Gaster [1]) with the Akkadian *erib biti*, 'he who enters the sanctuary'. The term *ṯnn* [2]) is probably connected with the root *ṯn*, 'two' and signifies repetition. The fact that in the text Gordon *UH* 52 the term is found in rubrics connected with catchlines of hymns suggests that it might denote those who sang antiphonal chants. In the same text *nsk ksp*, silver-casters, and *mkrm*, merchants, are grouped together. Again the functionaries might be secular. On the other hand, temple-monopoly of the working in precious metals was well known in the ancient Near East and the terms might be sacred. If *mkrm* denoted a sacral office we might have a reference to persons commissioned by the temple to trade abroad for precious metals, or to sell the produce from temple-lands, or even to sell animals for sacrifice, as those stigmatized for such traffic in the Temple by Our Lord (Matthew xxi, 12). Here we may note that in the account of the reforms of Joash in temple administration in Jerusalem *makkarim* were apparently attached individually to the priests (2 Kings xii, 6, 8, EVV. 5,7) as business assessors. Other such functionaries possibly attached to the temple who are named in these and similar fiscal texts are butlers (*ʿšrm*), who presumably served at communion-feasts, and measurers (*mdm*), who may have been surveyors of temple lands let out to tenants, persons who checked the goods produced from temple materials, or perhaps custodians of weights and measures, the sanctuary, as we know from the Old Testament phrase 'the shekel of the sanctuary', being the repository of standards of measurement. Potters (*yṣrm*), launderers (*kbšm*) and slaughterers (*mḫṣm*) are found in the same texts. The text Gordon *UH* 115, 8 mentions a class *trrm*. Connecting the word with the Hebrew root תּוּר, we may see a possible connection with those who inspected entrails or observed the stars. This would be a clear case of cultic officials. On the other hand, we prefer to regard the term as denoting caravan traders, the Hebrew אנשי התרים, [3]) who may or may not have been employed on behalf

---

'breeder of sheep' may be a late misunderstanding of the word, the statement about Mesha's tribute in sheep being a later gloss, as the extravagant round number 100,000 suggests.

1) Gaster, *Thespis*, p. 240.

2) Gordon *UH* Krt, 91 where *ṯnn* denotes trained regular soldiers. See p. 139, n. 1.

3) 1 Kings x, 15, 2 Chronicles ix, 14. The meaning is suggested by the association

of the temple. In the same texts it is possible that *ʾenšt* denotes the concubines attached to the fertility-cult. [1])

Lands were apparently entailed upon certain of these classes, namely *mdm* (GORDON *UH* 300, 1-6), *ʿšrm* (*ibidem*, 30), *šrm* (*ibidem*, rev. 9-11), *ṯġrm*, doorkeepers (*ibidem*, rev. 7-8), *nqdm* (*ibidem*, rev., 12-15), *trrm* (*ibidem*, rev., 16-21), *mḫṣm* (*ibidem*, rev., 25, 26), the entailment being, we think, on the guild rather than on individuals.

We gather from texts which record either state grants or taxes (GORDON *UH* 301, 303, and 400) that those guilds comprised certain families. Fifty families and six individuals are listed as *ytnm* (GORDON *UH* 301). We agree with GORDON [2]) in taking this word to mean 'temple servitors', the Hebrew נתינים. From GORDON *UH* 400 we have already pointed out that there were twelve families of priests (*khnm*), by which, no doubt, priests of the highest rank are denoted. These include the family of *Ṯʿ*. The word *Ṯʿ* is found repeatedly in the Krt text as a stock epithet of the king, and it may be a gentilic term, though it is probably an adjective, 'the Generous', from *ṯʿy* 'to present' (so. DRIVER, *op. cit.*, p. 33). [3]) Whether or not King Nqmd, the contemporary of Atnprln, was of the family of *Ṯʿ* is uncertain, but it does seem that the priestly office continued to be largely dominated by this family. The amount of silver noted against the name of this priestly family and its kin indicates a privileged status in the state. To judge by the same criterion a position almost equal is held by the families of *Dtn* and *Mglb*. Of the latter nothing is known, but the former is named in the Krt text where the hero is acclaimed as exalted

In the congregation of the land
In the assembly of the clan of Dtn. [4])

---

with סחרים and רכלים. The word is derived from a root cognate with the Akkadian *târu*, 'to turn about', cf. Arabic, تار (IV).

[1]) Females are obviously denoted. The word derives from the root *ʾenš* or rather *ʾanš* cognate with the Arabic أنيس, 'pleasant', 'sociable'.

[2]) GORDON *UH*, p. 237.

[3]) *ṯʿy* in the colophon to GORDON *UH* 62, 55-56 is not a gentilic referring to the family of Atnprln, but a verb, of which Nqmd is the subject. Here the reference is to the donation of the text, possibly from the royal library. In GORDON *UH* 2 the root as verb and noun refers to offerings for sacrifice, and is associated with old South Arabic *mṯʿy*, 'an offering' by AISTLEITNER (*Wörterbuch* 2907). *ṯʿ* as the stock epithet of Krt suggests Hebrew שׁוֹעַ, the sense 'generous' being suggested by the parallel נדיב in Isaiah xxxii, 5.

[4]) *Ibidem* 128, III, 2-4.

From this text we conclude that *Dtn* was a previous, or collateral, branch of the royal house which continued to exercise certain priestly functions proper to royalty like the ἀρχων βασιλευς in Athens.

The hereditary office implied in these texts suggests the establishment in the Jerusalem Temple, which the Chronicler (1 Chronicles xxiii-xxvi) ascribes to David, and the guilds designated by the names of the Sons of Asaph and the Sons of Korah in the Psalter. This is no doubt, at least as far as concerns Chronicles, a reflection of conditions of post-Exilic times, since the genuine pre-Exilic records do not know of such a rigidly confined priesthood. [1]) The Ras Shamra material, however, shows that such an establishment, if not actually demonstrable in the case of the pre-Exilic Temple in Jerusalem, was at least not an absolute anachronism in Canaan.

There is one most significant function of the Canaanite priest illustrated by the Ras Shamra texts. In the colophon to the text Gordon *UH* 62 the high priest Atnprln is cited as an authority for the version of the Baal-myth. The priests, then, were the custodians of literary tradition, and here again we may have an analogy in the ascription of certain Hebrew psalms to the Levitical Asaph or the Korahites, though these psalm headings may also indicate actual authorship. This passage is valuable as evidence of the manner of the transmission of tradition. It is said that Atnprln 'taught' (*lmd*) the particular version of the myth which was inscribed by El-mlk. Thus in the ancient Near East oral and written traditions were not mutually exclusive but both processes might go on *pari passu*, [2]) nor is there any reason to suppose that it was otherwise in Israel.

Apart from the Krt and Aqht texts from the heroic past, there is no evidence that the king continued to be the mediator of divine revelation. On the contrary, from Amorite texts of the 18th century

---

[1]) In the 11th century the chief priestly authority in Israel was exercised by Samuel who was not a Levite but a man of Ephraim, and in Solomon's establishment in the following century the Levitical family of Eli was demoted in favour of the family of Zadoq, who represented either the native priesthood of pre-Israelite Jerusalem, or a collateral Levitical family.

[2]) E. Nielsen cites evidence from Babylonia that, though the mythological texts there were inscribed, they were expected to be learned by heart. Similar evidence of the double preservation of sacred traditions by memory as well as in writing are cited from Judaism and Islam, *Oral Tradition*, (English Version), 1954, pp. 19 ff.

from Mari, [1] in Assyrian, [2] Aramaean, [3] and Hebrew texts [4] we find that the prophetic office was invested in certain officials who were, most significantly in our opinion, attached to the king. In Phoenicia itself about 1100 B.C. in the narrative of Wenamon at Byblos a case of prophetic ecstasy is described, through the medium of which an oracle was given to the king. [5] There is no instance known of such an office in Ugarit. Indeed it seems most significant that, with all that the Ras Shamra texts have to offer which is illustrative of the life and culture of Israel, they are absolutely silent on that feature which was so distinctive of Israel—the prophetic ministry of the word.

---

[1]) M. Noth, 'History and the Word of God in the Old Testament', *BJRL*, XXXII, ii, 1950. W. von Soden 'Verkündigung des Gotteswillens durch prophetisches Wort in den altbabylonischen Briefen aus Mari', *Die Welt des Orients*, 1950, pp. 396-403.

[2]) The divine will is communicated to Esarhaddon by the *maḫḫe*, the ecstatics, in connection with his restoration of the cult and temple of Marduk at Babylon, D. D. Luckenbill, *ARA* II, § 659 D. Another such instance is recorded on a text of Assurbanipal, *ibidem* II, § 989.

[3]) The will of Baalshemin was communicated to Zakar of Hamath 'by seers and soothsayers', ביד חזן וביד עדדן, M. Lidzbarski, *Ephemeris für semitische Epigraphik* II, 1909-1915, p. 3.

[4]) E.g. Nathan (2 Samuel vii, xii), Gad (2 Samuel xxiv, 11) and the canonical prophets. We note the close association of prophet with king in those instances and the designation of Gad as 'the king's seer'.

[5]) Gressmann, *Altorientalische Texte zum Alten Testament* 1909, 230.

CHAPTER V

THE SOCIAL ORDER

For a reconstruction of Canaanite society we are fortunate in the possession of legends such as the Krt and Aqht texts, which deal with the vicissitudes of kings and their entourage in the heroic past, and of administrative texts from the palaces of Ugarit and Alalakh, which deal with actual conditions at the end of the Bronze Age. In the light of these we may now appreciate similar matter in the Amarna Tablets, which, owing to their primary political significance, elucidate Canaanite society only indirectly. Social conventions are also reflected in the myths, which are rather naively anthropomorphic, and in legal texts from the palace of Ras Shamra.

We would emphasize the distinction between the data of the myths of the heroic past and the administrative texts, which relate to conditions in historical times. This makes possible a reconstruction of the historical development of the central institution in Canaan, the kingship, from its primitive ideal to its modification in actual practice at the end of the Bronze Age, from which point the study may profitably be pursued in the study of the kingship as it was adapted in Israel.

Among the ancient Semites there were two ideals of rule, charismatic and institutional. Characteristic of the first was the function of the Hebrew 'judge' and the Arab paramount sheikh, whose authority depended on their personal ability. The success of the Hebrew 'judge' in his spontaneous and often heroic reaction to a given crisis was taken as a token of divine endowment or blessing (*beraka*). The authority of such a leader might pass to a member of his family, as usual in Arab society, but was not bound to do so, and in the case of Solomon in Israel the convention of a special Divine sanction (by the oracle of Nathan, 2 Samuel vii, 12 ff.) and of the special revelation of endowment (Solomon's dream at Gibeon, 1 Kings iii, 5-15) had to be invoked to justify hereditary succession. Once probably among the Canaanites also authority depended upon personal ability and was not bound to be transmitted to the son of the ruler. But owing to the strength of the conception of the solidarity of the family, which was held to share the blessing of any one member, and to the practical advantages held by the ruler's family, the hereditary monarchy was early established, being in fact practically contemporaneous with sedentary civilization and the proprietary rights of the family rather than the tribe. In this connection a certain passage in the Krt text is significant as reflecting at one and the same time the conception that royal power depended on personal capacity and the natural claim of the king's son to succeed. In the grievous illness of King Krt his eldest son Yṣb claims that his father had forfeited the personal blessing, in virtue of which he ruled: [1])

> Thou hast let thy hands fall into error;
> Thou dost not judge the case of the widow,
> Nor decide the suit of the oppressed;
> Sickness is as thy bedfellow,
> Disease as thy concubine.
> Descend from thy rule that I may be king,
> From thy government that I may be enthroned.

Replenished repeatedly from the inner steppes by nomad stock with democratic tribal traditions, the Canaanites retained memories of charismatic leadership; long familiar with Egyptian ideas, they had already assimilated the conception of the special status of the king and the royal family, who moved in the orbit of the divine.

First and foremost then in the society of ancient Canaan as exemplified at Ugarit stood the king in all the strength of his unique sacral status, the son of former rulers and the father of rulers to come. The dynastic principle in Canaan must be emphasized in view of the fact that in Israel, particularly North Israel, it was never freely admitted. [2])

We shall have occasion to demonstrate that the status of the Canaanite king was considerably modified by the end of the Bronze Age, and it must be admitted, moreover, that Ugarit was in various

---

[1]) GORDON *UH* 127, 44-53.

[2]) H. FRANKFORT has emphasized that, in contrast to Egypt, where the hereditary principle was fundamental, royal succession in Mesopotamia in historical times was not mechanical, but, at least ideally, in consequence of special divine election, *Kingship and the Gods*, 1948, p. 238 ff. We subscribe to the view of ALT that the history of the monarchy in North Israel is only to be understood on the view that the dynastic principle was never accepted, but that the king was marked out by some special gift, or *charisma*, for office in a particular crisis, as the earlier judges. Attempts such as that of Omri to found a dynasty were private enterprises, and thus of short duration. The position of the line of David in Jerusalem was an anomaly, and was based on the personal power of the Davidic house with feudal support in Jerusalem, which was a crown possession, literally 'the city of David', A. ALT, *Die Staatenbildung der Israeliten in Palästina*, 1930, pp. 31 ff.; 'Das Königtum in Israel und Juda', *VT* I, 1951, pp. 2-22.

respects an exception among Canaanite city-states. The nexus of traderoutes between Mesopotamia, Anatolia, Egypt, and the Mediterranean, she was enormously wealthy. Strategically placed in the extreme North of Syria and of vital importance in the interplay of politics between Egypt and the Hittites, she was treated with consideration by both, and exploited this delicate situation by subtle diplomacy. In consequence her kings enjoyed an exceptional status among Canaanite kings under Egyptian suzerainty, and this is reflected in the palace and its archives, which are quite exceptional in Canaan in the Late Bronze Age. Further South the revival of Egypt in the 16th and 15th centuries had resulted in closer control with consequent modification of the powers of the local kings, as the Amarna Tablets indicate. It is not clear if all the local rulers who claim to hold the country for the Pharaoh are hereditary kings or not, and we suspect from the numbers of Aryan and Hurrian names that some at least were simply Egyptian commandants. Some, however, were certainly native kings, such as Addunirari of Nuḫašše in North Syria, who states that his grandfather had been anointed by Thothmes III. [1]) Abdi-Khipa implies that he was hereditary King of Jerusalem in his statement that..

> neither my father nor my mother has set me in this place, but the mighty hand of the King has installed me. [2])

Doubtless expediency dictated the policy of the confirmation of local kings and their families in office. But, whatever their hereditary status, the statement of Abdi-Khipa indicates that the accession of a Canaanite king was subject to confirmation by the suzerain, and that he might, like Aziru in central Syria, be deported to Egypt if he were not amenable to Egyptian policy. [3])

The Krt text expresses the conception that the king is the reflection of the royal authority of El, the supreme god in the Canaanite pantheon, whose 'son' and 'servant' par excellence he is: [4])

> Who is Krt that he should weep?
> The Gracious One, the Lad of El that he should shed tears?
> Is it the kingship of the Bull El his father that he desires?
> Or government like the Father of Men?

---

1) J. A. Knudtzon, *Die El-Amarna Tafeln*, no. 51, 4-6.
2) *ibidem*, no. 288, 13-15.
3) *ibidem*, no. 169.
4) Gordon *UH* krt, 38-43.

In the same text he is: [1])

> ...Krt the son of El,
> The offspring of the Kindly One and the Holy.

By the time the royal legends of Ugarit have taken shape this aura of divinity has extended to the royal family. The prince, the eldest son of Krt, is one

> Who sucks the milk of Aṯerat,
> Who sucks out the breasts of the Virgin Anat. [2])

This conception is familiar in Mesopotamian and Egyptian royal ideology, and is expressed in the ivory relief from the royal bed of Ugarit. [3])

Standing thus in a special relationship to God, and indeed himself regarded eventually in popular belief as invested with that 'divinity that doth hedge a king', the king in ancient Canaan was regarded as the special channel of divine power and blessing to the community.

In the more primitive age to which the Krt and Aqht texts refer the king, realizing in his person the sacramental union of his people and their god, personally represented the people as their priest, as we have already seen, and mediated the divine revelation. [4]) As mediator of the divine revelation and as representative of his people he personally dispensed justice. In the Krt text it is quite clear that unless the king could guarantee the order and well-being of society he was not fit to rule, a conception pointedly expressed by Krt's aspiring son *Yṣb*: [5])

> 'Thou dost not judge the case of the widow,
> Nor decide the suit of the oppressed.'

So distinctive of the royal office was this function of justice that in the Aqht text Dn'el's resumption of his normal routine after his ceremonial seclusion is described in the same terms: [6])

> He rises to take his seat at the opening of the gate
> In the place of the notables who are in the public place.

---

[1]) *ibidem*, 125, 20-22.

[2]) *ibidem*, 128, II 26-27.

[3]) C. F. A. SCHAEFFER, *Syria* XXXI, 1954, Pl. VIII.

[4]) Noting the exceptional absence of any prophet in the reign of Solomon, C. WESTERMANN makes the feasible suggestion that this indicates that Solomon affected this element in the pattern of Canaanite kingship, *A Thousand Years and a Day*, 1962, p. 142.

[5]) GORDON *UH* 127, 45-47.

[6]) *Ibidem* 2 Aqht, V. 6-8.

He decides the case of the widow,
He judges the suit of the orphan.

Here there is no question of professional judges, the local notables, presumably tribal elders, being in no sense judges, but rather witnesses to see the ethic of the community upheld. The king, however, as the favoured servant (*nʿmn ġlm* or *ʿbd*), or even 'the son', of El, the custodian of the moral order, stands in the intimate counsel of the god of his people and is thus peculiarly fitted to administer justice. The norm of justice is not explicit in the Ras Shamra texts even in the latest period. There is among the extant texts no formally codified system of law as in Babylon, Assyria, or among the Hittites, or as the codes such as eventually found a place in the Hebrew Canon. Whatever may have been the situation in Ugarit towards the end of the Bronze Age, when a regular system of civil law seems to have been in operation, [1]) in the earlier period to which the Krt and Aqht texts refer the king's judgments, ideally governed by direct divine revelation, were no doubt *ad hoc*, dictated by his own natural sagacity within the limits of communal custom, the actual scope of which we shall later consider. [2])

The ancient king was leader in war. There is unfortunately no Canaanite epic of the nature and volume of the Iliad to exemplify this aspect of the royal office. In the Krt text, however, where the bridal expedition of Krt is described in the fiction of a military expedition, [3]) we seem entitled to see the conditions of a normal military muster, where the fighting men gathered with infectious enthusiasm round the king and perhaps a core of regular soldiers. These conditions recall those in the days of the Hebrew judges and Saul when the people rallied in the time of crisis to the blast of the trumpet.

In the later administrative texts and certain letters from Ugarit there is no indication that the king was personal leader in war in the 14th century, though the feudal system that seems to be indicated there implies that the king remained the supreme authority. [4]) From two letters [5]) from one *ʾewrẑr*, [6]) which GORDON, rightly in our

---

[1]) *v. infra* p. 251.
[2]) *v. infra* pp. 239, 251, 254, 255 ff.
[3]) *v. supra* p. 138 ff.
[4]) *v. infra* pp. 236-239 ff.
[5]) GORDON *UH* 54, 138.
[6]) *v. supra* p. 6.

opinion, takes as military dispatches from a field commander, it is apparent that the day of the general rally under the personal leadership of the king was past at Ugarit and the professional soldier was in control of military operations. The presence and status of this class of military specialists is well illustrated in the administrative texts, especially GORDON *UH* 300 and 400, and the fact that texts which relate to the palace, as apart from the town and the realm at large, show a preponderance of non-Semitic names of such persons indicates where the strength of the royal authority really lay in the Late Bronze Age. The Amarna Tablets and contemporary Hittite documents [1]) also attest the power of non-Semitic professional soldiers at the same period in Central Syria. In the Amarna Tablets Rib-Addi of Byblos apparently relied on the strength of *Šardanu*, [2]) who are known from Egyptian inscriptions as Aegean mercenaries. In Palestine the situation was substantially the same. The nomenclature of the chiefs in the Amarna Tablets relating to Palestine shows a decided proportion of non-Semitic names, particularly in the commands at important strategic positions. [3]) Those chiefs were, of course, vassals of the Pharaoh, who, we believe, availed himself of the feudal system introduced by the Aryans to Western Asia to establish his control in Palestine and Syria. The employment of such professional soldiers either by native chiefs such as Rib-Addi of Byblos or the kings of Ugarit or by the Pharaoh did much to modify the ancient power of the Canaanite king as leader in war. With the irruption of the Aramaean barbarians in the Early Iron Age the king exercised his old

---

[1]) E. WEIDNER, *Boghazköi-Studien, Heft* 8; *Politische Dokumente aus Kleinasien*, I, 1923.

[2]) KNUDTZON, *Die El-Amarna Tafeln* 123, 15.

[3]) The approach to Palestine by way of the coastal plain was covered by Akhshapha, where Indaruta was in command, and by Akko, the command of Zurata and Zutatna (KNUDTZON, 85, 21; 232, 3; 245, 24, 31 etc.; 233, 4; 234, 3; 235, 5). The vital passes through the Carmel Range at Megiddo and Taanach were controlled by Biridiya (KNUDTZON 243; 244; 245; 246), and Taanach possibly by Yašdata (KNUDTZON 245; 248), and Šaruna, a key point on the pass from Tiberias to the great central plain, was controlled by Ruṣmania (KNUDTZON, 241), while Šuwardata was in command of Qelti, possibly in the vicinity of Hebron (KNUDTZON 278-284), and Widia at Askalon by the trunk highway from Asia to Egypt (KNUDTZON 320-326). None of these is a Semitic name and the majority are Indo-Iranian, A. DUMONT, 'Indo-Iranian Names from Mitanni, Nuzi, and Syrian Documents', *JAOS* LXVII, 1947, pp. 251-253; Idem, Appendix to R. T. O'CALLAGHAN, *Aram Naharaim*, 1948, pp. 149-155. The most common type of cylinder-seal found in Palestine is that from Mitanni in Upper Mesopotamia where the Aryans had settled with the Hurrians and developed their feudal system. B. PARKER, 'Cylinder Seals from Palestine', *Iraq* IX, 1949, pp. 1-42.

right as personal leader in war, as in the case of Saul and the warrior Kings of North Israel and Aram.

As we know from the records of Solomon's reign (1 Kings iv), and as we may infer from the office of Adoram, the controller of the *corvée* (2 Samuel xx, 24), and that of Shewa the scribe in David's reign (2 Samuel xx, 25), and from the fiscal dockets from the palace of Jeroboam II at Samaria, [1]) the king kept a close control of the economic resources of the realm through officials of his own household. In the account of Solomon's reign we see that these included the produce of the land, apportioned no longer strictly according to tribal divisions and tribally administered, but by districts, and controlled by the king's own officers. [2]) The land itself might even be considered as the personal property of the king, as in the case of the district of Kabul near Acco which Solomon handed over to Hiram of Tyre (1 Kings ix, 11-14). The king might exercise absolute rights over the persons of his subjects, using them in the *corvée* or even sending them abroad as mercenaries (Deuteronomy xvii, 16). There is much here which suggests conditions at Ugarit indicated in the administrative documents, which attest the *corvée* (Gordon *UH* 108, 109), the levy of archers, slingers, or their equipment (Gordon *UH* 321), and levies or payments of silver (Gordon *UH* 111, 112). Here the population was organized not in families, but in districts. Other texts attest land-grants (Gordon *UH* 300) and state-payments or burdens (Gordon *UH* 400) to certain families grouped by guilds. All this indicates a very highly-organized system of fiscal control. A dispatch from King Niqmad to his overlord the Hittite Šubbilu-

---

[1]) These are from the second palace at Samaria, first regarded as the palace of Ahab, but more likely that of Jeroboam II. J. Crowfoot, *Samaria-Sebaste* I, 1942, pp. 6-8. These, however, may relate to crown property.

[2]) The extent of this control is further indicated, apart from 1 Kings iv, in 1 Chron. xxvi, 30-32, which mentions Levites of Hebron in the royal service as well as over religious affairs throughout the land (לכל מלאכת יהוה ולעבודת המלך), to which Mazar ('The cities of the Priests and the Levites', *VT* Supplement VII 1959, pp. 193-205) relates the lists of Levitical settlements in Joshua xxi, many of which, as demonstrated by archaeology and on historical grounds, could not have been occupied before or after the time of David and Solomon, when 1 Chron. xxvi, 31 dates the organization of the administration. Mazar notes that such Levitical settlements were in border areas or Canaanite enclaves, and he plausibly suggests that they were designed to strengthen the defence of the realm or to extend the influence of Judah among the tribes, the leading Levitical family being from Hebron, the centre of David's power. He suggests that they were also fiscal officers and stewards of the crown properties, which the phrase עבודת המלך suggests.

liuma (GORDON *UH* 118), to whom, together with his family and notables, Niqmad sends a rich assortment of tribute, indicates that he no less than Solomon disposed of the resources of the realm as crown property. The picture is filled out by the numerous Akkadian deeds from the palace of Ugarit where it is clear that certain property disposed of by the king carries burdens to the palace such as tax in money and produce, cattle, corn, olives, fermented drink, or labour of serfs or beasts of burden. The extent to which the king maintained this economic control seems plainly demonstrated by the royal deeds of gift of land or goods, emancipation and remission of state dues so abundantly attested in the palace archives, where he arranges conveyance of property, promotes overseas trade, makes grants of land in return for capital [1]) or for services rendered, as, for instance, to officials, feudatories, or concubines.

We have already seen sufficient to convince us of the affinities and the significant differences between monarchy in Israel and in Canaan. In his excellent study *Sacral Kingship in Ancient Israel* A. R. JOHNSON does well to emphasize the conditional nature of the Divine grace by which the king reigns in Israel, and he has well emphasized the moral content of *ṣedeq*, the right norm of royal conduct before the king's Divine sponsor. The Canaanite kings also claimed to be מלכי צדק, 'right kings', as we know from the funerary inscriptions of the kings of Byblos Yeḥimelek (11th c.) [2]) and Yeḥawmelek (5th or 4th c.) [3]). Here, however, the phrase might mean no more than 'legitimate, as in the phrase *ʾaṯt ṣdq*. The word, that is to say, may have a non-moral connotation, 'proper', 'right' rather than 'righteous', as in the Hebrew כלי צדק, 'right tools', though the Yeḥimelek inscription, claiming the favour of the gods on the grounds that Yeḥimelek has been מלך צדק and מלך ישר, seems to imply more than mere legitimacy. There is one notable instance where *ṣedeq* applied to the king of Ugarit or the prince has apparently the connotation of 'righteousness'. That is in a short fragment from the palace of Ugarit (PRU II, 7) [4]), which apparently enumerates the titles of

[1]) Certain of these, however, may be fictitious grants, the king simply sanctioning the conveyance of property and thereby making the title more secure, while the sum paid to the king may be burdens attached to the property, as G. BOYER suggests, NOUGAYROL, *op. cit.*, p. 286.

[2]) M. DUNAND, *RB* XXXIX, 1930, pp. 321-33.

[3]) G. A. COOKE, *NSI*, 1903, pp. 18 ff.

[4]) (*n*)*qmpʿ*
(*bn.nq*)*md*
(*mlk*) *ʾugrt*

...Niqmepa‘
(the son of Niq)mad
(King) of Ugarit

Upholder of right,
Governor of the palace,
Guardian of the palace-gate,
Builder ( )
( ) heart of the king,
( ) scion.

SCHAEFFER has rightly emphasized this fragment [1]), which he takes to denote the absolute power of the King of Ugarit as supreme judge, head of the royal household, of the army as guardian of the frontier (*ṯġr*), builder, i.e. of the city and its temples and maintainer of settlements in the realm, and guarantor of the wellbeing of his subjects (reading ( ) *lb mlk* as '(rejoicing) the heart of the realm'), and also assuring the fertility of flock and field, suggested by the mention of *ṣ*(?)*mḫ* in the fragmentary end of the passage. He would therefore take the fragment as equivalent to the titulary which was an important part of the royal protocol in the Egyptian accession ritual, of which the throne-name of the king in Israel was also a reflection. [2]) This view is quite feasible, though we differ from VIROLLEAUD's translation [3]) on which SCHAEFFER's interpretation depends, and consider that the text and titles relate not to Niqmepa as king, but as prince [4]). We should agree with DE VAUX [5]) in relating this to the titulary of the royal scion in Isaiah ix, 5 (EVV, 6). As in the case of that passage, however, we regard the titulary as relating to the prince in his designation as heir-apparent or co-regent. The functions of 'Governor of the palace' and 'Guardian of the palace gate' would be of course nominal. The lacuna after *bny* might have denoted the prince as 'the propagator' of the royal line rather than literally a

bʿl ṣdq
skn bt
mlk . ṯġr
(m)lk . bny
( )*.lb . mlk*
( ) *ṣ*(?)*mḫ*

1) SCHAEFFER, *Le Palais royal d'Ugarit* II, 1957, pp. XVI-XVII.

2) A. M. HONEYMAN, 'The Evidence for Regnal Names among the Hebrews', *JBL* LXVII, 1948, pp. 13 ff.

3) C. VIROLLEAUD, *Le palais royal d'Ugarit*, ed. C. F. A. SCHAEFFER, II, 1957, p. 20.

4) We should emphasize, however, that the text is fragmentary, and *bʿl ṣdq* may be the proper name of a private official, as M. LIVERANI suggests (*Storia di Ugarit*, 1962, p. 68).

5) R. DE VAUX, *RB* LXV, 1958, p. 635.

'builder', a sense attested of *bny* in the mythological texts. *mlk* in 1.8, if this is complete, must mean 'king' and not 'kingdom', which, in the concrete, would be *mmlkt*. The combination *lb mlk* supports our interpretation. Niqmepa then is one who does something for 'the heart of the king', comforts it, or the like, with the hope of the continuance of the dynasty. The fragmentary nature of the text makes it impossible to tell whether *ṣmḫ* is to be read at all, though we consider this highly probable. In such a context referring to the adoption of an heir-apparent the term 'scion', lit. 'sprout', is highly intriguing in view of its usage in passages referring to the scion of the Davidic house in Jeremiah xxiii, 5; xxxiii, 15 and its technical significance in Zechariah iii, 8; vi, 12, cf. Isaiah xi, 1 (חֹטֶר מִגֶּזַע יִשָׁי).

There is a considerable amount of evidence from Ugarit for the *entourage* of royalty. In the Krt text the heir-apparent and the rest of the royal family stood close to the royal person. They do not seem, however, to have participated in government, and the claim of the king's heir Yṣb to a share in government is indignantly rejected. In the sickness of the king it is the queen and not the heir-apparent who entertains the notables of the realm, and we think that the queen, as among the Hittites, enjoyed a position of great respect and authority in Ugarit. In the Late Bronze Age the deferential way in which the king addresses his mother in a letter (Gordon *UH* 117) suggests the status of Bathsheba at the court of Solomon (I Kings ii, 19) and that of the Queen-mother generally in Judah, who was the first lady (הגבירה) in the realm.In the Krt text there are certain intimates admitted to a feast in the palace called the 'bulls' and 'gazelles' of the king or the 'bulls' and 'gazelles' of *ḫbr*, the city of Krt (Gordon *UH* 128, IV, 6-7, 8-9). The 'bulls' are described as seventy in number and the 'gazelles' eighty, though these numbers are not to be taken quite literally. The identity of these is uncertain. Two priestly orders may be denoted, that of Baal, whose cult animal was the bull and who is represented with bull's horns on his helmet, and that of Rešef, who is represented with gazelle-horns on his head-dress. Since Rešef was the deity of plague and the underworld, it may be that those were two orders which engaged in a ritual combat in the crisis of the king's health. The 'bulls', on the other hand, may have been chiefs representing the sedentary population of the realm and the 'gazelles' the nomad element. The situation in this case would be roughly analogous to that in Israel and Judah, where the Rechabites resolutely maintained the desert ideal in protest against assimilation to the sedentary life of Canaan. [1]) This, however, is a matter of conjecture. What is certain is that the 'bulls' and 'gazelles', whoever they were, were closely associated with the king and subservient to him.

Others who stand in equally close relation to the king and in a sacral capacity are the *rp'um*, whom we have already mentioned as a guild of limited number associated with the king in certain rites designed to promote the fertility of the crops, in which as we have already seen in the case of Dn'el, and probably of Krt, the King was the channel of divine blessing. [2])

A study of the monarchy in Ugarit thus reveals many features illustrative of the kingship in ancient Israel, and no doubt if royal psalms were extant from Ras Shamra the analogies between the institution in Canaan and Israel would be even more striking. Apart from the fact that the general imagery expressing the kingship of El and of Baal in the Ras Shamra texts suggests that the human kingship was a reflection of the divine rule and that the king was the temporal guarantee of the sovereign power of God, the mythological matter which is so richly employed in the Hebrew royal psalms suggests a source beyond the austere origins of the native faith of Israel.

The relation of the king to El, the divine king paramount, is expressed, as we have seen, in the Krt text, which terms El the father of the king, and Krt the son and servant (*'bd, ġlm*) of El, both conceptions being familiar in Israel, where the king is formally adopted as the son of God (Psalm ii) and designated the 'servant of Yahweh' *par excellence*. The 'servant' may designate the king as epitomizing the community of worshippers (עבדים). It may on the other hand signify one whose will was so much that of the master that he was the representative and deputy of God, almost in fact the *alter ego*, or, to borrow A. R. JOHNSON's phrase in speaking of the Davidic king as invested with the spirit of God, 'a potent extension of the Divine personality'. [3]) Royal psalms in the Old Testament which

---

[1]) A similar situation is indicated in the Aramaic inscription of Klmw from Šam'al, where there is reference to the population consisting of מֹשכבים ('settlers') and בעררים ('wild people'). Similarly, after the Moslem conquest of Syria and Palestine the Arab conquerors lived as a race apart in the desert or in military camps at Homs, Jabiya in the Hauran, and Amwas, Ramleh, and Tiberias in Palestine. At the present time there is definite self-consciousness on the part of Bedouin and fellahin (peasants) among the Arabs.

[2]) *v. supra* pp. 118 ff., 211.

[3]) A. R. JOHNSON, *Sacral Kingship in Ancient Israel*, 1955, p. 14.

reflect the ideology of Baal's kingship won in conflict with the powers of Chaos, e.g. Psalms ii, cx, cf. xviii, 5 (EVV, 4); lxxxix, 26 (EV 25), 39-46 [1]), suggest that there may well have been some comparable expression of the identity of purpose between the Canaanite king and Baal in his repeated assertion of his rule against the menace of Chaos. Such evidence, however, has not survived in the literature of Ras Shamra, though the relationship of the health, life, and death of the Canaanite king to the revival or decay of nature, obvious from the Krt and Aqht texts, suggests that the vicissitudes of Baal may well have been reflected in the ritual of kingship in Canaan, though there is not sufficient evidence for the ritual identification of the Canaanite king with the rising and dying god, which has been claimed by VIROLLEAUD, [2]) GRAHAM and MAY, [3]) ENGNELL, [4]) and MOWINCKEL. [5]) In the ritual of the Spring New Year festival at Babylon, which is so often cited in support of the view that the king in the Near East was identified with the dying and rising god of vegetation, it is well known that the king underwent a ritual humiliation. [6]) This certainly had a social significance, which is evidenced by the king's negative confession, exculpating himself from sins of omission and commision in his administration, whereas in the cult of Marduk in the historical period there is no certain evidence that the king's experience related to the cult of a dying and rising god. Marduk in fact throughout the festival was in the ascendant, with no question of his eclipse or death. A ritual text, attested in two copies from Ras Shamra, [7]) which

---

[1]) JOHNSON plausibly suggests on the basis of a careful citation and study of the texts that the king was a protagonist in a ritual representation of this theme of the New Year festival, *op. cit.*, pp. 93 ff.

[2]) C. VIROLLEAUD, 'Les poèmes de Ras Shamra', *Revue Historique* CLXXXV, 1939, pp. 1 ff.

[3]) W. C. GRAHAM and H. G. MAY, *Culture and Conscience*, 1936, p. 132.

[4]) I. ENGNELL, *Studies in Divine Kingship in the Ancient Near East*, 1943, pp. 18 ff.

[5]) S. MOWINCKEL, *NTT* 1941, pp. 129-158; 1942, pp. 24-26, having stated that Krt is no historical king, but an Adonis figure, a dying and rising vegetation deity, qualifies his statement by supposing that the original god has become the mythical founder of a dynasty. In his latest statement of the case (*He That Cometh*, 1959, pp. 52-55) MOWINCKEL emphasizes the historical element much more strongly, without, however, giving up the possibility that Krt was originally a divine figure. His view that the action of the Krt poem was influenced by the motifs of the Baal-myth is tenable, but does not prove more than literary influence.

[6]) e.g. J. G. FRAZER, *The Golden Bough* (*Adonis, Attis, Osiris*), 1914; A. M. HOCART, *Kingship*, 1927, and articles in *Myth and Ritual*, ed. S. H. HOOKE, 1933, and *The Labyrinth*, ed. S. H. HOOKE, 1935; S. H. HOOKE, *The Origins of Early Semitic Ritual*, 1938, 15 ff.

[7]) GORDON *UH* 9 and A. HERDNER, 'Un nouvel exemplaire du rituel RS 1929, no. 3', *Syria* XXXIII, 1956, pp. 104-112.

mentions the king in some ritual during the tenth month is unfortunately too fragmentary to support any theory.

We should be greatly misled in the study of kingship in Canaan and its relevance to the institution in Israel if we did not regard the kingship in Canaan as attested in the Ras Shamra texts as a developing institution. The kingship in Ugarit had undergone many modifications in the course of some four centuries which elapsed from the period described in the Krt text to that of the administrative texts. In the interim the feudal system had been firmly established with its class of professional soldiers and tactical specialists. Syria and Palestine had been reduced by repeated Egyptian expeditions to the status of provinces with local garrisons and commandants. The Hittites from Anatolia had reduced the kings of North Syria to vassalage. Just how seriously this affected the political and social situation in Palestine may be gathered from the Memphis stele of Amenhotep II (1448-1420 B.C.) who mentions among persons deported from *Rtnw*, or Southern Syria, 144 princes and 139 brothers of princes captured in his seventh campaign and 217 princes and 189 brothers of princes taken in his ninth expedition to Asia. [1]) A similar policy was pursued by Thothmes III, Seti I, and Ramses II. Finally we must reckon with the Philistine and the Aramaean invasions and settlement at the end of the Late Bronze Age and the beginning of the Iron Age. In the case of the Aramaean invasions, with which we associate the main phase of the Hebrew settlement in Palestine, we have confederacies of tribes whose polity was radically different from any monarchic system.

In Canaan, where the mass of the population was ultimately derived, and constantly replenished, from the great Arabian desert, we naturally expect the impress of tribal conditions to be strong on the social order. There is a certain amount of evidence that this tribal system once prevailed at Ugarit and that vestiges of it remained in the Late Bronze Age. The administrative text Gordon *UH* 400 names twelve priestly families, the chief of which are apparently *Ṯ*ʿ [2]),

---

[1]) A. M. Badawi, 'Die neue historische Stele Amenophis II', *ASAE* XLII, 1942, pp. 1 ff.

[2]) In the colophon to Gordon *UH* 62 (ll. 53-57), where *ṯʿy* was thought to refer to the clan of Atnprln, *Ṯ*ʿ, Driver after Ginsberg (*ANET* 1950, p. 141) translates *ṯʿy* as a verb 'he (i.e. King Nqmd) gifted' (the tablet), citing the Arabic cognate ثغى, 'to present', with which he connects Krt's stock epithet *ṯ*ʿ, which he renders 'the Munificent' (*Canaanite Myths and Legends*, p. 151).

Mglb, and *Dtn*, the last of which appears in the Krt text, probably signifying a family intimately related to the house of Krt. In the longer texts Krt and Aqht and in the Baal-cycle we shall later adduce instances of customs and observances which definitely imply a society based on the family or tribe. Those references again, however, carry us back rather to the heroic past. In texts which may be dated in the Late Bronze Age the scene has changed. The tribal system of society, if not quite defunct, had already broken down in Ugarit. We have already seen that the fiscal lists classify the population of the realm either territorially or by guilds, and not by tribes. This development may have been a consequence of the constitutional change from a primitive state of tribal oligarchy to that of monarchy. On the other hand, we think rather that it was due to the influx of a society whose organization differed from that of the native Semites. While in many respects Canaanite society reflects conditions of the tribes of the desert hinterland, it is equally true that Ugarit in particular in the extreme North of Canaan bore the impact of invasion of non-Semitic elements from the North and East, particularly of the Aryans who penetrated the area and imposed themselves as a military aristocracy on the native population about the end of the 19th century. It is our opinion that the classification of the population of Ugarit by vocations is a reflection of the caste system associated with the Aryans in India. There is, of course, no evidence in the Ras Shamra texts for the elaborate caste-organization of modern Hinduism with its four noble castes, each with its own taboos and food-restrictions. The system at Ugarit, in short, does not appear to have had any religious significance. The enumeration of families, however, under the heading of vocations and trades suggests this affinity.

In this connection the most significant text is Gordon *UH* 400, which records certain sums of money noted against the names of families listed under headings such as *mrynm*, *bdl mrynm*, *mrʾum*, *mrʾu sḳn*, *mrʾu ʾebrn*, *mž̮rġlm*, *bdl mž̮rġlm*, and *ḳhnm*. The first five classes, as we hope to demonstrate, are warriors, and the sixth and seventh probably also ranked with warriors. This would correspond to the second noble caste among the Hindus, the *Kshatriya*. The eighth class, the priests, would correspond to the *Brahmana*, the highest Hindu caste. In the text cited it is uncertain whether the sums listed against each family severally, and summed up by totals against the whole class, are a levy or a grant. Military specialists and priests, however, in virtue of what they have to offer, are most likely to be privileged classes, so that the sums might be regarded as state payments. On the other hand the Akkadian texts from the royal chancellery indicate rather that fiefs involved certain burdens. However this problem may be eventually solved, it is significant that by far the greatest amount is listed against the military orders, particularly the class *mrynm*. No family of this class, however, was more highly rated than the priestly family *Dtn*, which the Krt text associates with royalty. This suggests that the military duties in the kingdom of Ugarit by the 13th century B.C. were concentrated in the hands of military specialists whose status matched even that of the hereditary priesthood not excluding the royal kinship itself.

To turn more specifically to the various classes noted in the list, we may say that the significance of *mrynm* is beyond doubt. *Mariannu* was already known from Egyptian inscriptions of the XVIIIth Dynasty as a specialist in chariot warfare, [1]) and in an Akkadian text from Ras Shamra [2]) *mariannu* clearly bears the same meaning. This vocation, as well as the title, points directly to an Aryan origin, Indic *maria* signifying 'young man, hero', the *marias* being celebrated in Vedic literature as the attendants on the chariot of the storm-god Indra. As is well-known, the horse and two-wheeled chariot as an arm of war was introduced to Western Asia by the Aryan invaders c. 1800 B.C. [3]) The *mrynm* and other military orders owed their status directly to the king, as is clear from Akkadian texts from the palace archives where King Ammištamru makes one Adadšeni and his family *mrynm* (Nougayrol, *op. cit.*, 16.132, p. 140) and detaches Yanḫamu and his family from the status of *mu'ru* of Ibiranu and makes him *mudu* ('count') of the queen. [4]) The evidence from the Old

---

[1]) e.g. J. H. Breasted, *Ancient Records of Egypt* II, § 590.

[2]) Virolleaud, *Syria* XXVIIII, 1951, pp. 49-53.

[3]) In a text from the Hittite capital of Boghazköi on horse-training written by one Kikkuli, a professional from Mitanni, the numbers of laps (*vartana* = 'turns') are cited in a dialect which is very close to Sanskrit, e.g.

Hittite text, *aika*	=	1, cf. Sanskrit *eku*
tera	=	3, cf. Sanskrit *trayah*
pansa	=	5, cf. Sanskrit *panca*
satta	=	7, cf. Sanskrit *sapta*
nawa	=	9, cf. Sanskrit *nava*.

[4]) The status of *mudu* in this case involved not personal service, but a tax of 20 shekels of silver, Nougayrol, *op. cit.* 16348, p. 162. Conditions were the same at Atchana (ancient Alalakh) sixty miles North-East of Ras Shamra, where a tablet in Akkadian cuneiform and from the Late Bronze Age states:

'Seal of Niqmepa the King. As from this day forth Niqmepa the King has released Qabia to be a *mariannu*; as the sons of *mariannu* of the city-state of Alalakh

Testament of the relation of such professional soldiers to the king agrees with this data. Such texts as 1 Samuel xiv, 52., xviii, 13, and particularly xxii, 7 ff. indicate that Saul had already adopted the system, attaching professional soldiers to himself and granting them fiefs for their maintenance (1 Samuel xxii, 7). David was the outstanding example of such a professional soldier whose attachment was no longer to his ancestral land and community but to the king. As a mercenary commandant of the Philistine Achish of Gath David received the frontier town of Ṣiqlag, which remained in his family as a perpetual fief until the end of the monarchy of Judah (1 Samuel xxvii, 6). We think with De Langhe that the technical term *šd ʾubdy* in the text Gordon *UH* 300 signifies a grant of land *in perpetuum* [1]) where the *mrynm* or chariot-warriors might support themselves and their retainers and studs. At the zenith of Hittite power in Syria great feudal barons seem to have possessed lands commensurate with their authority, [2]) which on the collapse of the Hittite Empire at the end of the Bronze Age became nuclei of such states as Hamath, Arpad, and others in inland Syria. In the small realm of Ugarit, where the king was the vassal in turn of the Pharaoh and the Hittite King, the power and status of the barons was more limited.

Among other classes listed with *mrynm* in the text Gordon *UH* 400 and in the records of land-grants and conferment of status by the king are *bdl mrynm*, *nʿr mrynm* (*PRU* II, 31, 3-4), *mrʾum*, *mudu*, *mẓrġlm*, and *bdl mẓrġlm*. Of these *nʿr mrynm* recalls נערי שׂרי המדינות of 1 Kings xx, 14, a term which is generally, and we think satisfactorily, translated 'squires'. Here, as the etymology of the term suggests, they were young men, who were appropriately used as shock troops or commandos, which is also the rôle they play in the encounter of Joab

---

are so also are Qabia and his grandsons in perpetuity, and the priests of Enlil'. S. Smith, *Antiquaries Journal* XIX, 1939, p. 43.

[1]) Connecting *ʾubdy* with Arabic أبدى, 'perpetual', after R. De Langhe, *Les Textes de Ras Shamra et leurs Rapports avec le Milieu Biblique de l'Ancien Testament* II, p. 391. Tenancy of land in lieu of military service is a feature of the Middle and Late Bronze Ages in Mesopotamia and Anatolia, but the relevant texts from the palace archives of Ras Shamra show that fiefs which were originally inalienable were now disposed of as personal property to persons, such as women, who could not possibly give military service. The fiefs might exchange hands with a transference of the old state burden of service or produce, but there are many cases where those are expressly remitted. For an excellent study of feudal tenure in the Ancient East in the light of the palace archives of Ugarit see G. Boyer, in Nougayrol, *op. cit.*, pp. 293 ff.

[2]) E. Weidner, *op. cit.*

and Abner at Gibeon (2 Samuel ii, 14). *naʿaruna* is known as a military term in Egypt also, possibly referring to mercenaries recruited in Canaan, as DE VAUX suggests. [1]) *mrʾu* suggests to ALT [2]) the Egyptian term *mrʾ*, by which he understands 'horse-trainer'. In view of the verbal root *mrʾa* attested in GORDON *UH* 51, VII, 50, however, with the meaning 'to rule', this explanation is doubtful. The term is qualified by the person or office to which the *mrʾum* were attached, e.g. *murʾu* *amīlrabiṣi* (*PRU* III, 16.139, 14), cf. *mrʾu skn* (GORDON *UH* 400, V, 6), and *mrʾu ʾebrn* (*ibidem*, V, 17) cf. *murʾu Ibirana* (*PRU* III, 16.139, 14) respectively 'Governor's *mrʾum*' and Ibiranu's *mrʾum*, Ibiranu being the crown prince. [3]) Similarly qualified are *mudu*, as for instance 'King's *mudu*' (*PRU* III, 15.137, 12; 16.143, 21; 16.157, 20; 16.239, 18; 16.250, 16), and 'Queen's *mudu*' (*ibidem*, 16.353, 31; 16.14 verse, 3; 16.348, 6). J. NOUGAYROL explains the word as 'counts', i.e. 'those who know', or have personal dealings with, the King or Queen, and he suggests an analogy in 'the King's Friend' in Israel (1 Kings iv, 5). Their attachment to the Queen indicates that they had originally the function of palace staff, though in the case of one Abdu (*PRU* III, 16. 239), who also became a *mryn*, the office seems to have involved active service. In the list above cited *mẓrġlm* by its morphology suggests a non-Semitic word, for which we conjecture the meaning 'armourers'. [4]) Here again is a class of military specialists, who were consequently privileged. *bdl mrynm* and *bdl mẓrġlm* presents more of a problem. *bdl* suggests the Arabic بدل, 'to exchange, counterfeit', and we had previously suggested that it might denote 'substitutes' for equestrian feudatories or for *mẓrġlm*, whose status depended on their active service, but who might, as in

---

[1]) R. DE VAUX, *Ancient Israel*, 1961, p. 221.

[2]) A. ALT, *ZAW* N. F. XVII, 1941, p. 279.

[3]) cf. *murʾu ušriyani*,ʿ*m*. of the heir', cf. VIROLLEAUD, *Syria* XXI, 1940, p. 253. This suggests Adonijah's retinue which indicated his pretensions to succession (1 Kings i, 5).

[4]) DE LANGHE cites ALT's suggestion that this is a Hurrian word, as the termination *uḫlu* (the termination of the Hurrian *nomen agentis*) indicates. The consonant *ḫ* in the Akkadian cuneiform could be rendered by *ġ* in the Ugaritic alphabetic cuneiform. The root of the word might then be *ẓr*, which suggests to us the Hebrew שריון, 'coat of mail', surely a foreign loanword to the Hebrews who were so backward in the technical arts. The word *mšrġlm* may be a Semitized form of a Hurrian word after the pattern of the participle of an intensive verb, hence the initial *m* may be a preformative. SCHAEFFER found many scales of bronze coats of mail in the palace-complex at Ras Shamra and notes their affinity with such from Nuzu in the period of Hurrian domination. *Syria* XXVIII, 1951, p. 11, fig. 6.

feudal times in the Scottish Highlands, supply a substitute as a privilege of their craft. In administrative texts, however, dealing with these orders and guilds in the realm and their estates and lands, we note than *bdlm* occasionally appears absolutely (e.g. *PRU* II, 32, 1; 58, 20; 35, 4), and is listed as a category of *tamkaru* (merchant) in *PRU* III 16.257; II, 12. On this evidence we follow NOUGAYROL, who regards *bdl mrynm* and *bdl mẓrǵlm* as 'agents commerciaux' or financiers, [1]) bailiffs of the feudal estates or brokers for their produce, or perhaps merchants who financed the military orders in their horse-dealing and provision of arms for their retainers. To complete the picture of the military classes at Ugarit we may cite those of *ḫpṯ* and *ṯnn* which are mentioned in the Krt text. [2]) In the Amarna Tablets, which are contemporary with the administrative texts from Ras Shamra, the term is familiar in the form *ḫubšu.* [3]) Assyrian documents also mention a class *ḫubšu* which LEWY takes as feudal retainers or mercenaries. [4]) There were special officers of state appointed to look after the interest of wives of such persons if they were prisoners of war. DRIVER and MILES cite a text of Sargon II which describes five divisions of the army, apparently in order of attack. Here the *ḫubšu* are fourth, which suggests to DRIVER that they correspond to the infantry, [5]) or perhaps sappers. He does, however, agree with LEWY

---

[1]) J. NOUGAYROL, *PRU* III, p. 236.

[2]) GORDON *UH* krt 90-91.

[3]) The *ḫubšu* are mentioned eleven times in the correspondence of Rib-Addi of Byblos. He reports that in their extremity they have given up their property and their children to get corn (KNUDTZON, *op. cit.*, 85, 12; 114, 21 ff.), they try to get away and abandon him (*ibidem* 114 21 ff.; 81, 33), they plunder other cities in want of food (*ibidem* 125 ff.), and are thus a positive menace (*ibidem* 130, 41 ff.). Rib-Addi complains that he is in as much danger from his own *ḫubšu* as from his overt enemies (*ibidem* 112, 10 ff.; 117, 90). They abandon him for the sons of Abdi-Aširtu and in support of Sidon and Beirut (*ibidem* 118, 21 ff.). On the basis of this evidence PEDERSEN concludes that the term *ḫubšu* refers to the basic stock of the land, *JPOS* VI, 1926, pp. 103-105. ALBRIGHT connects the word with the Akkadian *ḫabašu*, Arabic حبس, and Hebrew חבשׁ, 'to bind', and suggests that the primary meaning was a serf bound to the land, the secondary meaning being a peasant landholder or freeholder as distinct from a serf. It was with the latter condition and meaning that the Hebrews were familiar by the time of the settlement in Palestine. *JPOS* VI, 1926, pp. 106-108. ALBRIGHT takes *ḫpṯ* in the Krt text as 'serfs', *BASOR* 63, 1936. GINSBERG also translates the term here as 'serfs', 'The Legend of King Krt', *BASOR* Supplement 2-3, 1946, p. 16. DRIVER, as we have seen, translates *ḫpṯ* as 'pioneers', and *ṯnn* as 'veterans', *v. supra*, p. 138, n.

[4]) J. LEWY, *ZA* XXXVI, 1925, p. 148, n. 3.

[5]) Arabic حَبَسَ, DRIVER and MILES, *op. cit.*, p. 485.

that the *ḫubšu* were 'irregular, probably mercenary, soldiers almost equally troublesome to both sides'. In this connection it is interesting to find the implication of a similar social order in Palestine in the time of Saul who undertook to make the family of Goliath's successful antagonist חפשי in Israel (I Samuel xvii, 25). This promise applied to the individual and his heirs. Saul did not promise emancipation in the commonly accepted sense, but undertook to release the prospective champion from the limitations of his local and family ties and invest him with the status and substance of a feudatory. In view of the currency of the word till much later in Assyria and also, on the evidence of I Samuel xvii, 25 in Israel, it is remarkable that the term *ḫpṯ* is not attested in the administrative texts from the palace of Ras Shamra. Obviously it has been replaced by another term, probably *ṯnn*, which is attested along with the military orders *mrynm*, *mr'um*, and *ḫsnm*. [1]) The Alalakh Tablets, however, which are much nearer to the Ras Shamra texts in time and place than the Hebrew and Assyrian texts, indicate that *ḫubšu* were small peasants, living on the outskirts of settlements perhaps as seminomads, scarcely integrated with the sedentary population, hence useful as mobile mercenary troops. *ṯnn*, on the other hand, are listed in census-texts in the Alalakh Tablets as regular members of military units. Their popular character is suggested by the fact that they far outnumber the charioteers of their units (WISEMAN, *op. cit.*, p. 11-12). ALBRIGHT is probably right in associating *šanannu* of the Alalakh Tablets with Akkadian *šananu*, 'to contest, strive', hence denoting trained troops (*v. supra*, p. 139 and n.).

These feudal relations are admirably illustrated from certain Akkadian texts from the archives of the palace of Ras Shamra, copies of deeds of investment of one Abdu ben Abinergal and of his sons Kalbu, Aziru, and Ilimilku under two kings of Ugarit, Arḫalbu and Niqmepa. In the first of these (*PRU* III, 16.239) Abdu, already a *mryn* and 'King's count', is granted certain lands as a perpetual heritable fief free from burdens except a certain sum of money due to the King on account of his status as 'count' (*mudu*). He is directly responsible to the King for the maintenance of his stud, which he is allowed formally to commit to the charge of his son Kalbu with certain property. Another document (*PRU* III, 16.431) dated in

---

[1]) This may indicate makers of חֹשֶׁן, 'a breastplate', cf. the high priest's pectoral with the sacred stones, Exodus xxv, 7; xxviii, 15, 29, 30.

the reign of Niqmepa, the successor and probably the brother of Arḫalbu, [1]) confers more lands upon Abdu, including, incidentally certain lands which had been the endowment of the god Šatran. Abdu's conveyance of these to his son Aziru, now a 'King's count' is sanctioned by the royal deed. As a 'King's count' Aziru is declared exempt from the authority of the mayor of the town, [2]) the official who was responsible for the conscription of chariotry, [3]) and another official *ubru*, who apparently had right of access to houses of subjects, probably to inspect arms and equipment of the feudal orders. We learn further that as 'King's count' 10 shekels of silver was due annually from Aziru to the King. NOUGAYROL [4]) plausibly suggests that such a comparatively small sum may have been to defray the cost of the maintenance of the 'count' in the discharge of such duties as involved his stay in the palace. In a third document (*PRU* III, 16.250) similar provision is made for a third son of Abdu Ilimilku (Hebrew Elimelech).

The civil administration in the realm of Ugarit was carried on by various officials directly appointed by the King and responsible to him. There was the *rabiṣu ekallim*, the palace governor or royal chamberlain, who, as appears from the alphabetic text *PRU* III, 16.145, 25-26, had authority to use the royal seal. This office appears to correspond to that of 'him who was over the house' (אשר על הבית) in Judah. As in Judah too in the case of Jotham the son of Azariah, Niqmepa, when heir-apparent in Ugarit, had the office of *skn bt mlk*, 'Governor of the Palace' (*PRU* II, 7, 5-6).

The districts with their towns or village centres throughout the realm were under the local administration of officials known as *ḫazanu* or *ḫazan ali*, which we may translate as 'mayor'. The power of the mayor seems to have been considerable since in royal deeds of investiture the 'count' is specially exempted from the authority of the mayor (e.g. *PRU* III, 15.137, 15-16; 16.157, 21-22; 16.250, 17-18).

[1]) The fact that one brother succeeded another probably reflects intervention in Ugaritic politics by Egypt and the Hittites about the middle of the 14th c. See C. F. A. SCHAEFFER, *PRU* III, pp. XXXVII-XXXVIII, n. 2, and his correspondence with S. SMITH.

[2]) The town may be Ugarit, but we think that local mayors are also indicated.

[3]) Cf. 'the scribe, the officer over the army' (הספר שׂר הצבא) in Judah on the fall of Jerusalem (2 Kings xxv, 19). This exemption from the royal authority in civil and military administration seems to us to elucidate the offer of Elisha to requite the hospitality of the Shunamite woman by speaking on her behalf to the King or to the commander of the army (2 Kings iv, 13).

[4]) J. NOUGAYROL, *PRU* III, p. 234.

Towns or village centres, however, might be made over by the King to whomsoever he pleased, as in *PRU* III, 15.114, where among other places a town Sakna is made over to one Takhulinu, apparently a Hittite agent from Carchemish who, in a period of Hittite pressure on Ugarit (cf. p. 237, n. 1), [1]) had been appointed palace governor (*rabiṣu ekallim*). In such a case the maintenance of the place was enjoined upon the tenant, but all state burdens of tax and *corvée* in men and beasts were waived. A grant of this nature is made to a daughter of the King, one Lady Apapa, and her husband (*PRU* III, 16.276), which recalls the Pharaoh's grant of Gezer to Solomon and his daughter (1 Kings ix, 16).

Already known from Mesopotamian and Hittite texts, the Amarna Tablets, and texts from Alalakh in the Late Bronze Age as an underprivileged class of displaced persons, who may live by mercenary service as soldiers or labourers or may even sell themselves into servitude, the *ḫabiru* are also mentioned in administrative texts from Ras Shamra. As in Hittite documents and the Amarna Tablets, they are named *ḫabiru* in Akkadian syllabic cuneiform and *SA GAZ* in ideogram, while the alphabetic texts term them *ʿprm*, cf. Egyptian *ʿprw*. A letter of a king of Carchemish to the King of Ugarit (*PRU* III, 16.03) indicates that they might be distributed from Ugarit to his realm on the Euphrates, though he states that he has none of them. Economic tablets from Ras Shamra (*PRU* III, 11.790; Gordon *UH* 110, 1; 112, 12) mention a town *ḫalpi* (alphabetic *ḫlb*) which had a quarter reserved for the *ḫabiru* or *ʿprm*. A royal deed of gift to Sinaranu (*PRU* III, 15.109), in exempting him from the visitation of the *ubru*, or royal overseer (*v. supra*, p. 237), also states that *ḫabiru* shall not enter Sinaranu's house. This leaves us in doubt as to whether this is an allusion to the *ḫabiru* as a kind of police force at the disposal of the *ubru* or a prohibition to Sinaranu to receive underprivileged persons under his patronage and so to abuse his influence. The main point is that here there is no question of an ethnic group. *ḫabiru* or *ʿprm* here as in other documents we have mentioned has a social or economic connotation. Known from texts from Mari[2], Alalakh [3] and Nuzu [4] as aliens who had left their native states for various reasons, they lived together, or were settled by the country where they

[1]) This correspondence is dated in the reign of Ammištamru son of Niqmepa. so after the death of Šubbiluliuma, and perhaps c. 1300.

[2]) J. Bottéro, *Le problème des Ḫabiru*, 1954, nos. 19-20.

[3]) *Ibidem*, no. 44.

[4]) *Ibidem*, nos. 49, 50, 56.

sojourned, in certain quarters, like *ḫlb* in Ugarit, or cantonments where they might be readily controlled and mobilized for military service, their common means of livelihood.

Apart from the professional classes of the military and ecclesiastical establishment, the people of the rural areas were conscripted for personal service (the *corvée*) or listed for conscription or, we believe, for the provision of a police force [1]) not by tribes or families, but by districts.

In these conditions, where the tribal organization of society had obviously been replaced, as far as concerned the influential classes at least, by a feudal order and a hierarchy of hereditary office, we can but speculate on the extent to which the old social values of the tribe or kinship group survived. Here our difficulty is that our documents for this subject relate without exception to the more primitive past. From the Late Bronze Age there are certain legal documents at Ugarit which imply a complex system of civil law in the interests of the individual on the principles of the urban system of Mesopotamia. [2]) This was probably superimposed on the system of ancient communal law or tribal custom. This situation is not unfamiliar in ancient Israel especially after the institution of the monarchy when, as the incident of David and the wise woman of Tekoa indicates (2 Samuel xiv, 4 ff.), the law on homicide executed by the kindred of the manslayer by unanimous consent could be abrogated, though not without compunction, by the king in the manifest interest of the individual.

In the Krt and Aqht texts the system of communal law or time-hallowed custom is often quite explicit and, indeed, these texts must have done much to preserve these social values. In the case of the Baal-cycle such principles find expression owing to the anthropomorphism of the texts. Here as in the case of agricultural ritual, which has its analogy in the ritual laws of the Torah, we cannot automatically find affinity between ancient Israel and Ugarit, but such affinity may nevertheless be established if one is aware of the implications of certain passages which are less apparent to the modern reader than to the native of Ugarit or ancient Israel.

---

1) This tablet is docketed as *TUPPU ṢABE ŠA QIŠATI*, 'tablet of archers'.

2) These comprise deeds of sale, conveyance of land, wills, and deeds of adoption. F. Thureau-Dangin, *Syria* XVIII, 1937, pp. 246-254, Virolleaud, *Syria* XXVIII, 1951, pp. 54-56, Schaeffer, *Syria* XXXI, 1954, pp. 30 ff. J. Nougayrol, *PRU* III (ed. Schaeffer), 1955, pp. 22-176 (Akkadian texts) with a special study by G. Boyer on Ugaritic law, pp. 283-308, and Virolleaud, *PRU* II ed. Schaeffer), 1957, pp. 17-35. Many of these documents cited the king either as witness or as judge and others were direct decrees of the king. Defaulters' fines were likewise paid to the king.

Documented history, language, and archaeology combine to attest the persistent influence of the desert upon the border-lands of Palestine, Syria, and both Upper and Lower Mesopotamia, the stock of which, whatever its original nature, was repeatedly replenished from the North Arabian steppe-land. In that semi-arid region property has not the same consequence as in the more favoured regions and in the nature of the case the community-sense is highly developed. From the dawn of conscience a man learns to know his duties and privileges as a member of the kingroup which protects him against those without. His code—the code of the group—rests upon a few very simple principles. Whatever menaces the physical strength or honour of the group, clan or tribe, must be resisted. The members have a very clear knowledge of what impairs the welfare or repute of the group and an equally clear knowledge of the particular reaction that this demands. In cases such as that of manslaughter a sheikh of repute may help to decide a case, but justice does not usually wait for such a decision, but is automatic, though often quite indiscriminate according to Western principles. A life is demanded for a life, though the life of any of the homicide's family to the fifth generation is deemed sufficient. The injured parties, individual or kinsmen, are their own executors, for there is no police-force in the open desert, and in place of criminal law the avenger has the sanction of tribal opinion and long-established custom.

This principle of communal responsibility was admitted in ancient Israel. In the instance we cited from 2 Samuel xiv, 4 ff., though appeal was made to the king in person, David was expected by the wise woman of Tekoa to have grave compunctions about abrogating the local community-law, which was depicted as being executed by the kinsmen of the homicide. [1]) Indeed even as late as Deuteronomy we find that, though cases were referred to the shrine where the priest and judge officiated, those were exceptional cases which were too hard for the elders of the community, who were the normal judges (Deuteronomy xvi, 18; xvii, 8). Again in Deuteronomy (xxi, 18) abuse of parents and insubordination were punished by stoning by the whole community if the father prosecuted the offending son before the elders. In this particular of communal responsibility for the execution of justice it is significant that the oldest code in the

[1]) Though this was a fictitious case it must have been true to life. It is noteworthy that the force of custom was so binding as to operate mechanically against the express wishes of the mother of the homicide.

Pentateuch, the Book of the Covenant (Exodus xx, 22-xxiii, 33), does not mention judges at all. [1]

In the Ras Shamra texts such a system of communal responsibility is implied in texts reflecting conditions of a more primitive period. In the mythological text GORDON *UH* 77, describing the marriage of the moon-god Yrḫ with the moon-goddess Nkl, the business of paying over the bride-price (*mhr*) is presided over by the lady's whole family. [2]

As in Bedouin justice and in ancient Israel, the law of blood-revenge was known in ancient Ugarit. In the Baal-texts Baal, having slain certain monsters who were actually his half-brothers, is condemned to die:

> 'Thou art appointed as satisfaction for (thy) kinsmen;
> I appoint thee to be spent for them.' [3]

In the main body of the Baal-texts the death of Baal at the hands of Mot is avenged by Baal's sister Anat, [4] and in the Aqht text the death of the hero is avenged by his sister 'the Maid', who declares:

> 'I will smite him who smote my brother,
> I will make an end of him who annihilated the child of my mother. [5]

An interesting case which combines the principle of the *lex talionis* and that of communal responsibility is that of homicide where the slayer is unknown. In such a case in ancient Israel the community nearest to the scene of the crime was held responsible and was obliged to undertake an oath of purgation over the blood of a heifer slain in a perennial wadi (Deuteronomy xxi, 1-9). [6] In the Aqht

---

[1]) So in North Israel in the time of Ahab (c. 860 B.C.) Naboth was condemned not by judges but by local notables and elders (1 Kings xxi).

[2]) This passage also illustrates the absolute right of the father. So also among the Bedouin in cases of adultery the father has the right of life and death over his offending daughter. In ancient Israel a new bride who is accused of adultery and cannot prove her virginity is stoned to death by the community at the door of her father's house (Deuteronomy xxii, 20-21).

[3]) *v. supra* p. 79.

[4]) *v. supra* pp. 124-125

[5]) We take *ʿl* in this passage as cognate with the Arabic عيل, 'family'. In *ʿl ʾumty*, 'child of my mother', it is explicitly stated that Baal was the uterine brother of Anat.

[6]) The spot of the ritual is more explicitly defined, אשר לא יעבד בו ולא יזרע The spring had not yet reached cultivable land, thus would be near its source (קור). The point would be that if the parties suspected had committed perjury the blood of which they were guilty would be carried down by the wadi and would

text GASTER would see a reflection of this practice [1]) in Dn'el's curse upon three sites when he learns of the death of his son Aqht. [2]) These localities are called *qr mym*, *qrt 'ablm 'ablm*, and *mrrt*, and are generally taken as place-names, [3]) presumably the three settlements nearest to the scene of Aqht's murder. We are not at all sure that all these are settlements, though in the case of *qrt 'ablm 'ablm* ('City of Many Streams') this seems probable. In the case of *qr mym* ('fountain of water') we may have a connection with the rite of slaying a heifer by a perennial wadi at a spot where cultivation was not yet possible, that is to say near the source. In the Aqht text there is no oath of purgation, a fact which indicates that communities are not in question. The curse on the water is intended to carry a penalty to the land through which it flows.

Whatever our interpretation of this passage may be, it does illustrate the principle familiar to anthropology that blood shed in violence and left uncovered pollutes the earth and occasions sterility.

In Bedouin society no distinction is made between wilful and unintentional homicide; blood demands blood. Even here, however, sanctuary may be offered. A fugitive from the avenger of blood may claim refuge in the tent of an Arab and once he has won to this flimsy sanctuary and claimed right of asylum his host is bound to give him protection at least for the space of three days and four nights. At the end of that period he may hazard his life again in the open desert, a perpetual wanderer like Cain (Genesis iv, 14), seeking continual refuge. In ancient Hebrew society this practice was known, as Psalm xxiii indicates. A significant advance was made in Israel, however, when the right of sanctuary at a shrine was admitted which should be effective in the case of accidental homicide (Exodus xxi, 13). This right of sanctuary, however, was not to be abused, and it is explicitly stated that not even the altar of Jahweh would protect the deliberate homicide from the avenger of blood (Exodus xxi, 14). [4])

---

pollute all that was watered by it. Hence it is not insignificant that Dn'el curses the fountain of water as well as the settlement by it.

[1]) GASTER, *Thespis*, p. 302.

[2]) *v. supra* pp. 122, 123.

[3]) GASTER, *Thespis*, p. 302.

[4]) According to W. R. SMITH (*The Religion of the Semites*, 3rd. ed., 1927, p. 148) this indicates the restriction of a custom of wider and more indiscriminate application. He cites Tacitus, Annals iii, 60 ff., where it is stated that Tiberius checked the abuse of the sanctuary in the Greek cities where all sorts of criminals found effective asylum.

A later development probably is the appointment of certain 'cities of refuge' (Numbers xxxv, 6 ff., Joshua xx, 2-3). [1])

It is claimed that the right of sanctuary is known also in ancient Ugarit. In view of the custom in ancient Israel, in primitive Arab society as shown in the pre-Islamic poets, and in Graeco-Roman Syria, where the coins of the period mention Askalon, Gaza, Sepphoris, [2]) Ptolemais (Akka), and Sidon as ΙΕΡΑΙ ΑΣΥΛΟΙ, [3]) it is extremely probable that the practice was known also at Ugarit. The evidence, however, is not quite so clear as we should wish. In the passage in the Aqht text where Dn'el pronounces a curse upon *qr mym*, *qrt 'ablm 'ablm*, and *mrrt* a regular formula is applied to each: [4])

'Away with thee now and for ever!'

In the case of *qr mym* the formula varies, a line occurring:

'amd gr bt 'el. Perpetually seeking sanctuary,

which we agree with GASTER in referring to *qr mym* 'the source of water', probably implying the neighbouring settlement. The term *gr* seems to be used in the sense of one who seeks shelter as a sojourner at a shrine in the short text GORDON *UH* 2 in the phrase *gr ḥmyt 'ugrt*. Here the qualifying word *ḥmyt* is significant, being associated by DHORME [5]) with the Akkadian *ḫamatu*, 'asylum', and by VIROLLEAUD [6]) with the Arabic root حمى, 'to protect'. Thus *gr ḥmyt* should probably be taken as a compound phrase meaning 'a sojourner of sanctuary' probably in the plural in the passage cited. There is no indication here that they were refuges from blood-revenge, but it is likely that they did include such.

The social convention of sanctuary in a private tent is bound up with the practice of hospitality. Public opinion is a powerful sanction of conduct in the desert and a man's generosity bears interest, while the niggard forfeits all credit. The guest of an Arab, or the refugee

[1]) ALBRIGHT believes that these cities of refuge were instituted in or immediately after the time of David, but were doubtless of earlier significance as sanctuaries. *The Biblical Period* (*The Jews: their History, Culture, and Religion*, ed. L. FINKELSTEIN) 1952, p. 25. Their institution, however, may be after the suppression of local sanctuaries by Josiah.

[2]) G. F. HILL, *A Catalogue of the Greek Coins in the British Museum* (*Palestine*), 1914, Pll. XII, XV, pp. xii, 107.

[3]) *Ibidem* (*Phoenicia*), 1910, pp. lxxxi, cvi, 158-161.

[4]) *v. supra* p. 122 n.

[5]) E. DHORME, *RB* XL, 1931, p. 39.

[6]) VIROLLEAUD, *La Légende Phénicienne de Danel*..., p. 37.

who is sojourning with him, enjoys the protection of his host and his tribe, which covers not only his person but his property. A famous instance of this is celebrated in Arab tradition as the War of el-Basūs. About 600 A.D. one had come as a refugee of the tribe Bakr and was living under the protection of el-Basūs, the aunt of the chief Jassās. Kulaib, the paramount chief of the tribe of Taghlib, had accidentally wounded the guest's camel and el-Basūs demanded that Jassās should exact satisfaction. The chief offered to replace the slain camel, but el-Basūs was adamant. After some delay she again urged the chief Jassās to vengeance, whereupon he replied that there should that day fall 'such a stallion of the Beny Taghlib' that the whole desert should resound. For that camel the son of the offending sheikh was slain and a bloody feud of forty years immediately broke out. While there is no such colourful instance from ancient Ugarit, a passage in the Aqht text clearly indicates that a similar convention of hospitality with protection of the guests obtained. In the catalogue of the virtues of the ideal son one of the duties is

> To drive away the oppressor of his father's night-guest.

It is noteworthy, however, that in settled Canaan in contrast to the open desert the security of the guest depended less on recognized communal custom than on the prestige or even physical strength of the host, as is implied in the instance of the angels entertained by Lot in Sodom (Genesis xix) and the case of the Levite and his concubine at Gibeah (Judges xix). This last instance is most illuminating as an illustration of the modification of the standards of the social ethic among the Hebrews on their settlement in Canaan. The spontaneous hospitality of the old man who entertained the Levite indicates that the old desert principles had not been entirely forgotten, but the fact that he alone in this Benjamite settlement offered to house the stranger, and the violation by the natives of the sanctity of the guest is a vivid commentary on the declension of the Hebrews from the unwritten social code of the desert. This is the more striking when we consider that, the Benjamites being among the last to penetrate the settled land, the offenders were removed from their desert life by little over a century.

Apart from ethical obligations which the Ras Shamra texts imply, there are a number of ritual obligations imposed on, or for, society. These relate to the crises of human life, the *passages* from one state to another, which in the conception of primitives both ancient and modern were fraught with peculiar dangers. These were regarded as periods when the individual and the community of which he formed an integral part were particularly exposed to supernatural influences, which the primitive mind views with distrust. Such phases are pregnancy, birth, puberty, marriage, sickness, and death, which demand a certain social readjustment. Originally this imposed a discipline on the whole community. By the time that the behaviour of Near Eastern societies is documented, however, this discipline has devolved upon the family or individual most intimately connected with the subject. Here, however, it must be emphasized that the rites so imposed, whether on a family or an individual, were on behalf of the community, which, at least ideally, remained in a state of suspension until the rites were duly completed. The fundamentally social aspect of such a discipline is of vital importance and underlies all such experiences in the Old Testament. This it is which explains the sometimes bewildering alternation between the singular and plural in the Psalms and the intimate relationship between Servant and community in Deutero-Isaiah.

We now proceed to consider those crises of life in detail and begin naturally with the experience of birth. Among modern primitives it has been observed by field anthropologists that the coming into society of a new member at birth is an event with a high potential of evil, and necessitates all kinds of precautions in order that the society may come safely through the crisis and eventually be properly readjusted to the new circumstances. Thus the society, either as a whole or vicariously through the mother of the child and those intimately associated with her, suspends its normal activities and above all abstains from its staple diet. Such 'rites of separation' are familiar to us from the ritual isolation imposed upon women after child-birth in ancient Israel (Leviticus xii). In the Ras Shamra texts there is no such specific regulation, but the same conception and practice are implied in the mythological texts Gordon *UH* 75 and 52. In the first of these texts the mother of the monster brood who are to cause the downfall of Baal is sent to bear in the desert:

'. . . . . take
Thy stool, thy settle, thy swaddling-bands,
And stoop, couch in pain
In the midst of the awful desert.' [1])

---

[1]) Gordon *UH* 75, I, 17-22, *v. supra* pp. 67, 77.

In the second text the two women who give birth to Šḥr and Šlm sojourn after the birth with their progeny in the desert: [1])

'O wives whom I wed,
O sons whom I beget,
Take your equipment to the awful desert.
There ye shall go around from stones to bushes.
Seven whole years,
An eighth circuit besides...'

Apart from such isolation at childbirth the further precaution was taken to employ women 'skilled' not only in midwifery but in singing incantations. These were the *kṯrt* and, from the fact that the adjective *kṯr* was applied to the craftsman-god Hyn, we are justified in concluding that they were 'skilled' not only in singing but in composing and improvising, an association familiar also in Hebrew in the case of קנה, 'to create', and קינה, 'lament, dirge'. [2]) The association of these females with birth is clear from the texts Gordon *UH* Aqht and 77. In the former text, after the revelation to Dn'el that he will beget a son and heir, the king entertains the *kṯrt* for 'seven' days between the time he ends his ritual seclusion in the temple and begets his son in the palace (2 Aqht II, 27-40). In the latter text, in spite of its fragmentary nature, the association of the *kṯrt* with birth is quite clear. [3])

Here, unfortunately, the state of the text does not permit us to determine precisely the rôle played by the *kṯrt*. From the second part of the text, which is a hymn to the 'Skilful Ones', we learn that

---

[1]) *Ibidem* 52, 64-67. For text and commentary *v. supra*, pp. 103, 104.

[2]) The word *snnt*, the stock epithet of *Kṯrt*, was associated with the Akkadian *sinuntu*, 'swallow' by Virolleaud, *La Légende Phénicienne de Danel...*, p. 106. In view of the association of the *kṯrt* with the marriage of the Moon-god and his consort, however, which we find in the text Gordon *UH* 77, *bnt hll* as an epithet of *kṯrt* might mean 'daughters of the new moon'. In this case *snnt* might mean 'shining ones', cf. Arabic سنى, 'to gleam', J. Obermann, *JAOS* Supplement 6, 1946, p. 26. Aistleitner (*Die mythologischen und kultischen Texte aus Ras Shamra*, p. 109) suggests that *snnt* means 'those who form' i.e. the embryo, cf. Arabic سَنَّ, 'to form in clay'. The association with *hll*, however, supports Obermann's view.

[3]) Gordon *UH* 77, 5-7.
tld btl(t
(lk)ṯrt
lbnt hll (snnt)
hl ġlmt tld b(n).

Driver considers that this passage relates to an actual human bride, and that the poem, though celebrating the marriage of the Moon-god and his consort, was used on the occasion of human nuptials of a girl Prbḫt, mentioned in the end of the text (*op. cit.*, pp. 24-25).

they were divine or at least sacral (*'elht*). [1] This passage is short and obscure, however, and does not convey any appreciable information about the 'Skilful Ones' beyond the fact that they are apparently interested in the dowry of the bride.

Here we should note the rôle played by women in those crises of life. It is perhaps natural that women should assist at birth, but there is a further reason, suggested by the fact, as among the modern Arab peasants, that the men including the father studiously avoid the very house where the birth is taking place. The fact is that in such a crisis the normal activity of the community is suspended and the men, who normally take the initiative, become for the moment nonentities. In the Book of Ruth not only do the women assist at the birth but they hold the initiative right through until the time when they actually name the child and so integrate the new life with the community. This is not only so at birth, but at death too it is the women who play the significant part as, for instance, the professional 'keeners' in Jeremiah ix, 16 ff. (EVV. 17 ff.), who incidentally, are also called חכמות, 'wise women', a term reminiscent of the Skilful Ones, *kṯrt* of the Ras Shamra texts.

Marriage in the Ras Shamra texts is singularly well documented. In the Krt text, relating to the older period, the memory of marriage by force is preserved. The King is depicted as mustering an army and laying siege to the fortress of the father or perhaps the grandfather of the bride. The latter eventually consents to a parley and offers gifts. This, of course, is a literary convention to enhance the value of the bride. It may, on the other hand, correspond to an actual practice whereby the bride's family conveyed a gentle hint of the amount of bride-price they expected. The bride-price is, of course, paid, possibly in the deposit which Krt vowed to make at the shrine of Aṯrt. [2] If our conjecture here were correct, the deposit being made at the shrine to avoid any impression of a commercial transaction and so to maintain the fiction of marriage by force, this might accord well with the convention among the Aneiza Bedouin

[1]) The word *'elht* might bear the sense not of 'goddesses' but of sacral persons in the Krt text, Gordon *UH* 126 IV, 13 which mentions *ngrt 'elht*. For the use of אלים denoting sacral persons and not gods cf. a late Phoenician inscription from Maʿsub where אלים is applied to the envoys, מלאכים, of the goddess Mlk-Astarte. The fact that they erected a portico to the goddess together with the citizens of Hammon indicates that these were human agents. G. A. Cooke, *NSI* 10, pp. 48 ff.

[2]) *v. supra* p. 145.

where the bride-price, according to BURCKHARDT, [1]) is not overtly accepted. The carefully regulated etiquette described in the Krt text was primarily designed to help an exogamous society to readjust itself to the introduction of an extraneous element. The element of force in marriage survives in certain marriage ceremonies in modern Arab societies and in the common Arabic expression for marriage خطف الابنة, 'snatching the girl'. In Arab communities as in ancient Israel the practice of giving the bride-price (Hebrew מהר, מלג) survives. The text Gordon *UH* 77, describing the marriage of Nikkal by the Moon-god, is a very full and interesting description of the process of marriage in ancient Canaan. As we have already suggested, it well illustrates the extent to which marriage was a family rather than a personal affair, as among the Arabs today.

First there is the proposal, probably by proxy, not to the girl herself but to her father: [2])

> The Moon, the Luminary of Heaven, sends
> To Hrhb, the Summer's King:
> 'Give Nikkal; the Moon will pay the bride-price;
> Let ʾ*eb* [3]) enter his house,
> And I will give [4]) her bride-price to her father,
> A thousand pieces of silver, yea ten thousand of gold;
> I will send gems of lapis lazuli;
> I will make her fallow-land into a vineyard,
> The fallow field of her love into orchards.' [5])

---

1) J. BURCKHARDT, *Bemerkungen über die Bedouinen und Wahaby*, 1831, p. 88.

2) GORDON *UH* 77, 16-23, *ylʾak yrḫ nyr šmm*
ʿm ḫr(ḫ)b mlk qẓ
tn nkl yrḫ ytrḫ
ʾeb tʿrbm bbhth
wʾatn mhrh lʾabh
ʾalp ksp wrbt ḫrṣ
ʾešlḥ ẓhrm ʾeqnʾem
ʾatn šdh krmm
šd ddh ḥrnqm

3) DRIVER points out that in Mesopotamia the Sumerian moon-goddess NIN.GAL was identified with the Akkadian *ilat inbi*, 'goddess of fruit', *op. cit.*, p. 125 n.

4) Reading *wʾatn mhrh* with A. Herdner for Gordon's transliteration *wʾat tmhrh* (►►► for ►—), so A. HERDNER, *Semitica* II, 1949, p. 18.

5) The figure of the bride's sexual charms as a garden or vineyard for cultivation was familiar in Israel, cf. Song of Songs i, 6; iv, 12-16; viii, 12. We suggest that in Isaiah's celebrated song of the vineyard (c.v, 1-7), which is also called 'my love song' (שִׁיר דּוֹדִי), there is a similar association of ideas, the prophet arresting attention by his announcement of such a love song, which however, was given a much more sober application.

There follows then a show of reluctance on the part of the bride's father, again a common convention among the modern Arabs: [1])

Then replied Hrhb the Summer's King:
'O Gracious One among the gods,
Affiance thyself [2]) to Baal,
Wed the Plump Maiden his daughter,
I will introduce thee to her father Baal.
Aṯtar is amenable [3]) in the matter of brideprice,
Go to *Ybrdmy* [4])
The Lion [5]) will give the daughter of his father [6]) in exchange.' [7])

The Moon-god himself presses his suit: [8])

'Nay but let Nikkal answer me, [9])
Then afterwards make me thy son-in-law.'

The bride-price is then paid under the supervision of the whole family of the bride: [10])

---

[1]) GORDON, *ibidem*, 23-30, *wyʿn ḫrḫb mlk qẓ*
lnʿmn ʾelm
lḫtnm bʿl
trḫ pdry b(th)
ʾaqrbk ʾabh bʿl
yġpr ʿṯtr trḫ
lk ybrdmy
bt ʾabh lbʾu yʿrr

[2]) We take the complex *lḫtnm* as an imperative with the enclitic *l* preformative as in Arabic, and *m* the enclitic afformative as in Akkadian. The root suggests the Hebrew חֹתֵן, 'father-in-law' and חָתָן, 'son-in-law'.

[3]) cf. Arabic غفر, 'to pardon', hence 'accept entreaty'.

[4]) *Ybrdmy*, possibly 'Cool Waters' (cf. Arabic برد. 'to be cool'), may either be the seat of Aṯtar or his sister. DRIVER (*op. cit.*, p. 166, n. 15) after GOETZE, cites Eusebius' mention of 'Ανωβρετ as the mother of one of the sons of El (*Praeparatio Evangelica* I, x, 400; IV, xvi, 156d-157a).

[5]) A title of Aṯtar. The lion was the cult animal of Ishtar in Mesopotamia and of Astarte in Canaan.

[6]) In may be noted that, though Bethuel the father of Rebeccah was evidently alive, it was her brother Laban and her mother that sanctioned the marriage. A. PARROT (*Abraham et son Temps*, 1962, p. 93) after R. H. PFEIFFER and E. A. SPEISER cites a text from Nuzu (15th c.) where a girl declares that with her consent her brother had given her in marriage.

[7]) We take *ʿrr* as cognate with a by form of Arabic, عار(و) meaning 'to exchange' in the VIIIth form.

[8]) GORDON, *ibidem*, 31-32, *wtʿn ʿmn nkl*
ḫtny ʾaḫr

[9]) It will be noted that we read *tʿn* for *nʿn* (again ►— for ►►►).

[10]) GORDON, *ibidem*, 33-37, *nkl yrḫ ytrḫ*
ʾadnh yšt mṣb mẓnm
ʾumh kp mẓnm
ʾeḫh yṯʿr mšrrm
ʾaḫtth lʾabn mẓnm

> The Moon paid the bride-price for Nikkal,
> Her father set the beam of the balances,
> Her mother set the pan of the balances,
> Her brothers arranged [1]) the standard weights, [2])
> Her sisters the weights of the scales.

In this text we are brought into intimate touch with actual marriage ceremonies in ancient Canaan, as we may reckon from modern analogies. Apart from the formalities which we have already noted, the most favoured season for marriage among the Arab peasants in Syria and Palestine is the end of harvest. Then the urgent seasonal work is over and the community has leisure for the occasion and the necessary affluence for the expenses of the brideprice, presents, and entertainment. [3]) This probably explains the theme which is taken as a prototype, the marriage of Nikkal the daughter of *Ḫrḫb*, 'the Summer's King', i.e. the goddess manifest in the new moon after harvest. The period of the waxing moon is still considered the most favourable for the undertaking of any new enterprise, particularly those associated with fertility such as sowing, planting, and marriage. [4]) As among modern Arab peasants the marriage ceremony is visualized as beginning at sunset (*bsġsġ špš*) [5]) the week-long celebrations being mostly nocturnal, as any who has lived in a Palestinian village has good cause to remember.

It is well known that natural processes, which are taken as the effects of divine activities, are supported in primitive societies by corresponding human activities as rites of imitative magic. Thus it may well be that this text celebrates a marriage or union as such a rite as the counterpart to the marriage of the Moon-god and his consort before the appearance of the new moon. In this case the bride, who is actually named, *prbḫṯ*, in l. 49, might be a priestess or temple prostitute of the Moon-god and his consort Nikkal. We think, however, that the myth of the divine marriage was recited as an element of imitative magic in support of an actual marriage. The

[1]) The root *ṯʿr* is used in the sense of 'arranging' seats and tables etc. in Gordon *UH* ʿnt, II, 20. It occurs possibly in Hebrew in the sense of 'arranging', 'disposing', e.g. Proverbs xxiii, 7, כמו שער בנפשו כן־הוא.

[2]) This meaning is suggested by the parallel *ʾabnm*, 'weights', lit. 'stones'. The root *šrr* is surely cognate with the Syriac ܫܪܪ, 'to be firm, genuine'.

[3]) G. Dalman, *Palästinische Diwan*, 1901, p. XII; M. Feghali, *Contes, légendes, coutumes populaires du Liban et du Syrie*, 1935, p. 79.

[4]) J. Scheftelowitz, *Alt-Palästinensischer Bauernglaube*, 1925, pp. 137 ff.

[5]) cf. Arabic سغسغ, 'to enter the earth'. But the reading is doubtful. See A. Herdner, *Corpus*, p. 102, n. 2.

survival of the text in the library of the temple of Baal at Ras Shamra probably indicates that the bride was a highborn maiden, a princess or the daughter of a noble or a priest.

The actual practice of marriage in its various implications is further illustrated in the Akkadian documents from the royal chancellery of Ugarit. From these texts it is plain that that the so-called 'bride-price' (*terḫatu*) is more than the conventional translation implies. It involves, certainly, the price paid by the bride-groom to the family of the bride, but it is given to the bride as a dowry. This is clearly indicated by the case of one Ananiḫebi, the daughter of Ilinaru, whose *terḫatu* was commuted into certain property belonging to her father which became her personal property (NOUGAYROL, *op. cit.*, 16.158, p. 62). The wife's *terḫatu* and other personal property she may possess were apparently used for the joint advantage of husband and wife during marriage, but on the death of the husband, or in case of divorce, the wife recovered her property intact, as is apparent from the case of Milka the wife of Yaṣiranu (NOUGAYROL, *op. cit.*, 15.92, pp. 54-56). This is an interesting case. Yaṣiranu is adopting a son and it is provided that, if he (Yaṣiranu) dies and his adoptive son wishes to break the association with his widow Milka, she is to receive 'the 80 shekels of silver which she brought to Yaṣiranu' (i.e. as *terḫatu*) and live in her father's house.

One of these documents, a disposition by King Arḫalbu (*PRU* III, 16.144, p. 76), attests a case of marriage of a man and his brother's widow. The king forbids the marriage of his wife Kubaba with any but his brother in the event of his death. On this evidence alone it is not possible to argue for the regular practice of levirate marriage as in Hebrew society. The fact that marriage of a widow with any but her brother-in-law is here expressly forbidden by special deed suggests that even if levirate marriage was regular in Ugaritic society it was certainly not compulsory. Indeed, since this is a royal disposition where the marriage of the king's widow might have possible political consequences, to say nothing of the infringement of the 'divinity that doth hedge a king', it may well be that levirate marriage in Ugarit was exceptional.

Death, like birth and marriage, was another event which disrupted the primitive community and demanded readjustment. This commonly took the form of ritual seclusion, as in the case of Krt on the extinction of his family. [1]) Dn'el also, being childless, withdraws to ritual

---

[1]) *v. supra*, p. 134.

seclusion in the sanctuary, though it is possible that he does so not as a mourning rite but as a means of securing revelation. [1] The period of ritual seclusion of the mourner formally ends by his washing, as in the case of Krt, who after washing was able to perform his normal functions as priest-king of the community. [2] Another instance is that of David, who observed similar rites of isolation in the illness of his son by Bathsheba, and when the ritual was over 'arose from the earth, and washed and anointed himself, and changed his apparel, and came into the house of the Lord and worshipped' (2 Samuel xii, 20).

The proper burial of the dead was a matter of the highest importance, not so much as a mark of respect for the departed, but rather as a matter touching the safety of the community. The locus classicus for the burial of the dead is in the Aqht text, [3] where the careful recovery and burial of the remains of Aqht from the gizzard of the vulture reflects the belief in the continued, though insubstantial, existence of the dead after life in the image of his living self. This belief obtained also in Israel, where the utmost disaster was that the dead should be left the prey of beasts (1 Kings xiv, 11; Jeremiah xvi, 4; xxii, 19; Ezekiel xxxiv 5). Similar evidence is furnished by the Baal-text, [4] which gives the fullest illustration of mourning rites in ancient Canaan, which in principle and in detail are substantially the same as in ancient Israel. The mourner, that is to say, sat on the ground, loosened his turban and the knot of his girdle (cf. Isaiah lviii, 6, *v. supra*, p. 62 n.), wallowed in the dust and sprinkled it on his head (cf. Ezekiel xxvii, 30; Micah i, 10), lacerated his face with his nails (cf. Jeremiah xvi, 6-7; xlvii, 5; Deuteronomy xiv, 1) [5] and dishevelled his hair, and wailed and repeated certain words of lamentation. Dancing was also a mourning rite, probably referred to in GORDON, *UH*, 1 Aqht, 189, reading *ltm mrqdm* ('when the dances were over'), and depicted in the peculiar flouncing of the skirts of mourning

---

[1]) Incubation at a shrine or a place associated with a *numen* as a means of securing revelation was known also among the Arabs. Instances in the Old Testament are Solomon at Gibeon and possibly Jacob at Bethel.

[2]) *v. supra* pp. 135-136.

[3]) *v. supra* p. 121.

[4]) *v. supra* pp. 64, 65.

[5]) The Deuteronomic prohibition against mourning rites was possibly occasioned by the association with ritual mourning for Baal (cf. Zechariah xii, 11; Ezekiel viii, 14), a seasonal rite in the fertility cult, as PEDERSEN suggests, *Israel* III-IV, 2nd ed., 1959, p. 484.

females with loosened bodices and dishevelled hair on the ends of Ahiram's sarcophagus from Byblos.

The text describing Anat's mourning and search for the dead body of her brother Baal, as well as illustrating those rites and the importance of proper burial, illustrates a 'rite of aggregation' whereby the mourning rite is concluded. That is the funeral feast where, at least according to the myth, wild oxen, tame oxen, sheep, deer, wild goats, and asses are slaughtered seventy-fold as a funeral due (*gmn*) [1]) to Baal. This too apparently survived in Israel, as is indicated by the disavowal demanded in Deuteronomy xxvi, 14 that the peasant on offering his tithe had invalidated it by offering any of the produce to the dead.

Thus on the evidence of the Ras Shamra texts the behaviour of the Canaanite community in the Bronze Age was regulated at every crisis of life from conception to the grave by customs designed to indicate a suspension of the normal state of society, 'rites of separation' as the anthropologist Van Gennep called them, until readjustment was effected, this being marked by 'rites of aggregation'.

The Ras Shamra texts indicate also the duties and responsibilities of persons in the family as well as in the community. Here the Aqht text is the most useful document. We learn there that maidenly duty consisted of drawing water, rising early like the good lady of the house in Proverbs xxxi, 15. The daughter of Dn'el, king though he is, is one

Who bears water on her shoulder,
Who sweeps the dew from the barley,
Who knows the course of the stars. [2])

The first duty of the maiden is the usual one of women in Syria, drawing water; the second probably refers to weeding and gathering fodder for the domestic animals from the growing crop, as the peasant women still do in Palestine. Again, like the industrious housewife in Proverbs xxxi, 18, she retires late to rest when the stars are already visible in their constellations. The maiden is also, we learn, familiar with the handling of beasts:

She straightway saddles an ass,
Straightway she harnesses a donkey,

[1]) *v. supra* p. 64, n. 5.
[2]) Gordon *UH* 1 Aqht, 50-52. *ṯkmt mym*
ḥspt lšʿr ṭl
ydʿt hlk kbkbm

Straightway she hoists her father,
Placing him on the back of the ass,
On the fair back of the donkey. [1])

Granted that the status and occupation of the princess did not remain in this condition of primitive simplicity, the status of women in ancient Canaan was apparently not much different from that in the Arab East today. They were literally hewers of wood and drawers of water as a passage in the Krt text indicates. [2]) Here again, however, we must discriminate between conditions in the heroic past and those in historical times. The Akkadian documents from the royal chancellery, as we have seen, reveal that even in matrimony a woman retains rights of property, being entitled to recover her *terḫatu* intact on the death of her husband or her divorce. The status of a wife is well illustrated by the will of Yarimanu, who leaves all his property together with all that he had acquired with his wife Bidawa to his wife with provisions for her security against any claims or ill-treatment by her two sons. Further Bidawa apparently has the right of disposing her goods to one or other of her sons at discretion. [3]) Women too might make legal transactions on their own account, as Ananaya, for instance, adopted as son Šubamma, this being possibly a case of sale-adoption, already familiar from the Nuzu Tablets, whereby for the sum of 500 shekels of silver Šubamma acquired a title to the property of his adoptive mother (Nougayrol, *op. cit.*, 16.200, pp. 64-65). Another tablet (Nougayrol, *op. cit.*, 16.261, pp. 159, 160) records the purchase of property by Laya and her family including a daughter Bathṣidqi. Such cases, of course, relate to the upper classes at Ugarit, and may not be quite representative of the general condition of women in ancient Canaan. On the other hand, even a slave-girl could aspire to emancipation and honourable matrimony, as the case of Eliawa indicates. [4]) In this case an officer of the queen's household emanci-

---

[1]) *Ibidem*, 57-60. *bkm tmdln ʿr*
bkm tṣmd pḥl
bkm tšʾu ʾabh
tštnn lbmt ʿr
lysmsm bmt pḥl

[2]) *v. supra* p. 142, n. 1,4

[3]) F. Thureau-Dangin, 'Trois Contrats de Ras Shamra', *Syria* XVIII, 1937, pp. 249-251.

[4]) *Ibidem*, III. This deed and other deeds of emancipation are of peculiar interest in that they attest anointing as a rite of emancipation. This is akin to anointing in marriage and betrothal in Egypt and Anatolia and in business transactions and conveyance of property among the Amorites at Mari, where, it signifies quittance

pates his slave-girl in view of her marriage. Her husband pays twenty shekels of silver to her master, which may serve at once as purchase-price of the slave-girl and as 'bride-price' to the master as head of her household. Another slavegirl of the royal household, Šaya, is emancipated and married to the governor (*rabiṣu*) (*PRU* III 16.267). From this case we learn that even a woman like Šaya could own property, since the deed provides that Šaya's house, lands, and other possessions passed to her husband in the event of her death. Provision for the restitution of a woman's dowry and other property on divorce, however, was probably a deterrent to divorce only among the less prosperous in the community. Among the wealthier Canaanites it was only a safeguard against destitution of the divorced women. The *mryn* and count Abdu, for instance, divorced his wife and first emancipated his slavegirl Ḫeyawa, whom he then married, apparently after she had borne him a son. The lady was formally installed as 'mistress of the house' with rights before her son, who, born to her before her emancipation, would have had prior right of inheritance (*PRU* III, 16.250, 21-24, p. 86).

The Aqht text defines the duties of an ideal son to his father. The son is [1])

> One who may set up the stele of his ancestral god [2])
> In the sanctuary which enshrines his forefather;
>
> Who may pour out his liquid offering to the ground,
> Even to the dust wine after him.

The son of the king as head of the community maintains the continuity of the common cult which gives the community cohesion. He also pays the due funeral rites to his father.

In his father's absence, or after his death, the son takes his place in the sanctuary at the communal meal whereby the community realizes its solidarity as a social and religious unit,

> Eating his slice in the temple of Baal,
> His portion in the temple of El. [3])

---

of further obligations or associations. This is the conception underlying the anointing of the priest, who is thus exclusively set apart for the service of God, E. Kutsch, *Salbung als Rechtsakt im Alten Testament und im Alten Orient*, *BZAW* LXXXVII, 1963.

[1]) Gordon *UH* 2 Aqht I 27 ff.

[2]) *v. supra* p. 109 n. 2

[3]) *Ibidem* 32-33, *v. supra* p. 110.

He maintains his father's good name for hospitality, a point of honour in Canaan of the heroic age as it is still in the desert:

> Heaping up the platters of his company,
> Driving away any who would molest his night-guest. [1]

The son's duty is to see that his father never falls into dishonour, as might well happen when he is drunk, either in social festivity or in religious observance as, for instance, at the feast of the Ingathering of the fruits. Then the son must support his father, [2]

> Holding his hand when he is drunk,
> Carrying him when he is sated with wine.

He literally must keep his father's roof above his head,

> Plastering his roof when it is muddy. [3]

The last duty of the son seems at first sight very peculiar,

> Washing his garment when it is dirty.

Here we must bear in mind the significance that the garment had for primitive man. As being in contact with a man's person and conformed to his shape it was a part of him and imbued with his power, as we see from the case of Elijah's mantle which, when cast upon Elisha, was the means of transferring the prophetic power of the former to the latter (1 Kings xix, 19). [4] Hence the garment—probably that worn next to the skin—of the father could be washed safely only by the son. This was a duty which could not safely be entrusted to a woman, through whom, for the primitive mind, invasive evil influences had more easy access.

The picture which the Ras Shamra texts present of social relationships, interesting and useful as it is, is nevertheless restricted. We are never dealing with individuals, as in the Old Testament, but always with types. Though we have definite indications of social obligations, morality never leaves the conventional level; there is no indication of a moral ideal apart from automatically binding

---

[1] *Ibidem* 29-30, *v. supra* p. 110.

[2] *Ibidem* 31-32, *v. supra* p. 110.

[3] *Ibidem* 33-34, *v. supra* p. 110.

[4] By cutting off the skirt of Saul's mantle David was probably regarded as having permanent power over Saul. The possession of someone's mantle was thought to involve the possession of the person of the owner. So in a Greek graffito from the 3rd century Phoenician tombs at Beit Jibrin a lover states that she has secured the garment of her lad. J. R. Peters and H. Tiersch, *Painted Tombs in the Necropolis of Marissa*, 1905, p. 57.

social custom. There was indeed a creditable standard of social justice as we see from the objection of Krt's rebellious son: [1])

> 'Thou hast let thy hand fall into error,
> Thou dost not uphold the case of the widow,
> Nor decide the suit of the oppressed.
> Thou dost not drive away those who prey upon the poor,
> Before thee thou dost not feed the fatherless,
> The widow is behind thy back.'

This conduct, however, as a similar passage in the Aqht text shows, relates to the office of the king rather than to the individual. The Canaanite literature never reaches the moral plane of the Old Testament. Indeed even in such a passage as that just cited and the description of the ideal son in the Aqht text the Canaanites were not at pains to present a *Fürstenspiegel* or pattern of a ruler such as is commonly found in Mesopotamian literature. [2])

The Ras Shamra texts may well be a fragment of the literature of ancient Canaan, and we have already hinted that there are traces of a more moral aspect of Canaanite religion. The limited conventional ethic which the texts illustrate, however, is probably typical of Bronze Age Canaan. Indeed the Hebrew ethic itself was largely a matter of communal convention until quite late in the Monarchic period. The moral limitation of Canaanite religion was probably due to its preoccupation with ritual related to the phases of the agricultural year. This religion was essentially magical and, as such, a-moral. Consequently, it was condemned by the Hebrew prophets not so much because of the immorality of its sexual excesses, but because as a substitute for the ancestral faith of the Hebrews, which rested on the moral basis of a covenant, it did nothing to conserve

---

[1]) Gordon *UH* 127, 44-50, cf. *supra*, p. 150.

[2]) e.g. the prayer of Nebuchadrezzar on his accession:

> 'O Eternal Ruler, Lord of the Universe,
> Grant that the name of the king whom thou lovest,
> Whose name thou hast mentioned, may flourish as seems good to thee.
> Guide him on the right path.
> I am the ruler who obeys thee, the creation of thy hand.
> It is thou who hast created me,
> And thou hast entrusted to me sovereignty over mankind.
> According to thy mercy, O Lord, which thou bestowest upon all,
> Cause me to love thy supreme rule.
> Implant the fear of thy divinity within my heart,
> Grant to me whatsoever may seem good before thee,
> Since it is thou who dost control my life'.

After M. Jastrow, *The Religion of Babylonia and Assyria*, 1898, p. 296.

the moral values which Israel had come to cherish, and indeed it positively undermined these. Such values must be conserved in the same spirit in which they are won.

In all the references in the Ras Shamra texts to social conceptions and practices we never touch more than the externals of behaviour. If we search behind them for the Canaanite view of the significance of life and death we find no preoccupation with the problem. Humanism in Israel, which produced the Wisdom literature, was comparatively late; in Ugarit, apparently, its voice was never heard. For the Canaanite as for the ancient Israelite it was sufficient that the community lived on. The conception of the dying and rising vegetation-god was, of course, familiar to the Canaanites from the cult, but they did not apply this ideology to the phenomenon of human life as was done in the case of the Egyptian and Greek variations of the same cult. The seasonal cults of Osiris, Dionysus, and Demeter and Kore developed into mystery-religions where the individual sought to appropriate the experience of the god in σωτηρία, or salvation from the power of death. The Canaanites, however, remained content with as negative a prospect after death as the ancient Hebrews with their current views of Sheol. On this subject the mind of ancient Canaan is unequivocally stated with brutal realism by Aqht, whom the goddess Anat tempts by glowing promises of immortality:

'Fabricate not O Virgin.
To a Hero thy lies are trash.
As for a mortal man what does he get as his latter end?
What does mortal man get as his inheritance?
Glaze will be poured out on my head,
Even plaster on my pate,
And the death of all men will I die,
Yea I will surely die.' [1]

---

[1]) GORDON *UH* 2 Aqht VI, 34-38. For text and philological notes *v. supra* p. 113 and notes *ad loc.*

CHAPTER VI

LITERARY AND LINGUISTIC

So far we have been mainly concerned with the content of Canaanite literature as revealed by the various texts from Ras Shamra. We now turn to the formal correspondence between the Ugaritic literature and the Old Testament in vocabulary, imagery, and literary style and form. Since the more obvious correspondences will no doubt have impressed the reader of the passages we have cited already, we shall here limit our study to less obvious cases.

In the first place there are single words in the Old Testament which, owing to their rarity, were only vaguely understood, if indeed they were not wholly misunderstood, until the discovery of the Ugaritic literature, where their higher frequency enables us to fill them out with more meaning.

The verb used for the 'creation' of woman in Genesis ii, 22 is **בנה**. Normally in Hebrew this verb means 'to build', but in the Ras Shamra texts it is used in the sense of 'to create', as, for instance, where El is called *bny bnwt*, 'Creator of created things' (Gordon *UH* 49, III, 5, 11; 51, II 11 etc.).

In Deuteronomy xxxiii, 29 we read:

יִכָּחֲשׁוּ אֹיְבֶיךָ לָךְ וְאַתָּה עַל־בָּמוֹתֵימוֹ תִדְרֹךְ׃

In the Old Testament **בָּמוֹת** is used of 'high places', specifically local Canaanite sanctuaries, and the word is taken in this sense in the passage in Deuteronomy xxxiii, 29 by the AV. The Ras Shamra texts prove, however, that **במה** had the primary meaning of the 'back' of a person or animal (Gordon, *op. cit.*, 51, IV, 14, 15; 62, 5; 67, VI, 22; 1 Aqht, 59, 60), which is far more suitable in Deuteronomy xxxiii, 29, which should be translated:

> 'Thy enemies shall be discomfited before thee, and thou shalt tread upon their backs.'

A hapax legomenon is the noun **דֹּבֶא**, which is given as 'strength' in BDB, or 'rest', after an Arabic etymology. The former sense would be more congruous with Deuteronomy xxxiii, 25, where it occurs:

בַּרְזֶל וּנְחֹשֶׁת נְעָלֶיךָ
וּכְיָמֶיךָ דָּבְאֶךָ

Iron and brass are thy bars,
And as thy days so thy strength.

This reading is, however, stated in BDB to be 'very doubtful'. Now the word is elucidated, and this meaning confirmed by the Ugaritic text Gordon, *UH* 76 II, 21-22, where *qrn db'atk* obviously means 'the horn(s) of thy strength', i.e. thy strong horn(s).

In 1 Samuel xxiii, 7 there is a rare word נכר in the phrase

נִכַּר אוֹתוֹ אֱלֹהִים בְּיָדִי

For נִכַּר the LXX reads πέπρακεν 'has sold', which gives excellent sense in the context. The verb, however, in this sense is unattested in Hebrew. Now in the Ras Shamra text Gordon *UH* krt 102, 191 we read

ybʿr ltn 'atth
lm nkr mddth

Here, unfortunately, the sense is in doubt, and it is possible to take *nkr* in the sense which it generally has in Hebrew as a 'stranger', to whom the newly-wed bridegroom in his ardour to follow the king abandons his bride. However, we share the belief of a number of scholars that *nkr* is a verb and the sense of the passage is:

Burning to claim his wife,
Yea, to acquire his beloved.

With Ugaritic *nkr* in this sense of 'to acquire' we might compare the use of נכר in Hosea iii, 2, וָאֶכְּרֶהָ, 'and I acquired her'. If this is a correct view then the Piel of נכר in Samuel would have the meaning 'to sell', as the LXX suggests. [1])

The evidence of the Ras Shamra texts suggests that Arauna the Jebusite of Jerusalem from whom David bought the site of the Temple was not a proper name but a title, as is proposed by J. A. Montgomery. [2]) So much is, in fact, suggested by the Hebrew text itself in 2 Samuel xxiv, 23:

הַכֹּל נָתַן אֲרַוְנָה הַמֶּלֶךְ לַמֶּלֶךְ

Here הַמֶּלֶךְ may be a Semitic gloss on the non-Semitic אֲרַוְנָה. The word *'ewr* appears independently or in compounds in Gordon *UH* 15, 5; 54, 1; 313, 7, and actually as *'ewrn* in *ibidem* 4, 51 and 28, rev. 9. In Gordon *UH* 54, 1 it is found in the name or title *'ewrẓr*, the writer

---

[1]) On the analogy of לָמַד, 'to learn' and לִמֵּד, 'to teach', cf. Aramaic זְבַן, 'to buy' and זַבֵּן, 'to sell'.

[2]) J. A. Montgomery, *JAOS* LV, 1935, p. 94 n.

of a military dispatch. It seems to us that it was a title expressing the dignity of a high feudal baron. This, however, is admittedly a matter of conjecture.

In 2 Kings x, 22 מֶלְתָּחָה, which in the context means clearly 'clothes store', has been taken as an Assyrian loanword, cf. Assyrian *meltaktu*. Now its cognate has been found in one of the administrative texts from the palace of Ras Shamra (Virolleaud, *PRU* II, 109),

spr npṣm dyṣ('a) bm'elḫ
A list of garments which went out from the clothes store.

The root *'elḫ* probably underlies the passage in Jeremiah xxxviii, 11, as Eissfeldt has suggested, in dealing with Ebed-melek's rescue of Jeremiah with rags obtained from אֶל־תַּחַת הָאוֹצָר. Here אֶל־תַּחַת or its original may well be the vestment department[1] of the store (אוצר) of the Temple.

In Isaiah's invective against women's fashions the word שְׁבִיסִים occurs (Isaiah iii, 18) as a *hapax legomenon*. Its conjunction with שַׂהֲרֹנִים (moons) suggests that it signified 'sun-ornaments'. This is now confirmed by the Ras Shamra texts where the word for 'sun' is *špš*. [2]

In the same passage the term בָּתֵּי־הַנֶּפֶשׁ occurs (Isaiah iii, 20). In discussing the meaning of this *hapax legomenon* BDB (p. 661) reject the possibility that נֶפֶשׁ means 'perfume', and suggest the meaning 'smelling-boxes'. In two offering-lists from Ras Shamra, however, (Gordon *UH* 5, 15; 9, 1) *npš* occurs as an item of offering, and in the former of these its association with *ṭb* (Arabic طيب) clearly indicates that it means 'perfume'.

The word נפש in Hebrew has several meanings which are now made more clear in the light of the Ugaritic evidence. In the figure of 'Hell opening wide its throat' in Isaiah v, 14 and Habakkuk ii, 5 and in the Ugaritic original of the figure [3] we see that the word could mean the throat or gullet. It might also mean 'appetite' as in Proverbs xxiii, 2, where the context makes it clear that בעל־נפש means 'a man of hearty appetite'. The word *npš* is found, we think,

---

[1]) O. Eissfeldt, 'The Alphabetic Cuneiform Texts from Ras Shamra published in "Le Palais Royal d'Ugarit" vol. II, 1957', *JSS* VI, 1960, p. 46.

[2]) J. W. Jack, *The Ras Shamra Tablets, their Bearing on the Old Testament*, 1935, p. 45.

[3]) *v. infra* p. 273.

in this sense in Gordon *UH* 127, 11, where the woman who heals the sick king Krt 'opens his appetite for food' (*bdʿt npšh llḥm*). A further instance of נפש in this sense may be Proverbs xix, 2:

גַּם בְּלֹא־דַעַת נֶפֶשׁ לֹא טוֹב

This verse, however, by בְּלֹא־דַעַת נֶפֶשׁ may refer to 'misguided enthusiasm', this sense of נפש being suggested by Proverbs xix, 18b:

וְאֶל־הֲמִיתוֹ אַל־תִּשָּׂא נַפְשֶׁךָ

Here the meaning of נפש is 'enthusiasm' or 'determination'. For this sense of נפש there is no evidence in Ugaritic.

In Isaiah xi, 10, וְהָיְתָה מְנוּחָתוֹ כָּבוֹד, conventionally rendered 'and his rest shall be glory', we suggest that מְנוּחָה should be translated 'dais'. We propose that מְנוּחָה is cognate with the Ugaritic noun *nḫt* which is parallel to *ksʾe mlkh*, 'his royal seat', and *kḥṯ drkth*, 'the throne of his sovereignty'. The word is obviously the cognate of the Arabic ناخ, 'to level', and means 'platform' or 'dais', so that we render Isaiah xi, 10 'And his dais shall be glory'. In this connection we may cite 2 Kings xvii, 29, where the Hiphil of נוח is used of setting idols up on pedestals.

The rare word שׁוֹעַ, found in Isaiah xxxii, 5 and Job xxxiv, 19, means 'noble' and this is suggested by the fact that in the first passage it is paralleled by נָדִיב, 'free', and in the second by דָּל, 'poor'. Its derivation, however, is uncertain. BDB (447b) suggest a connection with Arabic وسع, 'to be wide', which means also largeness of heart or generosity. In the Ras Shamra text of Krt the word *ṯʿ* appears as the stock epithet of the king, and a connection between the word and the Hebrew שׁוֹעַ has been suggested. [1]) The meaning of *ṯʿ* here is almost certainly 'the Generous', *ṯʿy* being attested in the texts as a verb meaning 'to give', *v. supra*, p. 230 n. 2.

In his famous passage in condemnation of idols and their makers Deutero-Isaiah says (Isaiah xl, 20):

הַמְסֻכָּן תְּרוּמָה עֵץ לֹא־יִרְקַב יִבְחָר

According to the Massoretic pointing the first two words have been translated 'He who is poor in respect of an offering', but it is well-known that the text is not undisputed. The LXX reads for these

---

1) Virolleaud, *La Légende de Kéret...*, p. 89.

two words ὁμοίωμα κατεσκεύασεν. This suggests the emendation תְּמוּנָה for תְּרוּמָה, which suits the whole context much better. It is further suggested that the Greek κατεσκεύασεν indicates the Hebrew הַמְכֹנֵן, 'he who would set up'. This is admittedly the meaning and a feasible emendation and one which is not too far from the Massoretic text. It is, however, unnecessary. In the inscription on a stele to Dagon at Ras Shamra (Gordon *UH* 69, 1,) *skn* is something which one has 'set up' (*dš'lyt*). In the text 2 Aqht I, 27; II, 16, also the verb *nṣb* suggests that its object *skn* is a stele. [1]) So in Isaiah xl, 20 we suggest the reading הַמְסַכֵּן תְּמוּנָה, 'he who would set up an image', or possibly הַמִסְכָּן יְרוֹמֵם, 'would one set up an image?'.

In Isaiah xlviii, 19 there is another *hapax legomenon* in the line

וַיְהִי כַחוֹל זַרְעֶךָ וְצֶאֱצָאֵי מֵעֶיךָ כִּמְעוֹתָיו

We suggest the connection of מֵעוֹת with the Arabic مَعِيَّة, 'multitude', giving the translation:

'And thy seed would have been as the sand,
And the issue of thy bowels as the multitudes thereof.' [2])

Here again an Ugaritic passage supports our interpretation. In Gordon *UH* krt, in the muster of the king's retinue, it is said (ll. 87// 177-178).

wyṣ'e 'dn m'.
'Forth comes the crowd athrong'.

In 1 Chronicles xii, 1 the phrase עֹזְרֵי הַמִּלְחָמָה occurs in a list of David's warriors. The word עזר is found in the Ras Shamra texts as *ġzr* meaning 'a young mettled lad', and is specifically used of warriors in the text Gordon *UH* 'nt, II, 22 where it is in parallelism with *mhr* and *ṣb'em*, both meaning 'soldiers'. Other possible instances of this word in the Old Testament are Ezekiel xii, 14:

וְכֹל אֲשֶׁר סְבִיבוֹתָיו עֶזְרֹה וְכָל־אֲגַפָּיו אֱזָרֶה לְכָל־רוּחַ

'And all his retinue, his warriors,
And all his bands will I scatter to all winds',

---

[1]) *v. supra* p. 109.

[2]) For the last word the LXX reads כַּעֲפַר הָאָרֶץ, 'as the dust of the earth', which is a good parallel to כחול, but may nevertheless be a case of paraphrase rather than translation, not being suggested at all by the Massoretic text.

and Psalm lxxxix, 20:

שִׁוִּיתִי עֹזֵר (עֵזֶר MT) עַל־גִּבּוֹר הֲרִימוֹתִי בָחוּר מֵעָם

'I have set a youth above the mighty man,
I have raised a young man above the people.' [1])

עֹזֵר in these passages and Ugaritic *ġzr* is elucidated by the usage of the verb עזר in I Chronicles v, 20. ויעזרו עליהם, 'and they attacked them', cf. Ethiopic *'zr*, 'to attack impetuously' cited by E. Ullendorff, 'Ugaritic Marginalia II', *JSS* VII, 1962, p. 347. In the light of such evidence the passage in Deuteronomy xxxiii, 26

רֹכֵב שָׁמַיִם בְּעֶזְרֶךָ
וּבְגַאֲוָתְךָ שְׁחָקִים (ובגאותו MT)

may be translated

Mounting the heavens in thine impetuous haste,
And in thy proud exultation the clouds.

In the psalm in Jonah הָאָרֶץ is used (ii, 7) meaning obviously 'the underworld', a sense which it also bears in the Ugaritic texts. This is beyond doubt in the text Gordon *UH* 62, 16-18:

tbkynh wtqbrnh	She weeps for him and buries him,
tštnh bḫrt 'elm 'arṣ	Putting him in the cavities of the deities of the underworld.

In the colophon to Gordon *UH* 62 (rev., 55) the high priest Atnprln is entitled also *rb nqdm*, 'chief of the herdsmen', and this has suggested the possibility that the prophet Amos, who is also associated with herdsmen, נוקדים, (Amos i. 1), was no common shepherd, but a cultic functionary. This we think most unlikely in view of the passage vii, 14 where Amos alludes to his actual occupation as a shepherd and moreover dresser of sycamore-figs. [2]) We think it probable, however, that the Ugaritic sense of *nqd* is present in the word when it is applied to Mesha the King of Moab in 2 Kings iii, 4.

---

[1]) Albright, *Archaeology of Palestine*, 1949, p. 233. We suspect the reading מֵעָם in the last word, and suggest מֵעָצֻם, 'than the mighty', as a good parallel to עַל גִּבּוֹר.

[2]) G. R. Driver (*ET* LXVII, 1955, pp. 91-92) maintains on good evidence that the particle לֹא in the phrase לֹא נָבִיא אָנֹכִי ... is not the usual negative, but is in fact interrogative for the more normal הֲלֹא, 'Am I not a prophet simply because I am a herdsman and a dresser of sycamores?'

The verb קנה, which means generally 'to buy', is used in Genesis iv, 1, קָנִיתִי אִישׁ, which the AV translated 'I have gotten a man'. In Genesis xiv, 19 in the phrase קונה שמים וארץ the verb obviously means 'creator'. [1]) This sense of the verb is also attested in Psalm cxxxix, 13:

כִּי אַתָּה קָנִיתָ כִלְיֹתָי תְּסֻכֵּנִי בְּבֶטֶן אִמִּי

'For thou it was who didst create my reins,
Weaving me in my mother's belly.'

In the Ras Shamra texts the stock epithet of the Mother-goddess is *qnyt ʾelm*, 'creatrix of the gods'. This usage is a very close parallel to that of קנה in Eve's statement in Genesis iv, 1, cf. Deuteronomy xxxii, 6:

הֲלוֹא־הוּא אָבִיךָ קָּנֶךָ
הוּא עָשְׂךָ וַיְכֹנְנֶךָ

Is he not thy Father, thy creator?
He is thy maker who fashioned thee

and Proverbs viii, 22:

יהוה קָנָנִי רֵאשִׁית דַּרְכּוֹ
קֶדֶם מִפְעָלָיו מֵאָז

Yahweh created me as the first of his ordered system
The oldest of his works from of yore. [2])

The few instances of the verb לחם, 'to eat', in the Old Testament are noted by BDB (p. 536b) as rare, poetic, and late. In Ugaritic the verb is quite regularly used, e.g. Gordon *UH* 52, 6

lḥm blḥm ʾay wšty bḫmr yn ʾay,
'Eat of the food, ho! Yea drink of the ferment of the wine, ho!' [3])

---

[1]) *qnʾ ʾrṣ wšmm* is predicated of El also in Azitawadd's inscription at Karatepe, col. iii, 18.

[2]) In Proverbs viii, 22: ..... יהוה קָנָנִי רֵאשִׁית דַּרְכּוֹ the fourth word should probably be emended to דְּרָכָתוֹ, as Albright suggests, 'Some Canaanite-Phoenician Sources of Hebrew Wisdom', *Supplements to Vetus Testamentum* III, 1955, p. 7. This is well-attested in the Ras Shamra texts Gordon *UH* 49, V, 6; VI, 35; krt, 41-42, where *drkt* (Arabic دَرَكٌ, 'government') is parallel to *mlk*, 'kingship', e.g. Gordon *UH* 68, 10,

tqḥ mlk ʿlmk	'Thou shalt take thine eternal kingship,
drkt dt drdrk	Thy government everlasting'.

[3]) Gordon takes the word *ʾay* to signify 'any', citing Proverbs xxxi, 4, אֵי שֵׁכָר (for Massoretic אוֹ), *Ugaritic Manual*, 1955, pp. 235.

This actual passage may well be echoed in Proverbs ix, 5:

לְכוּ לַחֲמוּ בְלַחְמִי וּשְׁתוּ בְּיַיִן מָסָכְתִּי

'Come ye, eat of my food, and drink of the wine which I have mixed.'

In Proverbs xxiii, 7, כְּמוֹ שָׁעַר בְּנַפְשׁוֹ כֶּן־הוּא, the difficulty of the text was felt by the Greek translators who rendered שער by τρίχα, 'a hair', obviously reading שֵׂעָר. The meaning would then be 'he is as a hair in the throat'. In the Wisdom of Amenemope, from which this section in the Book of Proverbs is so largely drawn, the same type of man is compared to a storm within one. [1]) This suggests that the reading of the Hebrew text may have originally been סַעַר corrupted to שַׂעַר during dictation of the text and subsequently read as שָׁעַר. The Massoretic reading, however, might be supported by the usage of *ṯʿr* in the Ras Shamra texts. In Gordon *UH* 77, 35 in the payment of the dowry of *Nkl* 'her brothers arrange (*yṯʿr*) the weights of the balances'. In Gordon *UH* ʿnt, I, 4-5 we read:

qm yṯʿr wʾašlḥmnh	'Rise, let preparation be made that I may feed him.'

Again in the same text (II, 20) the description of the banquet preparations of the goddess Anat contains the same word:

tṯʿr ksʾat lmhr	She prepares chairs for the warriors,
ṯʿr ṯlḥnt lṣbʾem	Arranging [2]) tables for the soldiers.

On lexical grounds then there is no reason why the Massoretic reading of Proverbs xxiii, 7 should not stand, 'as one purposes in his mind so he is'. The reading of the Egyptian text, however, suggests that after all emendation is necessary in this case.

In Esther i, 8 we apparently encounter a contradiction in the statement:

וְהַשְּׁתִיָּה כַדָּת אֵין אֹנֵס

And the drinking was by law; none compelled (EVV.).

The Ras Shamra texts prove doubly helpful here. כדת must be pointed כַּדּוֹת, 'by flagons', *kd* being well attested in the recurrent feasting scenes in the Ras Shamra myths and also in administrative texts. אנס a *hapax legomenon* in the Old Testament, though well attested in

[1]) H. Gressmann, 'Die neugefundene Lehre des Amen-em-ope und die vorexilische Spruchdichtung Israels', *ZAW* XLII, 1924, p. 277.

[2]) This is probably an infinitive absolute.

Aramaic and Syriac meaning 'restraint', is now illustrated, though with a phonetic variation, as DE VAUX noticed, [1] in the word *'unš*, which occurs in deeds of emancipation and conveyance of property from the palace of Ras Shamra (e.g. VIROLLEAUD, *PRU* II, 5, 8, and 9), the meaning being clearly 'feudal burden', as is apparent from fuller Akkadian texts on this subject from the archives of Ras Shamra. The passage in Esther, then, should be translated:

> And the drinking was by flagons without restraint.

In Job viii, 6 the verb יָעִיר, which generally means 'he awakes', occurs in what appears a curious context:

כִּי עַתָּה יָעִיר עָלֶיךָ
וְשִׁלַּם נְוַת צִדְקֶךָ

This is rendered in AV and RV:

> Surely he would awake for thee
> And make the habitation of thy righteousness prosperous.

The LXX is similarly unsatisfactory, merely paraphrasing

δεήσεως ἐπακούσεταί σου

The collocation of יָעִיר and שִׁלַּם suggests to EISSFELDT [2] the formula of greeting in letters from Ras Shamra:

'elm tġrk tšlmk (*PRU* II, 19), [3] 'may the gods protect thee and give thee peace'.

The passage therefore is to be translated:

> Then he will mount guard over thee
> And preserve thy righteous dwelling intact.

Isaiah xxxiii, 15 is probably also elucidated from the same Ras Shamra texts:

מֹאֵס בְּבֶצַע מַעֲשַׁקּוֹת
נֹעֵר כַּפָּיו מִתְּמֹךְ בַּשֹּׁחַד

which AV and RV render:

> He that despiseth the gains of oppression,
> That shaketh his hands from the holding of bribes.

נער, while not unintelligible in the sense 'shakes out', and indeed well attested in the Old Testament, is here, in our opinion, cognate with

---

1) R. DE VAUX, *RB* LXV, 1958, p. 636.
2) O. EISSFELDT, *JSS* V, 1960, p. 41.
3) cf. also GORDON *UH* 95; 101; 117; and 138.

the Ugaritic *nġr*, 'to keep guard', [1]) a byform of *ġyr*. Hence we translate Isaiah xxxiii, 15:

Who despiseth the gains of oppression
And guards his hands against the holding of bribes.

ġyr is probably also the root of יָעִיר in Deuteronomy xxxii, 11 which the LXX renders by σκεπάσαι. We propose the translation:

As a vulture guards its nest,
Hovering over its young.

We suggest that the root *ġyr* is the derivation of the Hebrew עִיר, which was properly a 'citadel' rather than a 'city', as suggested by 2 Samuel xii, 27, where we would translate עִיר הַמַּיִם (EVV. 'the city of waters') by

The tower guarding the water.

In Job xvi, 15 there is another *hapax legomenon*, the verb עלל in the phrase וְעֹלַלְתִּי בֶעָפָר קַרְנִי. This verb is now attested in the Ras Shamra texts. In Gordon *UH* 137, 23 the gods in shame 'lower their heads upon their knees' (*tġly 'elm r'ešthm lẓr brkthm*). The meaning of *ġly* is perfectly clear from the sequel where the gods in relief 'raise their heads from off their knees' (11. 29, *tš'u 'elm r'ašthm lẓ(r brkthm*).

In Job xxxi, 22 קנה occurs as a *hapax legomenon* in a context which admits no doubt as to its meaning as a part of the arm;

כְּתֵפִי מִשִּׁכְמָה (MT מִשִּׁכְמָה) תִפֹּל וְאֶזְרֹעִי מִקָּנָה תִשָּׁבֵר

'May my shoulder-blade fall from its shoulder and my arm be broken from its humeral bone.'

In the description of mourning rites in the texts Gordon *UH* 62, 4 and 67, VI, 20 the same two words *qn* and *ẓr'* or *ẓr'* are associated e.g.

qn ẓr'h yḥrṯ 'He scores the humeral joint of his arm'. [2])

In Psalm lxviii, 23 we read:

אָמַר אֲדֹנָי מִבָּשָׁן אָשִׁיב
אָשִׁיב מִמְּצֻלוֹת יָם

The Lord said, I will bring again from Bashan,
I will bring (them) again from the depths of the sea. (AV)

This is generally taken as a case of antithetic parallelism, Bashan,

---

[1]) e.g. Gordon, *UH* 52, 68, 69, 70, 73

[2]) A. Herdner, *RES*, 1942-45, p. 49.

the high plateau East of the Sea of Galilee, being contrasted with the Sea in the West. Here the difficulty is that if אָשִׁיב is taken in the usual sense 'I will bring back' there is no object in the first half of the line. The Ras Shamra texts attest *bṯn*, 'serpent', which corresponds phonetically to Hebrew בָּשָׁן. Metrical exigencies in the first half of the couplet suggested to CROSS and FREEDMAN that for מִבָּשָׁן we should read מִחוֹר בָּשָׁן [1]),

From the hole of the Serpent...

This proposal still does not overcome the main difficulty of the lack of an object for the transitive verb אָשִׁיב. Notwithstanding the arbitrary insertion of מִחוֹר, it is a feasible suggestion, which, however, we should translate rather

I shall bring back the Serpent from the hole
I shall bring back the Sea from the abyss.

Less violence would be done to the text, however, by omitting מ before בָּשָׁן as a dittograph, מ and ב being much alike in the 3rd-2rd c. B.C., and inserting the infinitive absolute הָשֵׁב, assuming its omission by haplography, and reading

אָמַר אֲדֹנָי בָּשָׁן הָשֵׁב אָשִׁיב
אָשִׁיב מִמְּצוּלוֹת יָם

I shall indeed bring back the Serpent
I shall bring back Sea from the abyss.

The Serpent and Sea are of course the powers of Chaos overcome by Baal in the Ras Shamra myth, the imagery of which is so often reflected in passages in the Hebrew Psalms, Prophets and Wisdom literature on the subject of the Kingship of God. The passage in Psalm lxviii, 23 thus interpreted reflects the sentiment of Amos ix, 3. The powers of chaos are imprisoned by God, but may still be used as instruments of his chastisement.

In Psalms lxviii, 28 (EVV. 27) in the phrase שָׂרֵי יְהוּדָה רִגְמָתָם, רִגְמָתָם, which finds no satisfactory explanation, least of all grammatically, becomes explicable in the light of the verb *rgm*, 'to speak', attested

---

[1]) F. M. CROSS and D. N. FREEDMAN, 'The Blessing of Moses', *JBL* LXVII, 1948, p. 208. 'The hole of the Serpent' (*ḥr bṯnm*) is actually mentioned in the Ras Shamra mythological fragment VIROLLEAUD *PRU* II, 1, 6, which F. C. FENSHAM uses in support of the reading of CROSS and FREEDMAN ('Ps. 68. 23 in the Light of the recently discovered Ugaritic Tablets', *JNES* XIX, 1960, pp. 292-3.)

passim in the Ras Shamra texts. A division of the letter-complex, as suggested by A. R. JOHNSON, [1]) gives רֹגֵם תָּם, which Professor JOHNSON happily renders 'honest-spoken'.

In Psalm xcvii, 3, an Enthronement Psalm which is strongly impregnated with the imagery and ideology of the Canaanite Baal-myth, Jahweh like the Canaanite Baal appears in cloud, thunder, and lightning, and it is said:

אֵשׁ לְפָנָיו תֵּלֵךְ וּתְלַהֵט סָבִיב צָרָיו

The last word causes some difficulty, and in its usual meaning, 'his adversaries', does not yield good sense. The emendation of this word to לְצְעָדָיו, 'his footsteps', is suggested, which would be not unsuitable in the context. In the Baal-cycle in the literature of Ras Shamra, however, the word *ṣrrt* is found in the phrase *ṣrrt ṣpn*, 'the cliffs of Ṣpn'. Now we have seen that Ṣpn is specifically the home of Baal, so we suggest that צריו be retained in Psalm xcvii, 3 in the same sense as in the Ras Shamra texts, the line being translated:

Fire goes before him and lights up his crags. [2])

Here probably we have the retention of the imagery and phraseology of some Canaanite hymn to Baal.

In Psalm lxv, 10 we read:

פָּקַדְתָּ הָאָרֶץ וַתְּשֹׁקְקֶהָ רַבַּת תַּעְשְׁרֶנָּה

The AV translates 'Thou visitest the earth and waterest it; thou greatly enrichest it'.

The English idiom in the last phrase blinds us to the peculiarity of the Hebrew, where הֶעֱשִׁיר is always used with a personal object when it means 'to enrich'. Actually the verb *'šr* is found in the Ras Shamra texts, notably in GORDON *UH* 'nt I, 9, where it means 'to serve with drink'. Here, moreover, it is, as in Psalm lxv, 10, in parallelism with *šqy*. Thus we should translate Psalm lxv, 10 as follows:

---

[1]) A. R. JOHNSON, *Sacral Kingship in Ancient Israel*, 1955, p. 75.

[2]) GORDON (*UM*, 1955, § 20, 1654) cites the suggestion of J. FINKEL that in Hosea xiii, 12, צָרוּר עֲוֹן אֶפְרָיִם צְפוּנָה חַטָּאתוֹ, the word may be connected with *ṣrrt*. Presumably then the meaning of the passage might be:

'The rock is the iniquity of Ephraim,
Saphon is his sin'.

This would refer to the worship of Baal the lord of Saphon. The collocation of צרר and צפן is certainly suggestive, but is, we think, no more than a coincidence. After all צרר in the sense 'to bundle up' and צפן, 'to lay up in store', are more regular in Hebrew and give excellent sense in the passage in Hosea.

'Thou hast visited the land and watered it,
Abundantly dost thou give it to drink'.

In Psalm xcii, 11 (AV 10) there is another *hapax legomenon* in the verb בלל in the phrase בַּלֹּתִי בְּשֶׁמֶן, for which the translation of the AV 'I am anointed with oil' is admittedly a *pis-aller* (BDB p. 117 b). The verb, however, seems cognate with the Arabic بَلَّ, 'to be wet', which has an Ugaritic cognate *bll*, which we take to be used as a verbal noun in the passage Gordon *UH* 129, 20-21, where Baal expostulates:

lblm 'ard bnpšny	'Am I to lay down my new-born offspring in dampness,
trḥṣn kṯrm ( )*bb*(*t*)*ym* [1])	And the Skilly Ones wash him in the house of Sea?'

Hence we render the phrase in Psalm xcii, 11 'I am drenched with oil'.

In Psalm cxlviii, 11 in the verse,

מַלְכֵי־אֶרֶץ וְכָל־לְאֻמִּים שָׂרִים וְכָל־שֹׁפְטֵי אָרֶץ,

the word לְאֻמִּים, which regularly in the Old Testament means 'peoples', is so translated in the English versions. The LXX renders the word here as λαοί, but in certain other passages (e.g. Genesis xxvii, 29; Isaiah xxxiv, 1; xli, 1; xliii, 4, 9; lv, 4) translates it by ἄρχοντες. The reason for the translation ἄρχοντες, 'rulers', is that there was another Hebrew word with the same consonants לאמים which meant 'princes'. This might have been conjectured from the Assyrian *limmu*, the title of the official who gave his name to the year. This obviously is the meaning demanded for לאמים in this context in association with מלכי־ארץ, שפטי ארץ, and שרים. Now in the Ras Shamra texts *l'emm* is found meaning 'people', notably in Gordon *UH* 62, 6, and less certainly in Gordon *UH* ʿnt II, 7, [2]) but in the phrase *ybmt l'emm*, the stock title of Anat, we think that *l'emm* signifies 'the Prince', i.e. Baal. [3]) Anat was the sister of Baal, whose royal status is well-known. The word *ybmt* is also interesting. In Hebrew it signifies generally a sister-in-law, for whom, of course, one had responsibility and the duty of marrying in the case of the husband's decease (Deuteronomy xxv, 7, 9). The term *ybmt* used of Anat with reference to her brother

---

[1]) For philological notes *v. supra*, p. 40.
[2]) *v. supra*, p. 23, n. 5 and n. 6.
[3]) *v. supra*, p. 40 n. 8.

Baal may express the relationship of an unmarried female to her male sponsor. [1])

In Psalm lxxxix, 19 we read:

כִּי לַיהוה מָגִנֵּנוּ וְלִקְדוֹשׁ יִשְׂרָאֵל מַלְכֵּנוּ

Here מָגִנֵּנוּ is taken as 'defence', literally 'shield', the sense it usually has in the Old Testament. In the Ras Shamra texts the verbal root *mgn* is found in parallelism with the verb *ġẓ y*, which is cognate with the Arabic غزى, 'to entreat', e.g. GORDON *UH* 51, I, 20-23:

'ap mṯn rgmm	'Yea, I repeat the word to thee,
'argmk šskn m'	I tell thee—establish it fast thereto—
mgn rbt 'aṯrt ym	The intercession of Lady Aṯrt of the Sea,
mġẓ qnyt 'elm	The entreaty of the Creatrix of the Gods.'

Thus in Psalm lxxxix, 19 מגננו might have the same sense, the translation then being 'For our intercession is unto Jahweh, even unto the Holy One of Israel our King'. This seems certainly to be the meaning of the word in the phrase מָגִנִּי אֶל־אֱלֹהִים מוֹשִׁיעַ יִשְׁרֵי־לֵב in Psalm vii, 11, a Plaint of the Individual Sufferer. [2])

A word which seems to us to require some explanation is שָׂרִים in Psalm lxxxii, 7: אָכֵן כְּאָדָם תְּמוּתוּן וּכְאַחַד הַשָּׂרִים תִּפֹּלוּ. Here it seems that the usual meaning of שׂרים, 'princes', is not appropriate, and we might suggest that the word is the masculine plural participle of a root שָׂרָה which is cognate with the Arabic شرى, 'to flash'. A reference to a comet would be appropriate, and the planet Jupiter is actually named المشترى in Arabic. The Ras Shamra text celebrating the birth of Šḥr and Šlm, the twin-deities manifest in the Venus star, begins:

'eqr'a 'elm n'(mm)
wysmm bn šr(   )

In view of the final lacuna we cannot be absolutely certain of the significance of *šr* (   ), which may or may not be complete as *šrm*. With this reservation we suggest the connection between *šr* (   )

[1]) In GORDON *UH* 'nt III, 9 the goddess is termed *ymmt l'emm*. This is probably simply a case of the assimilation of the labial *b* to the following labial *m* rather than a different term which GORDON suggests may be cognate with ימימה, the name of Job's eldest daughter (xlii, 14). *UM*, 1955, § 20, 789.

[2]) The Massoretic text reads מָגִנִּי עַל־אֱלֹהִים מוֹשִׁיעַ יִשְׁרֵי־לֵב. In the Syriac version על is omitted. It is suggested that עָלִי should be read with מָגִנִּי in apposition to אֱלֹהִים. Our reading assumes the frequent scribal error of עַל for אֶל.

and the Arabic شرى, the 'sons of brightness' being a fitting description of the Morning- and Evening-star. Now the text GORDON *UH* 49 I describes the futile attempt of Aṯtr, the Venus-star, to occupy the place of Baal, and his ignominious descent from the throne, a theme which, we believe, the Hebrew prophet borrowed when he compares the degradation of the King of Babylon to the fall of 'the Bright One, son of the Dawn' (הֵילֵל בֶּן־שָׁחַר). Our translation of Psalm lxxxii, 7 then would be:

'But ye die like men,
Like one of the bright (stars) fall ye'.

The plural שׂרים may refer generally to comets, or specifically to the fall of the Venus-star, which was sometimes thought of as the god Aṯtr and sometimes as Šḥr and Šlm, the twin-deities manifest in the star of the morning and evening.

In Psalm cxl, 11 we encounter a very awkward verse:

יִמּיטוּ עֲלֵיהֶם גֶּחָלִים בָּאֵשׁ יַפִּלֵם בְּמַהֲמֹרוֹת בַּל־יָקוּמוּ

Here the reading of the first half of the line is probably יַמְטֵר עֲלֵיהֶם גַּחֲלֵי אֵשׁ, as suggested by the LXX and by Jerome and by the figure in Psalm xi, 6.[1]) For the *hapax legomenon* מַהֲמֹרוֹת, however, no satisfactory explanation has been offered, and the emendation בִּמְהֵרוֹת, 'quickly', has been conjectured. In the Ras Shamra text GORDON *UH* 67, I, 7-8, however, the word *mhmrt* is found in a context which suggests the very figure the psalmist visualized. Mot, the deity of the underworld, threatens Baal:

lyrt bnpš bn 'elm mt	'Verily thou shalt go down into the throat of the god Mot,
bmhmrt ydd 'el ġzr [2])	Into the gullet of the Hero, Beloved of El.

In a later passage in the same text (II, 15) *hmry* ('Ruin') is the name of the city (*qrt*) of Mot. This obviously is in the mind of the psalmist in the passage which, without emendation of the consonants of במהמרות, may be read יַמְטֵר עֲלֵיהֶם גַּחֲלֵי אֵשׁ יִפְּלוּ בְּמַהֲמֹרוֹת בַּל־יָקוּמוּ and translated 'Let him rain coals of fire upon them, let them fall into ruin no more to rise'.

---

[1]) יַמְטֵר עַל־רְשָׁעִים פַּחִים אֵשׁ וְגָפְרִית. For פַּחִים Symmachos reads ἄνθρακας from Hebrew פַּחְמֵי, 'coals'.

[2]) For philological notes *v. supra* p. 56, n. 5.

Another text assumed to be corrupt and requiring emendation is Psalm lxxxviii, 5-6:

נֶחְשַׁבְתִּי עִם־יוֹרְדֵי בוֹר הָיִיתִי כְּגֶבֶר אֵין־אֱיָל
בַּמֵּתִים חָפְשִׁי כְּמוֹ חֲלָלִים שֹׁכְבֵי קֶבֶר

This again seems to us a direct reflection of the imagery of the two Ugaritic passages just cited, particularly Gordon *UH* 51, VIII, 7:

wrd bthptt 'arṣ	'And go down to the corruption of the underworld,
tspr byrdm 'arṣ [1])	Thou shalt be numbered among them that go down to the underworld.'

Hence in Psalm lxxxviii, 5-6 we should read:

נֶחְשַׁבְתִּי עִם־יוֹרְדֵי בוֹר הָיִיתִי כְּגֶבֶר אֵין־אֱיָל
כִּמְתֵי מַחְפֶּשֶׁת כְּמוֹ חֲלָלִים שֹׁכְבֵי קֶבֶר

and translate:

'I am reckoned as those who go down to the pit,
I am become as a man of no strength,
As men of corruption,
As mutilated men who lie in the grave.'

In the late book Ecclesiastes M. J. DAHOOD has, justly in our estimation, appraised the Phoenician character of the work over against the commonly-held thesis that its linguistic peculiarities are rather Aramaic. [2]) Here then are instances of words rare in Hebrew and on that account suspect and even mistranslated which may be defended and correctly translated in the light of the Ras Shamra evidence. In Ecclesiastes iii, 11 we read: גַּם אֶת־הָעֹלָם נָתַן בְּלִבָּם מִבְּלִי אֲשֶׁר לֹא יִמְצָא הָאָדָם אֶת־הַמַּעֲשֶׂה אֲשֶׁר עָשָׂה הָאֱלֹהִים. The word עֹלָם is translated in the RSV not as 'eternity', which ill accords with the general sense of the context, but as 'darkness', meaning thereby 'ignorance'. DAHOOD [3]) rightly adduces the Ras Shamra evidence of GORDON *UH* 125, 50 where *ġlm* means 'it had grown dark'. Further support for this interpretation is the phrase מַעְלִים עֵצָה in Job xlii, 3. The passage in Ecclesiastes might then be translated:

'Yea he set darkness in their hearts so that man discovers not the work which God has done'.

---

[1]) For philological notes *v. supra* p. 55.

[2]) M. J. DAHOOD, *Canaanite-Phoenician Influence in Qoheleth*, 1952, cf. GORDON, who proposes that such Canaanite features are due to the influence of N. Israelites in Babylonia, where the book was produced, *UM*, 1955, p. 81 n. 1.

[3]) *Op. cit.* p. 38.

Another possible instance of עלם in this sense is in Ecclesiastes xii, 5: כִּי הֹלֵךְ הָאָדָם אֶל־בֵּית עוֹלָמוֹ. Possibly the meaning of בית עולמו is 'his dark house', i.e. 'his grave', as the context indicates. The Egyptian expression for the grave, however, was 'house of eternity' and this may be the meaning of the phrase in question in Ecclesiastes.

In the following verse, Ecclesiastes xii, 6, וְתִשָּׁבֶר כַּד עַל־הַמַּבּוּעַ וְיֵרֹץ [1] הַגַּלְגַּל עַל [2]־הַבּוֹר DAHOOD has pointed out the disruption of the prevailing parallelism of the passage if גלגל is taken as 'wheel'. He cites the Akkadian *gulgullu* and the Ras Shamra text GORDON *UH* krt, 72//165, where *gl ḫrṣ* means 'a golden bowl'. The word *kd*, 'jar' is also well attested in the Ugaritic literature. The verse in Ecclesiastes then may better be translated:

> 'And the jar is broken at the spring,
> And the pot is shattered on the well-head'.

In the end of the book there is a beautiful case where an Ugaritic passage suggests a new meaning for two Hebrew words hitherto misunderstood. In Ecclesiastes xii, 12 there is no reference to 'the making of books... and much study' in the well-known passage:

עֲשׂוֹת סְפָרִים הַרְבֵּה אֵין קֵץ וְלַהַג הַרְבֵּה יְגִעַת בָּשָׂר

Both *spr* and *hg* occur similarly in parallelism in the Ugaritic text GORDON *UH* krt 90-91, cited by DAHOOD; [3]

> *ḫpṯ dbl spr*
> *ṯnn dbl hg.*

As this passage follows the hyperbolical enumeration of the king's retinue, it is to be translated:

> 'Peasant levies without number,
> Trained regulars beyond reckoning'. [4]

So for the passage in Ecclesiastes we suggest the translation:

> 'In much casting of accounts there is no end,
> And much reckoning is a weariness of the flesh'.

In the case of להג, incidentally, we have another feature fairly common in Ugaritic, namely the enclitic *l*, which is similarly used in Arabic

---

1) For the Massoretic reading וְנָרֹץ.

2) For the Massoretic reading אל.

3) DAHOOD, *op. cit.*, p. 51.

4) For philological notes *v. supra*, p. 138, n. 6, p. 139, n. 1.

before the adjective or noun as predicate in a nominal sentence. In such Wisdom books as Proverbs and Ecclesiastes it has long been customary to explain linguistic and grammatical peculiarities as Aramaisms, suggesting a late origin for the books in question. While there is every evidence that Ecclesiastes is late and Proverbs is a late compilation, the Canaanite features of these books in diction and literary style suggest that the latter contains matter from a much earlier date, and that the former, which has many later Phoenician features, may have been written in one of the Phoenician cities on the coast, perhaps such a place as Akka. [1])

In Psalm lxxviii, 48 we read of God's visitation upon the people, delivering the beasts up to the hail and afflicting the cattle:

וַיַּסְגֵּר לַבָּרָד בְּעִירָם וּמִקְנֵיהֶם לָרְשָׁפִים

The last word is generally taken to signify lightning, literally 'sparks'. The word is occasionally used in the Old Testament in this sense, but in Habakkuk iii, 5 it is found in the singular in parallelism with דֶּבֶר, 'plague', and in a similar context in Deuteronomy xxxii, 24. From the Ras Shamra texts we know that Rešef was the god of pestilence and he is specifically mentioned in Gordon *UH* krt, 19: *mḫmšt y'etsp ršp*,

At five years old Rešef gathered them to himself. [2])

In the verse in Habakkuk: לְפָנָיו יֵלֶךְ דָּבֶר וְיֵצֵא רֶשֶׁף לְרַגְלָיו we may have more than a personification of plague, the god Rešef himself being figuratively depicted as an attendant on Jahweh.

Apart from new meanings of such words revealed by the discovery of Ugaritic, the Canaanite texts attest new meanings of certain particles and conjunctions for which only one sense had been hitherto appreciated in their Hebrew cognates. In such cases the general sense of the context seemed to demand emendation, which in the light of the new evidence often proves unnecessary.

---

[1]) cf. Albright, 'Some Canaanite-Phoenician Sources of Hebrew Wisdom', *VT* Supplement III, 1955, p. 15, 'I therefore hold that the author of this Book was an influential Jew who lived on the Coastal Plain, probably in southern Phoenicia, about 300 B.C., and whose orally transmitted aphorisms were collected after his death and put into writing in Phoenicia. Though intended to be Hebrew, their written form betrays Phoenician influence in spelling, morphology, syntax, vocabulary, and content'.

[2]) *v. supra*, p. 133, n. 5.

In Deuteronomy xxxiii, 11, for instance, in the phrase מחץ מתנים קמיו, the sense of which is clearly indicated by the reading in the Samaritan Pentateuch מחץ מתני קמיו, 'Smite the loins of his enemies', CROSS and FREEDMAN proposed to retain the Massoretic reading taking the final ם of מתנים as a case of the enclitic *m*, [1]) which is commonly found between the construct and the absolute in Ugaritic. Here we agree, though in the cases which they cite in support of this reading (Psalms lxviii, 17; lxxvii, 18a; cxxv, 1) the final ם might equally well be the normal masculine plural afformative. In Psalm cx, 3, however, we would suggest that in place of the difficult reading מֵרֶחֶם שַׁחַר (for MT מרחם משחר) we should read מֵרֵחַ־ם שַׁחַר, 'From the breath of dawn'.

In Psalm xvi, 2 some difficulty is caused by the phrase טובתי בל עליך. The particle בל is taken as a negative, as generally in Hebrew, and haplography is presumed by Symmachus, the Targum, and Jerome, who obviously read טובתי בל בלעדיך, 'My good is not apart from thee'. [2]) This, it must be admitted, renders good sense, though, in the doubtful state of the sequel, it is hard to be certain of the reading. With this reservation, we may admit O'CALLAGHAN's proposition that the particle בל may here, as in Ugaritic and Arabic, introduce a strong asseveration in contrast with a negative expressed or implied, 'Nay but...' [3]) cf. Gordon *UH* 51 V, 123, *bl 'ašt 'urbt bbhtm*, 'Nay but I shall put a window in the house'. The phrase might, then, mean 'Nay but my profit is in thee', no emendation being necessary.

Another linguistic phenomenon which has been elucidated by the Ras Shamra texts is the asseverative כִּי. Before it was so understood this particle often seemed to invite emendation. Now the Ras Shamra texts demonstrate that it had the function of emphasizing a verb, which in any case was emphasized by being reserved till the end of the hemistich [4]) e.g. GORDON *UH* 51, II, 13-14:

hlk . bʿl . ʿṯtrt . ktʿn   Aṯtrt indeed eyed the going of Baal.

An excellent example, where the threefold repetition rules out the possibility of textual corruption, is Psalm cxviii, 10-12:

---

[1]) F. M. CROSS and D. H. FREEDMAN, 'The Blessing of Moses', JBL LXVII, 1948, p. 194, so also R. T. O'CALLAGHAN, *VT* IV, 1954, p. 170.

[2]) So also LXX, cf. the Vulgate, 'Thou hast no need of my goods'.

[3]) O'CALLAGHAN, *op. cit.*, pp. 166-167.

[4]) H. L. GINSBERG, 'Notes on "The Birth of the Gracious and Beautiful Gods"', *JRAS* 1935, p. 56.

כָּל־גּוֹיִם סְבָבוּנִי
בְּשֵׁם יהוה כִּי אֲמִילַם
סַבּוּנִי גַם סְבָבוּנִי
בְּשֵׁם יהוה כִּי אֲמִילַם
סַבּוּנִי כִדְבוֹרִים ....
בְּשֵׁם יהוה כִּי אֲמִילַם

Not only a final verb, but a final statement may be so emphasized by an introductory כִּי, e.g. Deuteronomy xxxii, 8-9:

בְּהַנְחֵיל עֶלְיוֹן גּוֹיִם
בְּהַפְרִידוֹ בְּנֵי אָדָם
יַצֵּב גְּבוּלוֹת עַמִּים
לְמִסְפַּר בְּנֵי יִשְׂרָאֵל
כִּי חֵלֶק יהוה עַמּוֹ
יַעֲקֹב חֶבֶל נַחֲלָתוֹ

When the Most High assigned the peoples their portion
When He separated the sons of men,
Fixing the bounds of the peoples
According to the number of the sons of El [1])
Yahweh's portion was His people,
Jacob the lot of his inheritance.

Ginsberg has further noticed that the enclitic *m* was found between a construct and its absolute. [2]) This suggests that in Psalm xviii, 16 (MT):

וַיֵּרָאוּ אֲפִיקֵי מַיִם
וַיִּגָּלוּ מוֹסְדוֹת תֵּבֵל

And the sources of the waters were made visible,
And the foundations of the world were disclosed

should be emended to

וַיֵּרָאוּ אֲפִיקֵי־ם יָם

And the sources of the sea were made visible...

This reading is supported by the parallel and by the MT of the psalm in 2 Samuel xxii, 16.

The enclitic *m* may also be used after a verb, as possibly in Psalm lxxxiii, 12:

שִׁיתֵמ(וֹ) נְדִיבֵמוֹ כְּעֹרֵב וְכִזְאֵב

Make their princes as Oreb and Zeeb,

---

[1]) So the LXX, Symmachos, and the Old Latin versions, reading בְּנֵי אֵל for MT בְּנֵי יִשְׂרָאֵל.

[2]) Ginsberg, *op. cit.*, pp. 47-48.

and Psalm xxix, 6:

וַיַּרְקִידֵם כְּמוֹ־עֵגֶל לְבָנוֹן

And he made Lebanon to skip like a calf. [1])

In לרשפים in Psalm lxxviii, 48 we suggest that the final ם was the final enclitic, used in Akkadian and Ugaritic as a substitute for, or a supplement to, the preposition, as DE LANGHE has demonstrated. [2]) When the early MSS were still written in *scriptio defectiva*, omitting י, this was mistaken for a plural ending, a mistake which is often made by the scribes. Hence we should translate:

And he delivered their beasts up to the hail,
And their cattle to the plague (or Reshef).

The reading of the last word further suggests to us that ברד ('hail') in the parallel position may well be a scribal error for דֶּבֶר ('pest'), as indeed Symmachos' Greek version suggests.

It often happens that an initial *l* presents a problem in the MT. This may readily be solved by Arabists, who are familiar with this enclitic introducing a noun or adjective as a predicate or the jussive of a verb. Akkadian also has this usage, and also Ugaritic, both with the perfect, e.g. *lrgmt lk* and imperfect indicative, e.g. *lymr'u 'elm wnšm* (GORDON *UH* 51, VII, 50-51) and jussive, e.g.

llṭpn.'el.dp'ed.ltbrk (*krt*) (GORDON *UH* 128, II, 13-15). [3])

This is also found in Hebrew, e.g. Gen. xxx, 34, cited by GORDON *UH*, § 9, 12:

הֵן לוּ יְהִי כִדְבָרֶךָ

May it be indeed as thou sayest.

This suggests to ALBRIGHT the reading of Habakkuk iii, 6-7 (MT):

הֲלִיכוֹת עוֹלָם לוֹ :
תַּחַת אָוֶן . . . .

ALBRIGHT, correctly in our opinion, notices that this is the last colon in a tricolon punctuating the bicola, the Massoretes having wrongly punctuated. With the omission of ו in לו the MT, apart from the punctuation, may be read, citing the whole tricolon:

---

[1]) In both instances the final ם (and ו in שִׁיתֻמוֹ may be written by scribal corruption and dittography of the following letters נ and כ, which closely resemble each other in the proto-Hebraic script.

[2]) R. DE LANGHE, 'L'enclitique cananéenne m(a)', *Muséon* LIX, 1946, pp. 89-111.

[3]) This passage illustrates in *llṭpn* another use of *l*, the vocative.

וַיִּתְפֹּצְצוּ הַרְרֵי־עַד
שַׁחוּ גִּבְעוֹת עוֹלָם
הֲלִיכוֹת עוֹלָם לְתַחַתֶּאנָה

While everlasting mountains broke up,
Eternal hills collapsed,
Eternal orbits were shattered. [1])

This is another instance of the Ras Shamra texts supporting the consonantal MT where previously emendation was considered imperative.

The particle אַל, which is regularly used with the jussive of the verb in prohibitions, is found occasionally in Hebrew with the indicative, e.g. Psalm cxxi, 3 אל־ינום, 'he will not slumber', cf. Jeremiah xlvi, 6; 2 Chronicles xiv, 10. Here again there is precedent in the Ugaritic texts for the usage of *'al* as a simple negative before a verb which is clearly indicative, e.g. Gordon *UH* 49, VI, 26, *'ek 'al yšm'k*, 'How will he not hear thee?'

In the words we have just studied we cannot fail to be impressed with the colour and content which their Ugaritic counterparts add to little known and even suspect words. The rarity of such words in extant Hebrew meant that their meaning was often a matter of conjecture, occasionally, to be sure, quite plausible and even certain in the context, but still conjecture. Not seldom scholars resorted to emendation, sometimes replacing the rare and unattested word by a similar one more familiar but much more prosaic. The evidence of the Canaanite literature which we have cited has in many instances supported the Massoretic text, making emendation unnecessary.

There are, however, instances where the same evidence has suggested emendation.

In David's lament for Saul and Jonathan, for instance, in 2 Samuel i, 21:

הָרֵי בַגִּלְבֹּעַ אַל־טַל וְאַל־מָטָר עֲלֵיכֶם וּשְׂדֵי תְרוּמוֹת

the last two words have occasioned much speculation. The literal translation 'fields of offerings' is meaningless and quite unsuitable to the context, and textual corruption is suggested by the great

---

[1]) W. F. Albright, *CBQ* VII, 1945, p. 24; 'The Psalm of Habakkuk', *Studies in Old Testament Prophecy*, ed. H. H. Rowley, 1950, pp. 11, 12, 14-15. הליכות in the sense of courses of the stars is also paralleled in Ugaritic, e.g. *hlk kbkbm* Gordon *UH* I Aqht, 52, 56, 200. The Hebrews visualized these courses or orbits as made roads, מסלות, which Albright appositely cites from Judges v, 20.

variety of readings in the ancient versions. Here then was wide scope for conjectural emendation.

After the passage in the Ras Shamra text GORDON *UH* 1 Aqht I, 44-45, which notes the three sources of moisture, in Syria,

bl ṭl bl rbb	'No dew, no rain!
bl šrʿ thmtm	No upsurging of the lower deep!' [1])

GINSBERG [2]) boldly proposed the reading:

הָרֵי הַגִּלְבֹּעַ אַל־טַל וְאַל־מָטָר עֲלֵיכֶם וְשֶׁרַע תְּהוֹמוֹת

'Ye mountains of Gilboa let there be neither dew nor rain upon you, nor upsurging of the lower deeps.'

And, indeed after the mention of dew (טַל) and rain (מָטָר) we normally expect mention of the subterranean sources.

Such a drastic emendation of the MT, however, may well be suspected. Actually R. GORDIS, [3]) inspired by GINSBERG's emendation, proposed to retain the consonants שדי, but to read שְׁדִי with the sense 'effluence', which is well attested in Aramaic. This verb and its verbal noun is attested also in the Ras Shamra text GORDON *UH* 52, 13, 28, where *šd* is taken as the 'effluence' of the breasts of the goddesses by DRIVER, [4]) who feasibly proposes the same meaning in Ezekiel i, 24: [5])

וָאֶשְׁמַע אֶת־קוֹל כַּנְפֵיהֶם כְּקוֹל מַיִם רַבִּים כְּקוֹל שְׁדִי (MT שַׁדַּי) בְּלֶכְתָּם

We accept GORDIS' emendation in 2 Samuel i, 21: שְׁדִי תהומות 'effluence of the lower deeps'.

In Ezekiel xxxii, 6 there is a verse containing no less than four questionable readings:

וְהִשְׁקֵיתִי אֶרֶץ צָפָתְךָ מִדָּמְךָ אֶל־הֶהָרִים וַאֲפִיקִים יִמָּלְאוּן מִמֶּךָּ

There is good authority in the LXX and Symmachos for emending the unintelligible צָפָתְךָ to צֹאָתְךָ, and the suggestion of the metathesis of צֹאָתְךָ and מִדְמֵי (for מִדָּמְךָ) is feasible, the resulting phrase דְּמֵי צֹאָתְךָ meaning 'thy filthy blood'. The last word in the line, meaning, as it stands in the Massoretic text, 'of thee', is not suitable and it has been

---

[1]) For philological notes *v. supra*, p. 118, n. 3.
[2]) H. L. GINSBERG, 'A Ugaritic Parallel to 2 Samuel i, 21', *JBL* LVII, 1938, pp. 209-213.
[3]) R. GORDIS, *JTS* XLI, 1940, p. 35.
[4]) G. R. DRIVER, *op. cit., ad. loc.*
[5]) G. R. DRIVER, *JTS* XLI, 1940, p. 168

suggested that it should be emended to מְדָמֶיךָ. Now in the Ras Shamra text Gordon *UH* ʿnt II, 13-15 the blood-bath of the goddess Anat is described:

brkm tġ(ll) bdm ẓmr	She plunges her knees in the blood of the soldiers,
ḫlqm bmmʿ mhrm	Her loins in the gore of the warriors. [1]

We suggest that ממך, the last word in the passage from Ezekiel, is a corruption of ממעך, 'thy gore' (Ras Shamra *mmʿ*), which gives the desired parallel with דְּמֵי צֹאָתְךָ in the first half of the line. Our restoration of the text in Ezekiel is:

וְהִשְׁקֵיתִי אֶרֶץ מִדְּמֵי צֹאָתְךָ (עַל־הֶהָרִים) וַאֲפִיקִים יִמָּלְאוּן מִמָּעֶךָ

Our translation is:

'And I will give the earth to drink of thy filthy blood (upon the mountains), [2]
And the wadis will be filled with thy gore.'

In Psalm xvi, 9 כבד is found in parallelism with לב. In the Massoretic text it is pointed as כָּבוֹד, 'glory', e.g.:

לָכֵן שָׂמַח לִבִּי וַיָּגֶל כְּבוֹדִי אַף־בְּשָׂרִי יִשְׁכֹּון לָבֶטַח

The pointing כָּבֵד, 'liver', is suggested by the text Gordon *UH* 75 I, 12-13:

ʾel yṣḥq bm lb	El laughs in his heart,
wygmẓ bm kbd	And is convulsed (with mirth) in his liver. [3]

Clearly, then, the liver was thought of among the ancient Semites as the seat of the emotions as the heart was thought of chiefly as the seat of cognition. Another passage where כָּבֹד of the Massoretic text must be emended to כָּבֵד is in Genesis xlix, 6:

בְּסֹודָם אַל־תָּבֹא נַפְשִׁי בִּקְהָלָם אַל־תֵּחַד כְּבֹדִי

'Into their society come not, my soul,
In their assembly rejoice not, my liver.'

Here the reading we adopt is suggested by the LXX, which reads ἥπατα for כבד.

In Psalm lxv, 10 the Massoretic text, ascribing to Jahweh the function of fertility, reads:

תָּכִין דְּגָנָם כִּי כֵן תְּכִינֶהָ

---

1) For philological notes *v. supra*, p. 41, n. 12, p. 42, n. 1.
2) As the metre suggests these two words are probably a gloss.
3) For philological notes see our article 'The Hunting of Baal...', *JNES* X, 1951, p. 148.

Here דְּגָנָם should probably be emended to דְּגָנָהּ, the pronoun referring to ארץ. The verb, used in the Hiphil and Po'lel means 'to prepare a crop', as is recognized in the LXX version of Psalm lxxx, 16 where כַּנָּה of the Massoretic text, probably a by-form of כּין, is rendered by κατάρτισαι. In Psalm lxv, 10, however, we propose that the last word, which we should read as תְּכֻנֶּה, has a different sense, namely 'thou art named'. The verb כנה is found in this sense in Isaiah xliv, 5, and is cognate with the Arabic كَنَى, whence كُنْيَة, 'patronymic'. Now in the Ras Shamra texts Baal is regularly termed *bn dgn*, 'the son of Dagon'. So in Psalm lxv, 10, reading the text תָּכִין דְּגָנָהּ כִּי כֵן תְּכֻנֶּה, we propose to translate

'Thou dost prepare the corn thereof
According to thy name.'

There is a double word-play here on the two meanings of כִּין and כָּנָה, and the word דָּגָן ('corn') and Dagon in Baal's title *bn dgn*. The psalm is otherwise redolent of the nature-cult of the peasant and may be an adaptation of a Canaanite hymn.

There is a similar word-play between two different meanings of שכח in Psalm cxxxvii, 5:

אִם־אֶשְׁכָּחֵךְ יְרוּשָׁלָ͏ִם תִּשְׁכַּח יְמִינִי

In the first case the verb means 'to forget'; in the second case the want of an object was felt, שָׁכַח, 'to forget', being a transitive verb. There were various efforts made in the ancient versions to overcome the difficulty and conjectural emendations have not been wanting. ALBRIGHT proposed the meaning 'waste away' or 'dry up' for שׁכח, which gives the translation:

'If I forget thee, O Jerusalem,
Let my right hand wither.'

This seems to be the sense of שׁכח in Psalm cii, 5 b:

הוּכָּה כָעֵשֶׂב וַיִּבַשׁ לִבִּי כִּי שָׁכַחְתִּי מֵאֲכֹל לַחְמִי

'My heart is stricken as grass and dried up,
For I am too parched to eat my bread.' [1])

No direct Ugaritic influence can be certainly cited, but the verb *ṯkḥ* in this general sense occurs in GORDON *UH* 67, I, 4, 31:

---

[1]) J. H. PATTON, *Canaanite Parallels in the Book of Psalms*, 1944, pp. 26-27.

t̲kḥ ttrp šmm krs [1]) *'epdk....*

The precise meaning is obscure here, but the reference is to the wilting and drooping of the sky under the influence of Mot, the deity of drought and sterility.

The text at Proverbs xxxi, 4,

אַל לַמְלָכִים שְׁתוֹ־יָיִן
וּלְרוֹזְנִים אֵו שֵׁכָר

is one of notorious difficulty, and is probably defective. The problematic או (Q אי) has been taken variously as a corruption of מסך or סבא ('to mix') or, what seems more likely, אוה ('to desire'). D. Winton Thomas [2]) suggests that או is correct, but that an initial ר has dropped out, which is quite possible after the preceding ם of רוזנים in the proto-Hebraic script. This, he suggests, may be a scribal error for רוו, or, as we think, may be a by-form of this verb. In any case the verb is parallel in form and meaning to שתו, though in both cases we should prefer to read infinitive absolutes שָׁתוֹ and רָאוֹ or רָווֹ, which Thomas admits, translating

'It is not for kings to drink wine,
Nor for rulers to imbibe strong drink'.

He would see the same verb in Ben Sirach xxxiv, 28,

יין נשתה בעת וראי

'Wine drunk at the right time and to satiety'.

Here, however, the initial ו may be a radical consonant and the final י the vowel of the genitive of the verbal noun in *scriptio plena*, the verb being cognate with Arab. ورأ. More aptly, in our opinion, he cites Proverbs xxiii, 31,

אַל־תֵּרֶא יַיִן כִּי יִתְאַדָּם
כִּי־יִתֵּן בַּכּוֹס עֵינוֹ

which he would render

'Drink not the wine when [3]) it is red,
When it gives forth its sparkle in the cup'.

Either ראה in the sense of 'drink' or ורא, cognate with Arab. ورأ,

---

[1]) The word *krs* may be read *kks* 'as the covering...' (Ugaritic *r* = ⊏⊏►, *k* = ⊏►), but *v. supra*, p. 30, n. 3.

[2]) D. W. Thomas, 'או in Proverbs xxxi, 4', *VT* XII, 1962, pp. 499-500.

[3]) Possibly concessive, 'though'.

'to be sated' (with drink), may be the cognate of *r'e* in the Ugaritic text GORDON *UH* 'nt I, 12-13,

bk rb.'ẓm.r'e
dn.mt.šmm

which we should render,

'A large goblet of mighty draught,
A jar of the folk of heaven'.

In Ecclesiastes vi, 10 DAHOOD [1]) proposes to read for the Massoretic text מַה־שֶּׁהָיָה כְּבָר נִקְרָא שְׁמוֹ וְנוֹדַע אַשְׁרֵהוּ. The verse, it is true, might render good sense as it stands, but DAHOOD is probably right in emending the last part of the text to אַשְׁרֵהוּ. This he does on the basis of the Ugaritic *'aṯryt*, 'destiny', 'fate', e.g. GORDON *UH* 2 Aqht VI, 35-36:

mt 'uḫryt mh yqḥ	'As for man what does he get as his latter end?
mh yqḥ mt 'aṯryt	What does a mortal get as his destiny?' [2])

In this passage in Ecclesiastes, incidentally, the phrase נִקְרָא שְׁמוֹ is suggestive of the passage in the Ras Shamra text GORDON *UH* 68 where the divine craftsman fashions two maces for Baal in his conflict with Sea. He declares their names (*yp'r šmt*) 'Expeller' and 'Driver'. From this passage it is clear that the names had reference to the purpose of the objects; it was a declaration of the destiny (Akkadian *šimtu*). In Ecclesiastes vi, 10, then, the phrase נוֹדַע אַשְׁרֵהוּ, 'its destiny is known', is a fitting parallel to נִקְרָא שְׁמוֹ, 'its name is declared'.

In Ecclesiastes vii, 12: כִּי בְּצֵל הַחָכְמָה בְּצֵל הַכָּסֶף DAHOOD [3]) is, in our opinion, right in seeing a word-play in צֵל, which means in the first case 'protection' and in the second instance 'glitter'. The phrase *ẓl ksp*, 'the glitter of silver', is found in the Ugaritic text GORDON *UH* 51, II, 27. In Ecclesiastes vii, 12 we follow the Greek version of Symmachos, the Syriac version, Jerome, and the Vulgate in reading: כִּי כְּצֵל הַחָכְמָה כְּצֵל הַכָּסֶף 'For the protection of wisdom is as the glitter of silver', meaning, we think, that wisdom gives that

[1]) DAHOOD, *op. cit.*, p. 40. (MT מַה־שֶּׁהָיָה כְּבָר נִקְרָא שְׁמוֹ וְנוֹדָע אֲשֶׁר־הוּא).
[2]) *v. supra*, p. 113, n. 4.
[3]) DAHOOD, *op. cit.*, pp. 41-42.

security which is also the result of wealth or perhaps of bribery. [1])

Another passage which has given rise to much speculation is Proverbs xxvi, 23:

כֶּסֶף סִיגִים מְצֻפֶּה עַל־חָרֶשׂ שְׂפָתַיִם דֹּולְקִים וְלֶב־רָע

The LXX λεῖα for דֹּולְקִים indicates that חוֹלְקוֹת, 'smooth' was read, and this must be preferred. It is suggested that סיגים, 'dross' was a gloss, and it must be admitted that, whereas סיגי כסף, 'dross of silver', would be intelligible, כסף סיגים would not. H. L. GINSBERG, however, has made the brilliant suggestion [2]) that the text should be read: כְּסַפְסַג מְצֻפֶּה עַל־חָרֶשׂ שְׂפָתַיִם חוֹלְקוֹת וְלֶב־רָע

'As glaze overlaid on a potsherd
Are smooth lips and an evil heart'.

In the word ספסג GINSBERG sees the Hittite *zapzaga*, which is actually attested in the Ras Shamra text GORDON *UH* 2 Aqht VI, 36-37, where the hero refers to grey hairs or the baldness of age:

spsg ysk lr'eš	'Glaze will be poured out on my head,
ḥrṣ lzr qdqdy	Even plaster upon my pate.' [3])

From our citation of the Ugaritic texts in cc. II and III the reader will doubtless have noticed many cases where the Hebrews appropriated the imagery of the Canaanite literature. Just as the theme of the conflict of the god Baal and the unruly waters was appropriated and adapted by the Hebrews, so Jahweh, particularly in those passages dealing with his triumph over the powers of Chaos, is invested with the features of the Canaanite Baal or Hadad, the deity manifest in rain, thunder, lightning, and the clouds of winter.

As Baal in the Ras Shamra texts, [4]) Jahweh makes the clouds his chariot. [5]) Jahweh like Baal 'utters his voice' [6]) in thunder and is manifest in the rainstorm. [7]) In Psalm xxix the Hadad-features of the

---

[1]) An alternative reading is that of DAHOOD, כִּי בְּצֵל הַחָכְמָה צֵל הַכָּסֶף taking ב as *beth essentiae*. The sense he proposes is that wealth, implying leisure, safeguards wisdom.

[2]) GINSBERG, *BASOR* 98, 1945, pp. 20-21, n. 55.

[3]) For philological notes *v. supra*, p. 113, 5, n. 6.

[4]) GORDON *UH* 51, III, 11, 18; V, 122; 67, II, 7; 68, 8, 29; 76, I, 7; III, 22, 37; 1 Aqht 43-44.

[5]) Psalm xviii, 11; lxviii, 5, 34; civ, 3; Deuteronomy xxxiii, 26.

[6]) יִתֵּן קוֹלוֹ, *ytn ql*.

[7]) GORDON *UH* 51, V, 70-71; Psalms xviii, 14-15; xxix, 3, 4, 5, 7, 8, 9; xlvi, 7; lxxvii 19; xcvii, 4; civ, 7; cxxxv, 7; cxliv, 6.

theophany of Jahweh are particularly in evidence, and it is now generally recognized that this is the Hebrew adaptation of a Canaanite ('Phoenician') hymn. [1]) As Baal in the Ugaritic text GORDON *UH* 137, Jahweh is pre-eminent in the 'assembly of gods', [2]) and his effectiveness is contrasted with their inefficiency. [3]) The triumph of Cosmos over Chaos, both in the case of Baal and that of Jahweh, is signalized by the assumption of kingship which is declared to be eternal. [4]) In such passages in the Old Testament, then, we are not free to consider the Sovereignty of God and his Judgement or related themes as if they were exclusively Hebrew insights. The Ras Shamra evidence compels us to study this matter in the wider context of the living Near East. As a result we shall find that the theme of the Kingship of God was to mean much more to the Hebrews than in the nature-cult of Canaan. Yet it is the recovery of the Canaanite prototype which enables us to recognize the main features of the theme throughout its various applications in the history of the Hebrews and to appreciate what in it is distinctively Hebrew.

A further echo of the Canaanite mythology in Hebrew literature is found in Psalm xlviii, 3 where Mount Zion is spoken of as יַרְכְּתֵי צָפוֹן 'the extremity (or 'height') of Saphon'. This seemed a strange description of Mount Zion in the South of Palestine as long as צפון was known in Hebrew only as signifying the 'North'. With the discovery of the Ras Shamra texts, however, came the discovery of a Canaanite 'Olympus', *ṣpn*, specifically the seat of Baal, the god who triumphed over the powers of Chaos and ruled as King in an ordered world. Zion, then, the seat of Jahweh, the sovereign power of Providence (קרית מלך רב), was a Palestinian *ṣpn*. The retention of the Canaanite place-name in remote Jerusalem indicates how firmly rooted was this myth, and probably also its ritual, in the life of Palestine and how indispensable it was deemed by the Hebrews in their settlement to the new life of the peasant.

Besides the application of specific features of the Canaanite Baal to Jahweh in the most important text which we have just cited, there are more sporadic uses of Canaanite imagery in the Old Testament.

---

[1]) T. H. GASTER, '*Psalm* 29', *JQR* XXXVII, 1946, pp. 54-67.
[2]) Psalms lxxxii, 1; lxxxix, 8.
[3]) Psalm lxxxii, 5-7.
[4]) GORDON *UH* 68; 10; Psalms x, 16; xxix, 10; xlv, 7; xciii, 2; cxlv, 13; cxlvi, 10 a.

Apart from the fall of the bright Venus-star, who proved an inadequate substitute for Baal, which is reflected in Isaiah xiv, 12 ff. in the taunt-song for the King of Babylon, [1]) and the victory of God over Leviathan, or the primaeval serpent (Isaiah xxvii, 1; Job xxvi, 12-13), the figure of Sheol opening wide its throat (Isaiah v, 14; Habakkuk ii, 5) seems definitely suggested by the passage in the myth of the conflict between Baal and Mt. [2])

The much-debated 'Immanuel' text which declares that the young child will eat butter and honey in his infancy (Isaiah vii, 15) seems to us to signify a reversion to desert conditions. [3]) This might refer to the anticipated devastation of Judah by Pekah and Rezin which would precede a better era when the young child—possibly the crown-prince—would grow to maturity. On the other hand this may be a case of the theme already known in saga of a period spent in the 'desert' in preparation for a special mission, as in the case of

---

[1]) So also Albright (*CBQ* VII, 1945), who, however, regards the Fall of הֵילֵל בֶּן שָׁחַר as an allusion to the fall of Aṯtar after the appearance of Baal, an episode from a myth now lost in the Ras Shamra texts. P. Grelot ('Isaie XIV 12-15 et son arrière-plan mythologique', *RHR* CXLIX, 1956, p. 18-48) endeavours to find support in the Ras Shamra texts in all passages mentioning Aṯtar for the myth of a presumptuous god Aṯtar, who like Phaeton of Greek mythology, fell through his presumption. It is doubtful if the Ras Shamra texts support such a view. We prefer to limit the reference in Isaiah xiv, 12 ff to this one incident, taking it as a case of literary borrowing and leaving the question of a Canaanite myth on the theme of presumption and retribution open. We should emphasize that the place on the vacant throne of Baal was not of Aṯtar's seeking. There was no question of the Titan theme of rebellion against El. A. Caquot ('Le dieu 'Aṯtar et les textes de Ras Shamra', *Syria* XXXV, 1958, pp. 44-59) would see here a reflection of the myth of fallen angels in Genesis vi, Psalm lxxxii, 7, and Ezekiel xxviii. In view of the dual character of the Venus star the reference in Genesis vi and Psalm lxxxii to a plurality of fallen angels may reflect the fall of Aṯtar in Gordon *UH* 49, especially if, as we suggest, the Hebrew tradition of the origin of these fallen ones from the union of gods and the daughters of men (Genesis vi) originated in the Ugaritic myth of the birth of *Šḥr* and *Šlm* (Dawn and Evening) from such a union.

[2]) Habakkuk ii, 5, אֲשֶׁר הִרְחִיב כִּשְׁאוֹל נַפְשׁוֹ וְהוּא כַמָּוֶת וְלֹא יִשְׂבָּע cf. Gordon *UH* 67, I, 18-22. For text, translation, and philological notes *v. supra*, p. 56.

[3]) It is suggested that, far from being a threat of privation (Gesenius, Ewald, Delitzsch, Dillmann, Duhm, Marti, Skinner, Cheyne, Peake), this denotes plenty, 'butter and honey' being the products of the promised land (G. B. Gray, *ICC*, *Isaiah* i-xxix, 1928, pp. 124, 129-30) after Grotius. We agree with Mowinckel (*Han som Kommer*, 1951, p. 80), who admits Gressmann's claim that this was the food of gods in mythology, but follows Budde in regarding it as nomadic fare. Mowinckel, citing A. Jaussen (*Coutumes des Arabes au Pays de Moab*, 1908, p. 17, n. 1) for the use of such food for a foster-child, sees in it a reference to the child in Isaiah as exceptional.

Moses, David, and Elijah. This motif is found also in the Ras Shamra texts GORDON *UH* 52, where the twin-gods Šḥr and Šlm spend their early years in the desert, [1]) and in GORDON *UH* 75, where the 'Voracious Devourers', who are to lure Baal to his doom, are born. [2])

The gargantuan appetite of Šḥr and Šlm is described in GORDON *UH* 52, 61-64, [3]) 'one lip to earth, the other to heaven', which we agree with H. RINGGREN, [4]) is probably adapted by the psalmist in Psalm lxxiii, 9:

שַׁתּוּ בַשָּׁמַיִם פִּיהֶם וּלְשׁוֹנָם תִּהֲלַךְ בָּאָרֶץ

It will have been noticed that Canaanite literature as attested at Ras Shamra consists mostly of poetry, prose being attested only in certain personal letters, military dispatches, and legal deeds, which by their nature are curt and to the point and not at all literary. The fact that such specimens of prose are limited by the formal cuneiform and by the comparatively exiguous dimensions of the clay tablets as well as by the nature of their contents makes it difficult to form an adequate impression of Canaanite prose. Doubtless if papyrus records, which we know to have been kept at Byblos at least as early as c. 1100, [5]) had survived we should have had an example of fluent Canaanite prose as vivid and expressive as Hebrew historical narrative, if lacking that maturity and vision which stamp this genre of Hebrew literature as unique in antiquity until the time of Thucydides. Canaanite poetry, however, is one of the major discoveries of archaeology in our time, and owing to its formal affinities especially with the older classical Hebrew poetry, which, from our citations from the Ras

---

1) GORDON *UH* 52, 65-68,

ybn ʾašld	'O sons whom I beget,
šʾu ʿdb tk mdbr qdš	Take tackle to the holy desert,
ṯm tgrgr lʾabnm wlʿṣm	There ye shall go around among stones and trees.
šbʿ šnt tmt	Seven whole years,
ṯmn nqpt ʿd	Yea an eighth anniversary moreover.'
ʾelm nʿmm ttlkn šd	The gracious gods go into the open country,
tṣdn pʾat mdbr	They range the desert marches.

2) GORDON *UH* 75, I, 19-23,

wẓʾe bʾaln tkm	'And stoop, couch in pain,
btk mdbr ʾel	In the midst of the awful desert.
šʾey kry ʾamt	Bear my burden, O Maid.'

For further citation from this text and philological notes *v. supra*, pp. 103, 104.

3) For text and translation *v. supra*, p. 103.

4) H. RINGGREN, 'Einige Bemerkungen zum lxxiii Psalm', *VT* III, 1953, pp. 267-8.

5) In the account of Wenamon at Byblos, *Golenischeff Papyrus* II, 9, translation by J. A. WILSON, *ANET*, p. 27. The reference is to business ledgers.

Shamra texts, will already have impressed the reader, invites closer analysis. Since Hebrew poetry was largely an adaptation of Canaanite prototypes, literary conventions, more strongly emphasized in the earlier Canaanite poems, are more easily recognized in Hebrew poetry in the light of Canaanite poetry than they would be if Hebrew poetry were studied in isolation.

The Ras Shamra poems show no regular strophic arrangement. The text runs straight on in the manner of the Greek epic. This continuity, however, tends to be broken by the alternation of direct speech and narrative, the intention of strophic arrangement, albeit irregular, being suggested by the close verbal repetition. The text may be punctuated by a break in the sequence of parallel couplets, which is the regular arrangement of the text. Here a tricolon may be introduced, where the parallelism of word and phrase may be used with a climactic effect. By such an arrangement and by the use of the graphic present or the simple past tense (preterite) the dramatic effect of the texts is achieved and sustained. This is particularly well exemplified in that part of the Baal-myth describing the conflict of Baal and the Waters.

This fragment opens with an unequivocal statement emphasizing the coming conflict and the cause at issue, the right to rule: [1])

wyʿn kṯr wḫss	Then up spake the Skilful and Percipient One.
lrgmt lk lẓbl bʿl	'Have I not told thee, O Prince Baal,
ṯnt lrkb ʿrpt	Have I not repeated, O thou who mountest the Clouds?
ht ʾebk bʿlm	Behold, thine enemy, O Baal,
ht ʾebk tmḫṣ	Behold, thine enemy thou shalt smite:
ht tṣmt ṣrtk	Behold, thou shalt subdue thine adversaries.
tqḥ mlk ʿlmk	Thou shalt take thine eternal kingdom,
drkt dt drdrk	Thy sovereignty everlasting.'

This might be regarded as the end of the first strophe, which is marked by a tricolon with climactic parallelism before the final couplet, which clearly states the theme of the whole text.

The next strophe, which for convenience we may call Strophe 2, describes the preparation of a weapon for Baal and the declaration of its name and purpose:

kṯr ṣmdm ynḥt	The Skilful One hews out a double mace,
wypʿr šmthm	And proclaims its name.

---

[1]) There is a lacuna in the text before this passage, so that here our analysis of the structure of the text must be provisional.

šmk ʾat ygrš	'Thy name is Driver;
ygrš grš ym	Driver, drive Sea,
grš ym lksʾeh	Drive Sea from his throne,
nhr lkḥṯ drkth	Even River from the seat of his sovereignty.
trtqṣ bd bʿl	Thou shalt soar and swoop in the hand of Baal,
km nšr bʾuṣbʿth	Even as an eagle in his fingers.
hlm ktp zbl ym	Strike the shoulders of Prince Sea,
bn ydm ṯpṭ nhr	Even the breast of River the Ruler.'

Strophe 3, resuming in identical language, describes the effect of the weapon in the actual conflict, adding, however, that it failed in its purpose. This first failure is a literary convention to increase the dramatic tension:

yrtqṣ ṣmd bd bʿl	Then soars and swoops the mace in the hand of Baal,
km nšr bʾuṣbʿth	Even as an eagle in his fingers.
ylm ktp zbl ym	It smites the shoulders of Prince Sea,
bn ydm ṯpṭ nhr	Even the breast of River the Ruler.
ʿz ym lymk	Sea is strong; he does not subside;
ltnġṣn pnth	His strength is not impaired;
lydlp tmnh	His dexterity fails not.

Strophe 4 describes in the same language as Strophe 2, with slight variation, the preparation of another weapon for Baal:

kṯr ṣmdm ynḥt	The Skilful One hews out a double mace
wypʿr šmthm	And proclaims its name.
šmk ʾat ʾaymr	'Thy name is Expeller.
ʾaymr mr ym	Expeller, expel Sea,
mr ym lksʾeh	Expel Sea from his throne,
nhr lkḥṯ drkth	Even River from the seat of his sovereignty.
trtqṣ bd bʿl	Thou shalt soar and swoop in the hand of Baal,
km nšr bʾuṣbʿth	Even as an eagle in his fingers.
hlm qdqd zbl ym	Smite the pate of Prince Sea,
bn ʿnm ṯpṭ nhr	Between the eyes of River the Ruler,
yprsḥ ym wyql lʾarṣ	That Sea may collapse and fall to the ground.'

In this case an odd line of four instead of the regular three beats marks the end of the strophe and, adding a further imprecation, increases the dramatic tension, and prepares the hearers for the final result.

Strophe 5 in identical language describes the effect of the weapon, which this time succeeded in its purpose:

wyrtqṣ ṣmd bd bʿl	Then soars and swoops the mace in the hand of Baal,
km nšr bʾuṣbʿth	Even as an eagle in his fingers.
ylm qdqd zbl ym	It smites the head of Prince Sea,
bn ʿnm ṯpṭ nhr	Between the eyes of River the Ruler.

yprsḥ ym yql lʾarṣ	Sea collapses and falls to the ground;
tnġṣn pnth	His strength is impaired;
wydlp tmnh	His dexterity fails.

The rest of the text describes Baal's treatment of the defeated enemy. The text is unfortunately fragmentary, but it seems unlikely that there was such careful strophic arrangement here, if indeed there was such arrangement at all. The dramatic climax obviously comes with the last passage we have cited, and probably the strophic arrangement ends there in order not to impair the dramatic effect.

Even in this text, however, taken as a whole, where there is a formal regularity rather exceptional in the Ras Shamra texts, the quasi-strophic arrangement relates more to sense than to form. There is a decided crescendo effect, and it may be said that the various strophes correspond to scenes or acts in a drama. Here and throughout the Ras Shamra myths and legends we find that where direct speech precedes narrative action a transition from one scene to another is usually indicated, a convention which L. Rost has noticed in the dramatic narrative prose of Israel. [1]) This use of direct speech to close one scene or act and introduce another may be practised on a great scale, as in the first tablet of the Krt text, where the whole tablet from the 21st couplet is divided between El's revelation to Krt of the course and outcome of his wooing and an almost verbatim account of that transaction.

As well as punctuating the action, direct speech here as in Hebrew narrative prose lends life to the text, and increases the impression of drama, an impression which, as we have noted, is heightened in the Ras Shamra texts by the use of the imperfect. So the general question of the building of a 'house' for Baal is the subject of overture and debate with much verbal repetition *in extenso* between Anat, Aṯerat, and El, and, in details, between Baal and the divine craftsmen, the Skilful and Percipient One: [2])

wyʿn.ʾalʾey(n bʿl)	Then up spake Baal the Mighty,
( )	( ),
ḫš̌.bhtm.tbn( )	'Hasten, houses [3]) shalt thou build,
ḫš̌.trmmn.hk(lm)	Hasten, thou shalt raise up palaces
btk.ṣrrt.ṣpn	In the midst of the crags of Saphon,
ʾalp.šd ʾaḫd bt	A house comprising a thousand fields,
rbt.kmn.hkl	A palace a thousand tracts'.

---

1) L. Rost, *Die Überlieferung von der Thronnachfolge Davids* (BWANT III, 6), 1926.
2) Gordon *UH* 51, V, 111... 115-VI, 9.
3) The plural may indicate the palace-complex of many buildings.

wyʿn.kṯr.wḫss	Then up spake the Skilful and Percipient One,
šmʿ.lʾalʾeyn bʿl	'Hear, O Baal the Mighty,
bn.lrkb.ʿrpt	Understand, O Thou who mountest the Clouds,
bl.ʾašt.ʾurbt.bbh(tm)	I shall surely put a shutter in the house,
ḥln.bqrb.hklm	A window in the midst of the palace'.
wyʿn.ʾalʾeyn bʿl	And Baal the Mighty answered,
ʾal.tšt.ʾurbt.b(bhtm)	'Put not a shutter in the house,
(ḥl)n.bqrb.hk(lm)	A window in the midst of the palace'.
wyʿn.kṯ(r wḫs)s	And the Skilful and Percipient One answered,
tṯb.bʿl.l(hwty)	'Thou shalt revert to my proposal, Baal',
ṯn.rgm k(ṯr w)ḫss	The Skilful and Percipient One again said,
šmʿ.mʿ.ʾalʾe)yn bʿl	'Hear, I pray, Baal the Mighty,
bl.ʾašt.ʾur(bt).bbhtm	Nay, but I will put a shutter in the house,
ḥln.bqrb(hk)lm	A window in the midst of the palace'.
wʿn.ʾalʾe(yn) bʿl	And Baal the Mighty answered:
ʾal.tšt ʾu(rb)t.bbhtm	'Put not a shutter in the house,
ḥln.bq(rb h)klm	A window in the midst of the palace'.

Needless to say the roof-shutter is installed in anticipation of the culminating act in the ritual reflected in the building of the house of Baal, the opening of the roof-shutter as an act of imitative magic: [1])

yptḥ.ḥln.bbhtm	He opens a window in the house,
ʾurbt.bqrb.hklm	A shutter in the midst of the palace.
ptḥ.bʿl.bdqt.ʿrpt	"Open, O Baal, the clouds with rain".

Canaanite poetry, like Hebrew, did not use end-rhyme. Instead short phrases, usually simple sentences, were grouped together, generally in couplets, but occasionally in tricola or even larger units. Each colon consisted usually of three stressed syllables, the strong emphasis on which discounted an irregular number of unaccented syllables. The cola were parallel to each other in general sense, and usually also in language, the subjects and objects of the cola being synonyms, and the same predicate, usually expressed in the first colon, serving also for the second. The second colon of a couplet or bicolon is thus generally the echo of the first, as in Hebrew poetry. So strongly was this a feature of early literature among the Canaanites, as in Israel, that it influenced even prose in the case of both, as may be observed, especially in direct speech in the Old Testament and in the letters from the Canaanite rulers in the Amarna Tablets. This gives a somewhat stilted effect to the literary texts of Ras Shamra, which, however, is a providential fault, since in the case of a new dialect the meaning of many unknown words is suggested by their

---

[1]) Gordon *UH* 51, VII, 25-28

parallels. The monotony which one might expect in this rather rigid parallelism is considerably relieved by the alternation of dialogue and narrative in the texts, by the swift action, and by vivid dramatization. In addition there are sundry variations in the parallelism, which we now proceed to illustrate.

The simplest form of parallelism, and the most common in Canaanite poetry, to judge from the Ras Shamra texts and passages in the Amarna Tablets where the correspondence lapses into poetry, is the arrangement in couplets with synonymous parallelism:

ks.yʾeḫd(ʾel.by)d	(El)takes a cup in his hand,
krpn.bm (ymn.)	A flagon in (his right hand)
	(GORDON *UH* 128, II, 16-18)
tšt ʾešt.bbhtm	Fire is set in the house,
nblʾat.bhklm	Flame in the palace.
	(GORDON *UH* 51, VI, 22-23)

In the couplet, however, the object or some other element in the second colon may be not a synonym but a complement to its parallel member in the first colon

h(lk l)bnn.wʿṣh	They went to Lebanon and its trees,
šryn.mḥmd.ʾarzh	To Širyon, even its choicest cedars.
	(GORDON *UH* 51, VI, 20-21)
tšty.krp(nm y)n	They drink wine by flagons,
(bks ḫrṣ dm ʿṣm)	The blood of trees in cups of gold
	(GORDON *UH* 51, VI, 58-59).

In the couplet again two corresponding members in each colon may complement each other by antithesis:

tmḫṣ.lʾem.ḫp ym	She smites the princes by the seashore [1])
tṣmt.ʾadm.ṣʾat.špš	She annihilates the folk in the direction of the sunrise
tḥth.kkdrt.rʾe(š)	Under her are heads like balls,
ʿlh.kʾerbym kp	Above her (fly) hands like locusts
	(GORDON *UH* ʿnt II, 7-10)

The parallelism may be chiastic, that is to say, the corresponding synonyms do not occupy the same position in their respective cola as

a   b
a^1 b^1

but as:

a   b
b^1 a^1:

---

[1]) i.e. the West.

ht ʾebk tmḫṣ	Behold thine enemy shalt thou smite,
ht tṣmt ṣrtk	Behold thou shalt subdue thine adversaries,
	(GORDON *UH* 68, 9)

Another variation in parallelism is the suspension of a certain essential member. This may be the object, as in the curse of Krt upon his presumptuous son:

yṯbr ḥrn.ybn	May Horon break, my son,
yṯbr.ḥrn rʾešk	May Horon break thy head.
	(GORDON *UH* 127, 54-56).

The member in suspension may be the verb:

ht.ʾebk bʿlm	Behold, thine enemy, O Baal,
ht ʾebk tmḫṣ	Behold, thine enemy shalt thou smite,

In the last case the suspension of the verb is a variation from the usual convention, where the verb is expressed in the first colon of a couplet, and understood, but not expressed, in the second:

yṯb lksʾe mlk	He took his seat on the royal throne
lnḫt.lkḥṯ.drkth	On the dais, the tribunal of his government.
	(GORDON *UH* 127, 23-24)

Both these instances of the suspension of a member introduce us to a further variation in parallelism. The sense may be extended beyond the simple couplet, the second colon being amplified by a third colon, which forms a couplet with it, something further always being added to the sense. This may be termed cumulative or climactic parallelism, as in the following instance, where the first additions are marked by italics and the second by heavy type in the translation:

yṯbr ḥrn.ybn	May Horon break, O son,
yṯbr.ḥrn.rʾešk	May Horon break *thy head,*
ʿṯtrt.šm.bʿl qdqdk	**Aṯtarat the Name of Baal** *thy pate*

One of the best instances of this variety of parallelism is from the much-quoted myth of the conflict of Baal and the Waters:

ht ʾebk bʿlm	Behold, thine enemy, O Baal,
ht ʾebk tmḫṣ	Behold, thine enemy *thou shalt smite,*
ht tṣmt ṣrtk	*Behold, thou shalt subdue* **thine adversaries.**

In both these instances another couplet amplifying the sense of the preceding lines closes the passage, giving it thus in form and content the appearance of a self-contained strophe. Krt's curse on his son, for instance, ends with the couplet, which employs chiastic parallelism:

tqln . bgbl šntk	Mayest thou fall in the exuberance of thy years,
bḫpnk . wtʿn	Even in the fulness of thy strength and be troubled.

(GORDON *UH* 127, 57-58) [1])

The passage from the Baal-myth is rounded out by a couplet with simple parallelism, which, amplifying the assurance of Baal's victory, declares:

tqḥ mlk ʿlmk	Thou shalt take thine eternal kingdom,
drkt dt drdrk	Thy sovereignty everlasting.

With this statement, which has the ring of finality, the proclamation of the divine craftsman, which conveys the theme of the text, is complete, and the next scene opens with the preparations of the weapons for the conflict.

This convention of cumulative parallelism in a tricolon clinched by a final couplet is employed in Psalm xcii, 10-11:

כִּי הִנֵּה אֹיְבֶיךָ יהוה
כִּי־הִנֵּה אֹיְבֶיךָ יֹאבֵדוּ
יִתְפָּרְדוּ כָּל־פֹּעֲלֵי אָוֶן

וַתָּרֶם כִּרְאֵים קַרְנִי
בַּלֹּתִי בְּשֶׁמֶן רַעֲנָן

Lo, indeed, thine enemies, O Yahweh,
Lo, indeed, thine enemies shall perish,
All workers of iniquity shall be scattered.

But my horn shall be exalted like (that of) the wild ox,
I have been drenched with fresh oil.

Similar instances of cumulative parallelism in the tricolon, but without the clinching couplet are Psalm xciii, 3:

נָשְׂאוּ נְהָרוֹת יהוה
נָשְׂאוּ נְהָרוֹת קוֹלָם
יִשְׂאוּ נְהָרוֹת דָּכְיָם

The rivers lifted up, O Lord,
The rivers lifted up their voice,
The rivers lift up their crashing roar,

and Psalm xciii, 4:

מִקֹּלוֹת מַיִם רַבִּים
אַדִּירִים מִמִּשְׁבְּרֵי (מִשְׁבְּרֵי MT) יָם
אַדִּיר(ים) בַּמָּרוֹם יהוה

---

[1]) For philological notes in support of our translation of this difficult passage see the writer's *The Krt Text in the Literature of Ras Shamra*, 2nd ed., 1964, p. 49.

Than the sounds of many waters,
More majestic than the breakers of the sea,
Majestic on high is Yahweh.

From Amos'

'For three transgessions of Damascus etc.,
Yea for four...'

we are familiar with what we might call numerical parallelism. The Canaanites too introduced passages by climactic numbers and then gave instances to correspond, as in the Baal-myth:

bm.ṯn.dbḥm.šnʾa.bʿl	There are two sacrifices which Baal detests,
ṯlṯ rkb.ʿrpt	Three (detested by) Him who Mounteth the Clouds,
dbḥ bṯt	A sacrifice of shame,
wdbḥ dnt	And a sacrifice of meanness [1]
wdbḥ.tdmm ʾamht	And a sacrifice of the lewdness [2] of handmaidens.

This recalls the passage in Psalm lxii, 12-13:

אַחַת דִּבֶּר אֱלֹהִים
שְׁתַּיִם־זוּ שָׁמָעְתִּי
כִּי עֹז לֵאלֹהִים
וְלַאֲדֹנָי חָסֶד (וּלְךָ אֲדֹנָי חָסֶד MT)
כִּי־אַתָּה תְשַׁלֵּם
לְאִישׁ כְּמַעֲשֵׂהוּ

One thing God has said,
Yea two are the things I have heard
That might pertains to God,
And loyal dealing to my Lord,
That thou dost pay unto a man
Full recompense for his works.

A development of this convention is found in the Wisdom literature in the Old Testament, where it may have been used in riddles as an engaging way of expounding empiric moral philosophy. Particularly good instances occur in the last section of the Book of Proverbs, e.g. Proverbs xxx, 18-19: [3]

שְׁלֹשָׁה הֵמָּה נִפְלְאוּ מִמֶּנִּי
וְאַרְבָּעָ(ה) לֹא יְדַעְתִּים

---

[1] cf. Arabic دنا, 'to be vile', after MONTGOMERY.

[2] cf. Hebrew זִמָּה, 'lewdness', Arabic ذَمَّ (IV), 'to commit a blameworthy act', after DRIVER (*op. cit.*, p. 153 n,).

[3] Similar instances of numerical climax are Proverbs xxx, 15-16, 21-23, 29-31.

דֶּרֶךְ הַנֶּשֶׁר בַּשָּׁמַיִם
דֶּרֶךְ נָחָשׁ עֲלֵי־צוּר
דֶּרֶךְ אֳנִיָּה בְלֶב־יָם
וְדֶרֶךְ גֶּבֶר בְּעַלְמָה

The numbers here of course are not to be taken literally as if these exhausted the things which Baal detested or those which God had revealed. In those cases that is accepted by all, yet such numbers have been interpreted literally in the passage in the Krt text where the journey of Krt's bridal retinue to the house of the bride is described as occupying seven days. This is simply a literary device to tide over an indefinite period, as in the case of the furnishing of the house of Baal:

hn ym . wṯn	Lo a day, two days
tʾekl ʾešt . bbhtm	Fire consumed in the house,
nblʾat bhklm	Flame in the palace,
ṯlṯ . rbʿ ym	A third, a fourth day
tʾekl(ʾe)št . bbhtm	Fire consumed in the house,
nblʾa(t) bhklm	Flame in the palace,
ḫmš . ṯ(d)ṯ . ym	A fifth, a sixth day
tʾekl ʾešt(b)bhtm	Fire consumed in the house,
nblʾat b(qrb hk)lm	Flame in the midst of the palace,
mk bšb(ʿ) y(mm)	Then on the seventh day
td . ʾešt bbhtm	Fire was removed from the house,
n(b)lʾat . bhklm	Flame from the palace;
sb . ksp . lrqm	Silver had turned into plates, [1])
ḫrṣ nsb . llbnt	Gold had turned into bricks . . .
	(Gordon *UH* 51, VI, 24-35)

Similarly in a rite associated with the conception of the prince Aqht Dnʾel entertains 'the Skilful Ladies' in the palace for this conventional period. The interval before the final conflict of Baal and Mot is similarly given as 'seven years', which in this case, however, may have a ritual significance, referring, as we have already suggested, to a seven-year cycle of agriculture such as was prescribed for Israel culminating in the Sabbatical year.

Simile is used in Canaanite poetry, a variation of the simple simile, developed probably under the exigency of parallelism, being what we might call cumulative simile. In the mourning of Krt, for instance,

tntkn . ʾudmʿth	His tears are poured out

[1]) Driver (*op. cit.* p. 155, n.) cites Akkadian *raqqu*, 'a thin plate of metal', cf. Arabic رقّ 'a sheet (of paper)'.

km.ṯqlm.ʾarṣh	As shekels to the ground,
kmḫmšt.mṭth	Even as pieces-of-five on his bed.

(GORDON *UH* krt, 28-30)

The parallel similes, on the other hand, may be used first, leading up with cumulative effect, to the main statement, as in the Baal-myth:

klb.ʾarḫ.lʿglh	As the heart of the cow after her calf,
klb.ṯʾat.lʾemrh	As the heart of the ewe after her lamb,
km.lb.ʿnt.ʾaṯr.bʿl	So the heart of Anat (yearns) after Baal.

(GORDON *UH* 49, II, 6-9)

Parallel similes are used with great effect to introduce a numerical climax in the description of Krt's bridal retinue:

kʾerby tškn.šd	As grass-hoppers which occupy the field,
km.ḥsn.pʾat.mdbr	As locusts the desert marches,
lk.ym.wṯn	Go a day, a second (day),
ṯlṯ.rbʿ ym	A third, a fourth day,
ḫmš.ṯdṯ.ym	A fifth, a sixth day,
mk.špšm bšbʿ	Then with the sun on the seventh day
wtmġy.lʾudm rbt	Thou wilt reach Udm the Great,
wlʾudm.ṯrrt	Yea Udm Abundant in Water.

(GORDON *UH* krt, 103-9)

The final combat between Baal and Mot is similarly described with a series of similes:

ytʿn.kgmrm	They glare at each other like glowing coals;
mt ʿz.bʿl.ʿz	Mot is strong, Baal is strong;
ynghn.krʾumm	They thrust at each other like wild-oxen;
mt.ʿz.bʿl.ʿz	Mot is strong, Baal is strong;
ynṯkn.kbṯnm	They bite like serpents;
mt.ʿz.bʿl.ʿz	Mot is strong, Baal is strong;
ymṣḫn.klsmm	They kick like stallions;
mt.ql.bʿl.ql ʿln	Mot is down, Baal is down on top of him.

(GORDON *UH* 49, VI, 16-22)

Here the series of similes is punctuated by the refrain 'Mot is strong, Baal is strong'. This marks the various stages of the sustained conflict, and anticipates the climax, which is an echo of the phrase, 'Mot is down, Baal is down on top of him'.

In other passages too we note the repetition of a certain word. Now in the great wealth of synonyms attested in these Canaanite texts the fact that the same word is repeated indicates that there was a particular point in such a repetition. It may have the effect of magical incantation, as in the imprecation of Krt:

May Horon break, O my son,
May Horon break thy head.

The stereotyped formula of imprecation is well exemplified in Dan'el's imprecation of localities adjacent to the scene of the murder of his son Aqhat:

qr.m(ym) mlk.yṣm	The King curses the Source of Water:
ylkm.qr.mym	'Out upon thee, O Source of Water,
dʿlk.mḫṣ.ʾaqht.ġẓr	For upon thee lies the guilt of the slaughter of Aqhat the Hero,
ʾamd.gr.bt.ʾel	Perpetually seeking sanctuary,
ʿnt.brḫ.pʿlmh	Away with thee now and for ever,
ʿnt.pdr.dr	Now and for every generation!'
ʿdb.ʾuḫry mṭ.ydh	(So says he), the staff in his hand signifying finality.
ymġy.lmrrt.tġll.bnr	He proceeds to the Myrrh-tree which emits its perfume when burned.
yšʾu.gh.wyṣḥ	He lifts up his voice and cries:
ylk.mrrt.tġll.bnr	'Out upon thee, O Myrrh-tree which emits its perfume when burned,
dʿlk.mḫṣ.ʾaqht.ġẓr	For upon thee lies the guilt of the slaughter of Aqhat of Aqhat the Hero,
šršk.bʾarṣ.ʾal.ypʿ	May thy root never grow big in the ground,
rʾeš.ġly.bd.nsʿk	Thy crown be brought low by the hand that plucks thee up,
ʿnt.brḫ.pʿlmh	Away with thee now and for ever,
ʿnt.pdr.dr	Now and for every generation!'
ʿdb.ʾuḫry.mṭ.ydh	(So says he), the staff in his hand signifying finality.
ymġ.lqrt.ʾablm.ʾablm	He proceeds to the City of Running Waters, Abilum,
qrt.ẓbl.yrḫ	The city of his lordship the Moongod,
yšʾu.gh.wyṣḥ	He lifts up his voice and cries:
ylk.qrt.ʾablm	'Out upon thee, O city Abilum,
dʿlk.mḫṣ.ʾaqht.gẓr	For upon thee lies the guilt of the slaughter of Aqht the Hero,
ʿwr.yštk.bʿl	May Baal make thee blind
lht.wʿlmh	From now and for ever,
ʿnt.pdr.dr	Now and for every generation' [1]
ʿdb.ʾuḫry.mṭ.ydh	(So says he), the staff in his hand signifying finality.

(Gordon 1 Aqht 151-169)

In Israel too this convention was known in such a context, as we may see from the introduction to the 'disabling oracle' in the series in Amos i, 3-ii, 5:

עַל־שְׁלֹשָׁה פִּשְׁעֵי דַמֶּשֶׂק
וְעַל־אַרְבָּעָה לֹא אֲשִׁיבֶנּוּ ...

---

[1]) For philological notes in support of this translation *v. supra*, pp. 122-123.

For three rebellious acts of Damascus,
Yea for four I will not revoke (the judgement) . . .

These oracles of doom as is well known follow a common pattern. After the introductory formula, the sins of the various peoples are stigmatized, and the particular doom of each is prefaced by the common formula with slight variation:

וְשִׁלַּחְתִּי אֵשׁ בְּ . . . .
וְאָכְלָה אַרְמְנוֹת . . . .

And I shall cast fire upon X,
And it shall devour the palaces of Y.

Here as in the passage from the Aqht text the verbal repetition is proper to solemn imprecation.

A similar use of verbal repetition in incantation and also to indicate persistence in ritual is exemplified in Dnʾel's fertility-ritual:

ydn dnʾel.ysb.pʾalth	Dnʾel investigates; he goes round his parched land;
bṣql yph bpʾalt	He sees a plant in the parched land,
bṣql.yph.byġlm	A plant he sees in the scrub.
bṣql.yḥbq.wynšq	He embraces the plant and kisses it.
ʾaḥl.ʾan bṣ(ql)	'Ah me for the plant!
ynpʿ.bpʾalt.bṣql	Would that the plant might flourish in the parched land;
ypʿ.byġl.ʾur	That the herb might flourish in the scrub,
tʾespk.yd.ʾaqht.ġẓr	That the hand of the hero Aqht might gather thee in,
tštk.bqrbm.ʾasm	That it might put thee in the granary'.
ydnh.ysb.ʾaklth	He investigates it; he makes a round of his blasted land;
yph.šblt.bʾaklt	He sees an ear of corn in the blasted land,
šblt.ypʿ.bḥmdrt	An ear of corn growing in the parched land.
šblt.yḥbq.wynšq	He embraces the ear of corn and kisses it.
ʾaḥl ʾan.šblt	'Ah me for the ear of corn!
tpʿ.bʾaklt.šblt	Would that the ear of corn might grow tall in the crop,
tpʿ.( ).ʾur	That the herb might grow tall ( ),
tʾespk.yd.ʾaqht.ġẓr	That the hand of the hero Aqht might gather thee in
tštk.bm.qrbm.ʾasm	And put thee into the storehouse'. [1]

(GORDON *UH* 1 Aqht, 61-74)

The recognition of this literary convention suggests the ritual significance of the description of the funeral offerings for Baal:

tṭbḫ.šbʿm.rʾumm	She slaughters seventy wild-oxen
kgmn.ʾalʾeyn.bʿl	As a funeral due to Baal the Mighty;
tṭbḫ.šbʿm.ʾalpm	She slaughters seventy oxen

[1]) For philological notes and commentary *v. supra*, pp. 118-120.

kgmn.ʾalʾeyn.bʿl	As a funeral due to Baal the Mighty;
tṭbḫ.šbʿm.ṣʾen	She slaughters seventy sheep
kgmn.ʾalʾeyn.bʿl	As a funeral due to Baal the Mighty;
tṭbḫ.šbʿm.ʾaylm	She slaughters deer
kgmn.ʾalʾeyn.bʿl	As a funeral due to Baal the Mighty;
tṭbḫ.šbʿm.yʿlm	She slaughters seventy wild-goats
kgmn.ʾalʾeyn.bʿl	As a funeral due to Baal the Mighty;
tṭbḫ.šbʿm.ḥmrm	She slaughters seventy asses
kgmn.ʾalʾeyn.bʿl	As a funeral due to Baal the Mighty. [1])

(Gordon *UH* 62, 18-29)

The repetition of a word or phrase may also indicate abundance, as in the passage just cited and in the description of Baal's house-warming:

špq ʾelm.krm y (n)	He supplied the gods with wether lambs and the appropriate wine. [2])
špq.ʾelht.ḫprt (yn)	He supplied the goddesses with ewe-lambs [3]) and the appropriate wine;
špq.ʾelm.ʾalpm.y(n)	He supplied the gods with oxen and the appropriate wine;
špq.ʾelht.ʾarḫt (yn)	He supplied the goddesses with cows and the appropriate wine;
špq.ʾelm.kḥṯm.yn	He supplied the gods with chairs and the appropriate wine,
špq.ʾelht.ksʾat)yn)	He supplied the goddesses with seats and the appropriate wine;
špq.ʾelm.rḥbt yn	He supplied the gods with casks of wine as was proper,
špq.ʾelht.dkrt (yn)	He supplied the goddesses with flasks of wine as was proper.

(Gordon *UH* 51, VI, 47-54)

The recognition of these various conventions of Canaanite poetry is of great significance for the interpretation of the text, and often for its relation to its *Sitz im Leben*. In many cases they serve to mark the punctuation, pause, and movement of the drama. At other times they are used for emphasis, to sustain suspense, or to mark progression. At all times they have to be appreciated as literary conventions, so

---

[1]) For philological notes and commentary *v. supra*, pp. 64-65.

[2]) *špq* is the Šafʿel of *wpq*, cf. Arabic وفق, 'to suit', also 'to find something to suit one'.

[3]) One thinks immediately of the Arabic خروف, 'a lamb', such metathesis between Semitic languages not being unknown, cf. Arabic حنش, Hebrew נחש. Driver, however, (*op. cit.*, p. 140) cites the Arabic verb خفر, 'to get the first teeth', from which the word is possibly derived.

that we may not forthwith conclude that a phrase is literal when in such a context it is only figurative, as in the case of numerical climax.

The affinities between Hebrew and Canaanite literature which we have noted throughout, and especially in the present chapter cannot fail to impress anyone familiar with the Old Testament and with an open mind, and since we have noted only the most striking correspondences more will doubtless occur to the reader. This remarkable correspondence is especially close in liturgical Hebrew poetry, notably in the Psalms and passages in the Prophets which reflect the liturgy. This is natural considering the common liturgical origin of much in the Psalter and the Baal-mythology of Ras Shamra, and MOWINCKEL is in our opinion right in supposing that with her settlement in Canaan, and especially after the elaboration of the cult in Solomon's Temple and the political development of the state with diplomatic relations with the contemporary powers in the Near East, Israel adopted and adapted the language and forms of liturgy in general use in the Near East and especially in Canaan. [1])

Canaanite influence in the Psalter has been the subject of several significant studies by PATTON, [2]) O'CALLAGHAN, [3]) and COPPENS, [4]) and, as far as concerns the psalm in Habakkuk iii, by ALBRIGHT, [5]) who emphasizes the influence of form as well as vocabulary in the arrangement of bicola and tricola with the variations of parallelism we have noted in the Canaanite prototypes.

On the basis of such evidence ALBRIGHT has ventured the opinion that such affinities provide a means of dating passages in Hebrew poetry, according as they are a feature of poems before and about the beginning of the Hebrew monarchy and from the end of the monarchy and the post-Exilic period. [6]) This view is developed by F. M. CROSS and D. N. FREEDMAN in studies of the Song of Miriam [7])

---

1) MOWINCKEL, *The Psalms in Israel's Worship* II, 1962, pp. 187-190.

2) J. H. PATTON, *Canaanite Parallels in the Book of Psalms*, 1944.

3) R. T. O'CALLAGHAN, 'Echoes of Canaanite Literature in the Psalms', *VT* IV, 1954, pp. 164-176.

4) J. COPPENS, 'La bénédiction de Jacob', *VT*, Supplement IV, pp. 97-115.

5) ALBRIGHT, 'The Psalm of Habakkuk', *Studies in Old Testament Prophecy*, ed. H. H. ROWLEY, 1950, pp. 1-18.

6) ALBRIGHT, *Archaeology and the Religion of Israel*, 3rd ed., 1953, p. 128.

7) F. M. CROSS and D. N. FREEDMAN, 'The Song of Miriam', *JNES* XIV, 1955, pp. 237-250. We admit the argument for the antiquity of this poem, which is really a test piece, on the basis of the archaic grammatical forms and orthography, which CROSS and FREEDMAN urge. The conceptions of the Kingship of God and

and the Blessing of Moses. [1]) The general influence here of Canaanite literature may be freely admitted, but a comparison with the Canaanite myths shows that the Hebrew poet employed little of the finesse of Canaanite prosody. The comparative rigidity of the arrangement of the cola in bicola and tricola shows none of the careful construction of Canaanite poetry for dramatic effect. On the contrary the staccato effect of the rigid parallelism, which to be sure has an echo in such a passage as that describing the final conflict between Baal and Mot, (Gordon *UH* 49, VI, 16-22), and may be deliberate, reveals the rude native vigour of a hymn to Yahweh militant in the cause of a warrior people. As the vigorous ballad poetry of the Bedouin tribesmen indicates, poetry is not the monopoly of the settled land and sophisticated society. The ruder strains of the tribesmen in fact may well be the origin of the elaborated prosody of Canaan.

Our conclusion therefore is that affinity between the metric system of a Hebrew poem and Canaanite poetry is not in itself an automatic criterion of date. General Canaanite influence in diction, imagery, and form, especially the former, may amount to strong cumulative evidence, but generally the matter of date must really be settled on other evidence. From the instances we have cited of the imagery, diction, and more elaborate metrical arrangements, as in numerical parallelism in Wisdom literature, the influence of the Canaanite prototype was not confined to the earlier period of the Hebrew

---

the establishment of his house are, we agree, thoroughly Canaanite motifs. This seems naturally to refer to the cult of God as King in the New Year festival at the Temple in Jerusalem, and it seems most natural to relate the reference to 'the mount of thine inheritance' to the Temple on Mt. Zion. This, however, might reflect the Canaanite conception of Mt Saphon as the royal seat of Baal. The building of the house also may refer to the theme of the Canaanite Baal-myth, the building of a 'house' confirming the establishment of Baal as King, as Cross and Freedman argue (p. 249) after Albright (*JBL* LXVII, 1948, p. 381 n., *Archaeology of Palestine*, 1949, pp. 232-3). We are prepared to admit that the general theme of the Kingship of God, which had its *Sitz im Leben* in the Autumnal New Year festival, was appropriated by Israel in the two centuries or so of the settlement, but the particular reference to the 'mount of God's inheritance' does suggest a date after the organization of the cult in Jerusalem, which had its own very vivid mythology, *v. supra*, p. 113, n. 11. Actually the date of the Song of Miriam is highly controversial. M. Rozelaar dates it in the 8th or 7th cent. (*VT* II, 1952, pp. 221-228) and R. Tournay associates it stylistically with Zephaniah, Deuteronomy and Psalms xx, xxi, dating it in the 7th c., and associating it with Josiah's Passover (*RB* LXV, 1958, p. 181).

[1]) F. M. Cross and D. N. Freedman, 'The Blessing of Moses', *JBL* LXVII, 1948, pp. 191-210.

settlement in Palestine, but may be characteristic of any age. [1])

The abundance of features in common with Canaanite poetry in post-Exilic Hebrew poetry, as in Ezekiel, Deutero-Isaiah, Job, Proverbs, and Ecclesiastes, which is generally admitted, has been explained by the assumption of a revival of interest in the literature of the ancient Near East including Phoenician literature with its rich imagery and mythological content. It is suggested that the rapprochement between the exiles of Judah and those from North Israel in the Neobabylonian and Persian periods introduced Phoenician elements to Hebrew poetry, which had already pervaded North Israelite literature. It is contended that Phoenician, or Canaanite, features including mythological motifs were now adapted with freedom by Hebrew prophets and psalmists since there was no longer any danger of contamination as in the days when they had had a deeper and more sinister significance when Israel was still in Palestine. This may be generally true, though the assumed antiquarian revival is still no more than an interesting hypothesis. The assumption of Canaanite influence in Israelite poetry, if it cannot be conclusively demonstrated, is at least feasible, especially in view of the Phoenician associations of the House of Omri, when there was a temple of Baal, implying his cult and mythology, in Samaria. [2]) But the influence of the imagery of Canaanite myth was equally strong in Jerusalem,

---

[1]) In such Psalms as xxix, lxvii, lxxvii, xcii-xcvi, for instance, where, as in Psalm xciii, we have noted close affinity of imagery, ideology, and form with the Canaanite Baal-myth, Mowinckel, noting the convention of bicola punctuated by tricola in what according to Albright are archaic hymns, argues that, though Psalm xxix is admittedly an Israelite readaptation of a Canaanite psalm, Psalm lxvii, with its conception of the world-domination of Yahweh, is late, as is Psalm xcii, with its conception of individual retributive justice (vv. 3, 13 ff.), and Psalm xciv, with its wisdom conception of the throne of iniquity which frames mischief against the established law ('"Psalm Criticism between 1900 and 1935" ', *VT* V, 1955, pp. 28 ff.). Mowinckel's conclusions as to the date of such passages are confirmed by the stylistic analysis of R. Tournay along the traditional lines of the older literary criticism, and the linguistic and stylistic affinity which he is able to establish with such datable passages is those in Zephaniah, Jeremiah, and Deuteronomy seems a more reliable criterion of dating than conventions familiar in the Ras Shamra poetry, but generally much less elaborate and meaningful in Hebrew.

[2]) Coppens (*op. cit.*) finds support for this view that Canaanite influence was mediated through North Israel in the view that in the Blessing of Jacob Canaanite features are to be noted only in the abnormally long blessing of Joseph. The imagery on which he builds so much in this uncertain and difficult passage does not convince us, and our own interpetation, with the same proportion of emendation as Coppens finds necessary, is quite different.

especially with the ideology of the Kingship of El in Jerusalem and that of Baal won in conflict with the powers of chaos. Leaving aside the vexed question of the date of the Psalms, which afford the most striking evidence of Canaanite influence in Hebrew poetry, the familiarity of Isaiah of Jersusalem with this theme and its characteristic imagery in the 8th century and the evidence of Nahum ii, 1 (EVV i, 15) (cf. Isaiah lii, 7) of the association of the New Year festival with the Kingship of God make it obvious that the cultic poetry of Canaan was familiar to poets in Israel throughout the monarchic period. To be sure, since they were conscious of the allurement of the Canaanite fertility-cult and its abuses, they used this matter advisedly with restraint, and, as we hope we have shown, selectively. They concentrated on the theme of the Divine triumph over chaos, the Kingship of God, symbolized by the establishment of his 'house' and expressed by the realization of his 'order' or 'government' (מִשְׁפָּט), a theme which, in its historical adaptation, was already appropriated by Israel in the Song of the Sea (Exodus xv) as late as the 7th century by the latest reckoning, and probably much earlier. In post-Exilic Hebrew literature this was still the main theme of Canaanite poetry which the Hebrew poets utilized. The increasing prominence of this theme in post-Exilic poetry and later Jewish apocalyptic may, in our opinion, be better explained by the acute tension of a stateless minority in face of pagan domination and by the intensification of eschatological hopes of the realization of the Kingship of God. The theme in its original Canaanite expression was familiar both long before and after the Exile. The comparative restraint on the subject in the earlier Hebrew literature is no more than the reflection of the difference between confident assurance and fervent hope. [1])

On this whole question of the extent of the influence of Canaan on Hebrew poetry the debate has proceeded mainly on the evidence of diction and imagery, though ALBRIGHT and his school have sought to extend the correspondence, as we have seen, to metric arrangement also. While appreciating the influence of Canaanite literature in respect of metric conventions in Hebrew, we must admit there is nothing extant in the Ras Shamra literature which corresponds to the Psalm as such in its various categories familiar in the Old Testament. Consequently in drawing analogies between the myths

---

[1]) We have studied this theme in earlier and later Hebrew literature in 'The Kingship of God in the Prophets and Psalms', *VT* XI, 1961, pp. 1-29.

of Canaan in narrative and epic style and the short, self-contained liturgic Psalms of Israel we must do so with reserve.

Nor in the Old Testament is there any exact replica of any of the literary types of Canaan extant in the Ras Shamra texts. We have contended that in the Ugaritic myth of the conflict of Baal and the Waters and that of Baal and Mot, for instance, we have functional myths related to ritual proper to seasonal crises. In spite of their essentially functional nature, however, these texts are highly elaborated; they have an aesthetic quality and a definitely literary character and a scope far beyond mere litanies. In the Old Testament the myth of the conflict of Cosmos and Chaos was particularly adapted by the Hebrews and used in its original context, we believe, at the New Year festival with the main features and much of the imagery familiar in the Canaanite myth. [1]) Here the influence of Canaanite literature and thought on that of the Hebrews is at its strongest. In the Psalms and the Prophets, however, though this myth may appear at considerable length, it is but an element in a larger context and is, we emphasize, not simply assimilated by the Hebrews, but adapted in a fashion which well reveals the ethos of Israel.

The Canaanite myths which we have cited in cc. II and III are cast in epic style and the narrative unfolds itself now with the leisurely dignity of epic and now with the restrained vivacity of classical drama. This applies not only to the Baal-myths, but also to the Krt and Aqht texts, both of which show decided features of saga. Here we find certain affinities with the narrative portions of the Old Testament. We do not claim that a Canaanite prototype has been quite reproduced in the patriarchal narratives, but, reading the patriarchal narratives, the traditions of the early monarchy, and prophetic narratives in Kings in the light of the Canaanite evidence, we discern certain features which suggest the influence of the Canaanite epic form, and may even point to original Hebrew sagas concerning the patriarchs, David, and Elijah and Elisha. As these, however, have been much revised and integrated into the Hebrew record of salvation (*Heilsgeschichte*) and the Deuteronomic philosophy of history, the epic or saga features are now merely sporadic, though none the less recognizable. The first point we must emphasize is the dramatic nature of such Old Testament passages as we have noted, which is produced by the employment of dialogue. This use of direct speech

---

[1]) *v. supra*, pp. 33 ff.

is a feature also of the Canaanite literary texts. This direct speech often conveys divine revelation, occasionally in the form of a dream. It may be used to describe a conflict in the mind of the hero, or to indicate his aspirations or intentions, and is well illustrated in the Krt and Aqht texts as also in the case of Abraham, Jacob, Moses, Gideon, Elijah, David, and Solomon. It may well be that we have the trace of an original saga in the revelation to Abraham in Genesis xii, 1-3 which, is in verse:

לֶךְ־לְךָ מֵאַרְצְךָ וּמִמּוֹלַדְתְּךָ וּמִבֵּית אָבִיךָ
אֶל־הָאָרֶץ אֲשֶׁר אַרְאֶךָּ
וְאֶעֶשְׂךָ לְגוֹי גָּדוֹל וַאֲבָרֶכְךָ
וַאֲגַדְּלָה שְׁמֶךָ וֶהְיֵה בְּרָכָה
וַאֲבָרֲכָה מְבָרְכֶיךָ וּמְקַלֶּלְךָ אָאֹר
(וְנִבְרְכוּ בְךָ כֹּל מִשְׁפְּחוֹת הָאֲדָמָה)

The verse-form seems to take us back to a very early stage in the tradition. Folk-oracles such as that to Rebeccah on the birth of Jacob and Esau (Genesis xxv, 23), Isaac's blessing of Jacob (Genesis xxvii, 27-29) and of Esau (Genesis xxvii, 39-40), Jacob's blessing of Ephraim and Manasseh (Genesis xlviii, 15-17), and the oracles of Balaam (Numbers xxiii, 7-10; 18-24; xxiv, 3-9; 15-24) are also in verse. This seems to have been the natural medium for such oracles in all ages, if we may judge from its use by the Hebrew prophets throughout the monarchic period. They may, nevertheless, still be features of primitive patriarchal or tribal sagas in verse after the style of the Krt text of Ugarit.

Certain motifs too are common to Hebrew narratives and the Canaanite myths in epic style. In the latter there are many passages verbally repeated. The course of action is often described in anticipation, and then in almost identical terms the action is described. The same device is used in the narrative of Moses and Aaron before Pharaoh in Exodus vii-xi, marking the various stages in the drama, which is plain when the J narrative is delimited and read without interruption. This expedient is well-known as a mnemonic in oral tradition, and was particularly useful in helping an audience to follow a cult-legend intelligently. Incidentally, the use of the Exodus passage as a cult-legend seems to be suggested by Exodus x, 2 where it is stated that the narrative has been recorded 'that thou mayest tell in the ears of thy son, and of thy son's son, what things I have wrought in Egypt and my signs which I have done among them, and that ye may know that I am the Lord'. Another instance of verbatim repetition in a passage which probably existed originally as a saga is the Elijah narrative in 2 Kings i where Elijah's words to the emissaries of the king to Ekron are repeated, and again in 2 Kings ii where there is a verbatim repetition of his warning to Elisha and the protest of the latter that he will not leave the master.

Conventional rather than actual numbers again indicate the saga. In his journey to the home of his bride, for instance, King Krt and his retinue go

.....a day, a second day,
A third, yea a fourth day,
A fifth, a sixth day,
Then at sunset on the seventh day.....

So Laban pursued Jacob seven days until he overtook him in Gilead (Genesis xxxi, 23), the Nile runs blood for seven days (Exodus vii, 25), the Ark is among the Philistines for seven months (1 Samuel vi, 1), and Elijah after the famous ordeal on Carmel sends his lad seven times to the top of the mountain to look for the rain-cloud (1 Kings xviii, 43-44). In the Ugaritic text King Krt's ill-fated progeny is mentioned in seven categories and eventually he begets seven sons and daughters and an eighth daughter, the latter probably indicating a renewal of his natural virility. David too is the eighth son of Jesse (1 Samuel xvi, 10-11).

In the epic style of the Ras Shamra texts a device employed in order to emphasize some particular point is to make it a matter of dispute. In the building of the 'house of Baal', for instance, the installation of a shutter in the roof in connection with the all-important rite of imitative magic to induce rain is a matter of argument between Baal and the divine craftsman *Kṯr wḪss*. Similarly God's mercy and the extreme depravity of the people of Sodom and Gomorrah are emphasized by the persistent intercession of Abraham (Genesis xviii, 23 ff.). The same emphasis may be made by a process of elimination from a larger number of elements, as in Samuel's choice of David after he had seen and rejected all his brothers. In the Krt text of Ugarit the king rejects

'.....silver and electrum,
Gold in token of her value,
And a perpetual henchman, three horses,
A chariot with yoke-fellows well-matched'.

Then his choice is stated:

> 'Nay but what I have not in my house do thou give,
> Give me the damsel *Ḥry*'.

So in the theophany to Elijah at Horeb (1 Kings xix, 11 ff.):

> 'And behold the Lord passed by and a great and strong wind rent the mountain and shattered the rocks before the Lord, but the Lord was not in the wind; and after the wind there was an earthquake, but the Lord was not in the earthquake. Then after the earthquake there was a fire, but the Lord was not in the fire, and after the fire, Hark! a gentle stillness'.

In narratives where such conventions are employed so freely the reliability of details is liable to be questioned. It is true that in the patriarchal narratives and those of the Exodus and the Hebrew settlement, David's escapades in the deserts of Judah, and the sagas of Elijah and Elisha there are indications that history was transmitted in saga form, each transmission of the oral tradition magnifying and schematizing the facts. At the other extreme there are the later editorial redactions of those traditions, where the primary facts are artificially related to ritual, social customs, moral or national ideals, theological doctrine, a plan of salvation, or merely to local place-names in a very puerile attempt at etymology. Nevertheless, between these two poles of the heroic and the tendentious it is not difficult to recognize the genuine stamp of historical fact, at least from the Exodus onward. The later adaptation of the tradition is easily recognized, and the conventional elements which we have pointed out are far outweighed by the particular details which are characteristic of history rather than saga. It is precisely such details that we feel bound to emphasize in the Old Testament. This respect for fact and historical perspective in the records of the people finds no parallel in the whole literature of the ancient Near East until the time of Herodotus of Halicarnassus.

The sudden exhumation of Canaanite literature at Ras Shamra, as well as confronting us with a new script, seemed also to have produced a new Semitic language. Many words had obvious cognates in Hebrew, Arabic, and other Semitic languages, but the affinity of many was not so obvious. Thus it is not surprising that attention should have tended to be focussed on single words as the unit of interpretation, and lexicons of the various Semitic languages seemed to be the interpreter's best friend. However rigorous a philological discipline these texts may impose, with salutary effect in all branches of Semitic linguistics and with fruitful results, pure linguistics cannot pronounce the final word. Quite apart from the vital importance of anthropology in the appreciation of the living situation in the social and religious life of the people to which these texts were functional, on the purely linguistic level we court disaster if we make the word the unit of interpretation. The word is only part of a larger whole, usually of the couplet, and, however much a Ugaritic word may resemble another which we know certainly in some cognate Semitic language, we must suspend our decision upon it until we have considered it in its context in the couplet, and particularly with relation to its parallel. The context may be, as we have already indicated, much larger than the couplet, extending even to what amounts to a strophe. In any case, the larger context, great or small, must be the unit of interpretation. With our eye on this larger unit we are able better to relate a word, phrase, or passage to the complete text, and, above all are able to delimit the literal and the figurative. In the Canaanite texts to be sure nothing more is at stake than the determination of the relevance of the texts to situations in the life of an ancient people which we study at an academic level, though, as the living context of life in ancient Israel, the life of Canaan has more than a mere academic interest for us. In the literature of Israel extant in the Old Testament our interpretation is of more vital significance insofar as it affects the substance of our living faith. Here again form-criticism on the same principles as in the Ras Shamra texts is the necessary instrument in delimiting the factual and the figurative and in relating given passages to their living context, so that, whatever their association in the context of Christian or Jewish faith, their ultimate relevance is appreciated, and they are redeemed from tendentious interpretation. In furnishing such abundant material, which so clearly elucidates the literary conventions which the Hebrews largely borrowed from their immediate neighbours and predecessors in Canaan, and so stimulating an intensification of form-critical study of Hebrew literature, the Ras Shamra discoveries, whatever their pure academic interest, have a most practical value.

BIBLIOGRAPHY

ABEL, F. M., *Géographie de la Palestine*, 1938.

AISTLEITNER, J., 'Zum Verständnis des Ras Schamra Textes ID', *Dissertationes in honorem Dr. Ed. Mahler*, 1937.

——, 'Die Anat-Texte aus Ras Shamra', *ZAW* LVII, 1939, pp. 193-211.

——, *Die mythologischen und kultischen Texte aus Ras Schamra*, 1959.

——, *Wörterbuch der ugaritischen Sprache*, 1963.

ALBRIGHT, W. F., 'The Syro-Mesopotamian God Šulman-Ešmun and Related Figures', *AfO* VII, 1931-32, pp. 164-169.

——, 'New Light on Early Canaanite Language and Literature', *BASOR* 46, 1932, pp. 15-20.

——, 'The North-Canaanite Epic of ʾAlʾêyân-Baʿal and Môt', *JPOS* XII, 1932, pp. 185-208.

——, 'More Light on the Canaanite Epic of ʾAlʾêyân-Baʿal and Môt', *BASOR* 50, 1933, pp. 13-20.

——, 'The North-Canaanite Poems of ʾAlʾêyân-Baʿal and the "Gracious Gods", *JPOS* XIV, 1934, pp. 101-140.

——, 'Zabûl Yam and Thâpiṭ Nahar in the Combat between Ba al and the Sea', *JPOS* XVI, 1936, pp. 17-21.

——, *The Archaeology of Palestine and the Bible*, 3rd ed., 1935.

——, 'New Canaanite Historical and Mythological Data', *BASOR* 63, 1936, pp. 23-32.

——, 'The Canaanite God Ḥauron (Ḥôrôn)', *AJSL* LIII, 1936, pp. 1-12.

——, 'Recent Progress in North-Canaanite Research', *BASOR* 70, 1938, pp. 18-24.

——, 'Was the Patriarch Terah a Canaanite Moon-god?', *BASOR* 71, 1938, pp. 35-40.

——, *From the Stone Age to Christianity*; *Monotheism and the Historical Process*, 1940.

——, 'Two Letters from Ugarit (Ras Shamra)', *BASOR* 82, 1941, pp. 43-49.

——, 'The Egypto-Canaanite God Hauron', *BASOR* 84, 1941, pp. 7-12.

——, 'Anath and the Dragon', *BASOR* 84, 1941, pp. 14-17.

——, (and MENDENHALL, G.), 'The Creation of the Composite Bow in Canaanite Mythology', *JNES* I, 1942, pp. 227-229.

——, *Archaeology and the Religion of Israel*, 2nd ed. 1942.

——, 'The Old Testament and Canaanite Language and Literature', *CBQ* VII, 1945, pp. 5-31.

——, *The Archaeology of Palestine*, 1949.

——, 'A Catalogue of Early Hebrew Lyric Poems (Psalm LXVIII)', *HUCA* XXIII, 1950-51, pp. 1-39.

——, 'The Psalm of Habakkuk', *Studies in Old Testament Prophecy*, ed. ROWLEY, H.H., 1950, pp. 1-18.

——, 'Dwarf Craftsmen in the Keret Epic and Elsewhere in North-West Semitic Mythology', *IEJ* IV, 1954, pp. 1-4.

——, *Recent Discoveries in Bible Lands*, 1955.

——, 'Some Canaanite-Phoenician Sources of Hebrew Wisdom', *VT* Suppl. III, 1955.

——, 'The High Place in Ancient Palestine', *VT* Supplement IV, 1957, pp. 242-258.

ALFRINK, B. J., 'De Opgravingen van Ras Sjamra', *Studia Catholica 21*, 1946, pp. 124-133.

ALT, A., *Die Landnahme der Israeliten in Palästina*, 1925.

ALT, A., *Die Staatenbildung der Israeliten in Palästina*, 1930.
——, 'Völker und Staaten Syriens im frühen Altertum', *AO* XXXIV, 1936.
——, 'Herren und Herrensitze Palästinas im Anfang des Zweiten Jahrtausends vor Christus', *ZDPV* LXIV, 1941, pp. 21-39.
——, 'Das Königtum in Israel und Juda', *VT* I, 1951, pp. 2-22.
BADAWI, A. M., 'Die neue historische Stele Amenophis II', *ASAE* XLII, 1942, pp. 1-23.
BARROIS, A. G., *Manuel d'Archéologie Biblique* I, 1939; II, 1953.
BARTON, G. A., 'A Liturgy for the Celebration of the Spring Festival at Jerusalem in the Age of Abraham and Melchizedek', *JBL* LIII, 1934, pp. 61-78.
——, 'Danel, a pre-Israelite Hero of Galilee', *JBL* LX, 1941, pp. 213-225.
VON BAUDISSIN, W., 'Der phönizische Gott Ešmun', *ZDMG* LIX, 1905, pp. 459-522.
——, *Adonis und Ešmun*, 1911.
——, *Kyrios*, 1929.
BAUER, H., 'Die Gottheiten von Ras Shamra', *ZAW* N.F. X, 1933, pp. 81-101; XII, 1935, pp. 54-59.
——, 'Safonisches', *OLZ* XXXVIII, 1935, cols. 129-133.
BAUMGARTNER, W., 'Krt, König der Sidonier ?', *JPOS* XVIII, 1938, pp. 50-53.
——, 'Ras Schamra und das Alte Testament', *TR* XII, 1940, pp. 163-188; XIII, 1941, pp. 1-20, 85-102, 157-183.
——, 'Ugaritische Probleme und ihre Tragweite für das Alte Testament', *TZ* III, 1947, pp. 81-100.
BEA, A., 'Archaeologisches und Religionsgeschichtliches aus Ugarit-Ras Schamra', *Biblica* XX, 1939, pp. 436-453.
BIČ, M., 'Der Prophet Amos, eine Hepatoscopos', *VT* I, 1951, pp. 293-296.
BIRKELAND, H., 'Zur Erklärung von ʾalʾeyn in den Texten von Ras Schamra'. *NTS* IX, 1938, pp. 338-345.
BOTTÉRO, J., *Le problème des Ḫabiru*, 1954.
BOYER, G., (in SCHAEFFER, C. F. A., *Mission de Ras Shamra VI; Le Palais Royal d'Ugarit III. Textes accadiens et Hourrites des Archives Est, Ouest, et Centrales*, 1955).
VON BRANDENSTEIN, C. G., 'Zum Hurrischen aus den Ras-Schamra Texten', *ZDMG* XCI, 1937, pp. 555-576.
BREASTED, J. H., *Ancient Records of Egypt*, 1906.
BRICE, W. (and LLOYD, S.), 'Harran', *AS* I, 1951, pp. 77-111.
BRINKER, R., *The Influence of Sanctuaries in Early Israel*, 1946.
BUBER, M., *Königtum Gottes*, 1932.
BUCHER, G. (and MONTET, P.), 'Un dieu cananéen à Tanis: Houroun de Ramsès', *RB* XLIV, 1935, pp. 153-165.
BURCKHARDT, J., *Bemerkungen über die Bedouinen und Wahaby*, 1831.
CANTINEAU, J., 'La langue de Ras Shamra', *Syria* XIII, 1932, pp. 164-170; XXI, 1940, pp. 8-61.
CAPART, J. (Preface to POSENER, G., *Princes et Pays d'Asie et de Nubie*, 1940).
CAQUOT, A., 'Le dieu ʿAthtar et les textes de Ras Shamra', *Syria* XXXV, 1958, pp. 45-60.
—— 'La divinité solaire ougaritique', *Syria* XXXVI, 1959, 90-101.
—— 'Les Rephaim ougaritiques' *Syria* XXXVII 1960, pp. 75-93.
CASSUTO, M. D., *From Adam to Noah*, 1953.
CASSUTO, U., 'The Seven Wives of Keret', *BASOR* 119, 1950, pp. 18-20.
——, האלה ענת, 1950.
——, 'Baal and Mot in the Ugaritic Texts', *IEJ* XII, 1962, pp. 77-86.
CAZELLES, H., 'Sur un rituel de Deutéronome', *RB* LV, 1948, pp. 54-71.
CHWOLSON, D., *Die Ssabier und der Ssabismus*, 1856.

Clay, A. T., *Amurru, the Home of the Northern Semites*, 1909.
——, *The Origin of Biblical Traditions*, 1923.
Contenau, G., *La Civilization des Hittites*, 2nd ed., 1948.
——, *La Civilization Phénicienne*, 2nd. ed., 1949.
Cook, S. A., *The Religion of Ancient Palestine in the Light of Archaeology* 1930.
——, 'The Yahu Coin', *ZAW* LVI, 1938, pp. 268-271.
Cooke, G. A., *A Handbook of North Semitic Inscriptions*, 1903.
Coppens, J., 'La bénédiction de Jacob', *VT* Supplement IV, 1957, pp. 97-115.
Cross, F. M. and Freedman, D. N., 'The Blessing of Moses', *JBL* LXVII, 1948, pp. 191-210.
——, 'Notes on a Canaanite Psalm in the Old Testament', *BASOR* 117, 1950, pp. 19-21.
——, and Freedman, D. N., 'The Song of Miriam', *JNES* XIV, 1955, pp. 237-250.
——, and T. O. Lambdon, 'A Ugaritic Abecedary and the Origins of the Proto-Canaanite Alphabet', *BASOR* 160, 1960 pp. 21-26.
Crowfoot, J. W., *Samaria-Sebaste* I, 1942.
Cumont, F., 'Adonies et Canicule', *Syria* XVI, 1935, pp. 46-49.
Dahood, M. J., *Canaanite and Phoenician Influence in Qoheleth*, 1952.
Dalman, G., *Arbeit und Sitte in Palästina*, 1928-37, reprint 1964.
Dhorme, E., *Textes Religieux Assyro-Babyloniens*, 1907.
——, 'Abraham dans le cadre de l'histoire', *RB* XXXVII, 1928, pp. 367-385, 481-511; XL, 1931, pp. 364-374, 503-518.
——, 'Les Amorrhéens', *RB* XXXVII, 1928, pp. 63-79, 161-179; XXXIX, 1930, pp. 161-168; XL, 1931, pp. 161-184.
——, 'Trouvailles sensationelles en Syrie', *RB* XXXIX, 1930, pp. 152-153.
——, 'Un nouvel alphabet sémitique', *RB* XXXIX, 1930, pp. 571-577.
——, 'Le déchiffrement des tablettes de Ras Shamra', *JPOS* XI, 1931, pp. 1-6.
——, 'Première traduction des textes phéniciens de Ras Shamra', *RB* XL, 1931, pp. 32-56.
——, 'Le dieu parent et le dieu maître', *RHR* CV, 1932, pp. 229-244.
——, 'Deux tablettes de Ras Shamra de la campagne de 1932', *Syria* XIV, 1933, pp. 228-237.
——, 'La lettre d'Ewir-shar', *Syria* XV, 1934, pp. 392-396.
——, 'Lettre du roi de Kargamish au roi d'Ugarit', *Mélanges syriens offerts à M. René Dussaud*, 1939, pp. 203-207.
——, 'Nouvelle lettre d'Ugarit en écriture alphabétique', *Syria* XIX, 1938, pp. 142-146.
——, *L'Évolution Religieuse d'Israël, I. La Religion des Hébreux Nomades*, 1937.
——, 'La question des Ḫabiri', *RHR* CXVIII, 1938, pp. 170-187.
——, 'Textes accadiens transcrits en écriture alphabétique de Ras Shamra', *RA* XXXVII, 1940, pp. 83-96.
——, *Les Religions de Babylonie et d'Assyrie*, 1949.
Dillmann, A., *Lexicon Linguae Aethiopicae*, 1865.
Diringer, D., *Iscrizioni antico-ebraiche palestinese*, 1934.
Dossin, G., 'Nqmd et Niqme-Had', *Syria* XX, 1939, pp. 169-176.
Doughty, C. M., *Travels in Arabia Deserta*, 1936.
Driver, G. R., 'The Original Form of the Name Yahweh, Evidences and Conclusions,' *ZAW* XLVI, 1928, pp. 1-8.
—— (and Sir John Miles), *The Middle Assyrian Laws*, 1935.
——, 'Ugaritic and Hebrew Problems', *Arch. Or.* XVII, 1949, pp. 153-157.
——, *Canaanite Myths and Legends*, 1956.
Dumont, A., 'Indo-Iranian Names from Mitanni, Nuzi, and Syrian Documents', *JAOS* LXVII, 1947, pp. 251-253.

DUMONT, A., Appendix to R.T. O'CALLAGHAN, *Aram Naharaim*, 1948, pp. 149-155.
DUNAND, M., 'La cinquième campagne de fouilles à Byblos (mai-juin 1926)', *Syria* VIII, 1927, pp. 93-104.
——, 'La sixième campagne de fouilles à Byblos (mai-juillet 1927)', *Syria* IX, 1928, pp. 173-186.
——, 'La septième campagne de fouilles à Byblos (mai-juin 1928)', *Syria* X, 1929, pp. 206-216.
DUSSAUD, R., *Topographie Historique de la Syrie Antique et Médiévale*, 1927.
——, 'Nouveaux renseignements sur la Palestine et la Syrie vers 2000 avant notre ère', *Syria* VIII, 1927, pp. 216-231.
——, 'Les missions archéologiques en Syrie en 1929', *Syria* X, 1929, pp. 368-370.
——, 'Brèves remarques sur les tablettes de Ras Shamra', *Syria* XII, 1931, pp. 67-77.
——, 'La mythologie phénicienne d'après les tablettes de Ras Shamra', *RHR* CIV, 1931, pp. 353-408.
——, 'Les fouilles et les recherches archéologiques en 1931 au Liban et en Syrie', *Syria* XIII, 1932, pp. 111-112.
——, 'Le sanctuaire et les dieux phéniciens de Ras Shamra', *RHR* CV, 1932, pp. 245-302.
——, 'Les Phéniciens en Negeb et en Arabie d'après un texte de Ras Shamra', *RHR* CVIII, 1933, pp. 5-49.
——, 'L'épopée de Keret roi des Sidoniens', *Syria* XV, 1934, pp. 215-216.
——, 'Baʿal et Ben-Dagon dans les textes de Ras Shamra', *Syria* XV, 1934, pp. 301-304.
——, 'Deux stèles de Ras Shamra portant une dédicace au dieu Dagon', *Syria* XVI, 1935, pp. 177-180.
——, 'Le mythe de Baʿal et d'ʾAlʾiyan d'après des documents nouveaux', *RHR* CXI, 1935, pp. 5-65.
——, 'Les éléments déchaînés. Une application des règles rythmiques phéniciennes', *Syria* XVI, 1935, pp. 196-204.
——, 'La notion d'âme chez les Israélites et les Phéniciens', *Syria* XVI, 1935, pp. 267-277.
——, 'Le vrai nom de Baʿal', *RHR* CXIII, 1936, pp. 5-20.
——, 'Le commerce des anciens Phéniciens à la lumière du poème des dieux gracieux et beaux', *Syria* XVII, 1936, pp. 58-66.
——, 'Le sacrifice šlm', *Syria* XVII, 1936, pp. 101-102.
——, 'Cultes cananéens au source du Jourdain d'après les textes de Ras Shamra', *Syria* XVII, 1936, pp. 283-295.
——, 'Encore le dieu Horon', *Syria* XVII, 1936, p. 394.
——, 'Ornithomancie et hépatoscopie chez les anciens Phéniciens', *Syria* XVIII, 1937, pp. 318-320.
——, 'À propos d'un protocole à Ugarit', *Syria* XIX, 1938, pp. 184-186.
——, 'Les combats sanglants d'Anat et le pouvoir universel d'El', *RHR* CXVIII, 1938, pp. 133-169.
——, 'Nouveaux textes d'exécration contre les peuples syriens', *Syria* XXI, 1940, pp. 170-182.
——, *Les Origines Cananéens du Sacrifice Israélite*, 2nd ed., 1941.
——, *Les Découvertes de Ras Shamra (Ugarit) et l'Ancien Testament*, 2nd. ed. 1941.
——, *La Religion des Phéniciens*, 1945.
——, *La Pénétration des Arabes en Syrie avant l'Islam*, 1955.
——, 'Yahwé, fils de El', *Syria* XXXIV, 1957, pp. 232-242.
——, J. GRAY, 'The Legacy of Canaan', (Review), *Syria* XXXV, 1958, pp. 372-374.
EBELING, E., *Tod und Leben nach der Vorstellungen der Babylonier*, 1931.

EISSFELDT, O., 'Jahweh als König', *ZAW* XLVI, 1928, pp. 1-105.
——, 'Baal Zaphon, Zeus Kasios, und der Durchzug der Israeliten durchs Meer', *Beiträge zur Religionsgeschichte des Altertums* Fasc. 1, 1932.
——, 'Die Wanderung palästinisch-syrischer Götter nach Ost und West im zweiten vor-Christlicher Jahrtausend', *JPOS* XIV, 1934, pp. 294-300.
——, *Molk als Opferbegriff im punischen und hebräischen und das Ende des Gottes Moloch*, 1935.
——, 'Ras Schamra und Sanchuniathon', *Beiträge zur Religionsgeschichte des Altertums*, Heft 4, 1939.
——, 'Zum geographischen Horizont der Ras Schamra Texte', *ZDMG* XCIV, 1940, pp. 59-85.
——, 'Mythus und Sage in den Ras-Schamra-Texten', *Arabistik, Semitistik, und Islamwissenschaft*, 1944, pp. 268-283.
——, 'El im Ugaritischen Pantheon', *Berichte über die Verhandlungen der Sächsischen Akademie der Wissenschaften zu Leipzig*, Phil.-hist. Klasse Band 98, Heft 4, 1951.
——, 'Partikularismus und Universalismus in der israelitisch-jüdischen Religionsgeschichte', *ThLZ* LXXIX 1954, cols. 253.
—— 'El and Jahweh' *JSS* I, 1956, pp. 25-37.
ENGNELL, I., *Studies in Divine Kingship in the Ancient Near East*, 1943.
——, 'The Text II K from Ras Shamra. A Preliminary Investigation', *Religion och Bibel. Nathan Söderbloms-Selskapets Årsbok*, 1943, pp. 1-20.
——, 'The Ebed Yahweh Songs and the Suffering Messiah in Deutero-Isaiah', *BJRL* 31, no. 1, 1948.
ERMAN, A., *The Literature of the Ancient Egyptians* (ET), 1927.
FEGHALI, M., *Contes, légendes, coutumes populaires du Liban et du Syrie*, 1935.
FENSHAM, F. C., 'Thunder-stones in Ugaritic', *JNES* XVIII, 1959, pp. 273-274.
——, Ps. 68. 23 in the Light of the Recently Discovered Ugaritic Tablets', *JNES* XIX, 1960, pp. 292-293.
FOHRER, G., 'Die wiederentdeckte kanaanäische Religion', *ThLZ* LXXVIII, 1953, cols. 193-200.
FRANKFORT, H., *Kingship and the Gods*, 1948.
FRAZER, Sir J. G., *Folklore in the Old Testament*, 1918.
——, *The Golden Bough* (one-vol. ed.), 1923.
FREEDMAN, D. N., see CROSS, F. M.
FROST, S. B., *Old Testament Apocalyptic*, 1952.
VON GALL, A., *Altisraelitische Kultstätten*, *BZAW* III, 1898.
GARDINER, A. H., 'New Literary Works from Ancient Egypt', *JEA* I, 1914, pp. 29-32.
——, 'The Astarte Papyrus', *Studies Presented to F. Ll. Griffiths*, 1932, pp. 74-85.
GASTER, T. H., 'The Beth-shemesh Tablet and the Origins of Ras Shamra Culture', *PEFQS* 1934, pp. 94-96.
——, 'Notes on Ras Shamra Texts I', *OLZ* XXXVIII, 1935, col. 473-477.
——, 'Notes on Ras Shamra Texts II', *OLZ* XXXIX, 1936, col. 401-405.
——, 'The Harrowing of Baal', *Acta Orientalia* XVI, 1937, pp. 41-48.
——, 'The Chronology of Palestinian Epigraphy II', *PEFQS* 1937, pp. 43-58.
——, 'A Note to Palestinian Epigraphy', *PEFQS* 1937, pp. 260-262.
——, 'The Service of the Sanctuary. A Study in Hebrew Survivals', *Mélanges syriens offerts à M. René Dussaud*, 1939, pp. 577-582.
——, ' "Baal is risen...". An Ancient Hebrew Passion-play from Ras Shamra-Ugarit', *Iraq* VI, 1939, pp. 109-143.
——, 'Notes on Ras Shamra Texts III', *OLZ* XL, 1937, col. 670-673.

GASTER, T. H., 'Notes on Ras Shamra Texts IV', *OLZ* XLII, 1939, col. 273-276.
——, 'The Canaanite Epic of Keret' (Review), *JQR* XXXVIII, 1947, pp. 285-293.
——, *Thespis*, 1950.
VAN GENNEP, A., *Les Rites de Passage*, 1909.
GIFFORD, E. H., *Eusebius, Praeparatio Evangelica*, 1903.
GINSBERG, H. L., 'Notes on "The Birth of the Gracious and Beautiful Gods" ', *JRAS*, 1935, pp. 45-72.
——, 'The Victory of the Land-god over the Sea-god', *JPOS* XV, 1935, pp. 327-333.
—— (and B. MAISLER), 'Semitized Hurrians in Syria and Palestine', *JPOS* XIV, 1934, pp. 243-267.
——, 'Women Singers and Wailers among the Northern Canaanites', *BASOR* 72, 1938, pp. 13-15.
——, 'Two North-Canaanite Letters from Ugarit', *BASOR* 72, 1938, pp. 18-19.
——, 'A Ugaritic Parallel to 2 Sam. i, 21', *JBL* LVII, 1938, pp. 209-213.
——, 'The Ugaritic Texts and Textual Criticism', *JBL* LXII, 1943, pp. 109-115.
——, 'The Legend of King Keret, a Canaanite Epic of the Bronze Age', *BASOR Supplementary Studies* 2-3, 1946.
——, 'Ugaritic Myths, Epics, and Legends', *Ancient Near Eastern Texts*..., ed. PRITCHARD, J. B., 1950, pp. 129-155.
GOETZE, A., *Hethiter, Churriter, und Assyrer*, 1936.
——, 'The Tenses of Ugaritic', *JAOS* LVIII, 1938, pp. 266-309.
——, 'The City Ḫalbi and the Khapiru People', *BASOR* 79, 1940, pp. 32-34.
——, 'Is Ugaritic a Canaanite Dialect?', *Language* XVII, 1941, pp. 127-138.
——, 'The Nikkal Poem from Ras Shamra', *JBL* L, 1941, pp. 353-374.
——, 'Hittite Myths, Epics, and Legends', *Ancient Near Eastern Texts*..., ed. PRITCHARD, J. B., 1950, pp. 120-128.
GORDIS, R., 'Biblical Root ŠDY-ŠD: Notes on 2 Sam. i, 21; Jer. xviii, 14; Ps. xci, 6; Job v 21, Isa. xiii, 6', *JTS* XLI, 1940, pp. 34-43.
GORDON, C. H., 'Parallèles nuziens aux lois et aux coutumes de l'Ancien Testament', *RB* XLIV, 1935, pp. 34-41.
——, 'A Marriage of the Gods in Canaanite Mythology', *BASOR* 65, 1937, pp. 29-33.
——, 'TRḪ, ṮN, and NKR in the Ras Shamra Tablets', *JBL* LVII, 1938, pp. 407-410.
——, *Ugaritic Handbook*, 1947.
——, *Ugaritic Literature*, 1949.
——, 'Sabbatical Cycle or Seasonal Pattern? Reflections on a New Book (A. S. Kapelrud, *Baal in the Ras Shamra Texts*, 1952)', *Orientalia* XXII, 1953, pp. 79 ff.
——, *Ugaritic Manual*, 1955.
GRAHAM, W. C., and MAY, H. G., *Culture and Conscience*, 1936.
GRANT, E., 'The Haverford College Excavation at Beth Shemesh 1928', *PEFQS* 1929, pp. 201-210.
——, 'Beth Shemesh 1930', *PEFQS* 1930, pp. 133-134.
——, 'Ain Shems', *PEFQS* 1931, pp. 167-170.
GRANQUIST, H., *Marriage Conditions in a Palestinian Village*, 1931, 1935.
GRAY, G. B., *Sacrifice in the Old Testament: its Theory and Practice*, 1925.
GRAY, J., 'The Canaanite God Horon', *JNES* VIII, 1949, pp. 27-34.
——, 'The Desert God Aṯtr in the Literature and Religion of Canaan', *JNES* VIII, 1949, pp. 72-83.
——, 'Cultic Affinities between Israel and Ras Shamra', *ZAW* LXII, 1949, pp. 207-220.
——, 'The Rephaim', *PEQ* 1949, pp. 127-139.

GRAY, J., 'The Hunting of Baal: Fratricide and Atonement in the Mythology of Ras Shamra', *JNES* X, 1951, pp. 146-155.
——, 'DTN and RPʾUM in Ancient Ugarit', *PEQ* 1952, pp. 39-41.
——, 'Canaanite Kingship in Theory and Practice', *VT* II, 1952, pp. 193-220.
——, 'Feudalism in Ugarit and Early Israel'. *ZAW* LXIV, 1952, pp. 49-55.
——, 'The Excavation of Ras Shamra, Past and Present', *ET* LXIV, 1953, pp. 205-208, 227-229.
——, 'The GOREN at the City Gate: Justice and the Royal Office in the Ugaritic Text Aqht', *PEQ* 1953, pp. 118-123.
——, 'The God YW in the Religion of Canaan', *JNES* XII, 1953, pp. 278-283.
——, 'Canaanite Mythology and Hebrew Tradition', *Transactions of the Glasgow University Oriental Society* XIV, 1953, pp. 47-57.
——, 'Arabic Affinities in the Dialect of Ras Shamra' (in Hebrew), *Melilah* 1955, pp. 1-14.
——, 'The Wrath of God in Canaanite and Hebrew Literature', *JMUEOS* XXV, 1947-53, pp. 9-19.
——, 'The Ras Shamra Texts: a Critical Assessment', *Hibbert Journal* LIII, 1955, pp. 115-126.
——, *The Krt Text in the Literature of Ras Shamra* (*Documenta et Monumenta Orientis Antiqui*, Vol. V), 1955, 2nd ed., 1964.
——, 'Royal Substitution in the Ancient Near East', *PEQ* 1955, pp. 180-182.
——, 'The Hebrew Conception of the Kingship of God: its Origin and Development', *VT* VI, 1956, pp. 268-285.
——, 'The Kingship of God in the Prophets and Psalms', *VT* XI, 1961, 1-29.
GRELOT, P., 'Isaie XIV, 12-15 et son arrière-plan mythologique', *RHR* CXLIX, 1956, pp. 18-48.
GRESSMANN, H., *Altorientalische Texte und Bilder zum Alten Testament*, 1909.
——, 'Die neugefundene Lehre des Amen-em-ope und die vorexilische Spruchdichtung Israels, *ZAW* XLII, 1924, 272-296.
DE GROOT, J., GUÉRINOT, A., 'Remarques sur la phonétique de Ras Shamra', *Syria* XIX, 1938, pp. 38-46.
GUNKEL, H., *Schöpfung und Chaos in Urzeit und Endzeit*, 1895.
——, *Genesis*, 3rd. ed., 1910.
GUSTAVS, A., 'Personennamen in den Tontafeln von Tell Taʾannek', *ZDPV* L, 1927, pp. 1-18; LI, 1928, pp. 169-217.
HARDING, G. L. (and TUFFNELL, O. and INGE, C. H.), *Lachish II*, 1940.
HARRIS, Z. S., *A Grammar of the Phoenician Language* (*American Oriental Series*, 8), 1936.
HEIDEL, A., *The Babylonian Genesis*, 1942.
HEMPEL, J., 'Glaube, Mythos, und Geschichte im Alten Testament', *ZAW* LXV, 1953, pp. 109-167.
HERDNER, A., J. PEDERSEN, 'Die KRT-Legende' (Review), *Syria* XXIII, 1942-43, pp. 275-285.
——, R. DE LANGHE, 'Les Textes de Ras Shamra-Ugarit et leurs Rapports avec le Milieu Biblique de l'Ancien Testament' (Review), *Syria* XXV, 1946-48, pp. 131-138.
——, 'Un nouvel exemplaire du rituel RS 1929, no. 3', *Syria* XXXIII, 1956, pp. 104-112.
——, J. GRAY, 'The Krt Text in the Literature of Ras Shamra' (Review), *Syria* XXXIV, 1957, pp. 357-361.
——, *Corpus des Tabléttes en Cunéiformes Alphabétiques*, 1963.
HERTZBERG, H. W., 'Die Melchisedeq Traditionen', *JPOS* VIII, 1928, pp. 169-179.

HILL, Sir G. F., *Catalogue of the Greek Coins of Palestine* (*Galilee, Samaria, and Judea*), 1914.
HOCART, A. M., *Kingship*, 1927.
HOOKE, S. H., (ed.), *Myth and Ritual*, 1933.
——, (ed.), *The Labyrinth*, 1935.
——, *The Origins of Early Semitic Ritual*, 1938.
——, 'Archaeology and the Old Testament', *Record and Revelation*, 1938.
HROZNY, B., 'Une inscription de Ras Shamra en langue churrite', *Arch. Or.* IV, 1932, pp. 118-129.
——, 'Les Ioniens à Ras Shamra', *Arch. Or.* IV, 1932, pp. 169-178.
HUMBERT, P., 'Le problème du livre de Nahoum, *RHPhR* 1932, pp. 1-15.
——, 'Une mention d'Asher dans les sources de Philon de Byblos', *RES*, 1941, pp. 61-66.
HVIDBERG, F. F., *Graad og Latter i det Gamle Testamente. En Studie i kanaanaeisk-israelitisk Religion*, 1938, ET, *Weeping and Laughter in the Old Testament*, 1962.
IBN EN-NEDIM, *El-Fihrist*, Cairo, A. H. 1348.
INGE, C. H., 'The Excavations at Tell ed-Duweir', *PEQ* 1938, pp. 240-256.
—— (and HARDING, G. L., and TUFFNELL, O.), *Lachish II*, 1940.
INGHOLT, H., *Studier over Palmyrensk Skulptur*, 1928.
JACK, J. W., *Samaria in Ahab's Time*, 1929.
——, *The Ras Shamra Tablets, their Bearing on the Old Testament*, 1935.
——, 'New Light on the Khabiru-Hebrew Question', *PEQ* 1940, pp. 95-115.
JAMME, A., 'D. Nielsen et le panthéon sud-arabe pré-islamique', *RB* LV, 1948, pp. 227-244.
JASTROW, M., *The Religion of Babylonia and Assyria*, 1898.
JIRKU, A., 'Die ägyptischen Listen palästinensischer und syrischer Ortsnamen', *Klio*, Beiheft XXXVIII, 1937.
——, *Kanaanäische Mythen und Epen aus Ras Schamra-Ugarit*, 1962.
JOHNSON, A. R., *The Cultic Prophet in Ancient Israel*, 1944.
——, *Sacral Kingship in Ancient Israel*, 1955.
KAISER, O., *Die mythologische Bedeutung des Meeres in Ägypten, Ugarit und Israel*, *BZAW* LXXVIII, 1962.
KAPELRUD, A. S., *Baal in the Ras Shamra Texts*, 1952.
——, *Ras Sjamra-Funnene og det Gamle Testament*, 1953.
——, Jahwes tronstigningsfest og funnene i Ras Sjamra', *NTT* 1940, pp. 38-88.
——, Baʿals kamp med havets fyrste i Ras Sjamra-tekstene' *NTT* 1960, pp. 241-51.
KING, L. W., *Legends of Babylon and Egypt in Relation to Hebrew Tradition*, 1918.
KLOSTERMANN, A., (ed.) *Eusebius*, *Onomasticon*, 1902.
——, *Die Bücher Samuelis und der Könige*, *Kurzgefasste Kommentäre* ed. STRACK, L.H. und ZÖCKLER, O., 1887.
KNUDTZON, J. A., *Die El-Amarna Tafeln*, 1908-15.
KRAELING, E. G. H., 'Light from Ugarit on the Khabiru', *BASOR* 77, 1940, pp. 32-33.
KRISTENSEN, W. B., 'De Rijkdom der Aarde in Mythe en Cultus', *Mededeelingen der Nederlandsche Akademie van Wetenschappen*, Afdeeling Letterkunde, 1942.
KUTSCH, E., *Salbung als Rechtsakt im Alten Testament und Alten Orient*, *BZAW* LXXXVII, 1963.
LAMBDON, T. O., see CROSS, F. M.
LAMON, R. (and SHIPTON, G. M.), *Megiddo I*, 1939.
LANGDON, S., *Semitic Mythology*, 1931.
DE LANGHE, R., 'Les textes de Ras Shamra-Ugarit et leurs apports à l'histoire des origines du peuple hébreu', *ETL* XVI, 1939, pp. 245-327.
——, 'Un dieu Jahweh à Ras Shamra?', *ETL* XIX, 1942, pp. 91-101.

De Langhe, R., *Les Textes de Ras Shamra-Ugarit et leurs Rapports avec le Milieu Biblique de l'Ancien Testament*, 1945.
——, 'Het Ugarietisch Keret-Gedicht, Legende, Mythus, of Mysteriespiel?', *Miscellanea Historica Alberti de Meyer*, 1946, pp. 92-108.
——, 'L'enclitique cananéenne m(a)', *Muséon* LIX, 1946, pp. 89-111.
——, *De Taal van Ras Schamra-Ugarit*, 1948.
——, 'Jahweh de wolkenrijder', *Handelingen van het zeventiende Flaamse Filologen-congres* (Louvain), 1948, pp. 92-97.
——, 'Myth, Ritual, and Kingship in the Ras Shamra Tablets', *Myth, Ritual, and Kingship*, ed. S. H. Hooke, 1958, pp. 122-148.
Largement, R., 'La naissance de l'Aurore, poème mythologique de Ras Shamra, Ugarit'. *Analecta Lovaniensia Biblica et Orientalia*, Ser. II, Fasc. ii, 1949.
van der Leeuw, G., *De Godsdiensten der Wereld*, 1948.
Leibovitch, J., 'Un nouveau dieu égypto-cananéen', *ASAE* XLVIII, 1948, pp. 435-447.
Lettinga, J. P., 'Ugaritica', *Ex Oriente Lux* IX, 1944, pp. 116-124.
——, *Oegarit* (*Cultuurhistorische Monografieen*, ed. Forbes, R. J., no. 11), 1948.
Lewy, J., 'Zur Amoriterfrage', *ZA* XXXVIII, 1929, pp. 243-272.
——, 'Les textes paléo-assyriens et l'Ancien Testament', *RHR* CX, 1934, pp. 28-65.
Lidzbarski, M., *Ephemeris für semitische Epigraphik*, 1902-15.
Liverani, M., *Storia di Ugarit*, 1962.
Lloyd, S. (and Brice, W.), 'Harran', *AS* I, 1951, pp. 77-111.
Lods, A., *Israël des Origines au Milieu du VIIIe Siècle*, 1930.
——, 'Archéologie et l'Ancien Testament', *RES* 1936, pp. xlviii-lxxi.
——, 'The Religion of Israel', *Record and Revelation*, 1938.
Loewenstamm, S. E., 'טכסטים חדשים בלשון אוגרית', *Tarbiz* XXVIII, 1959, pp. 244-250.
——, 'The Ugaritic Fertility Myth—the Result of a Mistranslation' *IEJ* XII, 1962, pp. 87-88.
Løkkegaard, F., 'A Plea for El, the Bull, and other Ugaritic Miscellanies', *Studia Orientalia Joanni Pedersen Dicata*, 1953.
Loud, G., *Megiddo II*, 1948.
Luckenbill, D. D., *Ancient Records of Assyria*, 1927.
Maag, V., *Malkût Jhwh*, *VT Supplement* Congress Vol. VII, 1960, pp. 129-153.
Maisler, B., 'Das vor-Davidische Jerusalem', *JPOS* X, 1930, pp. 181-191.
—— (and Ginsberg, H. L.), ('Semitized Hurrians in Syria and Palestine', *JPOS* XIV, 1934, pp. 243-267.
Mauchline, J., *Transactions of the Glasgow University Oriental Society* X, 1943., pp. 11-20.
May, H. G., see Graham, W. C.
Mazar (Maisler), B., 'The Cities of the Priests and the Levites', *VT Supplement* Congress Vol. VII, 1960, pp. 193-205.
Mendelsohn, I., 'The Canaanite term for "free proletarian" ', *BASOR* 83, 1941, pp. 36-39.
Mendenhall, G. E., *Law and Covenant in Israel and the Ancient Near East*, 1955.
——, (and Albright, W. F.), 'The Creation of the Composite Bow in Canaanite Mythology', *JNES* I, 1942, pp. 227-229.
Miles, Sir J. (and Driver, G. R.), *The Middle Assyrian Laws*, 1935.
Mishnah, *Menahoth*.
——, *Rosh ha-Shanah*.
——, *Sukkah*.
Montet, P., 'Tanis, Avaris, et Pi-Ramsès', *RB* XXXIX, 1930, pp. 5-28.
——, (and Bucher, G.), 'Un dieu cananéen à Tanis: Houroun de Ramsès', *RB* XLIV, 1935, pp. 153-165.

MONTET, P., *Le Drame d'Avaris*, 1941.
MONTGOMERY, J. A., 'Notes on the Mythological Epic Texts of Ras Shamra', *JAOS*, LIII, 1933, pp. 97-123.
——, 'Additional Notes on the Ras Shamra Texts', *JAOS* LIII, 1933, pp. 283-284.
——, 'Ras Shamra Notes II', *JAOS* LIV, 1934, pp. 60-66.
——, 'Ras Shamra Notes III', *JAOS* LV, 1935, pp. 89-94.
——, 'Ras Shamra Notes IV: the Conflict of Baal and the Waters', *JAOS* LV, 1935, pp. 268-277.
——, 'Ras Shamra Notes V', *JAOS* LVI, 1936, pp. 226-231.
——, 'Ras Shamra Notes VI: the Danel Text', *JAOS* LVI, 1936, pp. 440-445.
——, 'The New Sources of Knowledge', *Record and Revelation* (ed. H. W. ROBINSON), 1938.
——, *The Books of Kings* (ed. GEHMAN, H. S.), *International Critical Commentary*, 1951.
——, and HARRIS, Z. S., 'The Ras Shamra Mythological Texts'; *Memoirs of the American Philosophical Society* IV, 1935.
MOWINCKEL, S., 'Das Thronbesteigungsfest Jahwäs und der Ursprung der Eschatologie', *Psalmenstudien* II, 1922.
——, 'The Babylonian Matter in the pre-Deuteronomic Primeval History' *JBL* LVIII, 1939, pp. 87-91.
——, 'Immanuelprofetien Jes. 7. Streiflys fra Ugarit I', *NTT* XLII, 1941, pp. 129-158.
——, 'Til uttrykket "Jahves tjener". Streiflys fra Ugarit II', *NTT* XLIII, 1942, pp. 24-26.
——, 'Fra Israels omvaerden', *NTT* XLV, 1944, pp. 70-78.
——, *Han som Kommer. Messiasforventningen i de Gamle Testament og på Jesu Tid*, 1951. ET, *He that cometh* 1956.
——, *Offersang og Sangoffer. Salmediktning i Bibelen*, 1951, *The Psalms in Israel's Worship*, 1962.
——, 'Psalm Criticism between 1900 and 1935', *VT* V, 1955, pp. 13-33.
NAISH, J. P., The Ras esh-Shamra Tablets', *PEFQS* 1932, pp. 154-163.
NIELSEN, D., *Handbuch der altarabischen Altertumskunde* I, 1927.
——, *Ras Shamra Mythologie und Biblische Theologie* (*Abhandlungen fur die Kunde des Morgenlandes*, Band XXI, 4), 1936.
NIELSEN, E., *Oral Tradition*, 1954.
NOTH, M., 'Die syrisch-palästinische Bevölkerung des zweiten Jahrtausend vor Chr. im Licht neuer Quellen', *ZDPV* LXV, 1942, pp. 9-67.
——, 'The Word of God in the Old Testament', *BJRL* XXXII, ii, 1950.
——, *Die Welt des Alten Testaments* (2nd ed.), 1953.
NOUGAYROL, J. (in SCHAEFFER, C. F. A., *Mission de Ras Shamra VI. Le Palais Royal d'Ugarit* III, *Textes accadiens et Hourrites des Archives Est, Ouest, et Centrales*, 1955).
NYBERG, H. S., 'Studien zur Religionskampf im Alten Testament', *ARW*, XXXV, 1938, pp. 329-387.
OBERMANN, J., 'How Daniel was blessed with a Son', *JAOS* Supplement 6, 1946.
——, 'How Baal destroyed a Rival. A Mythological Incantation Scene', *JAOS* LXVII, 1947, pp. 195-208.
——, *Ugaritic Mythology*, 1948.
O'CALLAGHAN, R. T., *Aram-Naharaim*, 1948.
——, 'The Word *ktp* in Ugaritic and Egypto-Canaanite Mythology', *Orientalia* XXI, 1952 pp. 27-46.
——, 'Echoes of Canaanite Literature in the Psalms', *VT* IV, 1954, pp. 164-176.

OESTERLEY, W. O. E. (and ROBINSON, T. H.), *Hebrew Religion, its Origin and Development*, 1930, 2nd ed., 1937.
OESTERLEY, W. O. E. (and ROBINSON, T. H.), *A History of Israel* I, 1932.
——, 'Early Hebrew Festival Rituals', *The Labyrinth* (ed. HOOKE, S. H.), 1933.
OLMSTEAD, A. T., *History of Palestine and Syria*, 1931.
PARKER, B., 'Cylinder Seals from Palestine', *Iraq* IX, 1949, pp. 1-42.
PARROT, A., *Abraham et son Temps*, 1962.
PATTON, *Canaanite Parallels in the Book of Psalms*, 1944.
PEDERSEN, J., *Israel I-II*, 1934, 2nd ed., 1959.
——, *Israel III-IV*, 1940, 2nd ed., 1959.
——, 'Die KRT Legende', *Berytus* VI, 1941, pp. 63-105.
PETERS, J. R. (and THIERSCH, H.), *Painted Tombs of Marissa* (*PEF* publication) 1905.
POPE, M. H., *El in the Ugaritic Texts* (Supplements to *VT*, Vol. II), 1955.
POSENER, G., 'Nouveaux textes hiératiques de proscription', *Mélanges syriens offerts à M. René Dussaud*, 1939, pp. 313-317.
——, *Princes et Pays d'Asie et de Nubie, Textes Hiératiques sur des Figurines d'Envoûtement du Moyen Empire*, 1940.
——, 'Houroun, nouvelles mentions de cette divinité', *JNES* IV, 1945, pp. 240-242.
PRITCHARD, J. B., *Ancient Near Eastern Texts relating to the Old Testament*, 1950.
REIFENBERG, A., 'Ancient Jewish Coins', *JPOS* XIX, 1939, pp. 59-81.
REICKE, B., 'Analogier mellan Josefberättelsen i Genesis och Ras Shamra Texterna, *SEÅ* X, 1945, pp. 5-30.
REITZENSTEIN, R., *Die hellenistischen Mysterienreligionen*, 1927.
RINGGREN, H., *Word and Wisdom*, 1947.
——, 'Einige Bemerkungen zum lxxiii Psalm', *VT* III, 1953, pp. 265-272.
ROBINSON, H. W., *The Religious Ideas of the Old Testament*, 1934.
ROBINSON, T. H. (and OESTERLEY, W. O. E.), *Hebrew Religion, its Origin and Development*, 1930.
—— (and OESTERLEY, W. O. E.), *A History of Israel* I, 1932.
RONZEVALLE, A., *Mélanges de l'Université de St. Joseph* XV, 1930, pp. 235 ff.
ROST, L., *Die Überlieferung von der Thronnachfolge Davids* (*BWANT* III, 6), 1926.
ROWE, A., *The Topography and History of Bethshan*, 1930.
——, *The Four Canaanite Temples of Bethshan*, 1940.
ROWLEY, H. H., 'Zadok and Nehushtan', *JBL* LVIII, 1939, pp. 113-141.
——, 'Ras Shamra and the Habiru Question', *PEFQS* 1940, pp. 90-94.
——, 'Habiru and Hebrews', *PEQ* 1942, pp. 41-53.
ROZELAAR, M., 'The Song of the Sea (Exodus 15, 1b-18)', *VT* II, 1952, pp. 221-228.
SAARISALO, A., 'The Boundary between Issachar and Naphtali', *Finnish Academy of Science Publications*, XXI, 3, 1927.
——, 'Topographical Researches in Galilee', *JPOS* IX, 1929, pp. 27-40; X. 1930, pp. 5-10.
SCHAEFFER, C. F. A., 'Les fouilles de Minet el-Beida et de Ras Shamra (campagne du printemps 1929)', *Syria* X, 1929, pp. 285-297.
——, 'Les fouilles de Minet el-Beida et de Ras Shamra, deuxième campagne (printemps 1930)', *Syria* XII, 1931, pp. 1-14.
——, 'Les fouilles de Minet-el-Beida et de Ras Shamra, troisième campagne (printemps 1931)', *Syria* XIII, 1932, 1-27.
——, 'Les fouilles de Minet el-Beida et de Ras Shamra, quatrième campagne (printemps 1932)', *Syria* XIV, 1933, pp. 93-127.

SCHAEFFER, C. F. A., 'Les fouilles de Ras Shamra, cinquième campagne (printemps 1933)', *Syria* XV, 1934, pp. 105-131.
——, 'Les fouilles de Ras Shamra (Ugarit), sixième campagne (printemps 1934)', *Syria* XVI, 1935, pp. 141-176.
——, 'Les fouilles de Ras Shamra-Ugarit, septième campagne (printemps 1935)', *Syria* XVII, 1936, pp. 105-149.
——, 'Les fouilles de Ras Shamra-Ugarit, huitième campagne (printemps 1936)', *Syria* XVIII, 1937, pp. 125-154.
——, 'Les fouilles de Ras Shamra-Ugarit, neuvième campagne (printemps 1937)', *Syria* XIX, 1938, pp. 193-255, 313-334.
——, 'Les fouilles de Ras Shamra, dixième et onzième campagnes (automne et hiver 1938-39)', *Syria* XX, 1939, pp. 277-292.
——, *Ugaritica I* (*Mission de Ras Shamra* III), 1939.
——, *The Cuneiform Texts of Ras Shamra-Ugarit*, 1939.
——, *Stratigraphie Comparée et Chronologie d'Asie Occidentale*, 1948.
——, 'Reprise des Recherches Archéologiques à Ras Shamra-Ugarit. Sondages de 1948 et 1949: Campagne de 1950', *Syria* XXVIII, 1951, pp. 1-12.
——, *Reprise des Fouilles de Ras Shamra-Ugarit*, 1955.
SCHEFTELOWITZ, J., *Alt-Palästinensischer Bauernglaube*, 1925.
SCHMID, H., 'Jahweh und die Kulttraditionen von Jerusalem' *ZAW* N.F. XXVI, 1955, pp. 168-197.
SCHMIDT, W., *Königtum Gottes in Ugarit und Israel*, *BZAW* 80, 1961.
SCHRADER, E., *Die Keilinschriften und das Alte Testament*, 1903.
SELIGMAN, C. E., *Egypt and Negro Africa: A Study in Divine Kingship*, 1934.
VAN SELMS, A., *Marriage and Family Life in Ugaritic Literature*, 1954.
SETHE, K., *Die Ächtung feindlicher Fürsten, Völker, und Dinge auf altägyptischen Tongefässscherben des Mittleren Reiches* (*Abhandlungen der preussischen Akademie der Wissenschaft*, Phil.-hist. Klasse), 1926.
SMITH, Sir G. A., *The Historical Geography of the Holy Land*, 26th ed., 1935.
SMITH, S., 'A Preliminary Account of the Tablets from Atchana', *AJ* XIX, 1939, pp. 38-48.
——, *Alalakh and Chronology*, 1940.
——, 'On the Meaning of *Goren*', *PEQ* 1953, pp. 42-45.
SMITH, W. R., *The Religion of the Semites*, 1894.
——, *Kinship and Marriage in Early Arabia*, 1903.
SNAITH, N. H., *The Jewish New Year Festival*, 1947.
SPEISER, E. A., 'Ethnic Movements in the Near East in the Second Millennium B.C.', *AASOR* XIII, 1933, pp. 13-54.
——, 'Of Shoes and Shekels', *BASOR* 77, 1940, pp. 15-20.
STARKEY, J. L., 'Tell Duweir', *PEFQS* 1933, pp. 190-199.
——, 'Excavations at Tell Duweir, 1933-34', *PEFQS* 1934, pp. 164-175.
——, 'The Third Season's Work at Tell Duweir', *PEFQS* 1935, pp. 198-207.
——, 'The Fourth Season's Work at Tell Duweir', *PEFQS* 1936, pp. 178-189.
——, 'Excavations at Tell Duweir', *PEFQS* 1937, pp. 228-241.
STUMMER, F., ' "Convallis Mambre" und Verwandtes', *JPOS* XII, 1932, pp. 6-21.
SUKENIK, E. L., 'Paralipomena Palestinensia', *JPOS* XIV, 1934, pp. 178-184. XV, 1935, pp. 341-343.
——, 'Installations in connection with the cult of the Dead in Canaanite Ugarit and in Israelite Samaria', *Qedem* II, 1945, pp. 42-58 (in Hebrew).
SUKENIK (YADIN), Y., 'Note on ṯlṯ sswm in the Legend of Keret', *JCS* II, 1948, pp. 11-12.
THIERSCH, H. (and PETERS, J. R.), *Painted Tombs of Marissa* (*PEF* publication), 1905.

THOMAS, D. W., 'Mitteilungen. 1', *ZAW* LII, 1934, pp. 236-238.
——, 'או in Proverbs xxxi, 4', *VT* XII, 1962, pp. 499-500.
THUREAU-DANGIN, F., 'Vocabulaires de Ras Shamra', *Syria* XII, 1931, pp. 222-266.
——, 'Nouveaux fragments de vocabulaires de Ras-Shamra', *Syria* XIII, 1932, pp. 233-241.
——, 'Un comptoir de laine pourpre à Ugarit d'après une tablette de Ras Shamra' *Syria* XV, 1934, pp. 137-146.
——, 'Une lettre assyrienne à Ras Shamra', *Syria* XVI, 1935, pp. 188-193.
——, 'Trois contrats de Ras Shamra', *Syria* XVIII, 1937, pp. 244-254.
——, 'Une tablette bilingue de Ras Shamra', *RA* XXXVII, 1940, pp. 97-118.
TOURNAY, R., 'Le psaume et les bénédictions de Moïse', *RB* LXV, 1958, pp. 181-213.
——, 'Recherches sur la chronologie des psaumes', *RB* LXV, 1958, pp. 321-357, LXVI, 1959, pp. 161-190.
ULLENDORFF, E., 'Ugaritic Marginalia' I, *Orientalia* XX, 1951, pp. 270-274.
——, 'Ugaritic Marginalia II', *JSS* VII, 1962, pp. 339-351.
DE VAUX, R., 'Le cadre géographique du poème de Krt', *RB* XLVI, 1937, pp. 362-372.
——, 'Les textes de Ras Shamra et l'Ancien Testament', *RB* XLVI, 1937, pp. 526-555.
——, 'Études sur les Hurrites', *Vivre et Penser* 1941, pp. 194-211.
——, 'Les patriarches hébreux et les découvertes modernes', *RB* LIII, 1946, pp. 322-348; LV, 1948, pp. 321-347.
——, '*The Keret Text in the Literature of Ras Shamra*' (J. GRAY), review, *RB* LXIV, 1957, pp. 313-314.
——, 'Le Palais Royal d'Ugarit II, Textes en cunéiformes alphabétiques des archives est, ouest, et centrales (C. VIROLLEAUD) (ed. C. F. SCHAEFFER), 1957, review, *RB* LXV, 1958, pp. 635-637.
VINCENT, A., *La Religion des Judéo-Araméens d'Eléphantine*, 1937.
VINCENT, L. H., *Canaan d'après l'Exploration Récente*, 1907.
——, 'Le dieu cananéen de Beisan et sa parèdre', *RB* XXXIX, 1930, pp. 403-433,
VIROLLEAUD, C., 'Les inscriptions cunéiformes de Ras Shamra', *Syria* X, 1929. pp. 304-310.
——, 'Un poème phénicien de Ras-Shamra. La lutte de Môt, fils des dieux et d'Aleïn, fils de Baal', *Syria* XII, 1931, pp. 193-224.
——, 'Note complémentaire sur le poème de Môt et d'Aleïn', *Syria* XII, 1931, pp. 350-357.
——, 'Vocabulaire de Ras Shamra en langue inconnue', *Syria* XII, 1931, pp. 389-390.
——, 'Un nouveau chant du poème d'Aleïn-Baal', *Syria* XIII, 1932, pp. 113-163.
——, 'La naissance des dieux gracieux et beaux, poème phénicien de Ras Shamra', *Syria* XIV, 1933, pp. 128-151.
——, 'Proclamation de Seleg, chef de cinq peuples, d'après une tablette de Ras Shamra', *Syria* XV, 1934, pp. 147-154.
——, 'Fragment nouveau du poème de Môt et d'Aleïn-Baal (I AB)', *Syria* XV, 1934, pp. 236-243.
——, 'Table généalogique provenant de Ras-Shamra', *Syria* XV, 1934, pp. 244-251.
——, 'La mort de Baal. Poème de Ras Shamra (I AB)', *Syria* XV, 1934, pp. 305-336.
——, 'La révolte de Košer contre Baal. Poème de Ras Shamra (III AB A)', *Syria* XVI, 1935, pp. 29-45.
——, 'Les Chasses de Baal. Poème de Ras-Shamra (BH)', *Syria* XVI, 1935, pp. 247-266.
——, *La Légende phénicienne de Danel*, 1936.

VIROLLEAUD, C., *La Légende de Kéret, Roi des Sidoniens*, 1936.
——, 'Anat et la génisse. Poème de Ras Shamra (IV AB)', *Syria* XVII, 1936, pp. 150-173.
——, 'Hymne phénicien au dieu Nikal et aux déesses Kosarot provenant de Ras Shamra', *Syria* XVII, 1936, pp. 209-228.
——, 'La déesse Anat. Poème de Ras Shamra (V AB)', *Syria* XVII, 1936, pp. 335-345; XVIII, 1937, pp. 85-102, 256-270.
——, 'États nominatifs et pièces comptables provenant de Ras Shamra', *Syria* XVIII, 1937, pp. 159-173.
——, 'Textes alphabétiques de Ras Shamra provenant de la IXe campagne', Syria XIX, 1938, pp. 127-141.
——, '*La déesse Anat*', 1938.
——, 'Les poèmes de Ras Shamra', *Revue Historique* CLXXXV, 1939, pp. 1 ff.
——, 'Les villes et les corporations du royaume d'Ugarit', *Syria* XXI, 1940, pp. 123-151.
——, 'Lettres et documents administratifs de Ras Shamra', *Syria* XXI, 1940 pp. 247-276.
——, 'Textes administratifs de Ras Shamra', *RA* XXXVII, 1940, pp. 11-44.
——, 'Nouveaux textes administratifs de Ras Shamra', *RA* XXXVII, 1940, pp. 129-153.
——, 'Les Rephaim', *RES* 1940, pp. 77-83.
——, 'Les Rephaim. Fragments de poèmes de Ras Shamra', *Syria* XXII, 1941, pp. 1-30.
——, 'Le roi Kéret et son fils (II K). Poème de Ras Shamra', *Syria* XXII, 1941, pp. 105-136, 197-217.
——, 'La légende du roi Kéret d'après de nouveaux documents', *Mélanges syriens offerts à M. René Dussaud*, 1939, pp. 755-762.
——, 'Le mariage du roi Kéret (II K). Poème de Ras Shamra', *Syria* XXIII, 1942-43, pp. 137-172.
——, *Légendes de Babylone et de Canaan*, 1949.
——, *Reprise des Fouilles de Ras Shamra-Ugarit* (ed. SCHAEFFER, C. F. A.), 1955.
——, *Le Palais royal d'Ugarit II: Textes en cunéiformes alphabétiques des archives est, et centrales* (ed. C. F. A. Schaeffer), 1957 (abbrev. *PRU* II).
WEIDNER, E. F., *Boghazköi-Studien. Politische Dokumente aus Kleinasien* I, 1923.
WELLHAUSEN, J., *Reste des Arabischen Heidentums*, 1897.
WENSINCK, A. J., *Some Semitic Rites of Mourning and Religion*, 1917.
WIDENGREN, G., 'Psalm 110 och det sakrala kungadömet i Israel', *UUÅ* 7, I, 1941.
WILSON, J. A., 'Egyptian Texts' in *Ancient Near Eastern Texts* (ed. PRITCHARD, J. B.), 1950.
WISEMAN, D. J., *The Alalakh Tablets*, 1953.
WITZEL, M., *Tammuz-liturgien und Verwandtes*, 1935.
WORDEN, T., 'The Literary Influence of the Ugaritic Fertility Myth in the Old Testament', *VT* III, 1953, pp. 270-297.
al-YASIN, Izz ad-Din, *The Lexical Relation between Ugaritic and Arabic*, 1952.
YEIVIN, S., 'An Ugaritic Inscription from Palestine', *Qedem* II, 1945 pp. 32-41 (in Hebrew).

CONCORDANCE OF UGARITIC TEXTS

GORDON	VIROLLEAUD	BAUER	EISSFELDT	DE LANGHE	DRIVER	CORPUS
a			49	49		
b			50	50		
1	RS 1929, n° 1	1	1	1		34
2	RS 1929, n° 2	2	2	2		32
3	RS 1929, n° 3	3	3	3		35
4	RS 1929, n° 4	4	4	4		166
5	RS 1929, n° 5	5	5	5		33
6	RS 1929, n° 6	6	6	6		13
7	RS 1929, n° 7	7	7	7		168
8	RS 1929, n° 8	8	8	8		27
9	RS 1929, n° 9	9	9	9		36
10	RS 1929, n° 10	10	10	10		101
11	RS 1929, n° 11	11	11	11		98
12	RS 1929, n° 12	12	12	12		142
13	RS 1929, n° 13	13	13	13		54
14	RS 1929, n° 14	14	14	14		31
15	RS 1929, n° 15	15	15	15		107
16	RS 1929, n° 16	16	16	16		112
17	RS 1929, n° 17	17	17	17		29
18	RS 1929, n° 18	18	18	18		55
19	RS 1929, n° 19	19	19	19		39
20	RS 1929, n° 20	20	20	20		58
21	RS 1929, n° 21	21	21	21		56
22	RS 1929, n° 22	22	22	22		37
23	RS 1929, n° 23	23	23	23		38
24	RS 1929, n° 24	24	24	24		199
25	RS 1929, n° 25	25	25	25		151
26	RS 1929, n° 26	26	26	26		62
27	RS 1929, n° 27	27	27	27		180
28	RS 1929, n° 28	28	28	28		170
29	RS 1929, n° 29	29	29	29		130
30	RS 1929, n° 30	30	30	30		183
31	RS 1929, n° 31	31	31	31		175
32	RS 1929, n° 32	32	32	32		60
33	RS 1929, n° 33	33	33	33		47
34	RS 1929, n° 34	34	34	34		169
35	RS 1929, n° 35	35	35	35		170
36	RS 1929, n° 36	36	36	36		150
37	RS 1929, n° 37	37	37	37		196
38	RS 1929, n° 38	38	38	38		108
39	RS 1929, n° 39	39	39	39		211
40	RS 1929, n° 40	40	40	40		212
41	RS 1929, n° 41	41	41	41		138
42	RS 1929, n° 42	42	42	42		195
43	RS 1929, n° 43	43	43	43		54
44	RS 1929, n° 44	44	44	44		44
45	RS 1929, n° 45	45	45	45		169
46	RS 1929, n° 46	46	46	46		45
47	RS 1929, n° 47	47	47	47		43
48	RS 1929, n° 48	48	48	48		194

GORDON	VIROLLEAUD	BAUER	EISSFELDT	DE LANGHE	DRIVER	CORPUS
49	I AB	A	I AB	I AB	5. Baal III (ending in GORDON 62, vi, 38-57)	6 (I AB)
50		50	52	52		172
51	II AB	B	II AB	II AB	5. Baal II	4 (II AB)
52	SS	60	SS	SS	6. Shachar & Shalim	23 SS
53	53	51	53	54		30
54		52	54	55		53
55		53	55	56		160
56		54	56	57		161
57		66	57	58		207
58		65A	58	59		158
59		65B	59	60		159
60	PS	55	60	61		179
61		49	61	62		176
62	I AB i, 1-29 vi, 38-57	A i, 1-29 vi, 38-57	I AB i, 1-29 vi, 38-57	I AB i, 1-29 vi, 38-57	5. Baal I, 1-29 (-vi, 38-57)	6 (I AB), i, 1-29 vi, 38-57
63		59	62	63		77
64	TG	56	63	64		87
65	TGA	57	64	65		68
66	TGB	58	65	66		100
67	I* AB	*A	I* AB	I* AB	5. Baal I*	5 (I* AB)
68	III AB A	Ca	III AB A	III AB A	5. Baal . III* A	2 (III AB), iv
69		61 A	66	67		
70		61 B	67	68		
71		62	68	69		41
72		63	69	70		48
73		64	70	71		49
74		67	71	72		187
75	BH	D	BH	BH	4. Hadad	12 (BH)
76	IV AB		IV AB	IV AB	5. Baal IV	10 (IV AB)
77	NK		NK	NK	7. Nikkal & the Kathirat	24 (NK)
78: v. ʿnt						
79: v. ʿnt						
80			72	73		85
81			73	74		75
82			74	75		76
83			75	76		79
84			76	77		136
85			77	78		83
86			78	79		105
87			79	80		146
88: v. ʿnt						
89	Tl I		80	81		52
90			81	82		147
91			82	83		95

Gordon	Virolleaud	Bauer	Eissfeldt	De Langhe	Driver	Corpus
92			83A } 83B	84		137
93			83B }			
94			84	85		206
95	Tl II		85	86		51
96			86	87		148
97	RS 1929, n° 12		12	12		142
98			87	88		140
99			88	89		149
100			89	90		59
101			90	91		57
102			91	92		165
103			92	93		162
104			93	94		163
105			94	95		164
106			95	96		167
107 v. 53						
108			96	97		65
109			97	98		66
110			98	99		67
111			99	100		69
112			100	101		70
113			101	102		71
114			102	103		73
115			103	104		74
116			104	105		157
117			105	106		50
118			106	107		64
119			107	108		80
120			108	109		141
121 (=4 Aqht)	I Rp. (=IV D)		I Rp.	I Rp.		20 (I Rp.)
122	II Rp.		II Rp.	II Rp.	3. RephaimII	21 (II Rp.)
123	III Rp., A		III Rp., A	III Rp., A	3. Rephaim III, i	22 (III Rp.), A
124	III Rp., B		III Rp., B	III Rp., B	3. Rephaim III, iii	22 (III Rp.), B
125	II K, i-ii		II K, i-ii	II K, i-ii	1. Keret II, i-ii	16 (II K), i-ii
126	II K, iii-v		II K, iii-v	II K, iii-v	1. Keret II, iii-v	16 (II K), iii-v
127	II K, vi		II K, vi	II K, vi	1. Keret II, vi	16 (II K), vi
128	III K		III K; i-vi		1. Keret III	15 (III K)
129	III AB, C		III AB, C		5. Baal III* C	2 (III AB), iii (?)
130			V AB, var. A	V AB, var. A		7, II
131			V AB, var. B	V AB, var. B		7, I
132			IV AB, III*			11
133			I MF			9
134			145			40

Gordon	Virolleaud	Bauer	Eissfeldt	De Langhe	Driver	Corpus
135			II MF			26
136			III MF			25
137	III AB, B		III AB, B		5. Baal III* B	2 (III AB), i
138			146			
300			109	111		82
301			110	112		115
302			111	113		92
303			112	114		116
304			113	115		88
305			114	116		86
306			115	117		118
307			116	118		121
308			117	119		122
309			118	120		131
310			119	121		139
311			120	122		91
312			121	123		89
313			122	124		94
314			123	125		90
315			124	126		97
316			125	127		104
317			126	128		144
318			127	129		145
319			128	130		84
320			129	131		186
321			130	132		119
322 } 323 }			131	133		102
324			132	134		114
325			133	135		117
326			134	136		123
327			135	137		99
328			136	138		93
329			137	139		81
330			138	140		135
331			139	141		132
332			140	142		106
333			141	143		96
334			142	144		103
335			143	145		153
400	ES		144	110		113
1 Aqht	I D		I D	I D	2. Aqhat I	19 (I D)
2 Aqht	II D		II D	II D	2. Aqhat II	17 (II D)
3 Aqht	III D		III D	III D	2. Aqhat III	18 (III D)
4 Aqht: v. 121						
Krt	I K		I K	I K	1. Keret I	14 (I K)
ʿnt	V AB		V AB	V AB	5. Baal V	3 (V AB)
ʿnt, pl. IX-X	VI AB		VI AB	VI AB	5. Baal VI	1 (VI AB)

INDEX OF UGARITIC PASSAGES

(Numbers according to C. H. Gordon, *Ugaritic Handbook* unless otherwise stated)

1 6, n. 154, 188, 189, 192
196, 205, n.
2 6, n. 189, 204, 205, 206,
215
3 154, 188, 189
4, 51 260
5 6, n., 188, 212
9 6, n., 193, 204, 229
9, 1 261
9, 3 179, 189
9, 7 192, 193
12 205
15, 5 260
17 175, n.
17, 5 189
17, 12 184
17, 16 179, 189
18 197
18, 17 123, n.
19 6, n., 179, 189
19, 16 175, n.
22 6, n., 175
23 6, n., 175, n.
23, 6 196
27 197
28 260
41 6, n.
44 6, n.
45 197
47 6, n.
49 24, 288
I 273
11-13 177, 178
13-15 61, 62, 65
15-27 65, 66
28-37 66
30-36 174
II, 6-12 67, 299
12 ff. 174, n.
13-25 67, 68
30-37 68, 83, 95,
174
III, 1-21 70
5, 11 259
IV, 30-44 63, 71, 73
V, 1-6 72, 73
6 265
7-19 73, 84
VI, 11 76
14-15 74
16-22 74
23-31 74, 75
26 280
33-35 89
35 265
51 I, 20-23 272
II, 11 259
13-14 277
27 285
III, 11, 18 286
IV, 14, 15 259
20-26 156, 157
41 159, n.
43 86, 155
43, 44 49
50-51 178
59 24, n.
V, 68 ff. 49, 50
111-VI, 9 292, 293
122 286
123-124 50 n., 277
126-127 50, n.
VI, 4-6 51
8-11 51
15 51
15-18 51
16-22 299
20-21 294
22-23 259, 294
24-35 298
39 21, n.
47 ff. 147, 302
58-59 294
VII, 15-18 51
19-20 52
25 ff. 52, 168, 293
35-44 52
36-38 21, n.
43 88
47-52 54, 168
50-51 279
53-56 54
VIII, 1 ff. 55, 56
7 ff. 188, 274
34-35 164
edge 6, n.
52, 1-2 272
1-4 94
5 95
6 28, n., 95, 265
7 95
9-11 95, 96
11 96
12 96
13 96, 97, 281
14-15 96, 97
16-18 98
19-20 98
21-22 98
23-27 98, 99
28 281
30-35 100
35-49 100, 101
41-42, 44-46 99
49-57 101, 102
53, 60 31, n.
54 187
55 114, n.
57-60 101, 102
59 ff. 103, 104
61-62 58, 289
64-67 246
65-68 289
54 6, 222, 260
55 6, n.
56 6, n.
62, 4 268
5 259
6 271
9-18 63, 64
16-18 264
18-29 64, 302
42-52 187, 188
45-46 129, 130
53-57 151
54-56 211
56 6, n., 205
rev. 55 264

64, 12 189
67, I, 1-7 30, n., 32
1-8, 12-26 56, 57, 85
4, 31 283
7-8 273
II, 2-6 58
6-12 58
7 286
10-11 164
15 273
22 21, n.
V, 6-17 59
14 55, n.
17-22 60
VI, 8-25 61-62
20 268
22 259
25-31 62, 63, 201
68 23, n., 290-292
7 ff. 26-29, 168
9 295
10 265
27 45, n.
33-40 29
69 179, 189, 194, 263
70 179, 189
75 I, 12-13 282
12-41 76, 77, 78
17-22 245
19-23 289, n.
22 79
28-29 26, n.
41 21, n.
II, 6, 23 21
45-46 78
47-50 78
48 67
51-56 79
54-55 82
57-58 79
59-62 80, 81
76 81, 82
I, 7 286
II, 21-22 260
III, 22, 37 286
34-35 71, n.
77 38, n., 186
5-7 246
16-30 248
23-27 249
31-32 249
33-37 249, 250
35 38, n. 266
89 6, n.
95 266, n.
101 267, n.
107 6, n., 189, 190, 191, 205, n.
108 7, 224
109 7, n., 224
110 7, n., 238
111 224
112 224, 238
113 7, n., 213
114, 2 213
115, 8 213, 214
117 227, 267
118 6, n., 25, n., 225
120, 1, 4 198
121 II, 1 127
3-4 127
122 127, 211
123, 7 42, n., 211
13-18 127
124, 1-10 127, 128
8 42, n.
10-11 128, n
125, 6-11 148
20 ff. 149, 221
50 274
126 III, 12-17 149, 211
IV, 11 52, n.
13 274, n.
V, 11, 18, 21 188
127, 11 262
23-24 295
26 54
30-38 150
44-52 219, 221, 257
54-57 175, 295
54-58 150
57-58 296
128 II, 15 108, n.
16-18 294
16-27 146
26-27 221
27 174
III, 2-4, 13-15 146
IV, 6-7, 8-9 227
V, 19-20 148
129 23
19-20 23, 168
20-21 23, 173, 271
134 6, n.
137 23, 24, 287
18-19, 34-35 24
21 ff. 24, 25
23-24 268
24 ff. 36, n.
36 ff. 24, 25, n.
37 28, n.
39 ff. 25, n.
138 6, n., 222, 267
10 123, n.
300 7, 215, 223, 224
301 189, 215
303 215
306 189
313 260
321 7, n., 189, 224
322 179
400 189, 211, 215, 223, 224, 233, 234
II, 9 146
ʿnt, pl.vi, V, 38-51 49
pl. x, IV, 13-20 183
15, 17, 19 26, n.
V, 17 21, n.
I, 2 ff. 38, 39
4-5 266
9 270
12-13 285
II, 3 ff. 40-43
7 271
7-10 294
13-15 282
22 263
III, 2 ff. 45
9 272, n.
11 164
11-17 45, 46
17-28 46, 47
33 ff. 47, 48
34 ff. 30, n., 32
34-IV, 48 174
IV, 78-80 129
1 Aqht, 21-25 107
28-33 116
34-37 116, 117
37 67, n.
38-42 117
42-48 118
43-44 286
44-45 281
50-52 253, 254
51 44, n.
52, 56 280
55 44, n.
57-60 254

59-60 259
61-74 118, 119, 120, 301
75, 113 43, n.
134-147 120-121
145 43, n.
151 ff. 122, 123, 300
170-171 42, n.
170-179 123, 124
190-197 124, 125
199 44, n.
200 44, n., 280
214 195

2 Aqht I, 3-4, 8-9, 10-11, 13-14 108
16-34 108, 109, 110, 168
27 255, 263
29-30 256
31-32 256
33, 34 256
32-33 255
II, 10 70, n.
16 263
25 42, n.
27-40 246
V, 6-8 107, 221
23-31 189
25 42, n.
VI, 15-19 111
20-25 112
26-33 112, 113
31 39, n.
34-40 112, 258
35-36 285
36-37 286
43 40, n.
45 40, n.
46-54 113, 114, 115

3 Aqht, 27-37 115, 116
rev. 11-19 113, 114, 115

Krt 7 ff. 132, 133, 134
19 276
26-30 134
28-30 298-299
35-152 135-144
36, 297 70, n.
41-42 265
44-53 219
55, 127, 252 59, n.
68, 161 38, n.
72, 165 275
87, 177, 178 263
90-91 235, 275
102, 191 260
103-109 299
201 28, 70, n.
201-206 145

PRU II, 1 32, n., 189
1, 7 47, n.
3 47, n.
5 267
6 145, n.
7 225, n., 226, 237
8 267
9 267
12 235
16 104
19 267
24 59, n.
31 233
32 235
35 235
58, 20 235
109 261
289, 30 38, n.

PRU III, 11.790 238
15.109 238
15.114 238
15.137 234, 237
15. 70 127
15.88 127
16.03 238
16.132 232
16.139 234
16.143 234
16.144 251
16.145 237
16.148 234
16.157 127, 234, 237
16.158 251
16.200 254
16.239 234, 236
16.250 234, 237, 255
16.257 235
16.261 254
16.267 255
16.276 238
16.348 234
16.353 234
16.431 236

VIROLLEAUD, *Syria* XXVIII, 1951, pp. 25-27, text III 194

THUREAU-DANGIN, *Syria* XVIII, 1937, pp. 249-251 254, 255

INDEX OF UGARITIC WORDS

ʾeʾeṯt 55, n., 145, n.
ʾeb 116, n.
ʾab ʾadm 159
ʾubdy 233
ʾabn 62, n.
ʾebr 55, n.
ʾab šnm 114, n., 155, 156
ʾabynt 108, n.
ʾugr 77, n.
ʾagn 100, n.
ʾagẓr ym bn ym 98, n.
ʾadm (verb) 135, n.
ʾadr 107, n., 112, n.
ʾudr 32, n.
ʾawl 79, n.
ʾewr 260, 261
ʾewrẓr 260, 261
ʾuẓ 38, n.
ʾuẓr 108, n.
ʾaḫl 119, n.
ʾuḫryt 113, n.
ʾaḫ šmk 81, 82
ʾaṭm 47, n.
ʾuṭm 31, n.
ʾay 28, n., 265
ʾaymr 27, n.
ʾaklt 119, n.
ʾal 280
ʾul 138, n.
ʾelʾeb 109, n.
ʾalʾeyn 164
ʾall 67, n.
ʾell 60, n.
ʾaln 77, n.
ʾelnym 129, n., 130, n.
ʾalp 44, n.
ʾulp 204, n.
ʾelš 149, n.
ʾalt 75, n.
ʾamd 122, n.
ʾamt 143
ʾemt 57, n.
ʾumt 72, n.
ʾamtm 30, n.
ʾan 141, n.
ʾun (1) 61, n.
ʾun (2) 117, n.
ʾanhb 44, n.
ʾanḫr 57, n.
ʾanm 66, n.
ʾannḫ 97, n.
ʾanš 25, n.
ʾunš 266, 267
ʾap 204
ʾaplb 62, n.
ʾuṣbʿt 27, n.
ʾaqht 111, n.
ʾeqnʾe 144, n.
ʾar 39, n.
ʾur 119, n.
ʾurbt 50, n., 277
ʾargmn 25, n.
ʾarṣ 59, n., 264, 274
ʾarṣy 45, n.
ʾarš (1) 111, n., 135, n.
(2) 188, n.
ʾešd 46, n.
ʾušḫry 192
ʾušn 198
ʾaṯy 47, n.
ʾeṯ 70, n.
ʾeṯl 116, n.
ʾaṯm 197
ʾaṯr 62, n., 139, n.
ʾaṯryt 113, n., 285
b from) 43, n.
bdl 233
bhṯ 58, n.
bk 39, n.
bl 277
bll 23, n., 57, n., 271
bmt 41, n., 259
bny 70, 259
bny bnwt 33, 157, n., 259
bn ydy 27, n.
bnt hll 246
bʿl ṣdq 226
bʿr 47, n., 140, n.
bġy 47, n.
bṣqln 119, n.
bql 6, n.
bqr 194
brḫ 31, n., 122, n.
brẓl 198
bšm 28, n.
bt ḫrš 81, n.
btlt 43, n.
bṯ 29, n.
bṯn 31, n., 269
gbb 137, n.
ggn 54, n.
gẓr 98, n.
gl 275
glṯ 50, n.
gmn 64, n.
gmr 74, n.
gmẓ 76, n.
gnp 52, n.
gpt 52, n.
gr (verb) 141, n.
gr (noun) 122, n., 243
grgr 103, n.
grdš 132, n.
grn 107, n., 142, n.
dʾey 120, n.
dbʾat 260
dbḥ 195
dblt 6, n.
dbr 60, n.
dgn 283
dd 45, n.
dky 72, n.
dlp 27, n.
dmgy 76, n.
dn (1) 39, n.
dn (2) 118
dġṣt 125, n.
dgṯ 97, n., 125, n.
dqt 192
drkt 263, 265, n.
dtn 146
dṯ 115, n. 192, n.
hbr 114, n.
hg 275
hdy 62, n.
hll 246
hmlt 24, n., 62, n.
hmry 55, n., 56, n.
hrr 78, n.
ht 123
wdq 52, n.
whln 40, n.
wḥy 46, n., 77, n.

wkm 77, n.
wlš 76, n.
wsr 54
wpʿ 119, n.
wpq 79, n., 132, n.
wṣm 122, n.
wqb 72, n.
zbl (1) 71, n., 167
zbl (2) 140, n.
zbln (1) 133, n.
zbln (2) 150
ztr 109, n.
ḥbš 115, n.
ḥdg 77, n.
ḥdy 42, n.
ḥdṯ 140, n.
ḥwp 128, n.
ḥṭb 142, n.
ḥlqm 42, n.
ḥmdrt 119, n.
ḥmyt 206
ḥnn 190
ḥsp 44, n.
ḥpš 142, n.
ḥrṣ 113, n.
ḥrr 58, n.
ḥrš 81, n.
ḥrṯ 62, n.
ḥtk(noun) 71, n., 132
ḥtk (verb) 187, n.
ḫbr 137, n.
ḫbt 204, n.
ḫḫ 55, n. 113, n.
ḫlq 61, n.
ḫmt 136, n.
ḫnzr 59, n.
ḫnp 115, n.
ḫsn 236
ḫsp 138, n.
ḫpṯ 55, n.
ḫrṣ 47, n.
ḫrẓ 78, n.
ḫr(*ṯ*) 64, n., 121, 264
ḫṯʾa 56, n.
ḫẓẓ 139, n.
ṭb 261
ṭbn 118, n.
ṭbq 110, n.
ṭḥ 110, n.
ṭl 44, n.
ṭrd 47, n.
ẓʾe 76, n.
ẓʾu 44, n.
ẓl 136, n., 285
ybd 39, n.
ybl 25, n., 57, n., 195, 271
ybmt 43, 271
ybmt lʾemm 43, n.
ybrd 38, n.
ybrdmy 249
ygrš 27, n.
yd 100, n., 143, n.
ydlp 27, n.
ydty 57, n.
yly 79, n.
ym 23, ff.
ymk 26, n.
ymlk 33
ymm 51, n.
ymmt 272, n.
ymn 27, n.
yʿbdr 45, n.
yġlm 119, n.
yṣḥm 213
yṣm 122, n.
yṣq 61, n., 198, n.
yṣrm 214
yqṯ 28, n.
yr 117
yrq 143, n.
yšt 28, n.
ytnm 215
yṯb 61, n.
yṯʿr 38, n.
k 277 ff.
kbd 43, n., 282
kbšm 214
klʾat 136, n.
kms 79, n.
knkn 59, n., 121, n.
kst 67, n., 111, n.
kpp 41, n.
kr 77, n.
kšd 57, n.
ktp 72, n.
kṯrm 23, n.
kṯrt 246, n.
l (enclitic 143, n. 276, 279
(negative interrogative) 75, n.
(from) 123, n.
lʾa 68, n.
lʾay 165
lʾem 40, n., 43, n., 62, n.
lʾemm 43, n., 271
lbʾet 57, n.
lbnn 112, n.
lg 104, n.
lhn 104, n.
lḫ 62, n.
lḥt 110, n.
lyṭ 72, n.
ll 24, n.
lmd 216
lsm 46, n., 74, n.
lpš 62, n.
lṣb 70, n.
lqḥ 121, n.
lrmn 102
lšn 114, n.
ltn 48, n.
m 29, n., 171, 278
mʾelḫ 261
mbk 113, n.
mgn 272
mdb 100, n.
mdgt 121, n.
mdd ʾel 184, n.
mdl 47, n., 59, n.
mdm 214
mdnt 42, n.
mhmrt 56, n., 273
mhr (warrior) 41, n., 42, n., 113, n., 128, n.
mhr (brideprice) 248
mẓl 140, n.
mẓʿ 117, n.
mḫy 43, n.
mḫmšt 134, n.
mḫṣm 214
my 62, n.
myr 139, n., 55, n.
mkk 27, n.
mkrm 214
mlḥmt 45, n.
mmʿ 42, n., 115, n., 282
mnḫ 25, 198
mnn 100, n.
mswn 143, n.
mʿ 138, n., 263
mṣlt 81, n.
mṣb 249
mġy 42, n., 122, n.
mr 52, n.
mrʾu 233, n.
mrḫ 191, n.
mrynm 232
mrr 108, n.
mrrt 123, n.

mšdpt 142, n.
mšmš 79, n.
mšr (1) 45, n.
mšr (2) 205
mšrrm 249
mšt‘ltm 100, n.
mẓrġlm 233 ff.
mtn 195
mt rpʾe 108, 115
nʾet 191, n.
nbb 121, n.
nbt 136, n.
ngb 137, n.
ngy 144, n.
ngr 149, n., 150, n.
ngš 67, n.
ngṯ 78, n.
ndd 38, n.
ndy (1) 51, n.
ndy (2) 62, n.
ndr 127, n., 195
nẓl 136, n.
nḫt 48, n., 262
nks 62, n.
nkr 140, n., 141, n.
nkt 204, n.
nsk 198
n‘mn 135, n.
n‘r mrynm 233 ff.
nġṣ 27, n.
nġr 55, n., 105, n.
nġr mdr‘ 105, n.
npy 205, n.
npp 44, n.
npr 68, n.
npš 54, n., 261, 262
npšny 23, n.
nṣbt 191, n.
nqdm 213, 264
nšr 45, n.
ntk 80, n.
ntr 188, n.
nṯq (*wṯq*) 52, n.
sʾed 38, n.
sʾen 67, n.
swn 143, n.
skn 79, n., 109, n.
slḫ npš 193
slt 62, n.
snnt 246
s‘t 142
sġsġ 250
sp 144, n.
spsg 113, n., 286
spr 275
‘bṣ 46, n.
‘bš 128, n.
‘gl ‘el 31, n.
‘d (*w‘d*) 186, n.
‘db (1) 116, n.
‘db (2) 195
‘dd 54, n.
‘dn 49, n., 79, n., 137, n.
‘dt 51, n.
‘l (of liability) 122, n.
(family) 241
‘lm 58, n., 59, n.
‘m 109, n.
‘mmym 54, n.
‘ms 64, n.
‘mq 40, n.
‘mr 61, n.
‘n 72, n.
‘nn 24, n.
‘nt 71, n.
‘pr 77, n.
‘qb 115, n.
‘rbm 95, n., 214
‘rẓ 66, n., 169, n.
‘rr 249, n.
‘rṯ 192
‘šy 110, n.
‘šr 198, 214, 215, 270
‘tk 31, n., 41, n.
‘tn 55, n.
ġdd 43, n.
ġdyn 191, n.
ġẓr 41, n., 42, n., 193, 263, 264
ġẓy (*mġẓ*) 272
ġyr 195
ġly 25, n., 116, n.
ġll 123, n., 268
ġlm (darkness) 54, n., 134, n., 274
ġlm (lad) 135, n.
ġlmt 54, n.
ġpr 249
ġr (mountain) 40, n.
ġr (cave, inmost shrine) 40, n.
ġrmn 41, n.
pʾuy 74, n.
pʾalt 118, n.
pʾamt 98, n.
pbl 143
pdry 39, n., 192
pht 73, n.
pḫyr 134, n.
pḫr m‘d 24, n.
pll 71, n.
plṭ 115
plṯ 61, n.
pnt 27, n.
pslm 213
p‘r 26, n.
pġt 18, n., 125, n.
prṯl 47, n.
pr‘ 54, n.
pẓ 24, n.
ptḥ 104, n.
ṣʾat špš 41, n.
ṣbʾu 41, n.
ṣdynm 145, n.
ṣdq 132, n.
ṣḥ (*ṣwḥ*) 68, n.
ṣḥr 72, n.
ṣyd 63, n.
ṣly 117, n.
ṣmd 191, n.
ṣmdm 26, n.
(*ṣ*)*mḫ* 226, 227
ṣml 120, n.
ṣmt 41, n.
ṣ‘ 43, n.
ṣp 144, n.
ṣpr 143, 275
ṣrk 118, n.
ṣrm 144, n.
ṣrrt 270
ṣrt 24, n., 26, n.
qbt (*wqb*) 72, n.
qdš 25, n., 39, n.
qdšm 213
qṭṭ 204
qṭr 109, n., 110, n.
qll 42, n.
qn 56, n., 268
qny 177
qnyt ʾelm 265
qnṣ 102, n.
qṣm 41, n.
qrdm 164
qry 40, n., 45, n.
qrytm 40, n.
qrš 114, n.
qrt 94, n.
qšt 42, n.
rʾe 38, n., 285

rbb 39, n., 44, n.
rgm 141, n., 269, 270
rḥmy 175
rḥt 55, n.
rkb 26, n.
rkb ʿrpt 163
rnʾa 141, n.
rpʾe 18, n., 120, n., 146
rpʾum 120, 130, n., 187
rp̣y 30, n.
rṣy 104, n.
rṣṣ 66, n.
rr 193
rš 132
ršp 276, 279
rṯ 110, n.
šʾe 79, n.
šʾey 116, n.
šʾer 68, n.
šbm (1) 42, n.
šbm (2) 47
šd 72, n., 96., n., 281
šḫlmmt 60, n.
šlḥ 134, n.
šlḥm 38, n.
šlyṭ 31, n.
šlm 14, n., 43, n., 46, n.
šlmm 196
šmt 26, n.
šnm 155, 156, 205, n.
šnpt 196
šnst 41, n.
sʿtqt 150
špm 94
šqrb 195
šr (flash) 50, n., 94, n., 272
šr (verb) 128, n.
šr wmt 95, n.
šrg 112, n.
šrd 136, n.
šrʿ 118, n.
šrp (whole burnt offering) 193
šrp (generous) 191, n.
šrqm 31
št 45, n.
tʾenṯt 113, n.
tʾeṣ (*wʾaṣ*) 110, n.
tbʿ (1) 115, n.
tbʿ (2) 132-133, n.
thmt 281
tmn (*ymn*) 27, n.
tsm (*wsm*) 144, n.
tʿdt 24, n., 187
tġrk 267
tqh 24, n.
tqynh 24, n.
trbṣ 144, n.
trḫ 132, n., 140, n.
trp 30, n.
ṯʾeṭ 110, n.
ṯʾar 68, n., 133, n.
ṯd 38, n.
ṯkḥ 30, n., 283
ṯkm 128, n.
ṯkmn 128, n.
ṯlṯ (verb) 62, n.
ṯm 128, n.
ṯmq 128, n.
ṯn (verb) 140, n.
ṯnn 139, n.
ṯnnm 213, 214
ṯʿ 204, n.
ṯʿy 166, n., 191
ṯʿr 38, n., 42, n., 249, 266
ṯġr 226
ṯġrm 215
ṯpd 70, n.
ṯr ʾel 158
ṯrml 144, n.
ṯrt 50, n.
ṯtʿ 75, n.
ẓ̌d 114, n.
ẓ̌hrt 135, n.
ẓ̌mr (1) 41, n.
ẓ̌mr (2) 110, n.
ẓ̌rt 70, n.

SUBJECT INDEX

Abdu 236, 237
Adadšeni 232
Adonijah 234, n.
Adonis 16, 59, n., 61, n., 69, n., 114, n., 135, n.
Adoniṣedeq 186, n.
Aleyn 164
Alphabet xii, 6
Ammianus Marcellinus 69, n.
Ammištamru 232
Ananaya 254
Ananiḫebi 251
Anat 26, 31, 32, 40 ff., 48, 62 ff., 92, 98, 111 ff., 146, 174, 175
Anat-har 174
Anath-bethel 175
Anath-yahu 175
Anathoth 175
Anointing 254, 255, n.
Apapa 238
Aphrodite 61
Arauna 62, 260
Arḫalbu 236, 237
Armageddon 24, n.
Arsu 14, n., 185
Asaph 216
Asclepius 179
Ashdod 178
Asher 139, n.
Askalon 243
Astarte 26, 28, 29, 175, 176, 179, n., 212
Astarte Papyrus 28, n., 29, n., 176, 179
Astral worship 169 ff.
Asylum 242
Aṯerat 65, 72, 76, 145, 176
Atchana 138, n., 139, n. 232, n.
Athene 174
Atnprln 211, 213, 215, 216
Atonement 78 ff., 204 ff.
Aṯtar 14, n., 23, 24, 65, 66, 169 ff.
Aṯtar-Kemosh 171
Aṯtarat 26, 28, 29, 176, 212
Aṯtarat šm bʿal 150
Auronas 179
Aziru 236, 237
Azizu 14, n., 185
Baal 10, n., 20, 163 ff., 286 ff.
Baal-figurines 165, 203
Baal Saphon 203
Bathṣidqi 254
bdl mrynm 234 ff.
bdl mšrġlm 234 ff.
Beersheba 202
Beth-Anath 83, 175
Beth-Anoth 175
Beth-Dagon 178
Bethel 202
Beth-Horon 178
Beth-Shemesh inscription 3, n.
Bidawa 254
Birth 245 ff.
Bitch of the gods 31
Blood 44, 45
Blood-revenge 124, 125, 241 ff.
Bow 111
Bride-price 132, n., 241, 249, 251
Bull El 135, 158, 159
Bulls and Gazelles 147, 148, 227, 228
Burial 64, 65, 252
Burnt offering 192, 196
Cain 80, 117, 122, 242
Carmel 45, 148, 200
Caste 7, 231
Chalcol 207
Chariot 7, 144, 232
Coinage 1, 135, n.
Common meal 57, 110, 255
Communal responsibility 122, 123, 240 ff.
Communion 110, 196
Contactual magic 60
Corn-maiden 120
Corvée 224
'Count' 236, 237
Creation 22, 29, 30, 33
Creator, El as 33, 70, 159
Crooked Serpent 30, n., 31, n., 47, 48
Cup of the Lord's fury 125, n.
Dagon 178, 179, 189, 283
Dan 106, 107, 202
Dardar 207
David 212, 216, 219, n., 227, 252
Death 11, 12, 53 ff., 189
Dedication of the Temple 53
Delos 179
Demeter 61, 258

Desacralization 17, 68, 69, 137, n., 201, 210
Desert 288, 289
Devourers 77, 78
Dewy 39, 51
Dionysus 258
Dispenser of fertility 18, 108, 117 ff.
Divination 80, 81, 213, 214, n.
Divorce 254
Dn'el 18, 106 ff.
Dtn 146, 212, 215
Early rains 21, 52, n., 139, n.
Edessa 14, n., 185
Eighth 149
El 154 ff.
Elat 177 ff.
el-Basūs 244
Elephantine Papyri 175, 191, n.
Eliawa 254
Elijah 307, 309
Elyon 157
Emancipation 254, 255
Enthronement Psalms 11, 37
enuma eliš 11, 22
Eschatology 36, 70, n.
Eshmun 180
Ethanim 17, 53, 200
ʾetrḫ 15
Execration Texts 152 ff., 179, 185
Fallen angels 288
Fatherhood of El 155, 156, 159
Fertility of Golden Age 70
Feudal system 7, 222 ff.
First sheaf 68 ff., 201
Flood 47
Fratricide 78 ff.
Funeral feast 64, 253
Funeral rites 252 ff.
Gad 217, n.
Garden of Uzza 173
Gazelles and Bulls 147, 148, 227, 228
Gaza 243
gebīrā 227
Gezer tablet 117, n.
Gibeon 126, n., 202, 210
Gideon 308
Golenischeff Papyrus 148
Greek drama 13
Guild system 6, 7, 231
Hadad 21, 78, 79, 153, 163 ff., 201, 286
Hadad-rimmon 63
Hagar 76, n.
Ḫalubariḥ 153
Harran 22, n., 69
Harvest-sacrifice 68, 69, 70, 121, 122
Heavenly Twins 185
Herakles 179
Hesi-Nekht 175
Ḫeyawa 255
Hierombalos 180
hieros gamos 44, 101
Hinnom 172
Horites 3
Ḥoron 150, 179, 180
Ḥoronabi 153, 179
Hospitality 110, 243, 256
House of Baal 44, 49 ff. 168, 200
ḫubšu 138, n., 235, 236
Human sacrifice 121, 126, 170, 171, 202
Hurrians 17
Hyksos 174, n.
Hyn 48
Ibiranu 232
Ibn en-Nedim 69
Ilimilku 236, 237
Imitative magic 13, 45, 52, 120, 149, 199
Immanuel 288, 289
Incubation 108, 134, 210, 252, n.
Iolaus 179
Irrigation 66, 170
Ishtar 61, 173
Isis 61
Ittobaal 212
Iwer 6
Iwer-žarri 6
Jacob 308
Jahweh 180 ff.
Jamnia 179
Jebel el-Aqra 82
Jehu 174, 202
Jephthah 63, 201
Jerusalem 185, 202, 210
Jezebel 71, n.
Joseph 122
Josiah 172, 177, 202
Judges 222, 240, 241
Jupiter 180
Kalbu 236, 237
Kawkab el-Hawa 3, n.
Kerker 207
Kikkuli 232, n.
King and fiscal control 224 ff.
King as judge 107, 150, 218, 219
King as priest 136 ff., 209, 210, 211, 212

King as war-lord 138 ff., 222 ff.
King's Dale 173
King's Garden 173
Kingship of God 11, 29 ff., 86 ff., 156, 287
Kissing grain-stalks 119
Klmw 228
Korahites 216
Kore 61, 258
Ktr wḪss 26 ff., 48 ff., 111, 189
Kubaba 251
Kumarbi 154, 155
Laban 309
Larnax Lapethos 174
Last sheaf 69, 70, 201
Latakia 1
Latter rains 12
Laya 254
Leukos Limen 1
Leviathan 30, 31, 56
Levirate marriage 251
limmu 40, n
Lion, The 249
Lucian of Samosata 152
Maacah 177
Mace 26
maḫḫē 217
Manasseh 177
Marduk 11
mariannu 7, 231, 232
Marriage 133, 138 ff., 247 ff.
Mayor 237
Meal-offering 198
Mekal 133, n., 189
Melchisedeq 186, n.
Memphis 189
Memphis Stele 230
Mesha 171, 212, 213
Messiah 36
mglb 231
Milcom 171, 172, 173, 186
Milka 251
Minet el-Beida 1
Mitanni 2, 7
Molech 171, 172, 173
Monymos 14, n., 185
Monotheism 190 ff.
Moon-god 76, 123, 248 ff.
Moses 308
Mot 11, 12, 53 ff., 188, 189
Mother of the gods 178
Mount of Assembly 24, n.
Mourning rites 61 ff.. 200, 252
mudu 232
Murex 5
Mystery cults 258
Myth 20 ff.
Nathan 217, n.
Nathan-melech 172
Negeb 15, 137, n., 138, n.
Neirab 22
Nergal 180, 189
New Moon Festival 193
New Year Festival 9 ff., 22 ff., 199, 200, 306
Nikkal 22, n., 186
Niqmad 6, n.
Niqmepaᶜ 227, 236, 237
nᶜr mrynm 233
Numerical climax 297 ff.
Offering 196 ff.
Omen text 6, 194
Oracles 198, 210
Oral tradition 216
Orion 126
Osiris 61, 200, 258
Palmyra 14, n., 185
Parallelism, Variations of 293 ff.
Passover 201
Pentecost 69, 201
Perpetual offering 197
Philistines 8
Philo of Byblos 10, 152
Priesthood 209 ff.
Professional soldiers 224 ff.
Prophecy 216, 217
Prophets of Baal 45, 200
Prose, Canaanite 289
Prosody, Canaanite 289 ff.
Prostitution, Ritual 53, n., 215
Psalmody 207 ff.
Ptah 189
Ptolemais 243
Qadesh 15
Qenites 181
Qodšu 25, n.
rabiṣu ekallim 237
Rafat 180, n.
Rahab 32
Redemption 145, n.
Refuge 242, 243, 244
Repetition 299 ff.
Rešef 133, 179, 180, 189, 194, 227, 276
Restitution-offering 197
Revelation 210
Rites de passage 124

Ritual seclusion 108, 134
rp'um 126 ff., 211 ff., 228
Sabbatical Year 12, 75, 80
Sacred tree 176, 177, n.
Sale-adoption 254
Šalamanu 186
Samaritan Ostraca 7
Sanchuniathon 152
Sapon 47, 66, 82, 148, 287
Šardanu 223
Saul 212, 233, 236
Šaya 255
Scapegoat 80, 150
Sea 21 ff.
Sea Peoples 1
Search for Baal 61
Seasonal festivals 13, 203
Sedeq 186
Sepphoris 243
Servant of God 228
Seven year famine 118
Shamgar 175
Shechem 128, n., 145, n.
šḥr 14, 158, 170 ff., 184 ff.
Shrines of Canaan 202
Shutter 50 ff.
Sidon 243
Sin 22, n.
Sinaranu 238
Singers 207, 215
Sin-zer-abanu 22, n.
Skilful and Percipient One 26 ff., 48 ff., 111, 189
Skilly Women 23, 246
šlm 14, 158, 170 ff., 184 ff., 202, n., 289
šnm 189
Social crises 244 ff.
Solomon 210, 224, 225, 308
Son of God 136, 148, 149, 210, 220, 221
Spear as symbol of royalty 75
'Sprouts' 149
St. Nilus 170
Šubamma 255
Šubbiluliuma 6, 224, 225
Substitute 58, 194
Šulman 180
Sukkoth 16
Swine 59, n.
Tabernacles 17, 53, 200
Tablets of Destiny 22
Tabnith 212
Takhulinu 238
Tammuz 63, 64, 69, 85
Ta-net-not 207
Tanis 179
Tannin 30
Tell el-Kheleifeh 186
Terah 15
Theodulos 170
Threshing 68 ff., 192
Tiamat 11, 22
Tithe 198
ṯkmn 189
Tophet 172
*Ṯ*ᶜ 146, n.
Ṯrmn 192
Trumpet-blowing 53, n.
ubru 237
Udm 16, 144
Underworld 274
Unleavened Bread 201
Uriah 6, n.
Urušlmm 173, 185, n.
Uzza 173, 185
Veil 108, n.
Venus star 14, n., 65, 169 ff., 170 ff., 177, 185, 288
Veterinary text 6
Vine and Field 47, 54
Voracious Ones 77, 78
Vultures 116, 120, 121
Water-pouring 52, 149, 150
Wave-offering 196
Weeks, Feast of 69, 201
Wenamon 148, 217
Women in Canaan 178 ff., 253, 254
Yanḫamu 232
Yaṣiranu 251
Yarimanu 254
Yirpeel 180
yrḫ 22, n., 184, 186, 241, 249
yṣb 146, 150
yṭpn 115, 125
yw 180 ff.
Zakarbaal 148
Zamzam 81, n.
Zebulon 16, 133, n.
Ziqlag 8, 233

AUTHOR'S INDEX

ABEL, F. M., 83, n., 180, n.
AISTLEITNER, J., 3, 25, 39, n., 41, n., 43, n., 44, n., 50, 98, n., 102, n., 103, n., 116, n., 118, 119, n., 127, 128, 132, 137, n., 139, n., 140, n., 150, n., 184, n., 190, n., 204, 205, 215, 246, n.,
ALBRIGHT, W. F., 8, n., 15, n., 16, n., 24, n., 31, n., 45, n., 48, n., 51, n., 66, n., 103, n., 109, n., 111, n., 112, n., 125, n., 132, n., 133, n., 137, n., 139, n., 140, n., 141, n., 172, n., 174, n., 175, n., 179, 191, n., 235, n., 236, n., 243, 264, 265, 276, 280, 288, n., 303, 304.
ALT, A., 8, n., 89, 219, n., 234.
BADAWI, A. M., 230, n.
BARTON, G. A., 15, n., 106, 113, n., 121, n.
BAUDISSIN, W. VON, 161.
BAUER, H., 3, 164, 180
BAUMGARTNER, W., 14.
BIČ, M., 213, n.
BIRKELAND, H., 164, n.
BOTTÉRO, J., 238, n.
BOYER, G., 225, n., 233, 239, n.
BREASTED, J. H., 141, n., 232
BRICE, W. C. and LLOYD, S., 22, n.
BUBER, M., 89
BUDDE, K., 288, n.
BURCKHARDT, J., 248
CAQUOT, A., 23, 63, 127, 130, 170, 173, 187, 188, n., 288.
CANTINEAU, J., 3
CASSUTO, M. D., 46, n.
CASSUTO, U., 5, 9, 31, n., 39, n., 40, n., 41, n., 42, n., 43, n., 44, n., 51, n., 68, n., 83, 110, n., 117, n., 119, n., 133, n., 135, n., 154, n., 155, n.
CAZELLES, H., 65
CHEYNE, T. K., 288, n.
CHWOLSON, D., 22, n.
CLAY, J. C., 22, n.
CONTENAU, G., 132, n., 148, n.
COOK, S. A., 171
COOKE, G. A., 40, n., 129, 132, n., 149, n., 174, n., 212, n., 225, n., 249, n.
COPPENS, J., 303, 305.
CROSS, F. M. and FREEDMAN, D. N., 27, n., 269, 277, 303, 304, n.
CROWFOOT, J. W., 7, n., 224, n.
DAHOOD, M. 274, 275, 285
DALMAN, G., 96, 105, n., 117, n., 250, n.
DELITSZSCH, F., 288, n.
DHORME, E., 3, 107, 206, n., 243
DILLMANN, A., 288, n.
DIRINGER, D., 109, n.
DOUGHTY, C. M., 60.
DRIVER, G. R., 5, n., 9, 23, n., 25, n., 29, 31, n., 38, n., 39, n., 40, n., 41, n., 42, n., 43, n., 45, n., 46, n., 50, n., 51, n., 52, n., 53, n., 54, n., 55, n., 57, n., 58, n., 60, n., 66, n., 67, n., 70, n., 71, n., 72, n., 74, n., 79, n., 83, n., 95, n., 96, n., 100, n., 101, n., 102, n., 103, n., 104, n., 109, n., 111, n., 114, n., 118, n., 119, n., 121, n., 127, n., 128, n., 132, n., 133, n., 135, n., 137, n., 138, n., 139, n., 141, n., 143, n., 136, n., 150, n., 181, n., 235, n., 249, n., 264, 281, n., 297, 302, n.
DRIVER, G. R., and MILES, J., 235
DUHM, B., 288, n.
DUMONT, A., 223, n.
DUNAND, M., 132, n., 134, n., 225, n.
DUSSAUD, R., 4, 15, 16, 25, 39, n., 45, n., 50, n., 58, n., 64, n., 69, 82, 83, 93, 94, n., 100, n., 103, n., 133, n., 136, n., 137, n., 155, 172, 175, n., 181, 182, 184, 195, 196, 198, 199, 202, 203.
EBELING, E., 64, n.
EISSFELDT, O., 10, 14, 16, n., 38, n., 88, 90, 109, n., 136, n., 137, n., 141, n., 156, n., 161, 163, 172, n., 182, 189, n., 190, n., 191, n., 205, n., 261, n., 267, n.
ENGNELL, I., 16, 137, n., 139, n., 140, n., 229, n.
ERMAN, A., 6, n.
EWALD, H., 288, n.
FEGHALI, M., 250, n.
FENSHAM, F. C., 46, n., 269, n.
FINKEL, J., 270
FOHRER, G., 68, n., 163, n., 169
FRANKFORT, H., 13, 17, 130, n., 219
FRAZER, J. G., 131, n., 229, n.
FREEDMAN, D.N., and CROSS, F.M., 27, n., 269, 277, 303, 304, n.
FRIEDRICH, J., 4

FROST, S. B., 34, n.
GARDINER, A. H., 29, 176, n.
GASTER, T. H., 9, 10, 14, n., 16, n., 21, 23, n., 27, n., 32, n., 37, n., 41, n., 42, n., 43, n., 44, n., 51, n., 54, n., 55, n., 60, 61, n., 66, n., 68, n., 72, n., 75, n., 76, n., 77, n., 78, n., 79, n., 95, n., 98, n., 111, n., 112, n., 113, n., 115, n., 117, n., 119, n., 120, n., 122, n., 123, n., 125, n., 126, 133, 134, n.,, 135 n., 139, n., 140, n., 177, n., 195, 198, 203, 287.
GEHMAN, H. S., 138
GENNEP, A. VAN, 124, 253.
GESENIUS, W., 109, n., 288, n.
GIFFORD, E. H., 180, n.
GINSBERG, H. L., 5, 9, 16, n., 26, n., 40, n., 46, n., 51, n., 55, n., 62, n., 110, n., 112, 113, n., 117, n., 118, n., 119, n., 122, n., 124, n., 125, n., 132, n., 133, n., 134, n., 135, n., 138, n., 140, n., 142, n., 144, n., 235, n., 277, 278, 281, 286.
GLUECK, N., 186
GORDIS, R., 118, n., 281.
GORDON, C. H., *passim.*
GOETZE, A., 4, 155, n., 187, 249, n.
GRAHAM, W. C. and MAY, H. G., 229.
GRANQUIST, H., 142, n.
GRANT, E., 3, n.
GRAY, G. B., 197, n., 198, 288, n.
GRAY, J., 14, 26, n., 75, n., 106, n., 107, n., 135, n., 150, n., 194, n., 282, 296.
GRELOT, P., 288.
GRESSMANN, H., 148, n., 217, 266, n.
GROOT, DE, J. 180, n.
GUNKEL, H., 161.
HARRIS, Z. S. and MONTGOMERY, J. A., 4, n.
HEIDEL, A., 23, n.
HERDNER, A., 16, n., 57, n., 60, n., 62, n., 73, n., 99, n., 104, n., 118, n., 137, n., 193, n., 229, n., 243, n., 248, n., 250, n., 268, n.
HILL, G. F., 243, n.
HOCART, A. M., 229, n.
HOOKE, S. H., 229, n.
HONEYMAN, A. M., 226, n.
HUMBERT, P., 91
HVIDBERG, F. F., 13
INGHOLT, H., 185, n.
JACK, J. W., 261
JASTROW, M., 257
JAUSSEN, A., 71, n., 105, n., 288, n.
JIRKU, A., 137, n., 141, n.
JOHNSON, A. R., 92, 225, 228, 270.
KAISER, O., 30, 114, n.
KAPELRUD, A. S., 12, 29, n., 30, 37, 38, n., 76, n., 154.
KIRKBRIDE, A. S., 136, n.
KLOSTERMANN, A., 40, n., 141.
KNUDTZON, J. A., 28, n., 178, n., 194, n., 206, n., 208, n., 209, n., 220, n., 221, n.
KUTSCH, E., 146, n., 223, n., 255, n.
LAGARDE, P., 119, n.
LANDSBERGER, B., 79, n.
LANGHE, R. DE, 4, 9, 26, n., 37, 62, n., 63, n., 75, n., 124, n., 137, n., 139, n., 140, n., 141, n., 145, n., 233, n., 234, 279.
LAPP, P., 3
LARGEMENT, R., 94, 97, n., 98, n.
LEEUW, G. van der, 180, n.
LEWY, J., 235.
LEIBOVITCH, J., 133, n., 147, n.
LIDZBARSKI, M., 217, n.
LIVERANI, M., 226.
LLOYD, S. and BRICE, W. C., 22, n.
LOEWENSTAMM, S. A., 38, n., 68, n.
LØKKEGAARD, F., 163
LOUD, G., 207, n.
LUCKENBILL, D. D., 181, n., 217, n.
MAAG, V., 158, n., 183.
MARTI, K., 288, n.
MAUCHLINE, J., 170.
MAY, H. G. and GRAHAM, W. C., 229
MAZAR, B., 224.
MENDENHALL, G., 90, n.
— and ALBRIGHT, W. F., 111, 112, n.
MILES, J., and DRIVER, G. R., 235
MONTET, P., 179, n., 235, n.
MONTGOMERY, J. A., 4, n., 6, n., 113, n., 124, n., 138, n., 260, 297, 303.
MOWINCKEL, S., 11, 16, 26, n., 33, 34, 35, 37, 88, 92, 131, 135, n., 157, n., 167, 194, n., 207, n., 229, 288, n., 303, 305, n.
NIELSEN, D., 65, 154, 156, 177, n., 185, 216.
— E, 216.
NOTH, M., 2, 217, n.
NOUGAYROL, J., 5, n., 6, n., 8, n., 206, n., 225, n., 232, n., 233, n., 234, 235, 237, 239, n., 251.
OBERMAN, J., 28, n., 191, n., 246, n.
O'CALLAGHAN, R. T., 72, 233, n., 277, 303.

Otten, H., 158, n.
Parker, B., 223, n.
Parrot, A., 108, n., 249, n.
Patton, J. H., 283, n., 303.
Peake, A. S., 288, n.
Pedersen, J., 2, 16, n., 132, n., 133, n., 135, n., 136, n., 137, n., 138, n., 141, n., 144, n., 235, n., 237, 239, n., 252.
Peters, J. R., and Thiersch, H., 256, n.
Pfeiffer, R. H., 249, n.
Pope, M., 46, n., 113, n., 114, n., 154, 155, 156, n., 158, n., 190.
Posener, G., 118, 153, n., 165, 179, 185.
Reicke, B., 124.
Ringren, A., 191, n., 289, n.
Ronzevalle, A., 181, n.
Rost, L., 292
Rowe, A., 133, n., 147, n., 175, 203, n.
Rowley, H. H., 186, 280.
Rozelaar, M., 304.
Saarisalo, A., 141
Schaeffer, C. F. A., 1, n., 110, n., 135, n., 148, n., 165, n., 166, n., 177, n., 203, 213, 221, 226, 234, n., 237, n., 239, n.
Scheftelowitz, J., 250, n.
Schmid, H., 89, 157.
Schmidt, W., 155, 166.
Schrader, E., 186, n.
Seligman, E. G., 131, n.
Selms, A. van, 109, n., 110, n., 147, n.
Sethe, K., 152, n., 153, n., 165, 185, n.
Skinner, J., 288, n.
Smith, G. A., 83.
— S., 107, n., 233, n., 237, n.
— W. R., 10, 75, n., 242, n.
Snaith, N. H., 23, n.
Soden, W. von, 217, n.
Speiser, E. A., 196, n., 249, n.
Starkey, J. L., 165, n., 203, n.
Stummer, H., 77, n.
Thiersch, H. and Peters, J. R., 256, n.
Thomas, D. W., 156, n., 284.
Thureau-Dangin, F., 239, n., 254.
Tournay, R., 304, 305, n.
Ullendorff, E., 7, n., 38, n., 39, n., 42, n., 70, n., 71, n., 114, n., 121, n., 122, n., 264.
Vaux, R. de, 16, n., 124, n., 133, n., 141, n., 207, 226, 234, n., 267.
Vincent, A., 175, n., 180, n.
Virolleaud, C., *passim.*
Weidner, E. F., 223, n., 233, n.
Wellhausen, J., 173, n., 194, n.
Westermann, C., 221, n.
Wilson, J. A., 207, 289.
Wiseman, D. J., 138, n., 139, n., 236.
Witzel, M., 64, n.
Worden, T., 62, n.
Al-Yasin, Izz ad-Din, 114, n.
Yeivin, S., 3, n.

INDEX OF SCRIPTURAL PASSAGES

Genesis p.
ii, 6 63, n.
ii, 22 70, n., 259
iv, 1 265
iv, 11-12 80, 117, 131
iv, 14 242
vi 288, n.
vi, 1-4 158
vii, 11 50, n.
viii, 2 50, n.
ix, 4 45, n.
x, 2 308
xi, 7 143, n.
xii, 1-3 308
xiv 9, 161
xiv, 5 131
xiv, 7 81, n.
xiv, 18 186, n.
xiv, 19 265
xv, 9 133
xv, 20 131
xvi 76, n.
xvi, 7-14 120, 161
xviii 161, 162
xviii, 20 64, n., 203
xviii, 23 309
xix 244
xix, 11 123
xx, 17 18, n., 120, n., 129, n., 211, n.
xxv, 23 308
xxvii, 27-29, 40 308
xxvii, 28 44, n.
xxvii, 29 40, n., 271
xxvii, 39, 40
xxviii 120, 161, 308
xxx, 20 140, n.
xxx, 34 279
xxxi, 23 309
xxxi, 40 119, n.
xxxii, 23-33 161
xxxiii, 18-20 161
xli, 56 104, n.
xlvi, 11 111, n.
xlvii, 24 143, n.
xlviii, 15-17 308
xlix, 6 282
xlix, 7 185, n.
xlix, 10 111, n.
xlix, 24 158, n.

Exodus p.
vi, 3 163
vi, 16 ff. 111, n.
vii-ix 308
vii, 25 309
x, 2 308
xiii, 1-12 197
xv, 15 147
xix, 16 162
xx, 2-17 89
xx, 5 162
xx, 24 196
xx, 22-xxiii, 33 241
xxi, 13 242
xxi, 14 242
xxiii, 5 116, n.
xxiii, 10 73
xxiii, 19 97
xxiv, 5 196
xxv, 7 236, n.
xxviii, 15, 29, 30 236, n.
xxix, 20-21 136, n.
xxix, 27 196
xxxiv, 26 97
xxxiv, 33 108, n.

Leviticus
ii, 14 68, n., 121, n., 137 n., 149, n., 201.
vi, 10 198
vii, 22-24 136, n.
vii, 34 196
x, 14 196
xii, 245
xiii, 36 194, n.
xiv, 10, 24 104, n.
xvii, 14 45, n.
xxiii, 15, 17 196
xxv, 3-7 73
xxvi, 21 40, n., 253
xxvii, 31 198
xxvii, 33 194, n.

Numbers
v, 17-27 80, n.
viii, 16 197
xviii, 11 196
xviii, 24, 28 198
xxiii, 7-10, 18-24 308
xxiv, 3-9, 15-24 308

Numbers p.
xxviii, 6 197
xxxv, 6 ff. 243
xxxv, 33 117, n.

Deuteronomy
iii, 11 131
xii, 23 45
xiv, 1 124, n., 252
xiv, 21 97
xiv, 22 198
xvi, 18 240
xvii, 8 240
xvii, 16 224
xviii, 1 198
xx, 7 102, n., 140, n.
xxi, 1-9 122, 241
xxi, 18 240
xxii, 13 172
xxii, 20-21 241, n.
xxiv, 5 140, n.
xxv, 7, 9 271
xxvi, 14 61, n., 65, n., 183, 253
xxvii, 7 196
xxviii, 28 123, n.
xxviii, 30 140, n.
xxviii, 50 185
xxxii, 2 44, n., 162
xxxii, 6 265
xxxii, 8-9 161, n., 182, 278
xxxii, 11 268
xxxii, 24 276
xxxiii, 2 162
xxxiii, 3 27, n.
xxxiii, 5 90
xxxiii, 11 277
xxxiii 16 127, n.
xxxiii, 17 159
xxxiii, 25 259
xxxiii, 26 11, 26, n., 264, 286, n.
xxxiii, 29 259
xxxiv, 7 111, n.

Joshua
vii, 10 57, n.
viii, 31 196
x, 1, 3 186, n.

	p.
Joshua	
xii, 4	131
xiii, 12	131
xiii, 14	198
xv, 59	175
xvii, 15	131
xviii, 27	180
xix, 33	141, n.
xix, 38	83, n., 175
xx, 2-3	243
xxi	224, n.
Judges	
i, 33	83, n.
iii, 7	176
iii, 13	198
v, 4	162
v, 6	175
v, 17	141, n.
v, 20	280, n.
v, 30	96, n.
ix, 4	145
ix, 45	68, n.
x, 6	172, n.
xi, 24	171
xi, 37-40	63, 201
xiv, 18	185, n.
xviii, 7	83, 202
xix	244
Ruth	
iii, 16	62, n.
1 *Samuel*	
i, 24	133, n.
ii, 28	198
iv, 9	25, n.
v, 1-7	178
vi, 1	309
vi, 3, 4, 8, 17	197, n.
vii, 3-9	206
xi, 15	196
xii, 17	52, n.
xiii, 9	212
xiv, 35	212
xiv, 52	233
xvi, 10-11	309
xvi, 25	170
xvii, 17	137, n.
xvii, 25	236
xviii, 13	233
xxii, 6	75, n.
xxii, 7	233
xxiii, 7	141, n., 260

	p.
1 *Samuel*	
xxiii, 7	141, n., 260
xxv, 18	137, n.
xxvi, 7	75, n.
xxvii, 6	233
xxviii	109, n.
xxviii, 13	129
xxxi, 10	176, n.
2 *Samuel*	
i, 19	147, n.
i, 21	117, n., 118, n., 280-281
ii, 14	234
iii, 35	39, n.
vi	212
vii	217, n.
vii, 12 ff.	218
viii, 2, 6	25, n., 198
viii, 18	212
xii	217, n.
xii, 20	252
xii, 20-21	39, n.
xii, 27	268
xiv, 4 ff.	239, 240
xv, 10	88
xvii, 28	137, n.
xix, 44	143, n.
xx, 15	106, n.
xx, 24-25	224
xxi	202
xxi, 1 ff.	131
xxi, 1-9	126, n.
xxii, 16	278
xxii, 18	185, n.
xxiv, 11	217, n.
xxiv, 23	260
1 *Kings*	
i, 1-4	146, n.
i, 5	234, n.
i, 11, 18	88
i, 39	88
ii, 2	25, n.
ii, 19	227
iii, 4	202, n.
iii, 5-15	218
iv	224
iv, 5	234
iv, 7-19	7
v, 11	207
v, 13 ff.	7

	p.
1 *Kings*	
v, 13 ff.	7
vi, 5, 10	43, n.
viii, 2	17, n., 53
viii, 5, 62 ff.	49
ix, 11-15	224
ix, 15 ff.	7
ix, 16	238
x, 15	214, n.
xi, 7	171
xi, 8	172
xi, 25	204, n.
xi, 28	7
xiv, 11	252
xv, 13	177
xvi, 33	177
xviii	110, n., 200
xviii, 5	79, n.
xviii, 19	148, n., 177
xviii, 38, 45	46, n.
xviii, 43-44	309
xviii, 44-45	45, n.
xix, 11	310
xix, 19	256
xx, 14	233
xxi	241, n.
xxii, 10	142, n.
xxii, 11	159
xxii, 19	157
xx, 30	59, n.
2 *Kings*	
i	309
i, 11, 18	88
ii	309
ii, 19	96, n.
ii, 21	18, n., 120, n., 129, n., 211, n.
iii, 4	194, 213
iii, 27	172, 212, 213, n.
iv, 13	237
iv, 42	119, n.
vii, 2, 17, 19	138, n.
ix, 13	88
ix, 25	138, n.
x, 18	202
x, 22	261
x, 25	40, 138, n.
xi, 7	143, n.
xi, 14	88
xii, 6, 8	214
xii, 17	197

p.

2 *Kings*
xiii, 6 177
xv, 5 55, n.
xv, 25 138, n.
xvi, 3 172
xvi, 15 194, n.
xvii, 17 172
xvii, 29 262
xx, 7 6
xxi, 7 177
xxi, 18, 26 173
xii, 14 213, n.
xxiii, 4, 6 176, n.
xxii, 14 213, n.
xxiii, 5 172
xxiii, 11 172
xxv, 4 173
xxv, 19 237, n.

1 *Chronicles*
v, 20 42, n.
xii, 1 42, n., 263
xxiii-xxvi 216
xxvi, 30-32 224, n.

2 *Chronicles*
i, 3, 13 202, n.
ix, 14 214, n.
xiv, 10 280
xvi, 4 106, n.
xxvi, 21 55, n.
xxviii, 3 172

Ezra
iii, 5 197

Nehemiah
iii, 15 173

Esther
i, 8 266

Job
vi, 5 143, n.
viii, 6 267
xv, 23 103, n.
xvi, 15 268
xvii, 14 150, n.
xxiv, 24 27, n.
xxvi, 12-13 288
xxxi, 22 62, n., 268
xxxiv, 19 262
xxxvi, 13 115, n.

p.

Job
xxxvii, 3 50, n.
xxxviii, 7 158
xxxix, 21 40, n.
xlii, 3 274
xlii, 14 272, n.

Psalms
ii 158, 159, 228, 229
vi, 7 135, n.
vi, 8 144, n.
vii, 11 272, 273
xi, 16 278, n.
xi, 6 273
xvi, 2 277
xvi, 9 282
xviii, 5 (EVV 4) 229
xviii, 11 286, n.
xviii, 14-15 286, n.
xviii, 16 278
xviii, 18 185, n.
xx 304, n.
xxi 304, n.
xxi, 3 111, n., 135, n.
xxii 117
xxii, 3 78
xxiii 242
xxiv 157
xxvii, 4 194, n.
xxix 43, 286, 287, 305, n.
xxix, 3, 4, 5, 7, 8, 9 286, n.
xxix, 6 279
xxix, 10 33, 287, n.
xlv, 7 287, n.
xlvi 168
xlvi, 2-4 33
xlvi, 5 114, n.
xlvi, 7 286, n.
xlvii 86, 305, n.
xlvii, 2, 7 87
xlvii, 3, 8 87
xlviii 168
xlviii, 3 167, 168, 287
xlix, 16 64, n.
lxii, 12-13 297
lxv, 10 270, 271, 282, 283
lxvii 305, n.
lxviii, 5 11, 25, n., 286, n.
lxviii, 17 277
lxviii, 23 268, 269

p.

Psalms
lxviii, 28 269, 270
lxviii, 30 195
lxviii, 34 286, n.
lxxii, 8 114, n., 158
lxxiii, 9 289
lxxiv, 12-15 33
lxxiv, 12-19 21, 32
lxxv, 8 125, n.
lxxvii 305, n.
lxxvii, 18 277
lxxvii, 19 286, n.
lxxviii 207
lxxviii, 48 276, 279
lxxx, 6 63, n.
lxxx, 16 283
lxxxii, 1 287, n.
lxxxii, 5-7 94, n., 287 n.
lxxxii, 6 161 n.
lxxxii, 7 272, 288, n.
lxxxii, 8 161, n.
lxxxiii, 12 278
lxxxvi, 16 143
lxxxviii 207
lxxxviii, 5, 6 274
lxxxix 22, 207
lxxxix, 8 287, n.
lxxxix, 6-18 32
lxxxix, 8-19 33
lxxxix, 10-15 21
lxxxix, 19 272
lxxxix, 20 264
lxxxix, 26, 39-46 229
lxxxix, 37 (EVV 36) 208
xcii 305, n.
xcii, 10-11 296
xcii, 11 271
xciii 21, 86, 305, n.
xciii, 1 87
xciii, 2 287, n.
xciii, 3 296
xciii, 3-4 87
xciii, 4 296
xciii, 5 87
xciv 305, n.
xcv 305, n.
xcv, 3 84
xcv, 5 87
xcvi 305, n.
xcvi, 1 87
xcvi, 4 87
xcvi, 5 87

	p.
Psalms	
xcvi, 10	87
xcvi, 13	87
xcvii,	86
xcvii, 3	270
xcvii, 4	286, n.
xcvii, 9	87
xcvii, 7-9	87
xcviii	86
xcviii, 7-8	87
xcviii, 9	87
xcix	86
xcix, 2	87
xcix, 4	87
ci, 5	114, n.
cii, 5	283, 284
civ,	207
civ, 3	11, 26, n., 286, n.
civ, 7	286, n.
civ, 9	21
cx	158, 159, n., 229
cx, 3	277
cxviii, 10,11,12	277, 278
cxxi, 3	280
cxxv, 1	277
cxxix, 3	62, n.
cxxxii, 14	48, n.
cxxxv, 7	286, n.
cxxxvii, 5	283
cxxxix, 13	265
cxl, 11	273
cxliv, 6	286, n.
cxlv, 13	287, n.
cxlvi, 10	287, n.
cxlviii, 11	271
Proverbs	
iii, 13	132, n.
viii, 22	265 and n.
viii, 35	132, n.
ix, 5	266
xviii, 22	132, n.
xix, 2	262
xix, 18	262
xx, 25	194, n.
xxi, 9	137, n.
xxiii, 2	261
xxiii, 7	38, n., 205, n., 250, n.
xxiii, 31	172, n., 284
xxv, 24	137, n.
xxiv, 21	156,

	p.
Proverbs	
xxv, 24	137, n.
xxvi, 23	113, n., 286
xxx, 10	114, n.
xxx, 15-16	297, n.
xxx, 18-19	297
xxx, 21-23	297, n.
xxx, 29-31	297, n.
xxxi, 4	265, n., 284
xxxi, 15, 18	253
Ecclesiastes	
iii, 11	274, 275
vi, 10	285
vii, 12	285, 286
x, 9	79, n.
x, 18	27, n., 55, n.
xii, 5	275
xii, 6	275
xii, 12	275
Song of Songs	
i, 6	248, n.
iii, 6	123, n.
iv, 12-16	248, n.
vii, 3	119, n.
viii, 12	248, n.
Isaiah	
i, 2	159, n.
ii, 2-4	168
iii, 18	261
iii, 20	261
iv, 4	44
v, 1-7	248, n.
v, 14	261, 288
vi	158
vi, 5	90
vii, 14	135, n.
vii, 15	288
ix, 5 (EVV 6)	226
ix, 19	98, n.
x, 4	107, n.
xi, 1	227
xi, 8	62, n.
xi, 10	48, n., 262
xii, 6	24, n.
xiv, 9	147
xiv, 12	170, n., 288
xiv, 13	24, n.
xvi, 2	103, n.
xix, 4	185, n.
xxii, 18	41, n.

	p.
Isaiah	
xxv, 3	185, n.
xxv, 6	110, n.
xxvii, 1-2	32, 289
xxx, 14	44, n.
xxxii, 5	215, n., 262
xxxiii, 15	267
xxxiv, 1	40, n., 271
xxxviii, 21	6
xl, 12	100, n.
xl, 20	262, 263
xli, 1	40, n., 271
xli, 8	160, n.
xliii, 4, 9	40, n., 271
xliv, 5	283
xlvii, 9	96, n.
xlvii, 13	114, n.
xlviii, 19	263
li, 9 ff.	32, 34
li, 17	125, n.
li, 18	110, n.
lii, 7	33, 49, 87, 306
lv, 4	40, n. 271
lv, 10	63
lvii, 8	100, n.
lviii, 6	62, n. 252
Jeremiah	
iv, 11	94, n.
v, 17	132, n.
ix, 16 ff.	247
ix, 20	51, n.
xii, 12	94, n.
xvi, 4	252
xvi, 6	124, n.
xvi, 6-7	252
xxii, 19	252
xxiii, 5	227
xxv, 15-28	125, n.
xxxii, 35	172
xxxiii, 15	227
xxxviii, 11	261
xlvi, 6	280
xlvii, 5	252
Lamentations	
iv, 21	125, n.
Ezekiel	
i, 24	281
viii, 14	63, 201, 253, n.
xii, 14	201, 263
xiv, 14, 20	18, 107

p.

Ezekiel
xvi, 4 77, n.
xxiii, 3, 8 110, n.
xxvii, 6 114, n.
xxvii, 30 252
xxviii 288, n.
xxviii, 2 114 n.
xxviii, 3 107
xxviii, 14 24, n.
xxix, 3 ff. 34
xxix, 5 28, n.
xxxii, 2 ff. 34
xxxii, 4-5 28, n.
xxxii, 4-5 28, n.
xxxii, 6 281, 282
xxxiv, 5 252
xxxiv, 11-12 194, n.
xlvi, 15 197
xlvii 114, n.

Daniel
vii, 7 ff. 34
vii, 13 155
xi-xii 34

Hosea
iii, 2 141, n., 260
ix, 4 61
xi, 1 159, n.
xii, 2 25, n.
xiii, 12 270, n.

Joel
iv, 18 (Hebr. text) 70, n., 114, n.

Amos
i, 1 264
i, 2 52
i, 3-ii, 5 300, 301
ii, 7 53
iv, 4 198
v, 22 196
vii, 14-15 213, 264

p.

Amos
viii, 5 104, n.
ix, 2 208
ix, 3 269
ix, 13 70, n.

Jonah
ii, 7 264

Micah
i, 10 61, n., 252
i, 11 24, n.
iv, 1-3 168
v, 6 39, n., 44, n.
vii, 8, 10 24, n.

Nahum
i, 9 24, n.
ii, 1 (EVV i, 15) 33, 49, 87, 306

Habakkuk
ii, 5 31, n., 261, 276, 288
ii, 16 125, n.
iii 303
iii, 3 162
iii, 5 276
iii, 6-7 279, 280

Zephaniah
i, 5 172
iii, 9 128, n., 195, n.
iii, 10 25, n., 195

Zechariah
iii, 8 227
iii, 9 128, n.
vi, 12 227
ix, 9 114, n.
x, 1 139, n.
x, 9 68, n.
xii, 11 63, 201, 252, n.
xiv, 16-17 22, n., 34, 49, 87

p.

Malachi
i, 4 132, n.

2 *Esdras*
viii, 63-ix, 6 34
xii, 11 34

Ecclesiasticus
xxxiv, 28 284

Jubilees
xxiii, 11 ff. 34

Apocalypse of Baruch
2 *B.*
xxix, 4 36
xxxix, 7 35, 36
xl, 1 36
lxx, 1 ff. 35, 36
lxxii, 1 ff. 35
lxxiii, 1 ff. 36

Psalms of Solomon
ii, 28 35

Matthew
iv, 12-17 36
ix, 35 36
xii, 25 ff. 36
xxi, 12 214

Mark
i, 5 36
iii, 23 36

Luke
ix, 2 36
xi, 17 ff. 36

Revelation
xii 36
xiii 36
xvi, 16 24, n.
xxi, 1 87

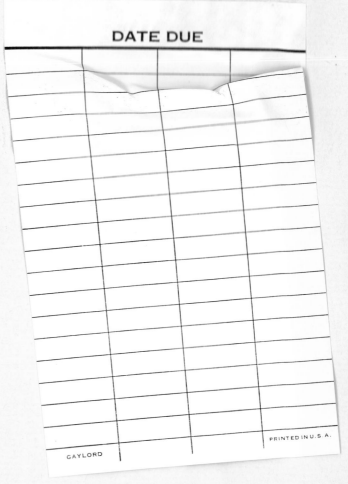